Lecture Notes in Artificial Inte

Subseries of Lecture Notes in Computer Sc
Edited by J. G. Carbonell and J. Siekmann

Lecture Notes in Computer Science

Edited by G. Goos, J. Hartmanis and J. van Leeuwen

Springer

Berlin
Heidelberg
New York
Barcelona
Hong Kong
London
Milan
Paris
Singapore
Tokyo

Matthew M. Huntbach   Graem A. Ringwood

Agent-Oriented Programming

From Prolog to Guarded Definite Clauses

Springer

Series Editors

Jaime G. Carbonell, Carnegie Mellon University, Pittsburgh, PA, USA
Jörg Siekmann, University of Saarland, Saarbrücken, Germany

Authors

Matthew M. Huntbach
Graem A. Ringwood
Department of Computer Science, Queen Mary and Westfield College
Mile End Road, London E1 4NS, UK
E-mail: {mmh/gar}@dcs.qmw.ac.uk

Cataloging-in-Publication data applied for

Die Deutsche Bibliothek - CIP-Einheitsaufnahme

Huntbach, Matthew M.:
Agent oriented programming : from prolog to guarded definite
clauses / Matthew M. Huntbach ; Graem A. Ringwood. - Berlin ;
Heidelberg ; New York ; Barcelona ; Hong Kong ; London ; Milan ;
Paris ; Singapore ; Tokyo : Springer, 1999
  (Lecture notes in computer science ; Vol. 1630 : Lecture notes in
  artificial intelligence)
  ISBN 3-540-66683-4

CR Subject Classification (1998): I.2, D.1.6, D.1.3, D.3, C.2.4

ISBN 3-540-66683-4 Springer-Verlag Berlin Heidelberg New York

© Springer-Verlag Berlin Heidelberg 1999
Printed in Germany

Typesetting: Camera-ready by author
SPIN 10703359   06/3142 – 5 4 3 2 1 0   Printed on acid-free paper

Preface

A book that furnishes no quotations is, me judice, no book – it is a plaything.

TL Peacock: Crochet Castle

The paradigm presented in this book is proposed as an agent programming language. The book charts the evolution of the language from Prolog to intelligent agents. To a large extent, intelligent agents rose to prominence in the mid-1990s because of the World Wide Web and an ill-structured network of multimedia information. Agent-oriented programming was a natural progression from object-oriented programming which C++ and more recently Java popularized. Another strand of influence came from a revival of interest in robotics [Brooks, 1991a; 1991b].

The quintessence of an agent is an intelligent, willing slave. Speculation in the area of artificial slaves is far more ancient than twentieth century science fiction. One documented example is found in Aristotle's *Politics* written in the fourth century BC. Aristotle classifies the slave as "an animate article of property". He suggests that slaves or subordinates might not be necessary if "each instrument could do its own work at command or by anticipation like the statues of Daedalus and the tripods of Hephaestus". Reference to the legendary robots devised by these mythological technocrats, the former an artificer who made wings for Icarus and the latter a blacksmith god, testify that the concept of robot, if not the name, was ancient even in Aristotle's time. Aristotle concluded that even if such machines existed, human slaves would still be necessary to render the little personal services without which life would be intolerable.

The name *robot* comes from the Czech words for serf and forced labor. Its usage originates from Karel Capek's 1920s play *Rossum's Universal Robots* in which Rossum, an Englishman, mass-produced automata. The play was based on a short story by Capek's brother. The robots in the play were not mechanical but grown chemically. Capek dismissed "metal contraptions replacing human beings" as "a grave offence against life". One of the earliest film robots was the replica Maria in Fritz Lang's 1927 classic *Metropolis*. The academic turned science fiction writer Isaac Asimov (1920–1992) introduced the term *robotics* when he needed a word to describe the study of robots in *Runaround* [1942]. Asimov was one of the first authors to depart from the Frankenstein plot of mad scientist creating a monster and to consider the social implications of robots.

An example of an automaton from the dark ages is a vending machine for holy water proposed by Hero of Alexandria around 11 AD. A modern reincarnation is Hoare's choc machine [Hoare, 1985] developed to motivate the computational model CSP (Communicating Sequential Processes). The word *automaton*, often used to describe computers or other complex machines, comes from the same Greek root as automobile meaning self-mover. Modern science owes much to the Greek tradition. Analysis of the forms of argument began with Empedocles and the importance of observation stems from Hippocrates. The missing ingredients of Greek science compared with the science of today were supplied by the Age of Reason. These were the need for deliberately contrived observation - experiments; the need for inductive argument to supplement deduction; and the use of mathematics to model observed phenomena. The most important legacy of seventeenth century science is technology, the application of science. Technology has expanded human capability, improved control over the material world, and reduced the need for human labor. Willing slaves are, perhaps, the ultimate goal of technology.

Industrial robots appeared in the late 1950s when two Americans, Devol and Engelberger, formed the company Unimation. Take-up was slow and Unimation did not make a profit for the first fourteen years. The situation changed in the mid-1980s when the automobile industry, dissatisfied with trade union disruption of production, turned to robot assembly. However, the industrial robot industry overextended as governments curtailed trade union power and the market saturated. Many firms, including Unimation, collapsed or were bought out by end product manufacturers. Today, the big producer is Japan with 400 000 installed robots compared to the US with over 70 000 and the UK with less than 10 000.

With pre-Copernican mentality, people will only freely admit that humans possess intelligence. (This, possibly, should be qualified to mean most humans on most occasions.) Humans can see, hear, talk, learn, make decisions, and solve problems. It seems reasonable that anyone attempting to reproduce a similar artificial capability would first attempt emulating the human brain. The idea that Artificial Intelligence (AI) should try to emulate the human nervous system (brain cells are nerve cells) was almost taken for granted by the twentieth century pioneers of AI. Up until the late 1960s talk of *electronic brains* was common place.

From Rossum's Universal Robots in Carel Kapek's vision to HAL in the film *2001*, intelligent machines provide some of the most potent images of the late twentieth century. The 1980s were, indeed, a good time for AI research. In the 1970s AI had become something of a backwater in governmental funding, but all that changed dramatically because of the Japanese Fifth Generation Initiative. At the beginning of the 1980s, MITI, the Japanese equivalent of the Department for Trade and Industry, announced that Japan was to concentrate on knowledge based systems as the cutting edge of industrial development. This sent tremors of commercial fear through the corridors of power of every country that had a computing industry. These governments had seen national industries such as shipbuilding, automobile manufacturing, and consumer electronics crumble under intensive Japanese competition. In what retrospectively seems to be a halfhearted attempt to target research funds to industrially relevant information technology, a few national and multinational research programs were initiated. A major beneficiary of this funding was AI. On short timescales, commercial products were supposed to spring forth fully armed from basic research.

Great advances in computer hardware were made in this decade with computing power increasing a thousandfold. A computer defeated the world backgammon champion and a computer came in joint first in an international chess tournament, beating a grandmaster along the way. This, however, did not augur the age of the intelligent machine. Genuine progress in AI has been painfully slow and industrial take-up has been mainly limited to a few well-publicized expert systems.

In the mid-1980s, it was envisaged that expert systems that contain thousands of rules would be widely available by the end of the decade. This has not happened; industrial expert systems are relatively small and narrowly focused on specific domains of knowledge, such as medical diagnosis. As researchers tried to build more extensive expert systems major problems were encountered.

There are two reasons why game playing is the only area in which AI has, as yet, achieved its goal. Though complex, chess is a highly regular, codifiable problem compared with, say, diagnosis. Further, the algorithms used by chess playing programs are not usually based on expert systems. Rather than soliciting knowledge from chess experts, successful game playing programs rely mainly on guided brute force search of all possible moves using highly powerful conventional multiprocessor machines. In reality, AI has made as much progress as other branches of software engineering. To a large extent, its dramatic changes of fortune, boom and bust, are due to fanatical proponents who promise too much. The timescale predictions of the Japanese now look very fanciful indeed. AI has been oversold more than once.

A common reaction to the early efforts in AI was that successful replication of human skills would diminish human bearers of such skills. A significant outcome of AI research is how difficult the simplest skills we take for granted are to imitate. AI is a long-term problem, a marathon, and not a sprint competition with the Japanese. Expert systems are only an early staging post on the way to developing intelligent machines.

AI pioneered many ideas that have made their way back into mainstream computer science. These include timesharing, interactive interpreters, the linked list data type, automatic storage management, some concepts of object-oriented programming, integrated program development environments, and graphical user interfaces. Whatever else it achieved, the Japanese Initiative provoked a chain of increased governmental funding for Information Technology reaction around the world from which many, including the authors, benefited.

According to Jennings et al. [1998], the fashion for agents "did not emerge from a vacuum" (who would have imagined it would?) Computer scientists of different specializations artificial intelligence, concurrent object-oriented programming languages, distributed systems, and human-computer interaction converged on similar concepts of agent. Jennings et al. [1998] state, "Object-oriented programmers fail to see anything novel or new in the idea of agents," yet they find significant differences between agents and objects. This is because their comparison only considers (essentially) sequential object-oriented programming languages such as Java. Had they considered concurrent object-oriented programming languages they would have found fewer differences.

Three languages have been promoted for agent development: Java, Telescript, and Agent-TCL. None of these are *concurrent* object-oriented languages. Java, from SUN Microsystems, is advocated for agent development because it is platform independent and integrates well with the World Wide Web. Java does, however, follow the tradition of interpreted, AI languages but is it not sympathetic to symbolic programming. Telescript, from General Magic, was the first commercial platform designed for the development of mobile agents. The emphasis is on mobility rather than AI applications. Agent-TCL [Gray et al., 1996] is an extension of TCL (Tool Command Language) which allows mobile code. While string based, TCL does not have a tradition of AI applications. Programs are not inductively defined, as is the case with Lisp or Prolog.

This monograph describes a concurrent, object-oriented, agent programming language that is derived from the AI tradition. A working knowledge of Prolog is necessary to fully appreciate the arguments. The monograph is divided into two parts. The first part, Chaps. 1–5, describes the evolution of the paradigm of Guarded Definite Clauses (GDC). If the paradigm is serious, and more than a fashion, then it is necessary to to describe its applications. This is done in the second part of the monograph, Chaps. 6–10. To set the paradigm in context, Chap. 1 provides an irreverent survey of the issues of AI. Chap. 2 completes the background to the paradigm with a retrospective rationale for the Japanese Fifth Generation Initiative. Chap. 3 describes how the paradigm evolved from Prolog with the environment change of multiprocessor machines. Included in this chapter is a chronology of the significant developments of GDC. Chap. 4 explores the manifestations of the vital ingredient of the paradigm - event driven synchronization. Chap. 5 compares and contrasts the language evolved with actor languages. The main difference is that GDC is an actor language with the addition of inductively defined messages.

The second part of the book begins with Chap. 6, which illustrates the advantages of GDC in parallel and distributed search. Chap. 7 describes the specialization to distributed constraint solving. Chap. 8 generalizes the chapters on search to meta-interpretation. An affinity for meta-interpretation has long been a distinguishing feature of AI languages. Chap. 9 describes how the overhead of meta-interpretation can be assuaged with partial evaluation. Chap. 10 concludes with the application of GDC to robotics and multi-agent systems.

While GDC as such is not implemented, it differs only marginally from KL1C, a language developed by the Japanese Fifth Generation Computer Systems Initiative. The Institute for New Generation Computer Technology (ICOT) promoted the Fifth Generation Computer Systems project under the commitment of the Japanese Ministry of International Trade and Industry (MITI). Since April 1993, ICOT has been promoting the follow-on project, ICOT Free Software (IFS), to disseminate the research:

> *According to the aims of the Project, ICOT has made this software, the copyright of which does not belong to the government but to ICOT itself, available to the public in order to contribute to the world, and, moreover, has removed all restrictions on its usage that may have impeded further research and development in order that large numbers of researchers can use it freely to begin a new era of computer science.*

AITEC, the Japanese Research Institute for Advanced Information Technology, took over the duties of ICOT in 1995. The sources of KL1 and a number of applications can be obtained via the AITEC home page: http://www.icot.or.jp/AITEC. KL1C runs under Linux and all the GDC programs in this monograph will run with little or no modification.

Despite their best efforts, the reader will find that the authors' cynicism shows through since they, like Bernard Shaw, believe that all progress in scientific endeavor depends on unreasonable behavior. In Shaw's view the common perception of science as a rational activity, in which one confronts evidence of fact with an open mind, is a post-rationalization. Facts assume significance only within a pre-existing intellectual structure that may be based as much on intuition and prejudice as on reason. Humility and reticence are seldom much in evidence and the scientific heroes often turn out to be intellectual bullies with egos like carbuncles.

The authors are very grateful to Jean Marie Willers and Peter Landin for the onerous task of proof reading earlier drafts of this monograph. Thanks are also due to our editors at Springer-Verlag, Ingrid Beyer, Alfred Hofmann, and Andrew Ross. Each author would like to say that any serious omissions or misconceptions that remain are entirely the fault of the other author.

January 1999   Matthew M Huntbach

                                                                    Graem A Ringwood

Contents

Chapter 1

The Art in Artificial Intelligence

Art is the imposing of pattern on experience, and our aesthetic enjoyment of it is recognition of the pattern.

AN Whitehead (1861–1947)

To better distinguish between historical precedent and rational argument, this first chapter gives an account of some of the intellectual issues of AI. These issues have divided AI into a number of factions – competing for public attention and, ultimately, research funding. The factions are presented here by an analogy with the movements of Fine Art. This is an elaboration of an idea due to Jackson [1986] and Maslov [1987]. The title of the chapter derives from Feigenbaum [1977].

The different movements in AI arose like their artistic counterparts as reactions against deficiencies in earlier movements. The movements of AI variously claim to have roots in logic, philosophy, psychology, neurophysiology, biology, control theory, operations research, sociology, economics and management. The account that follows is peppered with anecdotes. The more ancient anecdotes indicate that the issues that concern this product of the latter half of the 20th century have deep roots.

1.1 Realism

... used vaguely as naturalism, implying a desire to depict things accurately and objectively.

[Chilvers and Osborne, 1988]

A paper in 1943 by McCulloch and Pitts marks the start of the Realist Movement. It proposed a blueprint for an artificial neuron that claimed to blend the authors' investigations into the neurophysiology of frogs, logic – as represented in *Principia Mathematica* [Whitehead and Russell, 1910–13] and computability [Turing, 1936]. The state of an artificial neuron was conceived as

... equivalent to the proposition that proposed its adequate stimulus.

Artificial neurons are simple devices that produce a single real-valued output in response to possibly many real-valued inputs. The strength of the output is a threshold modulated, weighted sum of the inputs. An appropriate network of artificial neurons can compute any computable function. In particular, all the Boolean logic connectives can be implemented by simple networks of artificial neurons.

Parallel processing and robustness were evident in the early days of the Realist Movement. In an interview for the *New Yorker Magazine* in 1981, Minsky described a machine, the *Snarc*, which he had built in 1951, for his Ph.D. thesis:

We were amazed that it could have several activities going on at once in this little nervous system. Because of the random wiring it had a sort of failsafe characteristic. If one neuron wasn't working it wouldn't make much difference, and with nearly 300 tubes and thousands of connections we had soldered there would usually be something wrong somewhere ... I don't think we ever debugged our machine completely. But it didn't matter. By having this crazy random design it was almost sure to work no matter how you built it.

A war surplus autopilot from a B24 bomber helped the Snarc simulate a network of 40 neurons.

Minsky was a graduate student in the Mathematics Department at Princeton. His Ph.D. committee was not convinced what he had done was mathematics. Von Neumann, a member of the committee, persuaded them:

If it weren't math now it would be someday.

In 1949, Hebb, a neurophysiologist, wrote a book, *The Organization of Behavior,* which attempted to relate psychology to neurophysiology. This book contained the first explicit statement that learning can be achieved by modifying the weights of the summands of artificial neurons. In 1955, Selfridge devised a neurologically inspired network called *Pandemonium* that learned to recognize hand-generated Morse code. This was considered a difficult problem, as there is a large variability in the Morse code produced by human operators. At the first workshop on AI (which lasted two months) held at Dartmouth College, Rochester [1956], described experiments to test Hebb's theory. The experiments simulated a neural network by using a "large" digital computer. At the time, an IBM 704 with 2K words of memory was large and Rochester worked for IBM. Widrow and Hoff [1960] enhanced Hebb's learning methods.

The publication of *Principles of Neurodynamics* [Rosenblatt, 1962] brought the *Perceptron*, a trainable pattern-recognizer, to public attention. The Perceptron had various learning rules. The best known of these was supported by a convergence theorem that guaranteed the network could learn any predicate it could represent. Furthermore, it would learn the predicate in a finite number of iterations of the learning rule.

By 1969, while digital computers were beginning to flourish, artificial neurons were running into trouble: networks often converged to metastable states; toy demonstrations did not scale up. Minsky and Papert [1969], "appalled at the persistent influence of Perceptrons," wrote *Perceptrons: An Introduction to Computational Geometry* that contained a critique of Perceptron capability:

Perceptrons have been widely publicized as "pattern recognition" or "learning" machines and as such have been discussed in a large number of books, journal articles, and voluminous reports. Most of this writing is without scientific value ... The time has come for maturity, and this requires us to match our speculative enterprise with equally imaginative standards of criticism.

This attack was particularly damning because the authors ran an influential AI research laboratory at MIT. Minsky had, after all, done his Ph.D. in neural nets. The attack was only addressed at Perceptrons, which are, essentially, single layer networks. Although Perceptrons can learn anything they were capable of representing, they could represent very little. In particular, a Perceptron cannot represent an exclusive-or. Minsky and Papert determined that Perceptrons could only represent linearly separable functions.

Multiple layers of Perceptrons can represent anything that is computable (Turing complete [Minsky, 1967]), but general methods for training multilayers appeared to be elusive. Bryson and Ho [1969] developed back propagation, a technique for training multilayered networks, but this technique was not widely disseminated. The effect of the Minsky and Papert's critique was that all US Government funding in neural net research was extinguished.

1.2 Purism

They set great store by the lesson inherent in the precision of machinery and held that emotion and expressiveness should be strictly excluded apart from the mathematical lyricism which is the proper response to a well-composed picture.

[Chilvers and Osborne, 1988]

With the availability of analogue computers in the 1940s, robots began to appear a real possibility. Wiener [1948] defined *cybernetics* as the study of communication and control in animal and machine. The word cybernetics derives from the Greek *kubernetes*, meaning steersman. Plato used the word in an analogy with diplomats. One of the oldest automatic control systems is a *servo*; a steam powered steering engine for heavy ship rudders. Servo comes from the Latin *servitudo* from which English inherits servitude and slave. Cybernetics marked a major switch in the study of physical systems from energy flow to information flow.

In the period after Plato's death, Aristotle studied marine biology but faced with the enormous complexity of phenomena, despaired of finding explanations in Platonic rationalism. In opposition to his teacher, Aristotle concluded animate objects had a purpose. In 1943, Rosenbleuth et al. proposed that purpose could be produced in machines using *feedback*. The transmission of information about the performance back to the machine could be used to modify its subsequent behavior. It was this thesis that gave prominence to cybernetics.

Much of the research in cybernetics sought to construct machines that exhibit intelligent behavior, i.e. robots. Walter's Turtle [1950] is an early example of an autonomous robot. A finite state machine with four states can describe its behavior. In state 1, the robot executes a search pattern, roaming in broad loops, in search of a light source. If it detects a bright light source in state one, it changes to state two and moves towards the source. If the light source becomes intense, the robot moves to state three and swerves away from the light. The triggering of the bump switch causes transition to state four, where it executes a reverse right avoiding maneuver. Interest in cybernetics dwindled with the rise of the digital computer because the concept of information became more important than feedback. This was encouraged by Shannon's theory of information [Shannon, 1948; Shannon and Weaver, 1949]. Shannon was a Bell Telephones communication engineer. His investigations were prompted by the needs of the war effort, as was the development of computers and operations research.

1.3 Rococo

Style of art and architecture, characterized by lightness, playfulness ... a love of complexity of form.

[Chilvers and Osborne, 1988]

At the same first conference on AI at which Rochester explained his experiments with neural nets, Samuel [1959] described some game playing programs he had developed. Samuel had been working on checkers as early as 1948 and had produced a system that learnt to play checkers to Grandmaster level. The system had a number of numerical parameters that were adjusted from experience. Samuel's program played a better game than its creator and thus dispelled the prejudice that computers can only do what they are programmed to do. The program was demonstrated on television in 1956 creating great public interest. While the learning mechanism predated Hebb's mechanism for artificial neurons, the success of the checker player was put down to Samuel's expertise in the choice of parameters.

Samuel's achievement was overshadowed because checkers was considered less intellectually demanding than chess. An ability to play chess has long been regarded as a sign of intelligence. In the 18th-century a chess-playing automaton was constructed by Baron Wolfgang von Kempelen. Officially called the Automaton Chess Player, it was exhibited for profit in French coffeehouses. Its popular name, the Turk, was due to its form that consisted of a carved Turkish figurine seated behind a chest. The lid of the chest was a conventional chessboard. By rods emanating from the chest, the figurine was able to move the chess pieces on the board. The Turk played a tolerable game and usually won. While it was readily accepted it was a machine, curiosity as to how it functioned exposed a fraud. A vertically challenged human chess expert was concealed in the cabinet below the board. The Turk ended in a museum in Philadelphia in 1837 and burned with the museum in 1854. A detailed description of the Turk is given by Levy [1976].

In 1846, Babbage [Morrison and Morrison, 1961] believed his Analytical Engine, were it ever completed, could be programmed to play checkers and chess. The Spanish Engineer, Leonardo Torres y Quevedo built the first functional chess-playing machine around 1890. It specialized in the KRK (king and rook against king) endgame. Norbert Wiener's [1948] book, *Cybernetics,* included a brief sketch of the functioning of a chess automaton.

Zuse [1945], the first person to design a programmable computer, developed ideas on how chess could be programmed. The idea of computer chess was popularized by an article in *Scientific American* [Shannon, 1950]. Shannon had been instrumental in the rise of the digital computer. In his MIT master's thesis of 1938, Shannon used the analogy between logical operators and telephone switching devices to solve problems of circuit design. Shannon [1950] analyzed the automation of chess but he did not present a program. According to Levy and Newborn [1991], Turing and Champernowne produced the first chess-playing program, which was called Turochamp. However, pen and paper executed the program. Turing was denied access to his own research team's computers by the British Government because computer chess was considered a frivolous use of expensive resources.

Shannon [1950] argued that the principles of games such as chess could be applied to serious areas of human activity such as document translation, logical deduction, the design of electronic circuits and, pertinently, strategic decision making in military operations. Shannon claimed that, while games have relatively simple well-defined rules they exhibit behaviors sufficiently complex and unpredictable as to compare with real-life problem solving. He noted that a game could be completely described by a graph. Vertices of the graph correspond to positions of the game and the arcs to possible moves. For a player who can comprehend the whole graph, the game becomes trivial. For intellectually substantial games, the whole graph is too large or impossible to represent explicitly. It has been estimated [Thornton and du Boulay, 1992] that checkers has a graph with 10^{40} nodes while chess has 10^{120} nodes and the game of go has 10^{170} nodes.

The problem of the size of the graph can be approached piecewise. At each stage in a game, there is a multiset of open nodes, states of play, that have been explored so far but the consequences of which have not been developed. An exhaustive development can be specified by iterating two steps, *generate-and-test* (not in that order):

> While the multiset of open nodes is not empty
> > remove some node
> > if the node is terminal (a winning position)
> > > stop
> > else
> > > add the immediate successors of the node to the multiset

The object of the game then becomes to generate a terminal node while generating as few other nodes of the graph as is necessary.

Exhaustive search by generate-and-test is a long established method of problem solving where there is a need to filter out relevant information from a mass of irrelevancies. A classic example is Erastosthenes' Sieve for determining prime numbers. Erastosthenes was the Librarian of the Library of Alexandria circa 245–194 BC. He gave the most famous practical example of ancient Greek mathematics: the calculation of the polar circumference of the Earth. The Greek word *mathematike,* surprisingly, means *learning*.

Three immediate variations of generate-and-test can be realized:

- forward search in which the initial multiset of open nodes is a singleton, the start node;
- backward search in which the initial multiset of open nodes are terminal nodes and the accessibility relation is reversed;

- opportunistic search in which the initial multiset of open nodes does not contain the start node nor terminal nodes; the rules are used both forwards and backwards until both the start node and the finish node are produced.

Backward generate-and-test was known to Aristotle as means-ends analysis and described in *Nicomachean Ethics*:

> *We deliberate not about ends, but about means. For a doctor does not deliberate whether he shall heal, nor an orator whether he shall persuade, nor a statesman whether he shall produce law and order, nor does anyone deliberate his end. They must assume the end and consider how and by what means it is attained and if it seems easily and best produced thereby; while if it is achieved by one means only they consider how it will be achieved by this and by what means this will be achieved, till they come to the first cause, which in order of discovery is last ... and what is last in the order of analysis seems to be first in the order of becoming. And if we come on an impossibility, we give up the search, e.g., if we need money and this cannot be got; but if a thing appears possible we try to do it.*

Stepwise development does not reproduce the graph but a tree covering the graph. The search tree is developed locally providing no indication of global connectivity. Any confluence in the graph produces duplicate nodes in the search tree. Any cycles in the graph are unwound to unlimited depth. This leads to the possibility of infinite search trees even when the game graph is finite. At each node in the tree, there may be any number of successors. Shannon suggests generating the tree breadth-first. Breadth-first search chooses immediate descendants of all sibling nodes before continuing with the next generation. Breadth-first minimizes the number of generations that must be developed to locate a terminal node.

As noted by Shannon, when storage is limited, more than one successor at each node poses intractable problems for large (or infinite) game graphs. The number of open nodes grows exponentially at each generation, a phenomenon known as *combinatorial explosion*. Lighthill [1972] coined the name in an infamous report that was responsible for a drastic cutback of research funding for artificial intelligence in the UK:

> *One rather general cause for disappointments [in AI] has been experienced: failure to recognize the implications of the 'combinatorial explosion'. This is a general obstacle to the construction of a ... system on a large knowledgebase that results from the explosive growth of any combinatorial expression, representing the number of ways of grouping elements of the knowledgebase according to particular rules, as the base size increases.*

Leibniz was aware of combinatorial explosion some hundreds of years earlier [1765]:

> *Often beautiful truths are arrived at by synthesis, by passing from the simple to the compound; but when it is a matter of finding out exactly the means for doing what is required, Synthesis is not ordi-*

narily sufficient; and often a man might as well try to drink up the
sea as to make all the required combinations ...

Golomb and Baumbert [1965] gave a general description of a space saving form of generate-and-test called backtracking. The development of the tree is depth-first, with successors of the most recently chosen node expanded before considering siblings. On reaching the end of an unsuccessful branch, control *backtracks* to the most recently generated nodes. It has the advantage over breadth-first search of only requiring the storage of the active branch of the tree. Additionally, depth-first search generally minimizes the number of steps required to locate the first terminal node. Golomb and Baumbert do not claim originality for backtracking; it had been independently discovered in many applications. They cite Walker [1960] for a general exposition. Floyd [1967] noted that problems that can be solved by backtracking, may be simply described by recursively defined relations.

Golomb and Baumbert [1965] pointed out that there are numerous problems that even the most sophisticated application of backtracking will not solve in reasonable time. Backtracking suffers from pathological behavior known as thrashing. The symptoms are:

- looping – generating the same node when there are cycles in the game graph;
- late detection of failure – failure is only discovered at the bottom of long branches;
- bad backtracking point – backtracking to the most recently generated nodes which form a subtree of dead ends.

More seriously for automation, the search may never end; if a nonterminating branch of the search tree (even if the graph is finite) is relentlessly pursued, a terminating node that lies on some yet undeveloped branch will never be discovered.

1.4 Classicism

... a line of descent from the art of Greece and Rome ... sometimes
used to indicate a facial and bodily type reduced to mathematical
symmetry about a median axis freed from irregularities ...

[Chilvers and Osborne, 1988]

In contrast to game playing, the seemingly respectable manifestation of human intelligence was theorem proving. Two computer programs to prove mathematical theorems were developed in the early 1950s. The first by Davis [1957], at the Princeton Institute of Advanced Studies, was a decision procedure for Presburger arithmetic (an axiomatization of arithmetic with ordering and addition but not multiplication). This program produced the first ever computer-generated proof of the theorem that the sum of two positive numbers is a positive number. At the same first conference on AI at which Rochester explained his experiments on neural nets, Newell, Shaw and Simon [1956], from Carnegie Mellon University, stole the show with a theorem prover called the *Logic Theorist*. The Logic Theorist succeeded in demonstrating a series of propositional theorems in *Principia Mathematica* [Whitehead and Russell,

1910–13]. This often cited but seldom read tome attempted to demonstrate that all mathematics could be deduced from Frege's axiomatization of set theory. (*Principia Mathematica* followed the publication of *Principia Ethica* by another Cambridge philosopher [Moore, 1903].) McCarthy, one of the principal organizers of the workshop, proposed the name Artificial Intelligence for the subject matter of the workshop as a reaction against the dominance of the subject by cybernetics. The first 30 years of this shift in emphasis was to be dominated by the attendees of the conference and their students who were variously based at MIT, CMU, and Stanford.

By contrast with cybernetics, the goal of theorem proving is to explicate the relation $A_1, \ldots A_n \vdash A_{n+1}$ between a logical formula A_{n+1}, a theorem, and a set of given logical formulas $\{A_1, \ldots A_n\}$, the premises or axioms. There is an exact correspondence between theorem proving and game playing. The initial node is the set of axioms. The moves are inference rules and subsequent nodes are sets of lemmas that are supersets of the premises. A terminating node is a superset that contains the required theorem. Theorem proving suffers more from combinatorial explosion than recreational games. Since lemmas are accumulated, the branching rate of the search increases with each step.

The intimacy of games and logic is further compounded by the use of games to provide a semantics for logic [Hodges, 1994]. The tableau or truth-tree theorem prover can be interpreted as a game [Oikkonen, 1988]. The idea of game semantics can be seen in the Greek *dialektike*, Socrates' method of reasoning by question and answer (as recorded by Plato). Many aspects of mathematics, particularly the axioms of Euclidean geometry, derive from the Greeks. The Greek word *geometria* means *land survey*. Gelerntner [1963], a colleague of Rochester at IBM, produced a Euclidean geometry theorem prover. To combat the combinatorial explosion, he created a numerical representation of a particular example of the theorem to be proved. The system would first check if any lemma were true in the particular case. The program derived what at first was thought to be a new proof of the *Bridge of Asses*. This basic theorem of Euclidean geometry states that the base angles of an isosceles triangle are equal. Later, it was discovered that the same proof had been given by Pappus in 300 AD.

At the 1957 "Summer Institute for Symbolic Logic" at Cornell, Abraham Robinson noted that the additional points, lines or circles that Gelerntner used to focus the search can be considered as ground terms in, what is now called, the *Herbrand Universe*. In a footnote, [Davis, 1983] questions the appropriateness of the name. The Swedish logician Skolem [1920] was the first to suggest that the set of ground terms was fundamental to the interpretation of predicate logic. The same idea reappeared in the work of the French number theorist Herbrand [Herbrand, 1930; Drebden and Denton, 1966]. The fundamental result of model theory, known as the Skolem–Herbrand–Gödel theorem, is that a first-order formula is valid if and only if a ground instance of the Skolem normal form (clausal form) of the negation of the formula is unsatisfiable. A clause is a disjunction of literals (positive or negative atoms). Any set of formulas can be algorithmically transformed into Skolem normal form. Skolemization can be represented as a game [Henkin, 1959]. Hintikka [1973] extended Henkin's observation to logical connectives. The Skolem–Herbrand–Gödel theorem turns the search for a proof of a theorem into a search for a refutation of the negation.

The principal inference rule for propositional clausal form is *complementary literal elimination*. As the name suggests, it combines two clauses that contain complementary propositions, eliminating the complements. Complementary literal elimination is a manifestation of the chain-rule and the cut-rule. One of the first automatic theorem-provers to use complementary literal elimination was implemented by Davis and Putnam [1960]. The Davis–Putnam theorem prover has two parts: one dealing with the systematic generation of the Herbrand Universe (substituting variables in formulas by ground terms) and the other part concerned with propositional complementary literal elimination. The enumeration of all ground terms, *Herbrand's Property B*, is the basis of the Skolem–Herbrand–Gödel theorem.

Herbrand's Property B foundered on the combinatorial explosion of the number of ground instances. Enumerating the ground terms requires instantiating universally quantified variables at points in the search where insufficient information is available to justify any particular choice. A solution to the premature binding of variables appeared in a restricted form (no function symbols) in the work of the Swedish logician Prawitz [1960]. Prawitz's restricted form of unification enables a theorem prover to postpone choosing instances for quantified variables until further progress cannot be made without making some choice. Prawitz's restricted form of unification was immediately picked up and implemented by Davis [1963]. The work of Prawitz, Davis, and Putnam inspired a team of scientists led by George Robinson at Argonne National Laboratories (there are at least two other sons of Robin who worked in automatic theorem proving) to pursue a single inference rule for clausal form. A member of the team, Alan Robinson [1965], succeeded in combining complementary literal elimination with the general form of unification (including function symbols) in an inference rule called *resolution*. Martelli and Montanari [1982] present a more efficient unification algorithm. This *most general unifier* algorithm for solving a set of syntactic equality constraints was known to Herbrand (but obscurely expressed) as *Property A*.

Resolution only went some way to reduce the intolerable redundancies in theorem proving. It is common for theorem provers to generate many useless lemmas before interesting ones appear. Looping (reproducing previous lemmas) is a serious problem for automatic theorem provers. Various authors in the 1960s and early 1970s explored refinements of resolution. Refinements are inference rules that restrict the number of successors of a node. Model elimination [Loveland, 1968] is essentially a linear refinement. A resolution proof is linear if the latest resolvent is always an immediate parent of the next resolvent. Proofs in which each new lemma is deducible from a preceding one are conceptually simpler and easier to automate than other types of proof. The branching rate was remarkably reduced with SL (selective linear) resolution [Kowalski and Kuehner, 1971] which showed that only one *selected* literal from each clause need be resolved in any refutation. In SL resolution, literal selection is performed by a function. The necessity for fairness of the literal selection only became apparent with the study of the semantics of Prolog, a programming language. The selection can be made syntactic with ordered clauses [Reiter, 1971; Slagle 1971].

An ordered clause is a sequence of distinct literals. However, ordered resolution is not complete. Not all logical consequences can be established.

Efficiency was also traded for completeness with *input resolution* [Chang, 1970]. With input resolution, one parent of a resolvent must be an input clause (a premise). It is a special case of linear resolution that not only reduces the branching rate but also saves on the storage of intermediate theorems (they are not reused), an extra bonus for implementation. Kuehner [1972] showed that any (minimally inconsistent) clause set that has an input refutation is renameable as a set of Horn clauses. A *Horn Clause* is a clause with at most one positive literal. The importance of definite clauses for model theory was discovered somewhat earlier [McKinsey, 1943]. McKinsey referred to definite clauses as conditional clauses. Horn [1951] extended McKinsey's results. Smullyan [1956a] called definite clauses over strings Elementary Formal Systems, EFSs. EFSs are a special case of Post Production Systems where the only rewrite rules are substitution and modus ponens. Malcev [1958] characterizes classes of structures that can be defined by Horn clauses. He shows that in any such class, every set of ground atoms has a minimal model. Cohen [1965] characterizes problems expressible in Horn clauses, which include many problems in algebra.

Literal selection is fair if candidate literals are not ignored indefinitely. Kuehner imposed two further refinements on the theorem prover that he dubbed SNL for "Selective Negative Linear"; the name suggests a refinement of SL resolution. Kuehner anticipates resolvent selection by using ordered clauses. An ordered Horn Clause contains at most one positive literal, which must be the leftmost. One parent of a resolvent must be *negative*: that is each literal is a negated atom. Descendants of an initial negative clause are used in subsequent resolutions (linearity). This description of SNL will be familiar to readers with knowledge of the programming language Prolog. SNL retains the need for the factoring inference rule required by SL resolution and is incomplete if the clause literal selection is not fair. Factoring merges unifiable literals of the same sign in the same clause. Hill [1974] demonstrated for Horn Clauses that factoring was unnecessary and that the selected literal need not be selected by a function but can be chosen in an arbitrary manner. Hill called the resulting theorem prover LUSH for Linear resolution with Unrestricted Selection for Horn Clauses. This somehow became renamed as SLD [Apt and van Emden, 1982], the D standing for *definite* clauses. A definite clause is one with exactly one positive literal. The name suggests an application of SL to D that is misleading. SL requires both factorization and ancestor resolution for completeness. An ancestor is a previously derived clause.

1.5 Romanticism

*The Romantic artist explored the values of intuition and instinct ...
it marked a reaction from the rationalism of the Enlightenment and
order of the Neo-classical style.*

[Chilvers and Osborne, 1988]

Newell and Ernst [1965] argued that heuristic proofs were more efficient than exhaustive search. *Heuristics* are criteria, principles, rules of thumb, or any kind of device that drastically refines the search tree. The word comes from the ancient Greek *heruskin*, to discover and is the root of Archimedes' *eureka*. Newell and Simon satirically dubbed exhaustive search as the *British Museum Algorithm*. The name derives from an illustration of the possible but improbable by the astronomer Authur Eddington – if 1000 monkeys are locked in the basement of the British Museum with 1000 typewriters they will eventually reproduce the volumes of the Reading Room. The Romantics' belief that intelligence is manifested in node selection in generate-and-test is summed up in *An Introduction to Cybernetics* [Ashby, 1956]:

> *Problem solving is largely, perhaps entirely, a matter of appropriate selection.*

From an etymological point of view, that intelligence should be related to choice is not surprising. The word intelligence derives from the Latin *intellego* meaning *I choose among*. In 1958, Simon claimed that a computer would be world chess champion within 10 years.

Newell drew inspiration from the heuristic search used in the Logic Theorist. The Logic Theorist was able to prove 38 of the first 52 theorems in Chapter 2 of *Principia Mathematica*.

> *We now have the elements of a theory of heuristic (as contrasted with algorithmic) problem solving; and we can use the theory both to understand human heuristic processes and to simulate such processes with digital computers. Intuition, insight and learning are no longer the exclusive possessions of humans: any large high-speed computer can be programmed to exhibit them also.*

It was claimed that one of the proofs generated by the Logic Theorist was more elegant than Russell and Whitehead's. Allegedly, the editor of the *Journal of Symbolic Logic* refused to publish an article co-authored by the Logic Theorist because it was not human.

The principle heuristic of the Logic Theorist, means-end analysis was abstracted in the General Problem Solver, GPS [Newell and Simon, 1963]. On each cycle, best-first search chooses an open node that is "most promising" for reaching a terminal node. What is *best* might be determined by the cumulative cost of reaching the open node. Breadth-first search can be described by minimizing the depth of the tree. In means-ends analysis, selection is based on some measure of the "nearness" of the open node to a terminal node. This requires a metric on states. Wiener's [1948] book, *Cybernetics,* included a brief sketch of the functioning of a possible computer chess-playing program that included the idea of a metric, called an evaluation function, and minimax search with a depth cut-off. Assigning to each state the distance between it and some fixed state determines semantics (meaning) for the state space. (More generally, *semantics* is concerned with the relationship between symbols and the entities to which they refer.) The metric provides a performance measure that guides the search.

A common form of expression of a terminal state is a set of constraints [Wertheimer, 1945]. A *constraint* network defines a set of instances of a tuple of variables $<v_1 \ldots v_n>$ drawn from some domain $D_1 \otimes \ldots \otimes D_n$ and satisfying some specified set of relations, $c_j(v_1 \ldots v_n)$. This extra structure can be exploited for greater efficiency. The backtracking algorithm of Golomb and Baumbert [1965] was proposed as a constraint-solving algorithm. Backtracking searches the domain of variables by generating and testing partial tuples $<v_1 \ldots v_n>$ until a complete tuple satisfying the constraints is built up. If any one of the constraints is violated the search backtracks to an earlier choice point. Golomb and Baumbert [1965] describe a refinement of depth-first search, which they called *preclusion* (now known as *forward checking*) which leads to a more efficient search. Rather than testing that the generated partial tuple satisfies the constraints, the partial tuple and the constraints are used to prune the choice of the next element of the tuple to be generated. The partial tuple and constraints are used to specify a subspace, $E_{i+1} \otimes \ldots \otimes E_n$ with $E_j \subseteq D_j$, from which remaining choices can be drawn. Leibniz [1765] knew about preclusion:

> *... and often a man might well try to drink up the sea as to make all the required combinations, even though it is often possible to gain some assistance from the* method of exclusions, *which cuts out a considerable number of useless combinations; and often the nature of the case does not admit any other method.*

Constraint satisfaction replaces generate-and-test by generate and constrain. An example of constraint solving described in Section 1.4 is Herbrand's Property A in theorem proving.

Constraint satisfaction is often accompanied by the heuristic of *least commitment* [Bitner and Reingold, 1965], in which values are generated from the most constrained variable rather than the order of variables in the tuple. The principle asserts that decisions should be deferred for as long as is possible so that when they are taken the chance of their correctness is maximized. This minimizes the amount of guessing and therefore the nondeterminism. The principle of *least commitment* is used to justify deferring decisions. Resolution theorem proving is an example of the general principle of least commitment. Least commitment can avoid assigning values to unknowns until they are, often, uniquely determined. This introduces data-driven control that is known as local propagation of constraints. With local propagation, constraint networks are often represented by graphs. When represented as a graph, a constraint is said to *fire* when a uniquely determined variable is generated. The constraint graph and the firing of local propagation deliberately conjure up the firing of neurons in neural networks.

Constraint satisfaction was dramatically utilized in Sutherland's Sketchpad [1963], the first graphical user interface. A user could draw a complex object by sketching a simple figure and then add constraints to tidy it up. Primitive constraints include making lines perpendicular or the same length. Sketchpad monopolized a large mainframe and the system used expensive graphics input and display devices. It was years ahead of its time.

More general than preclusion is split-and-prune. Rather than directly generating instances for the variables, the search generates tuples of domains $<E_1...E_n>$ where $E_i \subseteq D_i$. At each step, the search splits and possibly discards part of the domain. Splitting produces finer and finer bounds on the values the variables can take until the component domains are empty (failure to satisfy) or sometimes singletons. The method of split-and-prune was known to the ancient Greeks in the form of hierarchies of dichotomous classification. Jevons [1879] argued that the procedure of cutting off the negative part of a genus when observation discovers that an object does not possess a particular feature is the art of diagnosis. This technique has subsequently been used in many expert systems. Aristotle strongly emphasized classification and categorization. His *Organon*, a collection of works on logic, included a treatise called Categories that attempted high-level classification of biology. He introduced the ontology genus and species but the sense now attached to the words is due to the work of 18th-century Swedish biologist Linnaeus.

Stepwise refinement, the process whereby a goal is decomposed into subgoals that might be solved independently or in sequence is a manifestation of split-and-prune. In the language of game playing, the game graph is divided into subgraphs (not necessarily disjoint). Search then consists of a number of searches. The first finds a sequence of subgraphs that join a subgraph containing the start node to a subgraph containing the finish node. Then for each subgraph a path traversing it has to be found. There is the complication that the terminal node of one subgraph must be the initial node of another. This can enforce sequencing on the search. If the subgoals can be further subdivided, the process becomes recursive.

The complexity-reducing technique of stepwise refinement was known to the Romans as *divide et impera* (divide and rule) but is known today as *divide and conquer*. (Its historical form suggests the Roman preoccupation with ruling; presumably, they found conquering a lesser problem.) Using loop checking, keeping a record of all nodes eliminated from the multiset of states, generate-and-test becomes a special case of divide and conquer. In this extreme case, the graph is partitioned into one set containing the current node and its nearest neighbors and another set containing all the other nodes of the graph.

Stepwise refinement excels in certain situations, such as chess endgames, where lookahead fails miserably. By design, the graph of subgraphs has fewer nodes than the original graph- searches are then less complex than the original. Stepwise refinement is a manifestation of Descartes' *Principle of Analytic Reduction,* an historic characterization of scientific tradition [Pritchard, 1968]. The principle attempts to describe reality with simple and composite natures and proposes rules that relate the latter to the former. The process of identifying the simple phenomena in complex phenomena was what Descartes meant by the word "analysis". Ockham's Razor, a minimization heuristic of the 14th century is often invoked to decide between competing stepwise refinements:

Entities should not be multiplied unnecessarily.

Interpreted in this context, it requires theories with fewer primitives be preferred to those with more. The psychological experiments of Miller [1956] suggest that in a diverse range of human activities, performance falls off dramatically when we deal with a number of facts or objects greater than seven. This limit actually varies between five and nine for different individuals. Consequently, it is known as the "seven-plus-or minus two principle".

Constraint solving and theorem proving were brought together in the planning system STRIPS [Fikes and Nilsson, 1971]. STRIPS was the planning component for the Shakey robot project at SRI. STRIPS overall control structure was modeled on Newell and Simons GPS and used Green's QA3 [1969] as a subroutine for establishing preconditions for actions.

1.6 Symbolism

The aim of symbolism was to resolve the conflict between the material and spiritual world.

[Chilvers and Osborne, 1988]

Within a year of Shannon's suggestion that the principles of game playing would be useful in language translation, the first full-time researcher in machine translation of natural language, Bar-Hillel, was appointed at MIT. The first demonstration of the feasibility of automatic translation was provided in 1954 by collaboration between Georgetown University and IBM. Using a vocabulary of 250 words, a carefully selected set of 49 Russian sentences was translated into English. The launch of the Russian Sputnik in 1957 provoked the US into large scale funding of automatic natural language translation.

During the next decade some research groups used ad-hoc approaches to machine translation. Among these were IBM; the US Air Force; the Rand Corporation and the Institute of Precision Mechanics in the Soviet Union. The Universities of Cambridge, Grenoble, Leningrad, and MIT adopted theoretical approaches. Influential among the theoretical linguistics groups was the one at MIT led by Chomsky [1957]. Chomsky's review of a book on language by the foremost behavioral psychologist of the day became better known than the book.

In the first half of the 20th century, American psychology was dominated by Watson's theory of behaviorism. Watson held that learning springs from conditioning and that conditioning is the most important force in shaping a person's identity (nurture not nature). The Russian Nobel Prize winner Pavlov was the first to demonstrate conditioning with his infamous experiments on dogs. In his book *Science and Human Behavior*, Skinner [1953] tries to reduce the psychology of organisms to stimulus response pairs. In 1957, Skinner published *Verbal Behavior*, a detailed account of the behaviorist approach to language learning. Chomsky had just published his own theory, *Syntactic Structures* [Chomsky, 1957]. In his review of Skinner's book, Chomsky argued that behaviorist theory did not address creativity in language – it did not explain how a child could understand and make up sentences it had not heard before. The review helped kill off research funding for behaviorism.

The symbolic movement represented linguistic grammars as rewrite rules. This representation was first used by ancient Indian grammarians (especially Panini circa 350 BC) for Shastric Sanskrit [Ingerman, 1967]. The oldest known rewrite grammar is the set of natural numbers. The number 1 is the single initial sentence and the single rewrite rule appends 1 to a previously constructed number. This method of counting, where there is a one to one correspondence between a number and the number of symbols used to represent it, appeared in many societies. Some historians of the written word (e.g., [Harris, 1986]) suggest that numeracy predates literacy. In evidence, Harris claims that societies that did not develop counting beyond the number three did not achieve literacy by their own efforts.

Rewrite rules require a notion of pattern matching which in turn requires the notions of subformula and an equivalence relation on formulas. Formulas are not restricted to strings; they can be graphs. Two formulas, p and q, can be matched if f is a subformula of p, g a subformula of q and f and g are in the same equivalence class. Construed in the terminology of game playing, one has an initial formula and a final formula. The goal is to find a sequence of symbol replacements that will transform the initial formula to the final formula.

Rewrite rules had been formalized by Post [1943] under the name of production systems. Maslov [1987] speculates on why many of Post's results were rediscovered in the 'Symbolic Movement':

> *There are times in the history of science when concrete knowledge is valued above everything else, when empiricism triumphs and abstract schemes are held in contempt. Then other periods come, when scientists are interested primarily in theoretical concepts and the tasks of growing a body of facts around these ideas are put aside. (These periodic changes in scientific fashion are an important component of the spiritual climate of a society and important correlations can be found between different aspects of these changes.) In this respect, science changed drastically after World War II, leading to the creation of the theory of systems, cybernetics and in particular the theory of deductive systems.*

The earliest reference to unification, in fact, dates back to Post. Post recorded his thoughts on the nature of mathematics, symbols and human reasoning in a diary (partially published in [Davis, 1973]).

Maslov [1988] uses the alternative names *calculus* or *deductive system* for rewrite rules. A deductive system has some initial symbols $\{A_1, \dots A_n\}$ and some schema for deriving new symbols from the initial ones and those already constructed. In correspondence with theorem proving, the initial symbols are called axioms, the schema are inference rules and the set of derivable symbols, theorems. For Post, symbols expressed a finite amount of information. As such, they could be encoded by words, finite sequences of typographical letters drawn from an alphabet. Each letter itself carries no information; their only property is the distinction of one letter from another.

The work of the 'Symbolic Movement', arguably, contributed more to computer science than it did to linguistics. A hierarchy of increasingly complex grammars were identified and classes of machine that can parse them developed:

Regular expressions	Finite state machine
Context free grammar	Stack machine
Context sensitive grammar	Linear bounded automata
Recursively enumerable set	Turing machine

An algorithm is a special case of a deductive system when at most one inference rule is applicable to each axiom or theorem. The theory of algorithms of Turing and Church has analogues in deductive systems. A set of words is said to be *recursively denumerable*, if its members can be derived by a deductive system. Enumeration can conveniently be achieved breadth-first with the inference rules used in a fixed order. Markov [1954] gives a theory of algorithms based on deductive systems where the rules are applied in a fixed order. The Church–Turing thesis [Church, 1936] is equivalent to the belief that any set that can be generated or enumerated by any constructive means is recursively denumerable.

A relatively complex deductive system is Gentzen's sequent calculus [Gentzen 1934; Szabo, 1970]. The well-formed formulas of predicate calculus are the theorems of a simpler deductive system (the rules of formation) which themselves use a deductively generated set of variables (e.g., the natural numbers) as the components of its alphabet. The hierarchy leads to two levels of implication, one material implication at the object level, the formal language, and another consequence at the metalevel. Once one level of implication is formalized, it is inevitable that its properties be discussed at the metalevel. Complementary literal elimination at the object level is reflected in the cut rule at the metalevel. Gentzen's calculus is typical of multilevel constructions whose theorems are the symbols of the uppermost layer of a hierarchy of deductive systems built from simpler deductive systems that generate the symbols [Maslov, 1988].

Gentzen was a student of Hilbert [Reid, 1970] who pioneered the formalization of mathematics as a symbol manipulation system. Hilbert's program was to provide a mathematical system that was *complete* (all truths should be provable), *consistent* (nothing false can be proved), and *decidable* (there should be a mechanical procedure for deciding if an assertion is true or false). Turing [1950] had proposed the idea that symbol manipulation was a sufficient process for artificial intelligence. Newell and Simon [1976] raised this view to the status of an hypothesis (in much the same sense as Church–Turing computability hypothesis):

A physical system exercises its intelligence in problem solving by search, that is, by generating and progressively modifying symbol structures according to rules until it produces a solution structure. The task of the symbol system is to use its limited processing resources to generate tentative solutions, one after another, until it finds one that satisfies the problem-defining test. A system would exhibit intelligence to the extent that solutions have a high likelihood of appearing early in the search or by eliminating search altogether.

The Physical Symbol Hypothesis had essentially been proposed earlier by the psychologist Craik [1943]:

> *My hypothesis then is that thought models, or parallels, reality –*
> *that its essential feature is not 'the mind', 'the self', 'sense data',*
> *nor propositions but symbolism, and that this symbolism is largely*
> *of the same kind as that which is familiar to us in mechanical devices which aid thought and calculation.*

Corresponding to the Universal Turing machine, there is a universal deductive system that can imitate any other deductive system by encoding its rules of inference as axioms. This universal deductive machine is (tersely) simplified by Smullyan [1956a]. A more leisurely exposition is given by Fitting [1987]. According to Smullyan, a string s is an element of a recursively denumerable set if and only if $p(s)$ is a theorem of a definite clause theory (with string concatenation as a primitive). *Universal modus ponens* (substitution and detachment) is the only inference rule required for definite clauses. (Smullyan's name for definite clauses over strings is Elementary Formal System.) Definite clause grammars were rediscovered by Colmerauer [1975] and developed in the context of logic programming by Pereira and Warren [1980]. Smullyan [1956b] gives, what is in effect, a minimal (Herbrand) model semantics for sets of definite clauses. Definite clauses are even more generous than is necessary. Tärnlund [1977] showed that binary clauses are Turing complete. A *binary* clause is a definite clause with one positive and one negative literal.

In the Symbolic Movement, optimism with machine translation was high but predictions of imminent breakthroughs were never realized. As the inherent complexity in linguistics became apparent, disillusionment grew. A disparaging anecdote of the time concerned an automatic Russian–English translator. Given the adage "out of sight out of mind" to translate into Russian and back to English it produced "the invisible are insane". The 'brittleness' of these small systems was claimed to be due to over-specialization. The problem is that natural language is ambiguous and leaves much unsaid. Understanding language was claimed to require understanding the subject matter and the context, not just the structure of the utterance. This may now seem obvious but was not obvious in the early 1960s. In a review of progress Bar-Hillel [1960] argued that the common-sense barriers to machine translation could only be overcome by the inclusion of encyclopedic knowledge. A report in 1966 by an advisory committee of the National Research Council found that:

> *There has been no machine translation of a general scientific text*
> *and none is in immediate prospect.*

All US government funding for academic translation projects was cancelled.

1.7 Neo-Classicism

> *... characterized by a desire to recreate the heroic spirit as well as*
> *the decorative trappings of the Art of Greece and Rome.*
>
> [Chilvers and Osborne, 1988]

Wang [1960], who claimed to have more success with the classical approach to proving the first 52 theorems in *Principia Mathematica*, than the Logic Theorist refuted the work of Newell and Simon:

> *There is no need to kill a chicken with a butcher's knife. Yet the impression is that Newell, Shaw and Simon even failed to kill the chicken.*

The authors are not quite sure what this means but the intention is clear. Wang was a prominent member of the classical school. The Neo-classical Movement proposed logic as a sufficient language for representing common sense. Hayes [1985] called this common-sense *naive physics*. In repost to claims that modern physics is not natural, Einstein claimed that common sense is the set of prejudices laid down in the first eighteen years of life.

The Neo-classical Movement grew, largely, out of the work of McCarthy. McCarthy was the principal organizer of the first workshop on AI held at Dartmouth College. In 1958, McCarthy put forward a computer program, the *Advice Taker* that like the Geometry Theorem prover of Gelerntner was designed to use knowledge to search for solutions to problems. The central theme of the Advice Taker was that first-order predicate calculus promised to be a universal language for representing knowledge. In this proposal, a computer system would perform deductions from axioms encoding common-sense knowledge to solve everyday problems. An example used by McCarthy to illustrate the point, the monkey and bananas problem, is a classic of AI. (In this problem, a monkey has to devise a plan to reach a bunch of bananas that are not directly accessible.) The Advice Taker was designed so that it could accept new axioms in the normal course of operation allowing it to achieve competence in new areas without being reprogrammed.

According to Gardner [1982], Leibniz was the first to envision a *Universal Algebra* by which all knowledge, including moral and metaphysical truths could be expressed. Leibniz proposed a mechanical device to carry out mental operations but his calculus, which was based on equality, was so weak that it could not produce interesting results. The development of logic has its roots in the 19th century with the disturbing discovery of non-Euclidean geometries.

Three of the early pioneers of logic were De Morgan, Boole, and Jevons [Kolmogorov and Yushkevich, 1992]. The word logic comes from the ancient Greek, *logike* meaning the art of reasoning. Historians have argued that logic developed in ancient Greece because of the democratic form of government. Citizens could shape public policy through rhetoric. Aristotle had tried to formulate the laws, Syllogisms, governing rational argument. After his death, his students assembled his teachings in a treatise, the *Organon* (meaning tool). Syllogisms allow one to mechanically generate conclusions from premises. While Aristotle's logic deals with generalizations over objects, the deductive system is weak because it does not allow the embedding of one generalization inside another. Aristotle did not believe that the entire mind was governed by deductive processes but also believed in intuitive or common sense reason.

A major barrier to the generalization of syllogisms was a fixation on one-place predicates. De Morgan [1846] gave the first systematic treatment of the logic of relations and highlighted the sorts of inferences that Aristotle's logic could not handle. Frege gave substance to Leibniz's dream by extricating quantifiers from Aristotle's syllogisms. In *Critique of Pure Reason*, Kant [1781] proposed that geometry and arithmetic are bodies of propositions that are neither contingent nor analytic. Frege did not accept Kant's philosophy that arithmetic was known synthetic a priori. Frege believed that the meaning of natural language was compositional and put forward a formal language, the *Begriffsschrift* (concept notation), to demonstrate his ideas. Frege's *Begriffsschrift* [1879] introduced the nesting of quantifiers but the notation was awkward to use. The American logician Peirce [1883] independently developed the same logic of relations as Frege but today's notation is substantially due to Peano [1889].

Frege's axiomatization of sets leads to paradoxes, the most famous of which was discovered by Russell:

> Let *S* be the set of elements that are not members of themselves. Is
> *S* a member of itself or not?

Both yes and no hypothesis to the question lead to contradictions. This paradox is similar to the Liar Paradox that was known to the ancient Greeks. The paradox concerns a person who asserts: "I am lying." The problem is again one of circularity. Although Whitehead and Russell duplicated an enormous amount of Frege's work in *Principia Mathematica*, it was through this work that Frege's ideas came to dominate mathematics. Russell at first thought the paradox he described was a minor problem that could be dealt with quickly. His collaborator on *Principia Mathematica*, Whitehead, thought otherwise. Quoting from Browning's poem, *The Lost Leader*, Whitehead remarked gravely:

> *Never glad confident morning again.*

Russell eventually proposed a hierarchy, a stratification of terms, which associates with each a *type*. The type partitions terms into atoms, sets, sets of sets etc. Propositions of the form "*x* is a member of *y*" are then restricted so that if *x* is of type atom, *y* must be of type set and if *x* is of type set *y* must be of type set of sets and so on. The hierarchy breaks the circularity in the paradox and is another manifestation of hierarchy in deductive systems as described by Maslov [1988].

Both Frege's and Whitehead and Russell's presentation of inference was axiomatic, also known as Hilbert style. Frege took implication and negation as primitive connectives and used *modus ponens* and substitution as inference rules. Whitehead and Russell used negation and disjunction as primitive connectives and disjunctive syllogism as inference rule. In 1935, Gentzen developed natural deduction, a more natural formulation of the Frege–Hilbert, axiomatic style. Natural deduction involves identifying subgoals that imply the desired result and then trying to prove each subgoal. It is a manifestation of the stepwise refinement formulation of generate-and-test.

McCarthy's ideas for using logic to represent common-sense knowledge and Robinson's resolution mechanism were first brought together by Green [1969]. Rather than a theorem prover, Green implemented a problem solving system, *QA3*, which used a resolution theorem-prover as its inference mechanism. His paper was the first to show how mechanical theorem-proving techniques could be used to answer other than yes-no questions. The idea involved adding an extra nonresolvable accumulator literal with free variables corresponding to the original question. If the refutation theorem proving terminates, the variables in the accumulator literal are bound to an answer, a counterexample.

Green, further, introduced state variables as arguments to literals in formulating robot-planning problems in predicate logic. Green's QA3 was the *brains* of Shakey [Moravec, 1981] an experimental robot at Stanford Research Institute. McCarthy and Hayes [1969] refined Green's ideas into *situation calculus* where states of the world, or situations were reasoned about with predicate logic. In such a representation, one has to specify precisely what changes and what does not change. Otherwise no useful conclusions can be drawn. In analogy with the unchanging backgrounds of animated cartoons, the problem is known as *the frame problem*. Many critics considered the problem insoluble in first-order logic. The *frame problem* led McCarthy and Reiter to develop theories of nonmonotonic reasoning – circumscription and default logic, where the frame axioms become implicit in the inference rules. Circumscription is a minimization heuristic akin to Ockham's Razor. In the model theoretic formulation, it only allows deductions that are common to all minimal models. The superficial simplicity and economy of nonmonotonic logics contrasts with the encyclopedic knowledge advocated in machine translation.

By a notoriously simple counterexample, the *Yale Shooting Problem* [Hanks and McDermott, 1986], the circumscriptive solution to the frame problem was later shown to be inadequate. In one form, the problem involves a turkey and an unloaded gun. In a sequence of events the gun is loaded, one or more other actions may take place and then the gun is fired at the turkey. The common-sense consequence is that the turkey is shot. The problem is that there are two minimal models one in which the turkey is shot and another in which it is not. In the unintended minimal model, the gun is unloaded in-between loading and shooting. As theories were elaborated to accommodate counterexamples, new counterexamples were elaborated to defy the new theories.

1.8 Impressionism

> *... they were generally in sympathy with the Realist attitude ... the primary purpose of art is to record fragments of nature or life.*
>
> [Chilvers and Osborne, 1988]

The frame and other problems of neo-classicism led to a general disillusionment with logic as a representational formalism. Crockett [1994] cites the frame problem as one symptom of the inevitable failure of the whole AI enterprise. The Yale shooting problem led to grave doubts about the appropriateness of nonmonotonic logics [McDermott, 1988]. Proposed solutions to the Yale shooting problem foundered on a further counterexample, the Stolen Car problem [Kautz, 1986]. The mood of disillusionment with logic is reflected in the satirical title of McDermott's [1988] article which was derived from Kant's *Kritik der reinen Vernunft*. It echoes an earlier attack on AI by Dreyfus [1972] under the title, *What Computers Can't Do: A Critique of Artificial Reason*. While logic as a computational and representational formalism was out of fashion, alternative ad hoc formalisms of knowledge representation were advocated.

The 'Rococo Movement' believed that the secret of programming computers to play good chess was look-ahead. If a program could develop the search tree further than any grandmaster, it would surely win. The combinatorial explosion limited the depth to which breadth-first tree development was able to produce a move in a reasonable amount of time. In the 1940s, a Dutch psychologist, de Groot [1946], made studies of chess novices and masters. He compared the speed with which masters and novices could reconstruct board positions from five-second glances at a state of play. As might be expected, chess masters were more competent than novices were. The mistakes masters made involved whole groups of pieces in the wrong position on the board but in correct relative positions. When chess pieces were randomly assigned to the chessboard, rather than arising from play, the masters faired no better than the novices did. This suggests that particular patterns of play recur in chess games and it is to these macroscopic patterns that masters become attuned.

Behaviorist mental models of long-term and short-term memory [Neisser, 1967] were a major influence on the Impressionist School of AI. In a simplified form [Newell and Simon, 1963], the memory model has a small short term memory (or database) that contains active memory symbols and a large long term memory that contains production rules for modifying the short term memory. *Production rules* take the form of condition-action pairs. The conditions specify preconditions that the short-term memory must satisfy before the actions can be effected. The actions are specific procedures to modify the short-term memory.

Production rules were grouped into decision tables and used in database management systems [Brown, 1962]. The rules are supplemented with a *control strategy* – an effective method of scheduling rule application. Rules are labeled and metarules control their application. Markov algorithms are a special case where a static precedence on use of the rules is given. For ease of implementation, the conditions of production systems are usually expressible with a small number of primitives such as syntactic equality and order relations. Boolean combinations form compound conditions. Using patterns in the working set to direct search was reflected in *pattern directed systems* [Waterman and Hayes-Roth, 1978]. Patterns in the working set determine which rule to fire next.

AI and associationist psychology have an uneasy alliance that comes from the observation that neurons have synaptic connections with one another, making the firing of neurons associate. In the late 1940s, a neurosurgeon, Penfield, examined the effects of operations he performed on patients by inserting electrodes into their brains. Using small electrical impulses, similar to those produced by neurons, he found that stimulation of certain areas of the brain would reliably create specific images or sensations, such as color and the recollection of events. The idea that the mind behaves associatively dates back at least to Aristotle. Aristotle held that behavior is controlled by associations learned between concepts. Subsequent philosophers and psychologists refined the idea. Brown [1820] contributed the notion of labeling links between concepts with semantic information. Selz [1926] suggested that paths between nodes across a network could be used for reasoning. In addition to inventing predicate logic, in the 1890s Peirce rediscovered the semantic nets of the Shastric Sanskrit grammarians [Roberts, 1973]. These ideas were taken up by Quillian [1968] who applied *semantic networks* to automatic language translation. The purpose was to introduce language understanding into translation to cope with examples like the previously cited "out of sight out of mind".

Semantic nets had intuitive appeal in that they represented knowledge pictorially by graphs. The nodes of a semantic net represent objects, entities or concepts. Directed links represent binary (and unary) relations between nodes. Binary constraint networks are one example. Storing related concepts close together is a powerful means of directing search. The emphasis of the model is on the large-scale organization of knowledge rather than the contents [Findler, 1979]. Semantic nets have a counterpart in databases in the network representation. A more recent manifestation of semantic nets is entity relationship diagrams, which is used in the design of databases [Chen, 1976; 1977].

Limitations of the use of early versions of semantic nets were quickly apparent. There was no information that guided the search for what you wanted to find. Simple semantic nets treat general and specific terms on the same level, so one cannot draw distinctions between quantifications; e.g., between one object, all objects and no such object. In the late 1860s, Mills showed that the use of a single concept to refer to multiple occurrences leads to ambiguity. Some arcs were regarded as transitive and others not. McDermott [1976] pointed out that the taxonomic, transitive *is-a* link was used for both element and subset relationships. Brachmann [1983] examined the taxonomic, transitive, *is-a* link found in most semantic networks. He concluded that a single representational link was used to represent a variety of relations in confusing and ambiguous ways.

1.9 Post-Impressionism

> *... both a development from Impressionism and a reaction against it. Post-Impressionism was based on scientific principles and resulted in highly formalized compositions.*
>
> [Chilvers and Osborne, 1988]

Minsky was one of the foremost critics of the use of logic for representing commonsense knowledge. A widely disseminated preprint [Minsky, 1975] had an appendix entitled *Criticism of the Logistic Approach* (the appendix did not appear in the published version):

> *Because logicians are not concerned with systems that will later be enlarged, they can design axioms that permit only the conclusions they want. In the development of intelligence, the situation is differ-*

ent. One has to learn which features of situations are important, and which kinds of deductions are not to be regarded seriously.

Some of the confusion with semantic nets was dispelled with *frames* [Minsky, 1975]. Frames were intended for the large-scale organization of knowledge and were originally introduced for scene representation in computer vision. They adopted a rather more structured approach to collecting facts about a particular object and event types and arranging the types into a taxonomic hierarchy analogous to a biological hierarchy. In frames, intransitive links were encapsulated in nodes. The fields (slots) of the frame are filled with the values of various default attributes associated with the object. Contrary to some opinion, frames are related to the frame problem of situation calculus. In the frame representation, only certain attributes need change their value in response to actions. Procedural knowledge on how the attributes are (or are not) updated as a result of actions are included in the frame. The restriction of links to *is-a* relations relates a class to a more general one. This produces a partial order on classes that organizes them into a hierarchy of specialization. Properties associated with general types can be inherited by more specialized ones. By adding a second (non-transitive) *instance* relation, the frame representation can be extended to allow the distinction to be made between general and specific. The instance relations allow default values to be inherited from generic class frames and the determination of all instances of a given class.

Minsky supervised a series of Ph.D. projects, known as microworlds, which used frames to represent limited domains of knowledge. Slagle's [1963] SAINT system solved closed form integration problems typical of college calculus courses. Evans' [1968] ANALOGY system solved geometric analogy problems that appear in IQ tests. Raphael's [1968] SIR (Semantic Information Retrieval) was able to accept statements in a restricted subset of English and answer questions on them. Bobrow's [1967] STUDENT system solved algebra story problems. The most famous microworld was the Blocks World. It consisted of a set of children's building blocks stacked on a tabletop. A task in this world is to rearrange the stack in a certain way using a robot arm than can only pick up one block at a time.

The Blocks World was the setting for many applications: Huffman's [1971] vision system; Waltz's constraint propagation vision system; the learning system of Winston [1975]; the natural language understanding program of Winograd and the planner of Fahlman [1974]. The use of constraint solving in Waltz's [1972] extension of Huffman's [1971] and Clowes [1971] computer vision systems was claimed to demonstrate that combinatorial explosion can be controlled. The system attempts to recognize objects in scenes from contours. Waltz's [1972] extension incorporated shadows to the scene analysis program. This contributed such an enormous increase in complexity to the problem that simple backtracking search became intractable.

Widely criticized as a trivial combination of semantic nets and object-oriented programming [Dahl et al., 1970], Minksy's frames paper served to place knowledge representation as a central issue for AI. Briggs [1985] suggests that knowledge representation research began with ancient Indian analysis of Shastric Sanskrit in the first millennium BC. Shastric Sanskrit grammatical theory proposed not only a formal syntax and vocabulary but also analysis of its semantics using semantic nets. In contrast, the linguist Schank [Schank and Abelson, 1977] claimed: *There is no such thing as syntax.* Schank and his students built a series of natural language understanding programs [Schank and Abelson, 1977; Schank and Riesbeck, 1981; Dyer, 1983] which represented stereotypical situations [Cullingford, 1981] describing human memory [Rieger, 1976; Kolodner, 1983], plans and goals [Wilensky, 1983]. LUNAR [Woods, 1972] allowed geologists to ask English language questions about rock samples brought back from the Apollo Moon Mission.

Although the original frame representation provided only single inheritance, later extensions allowed more than one superclass (this is called multiple and mixed inheritance). While multiple inheritance allows the user to gain further expressiveness, it brings a new range of problems. The inheritance network effectively becomes an arbitrary directed graph. Retrieving a value from a slot then involves search. Frames do not incorporate any distinction between 'essential' properties (those an individual must possess to be considered an instance of a class) and accidental properties (those that all instances of the class just happen to possess). The psychological intuition behind this is that conceptual encoding in the human brain is not concerned with defining strictly exhaustive properties of exemplars of some category. Categorization is concerned with the salient properties that are typical of the class. Brachmann [1985] pointed out that this makes it impossible to express universal truths, or even construct composite ideas out of simpler conceptual units in any reliable way.

A long-term research effort that attempted to build a system with encyclopedic knowledge using the frame representation is *Cyc* (from encyclopedia) [Lenat and Guha, 1990]. Cyc was a privately funded project at MCC that was part of the US response to the Japanese FGCS. Despite ten years effort and hundreds of millions of dollars in funding, Cyc failed to find large-scale application. The failure to choose a sufficiently expressive common representation language was admitted to be an oversight near the end of the project [Lenat, 1995]:

> *Another point is that a standard sort of frame-and-slot language proved to be awkward in various contexts: ... Such experiences caused us to move toward a more expressive language, namely first-order predicate calculus with a series of second order extensions ...*

Two years after Minsky's defining paper, Hayes [1977] gave a formal interpretation of what frames were about. Hayes argues that a representational language must have a semantic theory. For the most part, he found that frame representation is just a new syntax for a subset of first-order logic. While subsequently hotly disputed, Hayes' conclusion is that, except for reflexive reasoning, frames had not achieved much. *Reflexive* reasoning is one in which a reasoning agent can reason about its own reasoning process.

While generally not as expressive as first-order predicate calculus, semantic nets and frames do carry extra indexing information that makes many common types of inference more efficient. In defense of logic, Stickel [1982, 1986] and Walther [1984] give examples of how similar indexing can be done in implementations of systems that carry out inferences on predicate calculus expressions. One benefit of the frame organization of knowledge is economy of storage. Hierarchical organization gives improvement in system understanding and ease of maintenance. A feature of frames not shared by logic is object-identity, the ability to distinguish between two instances of a class with the same properties.

On the general endeavor of knowledge representation, Dreyfus [1988], an MIT philosopher, notes:

> *Indeed, philosophers from Socrates through Leibniz to early Wittgenstein carried on serious epistemological research in this area for two thousand years without notable success.*

With a slight exaggeration, Plato's theory of forms can be identified with frames: forms represent ideal perfect classes of object; earthly instances of forms are imperfect copies.

1.10 Precisionism

> *... in which urban and industrial subjects were depicted with a smooth precise technique.*

> [Chilvers and Osborne, 1988]

In the Precisionist Movement there was pressure from AI's principal funding agency, DARPA (the United States Defense Advanced Research Projects Agency), to make research pay off. DARPA's lead was followed by other governments' funding bodies that implicitly and explicitly directed AI to tackle real world, engineering problems instead of toy or mathematical problems. Feigenbaum and others at Stanford began the Heuristic Programming Project (HPP) to investigate the extent to which microworld technology could be applied to real world problems.

The first *expert system*, *Dendral*, was initiated in 1965 at Stanford University and grew in power throughout the 1970s [Lindsay et al., 1980]. Given data from mass spectroscopy, the system attempted to determine the structural formula for chemical molecules. The improvement in performance was brought about by replacing first level structural rules by second level (larger grain and possibly incomplete) rules elicited from experts. Dendral was followed by other successful expert systems in the 1970s that epitomized the 'Precisionist Movement'. *Mycin* [Shortliffe et al., 1973] gives advice on treating blood infections. Rules were acquired from extensive interviewing of experts who acquired their knowledge from cases. The rules had to reflect the uncertainty associated with the medical knowledge. Another probabilistic reasoning system *Prospector* [Duda et al., 1979] was a consultation system for helping geologists in mineral exploration. It generated enormous publicity by recommending exploratory drilling at a geological site that proved to contain a large molybdenum deposit. The first commercial expert system *Xcon* (originally called R1) [McDermott, 1981], is an advice system for configuring the DEC's VAX range of computers. By 1986, it was estimated to be saving the company $40 million a year.

The difficulty in building expert systems led to proprietary pluralist, high-level programming environments such as *Loops*, *Kee*, and *Art*. These environments provide the user with a myriad of tools that had been found useful in building expert systems. Such systems are criticized because they provide no guidance on how to compose the tools. This was claimed to encourage ad-hoc programming styles in which little attention is paid to structure. Clancey [1983] analyzed Mycin's rules and found it useful to separate base-level medical knowledge from metalevel diagnostic strategy. MetaX can be understood as "X about X." (This understanding does not apply to metastable states.) So for instance, metaknowledge is knowledge about knowledge, metareasoning is reasoning about reasoning. This separation followed a previous trend in program design. Wirth [1976], coined the adage

$$program = algorithm + datastructure$$

in the title of a book on programming. Kowalski [1979] continued the reductionist view with

$$algorithm = logic + control$$

in particular regard to the programming language Prolog. Using the separation of knowledge, *Meta-Dendral* [Buchanan and Mitchell, 1978] was able to learn rules that explain mass spectroscopy data used by the expert system Dendral [Buchanan et al., 1971].

A metareasoning facility allows reflection on the reasoning process that Hayes claimed was the only distinctive attribute of frames. The universal deductive system noted earlier is a meta-interpreter for a deductive system. More specifically, there are two theories: one, called the *object theory*, and another, the *metatheory* that concerns the object theory. Metaknowledge can be strategic and tactical, knowledge about how to use the base knowledge. An example is the metarule, *always try this rule before any other*. The base level knowledge could be from a conventional database or a set of production rules so that a distinction of degree arises. The term *expert system* is generally reserved for systems with many more rules than facts. *Deductive databases* have many more facts than rules. The term *knowledge-based system* was coined to encompass both extremes and dissociate the movement from the hyperbole that had become associated with AI. The distinction between a knowledgebase and a database is that in the former not all knowledge is represented explicitly. The emotive term *knowledge engineering* typifies the Movement. Feigenbaum [1980] defined it as the reduction of a large body of experience to a precise body of rules and facts.

The main difference between McCarthy's *Advice Taker* [1958] and Newell et al.'s *Logic Theorist* [1956] was the way in which heuristics were embodied. McCarthy wanted to describe the process of reasoning with sentences in a formally defined metalanguage, predicate calculus. For McCarthy the metalanguage and object language coincide. Hayes [1973] introduced a metalanguage for coding rules of inference and for expressing constraints on the application of those rules. He showed that by slightly varying the constraints it was possible to describe markedly different reasoning methods. He proposed a system called *Golux* based on this language, but it was never implemented.

According to Jackson [1986], successful expert systems are generally those with restricted domains of expertise. Here, there is a substantial body of empirical knowledge connecting situations to actions (which naturally lend themselves to production systems) and where deeper representations of knowledge such as spatial, temporal or causal can be neglected. With such systems it is known in advance exactly what external parameters are required to solve the problem (i.e., the items the system is expected to configure). The expertise of such a system is in making local decisions that do not violate global constraints and global decisions that allow local solutions (stepwise refinement).

By 1988, DEC's AI group had deployed 40 expert systems with more on the way. DuPont had 100 in use and 500 in development, saving an estimated $10 million a year. Nearly every major US corporation had its own knowledge engineering group and was either using or investigating expert system technology. A high point of the 'Precisionist Movement' came in 1981 with Japanese Fifth Generation National Initiative to build machines that give hardware support to knowledge-based systems [Moto-oka, 1982]. So as not to be left behind, other governments initiated national and multinational (EC) research programs of their own. In the US, the Microelectronics and Computer Technology Corporation (MCC) was formed as a research consortium. In the UK, the Alvey Report reinstated some knowledge-based systems funding that had been cut as a result of the Lighthill report. In Europe, Esprit supported industrial and academic collaborations. Industry sales of knowledge-based systems related components went from a $3 million in 1980 to $2 billion in 1988. Sales included software tools to build expert systems, specialized AI workstations based on Lisp and industrial robotic vision systems.

One of the difficulties of expert systems is eliciting knowledge from experts. Domain experts were visibly able to perform complex diagnostic tasks but found it difficult to explain how they had done so. With early systems, Dendral and Mycin, knowledge engineers conducted long interviews with domain experts to extract rules but the results often contained omissions and inconsistencies that had to be laboriously debugged. Quinlan [1982] observed:

> *While the typical rate of knowledge elucidation by this method is a few rules per man-day, an expert system for a complex task may require hundreds or even thousands of rules. It is obvious that the interview approach cannot keep pace with the burgeoning demand for expert systems.*

Feigenbaum [1977] had written:

> *... the acquisition of domain knowledge is the bottleneck problem in the building of applications-oriented intelligent agents.*

The problem has since become known as the Feigenbaum bottleneck.

1.11 New Realism

> *... used to cover a reaction from Abstract Expressionism in favor of*
> *a revival of naturalistic figuration embued with a spirit of objectiv-*
> *ity.*

[Chilvers and Osborne, 1988]

A new realism was heralded in the 1980s by a report of a team headed by Rumelhart and McClelland submitted to DARPA and its civilian counterpart the National Science Foundation. The report argued that parallel-distributed programming (PDP), a new name for artificial neural nets, had been seriously neglected for at least a decade. They advocated a switch of resources into the PDP arena. In 1985, a special issue of *Cognitive Science* was devoted to the subject of connectionism, another new name for the field. (When an area of endeavor has been disparaged, an important technique for erasing that memory and suggesting that there is something new is to give it a new name. This technique had been successfully deployed with knowledge-based systems.)

There were several reasons for the neural net renaissance, not the least of which was that it presented an opportunity for the US to regain the leading edge of computer science that had been seized by the Japanese Fifth Generation. The theoretical limitations identified by Minsky and Papert [1969] applied only to a single layer of neurons. In the intervening period, learning algorithms for multilayer systems such as the back propagation rule or generalized delta rule [Rumelhart, Hinton and Williams, 1986] emerged. (Ironically, back-propagation was discovered in the earlier movement [Bryson and Ho, 1969].) Hopfield's work [1982] lent rigor to neural nets by relating them to lattice statistical thermodynamics, at the time a fashionable area of physics. Lastly, demands for greater power appeared to expose the sequential limitations of von Neumann computer architectures.

An apparently convincing proof of concept was provided by the *Nettalk* system [Sejnowski and Rosenberg, 1987]. Nettalk is a text-to-speech translator that takes 10 hours to "learn to speak." The transition of Nettalk's childlike babbling to slightly alien but recognizable pronunciation has been described as eerily impressive. By contrast, a (symbolic) rule based system for the same task, DECtalk, required a 100-person years development effort.

By the mid-1980s, the connectionist renaissance was well under way. This prompted Minsky and Papert [1969, 1987] to issue a revised edition of their book. In the new prologue they state:

> *Some readers may be shocked to hear it said that little of signifi-*
> *cance has happened in this field* [neural nets].

Talk of a sixth generation of connectionism was stifled in Japan, so as not to compromise the much heralded, but late arriving, Fifth Generation.

The euphoria of the New Realism was short lived. Despite some impressive exemplars, large neural networks simulated on von Neumann hardware are slow to learn and tend to converge to metastable states. On training data Nettalk's accuracy goes down to 78%, a level that is intelligible but worse than commercially available programs. Other techniques such as hidden Markov models require less development time but perform just as well. Connectionist systems are unable to explain their reasoning and show little signs of common sense. An anecdotal example is a military application of tank recognition. A neural net had been trained to recognize tanks in a landscape. Testing with non-training data the system failed to recognize tanks reliably. It turned out that all the training photographs with tanks in the scene were taken on sunny days and those without tanks were taken on dull days. The network had learnt to reliably distinguish sunny days from dull days.

1.12 Baroque

> *The emphasis is on balance, through the harmony of parts in subordination to the whole.*
>
> [Chilvers and Osborne, 1988]

Brachmann [1985] claims that the use of frames for common-sense reasoning is fraught with difficulties. The formalism suggested by Minsky was widely criticized as, at best, a trivial extension of the techniques of object-oriented programming, such as inheritance and default values [Dahl et al., 1970; Birtwistle et al., 1973]. General problem solving systems like GPS [Newell and Simon, 1963] had faired no better than machine translation in naive physics. As the programs were expanded to handle more classes of problems, they performed less satisfactorily on any single one. Minsky [1975] remarked:

> *Just constructing a knowledgebase is a major intellectual problem ... We still know far too little about the contents and structure of commonsense knowledge. A "minimal" commonsense system must "know" something about cause-effect, time, purpose, locality, process and types of knowledge ... We need a serious epistemological research effort in this area.*

Expert systems are now so established in industry that they are rarely considered as AI. A general disillusionment with expert systems and AI grew because of the inability to capture naive physics.

That human intelligence is the result of a number of coordinating, possibly competing, intelligences grew out the work of the Swiss psychologist Piaget. Piaget's observations of his own children suggested they go through distinct stages of intellectual development. According to Papert:

> *... children give us a window into the ways the mind really works because they are open ... I think we understand ourselves best by looking at children.*

Piaget influenced Papert in the development of a programming language (*Logo*) for children. One of Piaget's well known experiments [Flavell, 1963] involves two drinking glasses, one tall and thin the other short and fat. A child's choice of the tall glass when the same volume of lemonade is contained in each is attributed to the intuitive mentality that develops in early childhood. In the second, kinesthetic stage, children learn by manipulating objects. In the final stage what they learn is dominated by language and becomes more abstract. The American psychologist Bruner developed Piaget's thesis to the point where these mentalities behave as semi-independent processes in the brain that persist through adult life. They exist concurrently and can cooperate or be in conflict.

A first attempt to coordinate multiple expert systems emerged in the 1970s, when DARPA launched a national effort to develop a natural speech understanding system. The result of this effort was *Hearsay*, a program that met its limited goals after five years. It was developed as a natural language interface to a literature database. Its task was to answer spoken queries about documents and to retrieve documents from a collection of abstracts of artificial intelligence publications. Hearsay gave a major push to the technology of speech understanding and additionally led to new sources of inspiration for AI: sociology and economics. Hearsay [Erman, 1976] comprised several knowledge sources (acoustic, phonetic, phonological, lexical, syntactic and pragmatic) and featured a *Blackboard System* for communication between them. In a blackboard system, a set of processes or agents, typically called knowledge sources (abbreviated KSs) share a common database. Each KS is an expert in a particular area and they cooperate, communicating with each other via the database. The blackboard metaphor refers to problem solving by a group of academics gathered around a blackboard to collectively solve a problem. Writing an idea or fact on the blackboard by one specialist can act as a trigger for another expert to contribute another part of the solution.

An early reference to the blackboard metaphor was Newell [1962]. The short-term memory of the Impressionist Movement can be viewed as a bulletin board that provides a channel of communication between rules. If autonomous agents use production rules, the workspace becomes a means of synchronization and communication. Newell pointed out that, in conventional single agent problem solving paradigms, the agent is wandering over a goal net much as an explorer may wander over the countryside, having a single context and taking it with them wherever they go. The single agent view led AI researchers to concentrate on search or reasoning with a single locus of control. As noted by Newell, the blackboard concept is reminiscent of Selfridge's (neural network) Pandemonium [Selfridge, 1955] where a set of demons independently look at a situation and react in proportion to what they see that fits their natures. Kilmer, McCulloch, and Blum [1969] offered a network in which each node was itself a neural network. From its own input sample, each network forms initial estimates of the likelihood of a finite set of modes. Then networks communicate, back and forth, with other networks to obtain a consensus that is most appropriate. The notion of organizing knowledge into unitary wholes was a theme of Kant's *Critique of Pure Reason* [1787], which was revived in the 20th century by Barlett [1932].

Hewitt [1977] developed the idea of control as a pattern of communication (message passing) amongst a collection of computational agents. Hewitt [1985] uses the term *open system* to describe a large collection of services provided by autonomous agents. Agents use each other without central coordination, trust, or complete knowledge. He argues that networks of interconnected and interdependent computers are qualitatively different from the self-contained computers of the past. The biologist von Bertalanffy expressed a similar sentiment in considering living organisms. In living systems, the whole is always more complex than the union of the parts. Von Bertalanffy drew attention to the distinction between systems that are open to their environment and those that are closed. He defined an open system [1940] as one having to import and export material from its environment.

In the same period after the war that Post published his results on deductive systems, von Bertalanffy proposed a holist view of biology: biology could not be reduced to chemistry. Biological evolution has developed one solution to the management of complex dynamic systems. In living things there is a hierarchy of structures: molecules, organelles (entities making up a cell), cells, organs, and organisms. By dissecting an organism into its representative parts, the form and function of each organ and chemical components can be discovered. In this reductionist process, the living entity vanishes in the search for elements. Reproduction is not within the power of any single molecule or organelle by itself. The reductionist philosophy of Descartes tries to explain social science with psychology, psychology with neurophysiology, neurophysiology with chemistry and chemistry with physics. Longuet-Higgins et al. [1972] satirically carries the argument further, reducing history to economics and economics to sociology.

Biological systems maintain control by confining processes and their data in self-contained cells. These cells act on each other by sending "messages" carried by chemical messengers. The cell membrane protects its data, DNA, from inappropriate processes. *General Systems Theory* is a logico-mathematical study whose objective is the formulation and derivation of those principles that are applicable to general systems, not only biological ones. The name is due to von Bertalanffy [1956]. Although von Bertalanffy introduced the terminology verbally in the 1930s, the first written presentations only appeared after World War II. General Systems Theory is founded on two pairs of ideas: hierarchy and emergence; communication and control. The theory challenges the use of reductionist philosophy in the theory of organizations and biology.

Organisms, von Bertalanffy pointed out, are unlike the closed systems usually studied in physics in which unchanging components settle to a state of equilibrium. Organisms can reach steady states that depend upon continuous exchanges with the environment. Whereas closed systems evolve towards increasing disorder (higher entropy), open systems may take up organized, yet improbable, steady states. Maintenance of a hierarchy, such as molecule to organism, entails a set of processes in which there is communication of information for purposes of regulation and control.

The blackboard technique is a form of opportunistic search. Partial information discovered by one knowledge base can be of sufficient use to guide another so that the two may solve a problem faster than by combining the knowledge. Hewitt and Kornfield [1980] have called this accelerator effect combinatorial implosion. The blackboard technique has the same problem as expert systems: it does not scale. If there is only one blackboard it becomes a severe bottleneck [Hewitt and Liebermann, 1984]. Cooperative Knowledge Based Systems (CKBS) exploit other forms of sociological cooperation. Axelrod [1984] explores the evolution of cooperation. The idea that competition through market forces is a more efficient search strategy than centralized control was an economic dogma of the same (Thatcher) decade.

1.13 Pre-Raphaelite Brotherhood

Their desire for fidelity to nature was expressed through detailed observation of flora etc.

[Chilvers and Osborne, 1988]

From his work on robotics with Papert, Minsky developed a theory of agent based intelligence that he laid out in the *Society of Mind* [1986]. Similar sentiments are to be found in Arbib's conception of the brain's information processing as a collection of concurrent "schemas" [Arbib, 1988]. Brooks [1986] suggests that the idea that intelligence can be split vertically into tasks such as search and knowledge representation is misguided. He claims a more suitable split is horizontal and based on function. The argument is that biological control is associated with the imposition of constraints and requires consideration of at least two hierarchical levels. At a given level, it is often possible to describe the dynamical properties of the system such as the possible transitions or search paths. Any description of control entails an upper level imposing constraints on the lower level. For example, the cell as a whole constrains the physicochemical possibilities available to DNA that makes it the bearer of information. The upper level is the source of an alternative (simpler) description of the lower level by specific functions that are emergent (epiphenomena) due to the imposition of constraints. Some otherwise undistinguished molecules in a cell are constrained to bear the function of repressor or activator. These functions are not available in the chemical properties of the molecules but are the result of hierarchical control.

According to Brooks [1991], AI should proceed as evolution does, beginning by constructing primitive autonomous artificial insects and progressing to more sophisticated mechanisms. Turing's universal computing machine suggested to von Neumann [1966] the idea of a universal construction machine: a machine which, given a sufficiently rich environment of components and furnished with suitable instructions, could replicate itself. While at Cambridge, John Conway invented an autonomous computer game, the *Game of Life* [Gardner, 1970]. A deterministic set of rules served as the physical laws and the microprocessor clock determined the time-scale. Designed as cellular automata, the screen was divided into cells whose states were determined by the states of their neighbors. The rules determine what happens when neighboring cells are alive or dead thereby triggering a cascade of changes throughout the system. One interesting discovery was a *glider*, a cell that moved across the screen. Conway proved that the Game of Life was not predictable; it was undecidable if the patterns were endlessly varying or repeating. Though it had a small number of deterministic rules, it had the capacity to generate unlimited complexity.

The aptly named computer virus is a recent manifestation of artificial life. Like its biological counterpart, a computer virus is incapable of replication without being incorporated in a host program [Ferbrache, 1992]. The code of the computer virus can be compared with the codon or nucleotide structure of DNA of a biological virus. The virus subverts the host program to infect other programs directly. Infection spreads through networks or files on discs. A virus arranges for its code to be executed by subverting machine or operating system initialization, termination, or demon code. Consequently, computer viruses are machine and operating system specific. A virus's behavior can be somewhat benign, only consuming space, or it can wreak havoc. Some computer viruses, such as the one that disrupted the Internet (the DARPA communication protocol that links defense, research, and educational sites in the US), operate from a predetermined, declarative instruction set. The Internet virus vividly demonstrated the vulnerability of computer networks to sabotage.

Random mutations of computer viruses caused by data corruption have been recorded so there is a possibility for evolution. However, computer systems try to prevent evolutionary behavior with error detecting and correcting codes. Genetic algorithms are a deliberate attempt to use evolution as a method of search. A caution against the speed of genetic search is expressed by McCulloch et al. [1962]:

> If you want a sweetheart in the spring, don't get an amoeba and wait for it to evolve.

1.14 Renaissance

> Term meaning 'rebirth' applied to an intellectual and artistic movement.
>
> [Chilvers and Osborne, 1988]

Growing commercialization of the Internet brought about a renaissance in AI with the distillation of the concept of *software agent*. According to Kay [1984]:

> The idea of an agent originated with John McCarthy in the mid-1950s, and the term was coined by Oliver G. Selfridge a few years later, when they were both at the Massachusetts Institute of Technology. They had in view a system that, when given a goal, could carry out the details of the appropriate computer operations and could ask for and receive advice, offered in human terms, when it was stuck. An agent would be a 'soft robot' living and doing its business within the computer's world.

The word agent derives from the Latin verb *agere*: to drive, lead, act, or do. The philosopher Dennett (1987) describes three ways of describing the behavior of systems that cause something to be done: physical, based on physical characteristics and laws; design, based on its functions; and intentional, based on the assumption of rational agent. Doyle [1983] proposed the design of rational agents as the core of AI. Horvitz et al. [1988] proposed the maximization of utility, in the sense of von Neumann and Morgenstern [1944], as the interpretation of rationality.

In *The Nature of Explanation*, Craik [1943] proposed a mental, deliberative, step between the behaviorists' stimulus and response. He argued that mental category such as goals, beliefs and reasoning are bulk properties of intelligence and are just as scientific as pressure and temperature used to describe gases, despite their being made of molecules which possess neither. Bratman [1987] introduced mental states of belief, desire and intention (BDI). Beliefs express an agent's expectation of its environment. Desire expresses preference over future states of the environment. Intentions are partial plans of actions that an agent can perform which are expected to achieve desired states. Craik proposed that intelligent systems execute a cycle: a stimulus is transformed into an internal representation; the representation is integrated with the existing mental representation and this is used to effect an action. This model was used as the basis of the influential robotics project, Shakey at SRI [Nilsson, 1984]. Shakey added a planning module to produce the sense-model-plan-act (SMPA) architecture. Shakey's world model was based on propositional logic.

Following Wittgenstein [1953], Austin [1962] noted that natural language utterances could be understood as actions that change the state of belief in the same way that actions change physical state. Searle [1969] derived necessary and sufficient conditions for the successful performance of speech acts, which distinguished five types of speech acts. Cohen and Perrault [1979] utilized this work on linguistic philosophy into an AI planning problem. Cohen and Leveque [1995] developed a theory in which rational agents perform speech acts in furtherance of their desires.

The Renaissance Movement is characterized by *situatedness*, which aims to build autonomous intelligent systems, embedded in real environments. This is exemplified by the *SOAR* agent architecture [Laird et al., 1987, Newell, 1990]. This can be seen as related to the empiricist movement started by Francis Bacon's *Novum Organum*. This philosophical movement is characterized by the philosopher John Locke's dictum:

Nothing is in the understanding, which is not first in the senses.

The theory was taken to extreme by Carnap [1928] and the Vienna Circle who introduced *logical positivism*. This doctrine holds that all knowledge can be characterized by logical theories ultimately connected to observation sentences that correspond to sensory input. Logical positivism held that all meaningful statements could be verified or falsified either by analyzing the meaning of the words or by experiment. Popper [1972] refuted this claim, with an argument which essentially comes from Hume's *A Treatise of Human Nature*. Hume proposed that general rules cannot be proved but are acquired by exposure to repeated associations between their elements – the principle of induction.

1.15 Hindsight

Everything of importance has been said before by somebody who did not discover it.

AN Whitehead (1861–1947)

The factions of AI have been presented by an analogy with the movements of Fine Art elaborating suggestions of Jackson [1986] and Maslov [1987]. Some may feel this is pushing an amusing metaphor too far, but like Fine Art, AI has its fashions and counterfashions, examples and counterexamples, claims and refutations. Papert now claims his and Minsky's attacks on connectionism have been misinterpreted. They were not directed against neural nets but against universality; the idea that there is a single mechanism that has universal application:

> *The desire for universality was fed also by the legacy of the scientists, largely mathematicians, who created AI, and it was nurtured by the most mundane material circumstances of funding.*

> [Papert, 1988]

Chapter 2

Fifth Generation Architecture

The architect should be equipped with knowledge of many branches of study and varied kinds of learning, for it is by his judgement that all work done by other arts is put to the test. This knowledge is the child of practice and theory.

Marcus Vitruvius Polio,
Roman architect and engineer of the first century BC

At the beginning of the 1980s, the Japanese Ministry of International Trade and Industry (MITI) usurped the *Fifth Computer Generation* with an initiative to commercialize knowledge-based systems.

Fig. 2.0.1 Fifth Generation tea party[1]

Advances in hardware had characterized the first four computer generations. This generation was to be different from previous ones. It was to be driven by software

---

[1] Any resemblance to a Macintosh is intentional.

technology and threatened to exploit expert systems, the fruits of US research. The initiative was intended to provide solutions to real-world engineering and commercial problems.

> *Fifth Generation computers are regarded as forming the corner-stone of so-called intelligent consumer electronics – sophisticated televisions, video recorders and learning aids etc. – the next generation of wealth-creating consumer products*

[Treleavan, 1983]

It is interesting to note that the same desire for smart consumer electronics motivated the design of Java.

The Fifth Generation initiative sent fearful tremors through the corridors of power of other members of the G7, the world's richest nations. The reaction was reasonable enough. Expert systems seemed to be the reward of AI research and the Japanese had a reputation of exploiting the inventions of other nations. National industries: shipbuilding, automobile manufacture and consumer electronics had crumbled under intense Japanese competition. Feigenbaum and McCorduck [1984] fuelled paranoia with their enthusiasm for knowledge engineering, portraying MITI's objective as a bid for world domination in information technology. As a reflex reaction to the Japanese threat, beleaguered governments initiated national and multinational research programs to channel research funds into information technology.

During the ten-year period of the project, MITI spent more than 50 billion yen (over $300 million). The research institute set up to direct the project, ICOT (Institute for New Computer Technology), had almost 200 researchers seconded from collaborating computer manufacturers such as Fujitsu, Hitachi, Mitsubishi and NEC. At any one time, there were about 100 researchers at ICOT, almost all under the age of 35. About 75 non-Japanese researchers from twelve countries visited ICOT for short periods and seven worked at the institute for one or more years.

At the outset, some believed the Japanese endeavor was doomed to fail because of the initial choice of Prolog as the machine programming language. A retrospective rationale for this design decision is presented in this chapter in a somewhat anecdotal form, since this is the nature of faith. As such, arguments cannot be expected to be irreproachable, original, or even consistent.

2.1 Architecture and Design

The problems of computer design are indicated by Lampson [1983]:

> *The designer usually finds himself floundering in a sea of possibilities, unclear about how one choice will limit his freedom to make other choices, or affect the size and performance of the entire system, or even any major part of it; much more important is to avoid choosing a terrible way, and to have clear division of responsibilities among the parts.*

At the height of the Precisionist Movement (Section 1.10), that a machine designed for knowledge-based applications might be radically different from previous machines, was readily argued:

> *Algorithmic procedures, such as Gaussian Elimination, are procedures about which properties such as efficiency and correctness can be proved mathematically. In contrast, artificial intelligence is mainly concerned with empirical procedures such as those required to drive from Palo Alto to Boston. In general, empirical procedures make use of empirical knowledge and require interaction with the physical world.*

[Hewitt, 1984]

It was argued that AI computations involve intensive memory accesses rather than ALU (arithmetic and logic unit) operations. The characteristics of symbolic processing are very different from numerical requirements for which conventional von Neumann computers were designed:

> *Von Neumann machines being sequential, are inadequate vehicles on which to base the development of large-scale artificial intelligence systems. We need architectures that are inherently parallel and sufficiently general to meet the requirements of distributed systems.*

[Hewitt, 1984]

The US was beginning to invest heavily in parallel machines hoping to steal a march over the Soviets.

Any radical departure from the status quo has to be designed:

> *... anyone who devises a course of action intended to change an existing state of affairs to a preferred one must engage in design ... Design distinguishes the artificial from the natural sciences.*

[Simon, 1981]

Architecture is the science and art of designing buildings and ships. The development of the IBM 7030 (known as STRETCH) computer extended the reference of the term *architecture* beyond buildings and ships to computers. In definition, Brooks [1962] suggests:

> *Computer architecture, like any other architecture, is the art of determining the needs of the user of a structure and then designing it to meet those needs as effectively as possible within economic and technological constraints.*

The goal of STRETCH was to produce a machine with 100 times the performance of the IBM 704. Only seven STRETCH machines were made but the technology developed was used in the IBM 7090 and 7094. The view of computer design as architecture was consolidated in experiences with the IBM System/360, a family of upwardly compatible computers. Computer architects accepted that to be commercially successful, designs must be able to survive developments in hardware components, software technology and application characteristics. Commercial and industrial customers are resistant to revolutionary change with every new feature because of the cost.

The problems of design are so similar across engineering disciplines that *design theory* has emerged as a discipline in its own right. The characterization of building design has been discussed at length [e.g., March, 1976]. Attempts to automate design processes have produced new models of design couched in the terminology of computer science and AI [Mostow, 1985; Coyne 1988; Mitchell, 1990]. Large software systems are described in terms of architecture. There is a trade-off between software and hardware. Software can be implemented in hardware with a gain in speed but with a loss of flexibility.

In the realm of numerical applications, it appeared that when it comes to performing highly specialized computations then, dollar for dollar, a tailor made computer could easily outstrip the biggest mainframe. Despite the noted affinity of main frames for numerical calculation a homemade computer, the *Dubners' machine* [Devlin, 1987] at the time of the article held several world records for natural number computation. The components of this machine, built by a father and son team in the US, cost around $1000. According to Devlin, this machine had found: the largest known palindromic prime (the same number read from left to right or right to left); the largest prime of the form n!+1; the largest known Euclidean prime (prime-factorial plus 1) and several other world records of a similar nature. For what it did, the Dubners' machine was claimed at the time to be only ten times slower than the fastest Cray of the day and the equal of anything that came out of IBM. This encourages the idea that specialized hardware might be appropriate in certain applications.

The same conclusion was to be drawn from computer chess. Progress in computer chess was initially slow. Chess programs of the 1970s became extremely complicated with various tricks and heuristics for pruning the search tree. The first significant increase in performance came in dedicated hardware with *Belle* [Condon and Thompson, 1982]. Belle used custom designed integrated circuits to implement move generation and position evaluation. On a scale where the average chess player is rated at a 1000 and the world champion at 2750, Belle's rating was 2250. In 1987, *Hitech* became the first chess computer to defeat a grandmaster [Berliner, 1989]. It ranked among the top 800 players. A team of CMU graduate students created *Deep Thought* which using two processors had a performance rating of 2450. It could examine 750 000 positions per second to a depth of 10 ply. Sponsored by IBM, Deep Thought 2 achieved a rating of 2600 in 1993 putting it in the top 100 players. In 1996, its successor, *Deep Blue*, won a game from the world chess champion, Kasparov. Kasparov won the match 4-2. Deep Blue uses 32 power PC2 chips to search two billion positions of the game tree per second to a depth of 14 ply. Kasparov – for some the greatest ever chess player – can evaluate no more than three positions per second. In a historic rematch in June1997, Deep Blue beat Kasparov 3.5 games to 2.5.

2.2 Design as Evolution

Popper [1972] likens the development of science to a Darwinian evolutionary process in the sense of continually eliminating errors. As the precision of scientific experiment increases with advances in technology, gaps between theory and experiment appear. Theory evolves to compensate for the discrepancies. Applying these ideas of evolution to the design process, a design begins with a problem. A tentative solution is proposed that constitutes an hypothesis or conjecture. How the initial design is arrived at is not dealt with by Popper's theory. The hypothesis is tested against observation and is modified to eliminate errors thus producing a new hypothesis.

Despite attempts to the contrary, testing is the way most computer programs are developed. For software design, the method is called the RUDE cycle. The acronym describes the stages of development:

- Run the current version of the system.
- Understand the observed behavior.
- Debug the underlying algorithm to eliminate undesired behavioral characteristics.
- Edit the program to introduce absent but desired characteristics.

As with Popper's theory, how the current version is arrived at is not dealt with by the method.

The computer architecture that has dominated since the mid-1940s is permanently associated with name of the Hungarian born mathematician von Neumann. The origin of the key component of the architecture, the stored program, is controversial. The idea appeared in a widely distributed report containing the blueprint for *Edvac* [von Neumann, 1945]. Edvac was the successor to *Eniac*, the first electronic computer built at the University of Pennsylvania. Eniac was not a stored program machine and von Neumann became a consultant to the project after the machine had been built.

Eniac established flashing lights as the outward sign of computer activity that is still a distinguishing feature of supercomputers (cf. Thinking Machines CM5). The big problem with Eniac was that it was difficult to program. The system of plugs and cables used for programming could take several days to program. This led the University of Pennsylvania team to the realization of the speed advantages of storing the program in the computer memory [Eckert, 1945]. Both Wilkes [1968], and Metropolis and Worlton [1980] insist that Eckert and Mauchly, the principal designers of Eniac, conceived the idea of stored program during development.

Somewhat earlier, Babbage had been aware of the possibility and potential importance of his Analytic Engine generating its own programs in the form of punched cards. He viewed this as a good means of reducing program bugs. It is the ability to calculate store addresses that is characteristic of the modern computer. Babbage is claimed to be the inventor of addressable memory, stored programs and conditional jumps [Bromley, 1987]. The von Neumann architecture was the first computer model that provided a foundation for both technological and programming language evolution. The stored-program concept is an engineering approximation to the theoretical universal Turing machine [Turing, 1936].

The early development of programming languages can be understood as the progressive automation of actions that were previously manual or explicit in the stored program machine. Early programs were written in binary. The introduction of simple input and output devices made input in octal possible. The next step allowed mnemonic codes that were mechanically translated to binary. Nevertheless, users were responsible for every detail of the store allocation. By the early 1950s this burden was transferred to macrocodes and assembly languages [Metropolis et al., 1990].

The introduction of Fortran [Backus et al., 1957] brought great simplification to the task of programming numerical applications. Fortran (FORmula TRANslation) was not revolutionary but a distillation of previous attempts to raise the level of programming. It was introduced:

> *to enable the programmer to specify a numerical procedure using a concise language like that of mathematics and obtain automatically from this specification an efficient (machine language) program to carry out the procedure*

[Backus et al., 1957]

Amongst other disagreeable features, Fortran is responsible for the convention of writing programming language names in upper case letters. Backus, one of the principal language designers, made it clear that the motivating factor behind the language was not the beauty of programming in a mathematical notation but economics [Wexelblat, 1981]. *Debugging*, the process of finding and fixing errors was thought to account for up to 50% of a computer's use. Faultfinding was not considered an economic use of what, at the time, was an expensive and exclusive resource. Fortran was predicted to reduce program development time to less than one-fifth of what it had been.

The store allocation policy used right up to Fortran77 was static: all identifiers are bound to fixed storage locations. This has three limitations:

- the size of data must be known at compile time;
- no procedure can be recursive since all activations use the same location;
- data structures cannot be created dynamically.

These restrictions were to some extent overcome by the block-structured languages *Algol-58* and *Atlas Autocode* by allocating data storage on the procedure-calling stack. An activation record or frame is pushed onto the call stack as each procedure is called and popped when it returns. In 1978, Backus [1978] suggested that the von Neumann architecture dictated the structural identity of programming languages. A program variable is an abstraction of a store location. Assignment statements reflect the underlying fetching and storing operations. Control statements, alternation and repetition, reflect test and jump instructions.

The evolution of processors over the years has followed a pattern familiar from the evolution of biological species. Processors became bigger with more complex machine instructions. Patterson and Dietzel [1980] called complex instruction set computers, *Ciscs*. This evolution came about partly to provide language and operating system support and partly because of the marketing strategy of upward compatibility. To ensure brand loyalty, a new processor should have all the functional capabilities of its predecessors and more. This allowed software written for the previous model to be run on later models. This philosophy was pioneered by IBM 360 series main frames and later exemplified by the Motorola 68x and Intel x86 microprocessor series.

2.3 Design as Co-evolution

Shannon [1950a; 1950b] proposed that the principles acquired from mastering games, like chess, were applicable to other areas of human intelligence such as language translation, logical deduction, strategic decision making in military operations and the design of electronic circuits. In the last of these, Shannon's foresight has been staggeringly successful. The detailed design of VLSI chip layout is now so complex that it would be impossible without CAD (Computer Aided Design). New models of computer are designed using software running on previous models. It is said that the Apple Macintosh was designed on a Cray and that the Cray was designed on an Apple Macintosh. This self-feeding spiral is partly responsible for the rapid evolution of computer technology.

An examination of the genealogy of programming languages reveals the nature of language design. Each successive language transfers new and more difficult cognitive skills from the programmer to the compiler and runtime system. As one shifts from one generation of language to the next, tasks that once required intellectual attention are reduced to algorithms that can be routinely and safely assigned to software and sometimes hardware.

The evolution of programming languages and hardware can be seen as co-evolution with developments in one driving development in the other. An early architecture to give hardware support for Algol's stacks was the Burroughs' 5000/6000 series. Using the stack for passing and returning parameters led computer architects to extend the von Neumann instruction set and registers to support such operations. The frame register of a machine is reflected in the scope of variables in block structured imperative languages. The influence of stacks even extends to the program design methodology. Top-down refinement abstracts the hierarchical structure of procedure and function calls [Dijkstra, 1972].

During the 1960s, many large software development efforts met with severe difficulties. Backus [1978] referred to this, later, as the *software crisis*. Computer system deliveries were typically late, exceeded budget and produced unreliable products [Brooks, 1975]. This tradition had been established by one of the first commercial computers, *Univac*. Univac was delivered to the US Census Bureau 15 months late and considerably over budget. This experience is typical of the situation with civil architecture: compare for example the Anglo-French Channel Tunnel.

Indiscriminate transfer of control emerged as one culprit for the software crisis and the finger of blame was pointed at *goto* statements [Dijkstra, 1968c]. This led to calls for an engineering approach to the production of software. Bohm and Jacopini [1966] demonstrated that all programs could be written with only three control structures: sequence, selection and repetition. There followed an avalanche of research activity that resulted in the paradigm of *structured programming*, a disciplined approach to writing clear, demonstrably correct programs. Knuth [1974] demonstrated structured programming with goto statements.

A much earlier software crisis had led Babbage to devise the Analytic Engine. Errors in mathematical tables produced by human calculators prompted the search for more reliable mechanical means of calculation. Babbage dreamed that logarithm tables could be computed by machine. More recently, the software used to control the 114 computers in the AT&T long-distance telephone network was held up as proof of the possibility of highly complex, yet flawless software. In January 1985 this Titanic system failed. Callers got busy signals and businesses dependent on communication descended into chaos. American Airlines claimed to have lost two thirds of its 300 000 daily calls. The malfunction was due to an error in one of two million lines of computer code. The error was introduced during an upgrade to reduce the time between dialing and ringing. A Peter Principle seems to apply in that demand for sophisticated software expands to exceed the limit by which it can be reliably produced.

The structured programming paradigm was intimately related with the programming language Algol. The term *Algol-like* language is testament to the dependence of a family of programming languages on a common ancestor. The main novelty of the family is the reservation of space for local variables on the function call stack. This implementation detail was reflected in the language in the abstraction of modular design. Modular design gives rise to variable scope and recursive procedure calls. The relationship between stacks and the paradigm is an incestuous one. Samelson and Bauer [1959] described how a stack store could be used to support the compilation of programs written in Algol-like languages.

The almost total replacement of assembly language by high-level languages laid the burden of use of the instruction set mainly on the compiler writer. Empirical investigations showed that compilers do not exploit most of the instructions provided by Ciscs. Alexander and Wortman [1975], for example, finds 10 instructions accounting for 80% of the code and 30 instruction for 99% of the code. Compiler writers prefer simpler architectures where the number of available choices is fewer and uniform.

Given the rapid development of technology, longer times for design and verification lead to situations where processors and compilers become obsolete before production. The inherent complexity of VLSI chips, measured in numbers of transistors, places formidable demands on debugging [Frank and Sproull, 1981]. Patterson and Dietzel [1980] claim that more cost-effective processors can be realized with simpler and more regular instruction sets, *Riscs* (Reduced Instruction Set Computers). Not only does regularity assist the compiler, it assists in algorithmic computer-aided design and verification. Purely on aesthetic grounds, an architecture that can be designed, implemented, and verified relatively automatically is appealing.

2.4 Design as Theorem

If an architecture survives a large, thorough testing regime then confidence in its design increases. Dijkstra [1972] captured the asymmetry of testing:

> *Program testing can be used to show the presence of bugs but never show their absence.*

Any number of tests will not guarantee the correctness but a single unsuccessful test will deny it. This is the same as Popper's objection to Logical Positivism. Many schemes continue to be proposed for debugging and increasing confidence in the correctness of hardware and software. Some deal with programming methodology and others with algebraic proofs that a program does what the specification intends of it. Formal specifications of AI architectures are rare. Craig [1991] gives a formal specification of blackboard architectures in the Z specification language.

Turing [1949] wrote a short paper in which he discussed the germinal ideas underlying what is now called *program verification*. Naur [1966] proposed an informal system for proving the correctness of programs. (Naur was editor of the Algol report and co-inventor with Backus of the *BNF*, a Post Calculus for specifying programming language syntax.) Better known, Floyd's [1967a] method associates a predicate with each arc in a flowchart. The flowchart was the earliest methodology for program design. Floyd introduced one of the most important components of program verification, the loop invariant. A loop invariant is a proposition that if true immediately before the start of a loop is true immediately after exiting. Floyd's work inspired Hoare [1969] to develop the first formal logic for proving partial correctness properties of sequential programs. The premises and conclusions of Hoare logics are triples consisting of a precondition, a program statement and a postcondition. Hoare [1988] claims that Turing was an early advocate of the assertional method:

> *On June 24, 1950 at a conference in Cambridge, he [Turing] gave a short talk entitled, "Checking a Large Routine" which explains the idea with great clarity. "How can one check a large routine in the sense of making sure that it's right? In order that the man who checks may not have too difficult a task, the programmer should make a number of definite assertions which can be checked individually, and from which the correctness of the whole program easily follows."*

That pre- and post-conditions could be used to synthesize a program came out of the work of Dijkstra [1975,1976]. To this end, Dijkstra contributed the weakest precondition for a given statement and postcondition. The problem of determining loop invariants has prevented a successful completion of this proposal. Hoare [1982] suggested:

> *A specification is a predicate describing all observations of a complex system ... Specifications of complex systems can be constructed from specifications of their components by connectives in the Predicate Calculus ... A program is just a predicate expressed using a restricted subset of connectives, codified in a programming language.*

Hehner [1984] presents a semantics of programming in which programs themselves are predicates manipulated according to the rules of predicate calculus.

Dijkstra [1968a; 1968b; 1971] was one of the first to emphasize the principle of separation of concerns and levels of abstraction in dealing with the complexity of software design. The principle, regarded as common sense, advocates partitioning concerns into strongly related components and then focusing on each component in isolation. Parnas pioneered most of the subsequent work on software design. Parnas [1972a] introduced the notion of module specification. A complex software system

may be divided into simpler components called modules. Modules are software fragments that may be a collection of routines, a collection of data, a collection of type
definitions or a mixture of all these. The benefit of modularity is that it allows the
principle of the separation of concerns to be applied in two phases. One phase deals
with individual modules in isolation and the other the integration of the modules.
Two relations between modules define the software architecture. One relation is M1
uses M2 for example when M1 calls a routine in M2. The other relation is *comprises*
when modules are composed of other modules. This relation is naturally a hierarchy.
Hierarchical relations are easier to understand than nonhierarchical ones. Hierarchy
defines the system through levels of abstraction.

The set of services that each module provides to other modules that use it is called its
interface. A clear distinction between the interface and the implementation of a module supports the separation of concerns. Parnas [1972b] introduced the concept of
information hiding. An interface may be viewed as a contract between a module and
its clients. As long as the interface remains fixed, the implementation may be
changed arbitrarily. The crucial aspect of the interface specification is what is visible
to clients and what is hidden. The hidden information is *encapsulated* in the implementation.

Britton, Parker, and Parnas [1981] discuss abstract interfaces for devices. Modules
can be categorized according to what their interface makes visible. *Procedural ab-
stractions* encapsulate algorithms. They were one of the first categories used in software design. A *library* is a module containing a number of related procedural ab-
stractions. It might seem that routines for random number generation are a library.
They are different in that successive calls with the same parameters do not return the
same result. Random number generators have encapsulated data, the seed that is only
visible to the routines. Modules that exhibit such state are called *abstract objects*.
With a shared data module, the structure of the data is visible to all clients. An *abstract data type* is a module that offers to supply data only through a number of visible routines. This hides the structure of the data and allows it to be implemented in
different ways.

Dijkstra and Parnas were leading figures in the foundation of software engineering.
Software engineering proposes that complex software systems can be developed in
the same way that engineers design cars, bridges, ships, airplanes and microprocessors. Engineering requires management, organization, tools, theories, methodologies
and techniques. Despite four technology generations, machine architecture did not
change very much. Microprocessors of the Fourth Generation were essentially instances of the same von Neumann architecture used in the first valve computers.
Backus [1982] argued that the effective use of VLSI was limited by current computer
architecture:

> *The key problem caused by the original [von Neumann] design of*
> *computers is in the connection between the CPU and the store.*
> *Since huge contents of the store must pass, one word at a time,*
> *through this connection to the CPU and back, one might call this*
> *the* von Neumann bottleneck.

Decreasing costs of hardware and increasingly available custom designed silicon chips make radically different hardware designs, such as neural nets, possible.

VLSI is a successful example of parallelism. The success is due in part to a hierarchy of interfaces for composing circuits: composing transistors to form memory units; composing functional units to form pipelined processors. Pipelining is a technique whereby multiple instructions are executed in parallel. A designer composing transistors has to be concerned with physical issues such as parasitic capacitance. A designer putting together functional units of pipelined processors has to be concerned with uninterrupted flows of instructions. Languages that give rise to fewer jump statements have increased performance on pipelined processors. The CDC (Control Data Corporation) 7600 was the first pipelined supercomputer.

Since the first working computer, architects have been striving to compose computers that are more powerful by connecting many existing smaller ones. The first computer from the Eckert-Mauchly Corporation (Eniac) had duplicate units to improve reliability (it was composed of valves that were considered unreliable components). Despite the innovation of VLSI, conventional machines were claimed to be reaching the limits of their power [Bouknight et al., 1972]:

> The turning away from conventional organization came in the middle 1960s, when the law of diminishing returns began to take effect in the effort to increase the operational speed of a computer... Electronic circuits are ultimately limited in the speed of operation by the speed of light ... and many of the circuits were already operating in the nanosecond [technological limit] range.

ILLIAC, a parallel array processor, was a result of the US Atomic Energy Commission's encouragement to manufacturers to research "radical" machine architectures [Hord, 1982].

Microprocessors, a product of Fourth Generation, seemed the ideal modules for composing parallel architectures [Bell, 1985].

> Multis are a new class of computer based on multiple microprocessors. The small size, low cost, and high performance of microprocessors allow design and construction of computer structures that offer significant advantages in manufacture, price performance ratio, and reliability over traditional computer families. Multis are likely to be the basis for the next, the Fifth Generation of computers.

The Transputer [INMOS, 1988] was a processor especially designed to be such a building block.

The immediate product of a design endeavor is a description of the artifact in some symbolic language such as a chip layout diagram. Interfacing many existing smaller designs forms the final design. Flip-flops can be composed from gates and shift registers from flip-flops. If these descriptions are thought of as inference rules in the sense of Post Calculi, then computers can be thought of as theorems of a deductive system. The same idea is used in the architecture of buildings [Mitchell, 1990]. Each rule dictates how shapes, standing for components or subsystems, combine in ways that accomplish some useful end. For example, an arch consists of two columns and a beam. Artifact designs are treated as expressions in languages specified by shape grammars, known as *artifact grammars*. These grammars are specialized Post Calculi.

Giloi [1983] proposed a classification scheme in which architectures are described by a formal grammar. For example, an inference rule of the form:

$$\frac{\text{operational principle} \qquad \text{hardware structure}}{\text{computer architecture}}$$

specifies that a *computer architecture* can be formed from an *operational principle* and *hardware structure*. The two rules:

$$\frac{\text{dispatch driven control}}{\text{operational principle}} \qquad \frac{\text{event driven control}}{\text{operational principle}}$$

specify that *operational principle* is either *dispatch driven control* or *event driven control*. Using the grammar, an architecture can be described by a parse tree of a sentence. Giloi's proposal suggests that to construct a comprehensive scheme it is first necessary to classify architectural features. Unfortunately, the lack of independence of concepts makes it less than useful for design purposes [Dasgupta, 1989].

The best known application of taxonomy is biology, where the development has a long history dating back to Aristotle. The earliest and most frequently cited classification incorporating parallel machines is Flynn [1966]. Flynn's scheme is non hierarchic and consists of four categories:

- SISD – single instruction stream, single data stream;
- SIMD – single instruction stream, multiple data stream;
- MISD – multiple instruction stream, single data stream;
- MIMD – multiple instruction stream, multiple data stream.

Because the taxons span a wide range of computers, they cannot make any reasonably accurate predications about the relative performance of SIMD and MIMD machines.

2.5 Design as Premise

The Japanese initiative was to be different from previous computer generations. At the outset, it was to be driven from the top by knowledge-based applications. The advantages that come from a goal directed approach to problem solving were apparent in the Romantic Movement (Section 1.5). Top-down design is a natural way of coping with design complexity. If interpretative knowledge can be used backwards, the design can be derived from the specification. This form of reasoning, called *abduction,* was identified by the American logician Peirce (co-discoverer of predicate logic) as especially important. Reggia [1983] suggested its use in diagnostic expert systems. Abductive inference allows one to infer Q as a possible explanation of P

given *P if Q*. To be useful *Q* needs be consistent with other beliefs. In this way, the design becomes a premise. Abduction is highly nonmonotonic and nondeterministic and this reflects the difficulty in design.

To see how abductive design might be done, consider the requirement for a real-time expert system for financial trading. (Thatcherism dominated the politics of the 1980s. The pursuit of profit was seen as an end in itself.) An essential feature of the requirement is that it will be couched in financial language with the intention that financial experts can evaluate it. In evaluating a design satisfying the requirements, it is necessary to reason about attributes that are not immediately evident from a description of the design. For example, one attribute might be how quickly the system can give advice in response to changes in the financial markets. Interpretative technological knowledge provides the mapping between symbols of the circuit diagram and performance. The price performance ratio gives semantics to the design. For example, if *ECL* (Emitter Coupled Logic) technology is used the cost per gate can be estimated and gate delays will be of the order of nanoseconds. Breal [1900] introduced the word semantics in the title of his book. It is one of a number of words derived from the Greek *semanio*, to mean. Other examples: *semiotic* and *semiology* refer to the relationship between signs and their meanings. Semantics refers to linguistic meaning. There is substantial literature on semantics in mathematical logic where it is known as model theory.

In October 1987, Black Monday was followed closely by Terrible Tuesday with computer "program trading" systems metaphorically screaming *Sell! Sell! Sell!* In "program trading" computers were programmed to issue sale demands when the Dow Jones, Nikkei Dow, Hang Seng or some other index reached a predetermined level. Economic commentators, eager to apportion blame, criticized computer systems for lacking intelligence and causing spiraling sell-offs in a downward market. Most of the programs were of the spreadsheet type on personal computers. Because of the crash, commentators rashly complained that computers do not think as humans do and artificial intelligence is technically impossible. As a basis for argument, the 1987 stock market crash is not entirely credible, since the Wall Street Crash of 1929 can hardly be blamed on the lack of intelligence of computers. Program trading systems in 1987, it seems, are already as intelligent as shareholders were in 1929. Indeed, it is thanks to modern technology that the 1987 crash was not worse than it was. It was reported that because of the unreliable and overloaded telephone exchanges shareholders were not able to instruct their brokers to sell.

A large part of the problem in developing AI applications is to obtain a formal understanding of the requirements. Fahlman [1980] listed some basic computing needs of AI researchers of the Precisionist Movement (Section 1.10).

> *AI programs tend to be very large ... any machine should have a large virtual address space to insulate the researcher from having to think about overlays. A 32-bit address space is comfortable for the immediate future... Most AI programs burn a lot of cycles. If your machine is slow and too heavily loaded, high-powered researchers will be spending all their time waiting for something to happen on their screens.... AI researchers spend most of their time*

editing and communicating with one another via computer mail.
First rate facilities for these activities should be provided.

Fahlman claimed that these requirements could be achieved by two architectures: time sharing systems and the personal workstations connected by high-bandwidth networks. This highlights the problem: there are many ways a specification may be met. Abduction gives no guidance as to which may be better. Additionally, new ways may be found during design and fabrication. Because abduction is nonmonotonic, abductive design does not lend itself to the later acquisition of knowledge.

A more fundamental problem limits the rationality of decisions – the specification may not be consistent. Some intended properties of a design can only be tested after the system has been fabricated or at least prototyped. Rationality is bounded by conflicts in the desired goals and imperfect knowledge of relevant information. There may be many performance indicators; one ubiquitous monitor is cost: cost of design, cost of fabrication and cost of distribution. Simon [1982] formulated the notion of bounded rationality. It is usually not possible to optimize all performance criteria simultaneously and some compromise is necessary. Simon called this compromise, *satisficing*.

Top-down design has a danger that it may be too specific. A design that would satisfy the requirements for financial investment may not be suitable for assisting VLSI layout. Different expert system applications require different inference engines and knowledge representation schemes [Chandrasekaran, 1983; 1985a; 1985b]. Interpretative knowledge is generally insufficient for producing designs from specifications.

2.6 Design as Paradigm

The software crisis was used to promote novel programming languages. Kuhn [1970] sees crises as the spur to the progress of science. Kuhn suggests that the establishment is uncritical of the paradigm in which it works and resists any changes to it. When the paradigm proves inadequate, a crisis arises. It is the young and ambitious that promote allegiance to some new paradigm. With the acceptance of the new paradigm, these pioneers go on to form the new establishment. For example, in logic programming Kowalski [1979], taking a lead from Wirth [1976] and expert systems, promoted the separation of logic and control. In contrast, a subsequent religion, object orientation, promotes the integration of data and algorithm.

The word *paradigm* derives from the Greek *paradeigma*, showing side by side. In ancient Greece, it described goods displayed for sale in the market place. From this, it acquired the meaning of sample, example and pattern. In science, it took on the meaning of a standard example for testing theories. For example, planetary motion in the solar system is used to test principles of mechanics. Because particular examples were associated with particular theories that explained them, the word *paradigm* was transferred to the principles of the theory. This is the interpretation of *paradigm* used by Kuhn [1970] in *The Structure of Scientific Revolution*. The paradigms of AI reflect the movements described in Chapter 1. Before the Japanese Initiative, design by programming language paradigm dominated all attempts to break away from design by evolution of the von Neumann architecture.

Algol-like programming languages were thought inadequate for the potential parallelism in AI applications:

> *Existing languages, which were designed for existing architectures, tend to be similarly inadequate. Languages designed for von Neumann machines are inherently sequential. Extensions of these restrict the amount of parallelism unnecessarily.*
>
> [Hewitt, 1984]

Landin's work in the mid-1960s [1964, 1965, 1966] was significant in the development of functional programming. Landin [1964] recognized that Algol-like languages could be approximated by syntactically sugared versions of Church's lambda calculus. Assignment could be approximated by substitution. Landin's thesis was that Algol and all past, present and future languages can be approximated by lambda calculus in one form or another. Landin designed an abstract stack based machine (*SECD*) for executing lambda calculus programs. Four stacks keep track of the syntactic structure of lambda expressions and the location of the leftmost redex (reducible expression).

Hoare's [1982] proposal that a program is a predicate is not consistent with Landin's interpretation of a program as a lambda term. Under the Brouer, Heyting and Kolmogorov interpretation, a closed lambda term represents the proof of a proposition and a proposition represents a type. Backus [1978] called for the functional style of programming, because of its simplicity, (sounder) mathematical foundations and reputedly higher expressive power. He argued that many so called architectures which support high-level languages are not driven by real language needs. Languages motivating the architecture were themselves a product of the architecture.

The first language specifically for AI was *IPL*, a list processing language, developed by Newell and Simon to write the Logic Theorist, the early heuristic theorem prover described in Chapter 1. IPL and the Logic Theorist were introduced at the first AI conference at Dartmouth College, of which McCarthy was co-organizer. The authors had no compiler and translated it into machine code by hand. It was an assembly level set of macros for list processing on a hypothetical stack machine (an abstract machine). Operations of *push* and *pop* were part of IPL.

FLPL (Fortran compiled List Processing Language) was McCarthy's first attempt to clean up the "untidiness of IPL". It was implemented on an IBM 704 [Gelerntner et al.., 1960]. With McCarthy's second attempt, *Lisp* (LISt Processing) [McCarthy, 1960], pairs rather than lists, were chosen as the primitive data type. From pairs, both lists and trees can be constructed. During the next few years, McCarthy refined the language. The computational model of Lisp is, like Algol, stack based. It is often claimed that lambda calculus was the theoretical basis of Lisp, but this appears not to be the case [McCarthy, 1978]. McCarthy's original motivation for developing Lisp was the need for list processing in artificial intelligence research. The presence of pragmatic features such as sequencing and assignment in Lisp had, doubtless, much to do with Fortran in which FLPL was written. The impact of lambda calculus on early Lisp development was minimal; it was only later that purged versions appeared, in particular *Scheme* [Abelson et al., 1985] and *ML* [Milner et al., 1990].

While array data structures are the dual of repetition, recursive data structures, such as lists, are the dual of recursion. A stack discipline is insufficient for dynamic data structures because their lifetime generally exceeds the lifetime of the procedure that created them [e.g., Wirth and Jensen, 1974]. Dynamic data structures require storage in a heap. Abstractly, the state of a computation that uses dynamic data structures can be understood as a rooted, connected, directed graph. The call stack acts as roots for the graph. As computation proceeds, the graph changes by the addition and deletion of vertices and edges. In this process some portions of the graph become disconnected from the roots. These disconnected subgraphs are known as *garbage*. Garbage collection is an unavoidable evil of computer languages that employ dynamic data structures. The earliest forms of store management placed the responsibility for allocation and reclamation on the programmer. Programmed garbage collection was error prone, if not burdensome and many languages, including Lisp, added automatic allocation and reclamation in a runtime system. One early variation of Algol, *Algol-W* included automatic garbage collection.

Although AI applications can be developed in Fortran, the higher level of Lisp with automatic garbage collection made programming easier and opened up implementation· to less mechanically inclined researchers. Lisp provided powerful metalevel facilities for manipulating programs. Because Lisp programs are syntactically the same as Lisp data structures, i.e., nested pairs, and the *eval* primitive had the quality of a universal Turing machine, Lisp was used as a metaprogramming language. Reynolds [1972] showed (in terms of lambda calculus) that it is impossible for a system to support itself in the same language it is written in. Languages have to resort to primitives to express some part of reflection. Languages that can represent programs as data make it natural to bootstrap new languages or control by metaprogramming. This makes it possible to solve complex problems by designing flexible problem or user-oriented programming languages. These can be implemented with only a small amount of effort. A tower of metalevels is an integral part of the meta-object protocol [Kiczales et al., 1991].

The utility of metalanguage in expert systems has been noted in many places [e.g., Davis and Buchanan, 1977; Davis, 1980; Bundy and Welham, 1981; Clancey, 1983; Aiello and Levi, 1984]. It had been argued that metalevel approaches, which separate control knowledge from domain knowledge, provide possibilities for an abstract expert system architecture that can be tailored to the problem at hand. A metalevel approach allows independent variation of control knowledge and domain knowledge. The separation permits domain knowledge to be completely declarative and this allows its use in different reasoning strategies, for example forward or backward chaining. Another application is the possible transformation of search intensive programs to search free programs using metacontrol knowledge.

One notable application of Lisp was *Saint* [Slagle, 1963]. Saint (Symbolic Automatic INTegrator) was an heuristic problem solver for first year university calculus problems. While differentiation can easily be expressed as an algorithm, integration cannot [Moses, 1967]. Several inference rules are available for symbolic integration (for example integration by parts and long division) that split the integrand into a sum of expressions that can be integrated separately. In first year MIT student examinations, Saint scored an *A*, a grade somewhat better than the average student. Saint evolved into *Macsyma*, an expert system for physicists and engineers to assist symbolic manipulation of mathematical expressions. Macsyma was, at one time, the largest symbol manipulation system.

Lisp programs like Macsyma, which consists of 230 KB of compiled code, need large virtual memories. The exclusive use of dynamically configured data structures makes an automatic storage mechanism with efficient garbage collection vital. Complaints about the speed of Lisp were met by specialized hardware. The earliest examples of hardware support for a high-level language were DEC's PDP-6 and its successors. The half-word and stack instructions were developed with Lisp in mind. In general, tag operations; stack operations and garbage collection present opportunities for hardware support. Proprietary *Symbolics* and *Xerox* Lisp workstations are epitomes of what can be achieved with a language paradigm. These machines came fully equipped with powerful AI application development environments, for example *Loops*, *Kee*, and *Art*. Such machines satisfied niche markets that required an AI programming language with computation speed that timesharing systems could not deliver. Language specific hardware all gave added support to the central role of Lisp for AI applications.

Kay [1993] was typical of the feelings about Lisp:

> *... there were deep flaws in its logical foundations ... its most important components – such as lambda expressions, quotes and conds – were not functions at all ...*

Kay's criticism would have been more accurate if he had concentrated his attack on name binding. Different interpretations led to a proliferation of incompatible versions of Lisp. Applications developed on one manufacturer's compiler would not run on another. A standardization meeting was convened at MIT for all interested parties including the Lisp workstation vendors. These manufacturers had large investments in software. Symbolics had recently acquired *Macsyma*, the algebraic manipulation application developed at MIT. Macsyma was considered a beautiful collection of algebraic manipulation algorithms coded extremely badly; the code was reputed to be unintelligible. It was alleged that Symbolics did not understand the algorithms but they had the source code in MacLisp. Xerox was in a similar situation, their workstation environment was written largely in Lisp. It was imperative for both manufacturers to protect their investments. The outcome of the meeting, chaired by Steele, was *Common Lisp*. The standard attempted to be catholic enough to support everyone's needs, but where it did not it put all manufacturers at equal disadvantage.

The Sapir–Whorf hypothesis asserts that it is possible for someone working in a natural language to imagine thoughts that cannot be translated or understood in another language. This is contrary to Church's thesis that any computation can be realized by partial recursive functions [Rogers, 1967]. Examples of computational languages have been proposed by Church [1936], Kleene [1936], Markov [Markov, 1954], Post [1936], Smullyan [1956] and Turing [1936]. An often cited, but erroneous [Pullham, 1991], example of the Sapir–Whorf hypothesis is that Inuit languages have many words for different types of snow. A weak form of Sapir–Whorf hypothesis is that different languages make some forms of problem decomposition and hence solution more natural than others.

2.7 Impressionist Design

According to Roberts [1973], in addition to inventing predicate logic, in the 1890s Peirce rediscovered the semantic nets of the Shastric Sanskrit. Semantic nets could be implemented reasonably efficiently in Lisp using property lists. Fahlman's (MIT) thesis [1979] proposed hardware architecture to support semantic networks. The architecture provides a tight coupling between a semantic network and parallel inference routines. In the Impressionist Movement (Section 1.8), when frame based representations of knowledge became popular, Lisp was naturally used as the language in which to implement them. Proprietary Lisp environments, Loops, Kee and Art, provided direct support for frames.

The concept of frames found counterparts in Algol [Stefik and Bobrow, 1986]. In particular, *Simula*, from the Norwegian Computer Center, was an extension of Algol that introduced class and instance concepts under the names of activities and processes. Although classes were introduced into Algol to describe the life cycles of the objects of discrete event simulation, encapsulation was later recognized as a general principle of program design [Dahl, 1972]. The idea that data structures and the operations on them should be encapsulated forms the concept of abstract data-type.

Sketchpad [Sutherland, 1963] was the first interactive graphics system and although it was not explicitly frame-based it boasted similar features. Sketchpad described drawings in terms of "master drawing" and instances. Control and dynamics were provided by constraints and represented in graphical form. Sketchpad had inheritance hierarchies and data structures with embedded references to procedures. According to Kay [1972], Sutherland's achievement in inventing interactive computer graphics was stunning:

> It was the first system that had a window, the first system that had icons, certainly the first system to do all its interactions through the display itself. And for a small number of people in this community, this system was like seeing a glimpse of heaven.

While a graduate student, Kay [1972, 1993] developed *Flex*, an Eulerized version of Simula for writing the operating system of the first portable computer, the *Dynabook* (dynamic book). Kay's undergraduate studies in biology influenced the design. Biological evolution had developed one solution to the problem of managing complexity. Biological systems maintain control by confining processes and data in self contained cells. These cells act on each other by sending "messages" carried by chemical messengers. The receipt of a message from other cells activates the processes within cells. The cell membrane and the nucleus protect its data, DNA, from access by untoward agents. Kay noted an operating system could be broken down into component parts similar to cells.

A purer form of Flex appeared in *Smalltalk* [Ingalls, 1978] under the funding of the Xerox Office Workstation Project [Kay, 1972; 1993]:

> *While Simula can be seen as an attempt to add object-oriented features to strongly typed Algol 60, Smalltalk can be viewed as an attempt to use the dynamic, loosely typed features of Lisp, but with methods and objects replacing functions and S-expressions.*
>
> [Norvig, 1992]

Kay was a founder member of the Learning Research Group at Xerox PARC. The workstation project was intended to create the iconic illusion of office organization, now so familiar in the Apple Macintosh and Microsoft Windows. Papert influenced Kay's idea that a workstation could be made easier to use by taking inspiration from child psychology. Papert reasoned that Piaget's development of child mentalities could be accelerated if abstract things such as geometry, could be made more concrete. The programming language Logo took advantage of young children's ability to manipulate objects – in this case a turtle – to perform abstract geometry. The cell-like programming units in Flex came to be called "objects" in Smalltalk.

The *Alto*, a Xerox graphics workstation, was the first hardware platform for Smalltalk. The Alto was designed for the paperless office but the more powerful *Dorado* soon succeeded it. The Dorado was designed to support both *Interlisp* and Smalltalk. Evidence of Lisp is apparent in the deeper structure of Smalltalk. Steele [1976a; 1976b] demonstrated how object-oriented programming can be done in Lisp using lambda. The MIT Lisp Group developed the idea in *Flavors* to support multiple inheritance [Moon, 1986]. Flavor was a slang word for type. In *New Flavors*, Symbolics produced a more efficient implementation and abandoned the message-passing paradigm. Xerox, continued the development with *Common Loops*. What remains is a set of macros, functions and data types for object-oriented programming that have been incorporated into Common Lisp under the name of *CLOS*.

Neither the Alto nor Dorado was sold commercially. The first commercially available object-oriented hardware architecture was the *Intel iAPX432*. The iAPX432 was a Cisc based symmetric multiprocessor machine designed by Intel. In contrast, *Soar*, Smalltalk on A Risc project, [Ungar and Patterson, 1987] places much of the burden of managing objects on software. Ungar and Patterson claim that much can be learned from what appear to be smart ideas in hardware that, in practice, do not contribute to a more efficient machine. They describe the salutary tale of the *computer architect's trap*:

> *... each idea was* clever *... each idea made a particular operation much faster ... not one idea significantly improved total performance! ... The primary impact of clever ideas was to increase the difficulty of building the machine and thus lengthen the development cycle.*

Lessons learnt from Soar were incorporated in the general purpose *Sparc* processor.

The semantics of object-oriented languages, like Smalltalk, is not altogether clear with different proponents emphasizing different features. Some propose abstract data types; for others message passing is considered a central tenet; for others it is hierarchy and program reuse. The problems of semantic nets and frames carry over to object-oriented programming, almost without change. Object-oriented programming leaves the programmer with difficult decisions to make regarding the epistemological status of the properties so encoded and their associated inheritance paths. The use of objects to code knowledge contrasts with the metalevel separation of control knowledge and object knowledge as advanced by expert systems. With metalevel architecture, it was argued that greater flexibility could be achieved by this separation. This distinction may be seen in the arguments for relational databases [Codd, 1970; Codd and Date 1974] as opposed to *CODASYL* [1978]. Criticism of the anarchy of network databases promoted the use of the relational model.

Lisp machines and Smalltalk machines provide powerful integrated program development environments. These are persuasive features of any system irrespective of the programming language. By the late 1960s, Lisp was almost exclusively the implementation language of choice for AI applications. With Lisp, novice students spent a considerable time developing pattern matchers for metaprogramming production systems. The first effective pattern matching and string manipulation language, *COMIT* was developed at MIT in the late 1950s. COMIT allowed substrings to be identified by their content rather than position. Newell and Simon [1963] designed a pattern directed production rule interpreter called *PSG* (Production System version G) specifically for use in simulating human problem solving. The psychological model of long and short memory inspired it. A PSG program consisted of an initial database and a collection of condition action rules, $C \Rightarrow A$, with an action A entailing one or more effects on the database. The interpreter tries rules in some order until one is found whose condition is satisfied by the database. The body of a rule is then executed which usually causes modification of the data. In this computational model, rules cannot call each other directly but only indirectly by placing appropriate triggers in the database.

Contrasting this method of behavior invocation with Lisp function calls gives production rules some advantage. With the looser coupling between invocations, incrementally acquired knowledge can be incorporated into the problem solving process. This is true even when the knowledge is fragmentary and heuristic. It was from this behavior that the exploratory, prototyping, approach to software development largely grew. PSG directly led to the influential *OPS* series of rule-based (cognitive modeling) languages [Forgy, 1981; 1982] from Carnegie Mellon University.

Production systems were used for the development of the first expert systems, like *Xcon*. The first version of OPS was implemented to test claims of the superiority of production systems over other representational schemes. Later versions were specifically adapted for the development of Xcon. DEC (Digital Equipment Corporation) started building Xcon, its first expert system in 1978 to configure PDP-11 computers. The first two attempts to build the system using Lisp and Algol-like programming languages were dismal failures. It was too difficult to manage the scale and complexity of the combinations of thousands of components in a procedural way. The first successful attempt was written in *OPS5*.

The OPS5 environment provided developers the capability to handle Xcon's scale and complexity. Additional flexibility came from a mechanism for focusing control on specific groups of rules. To prevent programmers from getting carried away with this feature, DEC developed a methodology, *Rime* (R1 Implicit Made Explicit), to control use of the mechanism. (R1 was the original name of Xcon.) The methodology is enforced by a toolset called *Sear*. Sear includes a graphical problem-solving method definer with its own OPS5 metalanguage. Using the metalevel language, Sear programmers can select a template for an appropriate control structure. Sear then compiles the OPS5 code for the desired control.

The use of production system languages has been restricted to expert systems. Not all human problem-solving methods are easily represented by forward chaining rules. For example, the principal of least commitment heuristic for constraint solving is naturally backward chaining. In production systems, condition testing with large antecedents is an inherently inefficient computational process and has serious implications for time-critical applications. Specialized algorithms such as *Rete* are used to overcome this difficulty. In addition, production rules have no intrinsic structure that makes for easier management of large knowledge bases. Most expert systems start as a prototype, with fewer than a hundred rules. Some grow to more realistic systems, with up to 1000 rules. Few expert systems become much bigger than this because of the difficulty of management.

Among the special architectures designed to speed execution of production systems is *Dado* [Stolfo and Miranker, 1986]. Dado consists of distributed processors connected as a binary tree by an underlying interprocessor communication network. The internal nodes are used to store production rules and as parts of the working memory. The root is used to select a matching rule and to broadcast resulting changes to the entire tree. Hardware support is provided for the Rete pattern-matching algorithm.

An advance on production rules came with the *planning* languages [Bobrow and Raphael, 1974]. These languages were designed specifically as vehicles to support top-down problem solving. The most notable, yet unimplemented, of these was *Planner* [Hewitt, 1969; 1972]. In the design of Planner, Hewitt was influenced by Floyd's [1967b] (so called) multivalued functions as a method of specifying search. Floyd [1967b] used chronological backtracking of Golomb and Baumbert [1965] to evaluate multivalued functions (recursively defined directed relations). It is interesting that Hewitt presented Planner at the same session of IJCAI 69 (International Joint Conference on Artificial Intelligence 1969) that Green presented QA3. The chair of the session was (Alan) Robinson.

Sussmann, Winograd, and Charniak [1971] were keen to use Planner but got so fed up with waiting for Hewitt to implement the language, they implemented their own cut-down version. *MicroPlanner* [Sussmann, Winograd and Charniak, 1971] was programmed in Lisp allowing access to Lisp constructs as primitives. A MicroPlanner program consisted of a database of *assertions* and a set of *conditionals*. An assertion is a tuple represented as a Lisp list. Assertions denote facts; conditionals are procedures or subroutines represented in the form P if Q. Searches are initiated by a *goal*, an assertion to be proved. A goal may be proved directly from a matching fact in the database or indirectly using a conditional as a procedure: to prove P prove Q. Because of nondeterminism, this sets up an automatic backward chaining mechanism to search the database in the style of [Floyd, 1967b]. This contrasted with the forward chaining of production systems.

Unlike production systems, the pattern matching of Planner was local to the goal; goals directly invoked other goals just like procedure calls. Goals took the form of a template containing variables. These variables could become instantiated during the search as envisaged in Green's QA3 [Green, 1969]. Assertions from the database or the consequent of conditionals are chosen in turn by their ability to match the goal template. Variables in a template are instantiated by any tuple they correspond to, in the pattern they are required to match. Whereas production rules separate data examination from modification, in Planner the two are integrated. This can be compared with the difference between Herbrand procedures and resolution in theorem proving. Planner provided additional primitives that allowed assertions and conditionals to be created and destroyed dynamically.

MicroPlanner was perceived as providing built-in facilities that everyone was to need for the next generation of AI systems. A notable application written in MicroPlanner was *Shrdlu* [Winograd, 1973], a natural language interface to the blocks microworld. The name Shrdlu came from ETAIONSHRDLU – the order of letters according to their frequency in English. Linotype printers stored their fonts in this order rather than alphabetically. Winograd was a student at MIT where for a period much research was focused on robot planners for the Blocks World. The Blocks World was a microcosm that consisted of a table with various toy blocks on it. The problem for a robot was to scan the scene, work out the relationship between and manipulate blocks to achieve some goal, such as building an arch. Winograd's Shrdlu made strong use of Planner's implicit attempted exhaustive search. Search failure was used as a procedural device to imitate negation. A justification for this was the nonmonotonic *closed-world assumption* [Reiter, 1980]. This is the hypothesis that the locally available knowledge is complete. Relational database systems make use of the closed-world hypothesis: if an entry is not found in a relational table, it is assumed false. Winograd [1973] claimed that:

> One basic viewpoint underlying the model is that all language use can be thought of as a way of activating procedures in the hearer. We can think of any utterance as a program – one that indirectly causes a set of operations to be carried out within the hearer's cognitive system.

This behavioral model is a natural product of the Impressionist Movement (Section 1.8). The operations of parsing, forming internal representations and reasoning about the model world were so deeply intertwined that critics charged the program with not contributing any insight into natural language processing or AI.

The initial euphoria created by Planner and Shrdlu quickly evaporated when basic deficiencies of the language became manifest. Backtracking search in MicroPlanner turned out to be hard to control and led to inefficiency. Planner's search fails to be exhaustive because of bottomless branches in depth-first search. To compound the problem, the language provided no support, beyond the conditional, for modular programming. This was, in part, intentional since it meant that programs could be developed incrementally in the exploratory style of production systems. Unfortunately, this led to programs that were difficult to understand and thus debug.

2.8 Classical Design

MicroPlanner effects another level of organization on top of Lisp. Because of the difficulties of controlling backtracking, Planner did not prove to be a replacement for Lisp. It only served to further establish Lisp as pre-eminent for metaprogramming. An effective method for the control of failure driven loops appeared with the much-criticized cut of *Prolog*. The Prolog (PROgrammation en LOGique) implementation was reported by Colmerauer and Roussel [1992] from Marseilles and evangelized by Kowalski [1974; 1979]. (Allegedly, Roussel's wife suggested the name Prolog.) The similarities of Planner and Prolog are readily apparent [Dowson, 1984] and much of the procedural terminology of *Logic Programming* such as *goal*, *head* and *body* of a clause seems to originate from Planner.

Abelson et al [1985] claims that logic programming grew out of a European attempt to understand Hewitt's impenetrable Ph.D. thesis. McCarthy [1988] expresses a similar sentiment:

> *MicroPlanner was a rather unsystematic collection of tools, unlike Prolog, a language that relies on one mathematically tractable kind of logic programming, but the main idea is the same. If one uses a restricted class of sentences, the so-called Horn clauses, then it is possible to use a restricted form of logical deduction.*

Colmerauer and Roussel [1992] deny this:

> *While attending an IJCAI convention in September 1971 with Jean Trudel, we met Robert Kowalski again and heard a lecture by Terry Winograd on natural language processing. The fact that he did not use a unified formalism left us puzzled. It was at this time we learned of the existence of Carl Hewitt's programming language, Planner [Hewitt, 1969]. The lack of formalization of this language, our ignorance of Lisp and, above all, the fact that we were absolutely devoted to logic meant that this work had little influence on our later research.*

Colmerauer's interest stemmed from natural language translation and in particular two-level grammars [Cohen, 1988]. The natural language group at Marseilles led by Colmerauer had developed a pattern matching, rewrite system called Q for natural language understanding. Between 1970 and 1972 this was extended to a French language query answering system, QA. The natural language processing was done in Q while the semantic part was written in predicate logic and used an SL resolution theorem prover [Kuehner and Kowalski, 1972] as its inference engine.

Prolog was born out of the motivation to find one system in which both natural language and semantic processing could be united. Despite linear input resolution's stack-like functioning, analogous to procedure calling in standard languages, SL had general computations (ancestor resolution and factoring) that seemed unnecessary for the natural language examples on which it was required to work. For efficiency, a restriction of SL resolution was adopted which fitted well with Colmerauer's preference for Floyd's [1967] method for managing nondeterministic search:

> *A draconian decision was made: at the cost of incompleteness, we chose linear resolution with unification only between the heads of clauses ... Robert Kowalski's contribution was to single out the concept of the "Horn Clause" which legitimized our principal heresy*

[Colmerauer and Roussel, 1992]

The relationship between linear input resolution and Horn clauses had been established earlier by Kuehner [1972] in his SNL theorem prover. With the exception of factoring, Kuehner's theorem prover is what came to be known as *SLD* (Selective, Linear, Definite) [Apt and van Emden, 1982]. Hill [1974] was the first to show that factoring was unnecessary for Horn clauses. Hill called the refinement *LUSH* for linear unrestricted selection of Horn Clauses.

The first version of Prolog was written in Algol-W. Boyer and Moore [1972] wrote an improved version in Fortran using the implementation technique of structure sharing. Colmerauer's group's purchase of an IBM 360 equipped with virtual memory dictated the switch to Fortran. It is interesting that the explanation of structure sharing appeared in the same issue of *Machine Intelligence* as Kuehner's SNL Horn clause theorem prover. As described in Chapter 1, apart from factoring, SNL is a proof system for Horn clauses.

The query answering part of Prolog was similar to Green's [1969] QA3. A list of nonresolvable predicates in the goal was used to record the variable bindings. Green [1969] presented his paper on *Theorem proving by resolution as a basis for question-answering systems* at the same Machine Intelligence Workshop in 1968 at which both *Absys* and Planner were announced. Absys stood for Aberdeen System and with the authors' hindsight, it was the first Logic Programming language [Foster and Elcock, 1969]. Absys later influenced Hewitt's Planner. Absys grew out of a desire to remove overspecification from procedural programming. Resolution appeared as a system for solving sets of equations after the fashion of Herbrand, thus separating complimentary literal elimination from unification that Robinson had so neatly sewn together. This route was later pursued by Colmerauer with *Prolog II* [Colmerauer, 1982] and developed into constraint logic programming [Jaffar and Maher, 1994].

Negation appeared in Absys as it does in Planner as negation by failure but it was interpreted using program completions rather than the closed world assumption. Clark [1978] later developed a completion semantic in the context of Prolog. Because resolution was effected by equation solving, negation as failure in Absys pre-empted constructive negation [Chan, 1988]. Prolog's longevity compared with Planner can be likened to the longevity of Lisp compared with IPL. Lisp was a rationalization of IPL that later was purified with lambda calculus. Although not central to Lisp, lambda calculus gave it credibility by providing underlying semantics. Prolog was a rationalization of Planner purified by Horn clause calculus. Smullyan [1956a] had shown that Horn clauses and *modus ponens* was a sufficient mechanism for all possible calculations (Turing complete). Kowalski and van Emden [1974] provided a fixed point semantics for Horn clause logic. The minimal model semantics was discovered earlier by Smullyan [1956b]. Negation as failure in Prolog extended the expressive power of the language. Semantics for negation as failure were given in terms of nonmonotonic logic [Apt, 1994]. For the Yale shooting problem (Section 1.7) identified by Hanks and McDermott [1986], both circumscription [McCarthy, 1980] and default logic [Reiter, 1980] give unintuitive inferences. Negation as failure gives the commonsense result [Evans, 1989]. Negation as failure has recently been identified as a form of argumentation [Dung, 1993]. Such reconstructions deepened understanding of both problems and solutions of nonmonotonic logic.

The Prolog phenomenon, perhaps, can be ascribed to at least three features. First, the semantics provided by Horn clause logic. Second, relatively efficient, Lisp-inspired (stack-based) implementations by Pereira et al. [1979] and subsequently Warren [1983]. Finally and much underrated in its contribution, is the provision of the cut operator to curb the onerous effects of unbridled depth first search which bedeviled Planner. In the Algol-W version of Prolog, there were four primitives to control the backtracking that appeared at the end of clauses. Planner had similar control primitives but they were not simple to use. In the later Fortran version, Colmerauer's reduction of the four to a single operator (cut) produced an enormous simplification:

> *Not only could the programmer reduce the search space according to purely pragmatic requirements he could also process negation in a way, which, although simplified and reductive in semantics, was extremely useful in most common types of programming.*

> [Colmerauer and Roussel, 1992]

2.9 Logic Machines

Before the Japanese initiative was announced, special purpose machines had been successfully built to support Algol-like languages. Special purpose machines had also been built to support Lisp and Smalltalk. Lisp workstations had been commercially profitable in providing unique development environments for AI applications. A special purpose workstation to support the latest AI language, Prolog, was a very natural consideration. The controversy and dogmas surrounding the paradigms of AI were all too clear in the *SIGART* Special Issue on Knowledge Representation [Brachmann and Smith, 1980]. The issue presented the results of an extensive survey on knowledge representation. The variety of answers to fundamental questions was notable. Logic Programming was promoted, in this issue, as the perfect arbiter between the declarative and the procedural [Kowalski, 1978] schism. With Logic Programming, Kowalski [1974] gave semantic credibility to Prolog by identifying the goal-directed procedural problem solver of Planner with the theoretical Horn clause SNL theorem prover of Kuehner [1972]. Hewitt had previously interpreted Planner both procedurally, goal driven, and as a theorem prover as witness the title of his paper and thesis [Hewitt 1969; 1972]. The assertions and conditionals of Planner correspond to Horn clauses written in the logically equivalent form P←Q. One difference between Planner and Prolog is that assertions are separate from conditionals in a database style in Planner. This allows sophisticated indexing optimizations for retrieving assertions.

The advantages of Planner [Sussmann and McDermott, 1972] apply equally well to Prolog. Both Planner and Prolog provide the same compact notation for encoding depth-first search. The gains of chronological backtracking are appealing. First, it provides a search mechanism generating alternatives one at a time. Second, it provides a mechanism for eradicating the consequences of alternatives later found to fail and so economizes on space. Thirdly, in negation by failure, by attempting exhaustive search, deduction effects a nonmonotonic form of negation.

One of the biggest applications that the Japanese Initiative had to consider was natural language processing. An advanced knowledge-based system would be expected to converse with its user in Japanese. Japanese is a regionally localized natural language but the *lingua franca* of commerce is (obtusely) English, so automatic translation between Japanese and English was a high priority application. Prolog was born out of natural language processing and so seemed an ideal candidate for a specialized machine.

The driving force of natural language processing for Prolog ensured that the Fortran version had the essential ingredients of a good metaprogramming language, uniformity of the program (clauses) and data (the terms) and a metacall predicate (reflexivity):

> One of the missing features of the preliminary Prolog was a mechanism that could compute a term that could then be taken as a literal to be resolved. This is an essential function needed for metaprogramming such as a command interpreter; this feature is very easy to implement from a syntactic point of view. In any event, a variable denoting a term can play the role of a literal.

> [Colmerauer and Roussel, 1992]

The Prolog metacall corresponds to the Lisp eval primitive. Prolog proved to be a better vehicle for metaprogramming than Lisp because of the additional attribute of pattern matching that unification offers.

The Fortran version of Prolog was widely distributed. Copies went to Leuven, Budapest, Waterloo (Canada) and Edinburgh. Prolog spread by people taking copies from Marseilles and its satellites.

> *Prolog was not really distributed; rather it escaped and multiplied*

> [Colmerauer and Roussel, 1992].

In 1976 Furukawa, who became deputy director of the Japanese Fifth Generation Computer System project (FGCS), was on a visit to SRI (Stanford Research Institute). From there he took a copy of Marseilles Prolog back to Japan. Before FGCS project started, more than a hundred Japanese researchers had been involved in discussions on new information processing technology. Out of the discussion, a proposal emerged to build a new software culture on languages for knowledge-based systems. The two candidates were Lisp and Prolog.

Lisp was a product of the USA. Although European, Prolog had not yet been commercially exploited. Furukawa was impressed by the metaprogramming capability:

I wrote a program to solve the Rubik cube problem in DEC-10 Prolog. It ran efficiently and solved the problem in a relatively short time (around 20 seconds). It is a kind of expert system in which the inference engine is a Production System realized efficiently by a tail-recursive Prolog program. From this experience, I became convinced that Prolog was THE language for knowledge information processing.

The simplicity of the Prolog *metacircular* interpreter is one of the most impressive features of the language. Reynolds [1972] coined the term metacircular for a lambda calculus interpreter that defines each feature of the defined language using the corresponding feature of the defining language.

One problem with meta-interpretation is that each level of interpretation gives extra overhead making multilayered meta-interpretation intolerably slow. The program transformation technique of partial evaluation [Futamura, 1971] offered a way of alleviating this drawback. This technique combines a meta-interpreter and an object program into a more efficient specialized program. The technique works by propagating constant values through the program, unfolding goals and branching at alternative clauses. Partial evaluation can be used to flatten the layers of meta-interpretation so that the overheads of multiply embedded interpreters are reduced. While applicable to any language, partial evaluation is particularly suitable for languages like Planner and Prolog that use pattern matching.

Partial evaluation provides a common framework for discussing program transformation, program control, programming language interpreters, compilers and a way for both compiling and automatically constructing compilers from interpreters. The result of partial evaluation of an inference engine with respect to the inference rules is a specialized inference engine just for those rules. Partial evaluation removes some inefficiency of meta-interpretation for designing problem solvers and application-specific programming languages. Prolog proved itself on small database applications, problem solving, expert systems, natural language parsing and compiler writing. However, to become established it had to overcome the inertia of Lisp. (The inertia of Fortran in numerical applications and *Cobol* (Common Business Oriented Language) in commercial applications still bedevils computer science.) Only in the 1990s did commercial sales of Prolog outstrip those of Lisp.

The idea of building a logic machine is aesthetically appealing and very much older than the Japanese initiative. In Plato's time, geometers speculated about machines that could support formal derivations in logic. According to Gardner [1982], the inventor of the world's first logic machine was the British diplomat Charles Stanhope (1753-1816), third Earl of Stanhope. Stanhope was a prolific inventor. His logic machine, in the form of a square slide rule, was known as the *Stanhope Demonstrator*. It demonstrated symbolically the inferences that follow from syllogisms in a manner similar to Venn diagrams, which the Earl's invention anticipated. A description of the machine was not published until 63 years after Stanhope's death. Another of his inventions, an improved calculator, may have had influence on computer science as two of them came into the possession of Babbage.

Boole [1847] introduced the first reasonably comprehensive and approximately correct logic based on an artificial language in his book *The Mathematical Analysis of Logic*. Boole's logic, which was guided by the algebra of arithmetic, subsumed the main parts of Aristotellian logic. The Megarian Stoics [Mates, 1953] appeared to have a comprehensive prepositional logic in the third century BC. The truth tables were rediscovered in fragments of Stoic writing by the American philosopher Peirce (1839-1914). Although Boole's logic fell short of today's propositional logic, other 19th century mathematicians, particularly De Morgan and Jevons, corrected the errors. Jevons proposed solving logical equations by reducing formulas to conjunctive normal form. The tedium of solving equations by this method led Jevons to the idea of performing the operations mechanically. Jevons' exhibited a logical machine [Jevons, 1870] at the Royal Society. The machine was called the *Logical Piano*, because, as the name suggests, it took the physical form of a piano. Premises and operations are fed into the machine by pressing keys. The machine also has a vertical board with slits and a collection of moving plates on which the results are displayed. The Logical Piano (now on display in the Oxford Museum of History) was in some ways a predecessor of the desktop computer.

Jevons' machine was based on a 'blackboard' method. Logical alphabets of problems (involving up to six variables) are written on an ordinary school blackboard with their constituents (conjunctive normal form) listed below. Premises of specific problems are written on the free portion of the board and are compared with the corresponding column of constituents. Corresponding contradictory combinations are erased. Post [1921] and Wittgenstein [1922] independently introduced Truth Tables as a method of calculation for propositional logic.

2.10 Hindsight

The Fifth Generation Initiative was brought together in the early 1980s to bring together two promising ideas. The first was the logic programming language Prolog. Prolog was claimed to be a declarative language. This meant that the order of evaluation was not significant to the result of the computation. This suggested it was suitable for the second ingredient, parallel processing, which could provide the computational power to tackle the huge computational needs that knowledge-based systems require. The ten-year program began in earnest in 1982 with an initial funding for five years. ICOT was organized into three semi-autonomous groups. One group was responsible for applications, including particularly natural language processing. A second group was responsible for the parallel hardware design. The third group, the broker between the two designed extensions to Prolog to facilitate the writing of operating systems and AI applications programs. These groups, however, did not interact well in the early years of the project, resulting in several parallel Prolog machines and language designs that did not fit them [Chikayama, 1993].

The Fifth Generation MITI project ended its ten-year research project with an international conference. Although some of the hardware, *PSI* (Personal Sequential Inference) machines and PIM (Parallel Inference Machines), were donated to researchers it was not commercialized. A *PIM* machine was used recently to solve a remarkable number of open problems in quasi group theory. The final version of the machine appeared on the verge of achieving 10^8 logical inferences per second. The software for the project was made public domain but, unfortunately, it only runs on PSI and PIM machines. Funding for a further three years was made available for scaled down project to port the software to *Unix* machines. Much of the FGCS project was concerned from the beginning with hardware and in particular Cisc microprocessor design. This went against the grain of the Risc thinking that appeared in the 1980s. The hardware part of the Fifth Generation Initiative was closed down and the researchers who were hired for the lifetime of the project were returned to their native companies (in Japan at the time, workers were seldom laid off).

ICOT's "Prolog Machines" (PSI and PIM) turned out to be slow, expensive, and clumsy in comparison with modern workstations or modern parallel supercomputers. The high cost of designing special purpose languagebased workstations with low-volume sales means that manufacturers are reluctant to redesign them to take account of more recent developments. Old special-purpose technology compares unfavorably with the most recent general-purpose technology. For example, Lisp runs faster on Riscs than it does on outdated Xerox and Symbolics workstations. Such language-based machines have only survived because of the luxury proprietary programming environments they provide.

In addition to Risc processors, computer technology developed very rapidly in other directions during the ten years of the Japanese project. Two significant changes in the marketplace in the 1980s made it relatively easy for small companies to enter computer manufacturing. Upward compatible microprocessor families made it easy to assemble computers from off-the-shelf components [Bell, 1985]. High-level languages meant almost an elimination of assembler programming and so reduced the need for object code compatibility. With *ANSI* standardization, *C* emerged as the universal assembler language. The emergence of *de facto* standard operating systems, such as *DOS* and *Unix*, lowered the cost and risk of bringing out new machines. Desktop-machines give greater flexibility and are more cost effective than large mainframes.

The principal design metric for the early advances in operating systems was efficient use of processors. In the late eighties, the *NSF* (National Science Foundation) realized that it could save money by creating just a few supercomputer centers and allowing university researchers remote access over telephone lines. *NSFNET* was based on the Internet Protocol developed for *Arpanet*. Arpanet was a computer network developed for the US Department of Defense whose design metric was survival from military attack. By dispersing the network over a wide area using a web of connections, the system could continue functioning even when portions were destroyed. Significant in the success of NSFNET was the release of 4.2 BSD Unix from the University of California at Berkeley, which provided a set of system calls (sockets) giving programmers access to the Internet Protocols. NSFNET was so successful it soon became saturated. The system was upgraded with faster telephone lines and node computers but it too became saturated. The US's information super highway project provided a further system upgrade.

When desktop computers became available, the same economics that prompted the use of networks shifted the focus of attention. Centralizing storage and I/O devices could save money. Early workstations came equipped with Berkeley Unix, which included Internet Protocol software. This readily adapted to local area networks. The need to manage multiple resources connected by a network led to distributed operating systems. Multis (computers based on multiple microprocessors) have not yet proved to be the basis for the next, the Fifth Generation, as Bell [1985] predicted. Driven by economic considerations, distributed systems emerged as the *de facto* Fifth Generation. Like previous generations, it was led by hardware advances.

Parallel machines have failed to make a big impact on commercial computer users despite products having been available for some time. The market has collapsed and most manufacturers have gone out of business. At its height, US federal government funding fueled the market. Every National Supercomputer Center was provided with the latest machine from the latest startup manufacturer. The end of the cold war put an end to such lavish spending. An argument that has been put forward for the failure is that different classes of architecture require radically different computational paradigms. There is no obvious winner and it is almost impossible to move applications from one class to another. With the evolution of pipelining into microprocessors, the predicted demise of the von Neumann computing model was premature and improved processor designs continued to extend the power of the architecture [Hennessy and Patterson, 1990]. Amdahl [1967] foresaw this:

> *For over a decade, prophets have voiced the contention that the organization of a single computer has reached its limits and that truly significant advances can be made only by interconnection of a multiplicity of computers in such a manner as to permit cooperative solution. Demonstration is made of the continued validity of the single processor approach.*

Amdahl's law [1967] gives a pessimistic estimate of the speed-up that can be obtained from parallelism. Assume that a program executes on a single processor in a time E. If the dependence between subtasks is accounted for by some time, C, spent in communication between the parts of the program, the total time for execution on N processors will be (C + E/N). The speed-up, the ratio of the execution time on a single processor to execution time using N processors, reduces to N /(1 + N/E') where E' = E/C. With increasing N, the asymptote, E', is a constant. With large communication costs, the speedup may even be less than unity. That communication cost is independent of the number of processors is a dubious assumption and refinements of Amdahl's law are possible [Genlebe, 1989].

The quotation at the beginning of this Chapter suggests that a computer architect requires breadth of knowledge of all areas of computer science: theory of computation, computer organization, operating systems, languages and applications. Deep knowledge of all the fields in one individual is rare. What seems important to one specialist is not usually important to another. Inadequate *knowledge in many branches of study and various kinds of learning* in the ICOT research team was readily admitted:

> *... when the research center [ICOT] was founded with some 30 researchers in June 1982 nobody had concrete research plans. ...*

> *Only a few had experience of any language systems or operating systems*

[Chikayama, 1993]

The companies collaborating in the Fifth Generation had little interest in the project. For them, the Fifth Generation was a design exercise in apprentice training. Seconded personnel were supposed to return to their parent companies after training but at the end of the project, many researchers found positions in Japanese universities.

Chapter 3

Metamorphosis

> *Human beings do not live in the objective world alone, nor alone in the world of social activity as ordinarily understood, but are very much at the mercy of a particular language which has become the medium of expression for their society. It is quite an illusion to imagine that one adjusts to reality essentially without the use of language and that language is merely an incidental means of solving specific problems of communication or reflection. The fact of the matter is that the 'real world' is to a large extent unconsciously built upon the language habits of the group ... We see and hear and otherwise experience very largely as we do because the language habits of our community predispose certain choices of interpretation – Edward Sapir*
>
> [Whorf, 1956]

In the Precisionist Movement (Section 1.10), Lisp proved to be the foundation of commercially successful Xerox and Symbolics workstations [Moon, 1987]. The FGCS decision to build Prolog multiprocessor workstations appeared, to some, a deliberate policy to be different from the US but this was not the whole story. The principal application for the project was Japanese natural language processing. Their language isolates the Japanese and automatic translation would be a major benefit in global commerce. Prolog designed specifically for the needs of natural language processing seemed a good choice for the Fifth Generation.

The bandwagon of Logic Programming caused by the FGCS choice was extensively criticized. Some doubted Prolog was up to the job:

> *There is a small class of problems for which Prolog works great (sic) and you can do beautiful demonstrations on these problems. But, when you have to deal with time-dependent behavior like an operating system, you get away from the nice qualities of Prolog, you have to use the ugly side effect features of input and output and you lose any advantage. For commercial users of a language it is such large operating system-type software that they most need to program. Will they want an interpreted language that can't usefully be used on most problems?*
>
> [Attributed to Winograd, The Guardian, 23 May 1985]

An operating system is the critical software that controls a machine's resources and supervises running programs. Without a flexible and supportive operating system a computer is virtually unusable. The symbiosis of the operating system and the hardware is a critical factor that a machine architect has to consider. A machine designed to support exclusively one particular language inherits the features and restrictions of the language. Some languages encourage some forms of expression at the expense of others. This has consequences for the operating system.

The first kernel language developed by the FGCS program *KL0*, Kernel Language Zero, was an extended version of Prolog. With feedback from what turned out to be the core application, the operating system, KL0 evolved into *KL1*. This chapter describes the difficulties of Prolog in a pedagogical fashion. The language derived, *Guarded Definite Clauses* (*GDC*) [Ringwood, 1987a] is not quite the Japanese successor KL1 but is generic.

3.1 Apparent Scope for Parallelism

Parallelism is sought at the language level to exploit multiple processors and so produce increases in execution speed, response-time and throughput. The declarative nature of a pure logic program guarantees that the result of a computation is independent of the order in which subcomputations are executed. This suggested to many that parallel evaluation would be immediate and straightforward. Closer examination reveals that the sequentiality embodied in chronological backtracking and the cut are crucial factors in Prolog's success.

The classic naive *quicksort* Prolog program serves to illustrate the problems.

```
%quicksort(UnsortedList, SortedList)
qsort([],[]).
qsort([Item],[Item]).
qsort([Pivot,Item|List],Sorted) :-
    part([Item|List],Pivot,Lesser,Greater),
    qsort(Lesser,LSorted),
    qsort(Greater,GSorted),
    conc(LSorted,[Pivot|GSorted],Sorted).

%partition(List,Pivot,LesserList,GreaterList)
part([],Pivot,[],[]).
part([Item|List],Pivot,Lesser,[Item|Greater]) :-
    Pivot=<Item,
    part(List,Pivot,Lesser,Greater).
part([Item|List],Pivot,[Item|Lesser],Greater) :-
    Item<Pivot,
    part(List,Pivot,Lesser,Greater).

%concatenate(List1,List2,List1List2)
conc([],List,List).
conc([Item],List,[Item|List]).
conc([Item1,Item2|List1],List2,[Item1,Item2|Lists]) :-
    conc(List1,List2,Lists).
```

The more sophisticated difference list version of quicksort is not used at this stage because the naive form better illustrates the points to be made. The % character indicates that what follows on the same line is a comment. The logical reading of the program is that the second argument of **qsort** is an ordered list, ordered by the relation =<, with precisely the same elements as the list in the first argument. For distinction, predicate names are printed in **boldface**. Lists are as usual in Prolog, denoted recursively, [Head|Tail], where Head is the first item of a list and Tail is the remainder of the list. By convention, the constant [] represents the empty list.

Procedurally, Prolog tackles a goal such as :- **qsort**([2,1,3],Sorted) by searching for matching clauses depth-first in textual order, backtracking to the most recent choice point on failure. The computational effect of the sequencing of clause subgoals is that the list to be sorted is first partitioned, the Lesser sublist is sorted, the Greater sublist is sorted and finally the two sublists are concatenated. Naively, the computation appears ripe to take advantage of multiprocessor architectures. If there were more than one processor, one could sort the Greater sublist and another could sort the Lesser in parallel.

If at some stage in a parallel computation **conc** is called with an uninstantiated variable as its first argument, it can resolve with the first or second clause of the relation. This may prematurely conclude the list so that the length of the sorted list is less than the list being sorted. This is illustrated by the following scenario where parallelism is simulated by interleaving [Pnueli, 1986; Chandy and Misra, 1988].

   :-   **<u>qsort</u>**(<u>[2,1,3],Sorted</u>), **ans**(Sorted).
   :-   **part**([1,3],2,Lesser,Greater), **qsort**(Lesser,LSorted),
       qsort(Greater,GSorted), **<u>conc</u>**(<u>LSorted,[2|GSorted],Sorted</u>),
       ans(Sorted)
   :-   **part**([1,3],2,Lesser,Greater), **qsort**(Lesser,[]),
       qsort(Greater,GSorted), **ans**([2|GSorted]).

The **ans** goal is used to accumulate the answer in the same way as Green's QA3 [1969]. The <u>underline</u> indicates the goal that is chosen to be resolved at each step. If the second or third clause for **conc** had been used, the list could overrun so that the length of the sorted list exceeds the length of the list being sorted. This *premature binding problem* is a consequence of the eagerness of clause invocation in Prolog. The previous sequential evaluation gave considerable control over of the flow of bindings.

The premature binding problem arises because **qsort** and **conc** can resolve asynchronously and they compete to instantiate the variable LSorted. Naively, it might be thought that if there is no explicit sharing by concurrent goals, there is no premature binding problem. That this is not the case is illustrated by the less complex example:

   p(X,Y) :- **q**(X), **r**(Y).

Since **q** and **r** do not share variables, it might be supposed that they could be safely executed in parallel, but the clause for **p** may be invoked with the goal :- **p**(Z,Z). The reason the parallelism of the quicksort seemed promising is that the calling pattern of **qsort** is controlled by the defining clause. The variables Lesser, LSorted, Greater and GSorted only occur in the body of the clause and not in the head. If only called from **qsort** there is no way that these body variables can be caused to share.

When unification is used for pattern matching and not for pattern generation, there is genuine data independence in conjunctive goals. If in the previous example the call to **p** is ground, such as :- **p**(a,b), the resolvent :- **q**(a), **r**(b) can be reduced in parallel. (Variable-free sentences and terms are said to be ground or closed). The calls to **q** and **r** are just tests that produce no bindings and so are independent. In general, only at runtime can independence of goals **q** and **r** be known. Compiletime analysis has been proposed to reduce the considerable overhead of dynamic independence testing [e.g., Delgado-Rannauro, 1992a].

3.2 Or-Parallelism

The problem with the above so-called *and-parallelism* is that shared variables are a form of dependency that can lead to conflicts of interest. At second look, a more promising task decomposition is *or-parallelism*. In depth-first evaluation, the alternative clauses for **partition** are tried in turn. Only if a clause fails is the next in textual order considered. Since, semantically, alternative solutions to a goal are independent, breadth-first search is a natural candidate for parallel execution. Each parallel branch is a *thread,* an independent locus of control. The problems of the combinatorial explosion of breadth-first search were elaborated in Chapter 1. Consequently, or-parallelism is usually only advocated when there are idle processors.

The terminology or-parallelism comes from AI search problems but as far as logic is concerned, or-parallelism is perhaps a confusing misnomer since clauses are, if anything, logically conjoined, not disjoined. This can be understood from Gentzen's *and* introduction rule on the left:

$$\frac{C1, C2 \vdash C}{C1 \wedge C2 \vdash C}$$

The term or-parallelism is used here at the control metalevel. A more appropriate name might be clause search parallelism. In this respect, the reader should not be confused by the Prolog or-operator (denoted by a semicolon in Edinburgh syntax [Bowen et al., 1981]) which is a metapredicate that exploits the nondeterministic search of Prolog to simulate logical disjunction.

From a conceptual viewpoint, the explorations of the alternative branches of the clause search tree are independent. From an implementation viewpoint, the alternative branches are highly dependent. Alternative clauses are invoked with the same initial conditions. In the usual WAM implementation [Ait-Kaci, 1991], the initial conditions are represented by a stack frame. A frame is associated with each instance of a clause invoked during execution. The frame serves to record the parent clause, the subsequent goal and the bindings of newly introduced variables. In general, alternative clauses lead to different variable bindings. The binding frame poses another conflict situation for parallel evaluation. With depth-first search, because only one branch of the search is explored at a time, at most one binding for each variable need be stored. These bindings are recorded in a trail stack. On backtracking, the trail stack is used to clear the binding frames of bindings caused by the previous clause choice. For breadth-first search, an obvious possibility for avoiding contention is to duplicate the binding frame for each clause; this is computationally expensive. More sophisticated methods have been proposed but these are complex [e.g., Delgado-Rannauro, 1992b] and still have considerable overhead. This situation illustrates that while theoretical decomposition of the problem may superficially suggest independent subtasks, the efficient implementation introduces hidden dependencies.

3.3 The Prolog Phenomenon[1]

The prospect of adapting Prolog for parallel execution stems from the intuition that if it takes n units of time for one agent to perform a task then n agents can perform the task in one unit of time. Brooks [1975] satirically provides a counterexample:

> *If it takes one woman nine months to produce a baby then nine women can produce a baby in one month.*

This is substantiated by naive attempts to parallelize Prolog. Prolog's success is intimately related to its stack control structure. Adapting Warren's implementation to take advantage of parallel hardware is much more complex than had been predicted by its advocates [e.g., Conery and Kibler, 1981].

Parker [1990] expressed concerns about Prolog's inflexible control mechanism for knowledge based applications, such as the hypothetical financial trading system considered in Section 2.5. It might be expected that such applications would need to access and import external knowledge incrementally from online information servers, such as Reuters. This data comes over a network, but other sources could be external devices, relational databases or, more simply, just files. Servers that handle input and output expect client programs to manage file descriptors and cursors. Nevertheless, Prolog, having declarative aspirations, encourages a style of programming that can abstract away such detail. Prolog has an inability to observe the arguments of a goal from outside a recursion without resorting to side effects. This means that in reading data from a database the whole relation must be imported wholesale into memory before it can be analyzed. For large databases Prolog requires large amounts of memory. Ideally, I/O processing programs must selectively read data items from multiple streams, process these items and selectively write multiple output channels. A stream is an incrementally constructed data structure. Streams are used in Unix for communication between processes and I/O devices. To handle streams requires an ability to suspend processing and interleave input with the data transformation and output. The consumer must wait for the producer. This is known as *condition synchronization*. Parker [1990] proposes meta-interpretation to solve this database interface problem. This solution suffers from busy waiting and the overhead of meta-interpretation. Busy waiting describes continuous testing of a variable waiting for some value to appear. Partial evaluation cannot be used to alleviate the problem of meta-interpretation because the input data is not known in advance.

Conway [1963] introduced a solution called coroutining as an improved way of executing multipass compilers:

> *A coroutine is an autonomous program that communicates with other coroutines as if they were input and output subroutines.*

In a multipass compiler, coroutines interleave successive passes of the source that incrementally transform a stream of input tokens into assembled code. The execution of coroutines is demand scheduled:

---

[1] Title borrowed from McDermott [1980].

> *When coroutines A and B are connected so that A sends items to B,*
> *B runs for a while until it encounters a read command, which*
> *means that it needs something from A. The control is then trans-*
> *ferred to A until it writes, whereupon control is returned to B at the*
> *point where it left off.*

Conway noted that coroutines could be executed simultaneously if parallel hardware were available. Simula and *Modula* both provide co-routines. Coroutining appeared in *IC-Prolog* [Clark and McCabe, 1979] for a somewhat different reason. Some Prolog primitives, such as arithmetic, are infinitely indeterministic. Edinburgh Prolog requires certain arguments to be ground to make them deterministic (functional). If a primitive is called with its arguments insufficiently instantiated, an exception is raised. The normal Prolog computation selects the literals to resolve in the textual order in which they appear in the body of a clause. Coroutining allows the computation rule to be changed so that such primitives are selected only when they are sufficiently instantiated or if there is no other choice.

Coroutining was used in Prolog to delay the evaluation of negations until all arguments are ground [Naish, 1985]. By their nature, definite clauses can only infer positive information. Negative atoms in goals were used by Absys [Foster and Elcock, 1969], Planner [Hewitt, 1969] and Prolog to extend the expressiveness of the languages through the nonmonotonic negation as failure. Negation as failure is a computable approximation to Reiter's [1978] closed world assumption. Negated goals that fail to be proved with exhaustive search are deemed to have established the negation. Negation as failure presents some control difficulties. It becomes unsound when the search is incomplete as it is using depth-first search and cuts. Unsoundness is also introduced by the existential quantification of variables in a goal. In practice, negations are usually placed towards the end of a Prolog goal so that they have a greater chance of being bound by the time they are called. If negative goals are unbound when called, an exception is raised. An *exception* is an undesirable state of the computation from which recovery is not possible and the computation has to be aborted. Even if coroutining is used to delay the evaluation of negative goals there are still problems. For some programs, no goal ordering can be relied on to produce ground negative goals. This situation is called *floundering*. Negation as failure is nonmonotonic and the semantics are not at all simple [e.g., Apt, 1994]. This detracts somewhat from the declarative claims of logic programming.

Coroutining was also proposed for Prolog for metalevel control [Dincbas, 1980; Gallaire and Lassere, 1980]. Criticism of the eagerness of clause invocation was noted for a predecessor of Prolog:

For some time we have been studying Planner and the uses to which it has been put, hoping to learn just what modifications would be desirable to the user community. These investigations have led us to decide that the basic control structure of Planner is wrong, though its success indicates that it contains many powerful (and seductive) ideas.

[Sussman and McDermott, 1972]

Sussman and McDermott complain that the eagerness of rules that may be invoked by Planner's pattern matching suggests independent ways of solving the same problem. Often, different clauses will duplicate solutions, fail with the same unacceptable variable bindings or run out of space because of unbounded depth of search trees. Novice programmers certainly find the duplication of solutions annoying and difficult to understand.

According to Newell [1981], a program cannot be described as intelligent if it does not make intelligent search. One might learn from mistakes by examining the assumptions that lead to failure. Backtracking suffers from many maladies and many refinements have been proposed. These can be classified as lookback and lookahead schemes. Lookback schemes attempt to improve on the choice of backtrack point by taking into account the causes of failure of previous branches. A failure to unify with any clause provides negative constraints on the variables in the failing goal. In logic programming, lookback is known as intelligent backtracking [Bruynooghe, 1991]. Intelligent backtracking has been a research topic for some time without leading to any acceptable working systems. A comprehensive bibliography was given in [Wolfram, 1986]. Lookahead schemes are concerned with restricting the choice of instantiation of variables and dynamic search rearrangement. Lookahead schemes include constraint satisfaction, as described in Chapter 1.

Constraint satisfaction and logic programming combine very naturally [Jaffar and Maher, 1994]. As Herbrand proposed [1930], unification of a clause head and a goal can be viewed as an equality constraint system. Constraint satisfaction was used in the first logic programming language, Absys [Foster and Elcock, 1969]. In Absys, a relation is defined by a bi-implication, known in logic programming as the *Clark Completion* [Clark, 1978]. The concatenate relation above would appear as the definition:

conc(List1,List2,List1List2) $\leftrightarrow$ (

    List1=[] $\wedge$ List1List2=List2)

  $\vee$ (List1=[Item] $\wedge$ List1List2=[Item|List2])

  $\vee$ (List1=[Item1,Item2|List4] $\wedge$ List1List2=[Item1,Item2|List3]

    $\wedge$ **conc**(List4,List2,List3)

)

All variables are assumed to be universally quantified. This presentation emphasizes the Absys designers' motivation of removing all forms of control and direction from a program. To provide a semantics for negation as failure, Clark [1978] used this form of closure of a definite clause. In Absys, equality relations are treated as coroutines and are reduced asynchronously. An equality predicate $X = Y$ is only reduced if one of the arguments is nonvariable. If both are variables, the goal suspends. The designers justified this by the symmetry of equality. By contrast in Prolog, recently introduced variables are bound to ones introduced previously (lower down the stack).

An attempt to overcome criticism of Planner's chronological backtracking was *Conniver* [Sussman and McDermott, 1972]. According to its developers, Conniver provides a more flexible form of control where arbitrary goals can suspend animation. A suspended goal is poised to continue where it left off. This makes it necessary to maintain a control tree, the leaves of which form a set of threads coperating to solve a problem. Sussman and McDermott complain that the search and data manipulation activities of Planner are too automatic. In Conniver, an active goal can relinquish control not only by returning to its parent but also by passing control to a goal in a suspended state (a coroutine). Two sorts of variables that act as producers and consumers of variable bindings provide synchronization. Besides moving up and down the hierarchical goal graph, flow of control may now also wander among the goals at the tree tips by suspending and resuming execution. Sussman and McDermott [1972] claim that backtracking search is of questionable use for applications in AI.

> *Programs that use exhaustive search are often the worst algorithms for problem solving ... The ubiquity of implicit search and the illusion of power that a query gives the user merely by use of invisible failure-driven loops encourage superficial analysis and poor programming practice.*

Conniver's generalized control structure allows programmer control over failure and backtracking. Variable bindings in one branch of the search tree are available to provide information to prune another. So that the speculation each clause indulges in does not interfere with a goal for some alternative clause, each clause has to have its own binding frame. This is the problem encountered with or-parallelism above; it leads to a tree of binding contexts rather than a stack. The alternative variable bindings produced by a clause are returned to a goal in the form of a list. All this makes the complexity of Conniver much greater than the difficulty of controlling failure driven loops. It never gained much of a following.

The trade-off between expressive power and implementation efficiency is at the heart of many arguments about the relative merits of different languages. At the start of the Fifth Generation initiative, The *Handbook of Artificial Intelligence* [Barr and Feigenbaum, 1982] proposed four language features that were deemed to be particularly important for AI applications:

- the ability to define data structures that are expressive and easy to handle;
- pattern directed procedure invocation;
- the existence of flexible control structures, in particular coroutining;
- an enhanced programming environment.

The earliest programming languages only permitted a programmer to process numbers first as scalars and then in arrays. A major contribution of the symbolic programming languages was the introduction of lists (IPL) and then binary trees (Lisp). The pattern directed procedure invocation advocated by Barr and Feigenbaum is probably a reference to Planner and rule-based systems. The requirement for flexible control structures is probably a reference to Conniver's criticism of Planner. The reference to enhanced programming environment stems from the facilities provided by Lisp and Smalltalk workstations.

3.4 Concurrency and Operating Systems

Concurrent programming encompasses nonhierarchical control such as coroutining, threads and processes and parallelism. A thread is a sequence of actions. Sometimes the word process is used in place of thread but may be better reserved for the case where an exclusive resource (address space) is associated with a thread. Concurrent programs have characteristics that differentiate them from other kinds. Harel and Pnueli [1985] drew the distinction between transformational and reactive programs. *Transformational* programs begin with the input of data, transform the input, output the result and terminate. This is the class of program most usually studied in computability theory. In contrast, *reactive* programs undergo continuous interaction with their environment. Sometimes reactive programs are effectively perpetual (they do not terminate). Operating systems, interactive graphical user interfaces with multiple windows, distributed systems and event driven real-time systems are all examples of reactive systems.

Earliest experience of concurrent systems was gained with operating systems. With Lisp, McCarthy devised a language needed to express the algorithms of AI. However, early versions of Lisp were inefficient and computing resources were scarce. While at MIT, McCarthy and others invented time-sharing to alleviate the problem of scarce resources. A number of graduate students formed the Digital Equipment Corporation, DEC, to market timesharing minicomputers. With the advent of timesharing, the emphasis of computing gradually changed from algorithms to systems. In the mid-1960s, Dijkstra [1968a] and colleagues developed the first multiprogrammed operating system, *THE*, at the University of Eindoven. The name THE derives from the name of the institution. The architecture of the operating system is hierarchical with a kernel and layers of virtual machines implemented by processes.

An early influential paper Dijkstra [1965] drew attention to the problem of mutual exclusion to resources shared between asynchronous processes. This was the first of many synchronization problems that have become classics. The mutual exclusion problem arises when testing and setting of shared resources is not atomic. Dijkstra credits Dekker with a solution for two processes that assumes load and store operations to be atomic but requires no other hardware. Contemporary microprocessors have at least one instruction that facilitates atomic test and set. Dijkstra extended Dekker's algorithm to any number of processes. Since then, numerous other versions that simplify the algorithm or improve fairness have been devised. Because the mutual exclusion problem is fundamental, there have been hundreds of papers and one entire book [Raynal, 1986] on the topic. The premature binding problem, exposed previously in trying to parallelize Prolog, is a manifestation of the mutual exclusion problem. Dijkstra [1968b] introduced and gave solutions for two further classic synchronization problems, the dining philosophers and the sleeping barber. Courtois et al. [1971] proposed solutions to another classic problem of concurrency, the readers and writers problem.

In the late 1960s, a few operating system architects realized that organizing an operating system as a collection of processes communicating by passing messages would avoid the mutual exclusion problem. This changed the problem of operating systems from one of sharing resources to one of cordination of processes. Brinch-Hansen's [1970] multiprogramming nucleus for the Danish RC 40000 was an early proposal for a message passing operating system. The similarity with biological systems is apparent. Biological systems maintain control by confining functionality and their data in self-contained cells. These cells act on each other by sending messages carried by chemical messengers. The cell membrane protects its data, DNA, from inappropriate processes. This analogy inspired Kay's [1972, 1993] Flex language and subsequently Smalltalk. Because it is more efficient to communicate using shared variables than message passing, most operating systems still use shared variables for process communication within a machine. Such operating systems, however, provide message-passing primitives so that processes can communicate with other machines over a network.

3.5 Concurrency and Distributed Systems

The process-message-passing concept developed in operating systems naturally lends itself to distributed systems. A distributed computing system consists of multiple von Neumann machines that coperate by sending messages over a communication network. A distributed architecture where computers are physically close, communication is fast and reliable, is said to be *closely coupled*. An example is a Transputer array. In contrast, systems with relatively unreliable communication between processors that are physically widely separated are *loosely coupled*. An example is a local area network (LAN).

Loosely coupled distributed systems are now favored over other architectures such as timesharing systems and shared memory multiprocessors for a number of reasons. First, for critical applications such as fly-by-wire aircraft or control of nuclear power installations, a single processor may not be reliable enough. Distributed systems are potentially more reliable because they have a *partial failure property*. Failure of one processor does not necessarily prevent the correct functioning of other processors. Second, they are scalable: greater power can be achieved by adding more devices. While increases in speed can be achieved with shared memory multiprocessors, such architectures do not easily scale to a large number of processors. Finally, there are applications where distribution is inherent such as sending electronic mail between workstations. Some applications are naturally structured as collections of specialized services. In control systems, it is natural to embody computation at the point of sensing, to filter irrelevancies and compress data.

Processes in a single computer that require the same resources can potentially interfere with one another. Control by mutual exclusion can lead to deadlock. Avoiding deadlock becomes particularly difficult in distributed systems because information about tasks and resources are distributed. In early operating systems, centralized resource management proved a more effective form of control. In a distributed system, any manager can become a bottleneck and centralized control is not fault tolerant to the failure of a manager. Having deputy managers take over when necessary can reduce this drawback. This has the overhead of having to keep the deputies informed of the current state of the manager.

More decentralized regimes grant access to resources based on local information. This reduces the overhead and bottlenecks, but might not prevent contention because local views may be inconsistent. In this case, mechanisms must be available to detect interference and recover from it. This may involve aborting and restarting some tasks. This is only feasible where recovery is relatively inexpensive (small tasks) and infrequent compared with the cost of maintaining global views.

In distributed scheduling, tasks arrive over time at nodes that have particular resource constraints: computation time, priorities and deadlines. Generally, nodes schedule tasks to maximize some performance criteria, such as servicing high priority tasks and meeting as many deadlines as possible. In a given time interval, some nodes may have more high priority tasks to perform than others and migrating tasks between nodes might improve the overall network performance. In decentralized control, local processing and task migration are possible. A local scheduler that cannot meet scheduling criteria might contract another node with fewer demands on it to perform the task. Distributed schedulers have borrowed techniques from distributed AI to do this contracting out [Ramamritham and Stankovic, 1984; Stankovic et al., 1985].

Managing consistency is essentially the same as controlling access to shared resources. Data could reside on a single node but this can become a bottleneck. Reliability is reduced if the node fails. If data is replicated, changes to the data have to be coordinated. If not, inconsistencies can be introduced. Cordination must either incur the overhead of continually insuring against inconsistency or the overhead of correcting the effects of inconsistencies. Nodes can modify local copies atomically and simultaneously or make local changes and detect when inconsistency arises. In the latter situation, nodes have to negotiate which of different views to converge on and activities based on inconsistent views rescinded.

Elementary distributed operating systems provide print services and a file archiving services. With resource sharing, the process model is refined to a client-server model. Servers are processes that act as resource managers. Clients are processes that require access to shared resources. The communication pattern is asymmetric. Clients initiate requests to servers. Generally, servers can receive requests from any client. When a request is received, a server queues the requests. Servers lie idle when the service queue is empty. In Unix systems, the client-server model has been successfully applied to the provision of permanent storage with NFS (Network File System) and the provision of a window interfaces in the X system. Client-server systems tend to have a few servers with much functionality built into each one. A refinement of the client server-model is the object model [Liskov and Zilles, 1975; Liskov et al., 1977]. An object can act as both server and client and consequently have smaller functionality. Any service an object cannot fulfil can be delegated to other objects.

Operating systems were initially concerned with independent tasks and the primary design objective was the efficient use of resources. Cordination is necessary to avoid contention and deadlock. Scheduling has to be controlled to meet performance requirements. Control is required to ensure the integrity of distributed data. These concerns of distributed systems are also concerns of distributed AI.

3.6 Symbiosis Between Programming Language and System Engineering

The resource management systems that make up an operating system need to cooperate to provide a virtual machine to a user. Attwood [1976] describes the enormous difficulty in designing an operating or distributed system. Operating systems are particularly difficult to construct and the advantage of using high-level languages for programming them proved itself in the symbiosis between C and Unix. High-level systems programming languages lead to significant reductions in coding effort, code size and bugs. They also provide portability and relative ease of modification. Although early versions of Unix were not multiprogramming, the operating system rapidly evolved to a multi-user, timesharing system. Unix users could create tasks consisting of two or more processes connected by pipes. A pipe is a one-way communication channel, the ends of which can be inherited by child processes. This allows two processes to communicate provided they have a common ancestor. Microkernel distributed operating systems like Mach [Baron et al., 1987], V [Cheriton, 1987] and *Chorus* [Rozier et al., 1987] are written mostly in C.

High-level languages like Prolog and Planner deliberately impose structure on the problem-solving behavior of the user making the expression of certain problems more natural and (hopefully) discouraging bad programming practice. They encapsulate high-level problem-solving concepts that generally make some forms of reasoning about programs simpler. Program design by stepwise refinement is a natural partner of modular design and hierarchical control of stack-based procedure calling. The drawback is that restriction on the allowed data structures, control structures and primitives make some algorithms more difficult to write than others. To handle system programming, a language needs to express dynamic process creation and termination, synchronization, communication and resource control.

In response to the growing costs of software development and maintenance of systems programs, the United States Department of Defense invited proposals for a new language. The winning proposal was called Ada [Ichbiah et al., 1979] after Augusta Ada Lovelace, daughter of the poet Byron. Lady Lovelace was a student of Jevons and a collaborator of Babbage and often said to be the first programmer. The *Ada* language extended *Pascal* (itself a derivative of Algol for teaching structured programming) to include features to support concurrency and programming in the large. Ada reflects the evident need to maintain very strict control over assignment in concurrent systems. Liskov et al. [1986] conclude that Ada's combination of synchronous communication and static process structure leads to complex solutions to common problems. Clarke et al's [1980] low opinion of procedure nesting in Ada (inherited from Pascal) is encapsulated in the title of the paper: *Nesting in Ada programs is for the birds*. Roberts et al. [1981] conclude that Ada does not meet the needs of real-time programming for which it was intended. Hoare [1981] who was employed as a consultant in the design of Ada gave a warning:

> *And so, the best of my advice to the originators of Ada has been ig-*
> *nored. In this last resort, I appeal to you, representatives of the*
> *programming profession of the United States, and citizens con-*
> *cerned with the welfare of your own country and mankind: Do not*
> *allow this language in its present state to be used in applications*

> *where reliability is critical, i.e., nuclear power stations, cruise missiles, early warning systems, anti-ballistic missile defense systems.*

Dijkstra [1972] and Brinch-Hansen [1972] proposed using the class structure of Simula for controlling access to shared variables in a concurrent program. Simula has control primitives, *call, detach* and *resume* which can be used to implement coroutines. In coroutines, synchronization is hidden in the input and output commands but the primitives of Simula allow other more obscure types of synchronization. The resume command, in particular, behaves like a goto command but with a moving target. Hoare [1974] describes solutions to the classic bounded buffer, interval timer and disk head scheduler (elevator algorithm) using a specific language proposal called *monitors*.

Smalltalk, inheritor of the Simula class structure, was further inspired by the biological analogy. Smalltalk was designed to be more than a programming language. Like the Fifth Generation, it was also a kernel language and used to implement computer operating systems. Objects in Smalltalk were viewed as both persistent and dynamic. Every object is always ready to receive and send messages and many objects can be active simultaneously. In Smalltalk, a user program can obtain an answer from an instance of a class by sending it a request but without knowing whether the information is data or a procedure. Kay [1973] exploited this in a distributed version of Smalltalk:

> *Though Smalltalk's structure allows the technique now known as data abstraction to be easily (and more generally) employed, the entire thrust of its design has been to supersede the idea of data and procedures entirely and to replace these with the more generally useful notions of activity, communication and inheritance.*
>
> [Kay, 1972]

3.7 Event Driven Synchronization

According to Arvind and Ianucci [1987] the two main issues that must be addressed by any successful exploitation of multiple processors are latency and synchronization. Latency is the elapsed time between the issue of a data request and its corresponding receipt. If data is situated on a nonlocal store, the access time is increased by transit through the communication network. This is compounded because requests are queued and not acted upon at once. The access time is typically orders of magnitude longer than an instruction cycle. This is particularly the case for Risc processors. Avoiding the processor idling while waiting for a response is vital. With synchronization, a process may wait for any one of a number of events and take different actions depending on the particular event. This is called *or-synchronization* by Maekawa et al. [1987]. Processes may require access to several resources simultaneously; this they call *and-synchronization*. It is sometimes convenient to synchronize processes using the absence of a condition instead of its presence. This is known as *not-synchronization*.

Petri's nets [Petri, 1962] was the first theory of synchronization. It is a generalization of the theory of automata studied in the 1950s [Shannon and McCarthy, 1956]. In classical automata, an automaton can be in one of any number of different states. The theory studies the nature and structure of transitions from one state to another. For Petri nets, changes also occur through transitions. A transition is characterized by preconditions, which must hold before it occurs and post-conditions, which must hold after it occurs. The (global) state of a Petri net is a simultaneous holding of a number of conditions. The nodes of the network represent the conditions. The literature on Petri nets is vast [Reisig, 1985].

Dijkstra [1975; 1976] argued that programmers should not be required to specify details such as synchronization that are not inherent in the problem. Not only is inessential detail wasteful of coding time, it may have adverse effects on the clarity of the program. It over specifies the required functionality. This is an argument for declarative programming. In imperative programming, programmers have to specify the sequences of tests. More often than not, such sequencing is a product of the computational model rather than the problem being solved. In Dijkstra's Guarded Command Language, the complex alternative (if) and iterative (do) statements are formed from guarded statements. Each guarded statement (command) has the form:

    <guard> -> statement.

The guard is a Boolean expression that evaluates to true or false. The alternative statement contains one or more guarded statements:

    if
        G_1 -> S_1
        G_2 -> S_2
        ...
        G_n -> S_n
    fi

Guards are not expected to be evaluated in any particular order. If only one guard G_i evaluates true, the command S_i is executed. If more than one guard evaluates to true, the choice of which statement to be executed is indeterministic. If no guard is true, execution of the if alternative has no effect. The iterative do statement is similar to the alternative statement except that guarded statements are repeatedly evaluated until all guards evaluate to false.

Many people including Hoare [1978] realized that Dijkstra's guards provided a basis for specifying synchronization in concurrent programs. In Hoare's experimental concurrent language *CSP* (Communicating Sequential Processes), both message send and receipt are guarded. CSP was not intended as a programming language but, rather, a paradigm. *Occam* is the most well known language based on CSP's synchronous communication. The concurrent programming language Occam was the result of *satisficing* (Chapter 2) the theoretical requirements with the difficulty of designing hardware to support it. The Transputer is significant in two respects regarding the FGCS: it provides direct hardware support for processes and communication and it was designed as a building block for parallel machines.

3.8 Earlier Manifestations of Guarded Commands

An earlier manifestation of guarded commands can be seen in database management systems. In 1958 the management services section of General Electric Company used decision tables to specify a prototype order processing system. A decision table is a tabular arrangement that specifies a combinational machine. Finite state machines are subdivided into combinational and sequential. Both current input and previous inputs determine the output of sequential machines. In other words, the machine has a memory. With combinational machines, the output is dictated solely by the input.

As an example, a simple decision table (adapted from [Subramanian et al., 1992]) for the hypothetical example of stock market trading in Chapter 2 takes the form of Figure 3.8.1.

Input	Rule1	Rule2	Rule3	Rule4
interest rate	down	down	down	up
exchange rate	up	–	down	down
	down	up	–	up
Action				
BT	buy	buy		sell
BA	buy	buy		sell
ATT	buy	sell	buy	sell

Fig. 3.8.1 Equity trading decision table

Rules are read vertically and conditions are separated fom actions. The underscores represent *don't care* conditions where the input is inconsequential on the output. Other arrangements are used, but the main principle is to cover all possible input combinations. Babbage used a number of graphical notations in the design of his analytic engine. One of these can be recognized as a state transition diagram.

Experimental interpreters for a decision table language *Tabsol* [Kavanagh, 1960] were developed by General Electric. General Electric's favorable experience with decision tables led to their inclusion in the company's procedure-oriented language *Geocom* [Sterbenz, 1971]. In the early 1960s, The Insurance Company of North America produced a decision table system to manage a large complex file system [Brown, 1962]. The system, called *Loboc* (Logical Business Oriented Language), inputs conditional statements and outputs an assembler language program. The porting of Loboc to a third generation machine is reported in Devine [1965].

The *Decision Logic Translator* [Reinwald, 1966] produced Fortran code for the IBM 1401 from a decision table specification. *Fortab*, developed by RAND for the IBM 7090, provided FORTRAN-embedded decision table entry [Armerding, 1962]. Fortab tolerated indeterminism in a table by prioritizing rules. It selected the first rule found to satisfy its condition in the order input by the programmer. The Systems Group of CODASYL introduced the decision table programming language *Detab-X* [CODASYL, 1962] for database management. Detab-X was designed to be compiled to Cobol but the full language was never implemented. A subset of Detab-X, *Detab/65*, was implemented and became widely successful.

A more recent manifestation of condition synchronization is seen in active databases. Rather than a repository of passive facts, active databases are able to react to the data they contain [Astrahan et al., 1976; Bunemann and Clemons, 1979; McBrien et al., 1991]. The actions are specified by a set of rules. Triggers are predicates that are the labels of rules.

trigger: Cond → Action

The conditions are tested against the database only when a trigger has been activated. Triggers remain active for only one evaluation cycle.

Decision tables and decision trees are established aids in decision making [Gregory, 1988]. They have proved indispensable techniques of systems analysis [De Marco, 1979] and real-time specification [Hatley and Pirbhai, 1987]. The expert system *Emycin* groups rules into decision tables. The tables are used to simplify the checking for errors within sets of rules. Entries in the table summarize cases of conflict, redundancy and missing cases.

3.9 Condition Synchronization in AI

Condition synchronization appeared in AI under the guise of *PDIS*. A Pattern-Directed Inference System (PDIS) [Waterman and Hayes-Roth, 1978] is a form of program control associated with the Impressionist Movement of AI (Section 1.8). It is still represented today by languages such as OPS5 [Forgy, 1981]. Pattern-directed systems refer to a method of procedure (or module) invocation. In a sequential computation, the procedures of the system call each other hierarchically. Each program module specifies precisely which module will be executed next by explicitly calling it. The corresponding flow of execution is deterministic and most naturally sequential. In a pattern-directed organization, rules are not directly invoked by other rules. Instead they are invoked by patterns that occur in the environment.

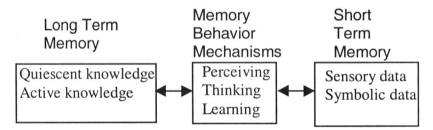

Fig. 3.9.1. A simple model of human cognition

A PDIS has three basic components: firstly, a collection of rules that can be activated, or fired, by patterns in the environment; second, zero or more data structures that form the environment; finally, an executive that controls the selection and activation of rules. In the Impressionist Movement, PDIS were justified by a simple model of cognition that consists of long term and short term memories with mental behavior mechanisms relating the two, Figure 3.9.1. The rules represent long term memory. The environment of data structures that can be examined and modified form the short-term memory. The executive comprises the mental behavior mechanisms of perceiving, thinking and learning.

In PDISs, rules consist of antecedent-consequent pairs. The examination of data takes place in the antecedent while the modification takes place in the consequent of the rule. The data structures in the environment can range over lists, trees, graphs and propositions. Data examination in PDIS consists of pattern matching portions of the environment with the antecedents of rules. The patterns may be defined in many ways: as simple strings, or complex graphs. The matching is not restricted to structural matching; evaluation of arbitrary constraints on the environment is allowed. Data modification can be as simple as asserting that some proposition holds, or as complex as arbitrary modifications of the environment. Even the executive structure can vary from a simple implicit ordering to complex heuristics and metarules.

The execution of PDISs can be defined as a series of recognize-act cycles. This is illustrated in Figure 3.9.2 by a hypothetical example of equity trading of Section 3.3.

PRIOR ENVIRONMENT	{DU, ID, XD}		
PRODUCTION RULES	CONFLICT SET	SELECTED RULE	ACTION
ID ∧XU ∧DD → A1			
ID ∧DU → A2	*	*	A2
XD → A3	*		
IU ∧XD ∧DU → A4			
POST ENVIRONMENT	{XD}		

Fig. 3.9.2. Simple RBS for equity trading

with the abbreviations:

IU: interest rate up
ID: interest rate down
XU: exchange rate up
XD: exchange rate down
DU: deficit up
DD: deficit down
A1: buy BT shares, buy BA shares and buy ATT shares
A2: buy BA shares, buy BT shares, and sell ATT shares
A3: buy ATT shares
A4: sell BA shares, sell BT shares and sell ATT shares

The "recognize" portion of the cycle consists of comparing rule conditions with the environment to find matches. The "conflict set" comprises all rules, the antecedent of which is satisfied by the current environment. Some form of conflict resolution, the process of deciding which satisfied rule to fire, is applied to the conflict set. Once a rule is selected, the cycle concludes with the "act" step during which the actions in the consequent of the rule are executed. The above example is for obvious reasons said to be antecedent driven.

The example can be transcribed to Prolog:

```
%market(InterestRate, XchangeRate, Deficit)
market(down,up,down) :-
    bt(buy), ba(buy), att(buy).
market(down,_,down) :-
    bt(sell), ba(buy).
market(down,down,_) :-
    att(buy).
market(up,down,up) :-
    bt(sell), ba(sell), att(sell).
```

The underscore is the Prolog anonymous variable. Multiple occurrences are considered distinct variables. Each definite clause can be viewed as a pattern-directed module. The environment is the current goal list to be satisfied. A clause guard corresponds to a rule antecedent. The conflict set is the set of clauses whose guards are satisfied. To execute a module means replace the goal in the environment with the list of goals in the body of a clause.

The analogy between PDIS and Prolog breaks down in a number of respects:

- In Prolog only clauses matching the head of the goal stack can be executed. This is not true of logic programming in general though; any clause that unifies with any goal in the resolvent can be executed.
- In PDISs, the flow of control is determined by patterns that occur in the environment. For Prolog the control is textual order, depth-first with backtracking on failure. That is, Prolog is in the above sense a conventional organization in which the procedures of the system call each other according to a fixed scheme. Each program procedure decides which other procedure will be executed next by explicitly calling them. The corresponding flow of execution is sequential and reproducible.
- Logic programming is nondeterministic while PDISs are usually indeterministic. The distinction between deterministic, indeterministic and nondeterministic comes from the theory of automata [Filman and Friedman, 1984]. A *deterministic* automaton traverses one fixed computation path for each possible input. An *indeterministic* automaton has points in the computation, branch points, where it is possible to follow any one of a number of alternative paths; the choice made is not dependent on the initial input. A *nondeterministic* automaton has similar branch points but attempts to traverse all possible branches, possibly in a breadth-first or depth-first manner. The potential for indeterminism in logic programming is made nondeterministic in Prolog by backtracking on failure; that is the Prolog evaluation of a program with the same input is always the same. In Production Systems the environment generally consists of many distinct data structures. A production rule can be used to modify any number of such data structures. In Prolog, the body of a rule is used to replace only one goal literal.
- In Production Systems, there is a total separation of data examination from data modification. With PDISs, examination takes part in the recognize part of the cy-

cle while modification takes part in the "act" part of the cycle. With Prolog, unification is eager; it combines data examination and data modification.

- The pattern matching of the data structures in PDIS is much more complex than Prolog. The environment of a PDIS is a multiset. Set inclusion of structured data is a highly nondeterministic computation. Restrictions on the allowed patterns and specialized algorithms, such as RETE [Forgy, 1982], have been developed to perform pattern matching efficiently.

- Pattern-directed systems are antecedent driven. Once a member of the conflict set is chosen the action taken is not rescinded. Since Prolog is consequent driven, bindings of variables accrued in a Prolog refutation proof are only considered useful if the empty clause is eventually derived. A Prolog program would modify the data in an attempt to derive the empty clause. If this attempt fails, all modifications to the environment since the last branch point are meaningless.

- With backwards reasoning, as used in logic programming, when the environment is empty the computation terminates with success. When the conflict set is empty, the goal fails. For a forward reasoning pattern-directed inference engine, as described in the example above, the computation certainly terminates when the conflict set is empty but not necessarily with failure. The nonempty environment represents the answer to the problem the program was designed to solve.

3.10 Guarded Definite Clauses

To some extent, a Prolog program can simulate pattern-directed inference by preventing backtracking using the cut as the first goal in a clause. By placing the cut further into the body, the clauses can often be made deterministic. In the intended mode of use of the **qsort** program above, the clauses for partition are deterministic. The pattern in the head distinguishes the first clause from the second and third clause. The comparison test in the body distinguishes the second and third clauses. Experienced Prolog programmers are often tempted to include a cut in each clause for partition to utilize this fact:

```
%partition(List,Pivot,Lesser,Greater)
part([],Pivot,[],[]) :- !.
part([Item|List],Pivot,Lesser,[Item|Greater]) :-
    Pivot=<Item, !,
    part(List,Pivot,Lesser,Greater).
part([Item|List],Pivot,[Item|Lesser],Greater) :-
    Item<Pivot, !,
    part(List,Pivot,Lesser,Greater).
```

The cut in the last clause is not, of course, necessary but is added for symmetry. The cuts are metalevel directives to the interpreter to take advantage of the mutual exclusion (between clauses) and prevent backtracking; the cut prunes the binding frame stack to the most recent previous choice point.

However, for pattern-directed inference systems, any output variable substitution would have to be considered as a component of the "act" part of the recognize-act cycle; with Prolog it is a component of the recognize part. The resolution mechanism of Prolog is intertwined with unification. The resolution mechanism of Robinson [1965] deliberately integrates unification with complimentary literal elimination (a manifestation of the cut rule). Unification can be thought of as a sophisticated two-way pattern matching. It is an integration of two data-manipulation operations: input term pattern matching and output variable substitution. Input term pattern-matching subsumes structured data component access, syntactic equality testing and parameter passing. Output variable substitution subsumes data construction and returning values.

By using the Prolog syntactic equality primitive, unification can be performed in the body of clauses but this really does not solve the problem of the eagerness of clause head unification. For some arguments, the syntactic equality tests are more like what is needed.

```
%partition(List,Pivot,Lesser,Greater)
part(List,Pivot,Lesser,Greater) :-
    List==[], !,
    Lesser=[], Greater=[].
part(List,Pivot,Lesser,Greater) :-
    List==[Item|List1], Pivot=<Item, !,
    Greater=[Item|Greater1],
    part(List1,Pivot,Lesser,Greater1).
part(List,Pivot,Lesser,Greater) :-
    List==[Item|List1], Item<Pivot, !,
    Lesser=[Item|Lesser1], part(List,Pivot,Lesser1,Greater).
```

But this is still not quite right. The Prolog syntactic equality primitive fails if the terms are not identical, variables and all. What is required is a primitive that will pattern match (data component access and parameter passing) and cause suspension, much like Absys [Foster and Elcock, 1969] until incoming variables are bound by other goals which share variables. As a first attempt, the desired condition synchronization is formalized by a decomposition of a definite clause into two parts: constraints that only test the input and the parts of the clause that can cause variable bindings.

```
<definite-clause> ::= <guard> | <body>
<guard>::= <head> :- <constraints>
```

The program for partition then becomes:

```
//partition(List,Pivot,Lesser,Greater)
part(List,Pivot,Lesser,Greater) :- []«List
    | Lesser=[], Greater=[].
part(List,Pivot,Lesser,Greater)
    :- [Item|List1]«List, Pivot=<Item
    | Greater=[Item|Greater1], part(List1,Pivot,Lesser,Greater1).
part(List, Pivot, Lesser, Greater)
    :- [Item|List1]«List, Item<Pivot
    | Lesser=[Item|Lesser1], part(List,Pivot,Lesser1,Greater).
```

In keeping with object-oriented programming, the // characters indicates that what follows on the same line is a comment. The primitive « is the instance relation: the left-hand argument (local variables) is an instance of the right hand argument (global variables). This can be interpreted in terms of ground (closed) instances. A non-ground term can be thought of as representing the set consisting of all ground (closed) instances of it. The instance relation is then the subset relation.

This instance relation more precisely explained as follows. Let F be the set of functor symbols used in the program, typically denoted by f. (Constants are functors of arity zero.) Let V be an enumerably infinite set of variable symbols including those in the program and typically denoted by X. Then $F^*(V)$ will denote the inductively defined set of terms of type F over V. A substitution is a mapping from V to $F^*(V)$ such that only a finite number of variables are not mapped to themselves. A substitution can be specified by a finite set pairs$\{X_1/t_1, \dots X_k/t_k\}$ where $t_i \neq X_i$ for $i = 1\dots k$. A substitution $\theta:V \rightarrow F(V)$ can be homogeneously extended to a map $\theta:F^*(V) \rightarrow F^*(V)$: $f(t_1,\dots,t_k)\theta = f(t_1\theta,\dots,t_k\theta)$. By convention, substitution application is written postfix. Let *vars* be the function that maps terms to the subset of variable symbols occurring in them. A term t' is said to be an immediate instance of a term t, written $t' \prec t$, if they are related by one of three elementary substitutions:

$t'=t\{X/f(X_1,\dots,X_k)\}$ & $X \in vars(t)$ & $\{X_1,\dots,X_k\} \cap vars(t)= \varnothing$ & (if $i \neq j$ then $X_i \neq X_j$) or

$t'=t\{X/X'\}$ & $\{X,X'\} \subseteq vars(t)$ or

$t'=t\{X/X'\}$ & $X \in vars(t)$ & $X' \notin vars(t)$.

The last elementary substitution is a single variable renaming. Let $\ll$ denote the transitive closure of $\prec$. If $t' \ll t$, then t' is said to be is an *instance* of t. Naturally enough, $\ll$ is transitive, $\ll^2 \subseteq \ll$, but it is also reflexive, $\Delta \subseteq \ll$, where Δ is the identity relation. In other words $(F^*(V)), \ll)$ forms a *preorder* [Reynolds, 1970].

The instance primitive $\ll$ does not cause any bindings of variables in its right hand argument but will bind variables local to the clause in its left hand argument. If the call to **part** is insufficiently bound to satisfy any guard constraint, the call suspends. The difference from a Prolog delay primitive is that the delay primitive only causes suspension. Here any call suspends if it is insufficiently instantiated to satisfy the guard of any of the defining clauses.

The body of a guarded definite clause represents subsequent action if the guard is satisfied. A goal is not reduced to the body of a clause until its guard is satisfied. The remaining part of the GDC (Guarded Definite Clause) program for the quicksort is:

```
//quicksort(UnsortedList, SortedList)
qsort(Unsorted,Sorted) :- []«Unsorted | Sorted=[].
qsort(Unsorted,Sorted) :- [Item]«Unsorted
    | Sorted=[Item].
```

qsort(Unsorted,Sorted):- [Pivot,Item|List]«Unsorted
  | **part**([Item|List],Pivot,Lesser,Greater),
  qsort(Lesser,LSorted),
  qsort(Greater,GSorted),
  conc(LSorted,[Pivot|GSorted],Sorted).

//**conc**atenate(List1,List2,List1+List2)
conc(List1,List2,List1List2) :- []«List1
  | List1List2=List2.
conc(List1,List2,List1List2) :- [Item]«List1
  | List1List2=[Item|List2].
conc(List1,List2,List1List2) :- [Item1,Item2|List11]«List1
  | List1List2=[Item1, Item2|List3],
  conc(List11,List2,List3).

3.11 Simulation of Parallelism by Interleaving

With the control provided by condition synchronization, **part** builds up its sublists item by item as they become available, **qsort** filters them item by item and **conc** consumes them item by item, as they become available. A reduction scenario for the goal

  :- **qsort**([2,1,3],Ss), **ans**(Ss).

best illustrates this. As in Prolog the convention is used that if a variable identifier ends with a letter **s** it is intended to be used as a list. Underscores will denote those goals that satisfy some clause guard and so can be reduced. As previously, the **ans** goal is used to accumulate the answer in the same way as previously.

Reducing the only goal satisfying a clause guard:

  :- <u>**part**([1,3],2,Ls,Gs)</u>, **qsort**(Ls,LSs), **qsort**(Gs,GSs),
    conc(LSs,[2|GSs],Ss), **ans**(Ss).
  :- <u>Ls=[1|L1s]</u>, **part**([3],2,L1s,Gs), **qsort**(Ls,LSs),
    qsort(Gs,GSs), **conc**(LSs,[2|GSs],Ss), **ans**(Ss).

(The word reduction sometimes seems to be inappropriate terminology for an action that may increase the complexity. The resolvent forms a network of goals connected by shared variables.)

Continuing, indeterministicly choosing the goal to reduce:

  :- <u>**part**([3],2,L1s,Gs)</u>, **qsort**([1|L1s],LSs),
    qsort(Gs,GSs), **conc**(LSs,[2|GSs],Ss), **ans**(Ss).
  :- <u>Gs=[3|G1s]</u>, **part**([],2,L1s,G1s), <u>**qsort**([1|L1s],LSs)</u>,
    qsort(Gs,GSs), **conc**(LSs,[2|GSs],Ss), **ans**(Ss).

While underscored goals can be reduced in any order, equality primitives will be given preference, for it is only through these that output variables become bound.

  :- <u>**part**([],2,L1s,G1s)</u>, <u>**qsort**([1|L1s],LSs)</u>, <u>**qsort**([3|G1s],GSs)</u>,
    conc(LSs,[2|GSs],Ss), **ans**(Ss).

:- **part**([],2,L1s,G1s), **part**(L1s,1,L2s,G2s), **qsort**(L2s,L2Ss),
   qsort(G2s,GS2s), **conc**(L2s,[1|GS2s],LSs), **qsort**([3|G1s],GSs),
   conc(LSs,[2|GSs],Ss), **ans**(Ss).
:- L1s=[], G1s=[], **part**(L1s,1,L2s,G2s), **qsort**(L2s,L2Ss),
   qsort(G2s,GS2s), **conc**(L2s,[1|GS2s],LSs), **qsort**([3|G1s],GSs),
   conc(LSs,[2|GSs],Ss), **ans**(Ss).
:- G1s=[], **part**([],1,L2s,G2s), **qsort**(L2s,L2Ss),
   qsort(G2s,GS2s), **conc**(L2s,[1|GS2s],LSs), **qsort**([3|G1s],GSs),
   conc(LSs,[2|GSs],Ss), **ans**(Ss).
:- **part**([],1,L2s,G2s), **qsort**(L2s,L2Ss),
   qsort(G2s,GS2s), **conc**(L2s,[1|GS2s],LSs), **qsort**([3],GSs),
   conc(LSs,[2|GSs],Ss), **ans**(Ss).
:- **part**([],1,L2s,G2s), **qsort**(L2s,L2Ss),
   qsort(G2s,GS2s), **conc**(L2s,[1|GS2s],LSs),
   conc(LSs,[2,3],Ss), **ans**(Ss).
:- L2s=[], G2s=[], **qsort**(L2s,L2Ss),
   qsort(G2s,GS2s), **conc**(L2Ss,[1|GS2s],LSs),
   conc(LSs,[2,3],Ss), **ans**(Ss).

There is a certain amount of concurrency available but it is severely restricted (as was the intention). Continuing to the bitter end:

:- G2s=[], **qsort**([],L2Ss),
   qsort(G2s,GS2s), **conc**(L2Ss,[1|GS2s],LSs),
   conc(LSs,[2,3],Ss), **ans**(Ss).
:- **qsort**([],L2Ss), **qsort**([],GS2s), **conc**(L2Ss,[1|GS2s],LSs),
   conc(LSs,[2,3],Ss), **ans**(Ss).
:- L2Ss=[], **qsort**([],GS2s), **conc**(L2Ss,[1|GS2s],LSs),
   conc(LSs,[2,3],Ss), **ans**(Ss).
:- **qsort**([],GS2s), **conc**([],[1|GS2s],LSs),
   conc(LSs,[2,3],Ss), **ans**(Ss).
:- GS2s=[], **conc**([],[1|GS2s],LSs), **conc**(LSs,[2,3],Ss), **ans**(Ss).
:- **conc**([],[1],LSs), **conc**(LSs,[2,3],Ss), **ans**(Ss).
:- LSs=[1], **conc**(LSs,[2,3],Ss), **ans**(Ss).
:- **conc**([1],[2,3],Ss), **ans**(Ss).
:- Ss=[1,2,3], **ans**(Ss).
:- **ans**([1,2,3]).

As can be seen, condition synchronization does appear to provide control over premature binding. There is no combinatorial explosion of parallel goals, as happens with unrestricted parallelism.

Condition synchronization tempers overeager nondeterminism. When there are choices to be made, goals are suspended until there is sufficient information on which to make a choice. In this example, the information uniquely determines the appropriate clause. This is a manifestation of the principle of least commitment used in constraint solvers as described in Chapter 1. Least commitment can avoid assigning values to unknowns until they are, often, uniquely determined. It minimizes the amount of guessing and therefore nondeterminism.

3.12 Indeterminacy

The syntax of GDC given above can be considerably simplified by representing the instance constraints by patterns in the head of a clause. The program for **qsort** then takes the form

```
//quicksort(UnsortedList, SortedList)
qsort([],Sorted) :- true
  |  Sorted=[].
qsort([Item],Sorted):- true
  |  Sorted=[Item].
qsort([Pivot,Item|List],Sorted):- true
  |  part([Item|List],Pivot,Lesser,Greater),
     qsort(Lesser,LSorted),
     qsort(Greater,GSorted),
     conc(LSorted,[Pivot|GSorted],Sorted).

//partition(List, Pivot, Lesser, Greater)
part([],Pivot,Lesser,Greater) :- true
  |  Lesser=[], Greater=[]
part([Item|List1],Pivot,Lesser,Greater) :- Pivot=<Item
  |  Greater=[Item|Greater1], part(List1,Pivot,Lesser,Greater1)
part([Item|List1],Pivot,Lesser,Greater) :- Item<Pivot
  |  Lesser=[Item|Lesser1], part(List,Pivot,Lesser1,Greater).

//concatenate(List1, List2, List1List2)
conc([],List2,List1List2) :- true
  |  List1List2=List2.
conc([Item],List2,[List1List2])
  |  List1List2=[Item|List2].
conc([Item1,Item2|List11],List2,List1List2):-
  |  List1List2=[Item1, Item2|List3], conc(List11,List2,List3).
```

The patterns in the head of a clause now denote pattern matching rather than unification. When the guard constraint can be completely captured by pattern matching, the empty condition is represented by the **true** condition.

What is lost from Prolog by condition synchronization is completeness not soundness. No unsound inferences can be made. The completeness sacrificed by replacing call-head unification in Prolog by condition synchronization manifests itself in the restricted mode of use of program clauses. For example, the relations for concatenate can only "fire" when the first argument of the call is a list. Unlike Prolog, the concatenate relation as it stands cannot be used to split a list; that is, with the third argument known but the first and second unknown.

While invertability is an attractive feature of Absys and Prolog, practical Prolog programs forgo this to avoid the bottomless pits of depth-first search or the use of cuts for the sake of efficiency. With condition synchronization, the patterns in the head of the clause are being used for metalevel control. Restricting the mode of use of relations in this way (directed relations), makes the semantics closer to functional languages.

PDISs and decision tables usually make no attempt at completeness. The lack of completeness of depth-first search was strongly criticized in Planner [Sussman and McDermott, 1972]. Hewitt's intention for Planner was a language for pattern directed invocation. Hewitt and Inman [1991] say:

> *The controversial decision to use backtracking served expediency,*
> *but moved the semantics of Planner-69 fundamentally away from*
> *the pattern-directed invocation metaphor in which it was grounded.*
> *What was needed was to take the metaphor that stood behind Plan-*
> *ner more seriously.*

Condition synchronization has severely crippled any prospect that GDC might be complete. There is no implicit search in functional programming but search can be programmed. In systems programming the problem is not to find all solutions to a problem but to find one efficiently. With an operating system, only one solution as to how a file might be written to disc is required. Like guarded commands in GDC, only one clause whose guard is satisfied is chosen to reduce a goal. The use of the guard in GDC makes the quicksort program deterministic so it is not affected by this decision. When more than one guard is satisfied, the programmer cannot be certain which one will be chosen. The guard allows one to express complex preconditions for the application of a rewrite. Variants of Prolog in which search is abandoned beyond the guard have been called committed choice languages.

3.13 The Premature Binding Problem Revisited

While there is no search beyond the guard, there is still search within the guard as the following GDC program to find a key at the node of a binary tree illustrates:

```
//onTree(Key, Tree, Found)
onTree(Key,tree(Left,Key1,_),Found)
    :- Key=/=Key1, onTree(Key,Left,Found)
    |  true.
onTree(Key,tree(_,Key,_),Found)
    :- true.
    | Found=found.
onTree(Key,tree(_,Key1,Right),Found)
    :- Key=/=Key1, onTree(Key,Right,Found)
    |  true.
```

The =/= primitive causes a call to suspend if either of its arguments are insufficiently instantiated to determine that they are different. If the root of the tree does not contain the key, two clauses are candidates for committal. Unlike previous examples, which only use primitives in the guard, the **onTree** example introduces user-defined goals in the guard. Determining the guard conditions, will necessarily recursively spawn other **onTree** goals. As the new goals invoke new guards, this can lead to a system of arbitrarily nested guards. As will be explained, nested guard conditions can cause premature binding.

With the logical infix implication symbol, $\leftarrow$, assumed to be left associative, the guarded clause

A :- B | C

is logically equivalent to $A \leftarrow B \leftarrow C$. Suppose an initial query:

$$\leftarrow a_1, a_2, \dots a_j, \dots a_n. \qquad (\leftarrow Q)$$

is given and where, for the sake of exposition, the arguments of the goals have been suppressed. Note that the initial query should not be considered as a list of atoms, no ordering is implied, rather it is a multiset set. Suppose for some clause

$$h \leftarrow c_1, c_2, \dots \leftarrow b_1, b_2, \dots, b_m. \quad (C)$$

in the program $a_j = h\theta_1$ (for some substitution θ_1). If θ_1 is an input match substitution and if the guard condition $(\leftarrow c_1, c_2, \dots)\theta$ is satisfiable with some substitution of variables θ which is an extension of θ_1 (i.e. $\theta = \theta_1\theta_2$, juxtaposition denoting composition of substitutions) then the clause is a candidate for committal. If this clause is the one selected, the goal a_j is replaced by the body $b_1, b_2, \dots b_m$ so that the resolvent of the initial goal and the input clause reduces to

$$\leftarrow (a_1, a_2, \dots b_1, b_2, \dots b_m, \dots a_n)\theta$$

If any of the bindings entailed by θ are due to recursive guards of the resolving clause C, they could well be communicated to other a_i $(i \neq j)$, which share variables with a_j, before committal.

$$\leftarrow (a_1, a_2, \dots a_j, \dots a_n)\theta \qquad (\leftarrow Q')$$

If by some chance the clause C is not committed but some other is, the communicated bindings will, in general, not relate of the chosen clause. It is then more likely that the query will fail because the variable bindings are more specific than is warranted. There is no need to worry about the substitution θ_1 since this is limited to pattern matching and only affects the local variables of the clause. We are then left with the bindings caused by the guard constraints:

$$\leftarrow (a_1, a_2, \dots a_j, \dots a_n)\theta_2 \qquad (\leftarrow Q'')$$

There will be no problem if the bindings generated by the guard θ_2 do not cause bindings of the variables in the call, the global variables.

$$a_i\theta = a_i\theta_2 = a_i$$

The possible inequality of $\leftarrow Q'$, $\leftarrow Q''$ and $\leftarrow Q$ is a formalization of *the premature binding problem*. The equality of $\leftarrow Q'$ and $\leftarrow Q''$ is guaranteed by pattern matching and the equality of $\leftarrow Q''$ and $\leftarrow Q$ can be thought of as the natural extension of pattern matching for guards with constraints other than pattern matching. This leads to the notion of *guard safety*: a guard is said to be safe if its evaluation does not incur any binding of nonlocal variables.

Safe guards can only test the input parameters since they produce no output bindings. For example, the membership relation defined by

```
//member(Element,List)
member(X,[X|Y]) :- true | true
member(X,[Y|Ys]) :- X=/=Y | member(X,Ys).
```

is clearly safe as can be easily recognized syntactically because there are no equality predicates in the body of any of its clauses or the bodies of any of the clauses of its subgoals. (Note that the recursive call to **member** in the second clause could equally well be part of the guard with the same declarative and operational effect. This gives another way of recognizing a safe guard: the body goals can *safely* be transferred to the guard.)

By comparison, the **onTree** relation defined previously is unsafe, as the variable Found in a top level call can be bound to found by a recursively invoked guard call before committal of the initial invocation. In this example, this does not cause an inconsistency because there is no conflict in what the variable Found can be bound to; it can only be bound to the constant found and nothing else. Furthermore, it will only be bound by a recursive guard call if the Key is on the tree so the conclusion will be sound. This example illustrates that the property of safety does not affect soundness. Because of indeterminism, the unrecognized presence of this problem can lead to unnecessary failure when greater care with the programming might circumvent the problem.

A simple way to make the **onTree** program safe is by making local copies (copies in the guard) of all endangered variables:

```
//onTree(Key, Tree, Found)
onTree(Key,tree(Left,Key1,_),Found)
    :- Key=/=Key1, onTree(Key,Left,FoundL)
    | FoundL=Found.
onTree(Key,tree(_,Key,_),Found) :- true
    | Found=found.
onTree(Key,tree(_,Key1,Right),Found)
    :- Key=/=Key1, onTree(Key,Right,FoundR)
    | FoundR=Found.
```

The local copy is only unified with the global parent after committal.

With the addition of an arbiter, **onEither**, the **onTree** goal can be moved out of the guard entirely:

```
//onTree(Key, Tree, Found)
onTree(Key,tree(Left,Key1,Right),Found):- Key=/=Key1
    | onTree(Key,Left,FoundL),
        onEither(FoundL,FoundR,Found),
        onTree(Key,Right,FoundR).
onTree(Key,tree(_,Key,_),Found) :- true
    | Found=found
onTree(_,emptyTree,Found) :- true
    | Found=notFound.
```

```
//onEither(FoundL,FoundR,FoundEither)
onEither(found,_,Found) :- true
    | Found=found.
onEither(_,found,Found) :- true
    | Found=found.
onEither(notFound,notFound,Found)
    | Found=notFound.
```

A hand trace of a call to the process **onTree** reveals that the data tree in the call is mimicked by a dynamically constructed tree of **onEither** processes and found or notFound eventually percolates to the top of the tree.

In the final version of **onTree,** only primitives appear in the guards. With unrestricted guards, a GDC program gives rise to a hierarchical computation. The computation is organized as an and/or goal tree, the depth of the or-tree corresponding to exhaustive search in the nesting of guards. Recursive guards describe a complex inference step of a nature similar to paramodulation or typed inference. Because the guards are recursive, in general, they will be undecidable. There is a sense where flat guards are modular with regard to synchronization whereas deep guards are not.

In PDISs and decision table languages, the conditions are often required to be primitive to make pattern matching and compilation tractable. If the guards only contain primitives, they can be guaranteed decidable and safe. The *flat* restriction only allows primitive (and consequently nonrecursive) predicates in the guard that test the input parameters and perform no output. In the flat regime the computation degenerates to an and-tree and hence the name flat. The possible primitives include syntactic equality-inequality testing, comparisons, and type checking none of which can perform any output. (In fact, the guard can be an arbitrary Boolean combination of constraints, not just conjunctions, but then the clause will not necessarily be definite, in the logical sense.) The language FGDC, so far specialized, is now an indeterministic conditional rewrite language. Deterministic (functional) conditional rewrite languages have been known for some time [Griesmer and Jenks, 1971; Hearn, 1971; Belia et al., 1980].

The restriction to a flat subset of the language is not debilitating as the final **onTree** program indicates. How expressive the language is will depend on the range of guard constraints. The restriction does require, however, a shift of programming style further away from Prolog. The GDC programmer cannot fall back on the exhaustive search of implicit failure driven loops or or-parallelism; search has to be programmed. Those programs that are not naturally flat and require search can be rewritten using suitably chosen recursive data structures, as will be seen in later chapters.

3.14 Decision Tree Compilation

When the guards are flat, there is even greater correspondence between FGDC and decision tables. Different strategies for translating decision tables into algorithms were discussed in Montalbano [1964]. The optimal methods of Rabin [1971] and Yasui [1971], reduce the number of constraints tested. In the first GDC partition relation defined above (not using pattern matching in the head of the clause), the test

[Item1|List1]«List1 occurs in the guard of two clauses. Composing guard constraints into decision trees can eliminate redundant tests:

```
//partition(List,Pivot,Lesser,Greater)
part(List,Pivot,Lesser,Greater)
      :-  []=List | Lesser=[], Greater=[].
  +   :-  [Item|List1]«List,
           {Pivot=<Item | Greater=[Item|Greater1],
           + Item<Pivot
              | Lesser=[Item|Lesser1], part(List,Pivot,Lesser1,Greater)
           }.
```

Alternative parts of clauses are denoted by a + symbol borrowed from *CCS* [Milner, 1980]. The heads of all clauses for partition are all the same and so are omitted.

Furthermore, the two constraints Pivot=<Item and Item<Pivot are exclusive and might be further coalesced into a single test:

```
//partition(List,Pivot,Lesser,Greater)
part(List,Pivot,Lesser,Greater)
      :-  []=List
        |   Lesser=[] | Greater=[]
      + :-  [Item|List1]=List,
           {Pivot=<Item
              |   Greater=[Item|Greater1],
              + otherwise
              |   Lesser=[Item|Lesser1], part(List,Pivot,Lesser1,Greater)
           }.
```

using otherwise (or else). The *otherwise* clause is only tried if all others are inapplicable.

3.15 A Brief History of Guarded Definite Clauses

To the uninitiated, the origins and relationships of logic programming languages may appear as shrouded in mystery as those of the Judaeo-Muslim-Christian religions. Both have had their prophets, heresies and schisms. (With logic programming the time-scale has been somewhat shorter.) At least six authors, Robinson [1983], Cohen [1988], Kowalski [1988], Elcock [1991] and Colmerauer and Roussel [1992] have chronicled the history of sequential Prolog. Early investigations into parallel Prolog were Pollard [1981] and Conery and Kibler [1981]. The parallel descendants of Prolog will not be mentioned further and it will be left to someone else to fill in this branch of the family tree.

1979   Van Emden and de Luceana [1979] embed the Kahn and MacQueen model
        of stream processing in logic programming. This gave a process interpreta-
        tion of goals in contrast to the previous procedural interpretation. Goals in a
        query or body of a clause are grouped into sequential and parallel conjunc-
        tions. Variables shared between parallel conjunctions are regarded as com-
        munication channels. Parallel processes suspend if shared variables are not
        instantiated to lists. Input and output modes are determined by the initial
        goal. The examples given are deterministic. The authors have great diffi-
        culty in getting their paper accepted for publication. It is not published until
        three years later as an invited contribution to a book [Clark and Tarnlund,
        1982].

        Dausmann et al. [1979] use a variable delay annotation /B to synchronize
        processes in concurrent logic programming. The occurrence of the annota-
        tion X/B delays reduction of the goal containing it until X is ground.

        Clark and McCabe [1979] produced IC-Prolog (a minor prophet), a version
        of Prolog that introduces a confusion of control facilities for synchronizing
        the concurrent evaluation of goals. IC-Prolog provides variable annotations
        to synchronize coroutines similar to Conniver [Sussmann and McDermott,
        1972]. However, both producer and consumer annotations are allowed. An-
        notations can appear in the head of a clause as well as the body. IC-Prolog
        introduces Dijkstra [1975] like guards that make clause head unification and
        guard constraints atomic. Unlike guarded commands, a clause with a suc-
        cessful guard is not exclusive. There is variable delay annotation '!', similar
        to Dausmann et al. [1980]. Stream primitives handle input and output.

1980   Hansson et al. [1980] propose a Kahn and McQueen interpretation of a logic
        language based on a natural deduction system of Prawitz [1965]. Producers
        and consumers are designated by an equational syntax. Nondeterminacy is
        handled by backtracking.

        Belia et al. [1980] describe FPL (Functional and Predicate Logic) a Horn
        clause equational functional setting for a deterministic language with guards
        (the word constraint is used instead of guard) and directed relations. Argu-
        ments of relations are designated as input and output. These modes are
        similar to the modes used in Edinburgh Prolog compiler [Warren, 1977] to
        improve the efficiency of compilation. The program is viewed as a set of
        conditional rewrite rules. Lazy evaluation semantics allows the use of
        streams.

1981   Conery and Kibler [1981] identified four prospects for parallelism in logic
        programs: and-parallelism, or-parallelism, stream-parallelism and search-
        parallelism. In search-parallelism, matching clauses are searched for in par-
        allel.

With the Relational Language, Clark and Gregory [1981] make the guard introduced in IC-Prolog indeterministic (committed choice) as happens with guarded commands. Variables in the guard must be ground by the call pattern for the guard to be satisfied. In the examples given, the guard constraints are primitives (flat) but this is not explicitly stated as a restriction. Producer occurrences of variables in goals are annotated. Data flows from annotated variables to unannotated variables. Unannotated variables are "read-only". An attempt to bind a read-only variable by clause head unification causes suspension of the clause. Output arguments are required to be unbound.

In this year, the first FGCS International Conference on Fifth Generation Computer Systems is held in Japan.

1982   Japanese launch FGCS initiative to build parallel knowledge-based machines using Prolog as a kernel language. Initial funding for five years is granted with a promise of renewal for a further five years subject to satisfactory progress.

1983   Shapiro [1983] attempts to clean up the Relational Language with Concurrent Prolog. Shapiro relaxes the restriction that the guard variables need to be ground and primitive. Allowing variables and user defined relations in the guard introduces the possibility of premature binding as described in Chapter Three. In Concurrent Prolog this is handled by having multiple binding environments as in or-parallel Prolog implementations. The guard controls the making of local environments public. Process synchronization is controlled by variable annotations. Rather than output variables being annotated, "read-only" variables are annotated á la Conniver [Sussman and McDermott, 1972]. As a visitor to ICOT, Shapiro persuades the FGCS project to switch allegiance from Prolog to Concurrent Prolog with a wealth of programming examples suitable for systems programming.

In response to Concurrent Prolog, Clark and Gregory [1981] propose *Parlog* by weakening the restrictions on the guard of the Relational language. Rather than use multiple environments they require guards to be safe; a property that is undecidable. They abandon producer annotations and use input/output modes assigned on a per relation basis as done by Belia et al. [1980].

1985   FGCS project produces first PSI (Personal Sequential Inference Machine) with *SIMPOS* (Sequential Inference Machine Personal Operating System) written in an object-oriented extension of Prolog, *KL0*.

Read-only unification turns out to be order dependent [Ueda, 1985a; Saraswat, 1986] and multiple environments are difficult to implement. Under the influence of Parlog, Ueda [1985b] transforms Concurrent Prolog into GHC (Guarded Horn Clauses). GHC uses a single binding environment and dispenses with read-only variables. The guard is used as a runtime safety check. Consequently, GHC programs have a greater tendency to deadlock. Body goals are allowed to be spawned before commitment, which causes a large amount of speculative computation.

Because of difficulties with implementation of multiple environments, Concurrent Prolog goes flat (only primitives in the guard). Semantic problems prompt the restricted use of read-only annotations [Mierkowsky, Taylor, Shapiro, Levy and Safra, 1985]. Even for the flat language, the principle difficulty with read-only variables as a method of synchronization is that relations fail to be modular with respect to synchronization: the program behavior depends on the form of the call.

1986   Ringwood [1986] cleanses Parlog under influence of GHC: GDC (Guarded Definite Clauses) replaces misleading mode declarations by pattern matching and explicit output. Like GHC the guard is the only form of synchronization. Unlike GHC the guard controls the synchronization of body goals. Safety is not the problem it was thought to be. It does not cause unsound inferences.

Vulcan [Kahn et al., 1986] is a simulation of *Actors* in FCP.

1987   FGCS secures funding for further 5 years, and produces first version of multi-PSI – a number of PSIs connected by a network. Multi-PSI is used to prototype the PIM (Parallel Inference Machine). The principle criticism of the GHC synchronization mechanism is that it fails to be modular with respect to synchronization: the behavior depends on the nesting of subsequent guard calls. This makes it difficult to implement. Chikayama at ICOT enhances GHC (by adding Parlog-like metacalls), while simplifying it (by making it flat, FGHC) to produce KL1 (Kernel Language 1), the kernel language of FGCS. Parlog86 is viewed as a set of indeterministic conditional rewrite rules [Ringwood, 1987a] similar to Belia [1980].

Following Jaffar and Lassez [1987], Maher [1987] interprets concurrent logic languages as constraint languages.

Mandala [Ohki et al., 1987] is a simulation of Actors in KL1.

1988   FGCS produce PIMOS (Parallel Inference Machine Operating System) for PIM, written in KL1 and tested on multi-PSI [Chikayama et al., 1988].

A'UM [Yoshida and Chikayama, 1988] is a further development of Mandala.

1989   Saraswat [1989] elaborates the constraint interpretation of Maher [1987].

AI Ltd produce Strand88 [Foster and Taylor, 1989] a commercial implementation of a restricted version of FGDC (previously known as Flat Parlog with Assignment).

1991   FGCS produce first working PIM.

Strand Software Technologies (remnant from collapse of AI Ltd) produce a distributed version of Strand88.

1992   FGCS complete the 10-year research program with an international conference. FGCS software is made public domain: IFS (ICOT free Software). Unfortunately, software only runs on PSI and PIMs that are not sold commercially. ICOT gets extension for further two years on much reduced scale to provide implementations for Unix.

POOL [Davison, 1992] is a simulation of Actors in Parlog. POOL is renamed POLKA because of a clash with a prior concurrent object-oriented language.

Gudemann and Miller [1992] produce a compiler for Linear Janus, a version of Strand with a constraint interpretation [Saraswat, 1989]. Variables are restricted to two occurrences, one in the guard, one in the body of a clause (linearity). The compiler compiles to C.

1993   Ericsson produce a version of Strand with a functional syntax called Erlang [Armstrong et al., 1993]. Erlang can be recognized as having a single implicit output argument for every relation. The language is targeted at real-time programming, in particular telephony applications.

1994   ICOT release KL1C, a version of KL1 that compiles to C.

SICS (Swedish Institute for Computer Science) develop AKL [Janson, 1994] merge a constraint interpretation of concurrent logic languages with OR-parallel Prolog.

1995   AITEC, the Japanese Research Institute for Advanced Information Technology established as a successor to ICOT. The main activities are dissemination of the ICOT Free Software (IFS) and forecasting the future of information technology. AITEC release the version 2 of KL1C.

DFKI (German Research Center for Artificial Intelligence) develop *OZ* [Smolka, 1995], a higher order functional extension of AKL. This can be compared with previous attempts to provide multiparadigm languages, e.g. POPLOG [Anderson, 1989]

1997   AITEC release version 3 of KL1C.

OZ2 [Henz, 1997] replaces the fine grain concurrency with explicit thread based concurrency.

1999   Ericsson announced the signing of a £270 million contract with British Telecom to deliver voice over ATM. "The large-scale network, integrating circuit-switched AXE and packet-switched ATM, will handle all of BT's national and international traffic as well as interconnect traffic." An integral part of the solution, AXD 301, was developed in Erlang.

OZ3 extends OZ2 with Concurrent Prolog like read-only variables called futures (following functional programming nomenclature) to assist Internet programming.

AITEC release source code of KLIC to be maintained by a body of interested users.

The principle difference between the three original branches of the church (transubstantiation) lies in the way in which synchronization is achieved. In GHC, a call suspends if call-head unification attempts to bind a nonlocal variable. For Concurrent Prolog, a call suspends if unification attempts to bind a read-only variable. In Parlog86, the head of a clause is only used for pattern matching. Term matching suspends waiting for nonvariable input. A call suspends until it satisfies some guard.

The development of the Guarded Definite Clause languages can be compared with the development of CSP [Hoare, 1978, 1985] and CCS [Milner, 1980]. Programming styles, expressiveness, examples, theoretical considerations and the clarity of one have led to modifications in another. This mutual monitoring has brought the strands of the GDC church closer together but has brought about political differences of opinion as who invented, or more truthfully introduced, what and when.

Chapter 4

Event Driven Condition Synchronization

> *By relieving the brain of all unnecessary work, a good notation sets it free to concentrate on more advanced problems, and in effect increases the mental power of the race. Before the introduction of the Arabic notation, multiplication was difficult, and the division even of integers called into play the highest mathematical faculties. Probably nothing in the modern world would have more astonished a Greek mathematician than to learn that ... a large proportion of the population of Western Europe could perform the operation of division for the largest numbers. This fact would have seemed to him a sheer impossibility. ... Our modern power of easy reckoning with decimal fractions is the almost miraculous result of the gradual discovery of a perfect notation.*
>
> *Alfred North Whitehead (1861–1947)*

The development of GDC was neither as analytical nor informed as Chapter 3 suggests. In that chapter, the premature binding problem was the motivation for the change of synchronization from control flow to condition synchronization. The present chapter shows how the combination of the logic variable and condition synchronization leads to stream processing. A stream is an incrementally constructed sequence of data objects, usually a linear list. Closer examination of the condition synchronization reveals a remnant of the premature binding problem, the binding conflict problem. The language is further refined as a result of this.

Stream processing was introduced by Landin [1965] in the context of functional programming. Landin proposed lazy evaluation as the appropriate mechanism for processing streams. Friedman and Wise [1976] showed the relation between lazy evaluation and coroutining with a designated producer. Earlier, Kahn [1974] proposed coroutines as a mechanism for processing streams. In Kahn's model, a parallel computation is organized as a set of autonomous threads that are connected to each other in a network by communication channels (streams). The model was suggested as suitable for systems programming. While the theory only allows deterministic programs, Kahn speculated that it would be possible to extend the idea to indeterministic programs. Kahn and McQueen [1977] extended Kahn's model to allow dynamic thread creation and termination. They proposed a functional syntax that relieved the programmer of the burden of programming the transfer of control. This subordinated the transfer of control between subroutines to the binding of variables (dataflow). In the paper, Kahn and McQueen suggest that streams may be broadened from linear lists to trees and tableaux. Dennis [1976] and Arvind et al [1977] augmented functional stream languages with a primitive indeterministic binary stream merge operator. The operator accepts two input-streams and produces an output stream that interleaves their elements. Park [1980], Brock and Ackerman [1981] and Smyth [1982] extensively studied the required properties of merge operators.

Van Emden and De Luceana [1979] used dataflow coroutining to embed streams in logic programming. Clark and Gregory [1981] added guards to further restrict the nondeterminacy. Streams will be illustrated with an archetypal example, the *Sieve of Erastosthenes*, used by Kahn and McQueen [1977]. Erastosthenes was a 3rd-century BC Alexandrine Greek philosopher who produced the first estimate of the circumference of the earth. This was calculated from the length of shadows cast by the sun. Erastosthenes' Sieve was at one time the basis of special purpose hardware for calculating large primes. The method has since been superseded by probabilistic methods.

4.1 Streams for Free

A Prolog version of Erastosthenes' Sieve is given by Clocksin and Mellish [1981, 2/e p170] (some of the predicate names have been changed to protect the innocent):

```
%primes(Limit, List_of_primes_less_than_limit)
primes(Limit,Ps) :- natNums(2,Limit,Ns), sieve(Ns,Ps).

%natNums(Low, High, List_of_consecutive_nats_between_low_and_high)
natNums(Low,High,[]) :- Low>High, !.
natNums(Low,High,[Low|Rest]) :- Low=<High, !,
    M:=Low+1, natNums(M,High,Rest).

%sieve(List_of_naturals, Sublist_of_primes).
sieve([],[]).
sieve([P|Ns],[P|Ps]) :- filter(P,Ns,Fs), sieve(Fs,Ps).

%filter(Prime, List_of_nums, Sublist_without_multiples_of_primes)
filter(P,[],[]).
filter(P,[N|Ns],[N|Fs]) :- 0=/=NmodP, !,
    filter(P,Ns,Fs).
filter(P,[N|Ns],Fs) :- 0=:=NmodP, !, filter(P,Ns,Fs).
```

In the example, Ns is an ordered list of consecutive natural numbers beginning with 2 and with final element Limit; Ps is an ordered list of all primes less than Limit. The list of primes is obtained by dynamically sieving the list of natural numbers for multiples of primes as they are discovered. This Prolog program is very algorithmic in nature not the least because of the cuts (one red and two green). The program exploits the ordering of clauses and goals in the bodies of clauses. It is a classic example of the use of Prolog for data construction. The functional decomposition is such that the list Ns is sieved in turn for multiples of primes starting with the smallest. The trawl for multiples of each prime is completed before the sieve for multiples of the next prime is begun. The first element of the list of natural numbers is 2. Multiples of 2 are excised from the rest of the list. The first element of the sieved list, 3, is not a multiple of 2 and, since the original list of natural numbers was ordered, must be prime. The rest of this list is sieved for multiples of 3 and so on. This would be regarded as a bad example of logic programming by purists, because of its use of a red cut and the implicit use of Prolog control features.

The GDC equivalent appears almost the same as the Prolog program:

```
//primes(Limit, List_of_primes_less_than_limit)
primes(Limit,Ps) :- true
    |   natNums(2,Limit,Ns), sieve(Ns,Ps).


//natNums(Low, High, List_of_consecutive_ints_between_low_and_high)
natNums(Low,High,Ns) :- Low>High
    |   Ns=[].
natNums(Low,High,Ns) :- Low=<High, M:=Low+1
    |   Ns=[Low|N1s], natNums(M,High,N1s).


//sieve(List_of_naturals, Sublist_of_primes).
sieve([],Ps) :- true
    |   Ps=[].
sieve([P|Ns],Ps) :- true
    |   Ps=[P|P1s], filter(P,Ns,Fs), sieve(Fs,P1s).


//filter(Int, ListOfInts, Sublist-multiples)
filter(_,[],Fs) :- true
    |   Ps=[].
filter(P,[N|Ns],Fs) :- 0=/=NmodP
    |   Fs=[N|F1s], filter(P,Ns,F1s).
filter(P,[N|Ns],Fs) :- 0=:=NmodP
    |   filter(P,Ns,Fs).
```

However, the operation of the GDC program for Erastosthenes Sieve is very different from the Prolog original. Firstly, the list of natural numbers does not have to be complete before the sieving begins. The sieving can begin as soon as its first argument becomes a list. That is, it is activated (fired) as soon as its first argument becomes instantiated. Similarly, the list of natural numbers does not have to be completely sifted for multiples of one prime before sifting can begin for multiples of the next prime.

The behavior of GDC arithmetic infix primitive :=, in the guard of the second clause for the generator **natNums** numbers, is somewhat different from its Prolog counterpart. The second clause is not a member of the conflict set until the right hand argument of the arithmetic constraint is ground (no variables) to an arithmetic expression. When the argument is ground the primitive evaluates the expression and binds the value to the variable in the left-hand argument. The left hand argument is not allowed to be a variable appearing in the head of the clause, because this would violate the condition that the guard has to be passive. In this way, expression evaluation does not cause any effect observable by other concurrent threads before the appropriate clause to reduce the thread has been determined. A filter thread can begin as soon as its first argument becomes a list and its second argument a natural number. The =:= operator is similar to the := primitive: its parent clause is not a member of the conflict set until both its arguments are bound to an arithmetic expression. The constraint is satisfied if the value of both arguments is the same.

The concurrent program dynamically sets up one filter thread for each prime detected so far. These threads filter multiples of their designated prime from their input lists and pass the remainder of the integers to their output lists. Thus, at any one time there can be a number of filter threads active each one disposing of integers that are non-prime or passing on to its neighboring filter integers that have not yet been established to be non-prime. An initial denial:

> :-   **answer**(Ps), **primes**(30,Ps).

will at some stage of a computation (it is deterministic) resolve into:

> :-   **answer**([2,3,5|Ps]), **natNums**(30,Ns), **filter**(2,Ns,F2s),
>   **filter**(3,F2s,F3s), **filter**(5,F3s,F5s), **sieve**(F5s,Ps).

The nascent list of natural numbers Ns is successively filtered (a dynamically changing pipeline) for multiples of primes. The synchronization in this program is totally administered by guard conditions and data availability. This is in contrast to the initial Prolog program where the synchronization is achieved by control flow.

This synchronization caused by the flow of binding of variables is a manifestation of condition synchronization. In the pattern-directed GDC program, a partial solution to the problem can be examined before it is complete. This allows the possibility of useful nonterminating threads. The natural number generator can be modified to produce an infinite sequence of naturals and the sequence of primes can be produced incrementally:

```
//primes(List_of_primes_less_than_limit)
primes(Ps) :- true
    |   natNums(2,Ns), sieve(Ns,Ps).

//natNums(Previous, List_of_consecutive_ints_following_previous)
natNums(M,Ns) :- M1:=M+1
    |   Ns=[M|Rest], natNums(M1,Rest).
```

This behavior is not possible in the original Prolog program because of control synchronization; the list of natural numbers has to be completed before any sieving begins. (Of course, a meta-interpreter can be written in Prolog to achieve this behavior.)

4.2 A Picture is Worth a Thousand Words

The stream threading of GDC lends itself to a diagrammatic *plumbing* representation. This representation is not intrinsic to the language but it does help novices to assimilate quickly this new computational model for logic programming. After several reductions (or partial evaluation steps) an initial denial:

> :-   **answer**(Ps), **primes**(Ps).

becomes:

> :-   **answer**([2,3,5|Ps]), **natNums**(6,Ns), **filter**(2,Ns,F2s),
>   **filter**(3,F2s,F3s), **filter**(5,F3s,F5s), **sieve**(F5s,Ps).

and is represented in Figure 4.2.1.

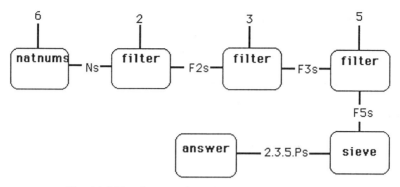

Fig. 4.2.1 The sieve pipeline after several reductions

Similar diagrams can be used to represent clauses. The clause:

sieve([P|Ns],Ps) :- **true**
    | Ps=[P|P1s], **filter**(P,Ns,Fs), **sieve**(Fs,P1s).

is pictorially illustrated in Figure 4.2.2.

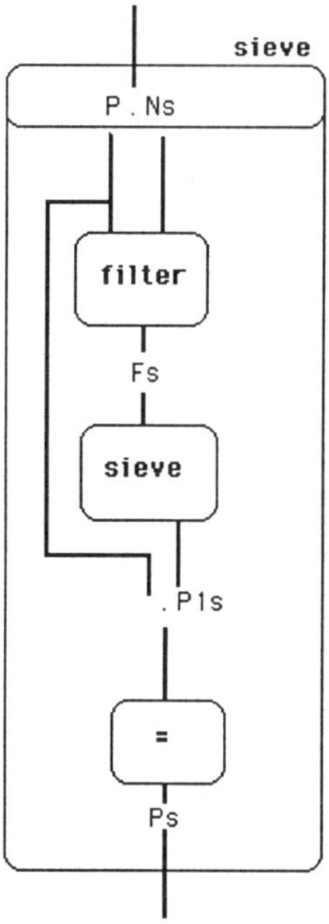

Fig. 4.2.2 The sieve Clause

The box at the top of Figure 4.2.2 denotes the guard. Further elaboration of the graphical representation of GDC is presented in Ringwood [1987] and Tanaka [1993].

Figure 4.2.1 would be familiar to a designer of signal processing systems. The building blocks of signal processing are generators, transducers, filters and integrators.
Generators produce signals: **natNums** is an example of a generator. Filters remove
part of the signal as **filter** does above. Transducers transform the signal; an example
of a transducer is **double** which doubles the integer elements of a stream:

```
//double(Integer_Stream, Two*Integer_Stream)
double([N|In],Out) :- N2:=N+N.
    |   Out=[N2|Out1], double(In,Out1)
double([],Out) :- true | Out=[].
```

Integrators accumulate signals; an example is a moving average of stock market share
prices. The following GDC program segment adapted from [Parker, 1990], is designed to calculate the five day moving average of closing share prices:

```
//movingAvg(#Items_averaged, Data_stream, Moving_average)
movingAvg(N,[Head|Tail],Mavs)
   :-  Mavs=[MavHead|MavTail],
       oneAvg(N,N,Tail,Head,MavHead),
       movingAvg(N,Tail,MavTail).

//oneAvg(#Items, Items_remaining, Data_stream, Running_total, Av)
oneAvg(N,M,[Head|Tail],Acc,Av) :- M>1, M1:=M-1, Acc1:=Acc+Head
    |   oneAvg(N,M1,Acc1,Av).
oneAvg(N,1,_,Acc,Av) :- A:=Acc/N | Av=A.
```

4.3 Dataflow Computation

The signal processing analogy and the pipeline diagrams proposed above are similar
to those used in constraint solving (Chapter 1) and dataflow computing. Dataflow
control claims to address the issues of latency and synchronization in distributed
programming (Chapter 3). Dataflow computing arose out of the graphical analysis of
program behavior called *dataflow graphs*. A dataflow graph is a directed graph consisting of named nodes that represent operations and arcs that represent data dependencies among nodes. A numerical example is depicted in Figure 4.3.1.

Dataflow computing was predicted in Brown [1962]. Petri nets [Petri, 1962] are another graphical based notation used to represent concurrent systems. A Petri net consists of a set of *places*, a set of *transition bars* and a set of directed edges, as in Figure
4.3.2. Each transition bar has an associated set of input places and an associated set of
output places. The presence or absence of tokens at places represents states of the
system. Transition bars represent possible changes of state. A transition bar can only
fire (i.e. change state) when each of its places holds at least one token. When a bar
fires, it removes one token from its input places and deposits one token at each of its
output places.

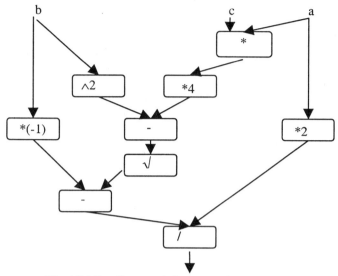

Fig. 4.3.1 Dataflow graph for a root of a quadratic

The Petri net in Figure 4.3.2 is easily modeled in GDC:

```
:-  bar1([1|P1],[1|P2],P3), bar2(P3,P1,P2).

bar1[[1|P1],[1|P2],P3) :- true
    |   P3=[1|P31], bar1(P1,P2,P31).
bar2[[1|P3],P1,P2) :- true
    |   P1=[1|P11], P2=[1|P21], bar2(P3,P11,P21).
```

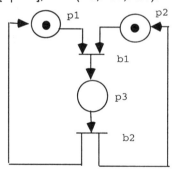

Fig. 4.3.2 An example Petri net

Karp and Miller [1966] used dataflow graphs to study parallel programs. In their model, a generalized program counter governs the control of operations. Rodriguez [1967] proposed that activations of operations are controlled by conditions on the input arcs. Independently, Adams [1968] added the notion of propagating operands over arcs of the graph. Tesler and Enea [1968] contributed the idea of a *single assignment language* for formulating dataflow programs.

Dennis and Misunas [1975] gave the first proposal for a computer architecture using dataflow principles. Dennis led the Computer Systems Group at MIT Lab where much of the early architecture work was done. Davis [1978] produced the first operational hardware dataflow processor. *Lucid* [Ashcroft and Wadge, 1975] was a language specifically designed for program proving. It is a first order functional language that predates Kahn and McQueen [1977]. While Lucid was developed for its formal properties, these properties were reportedly a great help in its efficient implementation on dataflow architectures [Ashcroft et al., 1985]. Another single assignment language designed to exploit dataflow architectures that claims to be a replacement *Fortran* is *Sisal* [McGraw et al., 1985]. Waters [1979] developed a program to analyze Fortran programs. He found that 60% of Scientific Fortran libraries could be formulated as generators, transducers, filters and integrators.

Lisp was given a dataflow implementation [Wathansian, 1978] on *FLO* [Egan, 1980], a decentralized dataflow machine. Early in the program, the Japanese Fifth Generation experimented with dataflow architectures for the implementation of FGHC [Yuba, et al 1990]. The first paper to propose dataflow execution for Prolog was [Morris, 1980]. Ito et al [1983; 1985] and Hasegawa and Mamnmiya [1984] took up this idea. The first reported dataflow implementation of Prolog was [Wise, 1986]. Although GHC is a dataflow language, the Japanese implementation was done in software. A hardware implementation of GHC was completed on the CSIRAC II dataflow architecture in Australia [Rawling, 1989].

The language GDC introduced in Chapter 3 is a condition-synchronized language. This is more than just dataflow synchronization. The input arguments of functions in dataflow languages are normally scalar datatypes. In contrast, the arguments of GDC are compound data structures. Guard satisfaction for compound data structures can run to several hundred machine instructions whereas for scalar datatypes they can be one machine instruction. In dataflow architecture the guard test for all operations is synchronized. There is no concept of thread. This is why specialized hardware is of concern in dataflow languages. The architecture of dataflow machines is not unlike that for parallel production systems. In the analogy operations correspond to production rules. The operations in dataflow languages are, however, usually deterministic. All operations that are in the conflict set are fired in parallel.

4.4 Dataflow Design

Dataflow diagrams (DFDs) have been exemplified as a tool for the analysis of software requirements [DeMarco, 1978; Gane and Sarson 1979]. Steer [1988] has shown how DFDs map directly onto GDC. DFDs model synchronously communicating threads that transform incoming streams to outgoing streams. The threads are hierarchically decomposed into primitive threads and data stores. A typical dataflow hierarchy is shown in Figure 4.4.1.

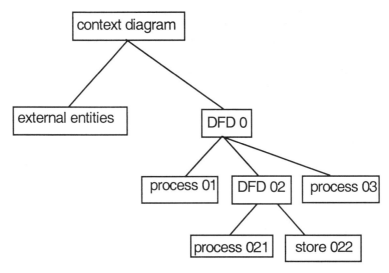

Fig. 4.4.1 A typical dataflow hierarchy of diagrams

The root of the hierarchy, the context diagram, isolates the domain of the problem and shows all flows from external entities. In the dataflow diagrams, the dataflows are made explicit. This can be illustrated in GDC:

:- contextDiagram

contextDiagram :- **true**
  | **externalEntities**(ArgE1,ArgE2,ArgE3),
      dfd0(ArgE1,ArgE2,ArgE3).

dfd0(ArgE1,ArgE2,ArgE3) :- **true**
  | **thread01**(ArgE1,Arg01,...,Arg0n),
      dfd02(ArgE2,Arg01,...,Arg0p,..., Arg0m),
      thread03(ArgE3,Arg0p...,Arg0q).

The new arguments show the dataflows between the subdiagrams of the level zero diagram:

dfd02(ArgE2,Arg01,...,Arg0p,...,Arg0m):- **true**
  | **thread021**(ArgE2,...,Arg0p,...,Arg1p),
      dataStore221(Arg1n,...,Arg1q).

A top level goal:

:- contextDiagram.

reduces directly to the primitive threads:

```
:-  externalEntities(ArgE1,ArgE2,ArgE3),
    dfd0(ArgE1,ArgE2,ArgE3).
:-  externalEntities(ArgE1,ArgE2,ArgE3),
    thread01(ArgE1,Arg01,...,Arg0n),
    dfd02(ArgE2,Arg01,...Arg0p,..., Arg0m),
    thread03(ArgE3,Arg0p...,Arg0q).
:-  externalEntities(ArgE1,ArgE2,ArgE3),
    thread01(ArgE1,Arg01,...,Arg0n),
    thread021(ArgE2,...,Arg0p,...,Arg1p),
    dataStore221(Arg1n,...,Arg1q),
    thread03(ArgE3,Arg0p,...,Arg0q).
```

Exactly how the primitive threads and data stores are implemented is shown in later sections.

4.5 Dataflow Programming

Abelson et al [1985] claim:

> ... streams can serve as standard interfaces for combining program modules. By using streams, we can formulate powerful abstractions that capture a variety of operations in a manner that is both succinct and elegant.

The Unix pipe exemplifies this sentiment. A Unix system call, *pipe()*, creates a one way communication stream, the ends of which can be inherited by child threads allowing two threads to communicate which have a common ancestor. The Unix pipe is a stream of characters (bytes). Unix pipes have a finite capacity (typically a few thousand bytes). If a thread tries to write to a pipe when it is full, the thread blocks until the downstream thread consumes some bytes. While there are similarities, the logic variable in GDC can be used to provide streams that are much more flexible than a Unix pipe. The GDC code for an amorous producer and coy consumer is:

```
eagerProducer(Stream) :- true
   |   Stream=beMine(TailStream),
       eagerProducer(TailStream).

dataDrivenConsumer(beMine(Stream)) :- true
   |   dataDrivenConsumer(Stream).

:- eagerProducer(Stream), dataDrivenConsumer(Stream).
```

Here, rather than use a list constructor for a stream, when the message protocol is prescribed a unary functor can be used. This emphasizes that it is not the list structure that gives rise to stream programming but the nondestructive assignment of variables. The reason for the long names of the producer and consumer will become clear below when alternative forms of producer and consumer program are derived. In this program, the producer is unrestrained, as the name suggests. Nevertheless, the consumer thread blocks waiting for its argument to be instantiated to the pattern in the head of the clause. When this constraint is satisfied, the consumer thread can reduce to a similar thread but with the tail of the stream as a parameter.

One possible evaluation scenario for the producer-consumer example is as follows:

:- **eagerProducer**(Stream), **dataDrivenConsumer**(Stream).

:- **eagerProducer**(TailStream), Stream=beMine(TailStream), **dataDrivenConsumer**(Stream).

:- **eagerProducer**(TailStream), **dataDrivenConsumer**(beMine(TailStream)).

:- **eagerProducer**(TailStream), **dataDrivenConsumer**(TailStream).

:- **eagerProducer**(TailStream1), TailStream=beMine(TailStream1), **dataDrivenConsumer**(TailStream).

:- **eagerProducer**(TailStream1), **dataDrivenConsumer**(beMine(TailStream1)).

:- **eagerProducer**(TailStream2), TailStream1=beMine(TailStream2), **dataDrivenConsumer**(beMine(TailStream1)).

:- **eagerProducer**(TailStream2), **dataDrivenConsumer**(beMine(beMine(TailStream2))).

.
.
.

If a clause guard is satisfied, the clause describes how a thread named by the clause head is transformed into the parallel composition of threads described by the body of the clause. In general, the thread behavior specifies dynamic thread creation:

oldThread(...) :- <constraint>
    | **newThread1**(...), **newThread2**(...), ...

In contrast to many languages where threads can only be declared statically and are persistent, e.g., Occam, GDC threads are dynamically created and are ephemeral. In this respect, thread behavior in GDC is much more like CCS [Milner, 1980] than CSP [Hoare, 1978].

Traditionally the proponents of logic programming have emphasized its stateless, side-effect-free nature. This emphasis is justified when the problem to be solved can be declared without reference to the environment. In concurrent programming, the very nature of the problem usually contains references to the state of the system. According to Abelson et al [1985], a thread is said to have state if its behavior is influenced by its history. In GDC, a thread cannot change its state but only reduce itself into other threads. From an intuitive point of view, a thread that reincarnates itself recursively can be thought of as a long-lived thread. Simulating long-lived threads by ephemeral recursive calls allows the interpretation of local (unshared variables) as states of a thread. In the following skeleton:

thread(State,[Message|InStream],...,OutStream)
    :- <Constraints(State,Message)>
    | **computeResponse**(State,Message,NewState,Response),
       OutStream=[Response|TailOutStream],
       thread(NewState,TailInStream,...,TailOutStream).

In general, the new state and the response depend on the initial state and the message. This skeleton suggests how, in a side-effect-free way, local variables and recursive ephemeral threads effect long-lived threads that can change state. Streams afford modularity without the need for state and multiple assignments to variables. The nonshared variables show how data stores can be implemented in GDC.

In this and a previous example, the effective threads are not just long lived but are persistent – they never die. Threads can be terminated by specifying an empty thread behavior:

thread(...) :- <constraints> | **true**.

The empty behavior can be contrasted with the Occam SKIP and STOP threads and the forwarder in Actors [Agha, 1986]. The constraints specify the conditions under which a long-lived thread is allowed to terminate.

A modification of the previous producer-consumer example that illustrates both state and thread termination is the following:

```
:-  finiteEagerProducer(5,Stream),
    terminatingDataDrivenConsumer(Stream).

finiteEagerProducer(N,Stream) :- N>0, N1:=N-1
    |   Stream=beMine(TailStream),
        finiteEagerProducer(N1,TailStream)
finiteEagerProducer(N,Stream) :- N=<0
    |   Stream=goodbye_cruel_world.

    terminatingDataDrivenConsumer(beMine(Stream)) :- true
    | terminatingDataDrivenConsumer(Stream).
    terminatingDataDrivenConsumer(goodbye_cruel_world) :- true
    | true.
```

The producer only issues five pleas before it withers and dies. The state of this producer is the number of outstanding messages. The producer commits suicide when it has sent the specified number of unrequited appeals. Upon receipt of knowledge of its suitor's demise ("Goodbye cruel world"), the consumer mortally regrets the rejection of its suitor.

Replies to messages can be engineered by adding extra variables:

```
:-  finiteEagerProducer(5,no,Stream),
    terminatingDataDrivenConsumer(0,Stream).

finiteEagerProducer(N,no,Stream) :- N>0, N1:=N-1
    |   Stream=beMine(Reply,TailStream),
        finiteEagerProducer(N1,Reply,TailStream).
finiteEagerProducer(N,ok,Stream) :- true
    |   bliss(TailStream).
finiteEagerProducer(N,Reply,Stream) :- N=<0
    |   Stream=goodbye_cruel_world.
```

terminatingDataDrivenConsumer(N,beMine(Reply,Stream))
   :- N1:=N+1, N<3
   | Reply=no, **terminatingDataDrivenConsumer**(N1,Stream).
terminatingDataDrivenConsumer(N,beMine(Reply,Stream))
   :- N >=3
   | Reply=ok, **joy**(Stream).
terminatingDataDrivencConsumer(N,goodbye_cruel_world)
   :- **true**
   | **true**.

Here, the consumer rejects the producer if less than three appeals are made. When more than three appeals are made, the consumer accepts the producers advances and they go onto a different phase of their relationship (which won't be pursued any further).

4.6 Message Passing

The top level of a GDC thread invocation takes the form of a negative clause:

   :-   <thread behavior>

Thread behavior describes a network of concurrent threads communicating via variables shared between the threads. These variables are not the usual form of shared variables in concurrent systems but are like message reception slots. The name *message reception slot* is cumbersome and the word *channel* will be used in its place. In concurrent programming two alternatives can be offered as mechanisms for thread communication: shared mutable data and message passing. With a shared address space, many threads can potentially assign the same variable. As is well known, competing threads trying to write to the same variable have race conditions, e.g., [Tanenbaum, 1987]. This can cause inconsistency in the final value of a variable. This final value is determined by whichever thread last assigns to it. In systems programming several solutions to race conditions have emerged, such as semaphores [Dijkstra, 1968].

The nature of the problem is made all too vivid by the bank balance example [Filman and Friedman, 1984], which if your bank is anything like ours, is not impossible. The bank account example has now become a classic illustration of object-oriented programming. Consider the C-like procedure:

deposit(Int Amount) {
   Balance:=Balance+Amount;
}

which might naively be used as an access routine to update a computerized bank account. Imagine that there is $10 000 in the account. Suppose two deposits of $1000 and $5 are made concurrently, a situation that might arise from two simultaneous transactions in different branches of the bank because of rebates from overcharge by different credit card companies. (The values of the starting balance and transactions are different from Filman and Friedman to allow for inflation and the 1987 stock market crash.) Executing two deposit routines in parallel can bring about the improved state:

```
par {
    deposit(1000);
    deposit(5);
}.
```

Although considered as primitive operations from the point of view of accessing the bank account, from a machine view the routine deposit is not atomic. Each operation of incrementing the account will consist of a sequence of machine instructions such as:

```
register Reg;
Reg:=Balance;
Reg:=Reg+Amount;
Balance:=Reg;
```

where Reg is deemed to be a hardware register. Concurrency can be modeled by the indeterministic interleaving of atomic actions [Pnueli, 1986; Chandy and Misra, 1988]. Assuming that each statement in the par statement is allotted its own processor, one possible scenario is:

```
Reg1:=Balance;      //Reg1 = 10000
Reg1:=Reg1+1000;    //Reg1 = 11000
Reg2:=Balance;      //Reg2 = 10000
Balance:=Reg1;      //Balance=11000
Reg2:=Reg2+5;       //Reg2 = 10005
Balance:=Reg2;      //Balance = 10005
```

which when you receive your next bank statement will send you scurrying to send a rude letter to your bank manager.

The bank account example illustrates that it can be unsound for two deposit threads to modify the variable balance simultaneously. A thread is in a *critical region* of a resource if it is testing and modifying the state of the resource. The problem of preventing threads from executing simultaneously in critical regions is called the *mutual exclusion* problem but this nomenclature does not describe the problem accurately. The mutual exclusion problem is one of the division of the test of the state of a resource from its modification. If the modification of the state depends on the result of the test, unsoundness can arise. Another thread can sneak in-between the test and the modification so that the state information on which the modification is based is no longer accurate. This explanation provides the more descriptive name of the *lost update* problem. In general, threads that arrange their activities so as not to interfere with another's activities are said to be *synchronized*. Synchronization is concerned with the ordering of actions. (Synchronization also has the connotation of co-operation of which non-interference is just one aspect.) The naive solution to the divisibility of test and modification is to make test and modification an atomic action. But therein lies a complex issue, not the least of which is deadlock, as will be illustrated later.

Communication by shared variables is an abstraction of processors sharing the same address space. As Bal et al [1989] points out, it is possible for a distributed programming language to have a logically shared memory while being implemented on a distributed system (where processors have distinct address spaces). Message passing is an abstraction of communication between processors that do not share the same address space. Message passing does not have race conditions as it involves data copying rather than data sharing. Some other agent, the operating system, is responsible for copying the data from the address space of one thread to that of the other. Consequently, message passing can be 100 times less efficient than data sharing [Hennessy and Patterson, 1990].

Whereas in communication by shared variables, a variable can be assigned any number of times, messages can be assigned only once. There is only one writer of each message but possibly many readers. The logical-variable of GDC lies somewhere between the two extremes of shared variable and message. It can be implemented by either. Logical-variables, like messages, can only be assigned once but there can be any (finite) number of potential writers. Whereas a message writer is determined at compiletime, the writer of a logical-variable is determined at runtime. After assignment of a logic-variable, all other threads sharing it will necessarily be readers; this is similar to multicasting. In a broadcast message system, any thread can read any message. In multicast message systems, only a prescribed subset of threads can be readers. In fact, only the equality primitive thread (illustrated in use above) can assign shared logical-variables. Of the competing equality threads, the successful writer is the one that gets there first. (By contrast, for shared multi-assignment variables, the successful writer is the one that assigns last. This is a *race condition*.) With nondestructive assignment variables, race conditions still exist but are somewhat less of a problem than with multiply assignable variables because the race can only occur once.

The following example illustrates this:

p(X) :- **true** | X=a.
p(X) :- **true** | X=b.

with the scenario:

   :-   **ans**(X), <u>p(X)</u>, <u>p(X)</u>.
   :-   **ans**(X), <u>X=a</u>, <u>p(X)</u>.
   :-   **ans**(X), <u>X=a</u>, X=b.
   :-   **ans**(X), <u>a=b</u>.

There is no flaw in the logic but it is purely a bug brought on by indeterminism. There are two possible bindings for X, a and b, but one part of the conjunction has made one choice as to which solution should be committed to and the other part of the conjunction has made the alternative choice. This is called the *binding conflict problem*. This is somewhat different from the premature binding problem. In the premature binding problem, the conflict can be resolved by condition synchronization. Here the guards are empty. It is not until after the threads have committed to their respective clauses that the conflict shows up. That is, the data examination and data modification are separate actions. Clause invocation bias or unfairness has definite advantages here. If rather than the choice of clause to reduce the goal being indeterministic, alternative clauses are always chosen in textual order this problem would not occur. This will be assumed to be the case. But clause priority would not solve the binding conflict problem with the similar program:

```
:-  ans(X), p(X), c(X).
p(a) :- true | true.
p(b) :- true | true.
c(X) :- true | X=a.
c(X) :- true | X=b.
```

where for perverseness, **p** is the consumer and **c** the producer. The difference between this and the previous example is that both threads are producers. The mutual
exclusion problem is a problem of multiple producers, sometimes called multiple
writers. Additionally, the two producers are calls to the same relation so that in GDC,
where synchronization is specified by the guard of a clause, one thread cannot be
made a producer and the other a consumer.

This suggests variable annotations in the body of a clause similar to Conniver [Suss-
man and McDermott, 1972]:

```
:-  ans(X?), p(X?), p(X).
```

This is the approach taken in Concurrent Prolog [Shapiro, 1983]. While this may
seem to solve this problem, there is a major drawback; by using this device, programs
lose modularity. The form of the call and not the program definition determines the
behavior of the program. Again, this is not the point at issue. It is not that multiple
producers are necessarily required, but it may not be known at compile time which
will be producer and which consumer. Exactly how such race conditions are dealt
with in GDC will be described below.

4.7 Eager and Lazy Producers

The only form of synchronization in GDC is condition synchronization as specified
by clause guards. This can manifest itself as pattern matching. An incrementally
instantiated logic variable can behave like an infinite message buffer. With such
asynchronous communication, if threads do not reduce at the same rate, producers
can run ahead of the consumers. The reduction scenario of the eager producer suggests this situation. In this example, the producer is totally unconstrained while the
consumer blocks waiting for data. This program will work as intended if the consumer consumes faster than the producer produces. If not, the list, a theoretically
infinite buffer, will eat-up the entire physical store.

GDC programs have a fine grain that permits a very high degree of parallelism, and
hence goals are eminently portable to different nodes of a network. In conventional
distributed systems the amount of parallelism available in the language usually exceeds the limited number of physical processors. In such circumstances, threads are
time-shared. The problem of the eager producer might be solved by giving the consumer a higher priority than the producer has. Primitives can be provided to facilitate
this:

```
:-  eagerProducer(Stream,-1)@priority(-1),
    dataDrivenConsumer(Stream).
```

Nonblocked threads are scheduled according to their priority. This corresponds to the
Occam prioritized parallel composition construct, **PRI PAR**. In GDC, processors

with the same priority form a FIFO queue in order of creation. The priority of a child thread, unless otherwise specified by an @ priority annotation, reverts to the default priority for the user. Dynamic control over priorities may be effected by passing the priority from parents to children as in:

eagerProducer(Stream,Priority) :- **true**
   | Stream=beMine(TailStream),
      eagerProducer(TailStream,Priority)@priority(Priority).

explaining the seemingly redundant second argument in the initial thread invocation above. This form of control is particularly useful for speculative search (Chapter 6).

When the number of threads exceeds the number of processors, (which is usually the case) or where the communication overhead would outweigh the benefits of distribution, some judicious mapping of threads to processors (load balancing) needs to be made. The problem of mapping threads to processors is, as it should be for maximum portability, orthogonal to the language. Thread distribution might be achieved in sympathy with the language in many ways. One possibility is to map a conceptual tree of threads onto a physical network of processors [Huntbach and Burton, 1988]. One can contemplate dynamic load balancing in shared memory systems or closely coupled distributed systems, where the cost of communication is low. In loosely coupled systems, it will be desirable for the programmer to express some control of the distribution of threads.

Although communication in Transputer networks is, compared to LANs, relatively inexpensive, it is not without cost. Occam provides placement instructions to enable the programmer to distribute threads over processors. In a similar way, GDC provides programmer annotations to facilitate thread distribution. By default, threads are scheduled on the processor on which their parent ran. Processor mapping annotations can be direct (specifying a particular processor) or indirect (specifying the *direction* (assuming some topology such as a matrix) of a nearest neighbor in which to migrate). An example is:

foo(State,...) :- <determine(State,NextProcessor)>
   | **bar1**(...)@processor(4),   // on specified processor
      bar2(...)@processor(next),   // on next processor (ring)
      bar3(...)@processor(east),   // in specified direction (mesh)
      bar4(...),   // stay put
      bar5(...)@processor(Next).   // on dynamically computed
                              // processor

Note that NextProcessor is determined dynamically. Partitioning processors among processors and scheduling is essentially orthogonal to the language. By combining partial evaluation (Chapter 9) with partitioning scheduling techniques it is expected that parallel architectures can be better exploited. The myths of load balancing are explained in Wikstrom et al. [1991]. Partial evaluation transforms a general program into a specialized program by taking advantage of information available at compiletime. Such information could be processor topology. This differs from conventional compilation techniques. Conventional compilers seek to optimize the execution of procedure calls and data-structure manipulations. Partial evaluation seeks to eliminate such operations by performing them in advance of runtime.

Thread priority will not solve the problem of the over eager producer if the producer and consumer are run on different processors. As an alternative, if the producer is known to be faster than the consumer is, the role of the producer and consumer can be reversed as in the program:

:-   **demandDrivenProducer**(Stream), **eagerConsumer**(Stream).

demandDrivenProducer([Message|Stream]) :- **true**
    | Message=msg(be_Mine), **demandDrivenProducer**(Stream)
eagerConsumer(Stream) :- **true**
    | Stream=[Message|TailStream], **eagerConsumer**(TailStream).

In this turnabout, the consumer solicits devotions from the producer by forming a list of message variables for the producer to instantiate. Now, the consumer can run arbitrarily far ahead of the producer.

If it is not known which of the producer and consumer is the faster, synchronous communication can be programmed by giving both the producer and consumer a pattern matching constraint:

:-   **dataDrivenConsumer**([Msg|List]),
     demandDrivenProducer([Msg|List]).

demandDrivenProducer([Message|Stream]) :- **true**
    | Message=msg(be_Mine), **demandDrivenProducer**(Stream).
dataDrivenConsumer([msg(Contents)|Stream]) :-
    | Stream=[Message|TailStream], **dataDrivenConsumer**(TailStream).

Here, the producer and consumer have to be hand started, otherwise they would both block (deadlock). With this program there is only one possible execution scenario:

:-   **demandDrivenProducer**([Message|List]),
     dataDrivenConsumer([Message|List])
:-   **demandDrivenProducer**(List), Message=msg(be_Mine),
     dataDrivenConsumer([Message|List]).
:-   **demandDrivenProducer**(List),
     dataDrivenConsumer([msg(be_Mine)|List]).
:-   **demandDrivenProducer**(List), List=[Message1|List1],
     dataDrivenConsumer([Message1|List1])
:-   **demandDrivenProducer**([Message1|List1]),
     dataDrivenConsumer(Message1|List1)
:-   **demandDrivenProducer**(List1), Message1=msg(be_Mine),
     dataDrivenConsumer([Message1|List1]).
:-   **demandDrivenProducer**(List1),
     dataDrivenConsumer([msg(be_Mine)|List1]).
:-   **demandDrivenProducer**(List1), List1=[Message2|List2],
     dataDrivenConsumer([Message2|List2]).

```
:-  demandDrivenProducer([Message2|List2]),
    dataDrivenConsumer([Message2|List2]).
        .
        .
        .
```

The producer and consumer are alternately blocked and progress lock step.

The synchronous communication programmed above with asynchronous communication effectively turns the infinite List buffer into a one-slot buffer. Given that there is only one consumer in this situation, a used slot can be garbage collected straight away and the old slot can even be re-utilized. It is possible to build some housekeeping of this kind into the compiler [Kemp and Ringwood, 1990]. Still, it is unlikely that all garbage collection can be done in this way and some runtime scavenging will be necessary.

Further modifying the code for the consumer in the one-slot-buffer program can produce a multislot buffer.

```
:-  Channel=[_,_,_,_|EndList], buffConsumer(Channel\EndList),
    dataDrivenProducer(Channel).

buffConsumer([msg(Contents)|List\EndList]) :- true
    |  EndList=[_|NewEndList], buffConsumer(List\NewEndList).
```

This program uses the Prolog notation of an underscore to denote an anonymous variable; repeated anonymous variables are taken to be distinct. This buffer program uses the familiar Prolog technique of a difference list [Colmerauer, 1992]. A difference list is just a manifestation of an accumulator. The difference list, denoted by an infix functor, \, at the consumer end acts as an N slot buffer. The equality thread in the initial thread invocation initializes N to four. The consumer maintains the length of the buffer by producing a new slot for every message consumed. Again garbage collection and slot reuse could be compiled into the code for the consumer.

For larger buffers, an auxiliary thread may be used to generate the slots:

```
:-  genBuffer(25,Stream,EndStream),
    buffConsumer(Stream\EndStream),
    dataDrivenProducer(Stream).

genBuffer(N, Stream, EndStream) :- N>0, N1:=N-1
    |  Stream=[_|TailStream],
        genBuffer(N1,TailStream,EndStream).
genBuffer(0,Stream,EndStream) :- true
    :-  Stream=EndStream.
```

Using difference streams, the quicksort program used to introduce GDC in Chapter 3 may be succinctly refined:

```
//quicksort(UnsortedList, SortedList)
qsort(Unsorted,Sorted) :- qsort(Unsorted,Sorted,[]).
qsort([],Sorted,Tail) :- true | Sorted=Tail.
```

```
qsort([Pivot|List],Sorted,Tail):-
    |   part(List,Pivot,Lesser,Greater),
        qsort(Lesser,LSorted,[Pivot|GSorted]),
        qsort(Greater,GSorted,Tail).
```

4.8 The Client-Server Paradigm

An important paradigm of distributed systems is the client-server. Many applications occur in systems programming in which several threads share a common resource.

```
server([Transaction|MoreTransactions],Data) :- true
    |   task(Transaction,Data,NewData),
        server(MoreTransactions,NewData).
```

Of the two arguments of **server**, the first is a stream of transactions from clients and the second a handle to the data administered by the server. This data is to be manipulated according to the form of transaction stipulated in the transaction message.

Alternative clauses to handle different transactions of the server show how abstract data types (objects) can be naturally implemented in GDC. A bank account accumulator provides a well-exercised example of an object.

```
accumulator([deposit(Amount)|More],Total) :- NewTotal:=Total+Amount
    |   accumulator(More,NewTotal).
accumulator([debit(Amount)|More],Total])
    :-  NewTotal:=Total-Amount, NewTotal>=0
    |   accumulator(More,NewTotal).
accumulator([balance(Amount)|More],Total)
    :-  Amount=total(Total), accumulator(More,Total).
```

For the sake of simplicity, the number of modes of access and functionality of the transactions has been kept small. In particular, the second clause, unrealistically, blocks indefinitely if the amount to be debited is greater than the balance. The third clause for accumulator illustrates how the server replies to its clients. The client provides the server with a variable as a reply paid envelope.

A client using the account server facility might appear:

```
client(...,ToServer) :- ...
    |   ToServer=[balance(Amount)|NewToServer],
        takeAction(Amount),
        client(...,NewToServer).
```

```
takeAction(total(Total)) :- ....
```

Here the client program interrogates the account held by the server with the incomplete message balance(Amount) . It spawns a child thread to act (earning some more money or asking for credit) on the return information. Note the **takeAction** thread will block until its argument is instantiated to total(Total).

Prolog primitives for reading from the keyboard and writing to the screen are side-effected. The sequencing of goals in the body of a Prolog clause is crucial in getting the required external behavior. In GDC, input/output is implemented in a natural way using primitive server threads. For example, a naive user defined transducer **double**:

```
:-   stdIn(integers_in, InStream),
     double(InStream, OutStream),
     stdOut(integers_out, OutStream).
```

The primitive thread **stdIn** instantiates a list of carriage-return separated terms typed at the keyboard. The input is closed by the constant term []. The primitive thread **stdOut** prints on the screen space separated terms that appear as list items on its argument. In a system where a user can invoke parallel threads, a multiwindowing environment is natural. In such an environment, each invoked **stdIn** thread would have its own input window (called "integers_in" in the above case) and each **stdOut** thread will have its own output window (called "integers_out" in the above example). Positioning the input/output primitives in the top-level thread invocation saves them from cluttering and interfering with the semantics of the program in lower levels. This is a modular approach to the problem of input/output in declarative languages.

The lazily instantiated dynamic data structure of a list used in GDC server communication is ideal for input/output as it behaves like an infinite message buffer. Lists used in this way correctly sequence the output to the windows though there is no sequential thread control construct in the language. As noted for functional programming, streams seem to be a particularly clean way to deal with input/output and reactive systems. What GDC offers over functional languages is better control over eagerness and laziness. Higher order functions can be embedded in GDC programming as shown by Reddy [1994].

Parker [1990] has elaborated the relevance of streams to interactive data analysis. Each client of a server could be allocated its own stream for communicating with a resource. More usually, it is convenient (particularly with input/output) to determine or change at runtime the number of threads communicating with the server. Although streams can be implemented in functional languages, there is a problem when it comes to merging streams fairly. It will not do to merge streams alternatively taking one item from each. An uninstantiated stream will block a stream with data items on it. Streams are true relations; there are many possible streams that are the fair merge of two streams. In functional languages, a stream is usually given as a primitive. In GDC a fair merge can be user defined:

```
//merge(Left_In_Stream,Right_In_Stream,Out_Stream)
merge([],InR,Out) :- true
    |   Out=InR.
merge(InL,[],Out) :- true
    |   Out=InL.
merge([Item|InL],InR,Out) :- true
    |   Out=[Item|NewOut], merge(InR,InL,NewOut).
merge(InL,[Item|InR],Out) :- true
    |   Out=[Item|NewOut], merge(InL,InR,NewOut).
```

A **merge** thread can be used to merge messages from two clients to a server. If a stream terminates the remaining, input is shorted with the output. In a message passing system the order of arrival of messages is not necessarily the order in which they were sent. However, with the merge thread, above, the relative order of terms produced by sources is preserved. To avoid starvation, when there are elements on the two input streams of merge, the arguments are reversed in recursive thread calls. With textual order of testing alternatives, changing the order of arguments causes the list from which an element is taken to alternate and serves to effect fairness of input arguments. A biased merge (without interchanging the arguments) gives a way of programming priority.

Table 4.8.1 summarizes the stream threading interpretation of a logic program:

Table 4.8.1 The thread interpretation of Logic Programs

Concurrent Programming	**Logic Programming**
network of threads	denial with shared variables
thread	negative literal
channel	logic variable
message queue	recursive data structure
thread state	unshared variable
thread creation	clause with more than one body goal
thread termination	unit clause
long-lived thread	recursion
indeterminacy	multiple candidate clauses
(condition) synchronization	clause guard

4.9 Self Balancing Merge

If more than two clients require access to a server, a tree of binary merges can be employed. Generally, the number of clients varies dynamically and the tree can become unbalanced giving rise to a linear merge tree. In the worst case, a message will take n reductions to work its way through an n way merge. Saraswat [1987] gives a self-balancing merge with logarithmic delay using splay trees [Sleator and Tarjan, 1985]. Balancing a binary tree requires information two nodes up in a tree. The problem with binary merge trees above is that this information on the tree structure is lost when the tree is splayed. The following implementation keeps trees of depth two as data structures retaining the information necessary to balance it. If a stream terminates, **merge**, as previously, shorts the input and output streams:

```
//merge(Left_In_Stream,Right_In_Stream,Out_Stream)
merge([],InR,Out) :- true
    |   Out=InR.
merge(InL,[],Out) :- true
    |   Out=InL.
```

On receipt of a data item the merge collapses the node to a data structure:

merge([item(I)|InL],InR,Out) :- **true**
   | Out=item(I,InR,InL).
merge(InL,[item(I)|InR],Out) :- **true**
   | Out=item(I,InL,InR).
merge(item(I,InL,InR),InR1,Out) :- **true**
   | Out=left(I,InL,InR,InR1).
merge(InL1,item(I,InL,InR),Out) :- **true**
   | Out=right(I,InL1,InL,InR).

which records the shape of the tree. At depth two the data structure is splayed:

merge(left(I,InL,InR,InR1),InR2,Out) := **true**
   | **merge**(InR1,InR2,InR3), **merge**(InR,InR3,InR4),
      Out=item(I,InL,InR4).
merge(InL,left(I,InL1,InR,InR1),Out) :- **true**
   | **merge**(InL,InL1,InR2), **merge**(InR,InR1,InL2),
      Out=item(I,InL2,InR2).
merge(right(I,InL1,InL,InR,),InR1,Out) :- **true**
   | **merge**(InL1,InL,InL2), **merge**(InR,InR1,InR2),
      Out=item(I,InL2,InR2).
merge(InL,right(I,InL2,InL1,InR),Out) :- **true**
   | **merge**(InL,InL2,InL3), **merge**(InL3,InL1,InL4),
      Out=item(I,InL4,InR).

4.10 Synchronization

The transaction facilities of GDC can be used for many purposes; below is a client of the bank balance server that sends a pair of abstract datatype transactions to double the current account total:

client(..., ToServer) :- . . .
   | ToServer=[balance(Amount),add(Amount)|TailToServer],
     client(...,TailToServer).

Underlying the doubling operation is some sophisticated synchronization: the two messages are both sent with the same uninstantiated argument. Once the server has received the first transaction, it may receive the second before the reply to the first has been instantiated. This is legitimate because the condition synchronization of the arithmetic primitives ensures that Amount will not be added to the balance until it is ground. The use of GDC clearly allows the programmer to express higher levels of abstraction without having explicitly to code the synchronization.

This example raises the specter of atomic transactions. If the streams from the above client and any other clients (joint accounts) are merged as above, there is the possibility that another transaction, say a withdrawal, could sneak (God forbid) between the two parts of the double transaction. In such a situation, if the amount to be debited is greater than the current balance the transaction will deadlock. Whereas, if the amount to be debited was less than twice the total and the double transaction had taken effect atomically, it could have paid out the requested amount. This is a variation on the "lost update" problem. A general approach to the problem is the provision of an atomic transaction protocol for the server. Transactions that must be threaded atomically are bundled together into a single compound transaction:

```
client(...,ToServer) :-...
  |  ToServer=[[balance(Amount),add(Amount)]|NewToServer],
     client(...,NewToServer).
```

which is unbundled by an additional server clause:

```
accumulator([[X|Y]|Rest],Total) :- true
  |   concatenate([X|Y],Rest,Stream),
      accumulator(Stream,Total).
```

The contrast between the alternatives of merging and concatenating streams can be important for input/output. As with Prolog, difference lists can be used to produce the effect of concatenation in constant time.

A set of threads that require exclusive access to a server can be connected through a fair merge to a mutual exclusion thread:

```
mutex(free,[do(Job)|In],Out) :-
  |  Out=[do(Job,Free)|NewOut], mutex(Free,In,NewOut).
```

Clients send transaction messages to **mutex** and wait for access to be granted. Messages are only forwarded to the server if it is free:

```
server([do(Job,Free)|Trans]) :- true
  |  task(Job,Free), server(Trans).
```

The **task** thread binds the variable Free to free when it terminates, thus only allowing one transaction to enter the server at a time.

In procedural languages, remote procedure calls are often used to implement servers. With a remote procedure call, an answer is returned to a client only after the remote call completes. In GDC developed so far, there is no explicit sequencing and the mutual exclusion above does not achieve what is required. If the task were just a reply to the client:

```
task(Job,Free) :- true
  |  Job=done, Free=free.
```

Free may be assigned to free before Job is assigned to done. This requirement for sequencing may be generalized as a *continuation*. Continuations are used in denotational semantics [Strachey and Wadsworth, 1974; Milne and Strachey, 1976] to describe control mechanisms. They have their origins in the tail functions of Mazurkiewicz [1971]. Continuations are used in the compilation of Prolog programs to binary metaclauses [Tarau and Boyer, 1990]. In this scheme an extra argument, the continuation, is added to each goal and is used to represent a following computation. The following program and scenario illustrates this:

```
q(X,Cont):- true | Cont.
r(X,Cont):- true | Cont.
s(X):- true | true.
```

```
:- q(a,r(b,s(c))).
:- r(b,s(c)).
:- s(c).
:- true
```

Here Cont is a metavariable that ranges over goals. As equality is a primitive, a new equality primitive with an extra argument is necessary. The primitive **eq**(A,B,Cont) assigns (unifies) A to B and continues with Cont. By nesting continuations, the sequencing of variable bindings can be obtained: **eq**(A,B,eq(C,D,Cont)). With this primitive, the appropriate form of the **task** clause becomes:

```
task(Job,Free) :- true
    |  eq(Job,done, Free=free).
```

The introduction of this new primitive, allows remote procedure call to be programmed much more simply:

```
server([do(Job,Free)|Rest]) :- true
    |  eq(Job,done,server(Rest)).
```

avoiding the mutual exclusion protocol above. The use of metapredicates goes outside first order logic but it is encompassed by Elementary Formal Systems [Smullyan, 1956].

4. 11 Readers and Writers

Readers and writers [Courtois et al., 1971] is a classic synchronization problem. Two kinds of accesses, readers and writers, are allowed to a server. Writers modify the state of the server and are allowed exclusive access. Readers do not modify the server and have nonexclusive access. If the state of the server is not mutable, this is not a problem in GDC:

```
server([read(Query)|Trans],Data) :- true
    |  read(Query,State), server(Trans,Data).
server([write(Update,Free)|Trans],Data) :- true
    |  write(Update,Data,NewData), server(Trans,NewData).
```

However, if the server is external and has a mutable state a combination of merge and mutual exclusion can be used to solve the problem. Reader and writer requests are segregated to give priority to writers:

```
//dispatch(In_Stream,Readers_Out,Writers_Out)
dispatch([read(Query)|In],ROut,WOut) :- true
    |  ROut=[read(Query)|NewROut], dispatch(In,NewROut,WOut).
dispatch([write(Update)|In],ROut,WOut) :- true
    |  WOut=[write(Update)|NewWOut], dispatch(In,ROut,NewWOut).
```

These two streams are fed into a **mutex**, which gives exclusive passage to writers:

```
//mutex(Free, Readrs_In, Writers_In, Out)
mutex(free,Rin,[write(Update)|Win],Out) :- true
    |  Out=[write(Update,Free)|NewOut],
       mutex(Free,Rin,Win,NewOut).
```

```
mutex(free,[read(Query)|Rin],Win,Out) :- true
    |   Out=[read(Query)|NewOut], mutex(free,Rin,Win,NewOut).
```

mutex blocks the entry of further reader and writer requests until the write request just entered has signaled completion. Priority is given to writers by placing this clause first. The server spawns concurrent readers chaining them together in order to detect termination.

```
server([read(Query)|Trans],Head,Tail) :- true
    |   read(Query,Tail1=Tail),
        server(Trans,Head,Tail1).
server([write(Update,Free)|Trans],Head,Tail) :- true
    |   Tail=done, wait(Head,Update,Free,Trans).
```

A writer sets Tail to done and waits for all the readers to complete. The second argument of **reader** is a continuation. When a reader completes, it shorts two variables. When all the readers have finished the chain connecting all the readers is shorted and Head is bound to done. Takeuchi [1983] invented this technique of ascertaining distributed termination. The shorting of this circuit activates the writer, which then has exclusive access:

```
wait(done,Update,Free,Trans) :- true
    |   write(Update,Free,Trans), server(Trans,Head,Tail).
```

When **write** terminates it binds its second argument to free allowing more read and write requests to enter the server. Using continuation, for the writer, the mutual exclusion protocol can be avoided altogether:

```
server([write(Update)|Win],Rin,Head,Tail) :- true
    |   wait(Head,write(Update,server(Win,Rin,NewHead,Tail))).
server(Win,[read(Query)|Rin],Head,Tail) :- true
    |   read(Query,Tail1=Tail), server(Win,Rin,Head,Tail1).
```

4.12 The Dining Philosophers

At first sight, the problem of the dining philosophers [Dijkstra, 1971] appears to have greater entertainment value than practical importance. In fact, it provides a benchmark of the expressive power of new primitives of concurrent programming. It stands as a challenge to proposers of concurrent programming languages. Attempts to develop a solution reveal many of the difficulties of concurrent programming [Gingras, 1990]. Many nonsolutions have been proffered, e.g., [Tanenbaum, 1987, Shapiro 1989, Carriero and Gelerntner, 1989].

The problem is set in a Buddhist monastery of a contemplative order of five monks. Each monk is a philosopher who would be content to engage solely in deep thought if it were not occasionally necessary to acquiesce to the worldly desire for sustenance; the life of a philosopher is an endless round of eating and thinking (a sort of US National Security Council). Each philosopher behaves independently of his brothers. Thus, the activities of the inmates of the monastery are, in general, asynchronous.

A philosopher wishing to eat enters the refectory, takes a seat, eats and then returns to his cell. The communal dining arrangements are shown in Figure 4.12.1.

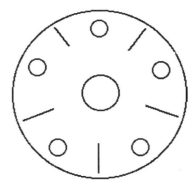

Fig. 4.12.1 The Refectory Seating Arrangements

Five bowls and five chopsticks are arranged alternately around a circular table. Each philosopher has his own place at the table. In the center of the table is a large bowl of rice that is continually replenished. To eat rice requires two chopsticks. (In the original description of the problem, the food in the bowl was spaghetti and the eating implement was a fork. In the authors' experience, eating spaghetti with one fork can be accomplished but eating rice requires at least two chopsticks.) A philosopher may use only those two chopsticks that are either side of his bowl. A chopstick can only be used by one philosopher at a time.

The following scenarios in the monastery illustrate three classic difficulties encountered with synchronization: mutual *exclusion, deadlock* and *starvation.* Clearly, while one philosopher is using a chopstick to eat it cannot be used by another philosopher. Thus, two philosophers are competing for each chopstick. This is an example of the need for mutual exclusion; no two philosophers may use the same chopstick simultaneously.

A philosopher can take one chopstick (thus preventing his neighbor from using it) while waiting for a second chopstick to become available. When a philosopher gets possession of a chopstick he can retain it until he has finished eating. Given perfect synchronization (the philosophers have pondered the vexed question of the suitability of synchronized swimming for inclusion in the Olympic Games) a scenario could occur in which each philosopher simultaneously takes the chopstick on his left. All philosophers are then waiting for the chopstick on their right and no philosopher (typically) is prepared to give up the chopstick they already hold. (Philosophers and academics are not generally noted for their social graces.) This is an example of *deadlock*: all philosophers die waiting for a situation that will never occur, their neighbor to give up the chopstick on their right.

Deadlock is a situation in which through obduracy all the philosophers starve to death. A more sinister scenario can occur in which two philosophers conspire to starve their mutual neighbor. Suppose, to avoid the above deadlock situation the philosophers agree (détente) that no one will lay claim to a chopstick unless claim can be made to both required chopsticks simultaneously. A scenario can occur in which philosophers 0 and 2 (the philosophers have also considered the advantages of modulo numbering systems) eat alternately. This prevents philosopher 1 from eating since when philosopher 0 is eating philosopher 1's chopstick on the left-hand side is occupied and when philosopher 2 is eating, philosopher 1's chopstick on the right-hand side is in use. Again perfect synchronization between philosophers 0 and 2 will ensure that the two chopsticks that philosopher 1 requires to eat will never be available at the same time. This is an example of *starvation* or *fairness*; philosophers 0 and 2 conspire in the demise of philosopher 1.

Fig. 4.12.2 Another day in the life of a monastery[1]

These difficulties are illustrated by the following attempted GDC nonsolution to the problem:

```
:-   phil(Left0,Right0), chopstick(free,Right0,Left1),
     phil(Left1,Right1), chopstick(free,Right1,Left2),
     phil(Left2,Right2), chopstick(free,Right2,Left3),
     phil(Left3,Right3), chopstick(free,Right3,Left4),
     phil(Left4,Right4), chopstick(free,Right4,Left0).

phil([FreeL|Left],[FreeR|Right]) :- true
     |    FreeL=free, FreeR=free, phil(Left,Right).
```

In this simulation, a philosopher eats when he has both chopsticks as indicated by the list pattern in each argument. After eating, a philosopher releases both chopsticks and is immediately ready to eat again (these philosophers do no thinking):

```
chopstick(free,Left,Right) :-
     |    Left=[Free|Left1], chopstick(Free,Right,Left1).
```

---

[1] Inspired by Holt [1983].

This is an example of a chain of demand driven producers and data driven consumer (Section 4.7). What is significant is that the chain is cyclic.

A chopstick can be in a state free or in use. The chopstick thread behaves as a combined mutex thread and a fair merge of the streams from its two philosopher neighbors. As described, this can lead to deadlock when a chopstick is offered simultaneously to all the philosophers on the left, say, of the chopsticks. This symmetry can be broken (credited to Toscani in [Holt, 1983]) by making alternate chopsticks initially prefer a philosopher different from its neighbor. This is achieved by changing the arguments around in one of the chopstick threads in the initial goal:

    :- **phil**(Left0,Right0), **chopstick**(free,Right0,Left1),
        phil(Left1,Right1), **chopstick**(free,Left2,Right1),
        phil(Left2,Right2), **chopstick**(free,Right2,Left3),
        phil(Left3,Right3), **chopstick**(free,Left4,Right3),
        phil(Left4,Right4), **chopstick**(free,Right4,Left0).

For three philosophers, they take turns in eating as indicated Figure 4.12.3.

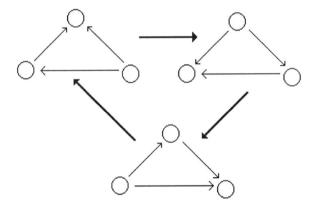

Fig. 4.12.3 Three philosophers taking turns

The circles represent philosophers seated at the table. The thin arrowed lines represent chopsticks offered. The philosopher with two chopstick offers is eating. The thick arrowed line represents three goal reductions: one philosopher and two chopsticks.

While this solution provides mutual exclusion, deadlock and starvation avoidance it is not maximally parallel. When philosophers think for arbitrary amounts of time scenarios can arise when there are philosophers ready to eat and chopsticks available but they are offered to thinking philosophers. To obtain maximal parallelism requires more complex solutions [Ringwood, 1986; Gingras, 1990].

4.13 The Brock–Ackerman Anomaly

There is a problem with indeterministic dataflow languages in that functional semantics (input-output relation) is not compositional [Keller, 1977; Kosinski, 1978]. The
Brock-Ackerman [Brock and Ackerman, 1981] counterexample in GDC is essentially:

```
first2(0,[A|In],Out) :- true
    |   Out=[A|Out1], first(In,Out1).
first2(1,[A,B|_],Out) :- true
    |   Out=[A,B].
first([A|_],Out):- true
    |   Out=[A].

dup([A|In],Out) :- true
    |   Out=[A,A|Out1], dup(In,Out1).

ba(N,Ix,Iy,Out) :- true
    |   dup(Ix,Ox), dup(Iy,Oy), merge(Ox,Oy,Oz), first2(N,Oz,Out).
```

The clause for **ba** is usefully illustrated in Figure 4.13.1.

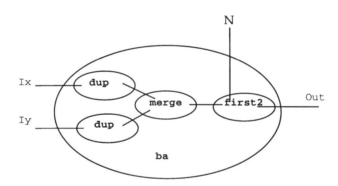

Fig. 4.13.1 Brock–Ackerman clause

where **merge** is the simple nonbalancing merge given previously. The success set of
a goal is the set of literals with arguments with their final bindings after the descendants of a goal successfully terminate. In logic programming, such a success set records the input-output semantics of a goal. The input-output semantics of the goal **ba**
is independent of its first argument.

```
{ba(_,[X|_],_,[X,X]), ba(_,_,[Y|_],[Y,Y]),
    ba(_,[X|_],[Y|_],[X,Y]), ba(_,[X|_],[Y|_],[Y,X])}
```

Consider now the feedback loop:

```
feedback(N,Out) :- true | ba(N,[5],Mid,Out), mapPlus1(Out,Mid)
```

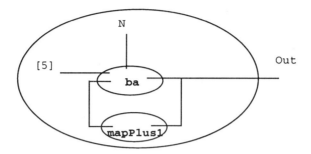

Fig. 4.13.2 Feedback loop

where:

mapPlus1([[A|In],Out) :- A1:=A+1
  | Out=[A1|Out1].

The input-output semantics of the composition **feedback** of **ba** and **mapPlus1** is dependent on its first argument:

{**feedback**(0,[5,5]),**feedback**(0,[5,6]),**feedback**(1,[5,5])}

Thus, while the input and output semantics of **ba**(0,_,_) and **ba**(1,_,_) are indistinguishable, they can be distinguished in a composition with a feedback loop.

4.14 Conditional Semantics

The state of a GDC computation can be described by a triple $<R,B,I>$ of multisets of reducible, blocked and irreducible goals, where the terminology will be explained. In the initial state, R, B and I are a partition of the goals in the initial network invocation:

$\leftarrow a_1, a_2,...a_n.$

Excluding for the moment the equality primitive threads, the reducible set R consists of those threads that satisfy the guard of some clause. That is, for each nonprimitive (equality and its continuation variant are the only primitives) thread a_j in R there is an instance of some clause:

$h \leftarrow c_1, c_2,... c_p \leftarrow b_1, b_2,... b_m.$

in the program for which a_j and h are syntactically identical and the constraint $c_1,c_2,...c_p$ is satisfiable. The blocked set B contains those threads a_j that are not reducible but have a reducible instance, a_j'. These threads are blocked waiting for instantiations. All other nonequality threads are members of the irreducible set, I. For them, there is no instance of the thread and clause of the program for which the guard is satisfiable.

There are no equality primitive threads allowed in B. If a_j is an equality primitive of the form $f(t_1,... t_k)=f(t_1',...t_k')$, k nonzero, then it is reducible and a member of R. A computation step is one of the following:

- For a nonequality thread a_j in R and a *least* instance

  $$h \leftarrow c_1, c_2,... c_p \leftarrow b_1, b_2,... b_m.$$

  of some clause in the program for which a_j and h are syntactically identical, a_j is removed from R and the instance of the behavior of the clause, $b_1, b_2,... b_m$, is partitioned appropriately between the subsets R, B and I.
- An equality primitive $f(t_1,... t_k)=g(t_1',...t_k')$ is transferred to B. An equality primitive $f(t_1,... t_k)=f(t_1',...t_k')$ R is removed and the network of primitive equality threads $t_1=t_1',...t_k=t_k'$ are appropriately partitioned between R and I. Thus, in GDC the equality thread is a unification thread that reduces implicitly and concurrently.
- Equality primitives of the form $X=t$ or $t=X$ in R are transferred to I if there is no occurrence of the variable X in other threads. If there are other occurrences of X in the sets R and B, they substituted by t. This is also accompanied by a redistribution of those nonequality threads from B to R, which because of the substitution have become reducible.

The denotation of each GDC thread is a logical atom. Primitive constraints can be thought of as semantic attachments in the sense of Weyrauch [1980]. The primitive equality thread, which implements syntactic equality also, can be thought of as a semantic attachment. In the same way, the primitive input/output threads are semantic attachments. Each clause denotes a first order, universally quantified, logic formula. Each step of the computation denotes a deduction. The deduction steps are complex of the like of paramodulation. Computation steps can be described as guarded complex deductions by analogy with Dijkstra's guarded commands.

The denotation of the initial thread network is given by abduction. Given a theory T expressed by logical formulae and a possible conclusion C, an abductive explanation of C is a set of sentences D such that T, D $\vdash$ C. Using the deduction theorem, this can be expressed as T $\vdash$ C $\leftarrow$ D. The initial goal:

$$\leftarrow a_1, a_2,... a_n.$$

is the initial abductive answer:

$$a_1, a_2,..a_n \leftarrow a_1, a_2,... a_n.$$

and resolvents form a denotation of subsequent program states:

$$a_1, a_2,...a_n \leftarrow R \leftarrow B \leftarrow I.$$

The reduction scenarios depicted in previous sections denote derivations. A program is thus denoted by the set of possible derivations. As such, GDC programs are amenable to formal reasoning and program transformation. More precisely, GDC programs are easy to reason about and transform because variables may be freely replaced by their values (single assignment).

4.15 Open Worlds and Abduction

A computation terminates when R is empty, but unlike Prolog, a GDC computation may never terminate. (Abductive answer semantics for GDC programs were first introduced to provide a semantics for perpetual threads in [Ringwood, 1987].) Unlike Prolog, with abductive answer semantics there is no concept of goal failure. If at any stage of the computation the irreducible set I contains an equality of, say, the form jehovah=allah a Prolog computation would have been deemed to have failed. In GDC the conclusion to be drawn is that jehovah and allah are different names for the same entity, that is, aliases. The equalities of the irreducible set I establish a congruence relation on the Herbrand base.

The term *reducible equality* is used in the sense of Herbrand's (syntactic) equality axioms over a universally quantified term algebra. If at any stage of the computation I contains an equality of the form X = t, where X is a variable and t is a term that contains X and t is not equal to X, the usual logic program would have been deemed to have failed. (This is not so for Prolog where the occur check is, usually, not implemented.) As some threads are deliberately nonterminating, it is more appropriate to consider rational rather than finite terms [Lalement, 1993].

It will generally be the case that constraints in I can be further reduced by additional equality axioms. For example, the constraints f(f(f(f(f(a)))))=a and f(f(f(a)))=b could be further reduced to f(f(b))=a, by substituting the second constraint in the first. There exist fast decision procedures for determining the congruence closure of quantifier free equations, e.g., [Nelson and Oppen, 1980]. These could be provided as a user defined extension of the equality primitive, but this idea will not be pursued here.

If at any stage of the computation the irreducible multiset of threads, I, contains predicates other than equalities, the corresponding Prolog program would have failed. The irreducible user defined goals are not assumed to be false, as is the case with negation as failure, but form part of the conditional answer. This has been called the *Open-World Assumption* [Ringwood, 1987] and is a desirable semantics where recovery from hardware failure is a promised attribute of distributed systems [Bal et al., 1989].

An additional control mechanism can be added to prevent nonequality threads becoming members of the irreducible set. This is the *otherwise* constraint as introduced in the previous chapter:

```
thread(State,[Message|InStream],...,OutStream)
    :- <constraint(State,Message)>
    |  computeStateResponse(State,Message,NewState,Response),
       OutStream=[Response|TailOutStream],
       thread(NewState,InStream,...,TailOutStream).
thread(State,InSt,...,OutSt) :- otherwise
    |  exceptionHandler(State,InSt,NewState,TailInSt,Response),
       OutSt=[Response|TailOutSt].
```

The *otherwise* clause is only used for thread reduction if all other clause guards for the thread are unsatisfiable. That is, were it not for the *exception* clause the thread would be irreducible. A thread that has an otherwise clause can never be a member of the irreducible set, I, but it can be a member of the blocked multiset B. A situation in which this might be needed is when the thread receives a message whose type it is not programmed to expect. Delegating a message is a technique of object-oriented programming. The guard of the *otherwise* clause is, in effect, the negation of the conjunction of the guards of all the other clauses describing the possible thread behaviors. *Otherwise* negation does not have the problems of Negation as Failure. This is because all the guard constraints are decidable primitives so the alternatives are exhaustive. Guard constraints only test the input, they do not cause any bindings to the call variables.

If, at a stage of the computation the multiset of reducible threads, R, is empty, there may still be threads that are not irreducible yet have instances that are reducible. These threads will be in B. Such a state is called *deadlock termination*; the threads in the multiset B are waiting for conditions that will never hold. This predicament may occur because of cycles in the dataflow [Burt and Ringwood, 1988] or because of incomplete guards or because a node of the distributed system fails. Another control mechanism may be introduced which ensures that threads do not remain indefinitely in B. This is the *after* guard that is illustrated as follows:

thread(State,[Message|InStream],...,OutStream)
    :- <constraint(State,Message)>
    | **computeStateResponse**(State,Message,NewState,Response),
       OutStream=[Response|TailOutStream],
       thread(NewState,InStream,...,TailOutStream)
thread(State,InSt,...,OutSt) :- after(5)
    | **timeOutResponse**(State,InSt,NewState,TailInSt,Response),
       OutSt=[Response|TailOutSt],
       thread(NewState,TailInSt,...,TailOutSt).

A thread with an *after* clause will remain in a blocked state for a maximum time indicated by the parameter of the primitive after constraint (a *time-out*). The timer starts the first occasion the thread is scheduled. If at the end of the time-out period, none of the guards of the other clauses are satisfiable, the behavior of the time-out clause will be used to reduce the thread. The time-out clause will most naturally be used in conjunction with priority scheduling.

The time-out guard may be compared with the Occam delay guards. As with Occam, the parameter of after can be dynamic and passed as a parameter by the call:

thread({State,N},InSt,...,OutSt) :- after(N)
    | **timeOutResponse**(State,InSt,NewState,TailInSt,Response),
       OutSt=[Response|TailOutSt],
       thread(NewState,TailInSt,...,TailOutSt).

4.16 Implementation Issues

For the implementation of GDC, a functor of the form $f(X1,...XN)$ is represented as a tuple or array $\{f,X1,...XN\}$; that is a contiguous block of $N+1$ references in memory. Access to the elements of the array so far has been by pattern matching but for large arrays this becomes impractical. For such large arrays three primitive constraints are provided to effect indexed access. (Proposals to incorporate arrays into logic programming have been around for some time [Eriksson and Raynes, 1984]. The constraint array(FA,NA,A) causes a thread to block until NA is instantiated to a natural number. As with the arithmetic constraint, is, the variable A must not be contained in the head of a clause. When this condition is satisfied the variable A is instantiated to an array $\{FA,A1,...AN\}$.

Dual to the array primitive is the constraint functor(A,FA,NA) which causes a thread to block until A is instantiated to a nonvariable term. When this holds, FA is instantiated to the name (functor) of the array (term) and NA to the arity. This primitive is restricted in a similar way to the array primitive and expression evaluation primitive, in that FA and NA must be variables that are not contained in the head of the clause. If A is a constant (functor of arity 0) then FA is bound to the same constant and NA is bound to 0.

The final primitive of the trio arg(A,N,AN), provides indexed access to the elements of an array without pattern matching. The argument A is the array and the argument N is the index of the array element being sought. Both these variables must be bound if the thread is not to block. When this condition is satisfied, the arg primitive binds the variable AN to the N-th element of the array A. Like the constraints array and functor, arg is restricted in a similar way to the expression evaluation primitive, is, in that AN is not allowed to be a variable in the head of the clause.

The cost of representing arrays in this way is the need to copy nearly all the array to update a single element. If any other thread does not require the old element value it can be garbage collected and its storage reused by the new. This will require the somewhat sophisticated program analysis envisaged in Kemp and Ringwood [1990] if it is to compete with the efficiency of mutable arrays.

With the above primitive array constraints, the proposed attachment semantics of equality is almost implementable in GDC:

```
X=Y :- functor(X,FX,NX), functor(Y,FY,NY), FX=FY, NX=NY
    |   equalArgs(X,Y,NX)
X=Y :- testCommitAndSet(X,Y) | true.
```

```
equalArgs(X,Y,0) :- true | true.
equalArgs(X,Y,N) :- /(N=<0), arg(N,X,XN), arg(N,Y,YN) & N1:=N-1
    |   XN=YN, equalArgs(X,Y,N1).
```

The symbol / negates a constraint. The constraint, /(N=<0), suspends until N is instantiated to something other than 0. The unexplained testCommitAndSet primitive in the second clause for the equality thread is a manifestation of the race condition associated with shared variables noted previously. If such a primitive was to be provided for programmers it would correspond to an atomic test-commit-and-set action. It tests to see whether the first argument is a variable and if so commits the clause and instantiates the first argument with the second argument as an all-or-nothing action. Burt and Ringwood [1988] first introduced the idea of this primitive. It violates a previous rule that guards cannot instantiate variables in the call. This condition has to be modified to allow instantiation of a thread variable only as part of an atomic guard-variable test, clause commit and variable instantiation. (It does not conflict with the semantics where the guard is assumed atomic.)

In a distributed implementation, the way that the atomic test-commit-and-set action is achieved is as follows. Each yet unbound variable, X, occurs only once in the distributed system, at the node where it was first created. All other references to it are indirections. An equality thread of the form $X=t$ has to migrate to the node where the variable X is stored to bind it.

If the constraints provided by the system are insufficient or inappropriate, new ones can be user defined in a lower level language and linked into the system. Primitive threads can also be defined by the user as required and added to the system. In this respect GDC is like *ISWIM* [Landin, 1966], in that it is really a family of languages, the individuals being determined by the set of guard primitives and thread primitives provided as semantic attachments.

Chapter 5

Actors and Agents

Even while it changes, it stands still

Heraclitus

Hewitt and Agha [1988], in a Fifth Generation conference, asked if Guarded Definite Clause languages were logical. That they are sound but not complete should be clear from previous chapters. Hewitt made a similar previous reappraisal of Planner. The similarity of Planner with Smalltalk [Hewitt 1973, 1974] led Kornfield and Hewitt to develop a pattern-directed invocation language, Actors, to build multi-agent systems. Programming in the Actor formalism requires first deciding the messages each actor can receive and then what each actor should do when it receives such a message. The idea that single assignment variables can be considered as message channels was raised in the previous chapter. The correspondence of GDC and Actors is explored in this chapter. The superficial difference between Actors and GDC is one of ontology. Actors names behaviors, message queues and local variables while GDC names only behaviors and channels. The essential difference between the two languages is that messages are defined inductively in GDC and message queues are implicit in Actors.

Like GDC, the process structure of Actors is small and therefore scalable. In concurrent object-oriented programming, the uniformity of communication and encapsulation, enable combination and co-operation of various levels and grains of agents. This helps in constructing multi-grain intelligent architectures such as an architecture for brain simulation [Weitzenfeld and Arbib, 1991]. In a similar way, GDC programs can model fine entities such as neurons [Kozato and Ringwood, 1992]. This is illustrated in this chapter. The elegance with which process based languages can be used to build neural networks indicates both the advantages of implementing neural nets in a concurrent programming language and the innate potential for massive parallelism with such languages. This Chapter also explores new directions for both connectionism and symbolic AI research with a view to fusion. For those readers who have managed to avoid connectionist propaganda until now, the chapter introduces neural networks. In Section 5.8, an example indicates how a self-replicating network of generic neurons can be produced. The neuron type is specialized in Section 5.9 where its response behavior is programmed. Section 5.10 describes how such a neural network can be taught a simple recognition task, parity determination. Parity recognition is an *example celebre* that presents a hard learning exercise for most neural networks [Minsky and Papert, 1969].

Conway's *Life* game provides a rich source of insight into how simple rules lead to complex "social" behavior. Until the development of GDC languages, Logic programmers were somewhat disadvantaged in this game. The chapter illustrates how, with such Logic Languages, Logic programmers can readily join in. In particular, the chapter reports a new asynchronous implementation of the Life game on distributed workstations. This chapter is envisaged as the first step in the investigation of the use of GDC languages for building self-replicating multi-agent systems.

5.1 The Actor Model

Newell [1962] pointed out that with conventional AI, a single agent appears to be wandering over a goal net much as an explorer wanders over the globe. The agent has a single context that it takes with it wherever it goes. This single agent view focuses attention on the internal process of search with a single locus of control and attention. This leads to preoccupation with control structures such as goal stacks and queues for making decisions and changing contexts. Rather than a sequence of choices made by a decision maker on a web of choice points, Hewitt [1977] envisages control as a pattern of messages among a collection of computational agents he called Actors.

According to Hewitt [1985], incomplete knowledge is typical of AI and as such requires an approach that allows continuous acquisition, refinement and toleration of inconsistency. Hewitt claims open systems uncover important limitations in current approaches to AI. Such systems require an approach more like organizational behavior embodied in general systems theory [Skyttner, 1996]. Minsky [1986] has claimed that intelligence in humans is a result of the interaction of a very large and complex assembly of loosely connected subunits operating much like a society but within a single individual. More generally, Hewitt argues that the agents in an organization are open in the sense that they are embedded in an environment with which they interact asynchronously. Open systems are not totally in control of their fate. They consist of agents, conceptually parallel threads, which communicate with each other and co-operatively or competitively respond to events that occur indeterministicly in real-time.

Refinement of these ideas produced the Actor language [Agha, 1986] that attempted to address the needs of distributed AI. The example of a stack is used to introduce Actors in [Agha, 1986] using the Simple Actor Syntax:

```
def node(Item, Link)
    [case operation of
        push: (NewItem)
        pop: (Customer)
    end case ]
    if operation = push then
        let L = new node(Item, Link)
        become node(NewItem, L)
    fi
    if operation = pop then
        send Item to Customer
        become forward(Link)
    fi
end def
```

The case statement clearly corresponds to GDC guards. Besides the conditional, actors are defined inductively with four primitive actions: **send**; *become; create* and **forward**. The arrival order of messages is nondeterministic but the underlying message passing system is assumed to guarantee eventual delivery. To send a message, the identity (mail address) of the recipient needs to be specified. The *become* directive specifies the subsequent behavior of the actor. The **send** action causes a message to be put in the recipient's mailbox (message queue). The *create* primitive (*let and new*) is to Actors what procedural abstraction is to sequential programming. Newly created actors are autonomous and have unique mail addresses specified in the create command.

The **forward** primitive actor passes on received messages to the mailbox named in its argument. It is left to a garbage collector to detect and finesse forwarders. Both channels, such as Item and message queues, such as Link, are named in the language. The **forwarder** can be understood in GDC as shorting two streams as in **merge**. To better understand the Actor language, a GDC program for the stack example corresponding closely to the Actor program is given:

```
//node(Item, Task ,Link)
node(Item, push(NewItem, Task),Link) :- true
    | node(Item, L, Link), node(NewItem, Task,L)
node(Item,pop(Customer,Task),Link) :- true
    | send(Task, Link) send(Item, Customer)
```

where **send**(Message, Channel) is used as a synonym for Channel=Message.

The first clause can be represented pictorially as in Figure 5.1.1 and the second clause as in Figure 5.1.2. The essential difference between this and the previous program is that Actors names message queues and channels, while GDC names only channels. In Actors, variables are local variables and only message queues are shared. The behavioral identity of an actor is ephemeral, as are GDC goals and lasts only one reduction. Actor destruction is thus implicit.

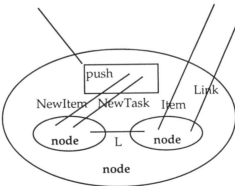

Fig. 5.1.1 First node clause

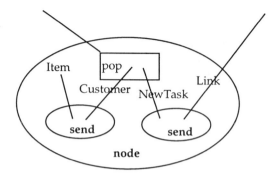

Fig. 5.1.2 Second node clause

A scenario illustrating how the stack grows and collapses is the following.

:- **node**(empty, Task, nil), **send**(push(m1,Task1),Task),
   send(push(m2,Task2),Task1), **send**(pop(Top,Task3),Task2).
:- **node**(empty,push(m1,Task1),nil), **send**(push(m2,Task2),Task1),
   send(pop(Top,Task3),Task2).
:- **node**(empty,push(m1,push(m2,Task2)),nil),
   send(pop(Top,Task3),Task2).
:- **node**(empty, push(m1,push(m2,pop(Top,Task3))),nil).
:- **node**(m1,push(m2,pop(Top, pop(Top,Task3))),L1),
   node(nil,L1,nil).
:- **node**(m2,pop(Top,Task3),L2), **node**(m1,L2,L1),
   node(empty,L1,nil).
:- **node**(m1,L2,L1), **node**(empty,L1,nil), **send**(m2,Top),
   send(Task3,L2).
:- **node**(m1,Task3,L1), **node**(empty,L1,nil), **send**(m2,Top).
.
.
.

Before the pop operation the initial **node**(empty,Task,nil) has evolved into three nodes as in Figure 5.1.3.

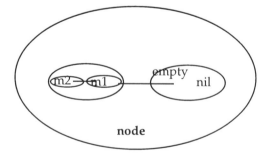

Fig. 5.1.3 Node evolution

Here the identity of the stack is inherited from the initial **node**(empty,Task,nil). That is, agent identity is emergent, in the sense of general systems theory and not exhibited by a single node.

In the conditional semantics of GDC (described in Chapter 4):

$a_1, a_2,...a_n \leftarrow R \leftarrow B \leftarrow I$

lends itself to this idea of agent identity. If an actor a_i in the initial network reduces to a set of actors:

$\leftarrow b_1, b_2,... b_m$

the parent relation conveys a connotation of identity.

In the Actor interpretation of GDC, actors are defined inductively using a single primitive agent **send**. The action is one of substitution of an actor by a network of actors specified in the body of a clause. As actors in GDC are ephemeral, there is no need for **fowarders**. This is summarized in the following table:

Table 5.1.4 Actor interpretation

behavior	named set of condition action pairs (guarded clauses)
condition (guard)	**node**(Item, Task, Link) if **receive**(push(NewItem,NextTask),Task)
action – substitution by network of agents	become **node**(NewItem, NextTask, L) | **node**(Item,L,Link)

Yet again, the syntax of GDC has been changed to illustrate the actor interpretation. The notation | for the concurrent composition of actors is borrowed from CCS [Milner, 1980].

One problem with Actors is the combinatorial explosion in their number of actors. Constructing message queues using data structures gives more flexibility and avoids some of the explosion:

```
//node(Task, Stack)
node(Task, Stack)
    if receive(push(NewItem, Task),Task)
    become send(stack(NewItem, Stack),St1) | node(Task,St1).
node(Task, stack(Item, Stack))
    if receive(pop(Customer, Task), Task),Item)
    become send(Item, Customer) | node(Task, Stack)
```

In this revised implementation, a stack is formed by a message queue and **node** becomes a server of the message queue. In the first behavior for **node**, the node sends itself a message. This can be finessed:

```
node(Task,Stack) if receive(push(NewItem, Task),Item)
    become node(Task, stack(Item, Stack)).
node(pop(Customer, Task),stack(Top, Stack))
    if receive(pop(Customer, Task), Task),Item)
    become send(Item, Customer) | node(Task, Top)
```

Figure 5.1.5 illustrates the revised first behavior.

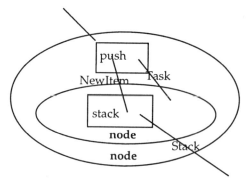

Fig. 5.1.5 Revised node behavior

The diagram for the second behavior is similar. This solution is not possible in Actors because, essentially, it requires two message queues.

5.2 Haggling Protocols

Interaction is a basic concept in multi-agent systems. Several agents can combine their efforts by means of interaction. In an interaction, one agent takes an action or decision that is influenced by the presence or knowledge of other agents. Each interaction can cause revisions in an agent's model of other agents. The example below (illustrated in Figure 5.2.1) is a GDC program for the Winograd and Flores *haggling protocol* [Winograd and Flores, 1986]:

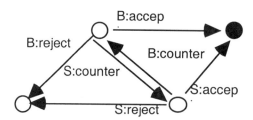

Fig. 5.2.1 Winograd Flores labeled digraph

The buyer and seller start concurrently with a message for the buyer, the seller's asking price, already waiting:

become **seller**(100,Haggle,50) | **buyer**(30,counter(100,Haggle),60).

If the buyer receives an offer less than its upper limit, a message agreeing to the price is sent:

```
//buyer(CurrentOffer, NewOffer, UpperLimit)
buyer(Offer, NewOffer, UpperLimit)
    if receive(counter(Ask, Haggle),NewOffer) & Ask<UpperLimit
    become send(accept(Ask),Haggle).
```

If the buyer receives an offer greater and the difference between its previous offer and the new asking price is less than its upper limit, it proposes a counter offer:

```
buyer(Offer, NewOffer, UpperLimit)
    if receive(counter(Ask, Haggle),NewOffer) & Ask>UpperLimit
        & NewOffer:=(Ask+Offer)/2 & NewOffer<UpperLimit
    become send(counter(NewOffer, NewHaggle),Haggle)
        | buyer(NewOffer, NewHaggle, UpperLimit).
```

If splitting the difference is greater than the buyer is prepared to pay it rejects the offer:

```
buyer(Offer, NewOffer, UpperLimit)
    if receive(counter(Ask, Haggle),NewOffer) & Ask>UpperLimit
        & NewOffer:=(Ask+Offer)/2 & NewOffer>UpperLimit
    become send(reject(Ask),Haggle).
```

The code for the seller is similar:

```
//seller(CurrentAskingPrice, Offers, LowerLimit)
seller(Ask,Offers, LowerLimit)
    if receive(counter(Offer, Haggle),Offers) & Offer>LowerLimit
    become send(agreed(Offer),Haggle).
seller(Ask, Offers, LowerLimit)
    if receive(counter(Offer, Haggle),Offers) & Offer<LowerLimit
        & NewAsk:=(Ask+Offer)/2 & NewAsk>LowerLimit
    become send(counter(NewAsk, NewHaggle),Haggle)
        | seller(NewAsk, NewHaggle, LowerLimit).
seller(Ask, Offers, LowerLimit)
    if receive(counter(Offer, Haggle),Offers)
        & Offer<LowerLimit & NewAsk:=(Ask+Offer)/2
        & NewAsk<LowerLimit
    become send(reject(Offer),Haggle).
```

The comparison of the Winograd Flores network and finite-state-machine diagram is readily apparent. A comparison of GDC and the specification of finite state machines, decision tables was made in Chapter 4.

The given initial object network results in the following scenario:

```
become seller(100,Haggle,75) | buyer(40,counter(100,Haggle),80).
become seller(100,Haggle,50) | send(counter(0,Haggle1),Haggle)
    | buyer(70,Haggle1,80).
become seller(100,counter(70,Haggle1),75) | buyer(70,Haggle1,80).
become seller(85,Haggle2,75) | send(counter(85,Haggle2),Haggle1)
    | buyer(70,Haggle1,80).
become seller(85,Haggle2,75) | buyer(70,counter(85,Haggle2),80).
```

become **seller**(85,Haggle2,75) | <u>**send**(counter(77.5,Haggle3),Haggle2)</u>
    | **buyer**(77.5,Haggle3,80).
become <u>**seller**(85,counter(77.5,Haggle3),75)</u>
    | **buyer**(77.5,Haggle3,80).
become <u>**send**(agreed(77.5),Haggle3)</u> | **buyer**(77.5,Haggle3,80).
become **buyer**(77.5,agreed(77.5),80).

5.3 Consensus Protocols

There are three equivalent agreement problems that illustrate the potential for fault tolerance of distributed systems: the Byzantine agreement, the consensus problem and the interactive consistency problem [Singhal and Shivaratri, 1994]. They are equivalent in the sense that a solution to any one can be used to solve the others. The *Byzantine Generals problem* [Dolev, 1982] is so called because it resembles a team of army generals trying to agree an attack plan. The generals are located on different hilltops around the battlefield and communicate by sending messages (by semaphore). Some of the generals are traitors (faulty processors) who by sending conflicting messages, deliberately try to prevent the loyal generals agreeing.

Lamport et al.'s [1982] Oral Message algorithm is one solution to the problem. The following illustrates the situation of four generals, one of which is a traitor:

    become **source**(1,[A,B,C]) | **general**(A) | **traitor**(B) | **general**(C).

An arbitrarily chosen source general broadcasts its plan to all other generals:

    //**source**(Value, List_of_Messages)
    source(N,[G1,G2,G3]) if **true**
        become **send**(plan(N,[{G12,G21},{G13,G31}]),G1)
        | **send**(plan(N,[{G21,G12},{G23,G32}]),G2)
        | **send**(plan(N,[{G31,G13},{G32,G13}]),G3).

In doing so, the source sets up the mutual channels.

In the Lamport–Shostak–Pease [1982] solution, the generals send the plan they received from the source to the other generals and choose the majority plan:

    //**general**(Plans)
    general(Plans) if **receive**(plan(N,[{TA,FA},{TB,FB}]),Plans)
        become **send**(N,TA) | **send**(N,TB)
        | **majorityGeneral**([N,FA,FB]).

    //**traitor**(Plans)
    traitor(Plans) if **receive**(plan(N,[{TA,FA},{TB,FB}]),Plans)
        become **send**(N,TA) | **send**(0,TB) | **majorityTraitor**([N,FA,FB])

In this scenario, the faithful generals agree on the Plan 1:

    become <u>**source**(1,[A,B,C])</u> | **general**(A) | **traitor**(B) | **general**(C)

become **send**(plan(1,[{AB,BA},{AC,CA}]),A)
   | **send**(plan(1,[{BA,AB},{BC,CB}]),B)
   | **send**(plan(1,[{CA,AC},{CB,BC}]),C)
   | **general**(A) | **traitor**(B) | **general**(C).
become **general**(plan(1,[{AB,BA},{AC,CA}]))
   | **traitor**(plan(1,[{BA,AB},{BC,CB}]))
   | **general**(plan(1,[{CA,AC},{CB,BC}]),C)).

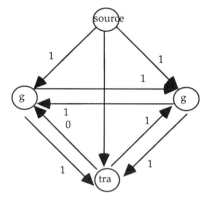

Fig. 5.3.1 Four Byzantine generals

The three sends have been done simultaneously. Continuing:

become **general**(plan(1,[{AB,BA},{AC,CA}]))
   | **traitor**(plan(1,[{BA,AB},{BC,CB}]))
   | **general**(plan(1,[{CA,AC},{CB,BC}]),C)).
become **send**(1,AB) | **send**(1,AC) | **majorityGeneral**([1,BA,CA])
   | **traitor**(plan(1,[{BA,AB}|{BC,CB}]))
   | **general**(plan(1,[{CA,AC}|{CB,BC}]),C)).
become **majorityGeneral**([1,BA,CA])
   | **traitor**(plan(1,[{BA,1},{BC,CB}]))
   | **general**(plan(1,[{CA,1},{CB,BC}]),C)).
become **majorityGeneral**([1,BA,CA])
   | **traitor**(plan(1,[{BA,1},{BC,CB}]))
   | **general**(plan(1,[{CA,1},{CB,BC}]),C)).
   send(1,CA) | **send**(1,CB) | **majorityGeneral**([1,1,BC]).
become **majorityGeneral**([1,BA,1])
   | **traitor**(plan(1,[{BA,1},{BC,1}]))
   | **majorityGeneral**([1,1,BC]).
become **majorityGeneral**(1|BA|1)
   | **send**(1,BA) | **send**(0,BC) | **majorityTraitor**([N,FA,FB])
   | **majorityGeneral**([1,1,BC]).
become **majorityGeneral**([1,1,1])
   | **majorityTraitor**([1,1,0]),
   | majorityGeneral([1,1,0]).

5.4 Market Forces

In the much vaunted *Contract Net Protocol* [Smith, 1980], a customer requests Contractors to tender for a specified job.

    //**contractNet**(SpecifiedJob, SetOfContractors, Chosen)
    contractNet(Job, Contractors, Chosen) if **true**
        become **tender**(Job, Contractors,[],Time,Tenders)
            | **time**(5,Time) | **select**(Tenders, Chosen).

The actor **time/2** is a primitive that immediately it is spawned initializes a real-time clock. After the designated five periods has elapsed, it sends a message timeUp on the channel Time. (Man [1992] describes concurrent analysis techniques that, he claims, make GDC programming suitable for hard realtime systems.) The actor **select/2**, which is not specified, choses the contractor on the basis of the tenders received (usually the lowest cost.)

After the timeout has expired, **tender/4** sends the received bids on Tenders to the selector actor. In the meantime it distributes the Job description to the set of Contractors with a unique reply channel (as in the **client** actor in Chapter 4):

    //**tender**(SpecifJob, Contractors, ReplyAcc, Time, TenderReplies)
    tender(Job, Contractors, Accum, Time, Tenders)
        if **receive**(timeUp,Time)
        become **send**(Accum, Tenders).
    tender(Job, Contractors, Accum, Time, Tenders)
        if **receive**([Contractor|Cs],Contractors)
        become **send**(offer(Job, Reply),Contractor)
            | **tender**(Job, Cs, [Reply|Accum], Time, Tenders).

5.5 Poker Faced

A poker game can be seen as a combination of a contract net and the haggling protocol. The auctioneer raises the stakes until there is only one punter left in the game:

    //**auction**(CurrentOffer, SetOfPunters)
    auction(CurrentOffer, Punters) if Offer:=CurrentOffer+1
        become **request**(Offer, Punters, Accum, Replies)
            | **time**(5,Time) | **wait**(Time, Offer, Replies)

Punters are connected to the auction via fair merges. The punter is simplified to remain bidding while Offer is less than some punter chosen limit:

    //**punter**(Requests, UpperLimit)
    punter(Requests, UpLimit)
        if **receive**([bid(Offer, Reply)|Round],Requests)
            & Offer=<UpLimit
        become **send**(in(More),Reply) | **punter**(More, UpLimit).

```
punter(Requests, UpLimit)
    if receive([bid(Offer, Reply)|Round],Requests)
        & Offer>UpLimit
    become send(out,Reply).

//request(Offer, SetPunters, Accumulator, SetBidReplyPairs)
request(offer, SetPunters, Accum, Replies)
    if receive([in(Punter)|Ps],SetPunters)
    become send(bid(offer,Reply),Punter)
        | request(offer, Ps,[Reply|Accum],Replies).
request(offer, SetPunters, Accum,Replies)
    if receive([out|Ps],SetPunters)
    become request(offer,Ps,[Reply|Accum],Replies).
request(Job, SetPunters, Accum,Replies)
    if receive([],SetPunters)
    become send(AccumReplies).
request(offer, SetPunters, Accum, Replies)
    if receive([X|Ps],SetPunters) & unknown(X)
    become request(offer, Ps,[Reply|Accum],Replies).

wait(timeUp, offer, Replies) if true
    become auction(Bid, NewPunters).
```

5.6 Virtual Neural Networks

Weitzenfeld and Arbib [1991] propose building a brain from a host of actors in much the same way a biological brain is made up of neurons. That organic brains and computers have approximately the same number of processing elements, 10^{11}, might initially suggest that the perceptive power advantage of organic brains over computers must be due to the speed of its electrochemical processing elements, neurons. This is not so. Neurons are significantly slower at firing than logic gates are at changing state. Neurons fire in milliseconds whereas off-the-shelf solid-state technology can switch state in nanoseconds. If raw processing power is calculated as the product of the number of processing elements and the response rate, the computer has an apparent power advantage of ten thousand. Nevertheless, this advantage is not realized because only small fractions of logic gates change state simultaneously. It is one thing to have the capacity for parallel processing, it is another to be able to exploit it efficiently. It would seem to be the way in which potential parallelism is exploited in organic brains that gives them greater power than conventional computers.

Conscious thought, examined on time-scales of seconds or minutes has sequential characteristics. Current psychological thinking on perception is that humans relate fragmentary stimuli to knowledge familiar from various experiences and unconsciously test and reiterate perceptions at different levels of abstraction. In other words, what beings believe they perceive, is, in fact, only a mental reconstruction of fragments of sensory data. This is reminiscent of the philosophy of Husserl and Heidegger. This suggests that symbolic AI is not made redundant by artificial neural machines but is only part of the solution to Artificial Intelligence. Symbolic AI corresponds to the higher conscious levels of human thought processes.

Linguists have speculated that higher levels of thought processes are only possible with the aid of phonograms and ideograms. The superiority of ideograms over phonograms has proved itself in mathematics and science. Uncritical surrender to neural fever (or *mad cow disease* as it is known in the UK) threatens the transparency and maintainability that software engineering is striving to achieve. An alternative to surrender is compromise; the two approaches to AI should form different layers in the pursuit of Artificial Intelligence. If thought processes are organized in hierarchical layers of abstraction then the interface between symbolic AI and artificial neural networks is a legitimate area of study. The combination of artificial neural networks and computer symbolic processing holds the promise of being better than the sum of the parts.

5.7 Biological and Artificial Neural Networks

Neurons are the primitive constituents of organic brains. A neuron is a nerve cell that consists of a nucleus, dendrites, axon and synapses, as depicted in Figure 5.7.1. The synapses form the connection between the axon of one cell and the dendrite of another. Functionally, the dendrites are receptors and the axon an emitter of bursts of electrochemical pulses generated by the cells. A neuron produces pulses along its axon in response to pulses received from other neurons at its synapses. Whether a neuron decides to 'fire', produce a pulse, depends on the combination of the present state of the neuron and the pulses received from its immediate neighbors. The similarity with Petri nets is clearly apparent. (For a better informed description of the physiology of nerve cells the reader is referred to [Crick and Asanuma, 1986].)

Neurons in organic brains are autonomous computational units and each may be directly connected with up to several thousand other neurons forming a network. The computational mechanism of each neuron is local and simple. It can only be the autonomy of neurons, as processing elements and the complexity of interconnections wherein lies the ability to explore simultaneously many competing hypotheses. The way neurons interconnect and fire allows the possibility of chain reactions in much the same way as chain reactions occur in an atomic explosion. This analogy reveals the way in which explosive parallelism can be achieved by neural systems.

Artificial neural networks are characterized by network topology, node characteristics and training or learning rules. Though in what follows the three components are explained separately for pedagogy, they are not independent. Neuron connectivity can be represented as a directed graph with neurons as the vertices and directed edges synaptic connections. In general, there can be cycles, closed loops, so that feedback is possible as depicted in Figure 5.7.2. An artificial neural network adopting this type of topology [Hopfield, 1982], was partly responsible for the renewed enthusiasm in connectionist systems.

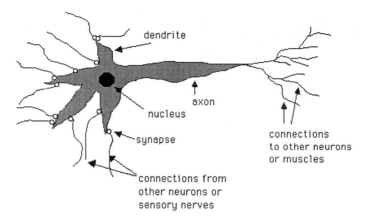

Fig. 5.7.1 A simplified organic neuron

If there is no feedback the network forms a DAG (directed acyclic graph) and is stratified, as illustrated in Figure 5.7.3. This form of topology is exemplified by, *Nettalk* [Sejnowski and Rosenberg, 1985]. Nettalk's ability to read text aloud contributed to the revival of interest in connectionist systems. External stimuli feed into a bottom layer of neurons and the output is taken from the top layer; there can be many layers of hidden neurons in-between. There may be different numbers of nodes in each layer and such networks can be used to classify input patterns, the number of output nodes reflecting the number of classes.

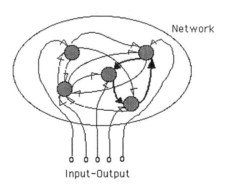

Fig. 5.7.2 The 'feed-all' network

It is in the DAG topology that the potential for explosive parallelism can best be seen when the hidden layers have increasing numbers of neurons. The way neurons interconnect and fire in this topology allows the possibility of chain reactions in much the same way as chain reactions occur in an atomic explosion.

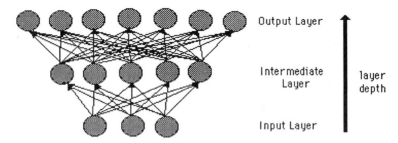

Fig. 5.7.3 The feed-forward network

5.8 Self-Replicating Neural Networks

For the sake of definiteness, the network topology chosen for implementation is a binary tree, but other arrangements can be accommodated as easily. As will be illustrated, such a neural network can be taught to recognize the parity of input bit vectors. A binary tree of protoneurons with three layers can be brought into existence by the GDC process invocation:

become **tree**(3, O, Is).

where the **tree** relation is defined by:

//**tree**(NumberOfLayers, OutputStream, ListOfInputStreams)
tree(NumberOfLayers,A,Ss) if **receive**(1,NumberOfLayers)
    become **send**([S1|S2],Ss) | **protoNeuron**(A,S1,S2)
tree(N,A,Ss) if N>1 & N1:=N-1
    become **protoNeuron**(A,A1,A2) | **tree**(N1,A1,S1s)
    | **tree**(N1,A2,S2s) | **concatenate**(S1s,S2s,Ss).

A graphical trace of a parallel reduction of the initial agent [á la Ringwood, 1989a] is given in Figures 5.8.1a and 5.8.1b; active (reducible) agents at each stage are shaded. The tree process evolves into a tree of generic neurons (the type of neuron will be specified in the next section).

5.9 Neuron Specialization

There are essentially two types of artificial neurons: analogue neurons [Pitts and McCulloch, 1947], which are weighted sum threshold activation models, and the earlier discrete logic gates [McCulloch and Pitts, 1943], which are motivated by digital hardware (Figure 5.9.1).

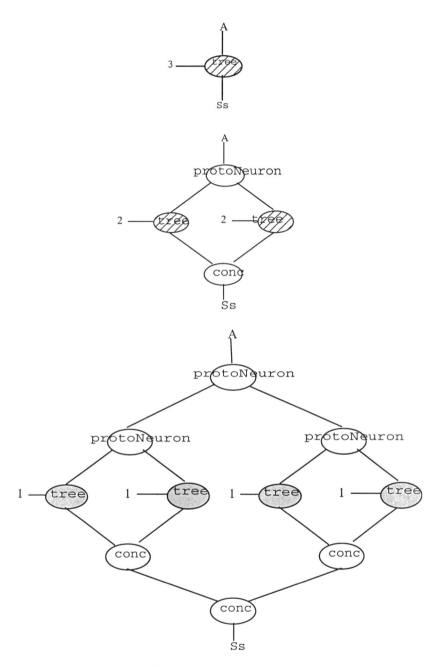

Fig. 5.8.1a Evolution of the net

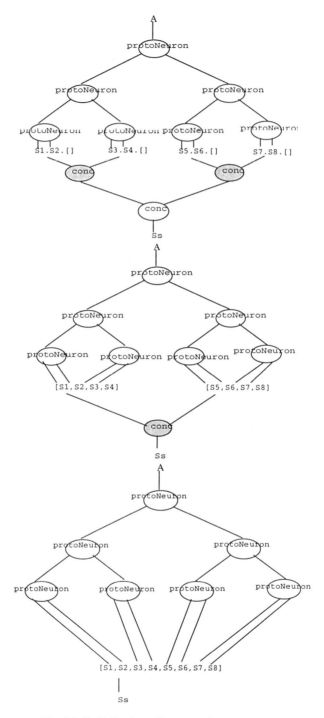

Fig. 5.8.1b Collection of inputs to the net.

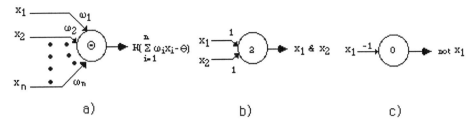

Fig. 5.9.1 a) 1947 Pitts–McCulloch artificial neuron where H, is the Heaviside's step function and the weights ω_i and threshold Θ are arbitrary real numbers; b) and c) 1943 McCulloch–Pitts threshold logic gate neurons where the possible weights are +1 or -1 and the thresholds Θ integer.

Discrete logical neurons are, of course, ideally suited to implementation in conventional hardware. One mutable form of a logic gate, *Probabilistic Logic Neuron* [Aleksander, 1988] (PLN), was chosen for the present chapter for the sake of definiteness. There is a sense in which the PLN is biologically more realistic than the analogue McCulloch–Pitts [1947] neuron. In biological neurons it is widely believed that, before adaptation, a neuron fires or does not with roughly equal probability. The probability edges towards certainty as the learning process progresses [Sejnowski, 1981; Aleksander, 1988]. Any other form of artificial neuron or network can be implemented by the same techniques used below.

The PLN is essentially a programmable, probabilistic, logic gate.

```
//protoNeuron(Axon,Synapse1,Synapse2)
protoNeuron(A,S1,S2) if true
    become
        pLN(table(Seed,unknown,unknown,unknown,unknown),S1,S2,A).
```

Initially, the gate type is unspecified (Figure 5.9.2). The constant unknown in the table is used to indicate that the neuron will produce an indeterministic response (0 or 1) to a binary input pattern. The first parameter of table is used as the seed of a pseudo random number generator to produce this effect. In this situation, the PLN produces a 1 or 0 output with equal probability. This stochastic nature endows the PLN with indeterministic properties that biological neurons are speculated to possess [Sejnowski, 1981]. (By modifying the tree clause it can be arranged that the different neurons do not have the same initial seed.)

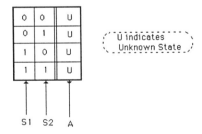

Fig. 5.9.2 Initial State of the PLN

As the neural network undergoes training, undetermined truth table entries become *learnt* responses to controlled input (Figure 5.9.3).

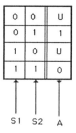

Fig. 5.9.3 Some partially learnt state

The response behavior is captured by the actor **pLN**:

```
//pLN(State,InputStream1,InputStream2,OutputStream)
pLN(State,InputStream1,InputStream2,Output)
    if receive([o(S1)|S1s],InputStream1)
       & receive([o(S2)|S2s],InputStream2)
    become send([o(A)|S3s],Output)
       | gate({S1,S2},State, NewState,A)
       | pLN(NewState,S1s,S2s,S3s).
```

The response consists of truth table lookup. If the table value has been learnt, this value is returned:

```
//gate(InputPairState, LookUpTable, OuputState, Output)
gate(InputPairState, table(Seed, learnt(T),U,V,W),NewState,A)
    if receive({0,0},InputPairState)
    become send(T,A) | send(table(Seed,learnt(T),U,V,W),NewState).
gate(InputPairState, table(Seed,unknown,U,V,W),NewState,A)
    if receive({0,0},InputPairState)
       & NSeed:= if Seed<0 then shiftleft(Seed)XOR3
    else shiftleft(Seed) & B:=NSeedmod2
    become send(B,A) | send(table(NSeed,unknown,U,V,W),NewState).
gate({0,1},table(Seed, T, learnt(U),V,W),NewState,A) if true
    become send(U,A) | send(table(Seed,T,learnt(U),V,W),NewState)
gate({0,1},table(Seed,T,unknown,V,W), NewState,A)
    if NSeed:= if Seed<0 then shiftleft(Seed)XOR3
    else shiftleft(Seed) & B:=NSeedmod2
    become send(B,A) | send(table(NSeed,T,unknown,V,W),NewState)
gate({1,0},table(Seed,T,U,learnt(V),W),NewState,A) if true
    become send(V,A) | send(table(Seed,T,U,learnt(V),W),NewState)
gate({1,0},table(Seed,T,U,unknown,W),NewState,A)
    if NSeed := if Seed<0 then shiftleft(Seed)XOR3)
    else shiftleft(Seed) & B := NSeedmod 2
    become send(B,A) | send(table(NSeed,T,U,unknown,W),NewState)
```

gate({1,1},table(Seed,T,U,V,learnt(W)),NewState,A) if **true**
  become **send**(W,A) | **send**(table(Seed,T,U,V,learnt(W)),NewState)
gate({1,1},table(Seed,T,U,V,unknown),NewState,A)
  if NSeed := if Seed<0 then shiftleft(Seed)XOR3
    else shiftleft(Seed) & B := NSeed mod 2
  become **send**(B,A) | **send**(table(NSeed,T,U,V,unknown),NewState).

The algorithm for calculating random bits is taken from Knuth [1969].

A trace of how inputs propagate in parallel through a PLN tree network is shown in Figure 5.9.4. (The word *propagate* does not really convey the sense of urgency associated with combinatorially explosive parallelism.)

5.10 The Teacher Teaches and the Pupil Learns

In artificial neural networks, there is no conventional stored database, no carefully worked out application specific rules. The only principle that guides the system is that it incorporates some notion of a *right* and *wrong*. It is constructed to strive to respond correctly. In this way, the network can be self-taught: each input produces an output. Correct outputs are reinforcing, incorrect outputs cause internal adjustments. By modifying its internal state, the network strives to achieve favorable responses. At first, the response is by trial and error; later, as the learning process continues, it becomes a mixture of trial, error and experience. Eventually the machine behaves as if it "knew" exactly what it was the instructor was trying to tell it. When the neural machine has learned something, the instructor does not know at the conceptual level what is going on inside the machine – it is generally far too complex for that.

Training for a PLN neuron can be effected by a second clause for **pLN**: the functors t on the input are used to indicate that the training mode is operating:

pLN(Table,[t(S1,R1)|S1s],[t(S2,R2)|S2s],Output) if **true**
  become **send**(t(A,R)|S3s,Output) | **gate**({S1,S2},Table,A)
    | **training**({A,R},Table,{{S1,R1},{S2,R2}},NewTable)
    | **pLN**(NewTable,S1s,S2s,S3s).

Here, the recursive **pLN** clause simulates a perpetual actor that changes state according to the training relation. Output response pairs {S1, R1}, {S2, R2} and {A, R} are used to direct the responses to the proffered inputs back to the nodes responsible for them. Back-communication naturally lends itself to back-propagation [Rumelhart et al., 1986], a learning technique for networks with hidden layers of neurons that was partially responsible for the neural network renaissance. The training process records the output and amends the lookup table as dictated by the response for the recursively-reincarnated neuron.

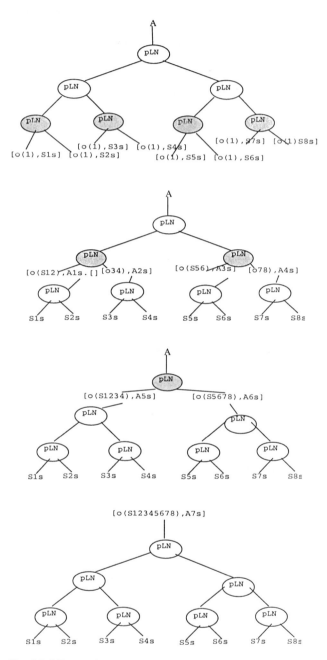

Fig. 5.9.4 Trace of virtual neurons firing in response to input

It then remains to specify the training algorithm. The method chosen for the present work, is one of several possibilities [Myers and Aleksander, 1988]:

- Step 1: Choose an input pattern from some training set and apply it to the input nodes.
- Step 2: Allow values to propagate through all neurons in the network. (Each PLN responds according to the state of its truth table.)
- Step 3: If the values on the output connections are the ones expected, the output of each neuron becomes established (learnt).
- Step 4: Otherwise, return to Step 2 and try again (because the output of each neuron is stochastic the output will generally be different) until a correct output is generated or
- Step 5: A 'sufficient' number of errors has been made suggesting the possibility of succeeding is effectively zero. In this situation, all nodes are returned to their initial indeterministic state.
- Step 6: Repeat steps 1 to 5 until 'consistent' success indicates that all patterns have been learned:

```
//training(OutputPair, OldTbl, InputPairs, NewTbl)
training({A,confirmed},table(Seed,T,U,V,W),{{0,R1},{0,R2}},Tbl1)
    if true
    become send(Tbl1,table(Seed,learnt(A),U,V,W))
       | send(R1,confirmed) | send(R2,confirmed)
training({A,incorrect},table(Seed,T,U,V,W),{{0,R1},{0,R2}},T1)
    if true
    become send(T1,table(Seed,unknown,U,V,W))
       | send(R1,incorrect) | send(R2,incorrect)
training({A,confirmed},table(Seed,T,U,V,W),{{0,R1},{1,R2}},T1)
    if true
    become send(T1,table(Seed,T,learnt(A),V,W))
       | send(R1,confirmed) | send(R2,confirmed)
training({A,incorrect},table(Seed,T,U,V,W),{{0,R1},{1,R2}},T1)
    if true
    become send(Tbl1,table(Seed,T,unknown,V,W))
       | send(R1,incorrect) | send(R2,incorrect)
training({A,confirmed},table(Seed,T,U,V,W),{{1,R1},{0,R2}},T1)
    if true
    become send(T1,table(Seed,T,U,learnt(A),W))
       | send(R1,confirmed) | send(R2,confirmed)
training({A,incorrect},table(Seed,T,U,V,W),{{1,R1},{0,R2}},T1)
    if true
    become send(T1,table(Seed,T,U,unknown,W))
       | send(R1,incorrect) | send(R2,incorrect)
training({A,confirmed},table(Seed,T,U,V,W),{{1,R1},{1,R2}},T1)
    if true
    become send(T1=table(Seed,T,U,V,learnt(A))
       | send(R1,confirmed) | send(R2,confirmed)
```

training({A,incorrect},table(Seed,T,U,V,W),{{1,R1},{0,R2}},T1)
    if **true**
    become **send**(T1,table(Seed,T,U,V,unknown))
      | **send**(R1,incorrect) | **send**(R2,incorrect)

5.11 Neural Simulation

The implementation of a neural net described in the previous section has been successfully taught to recognize the parity of input bit vectors [Kozato, 1988]. Clearly, this means that each PLN has learnt to behave as an Exclusive-Or gate. The implementation was slow, not the least because of the overhead of process switching. The speed of process switching is of the order of the response rate of biological neurons, that is microseconds. Organic neural nets illustrate how fast processing can be achieved even by such slow processing elements. This is due to the way in which parallelism is organized into small, equal sized portions without any synchronization problems. The feed-forward network topology is amenable to explosive computational parallelism of which organic brains are capable. With this topology of actors, there is only one producer and ideally many consumers so there is no binding conflict problem.

As the number of processors is increased, there will be less demand for process switching. In this regime, the implementation of neurons by software processes could be a viable proposition. However, to expand this model to a real application on multiple processors the further factor of processor communication cost must be considered. Since the communication is only an activation signal, this cannot be too expensive. Judicious partitioning of neurons across processes minimizes the cost and this will be particularly beneficial when there are highly interconnected clusters with few connections between clusters. These virtual neurons can even be allowed to migrate between processors.

The choice of illustration, a tree network of PLN neurons, was purely for the sake of explanation and definiteness; the techniques presented here are capable of implementing any topology, any type of artificial neuron and any training rules. It can be seen that the computational model of GDC corresponds largely with a connectionist one. Actors fire or not depending on their internal state and on data received from other actors. While shared variables do give potential synchronization problems in GDC when there are multiple producers, a style of programming can be adopted, such as the feed-forward network, where there are only single producers for shared variables.

Some features of a neural network implementation in GDC are unusual. It is generally believed that neural nets should ultimately be built in hardware. Yet experience has revealed many difficulties with this philosophy. For example, training a network is a very slow and painful business. For the network described above, learning proceeds by a process of trial and error. For each input-output pair, trials are made a predetermined number of times. This is the accepted regime because the intended implementation medium is hardware. When the implementation medium is software, as herein, the number of trials can be adjusted to reflect the number of *unknown* entries in the lookup tables. This is achieved by making the propagation signals carry information on the internal states of the neurons. This modification for the above implementation is simple but would be impractical if not impossible to achieve in a hardware implementation. Thus, for software implementations the learning phase can be dramatically shortened [Kozato, 1988].

There is some belief that sophisticated cognitive systems can only be built from a suitable combination of neural networks and symbolic AI techniques [Hendler, 1989]. From this point of view, the advantages of implementing neural nets in a programming language that is suitable for symbolic manipulation are clear. Furthermore, for hardware implementations, reconfiguring neural nets and adding new nodes to accommodate more concepts seems impossible without having great redundancy. In software, for languages like GDC, this presents no difficulty. GDC allows dynamic process creation and this allows dynamic neuron creation. The above section illustrating the dynamic construction of a neural net exemplifies this. Thus, in a learning situation, new neurons can be created as necessary. This increases the potential of the system to learn new concepts. Because the language GDC, by inheritance from Prolog lends itself to partial evaluation, the training sessions could be viewed in this light. After a training session, a virtual neural net will have acquired some knowledge. Viewed as partial evaluation, this new goal has been specialized for the training data. Once a particular neural net has acquired some knowledge, the resolvent can be saved as a partially evaluated goal. Goals can be composed to give more complex nets that accumulate knowledge.

The implementation of neural nets in GDC is not just a simulation. It offers an executable language for describing neural networks and opens the possibility of dynamically evolving neural systems. This research suggests a new direction for both neural network research and conventional symbolic AI with a view to their fusion.

In general, neural networks tend to be regarded with disdain by the symbolic AI community: they are seen as a rival technology. This attitude overestimates the capability of both connectionist and symbolic systems and as an alternative, the two technologies might be more usefully viewed as complementary. Hybrid systems could provide a fruitful line of research for constructing more sophisticated, artificial cognitive systems. There are of course many possible variations for hybrid systems, e.g. on the symbolic side rule-based systems or semantic networks, discrete or analog neurons implemented in software or hardware on the connectionist side. Some tentative hybrid neural networks have already been proposed, e.g. [Ballard, 1986; Derthick, 1988; Touretzky and Hinton, 1988; Shastri, 1988 and Shastri, 1989], but the software-hardware implementation issue of neural networks has not received any attention. This is because it has naturally been assumed that software implementation is a temporary expedient and connectionist systems eventually, when the technology catches up, will be totally implemented in VLSI.

The neural simulation represents an initial step investigating a language-based approach to hybrid symbolic connectionist systems. By implementing a neural network in the language GDC, the correspondence between the computational models of neural networks and Actors are brought to light. Some of the advantages of a software implementation of connectionist systems are discovered and the simplicity with which the construction can be achieved indicates the potential capacity for parallel processing which GDC languages possess.

5.12 Simulated Life

Conway's *Life* game is not as its name might suggest, competitive, nor a game of chance. Rather it is a deterministic simulation of the evolution of a population of interdependent individuals. The only randomness is in the choice of the initial state. Evolution proceeds according to a small number of simple, fixed rules. Life is played out on a square board in the fashion of chess. Each square or cell may be occupied or unoccupied. The board is assumed infinite but initially (and subsequently) only finitely many cells are occupied. The rules describe the evolution of an individual in terms of the occupancy of neighboring cells.

A *cell* has four nearest neighbors and a further four next nearest diagonal neighbors. Each cell passes through a sequence of generations. The occupant of a cell with two or three occupied neighbors survives to the next generation. A cell with less than two occupied neighbors dies of loneliness. A cell with four or more contemporaries dies from overcrowding. Exactly three neighboring cells of an unoccupied cell give birth (triolism) to a new occupant.

The board is taken to be infinite to avoid introducing special rules for boundary conditions. Given that there are only going to be a finite number of occupied cells in any one generation, simulation on an infinite board is approximated by taking a finite array with cyclic (or twisted) boundary conditions. This means that the simulated Life Game is played out on a torus or Klein bottle. Such a board on a closed surface can be thought of as an infinite flat board on which the pattern of the finite colony is repeated as with a wallpaper pattern. The boundary effects are then explicable in terms of the state of the neighboring colonies.

The rules that determine the life and death cycle of cells are local. Nevertheless, given the generational life of a cell the dynamics can be extrapolated to determine the state of the whole board in successive generations. Such a lock-step simulation can easily be programmed in an imperative language such as C using arrays to represent the board. What tends to exclude Prolog programmers from this form of the game is that the problem domain is naturally expressed in terms of an array of cells. The tree-like data structures in logic programs do not prevent the representation of arrays but it is not particularly sympathetic to it. The single assignment of logic variables can make updating a single element an expensive business [e.g., Eriksson and Rayner, 1984].

GDC having a rather different computational model from Prolog allows computation via concurrent processes organized by local communication. An actor that accepts messages to lookup and update its elements can model a mutable array:

arrayn((trans(lookup(1,Element),Rmgs),E1,E2,...,En) if **true**
    become **send**(E1,Element) | **arrayn**(Rmgs,E1,E2,...,En);

...

arrayn(trans(update(1,Element),Rmgs),E1,E2,...,En) if **true**
    become **arrayn**(Rmgs,Element,E2,...En)

...

This is implemented using tail-recursion so that the recursive actor takes over the process descriptor of the parent, thus saving the copying of most of the arguments. Another possibility is to simulate each element of the array by an actor. This will be demonstrated with the Game of Life below.

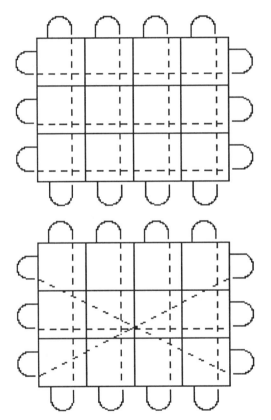

Fig. 5.12.1: Representation of a 3x4 torus and Klein board

5.13 Life Yet in GDC

Each cell need never know where it is in the array. For simplicity, only four nearest neighbors: North; South; East and West will be represented. Each cell of the array has a small amount of transitory state, occupation, which it communicates to its neighbors. The rule concerning a cell dying by overcrowding is simulated by the definite clause:

```
//cell(State, North, South, East, West, OutputStream)
cell(State,[occpd|RNs],[occpd|RSs],[occpd|REs],[occpd|RWs],Os)
    if true
    become send([unoccpd|ROs],Os)
        | cell(unoccpd, RNs, RSs, REs, RWs, ROs)
```

The first argument of **cell** is its current state. This actor blocks waiting for its middle four arguments to be instantiated to streams such that the head of each list is the constant occpd. When this constraint is satisfied, the **cell** actor can metamorphose into a similar actor and output its new state on the stream Os.

The other conditions that govern the life of a cell can be represented in a similar way. As there are a large number of combinations, a more succinct representation is obtained by denoting the state of the cells by integers: 0 for unoccupied and 1 for occupied:

```
cell(State,[Nn|Ns],[Sn|Ss],[En|Es],[Wn|Ws],Os)
    if Nn+Sn+En+Wn<2
    become send([0|ROs],Os)
        | cell(0,Ns,Ss,Es,Ws,ROs)
cell(State,[Nn|Ns],[Sn|Ss],[En|Es],[Wn|Ws],Os)
    if Nn+Sn+En+Wn=:=2
    become send([State|ROs],Os)
        | cell(State,Ns,Ss,Es,Ws,ROs)
cell(State,[Nn|Ns],[Sn|Ss],[En|Es],[Wn|Ws],Os)
    if Nn+Sn+En+Wn=:=3
    become send([1|ROs],Os)
        | cell(1,Ns,Ss,Es,Ws,ROs)
cell(State,[Nn|Ns],[Sn|Ss],[En|Es],[Wn|Ws],Os)
    if Nn+Sn+En+Wn>=4
    become send([0|ROs],Os)
        | cell(0,Ns,Ss,Es,Ws,ROs).
```

In this situation the guards of the clauses are disjoint and so deterministic.

5.14 Cheek by Jowl

In operation the simplified four nearest neighbor game, a cell is connected to its neighbors by shared logic variables:

```
become ...| cell(N,NNs,Os,NEs,NWs,Ns) | ...
        | cell(E,ENs,ESs,EEs,Os,Es) | ...
        | cell(M,Ns,Ss,Es,Ws,Os) | ...
        | cell(W,WNs,WSs,Os,WWs,Ws) | ...
        | cell(S,Os,SSs,SEs,SWs,Ss) |...
```

A recursively-defined actor may easily generate a (one-dimensional) chain of N cells connected with two nearest neighbors:

```
chain(1,Es,Ws,Os) if true
    become cell(State, Es, Ws, Os);
chain(N, Es, Ws, Os) if N>1 & N1:=N-1
    become cell(State, Es, Ws, Os) | chain(N1,Os,W1s,Ws).
```

amended to get the connectivity required for a one-dimensional Life game of N cells on a circle:

```
cycle(N) if N>1
    become cycle1(N, Es, Ws, Os, Es)
cycle1(1,Es,Ws,Os,Ts)
    become send(Ws, Ts) | cell(Es, Ws, Os)
cycle1(N, Es, Ws, Os, Ts) if N>1 & N1:=N-1
    become cell(Es, Ws, Os) | cycle1(N1,Os,W1s,Ws,Ts).
```

A two-dimensional generalization of this idea can be used to produce an M by N array of cells with four nearest neighbors connected as a torus:

```
torus(M,N) if N>1
    become torus(M, N, Es, Ws, Os, Es)
torus(M,1,Es,Ws,Os,Ts)
    become send(Ws, Ts) | col(M, s, Ws, Os)
torus(M, N, (M, Es, Ws, Os) | torus(M,N1,Ns,Ss,Os,W1s,Ws,Ts)
```

This forms a cycle of columns. The columns are then unfolded into a torus:

```
col(1,Es,Ws,Os)
    become cell(Es,Ws,Os)
col(M,Ess,Wss,Oss) if M>1
    become send([Os|ROss],Oss) | col1(M,Ns,Ss,Ess,Wss,Os,ROss,Ns)
col1(1,Ns,Ss,[Es|Ess],[Ws|Wss],Os,Oss,Rs) if true
    become send(Ss,Rs) | cell(Ns,Ss,Es,Ws,Os)
col1(M,Ns,Ss,[Es|Ess],[Ws|Wss],Os,Oss,Rs) if M>1 & M1:=N-1
    become send([Ss|ROss],Oss) | cell(Ns,Ss,Es,Ws,Os)
        | col1(M1,Os,S1s,Ess,Wss,Ss,ROss,Rs)
```

While the suffix s denotes a stream the suffix ss denotes a stream of streams.

5.15 Distributed Implementation

The GDC program for Life described in the previous section has been has been implemented [Linney and Ringwood, 1992] on a distributed system of workstations. The game is started with an actor **life/3** that has three channels. These are the size of the board; the maximum number of iterations a cell may go through and a list of the coordinates of the cells that are initially occupied. To initialize and observe the game a controller actor is required. Besides the code given above, each cell shares a command stream with the controller. To initialize particular cells each cell must carry its identity (x-y coordinate pair) as part of its state. Commands can then be broadcast to the cells; only those cells with the same identity will change state according to the commands. To observe the output of the game, a display thread must also share stream of each cell. The Life program is inherently concurrent, and so is suited to execution on multiprocessor systems.

At the 1948 Hixon Symposium, von Neumann [1951] reflected on McCulloch and Pitts' work on the design of digital computers. Turing's result of a universal computing-machine suggested to him that there might be a universal construction machine. A machine which when provided with a description of an automaton and a component rich environment could construct a copy of itself.

In a manuscript published after his death [1966] von Neumann demonstrated a Turing-like machine that could reproduce itself. To do this von Neumann imagined an infinite "chess board" in which each cell is either empty, or contains a single component. Each component can be in one of several states. A group of occupied cells in the plane is interpreted as an organism. Such systems have become known as cellular automata [e.g., Toffli and Margolis, 1987].

The present chapter describes the use of GDC Languages for simulating a particular cellular automaton, Conway's Life, on a distributed collection of workstations. The simulation has a similar structure to the simulation of artificial neurons in GDC Languages as described by Kozato and Ringwood [1990]. The traditional implementation of the Life game is played in a lock-step fashion. Typically, the grid of cells being stored as a two-dimensional array with the algorithm updating all the cells at each generation. This version is very different in that each cell is a process and cells asynchronously communicate their states to each other. This inherently concurrent behavior allows cells to be updated in parallel.

Newman [1990] describes an implementation in Parlog of the Life Game, which came to the attention of the authors after the present simulation was designed. Newman's implementation lies somewhere in between the conventional implementation and the one described here in that while the cells are modeled as processes, they are updated lock-step generation by generation. Newman generates the cells in two phases. First the cells are generated; then the streams are connected to nearest neighbors. In this chapter, generation and connection is performed in one step.

The present asynchronous implementation makes the program much simpler. Despite the asynchronous communication, a cell cannot advance more than one generation in front of a neighbor because the next state is determined by the cumulative state of its neighbors. Generations by generation then, the expected patterns associated with the sequential implementations of the Game are exhibited.

The original idea that self-replicating automata should be cellular arose from its origins in the Turing machine and the need to supply a component rich environment from which to build replicas. With concurrent languages such an environment is not necessary, as can be seen from the array program that generates the matrix of cells (from thin air), so that restriction to an array is unnecessary. Systolic algorithms [Kung, 1982] can be seen as a generalization to other tessellations of the plane. They were developed to exploit pipeline parallelism, inherent in many algorithms, by the use of special purpose hardware. Shapiro [1984] saw the advantages of the use of GDC for the implementation of such algorithms.

Given that systolic automata can be built in software, there is no necessity for them to be simple. For example, reactive problem solving agents can be constructed dynamically. In a real-world situation, things do not usually proceed as planned. The traditional assumptions made by planning systems, for example *STRIPS* [Fikes et al., 1971], are that the environment is totally predictable. The world model is totally complete and correct, and primitive actions are instantaneous and can never fail. Such an environment is termed *static*. In the real world, this is rarely the case, it is a dynamic, on-going, real-time and unpredictable environment. An agent interacting with it must be able to behave appropriately - this suggests that the agent should possess a degree of *reactivity* and should be created dynamically when demand arises. The Life simulation should be viewed as an initial investigation into the possibility of using GDC for building self-replicating agents.

5.16 Agent Micro-Architectures

The notion of a rational agent is that of an agent that has explicit representation of its own goals and beliefs about its environment. Two lines of approach to multi-agent systems can be distinguished: macro and micro. The macro-micro distinction is common to disciplines such as economics and sociology that are metaphors for multi-agent systems. Microsystems focus on the architecture of an individual. Macrosystems are concerned with interagent dynamics. The examples so far have been about macrosystems.

Shoham [1990] proposes an architecture as a specialization of Actors. Following Dennett [1987] and McCarthy [1979] Shoham endows agents with a state consisting of mentalistic components: beliefs, capabilities, choices, commitments etc. Following Searle [1969], Cohen and Perrault [1979], agents communicate with other agents by Speech-acts. Speech-act theory categorizes communication as informing, requesting, offering and so on. In GDC, a Shoham agent would be similar to the client actor described in the previous chapter:

```
//agent0(MessageStream, Beliefs, Commitments)
agent0([inform(Fact)|Stream], Beliefs, Commitments) if true
    become
        inform(Fact,Beliefs,NewBeliefs,Commitments,NewCommitments)
        | agent0(Stream,NewBeliefs,NewCommitments)
agent0([request(Action)|Stream],Beliefs,Commitments) if true
    become request(Action,Beliefs,NewBeliefs,Commitments,
        NewCommitments)
        | agent0(Stream,NewBeliefs,NewCommitments)
```

agent0([offer(Action)|Stream],Beliefs,Commitments) if **true**
    become
        offer(Action,Beliefs,NewBeliefs,Commitments,NewCommitments)
        | **agent0**(Stream,NewBeliefs,NewCommitments)
etc

The actors **inform, request** and **offer** etc execute commitments. Shoham uses a real-time clock to time the actions, but in GDC time is measured by events and events are the sending (or receipt) of messages. A real-time clock is a concept, like inheritance, that does not fit well in distributed systems. Rather than regarding history as the passage of time, time is considered as the passage of history. If no events have taken place, no time has passed. This is the philosophy of discrete event simulation. A local clock is just a monotonic counter:

    become **clock**(A)|**send**(s(B),A)|**send**(s(C),B)|**send**(s(D),C) ...
    become **clock**(s(B)) | **send**(s(C),B) | **send**(s(D),C) ...
    become **clock**(s(s(C))) | **send**(s(D),C) ...
    become **clock**(s(s(s(D)))) | ...

5.17 Metalevel Agent Architectures

An agent's belief typically includes beliefs about actions the agent can perform and beliefs about the other agents. Reflexive or meta-level architectures where an agent reasons about itself and other agents [Maes, 1988] is another micro-architecture.

Being symbolic, GDC shares with Prolog and Lisp an affinity for meta-interpretation. In Prolog, a simple propositional Prolog meta-interpreter would take the form:

    //**demo**(Program, Goals)
    demo(G) if **true**
        become **clause**(G:-G1) | **demo**(G1).
    demo(G1|G2) if **true**
        become **demo**(G1) | **demo**(G2).
    demo(**true**) if **true** become **true**.

Here, the **demo** predicate expresses that the goal G can be demonstrated from the program P. A clause is represented as a conjoined list terminated by true:

    clause(g:-[g1 , g2 , . . . , gn|true])

While this is propositional, it can be generalized to the first order case:

    demo(G1) if **true**
        become **demo**(forall(X,G)) | **substitute**(X,G,Y,G1).

The predicates hold when G1 results from substituting the term Y for the variable X in G. The Prolog meta-interpreter is nondeterministic, because it is not determined which clause might demonstrate the goal G. The inbuilt depth-first engine performs the search.

Because there is no backtracking in GDC, the search has to be programmed. This is achieved by organizing the alternative search branches as a stream. As a simple illustration, a resource bounded meta-interpreter for propositional Prolog in GDC follows. It is adapted from [Kowalski, 1995]:

```
//demo(KB,InGoals,Result)
demo(KB,fail,Result) if true
    become send(fail,Result).
demo(KB,[]+AltGoals,Result) if true
    become send(true,Result).
demo(KB,fail+AltGoals,Result) if true
    become demo(KB,AltGoals,Result).
demo(KB,[G|Rest]+AltGoals,Result) if true
    become ask(KB,G,D) | dnf([D|Rest],AltGoals, DNF)
        | demo(KB,DNF,Result)
```

Here, the **demo** agent reduces a stream of InGoals with respect to the definite clauses in a knowledgebase, KB. Alternative branches of the search space are represented by disjuncts. That is, the clauses having conclusion G, are represented by a single list of alternative body goals terminated by fail, e.g.

G←D where D=Alt1+Alt2+...+fail and Alti=[Gi1,Gi2,...,Gin]

Thus, every disjunct is terminated by fail and if a goal G is the conclusion of no clause in the knowledgebase, **ask** returns the value fail in its third channel. The actor **dnf** computes the disjunctive normal form of its first argument. As the disjunctive normal form is not unique, this actor behaves as a selection rule.

In the above program, the agent persists until it reduces the goal to true or fails in the attempt. In practice, agents will have a limited time to reach a conclusion; they will be resource-bounded. A resource-bounded agent can easily be formed by a slight modification of the previous program:

```
//demo(KB,InGoals,OutGoals,Resource)
demo(KB,fail,OutGoals,R) if true
    become send(fail,OutGoals).
demo(KB,[]+AltGoals,OutGoals,R) if true
    become send(true,OutGoals).
demo(KB,InGoals,OutGoals,0) if true
    become send(InGoals,OutGoals).
demo(KB,[G|Rest]+AltGoals,OutGoals,R)
    if R>0 & R1:=R-1
    become ask(KB,G,D)
        | dnf([D|Rest],AltGoals, DNF)
        | demo(KB,DNF,OutGoals,R1)
demo(KB,InGoals,OutGoals,R) if otherwise
    become send(InGoals,OutGoals)
```

Here, the **demo** agent reduces a stream of InGoals to a stream of OutGoals with respect to the definite clauses in the knowledgebase, KB. This is done within Resource backward chaining steps, so this agent is bounded. The work that **dnf** does is not included in the resource count but probably should be.

The **demo** agent can be modified to include abducibles:

```
//demo(KB,Abducibles,InGls,OutGls,Resource)
demo(KB,Abs,{fail,Beliefs},OutGls,R) if true
    become send({fail,Beliefs},OutGls).
demo(KB,Ab,{[],Beliefs}+AltGls,OutGls,R) if true
    become send({true,Beliefs},OutGls)
demo(KB,Ab,InGls,OutGls,0) if true
    become send(InGls,OutGls).
demo(KB,Ab,{[G|Rest],Beliefs}+AltGls,OutGls,R)
    if R>0 & R1:=R-1
    become ask(KB,Ab,{[G|Rest],Beliefs},D)
    | dnf([[D|Rest]+AltGLs, DNF)
      | demo(KB,Ab,DNF,OutGls,R1)
demo(KB,Ab,InGls,OutGls,R) if otherwise
    become send(InGls,OutGls)
```

The knowledge base is extended with a set of abducibles, Ab. The **ask** agent returns
true if the goal is a belief or an abducible. If not already a belief, the abducible is
added to the set of beliefs. The actor **dnf** also has to be modified to handle beliefs
appropriately.

5.18 Actor Reconstruction of GDC

Hewitt [1985] argues that systems of interconnected and interdependent computers
are qualitatively different from the self-contained computers of the past. The
argument goes as follows: if, to avoid the von Neumann bottleneck, decision making
is decentralized, no system part can directly control the resources of any other system
part (otherwise it would itself become a bottleneck). The various autonomous parts
must necessarily communicate with one another if anything is to be co-operatively
achieved. Response from a remote service typically has latency. Consequently,
communication should be asynchronous so that the local computation can continue
and do something useful rather than waiting for a response. This contrasts with CSP
where communication is synchronous.

Kahn and Miller [1988] argue that most current programming languages are
inadequate for large-scale open systems. They say there are two notable exceptions
Actors and GDC. In distributed systems the remote procedure call (RPC) is favored
because it to some extent it imitates the procedure call of third generation languages.
However, the synchronous call/return of RPC can cause an inefficient use of
resources. A response from a remote server typically has a long latency. While
asynchronous message passing is possible, it is difficult to integrate with third
generation languages.

RPC differs from procedure call in that it is call by value. Call by reference cannot be
achieved because remote nodes do not share the same address space. A local
procedure call cannot usually be replaced by an RPC. It cannot easily transmit
mutable values.

One approach to the problem is at the operating system level. Mach [Rashid, 1988], for example, distinguishes between threads and tasks. While threads are loci of control sharing the same address space, tasks are not. Processes (threads or tasks) send messages to named ports (message queues). Port names can be passed in messages but the message queue is mutable.

However, an operating system is not a programming language. In an operating system, the criterion of locality is address space while for procedure calls it is local variables. A programming language allows a decoupling of concurrency and the allocation of processes to processors. This transparency between local and remote affords scalability.

Both Actors and GDC can be rationalized from the starting point of asynchronous message passing agents. According to Russell and Norvig [1995], an agent can be viewed as anything perceiving its environment through sensors and acting upon that environment through effectors. The actions are not generally random: there is some correlation between percept and action. For software agents, perceptions are received messages. The characteristics of a software agent are:

- asynchronous message passing;
- local decision making.

Point-to-point asynchronous communication allows locality to be expressed and optimized. The local decision making decides which actions, if any to perform. A primitive action is to send a message. In its primitive form, the reactive agent, the behavior can be specified by a set of stimulus response pairs, such as the decision tables of Chapter 3. Alternative behaviors are discriminated by the message received.

Subsequent behaviors can be defined inductively by a network of agents that replace the agent. In Actors, the replace is specified by become and create. In GDC it is only specified by create. The action become is distinguished from create in Actors by the inheritor of the message queue. The speculation is that rational agents can be built up from herds of reactive agents by programming. A rational agent is one that behaves logically or maximizes its own utility.

Kornfield and Hewitt [1981] extend the principles of Actor theory, to provide what they call a scientific community metaphor. They claim that scientific communities behave as parallel systems, with scientists working on similar problems concurrently with other scientists. This is reminiscent of the blackboard metaphor described in Chapter 1. Hewitt [1985] explains the idea of open systems in distributed AI; an *open system* is a large collection of computational services that use each other without central co-ordination, trust or complete knowledge of each other. This is reminiscent of open systems theory [von Bertalanffy, 1968]. It contrasts with, closed systems and conjures up completeness and the Closed-World assumption of databases as invoked by Absys, Planner and Prolog to explain negation as failure.

Agent identity is recognised as an essential problem of multi-agent systems [Gasser and Briot, 1992]. Fixed boundaries for objects are considered to be too inflexible and do not reflect theoretical positions in which agents are dynamically defined by reference to their changing position in the community. Computational units may participate in different agents. It is thus necessary to distinguish between agents and actors. There is nothing to maintain a stable identity when an agent is composed of ever changing definitions and patterns of interaction.

When the number of agents becomes large, individual referencing becomes difficult so it becomes necessary to organize them into larger entities. Most conceptions of group employ a representative agent that serves as a surrogate for the group. This surrogate becomes a bottleneck and conflicts with the initial intentions.

With Actors, the notion of identity is somewhat confused because identity is manifested in different ways. To send a message an agent must be able to take for granted some predictable stable quality of the recipient, such as the name of the mailbox. An agent can also be identified by its behavior: the messages it is prepared to accept and its subsequent behavior. In Actors, a name is associated with an inductively defined behavior. A name is also associated with a mailbox (a message queue). The two are associated by the create action. The become action relates the mailbox name to subsequent behavior. While the inductively defined behavior is shortlived, a message queue is long lived. The forward actor that serves no useful purpose (no decisions to make) exemplifies the problem and it is left to the garbage collector to remove. There is no explicit destruction of actors in the Actor language.

The message queue has a long-lived identity whereas process behavior has a short-lived identity. Tomlinson and Singh [1989] suggest reifying the message queue in Actors to gain some control over the acceptance of messages. That is, the queue may be accessed other than by its head. Other authors suggest multiple message queues. This was noted in the previous chapter where it was shown how in GDC languages a message queue can be built up from a nesting of channels.

The essential difference between Actors and GDC is that Actors names local variables and message queues while GDC only names channels. Message queues or mailboxes allow many to one communication. In GDC, this must be done with an explicit merge. Channels have the same lifetime as behaviors; they can only receive one message.

There have been a number of attempts to simulate Actors in GDC languages: *Vulcan* [Kahn et al., 1986]; *Mandala* [Ohki et al., 1987] and *POLKA* [Davison, 1992]. As can be understood from above, this simulation essentially consists of implementing a message queue as a list of channels and hiding from view. As can also be seen from this section and as Kahn [1989] admits, this is not necessarily an advantage.

5.19 Inheritance Versus Delegation

A common feature of object-oriented languages is encapsulation (locality). Inheritance is an additional feature of sequential object-oriented languages such as *Smalltalk* and *C++*. Object-oriented languages such as Actors and *ABCL* [Yonezawa, 1990] emphasize concurrency as a characteristic. ABCL [Yonezawa, 1990] provides two message queues with each object, a normal one and an express one. These languages are sometimes referred to as object-oriented concurrent languages, OOCLs. Numerous authors [America, 1987; Briot and Yonezawa, 1987; Chaffer and

Lee 1989; Papathomas, 1989; Tomlinson and Singh, 1989] have pointed out the conflicts between inheritance and concurrency that break encapsulation. Matsuoka and Yonezawa [1993] call the phenomenon *inheritance anomaly*.

In most OOCLs, the programmer explicitly programs the synchronization, the guard in GDC, to restrict the set of acceptable messages. The inheritance anomaly is that the synchronization code cannot be effectively inherited. This is illustrated with the bounded buffer example of Matsuoka and Yonezawa:

b_buf([put(Item)|Tasks],List\EndList) if **true**
    become **send**([Item|NewEndList],EndList)
      | **buffConsumer**(Tasks,List\NewEndList)
b_buf([get(Contents)|Task],[Item|List]\EndList) if **true**
    become **send**(Item,Contents)
      | **buffConsumer**(Tasks,List\NewEndList).

A put message stores an item in the buffer, a get message removes it. Upon creation, the buffer is in the empty state.

    become **b_buf**(Tasks,EndList\EndList) | ....

Now consider the a subclass **gb_buf** which accepts an additional message gget(). The behavior of gget() is almost identical to that of get(), with the exception that it cannot be immediately accepted after a put() message. This can only be handled by adding a state variable, afterPut. That is **b_buf** must be redefined to account for the newly added method. The problem is that gget() is history sensitive. This is similar to the Brock–Ackerman anomaly [1981] described in Chapter 4.

Chapter 6

Concurrent Search

Half the money I spend on advertising is wasted, and the trouble is I don't know which half.

Lord Leverhulme (1851–1925)

As noted in Chapter 1, search had a prominent role in the beginning of artificial intelligence. Early textbooks on the subject (e.g. [Nilsson, 1971]) devote a great deal of space to search. Improved search methods were considered worthy subjects for inclusion in artificial intelligence conferences and journals. While consideration of search in the abstract has tended to move from the field of artificial intelligence to mainstream computer science and operational research, search continues to be an important tool for artificial intelligence practitioners. Parallel and distributed search continues to be an active field of research in computer science, much of the interest coming from the fact that search algorithms designed for sequential computers rarely map easily onto distributed and parallel architectures. The challenge for programming language design is to invent languages which free the programmer from having to consider low level details of the parallel architecture. This allows the programmer to concentrate on the more abstract aspects of concurrent algorithms, while retaining sufficient control to efficiently exploit the parallelism available in the architecture.

In logic programming, Prolog was notable for incorporating a search mechanism as a built-in part of the language. The indeterministic logic languages have been criticized for abandoning this built-in search, resulting in various attempts to create hybrid languages that can revert from indeterminism to nondeterminism [Clark and Gregory, 1987; Haridi, 1990]. However, the lesson that can be learned from any good Prolog textbook (e.g. [O'Keefe, 1990]) is that Prolog's built-in search is often subverted and search explicitly programmed. Thus, it is the ability to program search in Prolog rather than its built-in search that makes it suitable for artificial intelligence programming. Stream parallel logic languages inherit this metaprogramming ability. This chapter builds on this theme and further explores the nature of the stream parallel logic languages, by developing some simple search programs.

6.1 A Naive Prolog Solution to the 8-Puzzle

The 8-puzzle is a familiar example used to illustrate state space search problems [Nilsson, 1971]. The problem consists of a 3×3 matrix of eight cells marked with the numbers "1" to "8" and one space. A state of the puzzle is represented by a particular matrix of the cells. The successors of a state are generated by up to four different ways in which a marked cell may be moved into the space. Only if the space is in the center will there be four successors. The actions of marked cells turn out to be more conveniently thought of as actions of the space: left, right, up and down. A solution to the puzzle is a sequence of actions that will transform some initial state to some desired goal state. The goal state conventionally used is shown if Figure 6.1.1.

An arbitrary initial state is given in Figure 6.1.2. There are three possible actions from this state with the three successor states given in Figure 6.1.3. A complete solution to the 8-puzzle with the given initial state is the sequence of actions

[left, down, right, down, right, up, left].

In abstract, this problem is similar to the **onTree** problem of Chapter 3, where the nodes in the tree are the states and their descendants are the states obtainable from them by legal actions. In the present case, however, the tree is constructed dynamically while it is searched. Part of the search tree for the problem above, including the sequence of actions taken to reach the leaves is given below in Figure 6.1.4.

1	2	3
8		4
7	6	5

Fig. 6.1.1. The goal state of 8-puzzle

2	8	3
1	4	5
7		6

Fig. 6.1.2 An arbitrary initial state of the 8-puzzle

2	8	3
1	4	5
7	6	

Left

2	8	3
1	4	5
	7	6

Right

2	8	3
1		5
7	4	6

Down

Fig. 6.1.3 Successor states

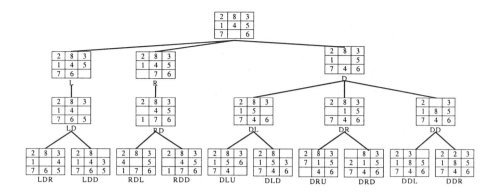

Fig. 6.1.4 Search tree for the 8-puzzle to depth 3

Consider a naive Prolog program to solve this puzzle:

search(State,State) :– **goal**(State).
search(State, Soln) :– **left**(State,Left), **search**(Left,Soln).
search(State, Soln) :– **right**(State,Right), **search**(Right,Soln).
search(State, Soln) :– **up**(State,Up), **search**(Up,Soln).
search(State, Soln) :– **down**(State,Down), **search**(Down,Soln).

The predicates **left**, **right**, **up** and **down** give the successor states of the state given as their first argument, or fail if there is no such successor state.

This program, though declaratively correct, will most likely fail to terminate since it will perform a depth-first search of a tree with infinite branches. To avoid this, the information stored by each state can be extended to include the sequence of actions used to reach the state from the initial state and the predicates refined to fail if the successor is a previously encountered state. This would limit search to a finite tree, but would still be grossly inefficient. There are well known heuristics to better direct the search for this problem [Nilsson, 1971]. The naive program works poorly because it transfers the built-in left-to-right depth-first scheduling of Prolog directly to the search of the problem that really requires a more sophisticated scheduling.

Notwithstanding the naive nature of the program above, consider a similar solution in GDC:

search(nostate,Soln) :- Soln=none.
search(State,Soln) :- State=/=none
    | **isgoal**(State,Flag), **expand**(Flag,State,Soln).

```
expand(true,State,Soln) :- Soln=State.
expand(false,State,Soln)
    :- left(State,Left), search(Left,SolnL),
       right(State,Right), search(Right,SolnR),
       up(State,Up), search(Up,SolnU),
       down(State,Down), search(Down,SolnD),
       choose(SolnL,SolnR,SolnU,SolnD,Soln).

choose(SolnL,_,_,_,Soln) :- SolnL=/=none | Soln=SolnL.
choose(_,SolnR,_,_,Soln) :- SolnR=/=none | Soln=SolnR.
choose(_,_,SolnU,_,Soln) :- SolnU=/=none | Soln=SolnU.
choose(_,_,_,SolnD,Soln) :- SolnD=/=none | Soln=SolnD.
choose(none,none,none,none,Soln) :- Soln=none.
```

A number of points may be noted. Firstly, the OR-parallelism, which was implicit in the Prolog program, is converted to GDC AND-parallelism with the termination of any of the OR-parallel branches indicated by the return of the dummy solution none. Secondly, the actor **choose** is introduced to make an indeterminate choice between solutions in OR-parallel branches, returning none if no sub-branch returns a solution. This technique of converting conceptually OR-parallelism to AND-parallelism is a cliché in concurrent logic programming, proposed by Codish and Shapiro [1986] and Gregory [1987]. In fact, the same technique is frequently used in Prolog.

Returning all solutions to a problem where a solution is obtainable by method A *or* method B is equivalent to combining the solutions obtained from method A *and* method B. The Prolog all-solutions program for this problem is:

```
search(nostate,[]) :- !.
search(State,[State]) :- goal(State),!.
search(State,Solns) :-
    left(State,Left), search(Left,SolnsL),
    right(State,Right), search(Right,SolnsR),
    up(State,Up), search(Up,SolnsU),
    down(State,Down), search(Down,SolnsD),
    append4(SolnsL,SolnsR,SolnsU,SolnsD,Solns).
```

where **append4** simply appends its first four arguments to give its fifth. It is assumed that rather than fail, **left**(State,Left) will bind Left to nostate if there is no left successor state and likewise with the other actions. The same assumption is made in the original GDC program. The closeness of the two programs is apparent. The main difference is the use of **choose** as an-indeterministic OR operation picking one of its inputs, as compared with **append4**, an AND operation which combines its inputs. This is due to the flat nature of GDC: backtracking has to be replaced by an explicit choice. The Prolog test predicate **goal** is converted to the GDC actor **isgoal**, which returns true or false in a second argument. This is combined with the introduction of a new actor to cover the search beyond the test, which takes the Boolean value from **isgoal** and reacts appropriately. For simplicity, it is assumed that goal states in the search tree are leaves. Hence the cut in the Prolog program is a green cut. A more complex Prolog program would be required to deal with cases where goal states in the search tree have descendants that are also goal states.

The **choose** actor explicitly represents the independent binding frames for each non-determinately choosable behavior which are implicit in the Prolog program. This corresponds to the **onEither** actor of Chapter 3. The indeterminism of GDC maps directly onto an indeterministic choice of solutions. The nondeterminism of Prolog is managed by cutting back the binding frame stack on backtracking. In an OR-parallel logic language an unbound channel, like the one that returns the solution in our search example, is duplicated for each OR-parallel computation. Explicit distinct channels in the GDC program replace this implicit copying. It will be assumed that:

   :-   **choose**(SolnL,SolnR,SolnU,SolnD,Soln)

is reducible as soon as any of its first four arguments are bound to anything but none, or when all its first four arguments are bound to none.

The result of executing the GDC program will be to create a tree of **choose** actors, replicating the search tree of the problem. The actor **search**(State,Soln) will first reduce to

   :-   **isgoal**(State,Flag), **expand**(Flag,State,Soln).

If **isgoal**(State,Flag) causes Flag to be bound to true, following the reduction of **expand**(Flag,State,Soln) the situation will be as in Figure 6.1.5.

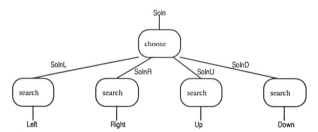

Fig. 6.1.5 Tree of search actors

This is the diagrammatic representation of Chapter 4, where the nodes are actors and the arcs communication channels. Unless either a goal node is found or no successor states are generated, each of the descendants of the root **choose** actor will become a further **choose** actors and so on.

The major difficulty with the program given is that the number of actors will grow exponentially, until any practical distributed or parallel architecture would be overwhelmed. In problems like this there are usually heuristics which indicate a goal state is more likely to be found in one subtree than another, but in GDC as described so far there is no way of giving preference between leaves in the search tree to expand.

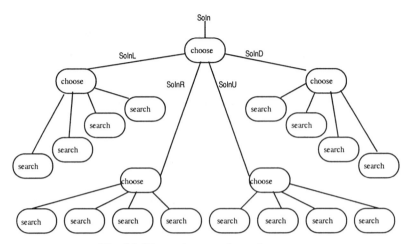

Fig. 6.1.6 Recursive tree of search actors

6.2 Speculative Parallelism

Another problem with the naive GDC search program is that it omits to describe a mechanism for halting actors that are not going to contribute to a solution. As soon as any of the first four arguments of the actor

:-   **choose**(SolnL,SolnR,SolnU,SolnD,Soln)

is bound to something other than none, it reduces and the continuing execution which is determining the values of the other arguments is redundant. This sort of parallelism is known as *speculative parallelism*, since in effect any computation of the solution returned from a subtree is a speculation on that solution being necessary for the overall solution. In an ideal parallel architecture, we speculate because we have nothing to lose – the processors engaged on the speculative computation would otherwise be idle. In practice, the overhead of managing speculative parallelism means that it is too glib to say there is "nothing to lose". Speculative parallelism should only be engaged in if the likelihood of it being needed outweighs the overhead. As shown by Lai and Sahni [1984], in a search on a multiprocessor system where there are more possible node expansions than processors and node expansion choice is guided by heuristics, even in the absence of communication overheads it is possible for anomalous results to occur. These range from slowdowns to speedups greater than the number of processors. These anomalies are discussed in Section 6.9. Given that in practice there are a limited number of processors available, it makes sense to cut off work known to be unnecessary. Processors that are available can be dedicated to work that is known to be necessary (to avoid speculation) or has not been shown to be unnecessary (allowing speculation).

Grit and Page [1981] discuss the possibilities of incorporating a mechanism into a functional programming language for automatically cutting off speculative computations which have been found unnecessary. Without this sort of facility such a mechanism must be programmed in explicitly by the programmer. This problem is analogous to the consideration of whether garbage collection should be automatic or programmer-defined. It is essential that any mechanism that passes on the information that a solution has been found has priority over further computations. Otherwise, there is the possibility of actors in the search tree monopolizing the computational resources even though actors elsewhere in the search tree could show them to be redundant. The monopolization would prevent the message notifying that these are redundant being sent. This situation might aptly be described as *livelock*.

Speculative parallelism is associated particularly with OR-parallelism [Burton, 1988], indeed, it could be argued that the two are the same thing, the former term being used in a functional language context, the latter in a logic language context. However, as our search example shows, speculative parallelism is a real issue in AND-parallel languages, since metapredicates like **choose** which make OR choices between their arguments can be exploited. These might be considered generalizations of functional programming's **cond** operator [Turner, 1979]. This operator has three arguments, a Boolean V and A and B, evaluating to A if V evaluates to true and to B if V evaluates to false.

In functional languages, the operation **cond** is usually evaluated lazily, that is its second and third arguments are not evaluated before the condition is evaluated. A similar suspension of evaluation can be programmed in GDC using its suspension mechanism:

```
eval_cond_lazily(V,A,B,Val)
  :- eval(V,VVal),
     cond(VVal,A,B,Val).


cond(true,A,_,Val) :- eval(A,Val).
cond(false,_,B,Val) :- eval(B,Val).
```

This is not full lazy evaluation, since either A or B is evaluated rather than returned as an unevaluated reference, but for now it serves to illustrate the point. Speculative parallelism in functional languages requires a rejection of the evaluate **cond** lazily convention, generally involving special language constructs. No special mechanisms are required in GDC:

```
eval_cond_speculatively(V,A,B,Val)
  :- eval(V,VVal), eval(A,AVal), eval(B,BVal),
     cond(VVal,AVal,BVal,Val).


cond(true,AVal,_,Val) :- Val=AVal.
cond(false,_,BVal,Val) :- Val=BVal.
```

It is clear here that **eval_cond_lazily** and **eval_cond_speculatively** represent two extremes: in the former no potential parallelism is exploited; in the latter parallelism is exploited perhaps inappropriately. In fact, although it is made clear above, these two opposite approaches to potential speculative parallelism may occur less obviously in GDC programs in that general and fairly subtle changes to a program may cause a switch from overabundant parallelism to no parallelism at all. This is one of the reasons why, as noted in [Tick and Ichiyoshi, 1990], a straightforward translation of a sequential logic program to a concurrent logic program does not always result in a good parallel program. The issue of over abundant versus no parallelism is discussed in further detail later in this chapter.

6.3 Non-speculative Non-parallel Linear Search

Note that a simple attempt to remove the speculative element from our search program can result in losing parallelism in the search altogether. For example, the following GDC program for the 8-puzzle starts search of one branch of the tree only if no solution has been found in the previous branch:

```
search(nostate,Soln) :- Soln=none.
search(State,Soln) :- State=/=nostate
    |  isgoal(State,Flag), expand(State,Flag,Solution).

expand(true,State,Soln) :- Soln=State.
expand(false,State,Soln)
    :-  lsearch(State,Soln1),
        rsearch(Soln1,State,Soln2),
        usearch(Soln2,State,Soln3),
        dsearch(Soln3,State,Soln).

lsearch(State,Soln)
    :-  left(State,Left), search(Left,Soln).

rsearch(none,State,Soln)
    :-  right(State,Right), search(Right,Soln)
rsearch(InSoln,State,Soln) :- InSoln=/=none | InSoln=Soln.

usearch(none,State,Soln)
    :-  up(State,Up), search(Up,Soln).
usearch(InSoln,State,Soln) :- InSoln=/=none | InSoln=Soln.

dsearch(none,State,Soln)
    :-  down(State,Down), search(Down,Soln)
dsearch(InSoln,State,Soln) :- InSoln=/=none | InSoln=Soln.
```

This will result in a strict depth-first left-to-right search of the tree. Consideration of any actor in the tree is suspended on the result of the previous one in the search order. The actor structure created by execution will be a chain of actors, all except for the first waiting for either a solution or none message. In the former case, the solution is passed straight down the chain and its length is reduced by one. In the latter the front of the chain is expanded. This can be compared with the stack of actors described in Chapter 5. After the first expansion, the actor is shown in Figure 6.3.1.

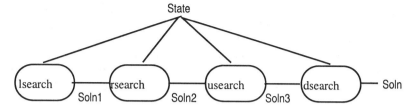

Fig. 6.3.1 Actor structure after the first expansion

After the next expansion the actor structure is depicted in Figure 6.3.2. This form of search program is called *linear search* from the linear form the actors link into during execution. In effect, the actors linked by channels are equivalent to a linked list forming a stack of states that would be formed in conventional depth-first search of a tree.

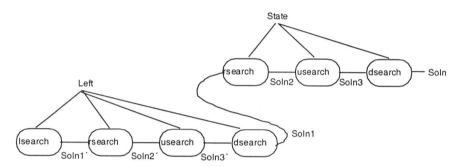

Fig. 6.3.2 Actor structure after the second expansion

6.4 A Practical Prolog Solution to the 8-Puzzle

In practice, Prolog programs for search problems, where left-to-right depth-first search is not the optimal strategy, abandon attempts to effect the search by Prolog's built-in search mechanism. Instead, a metaprogramming approach is used, in which some explicit representation of the global search space is manipulated. This gives us the following Prolog program for the 8-puzzle, in which search is specifically programmed:

```
search([State|States],State) :- goal(State).
search([State|States],Soln) :-
    left(State,Left), right(State,Right),
    up(State,Up), down(State,Down),
    insert(Left,States,States1), insert(Right,States1,States2),
    insert(Up,States2,States3), insert(Down,States3,States4),
    search(States4,Soln).
```

Like previous programs, this one simulates disjunction in the problem with conjunction in the program. The first argument to the **search** predicate is a list of states representing the frontier of the search – the leaf nodes of the search tree. It will be assumed that **insert** inserts a state into its appropriate place in the list. It will also be assumed that **left, right, up** and **down** return the dummy value none for those states that do not lead to a successor or where the successor to which they lead has already occurred as an intermediate state. Attempting to insert none into the list of states leaves the list unchanged. The program is initially called with the list of states consisting of just the initial state as its single element.

The reason such a program is preferred is that it is generally possible to find *heuristics* [Pearl, 1984] which are estimates of the likely cost of a solution through any state. The list of states is kept in order of the heuristic value for each state, so that, in the above program, **insert** maintains the active list of states in heuristic order. A simple heuristic, the *Manhattan distance,* in the 8-puzzle is to count the number of cells each cell is away from its goal position. (Those familiar with this puzzle will know that this heuristic, while useful, is not accurate. It is sometimes necessary to move a cell away from its correct position in order to make corrections elsewhere and then move it back again.) Using this simple heuristic is an improvement on the fixed search order of Prolog.

The Prolog metaprogramming program is already very close to a GDC solution. The only backtracking involved is in the testing for goal states. This is also the only case of output by unification. Removing this gives the GDC version:

```
search([State|States],Soln)
    :- isgoal(State,Flag), expand(Flag,State,States,Soln).
```

```
expand(true,State,States,Soln) :- Soln=State.
expand(false,State,States,Soln)
    :- left(State,Left), right(State,Right),
       up(State,Up), down(State,Down),
       insert(Left,States,States1, insert(Right,States1,States2),
       insert(Up,States2,States3), insert(Down,States3,States4),
       search(States4,Soln).
```

This program is deceptive. It appears to offer concurrent heuristic search. In fact, it is a good example of the problem of parallelism disappearing. An actor

```
:-  search(States1,Soln)
```

will only reduce to

```
:-  isgoal(State,Flag), search1(Flag,State,States,Soln)
```

when States1 has become bound to [State|States]. This means that although the four descendant states of State can all be calculated concurrently, any further state expansion is left until the head of the subsequent list of actors is known: that is, after all the insertions. The actor **search**(States4,Soln) will not reduce until that is the case. Any search before this would have to speculate on which goals would be at the head of the list.

Concurrency can be pursued a little further with the above approach. Suppose there are N processors available and we use actor mapping notation of Chapter 4. The actor **actor**(Args)@p, 1≤p≤N, indicates that **actor**(Args) should be executed on processor p. Then, the first N states in the list can be expanded simultaneously, distributing each state to a separate processor. Expanding only the first state gives the following program:

```
search(N,States,Soln)
    :- distribute(N,States,OutStates,Soln1),
       search_if_no_soln(N,Soln1,OutStates,Soln).

search_if_no_soln(N,none,States,Soln)
    :- search(N,States,Soln).
search_if_no_soln(N,Soln1,States,Soln) :- Soln1=/=none
    |  Soln=Soln1.

distribute(N,[State|States],OutStates,Soln) :- N>0, N1:=N−1
    |  try_state(State,OutStates1,OutStates,Soln1)@N,
       distribute(N1,States,OutStates1,Soln2),
       choose(Soln1,Soln2,Soln).
distribute(0,States,OutStates,Soln)
    :- OutStates=States, Soln=none.
distribute(N,[],OutStates,Soln) :- OutStates=[], Soln=none.

choose(none,none,Soln) :- Soln=none.
choose(Soln1,_,Soln) :- Soln1=/=none | Soln=Soln1.
choose(_,Soln1,Soln) :- Soln1=/=none | Soln=Soln1.

try_state(State,InStates,OutStates,Soln)
    :- isgoal(State,Flag),
       expand(Flag,State,InStates,OutStates,Soln).

expand(true,State,InStates,OutStates,Soln)
    :- Soln=State, OutStates=InStates.
expand(false,State,InStates,OutStates,Soln)
    :- left(State,Left), right(State,Right),
       up(State,Up), down(State,Down),
       insert(Left,InStates,States1),
       insert(Right,States1,States2),
       insert(Up,States2,States3),
       insert(Down,States3,OutStates),
       Soln=none.
```

There are several problems with this program. Firstly, it is dependent on a specific architecture: one in which all processors may be accessed from a central controller, although it does allow flexibility in the number of processors. Secondly, it involves considerable communication costs: at each cycle states are sent out to each processor and their descendants are collected together again on one processor. Thirdly, it does not give optimal use of the multiprocessors. If one processor finishes work on the state it has been sent while the others are still busy, it cannot go on to search further states. Rather, it must wait until all processors have finished and work is distributed again. The main problem, however, is that it does not separate algorithm from control. The abstract consideration of expanding the search tree is mixed up with the lower level control considerations. The resulting program is a long way removed from the abstract control-free program we started with. It would be preferable to start with a simple declarative program and add annotations, where necessary, to obtain a practical parallel program.

This latest program may be regarded as a metaprogramming solution to the problem, since the actual tree expansion of the task can be considered a metaprogram running on top of the main program which covers the control aspect. The metaprogramming aspect would become even more dominant on a more complex architecture such as a distributed network of processors. Taking this metaprogramming approach further leads to the replicated worker approach to parallel search [Bal, 1991].

6.5 A Generic Search Program

Before continuing, let us generalize the 8-puzzle to a general search problem into which actors could, as necessary, be instantiated to specialize an 8-puzzle or any other state-space search. An actor **isgoal**(State,Flag) is needed which takes the representation of a state in the search and sends true on Flag if it is a goal state and false otherwise. In addition, an actor **successors**(State,Succs) is needed which sends the list of successor states of State on Succs. This will give us the following general declarative search program:

```
search(State,Sols) :- isgoal(State,Flag), expand(Flag,State,Sols).

expand(true,State,Sols) :- Sols=[State].
expand(false,State,Sols)
    :- successors(State, Succs), branch(Succs, Sols).

branch([], Sols) :- Sols=[].
branch([State|Siblings], Sols)
    :- search(State,Sols1),
       branch(Siblings,Sols2),
       combine(Sols1,Sols2,Sols).
```

The italic **combine** is meant to indicate that a number of different actors could be put here, resulting in a variety of search programs with different properties.

To get a behavior similar to the initial search program, a simple indeterminate **choose** actor, similar to before, is used for **combine** except it takes only two inputs:

choose([Sol], _, OutSols) :- OutSols=[Sol].
choose(_, [Sol], OutSols) :- OutSols=[Sol].
choose([], Sols, OutSols) :- OutSols=Sols.
choose(Sols, [], OutSols) :- OutSols=Sols.

Note that in the place of the previous none, the empty list [] is used and the solution is returned inside a single element list. This enables us to obtain a greater variety of programs, including multiple solution programs just by varying **combine**.

The result of using **choose** for **combine** is that program execution will result in a binary tree of **choose** processes. This represents the search tree of the problem using the standard n-ary to binary tree mapping that can be found in any good data structures textbook. The left branch represents the relationship *first child* and the right branch the relationship *next sibling*. Declaratively, the solution obtained is as before, though pragmatically the change would mean that the bias between indeterminate choices would change the likelihood of any particular solution being returned in the case of multiple solutions. For example, if a solution is obtainable through all four branches of the 8-puzzle and the choice is made when all four solutions are available, time-related factors can be discounted. In our initial program, there appears to an equal chance of any of the four solutions being returned. In this version, the first solution has only to get through one **choose**, the second has to get through two and the third and fourth through three. So there is a 50% chance of the first solution being returned, a 25% chance of the second and a 12.5% chance for each of the third and fourth.

If **combine** is standard list append, the output will be all solutions in left-to-right order from the search tree. If it is stream merger, the output will be all-solutions in an indeterminate order, but ignoring communications factors, in the order in which they are found temporally. Other possibilities are:

leftmost([Sol], _, OutSols) :- OutSols=[Sol].
leftmost([], Sols, OutSols) :- OutSols=Sols.

which will result in the leftmost solution in the search tree being returned and

indeterminate(Sols, _, OutSols) :- OutSols=Sols.
indeterminate(_, Sols, OutSols) :- OutSols=Sols.

which maps the indeterminacy of GDC straight into an indeterminate return of any solution. (This is not an option to be considered unless every leaf in the search tree is a solution!). If there are costs associated with solutions and **cost**(Sol,Cost) gives the associated cost, then using **lowestcost** as given below for **combine** will result in the lowest cost solution being returned:

lowestcost([], Sols, OutSols) :- OutSols=Sols.
lowestcost(Sols, [], OutSols) :- OutSols=Sols.
lowestcost([Sol1], [Sol2], OutSols)
    :- **cost**(Sol1,Cost1), cost(Sol2,Cost2),
       cheapest(Sol1, Cost1, Sol2, Cost2, Sol), OutSols=[Sol].

cheapest(Sol1,Cost1,_,Cost2,Sol) :- Cost1<Cost2 | Sol=Sol1.
cheapest(_,Cost1,Sol2,Cost2,Sol) :- Cost1>=Cost2 | Sol=Sol2.

A generic version of the linear search program may also be written, using the principle that a branch in the tree is searched only if search of the branch to its left has completed and no solution was found in it. Unlike the linear search version of the 8-puzzle, however, this program generates the successors of a node in advance rather than when needed:

```
search(State,Sols)
    :- isgoal(State,Flag),
       expand(Flag,State,Sols).

expand(true,State,Sols) :- Sols=[State].
expand(false,State,Sols)
    :- successors(State, Succs), branch(none, Succs, Sols).

branch(Sol1, [], Sol) :- Sol=Sol1.
branch(Sol1, _, Sol) :- Sol1=/=none, Sol=Sol1.
branch(none, [State|Siblings], Sol)
    :- search(State, Sol1),
       branch(Sol1, Siblings, Sol).
```

The all-solutions program which instead of appending lists of solutions adds them to an accumulator, is a form of linear search. Rather than have a separate **combine** actor, the solutions from one branch are passed as input to the actor working on its sibling. In concurrent logic programming, this is known as a *short-circuit*, since it amounts to the various solutions eventually being linked together like an electric circuit. In this case, the program is fully parallel. The generic version is:

```
search(Acc,State,Sols)
    :- isgoal(State,Flag), expand(Flag,Acc,State,Sols).

expand(true,Acc,State,Sols) :- Sols=[State|Acc].
expand(false,Acc,State,Sols)
    :- successors(State, Succs), branch(Acc,Succs,Sols).

branch(Acc,[],Sols) :- Sols=Acc.
branch(Acc,[State|Siblings],Sols)
    :- search(Acc,State,Sols1),
       branch(Sols1,Siblings,Sols).
```

In Prolog, this technique is known as *difference-lists* [Clark and Tärnlund, 1977] (*or accumulators*), with the convention being that the pair Acc and Sols is written Sols−Acc, indicating that a conceptual way of viewing it is as the solutions returned are those in Sols less those in Acc.

6.6 Layered Streams

So far, it has been assumed that goals are delivered only at leaves of the search tree. If this is not the case, an alternative method – *layered streams* [Okumura and

Matsumoto, 1987] can be used. Layered streams are used if the solutions to some search problem consist of a sequence of actions. The head of the sequence is derived from the current state independent of subsequent actions and the tail of the list being the remaining actions. Then, the set of solutions can be returned in a tree form matching the tree structure of the search space. Using the notation convention introduced by Okumura and Matsumoto [1987], a set of solutions with a common first action M is stored in the form $M^*[T_1,...,T_n]$ where T_i is a tree in similar form representing a set of possible tails to the list of actions. A layered stream representing the set of actions from a given state takes the form of either a set of these sets of solutions or two special atomic values. The atomic message begin indicates that the state is itself a goal state and so a solution is found with the empty list of actions. The message [] indicates a state which is not a solution and there are no possible actions from it that will lead to a solution. For example, the layered stream

[1*[2*[3*begin,4*[]],5*[6*begin,7*[],8*begin]],9*begin]

is a representation of the set of solutions {[1,2,3],[1,5,6],[1,5,8],[9]}, which is more intuitively pictured as the tree in Figure 6.6.1.

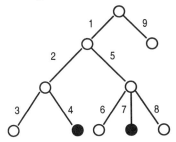

Fig. 6.6.1 A layered stream

The arcs are labeled with the actions they represent and the black circles represent nodes that are not solutions and have no descendants.

The generic search program, which produces a layered stream representing the set of possible solutions, is:

```
search(State,Sols)
    :- isgoal(State,Flag), expand(Flag,State,Sols).

expand(true,State,Sols) :- Sols=begin.
expand(false,State,Sols)
    :- successors(State, Succs), branch(Succs, Sols).

branch([], Sols) :- Sols=[].
branch([(State,Action)|Siblings], Sols)
    :- search(State,Sols1),
       branch(Siblings,Sols2),
       join(Action,Sols1,Sols2,Sols).

join(Action,Sols1,Sols2,Sols) :- Sols=Action*[Sols1|Sols2].
```

where it is assumed that states are returned paired with the action that generated them from their parent in **successors**.

A slightly more complex form of **join** removes dead-end branches from the tree as they are constructed:

```
join(Action,Sols1,Sols2,Sols) :- Sols1=/=[]
    | Sols=Action*[Sols1|Sols2].
join(Action,[],Sols2,Sols) :- Sols=Sols2.
```

A version of **join** that returns a single solution indeterminately is easy to define:

```
join(Action,Sols1,_,Sols) :- Sols1=/=[] | Sols=[Action|Sols1].
join(Action,_,Sols2,Sols) :- Sols2=/=[] | Sols=[Action|Sols2].
join(Action,[],[],Sols) :- Sols=[].
```

Further variants of **join** may be considered in a similar way to the variants of **combine** considered previously. Some of these will appear later in the chapter. Layered streams may seem complex when combined in an undisciplined way with other elements of search (for example in some of the programs in [Tick, 1991]). However, when analyzed in this generic way they are a natural extension to the techniques already introduced. The complexity comes about because in the interests of efficiency elements of the search, which have been split up here into separate actors, may in practice be interlinked in single multi-purpose actors. Our preferred mode of programming would be to encourage the use of generic programming patterns or clichés [Waters, 1985] in program development, but to use program transformation methods, such as partial evaluation (Chapter 9) to produce more efficient but less understandable programs.

6.7 Eliminating Redundant Search

A simple way of eliminating redundant speculative search is through the use of a *termination message*. The idea is that search may only continue while a channel remains unbound. When a solution is found, the channel is bound to some constant found. This channel is checked before each expansion of the search tree takes place. Of course, objections may be raised that this technique requires the use of an extra-logical test for whether a message has arrived. For the moment, these objections will be overridden. A generic search program using the termination message technique is given below:

```
search(Term, State, Sols)
    :- isgoal(State, Flag),
       expand(Flag, Term, State, Sols).

expand(Flag, found, State, Sol) :- Sol=none.
expand(true, Term, State, Sol) :- unknown(Term) | Sol=State.
expand(false, Term, State, Sol) :-unknown(Term)
    | successors(State, States),
      branch(Term, States, Sol).
```

```
branch(Term, [], Sol) :- Sol=none.
branch(Term, [State|Siblings], Sol)
   :- search(Term, State, Sol1),
      branch(Term, Siblings, Sol2),
      choose(Sol1, Sol2, Sol).
```

The exact nature of the test for a message being unbound in a concurrent and potentially distributed program is an issue for discussion. The constraint **unknown** is used to indicate an inexpensive test that simply checks whether the channel is known to be bound at the processor on which the test takes place. It may be that it has been found elsewhere, but news of that binding has not yet reached the processor. The distinction between this test and a **var** test which locks the channel and makes a full check for lack of a binding throughout the system is noted in [Yardeni et al., 1990]. This reference also suggests a "test-and-set" operator, that is an atomic operation which checks the whole system for whether a channel is unbound and if it is unbound sets it to a value, otherwise it has no effect. The advantage of this operator is that it can overcome the binding conflict problem and allow us to have a single shared channel to return a solution.. In effect, this channel has the dual role of returning a solution and acting as a termination message. This version is given below:

```
search(State, Sols)
   :- isgoal(State, Flag),
      expand(Flag, State, Sols)

expand(Flag, State, Sol) :- nonvar(Sol) | true.
expand(true, State, Sol) :- test_and_set(Sol,State).
expand(false, State, Sol) :- var(Term)
   |  successors(State, States),
      branch(States, Sol).

branch([], Sol) :- true.
branch([State|Siblings], Sol)
   :- search(State, Sol),
      branch(Siblings, Sol).
```

The version using **test_and_set** enables us to dispense with the hierarchy of **choose** actors that are necessary in the version of the program using **unknown**. This is because without a **test_and_set** we cannot tell whether a channel we are binding has been bound elsewhere. Even with **var** it cannot be guaranteed that in between **var**(X) succeeding and the execution of X=value, X has not been bound elsewhere. This problem does not occur with the termination message so long as = is unification rather than assignment since then Term=found will succeed even if Term has been bound elsewhere to found. If multiple writers to the termination message is a problem, or to avoid the bottleneck of every process over a distributed system needing access to a single global termination channel, we can use a version in which each actor has its own termination channel. Then, **choose** has a multiple role – as well as passing solutions upward in the tree, it passes termination signals downwards. The following program does this:

search(Term, State, Sols)
   :- **isgoal**(State, Flag),
      expand(Flag, Term, State, Sols).

expand(Flag, found, State, Sol) :- Sol=none.
expand(true, Term, State, Sol) :- **unknown**(Term) | Sol=State.
expand(false, Term, State, Sol) :- **unknown**(Term)
   | **successors**(State, States),
      branch(Term, States, Sol).

branch(Term, [], Sol) :- Sol=none.
branch(Term, [State|Siblings], Sol)
   :- **search**(Term1, State, Sol1),
      branch(Term2, Siblings, Sol2),
      choose(Term, Term1, Term2, Sol1, Sol2, Sol).

The six argument version of **choose**, including termination channels is:
choose(found, Term1, Term2, _, _, Sol)
   :- Term1=found, Term2=found, Sol=none.
choose(_, _, Term2, Sol1, _, Sol) :- Sol1=/=none
   | Term2=found, Sol=Sol1.
choose(_, Term1, _, _, Sol2, Sol) :- Sol2=/=none
   | Term1=found, Sol=Sol2
choose(_, _, _, none, none, Sol)
   :- Sol=none.

The effect of executing this program, as shown in Figure 6.7.1, is to set up a binary tree of **choose** actors in which each arc is represented by two channels. The arrows show the direction of the flow of data in these channels.

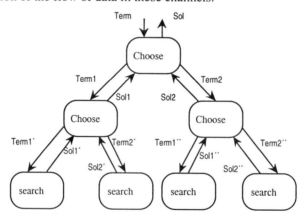

Fig. 6.7.1 Duplex communication between **choose** actors

A short-circuit all-solutions search program may also be used as the basis for a speculative search program with a cutoff when a solution is found. The following version of it program will accomplish this:

```
search(Acc,_,Sols) :- wait(Acc) | Sols=Acc.
search(Acc,State,Sols) :- unknown(Acc)
    | isgoal(State,Flag), expand(Flag,Acc,State,Sols).

expand(true,Acc,State,Sols) :- Sols=[State|Acc].
expand(false,Acc,State,Sols)
    :- successors(State, Succs), branch(Acc,Succs,Sols).

branch(Acc,[],Sols) :- Sols=Acc.
branch(Acc,[State|Siblings],Sols)
    :- search(Acc,State,Sols1),
       branch(Sols1,Siblings,Sols).
```

where **wait**(X) cannot fail, but if X is unbound suspends until it becomes bound. The initial call to this program should be

```
:- search(Acc,State,Sols), complete(Sols,Acc),
```

where **complete** is defined by:

```
complete(Sols,Acc) :- wait(Sols) | Acc=[].
complete(Sols,Acc) :- Sols==Acc | Acc=[].
```

The result is that when a solution is found, any search which remains to be done is cut off and the circuit is linked up to the right of the solution in the search tree. The **complete** actor completes the circuit halting any remaining search to the solution's left. It is assumed the **==** test in the second behavior for **complete** will succeed if its two arguments are the same unbound channel and suspend if they are two different unbound channels. This will prevent deadlock in the case where there are no solutions. It is possible for a solution to be found in one place and linked into the list of solutions before news of the finding of a solution elsewhere is received. Unless there are no solutions, the output of this search will be a short list containing at least one but possibly more solutions.

6.8 A Direct GDC Solution Using Priorities

The problem of unrestricted parallelism has not yet been dealt with. At any point in the execution of a search, any actor that is sufficiently bound to reduce could do so. In practice, **choose** actors will remain suspended waiting for solutions or termination channels, so it will be the **search** actors at the leaves of the tree that will be reducing. Generally, some of the **search** actors are more likely to lead soon to a solution state than others. In the absence of architectural limitations on the amount of parallelism available, we would prefer that if a processor has a choice of **search** actors which it can expand, it will pick the one most likely to lead to a solution. In many problems there is a heuristic that indicates which one it is.

Once a solution is found, the **choose** actors, which pass the solution upwards and termination values downwards to the rest of the tree, need priority over the **search** actors which are expanding the tree. Otherwise livelock occurs where expanding **search** actors take over the resources that ought to be used by the **choose** actors, to send messages that a solution has been found and no further expansion is necessary.

The preferred solution is to control the parallelism through the priority pragma of GDC introduced in Chapter 4. The idea of introducing priorities into concurrent logic languages was arrived at independently by one of the authors [Huntbach, 1988; 1991], influenced by Burton's use of a similar priority pragma in functional languages [Burton, 1985] and the ICOT group developing the parallel language KL1 [Ueda and Chikayama, 1990]. The priority pragma may be considered a practical implementation of the precedence relationship between subproblems in a General Problem Solving Algorithm [Rayward-Smith et al, 1988]: the precedence relationship establishes a partial ordering among subproblems, which in practice may be modeled by assigning them a numerical priority. The precedence gives an ordering of the likelihood of a subproblem contributing to the overall solution.

The idea is that should two actors be located on a single processor with its own memory and both actors have channels sufficiently bound so that they can reduce, the one with the highest priority will always be reduced first. If N processors share a memory store and there are more than N reducible actors in that store, then the N highest priority actors will be reduced. It is assumed that an underlying load-balancing mechanism will give a reasonable distribution of high priority actors across processors. The alternative would be a global priority list shared out across the processors, but this would be an expensive bottleneck on a non-shared memory system. Otherwise the programmer need not be concerned with actor-mapping. This means that a program employing priorities may be ported with ease between a variety of architectures.

Load-balancing between processors in a parallel architecture may be compared to such things as register allocation in a standard sequential system. In both cases, although a program could be made more efficient by giving the programmer direct control over allocations, it is best to free the programmer from such low-level considerations. At least it would be preferable to confine them to a separate program layer so that the abstract structure of the algorithm is not buried within code dealing with the allocations.

The syntax for priorities writes actors as **actor**@priority(P) where **actor** is any GDC actor and P is a real number, or a GDC channel that will be bound to a real (in the latter case the actor will be suspended until P is bound). When **actor** is sufficiently bound to reduce, **actor**@priority(P) will reduce in just the same way as **actor** would, providing there are no other reducible actors with higher priorities sharing the same processor. Any actor without a priority call is termed *mandatory* (following Burton [1985]) and in effect has infinite priority. Note that our intention, unlike the ICOT team, is that priorities should be attached only to current actor and not to subsequent subactors. This gives the maximum flexibility – if it is desired that the children of an actor should share that actor's priority this can easily be arranged by passing the priority down to them as a parameter.

The priority call is an unobtrusive addition to a program that enables the programmer to write the program as if the maximum parallelism is available and add annotations at a later stage to cover the fact that in practice parallelism is limited. To add priorities to the existing search programs, a simple change is needed to the behavior that sets up a search actor in a branch. With an actor **heuristic** that takes as its first argument a state in the search space and returns in its second argument a heuristic value associated with that state, the following new clause for **branch** suffices:

```
branch(Term, [State|Siblings], Sol)
  :- heuristic(State,H),
     search(Term1, State, Sol1)@priority(H),
     branch(Term2, Siblings, Sol2),
     choose(Term, Term1, Term2, Sol1, Sol2, Sol).
```

Note that although the priority is attached only to the **search** actor, this will affect the whole program since, as shown, the program reduces to a tree with **search** actors at the leaves being the only reducible actors. The internal **choose** actors suspend. Thus, every reducible actor will have a priority. Since **choose** actors do not have priorities they are mandatory as required; they will always be executed before **search** actors. This gives the desired property that passing on a termination signal will always have priority over expanding the tree.

The use of priorities fits in best with the AND-parallel languages like GDC where program execution may be viewed in terms of concurrent actors. Although it is possible to introduce user-defined priorities into OR-parallel languages, it seems to be more complex. Szeredi [1991], for example, introduces priorities into *Aurora* to solve heuristic search problems similar to that considered here, but requires a further four additional primitives.

Saletore [1990] has also considered the introduction of priorities into parallel logic programs in order to control speculative computations. His priorities are inferred by the system rather than given by the user and are thus less flexible than those given here. However, Salatore's detailed consideration of methods for implementing priorities and load-balancing schemes, together with encouraging practical results, offers further support for the priority construct.

6.9 Search Anomalies

On a single processor system, the search program with priorities will degenerate to a situation where the implicit priority queue of **search** actors matches exactly the explicit priority queue of states in the metaprogramming approach above. It is well known that if the heuristic associated with any state is a lower bound on the cost of all solutions reachable through that state (a heuristic with this property is termed *admissible*), the first solution found by expanding the search tree in the heuristic order will be optimal. However, this cannot be guaranteed on a multi-processor system, even if the priority list is shared. Consider the situation where the subtree in Figure 6.9.1 is part of the search tree, where double circled nodes indicate solution nodes, the values in the nodes are the heuristics and no node anywhere else in the tree has a heuristic less than N+5. Here, by convention, nodes with the lowest heuristic are expanded first (the GDC priority would be the inverse of the heuristic):

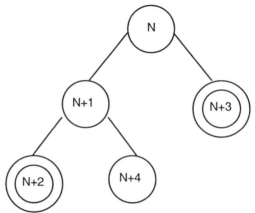

Fig. 6.9.1 Actors prioritized by heuristic valuations

On a single processor system, the node with heuristic N will be expanded first, leading to the two nodes with heuristic N+1 and N+3 being at the head of the priority queue. The node with heuristic N+1 will then be expanded leading to the three nodes with heuristic N+2, N+3 and N+4 being at the head of the priority queue. The node with heuristic N+2 will then be expanded and found to be a solution.

On a two-processor system, however, the node with heuristic N and some other node (with, as said, heuristic N+5 or more) will both be expanded. This will lead to the nodes with heuristics N+1 and N+3 being at the head of the priority queue. Both will be expanded and the node with heuristic N+3 found to be a solution rather than the better solution with heuristic N+2. There is more scope for this sort of anomaly if there is a separate priority queue for each processor. Suppose there are three nodes with heuristics N, N+1 and N+2 on a two-processor system. It may be the case that the nodes with heuristics N and N+1 are on the same processor and so the nodes with heuristics N and N+2 are expanded, so the strict order of priority is lost.

To see how a multiprocessor search can lead to arbitrarily large speedup or slowdown, consider first the case where the children of a state with heuristic N are a solution state with heuristic N+2 (Figure 6.9.2) and a non-solution state with heuristic N+1. This non-solution child has an arbitrarily large number of non-solution descendants all of heuristic N+1 with no other state having a heuristic less than N+3 (Figure 6.9.2).

On a single processor, the state with heuristic N will be expanded, putting the top state with heuristic N+1 and the state with heuristic N+2 at the head of the priority queue. The state with heuristic N+1 will then be expanded putting two more states with heuristics N+1 at the head of the priority queue and so on for an arbitrary length of time. Only when the N+1 heuristic states are exhausted is the N+2 heuristic state tried and found to be a solution. On a two processor system the top N+1 and the N+2 heuristic state will be expanded and the N+2 heuristic state found to be a solution and returned, without any further search needed. Since the number of N+1 nodes that are no longer considered is arbitrarily high, the speedup with two processors is arbitrarily high.

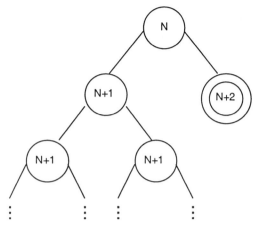

Fig. 6.9.2 Acceleration anomaly

Deceleration anomalies or slowdowns occur when a multiprocessing system causes a node to be expanded that would not be considered in a single processor system, but on expansion reveals promising-looking descendants which do not though have any solutions in them. For example, suppose in the tree in Figure 6.9.3, the N+1 heuristic states have an arbitrary number of descendants all with heuristic N+1 but with no solutions among them. On a single processor they would never be reached since on expansion of the N heuristic node, the N+2 and N+3 heuristic nodes would be produced and the N+2 expanded first. This would reveal its successor N+2 heuristic node, which again would be expanded before the N+3 node and found to be a solution.

On a two processor system, however, after the expansion of the initial N heuristic node, both its successors would be expanded, resulting in the top two N+1 heuristic nodes being at the head of the priority queue, followed by the N+2 heuristic goal state. Since there are an arbitrary number of N+1 heuristic descendants of the top N+1 heuristic nodes, the two processor system would spend an arbitrarily long amount of time searching them, before finding the N+2 heuristic solution.

As Lai and Sahni [1984] point out, although the conditions which produce these anomalies look unusual, in practice it is quite common for nodes in a search tree surrounding a solution to have heuristic values which are very close to each other. Therefore, they are a factor that needs to be taken into account. Fortunately, the conditions that lead to superlinear speedup are more common than those that lead to slowdown are. As McBurney and Sleep [1987] show experimentally, it is not unusual for state space search with N processors to result in a speedup of more than N. Lie and Wah [1984] describe conditions on heuristics that assure that the detrimental slowdowns that are possible with parallelism cannot occur and also conditions that are necessary for superlinear speedup. The possibility of superlinear speedups led

Kornfeld [1982] to suggest that the use of a parallel language and pseudo-parallel execution could improve algorithm efficiency, even when actually executed on a single processor. The improvement which Stockman [1979] notes in his *SSS** algorithm gives over the standard alpha-beta search of game trees is due to the pseudo-parallel search of the game tree which SSS* uses in the place of alpha-beta search's strict depth-first left-to-right approach.

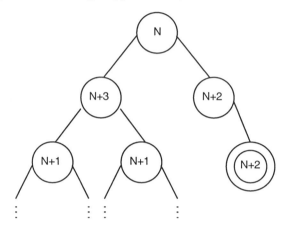

Fig. 6.9.3 Deceleration anomaly

The more usual situation, however, is that search on a multiprocessor system will yield some speedup but a speedup less than the number of processors. In addition to dealing with the overhead of the parallelism, if some of the parallelism is speculative the total amount of work done in a parallel search will be greater than that done with the same problem on a single processor. This is due to parts of the tree being searched that would not be considered in a single processor search. If there is no speculative computation, for example in a search for all solutions, any failure of the speedup to reach the number of processors will be due just to the overhead of parallelism, since the total amount of work done on the problem itself will not change.

6.10 Branch-and-Bound Search

As shown above, on a multiprocessor system, even if an admissible heuristic is available, we cannot guarantee that the first solution found is the lowest cost one. The cost of the first solution is, however, an upper bound on the lowest cost solution. If there is a way of determining a lower bound on the cost of any solution reached through a particular state and if that lower bound is greater than or equal to the cost of the best solution so far, the state need not be expanded. This is because it will not give us a better solution. The point at which search of a subtree is abandoned because its lower bound is greater than a known upper bound is known as a *cut-off*. This method of searching with bounds is known as *branch-and-bound* search [Lawler and Wood, 1966]. Often, a heuristic used for search is also a lower bound. That is so with the heuristic for the 8-puzzle described in Section 6.4, since, to move all cells into position requires at minimum the number of squares each cell is out of position.

A branch-and-bound search program can be based on an all-solutions program, returning a stream of solutions. Cutoffs will stop many of the solutions being reached and joining the stream. A simple version of a branch-and-bound program has a manager actor to which all solutions are sent and which keeps an account of the lowest cost solution found so far. Since the cost of this solution is an upper bound, the manager also receives requests from the search processes for the current upper bound. The manager deals with **sol** type messages, which pass on new solutions and their associated costs and **request** messages, which request the current upper bound and return it in a reply channel. Replacing **choose** actors of the single-solution search with stream merges, there is no need for any other termination mechanisms. There is no need to use the extra-logical **unknown**.

The following program implements this:

```
search(State,Msgs)
   :- Msgs=[request(UpBound)|Messg1],
      lowerbound(State,LoBound),
      cutoff(State,LoBound,UpBound,Msgs1).

cutoff(State,LoBound,UpBound,Msgs) :- LoBound>=UpBound
   | Msgs=[].
cutoff(State,LoBound,UpBound,Msgs) :- LoBound<UpBound
   | isgoal(State,Flag), expand(Flag,State,Msgs).

expand(true,State,Msgs)
   :- cost(State,Cost), Msgs=[sol(State,Cost)].
expand(false,State,Msgs)
   :- successors(State, Succs), branch(Succs, Msgs).

branch([], Msgs) :- Msgs=[].
branch([State|Siblings], Msgs)
   :- heuristic(State,H),
      search(State,Msgs1)@priority(H),
      branch(Siblings,Msgs2),
      merge(Msgs1, Msgs2, Msgs)
```

It is assumed that **cost** gives the cost associated with a solution state and **lowerbound** gives the lower bound on solutions reachable through a given state. Note that, since **cutoff**, the actor that either cuts off search or continues as appropriate, contains an arithmetic test using LoBound in its guards, it will suspend until the lower bound has been returned in the reply channel from the manager. The **manager** behaviors are:

```
manager([],ASolution,ACost,BestSol,LowestCost)
   :- BestSol=Solution, LowestCost=Cost.
manager([request(UpBnd)|Msgs],ASol,ACost,BestSol,LowestCost)
   :- UpBnd=ACost,
   manager(Msgs,ASol,ACost,BestSol,LowestCost).
manager([sol(Sol1,Cost1)|Msgs],Sol2,Cost2,BestSol,LowCost)
   :- Cost1<Cost2
   |  manager(Msgs,Sol1,Cost1,BestSol,LowestCost).
manager([sol(Sol1,Cost1)|Msgs],Sol2,Cost2,BestSol,LowCost)
   :- Cost1>=Cost2
   |  manager(Msgs,Sol2,Cost2,BestSol,LowestCost).
```

The system is set up with initial actors:

```
:- search(InitState,Msgs),
   manager(Msgs,Dummy,_,BestSol,LowestCost)
```

where Dummy is a value, which is known to be above any solution cost that might be found.

Here normal stream merger can be used, but some efficiency gains can be made with a more sophisticated merger. If two request messages are sent, they can be merged into one by unifying their reply channels, thus reducing the number of messages that need to be dealt with. If two solution messages are being sent, only the one with lowest cost needs to be sent further. These considerations give rise to the following version of **merge**:

```
merge([request(R1)|S1], [request(R2)|S2], S)
   :- R1=R2, merge([request(R1)|S1], S2, S).
merge([request(R1),request(R2)|S1], S2, S)
   :- R1=R2, merge([request(R1)|S1], S2, S).
merge(S1,[request(R1),request(R2)|S2],S)
   :- R1=R2, merge([request(R1)|S1], S2, S).
merge([request(R)|S1], S2, S)
   :- S=[request(R)|S3], merge(S1,S2,S3).
merge(S1, [request(R)|S2], S)
   :- S=[request(R)|S3], merge(S1,S2,S3).
merge([sol(Sol1,Cost1)|S1], [sol(Sol2,Cost2)|S2], S)
   :- Cost1<Cost2
   |  merge([sol(Sol1,Cost1)|S1],S2,S).
merge([sol(Sol1,Cost1),sol(Sol2,Cost2)|S1], S2, S)
   :- Cost1<Cost2
   |  merge([sol(Sol1,Cost1)|S1],S2,S).
merge(S1, [sol(Sol1,Cost1),sol(Sol2,Cost2)|S2], S)
   :- Cost1<Cost2
   |  merge([sol(Sol1,Cost1)|S1], S2, S).
merge([sol(Sol1,Cost1)|S1], [sol(Sol2,Cost2)|S2], S)
   :- Cost1>=Cost2
   |  merge([sol(Sol2,Cost2)|S1], S2, S).
```

```
merge([sol(Sol1,Cost1),sol(Sol2,Cost2)|S1], S2, S)
    :- Cost1>=Cost2
    |  merge([sol(Sol2,Cost2)|S1],S2,S).
merge(S1, [sol(Sol1,Cost1),sol(Sol2,Cost2)|S2], S)
    :- Cost1>=Cost2
    |  merge([sol(Sol2,Cost2)|S1],S2,S).
merge([sol(Sol,Cost)|S1], S2,S)
    :- S=[sol(Sol,Cost)|S3], merge(S1,S2,S3).
merge(S1, [sol(Sol,Cost)|S2], S)
    :- S=[sol(Sol,Cost)|S3], merge(S1,S2,S3).
```

A single manager holding the current best known solution is clearly a bottleneck, since it has to respond to every search call checking for the current upperbound. The above version of **merge** makes some improvements by merging multiple requests for the upperbound into one. An alternative way of dealing with parallel branch-and-bound search takes a similar approach to that used to avoid the bottleneck of a global termination channel on the search for a single solution. In this case, each node in the tree of **merge** actors created by the search stores its own upperbound limit. When a lower cost solution is received from one branch, the limit is updated, the new solution sent upwards in the tree and the new lower bound sent downwards on the other branch. When a solution reaches a **merge** actor with a cost higher than the current limit, it is not sent any further. It can be seen that when it is found, a lower bound will gradually diffuse through the tree. The complete program for this branch-and-bound search with distributed limits is:

```
search(InCosts,State,Sols)
    :- lowerbound(State,LoBound),
       cutoff(LoBound,InCosts,State,Sols).

cutoff(LoBound,[UpBound1,UpBound2|UpBounds],State,Sols)
    :- LoBound<UpBound1
    |  cutoff(LoBound,[UpBound2|UpBounds],State,Sols).
cutoff(LoBound,[UpBound|UpBounds],State,Sols)
    :- LoBound>=UpBound
    |  Sols=[].
cutoff(LoBound,[UpBound|UpBounds],State,Sols)
    :- unknown(UpBounds), LoBound<UpBound
    |  isgoal(State,TV), expand(TV,[UpBound|UpBounds],State,Sols).

expand(true,Bounds,State,Sols)
    :- cost(State,Cost), Sols=[(State,Cost)]
expand(false,Bounds,State,Sols)
    :- successors(State,States), branch(Bounds,States,Sols).
```

```
branch(Bounds,[],Sols) :- Sols=[].
branch([Bound|Bounds],[State|Siblings],Sols)
    :- heuristic(State,H),
       search([Bound|Bounds1],State,Sols1)@priority(H),
       branch([Bound|Bounds2],Siblings,Sols2),
       merge(Dummy,[Bound|Bounds],Bounds1,
             Bounds2,Sols1,Sols2,Sols).


merge(Lim,[Bnd1,Bnd2|InBnds],Bnds1,Bnds2,Sols1,Sols2,Sols)
    :- merge(Lim,[Bnd2|InBnds],Bnds1,Bnds2,Sols1,Sols2,Sols).
merge(Limit,[Bnd|InBnds],Bnds1,Bnds2,Sols1,Sols2,Sols)
    :- unknown(InBnds), Bnd<Limit
    |  Bnds1=[Bnd|NewBnds1], Bnds2=[Bnd|NewBnds2],
       merge(Bnd,InBnds,NewBnds1,NewBnds2,Sols1,Sols2,Sols).
merge(Limit,[Bnd|InBnds],Bnds1,Bnds2,Sols1,Sols2,Sols)
    :- unknown(InBnds), Bnd>=Limit
    |  merge(Limit,InBnds,Bnds1,Bnds2,Sols1,Sols2,Sols).
merge(Limit,InBnds,Bnds1,Bnds2,[(Sol,Cost)|Sols1],Sols2,Sols)
    :- unknown(InBnds), Cost<Limit
    |  Bnds2=[Cost|NewBnds2], Sols=[(Sol,Cost)|NewSols],
       merge(Cost,InBnds,Bnds1,NewBnds2,Sols1,Sols2,NewSols).
merge(Limit,InBnds,Bnds1,Bnds2,Sols1,[(Sol,Cost)|Sols2],Sols)
    :- unknown(InBnds), Cost<Limit
    |  Bnds1=[Cost|NewBnds1], Sols=[(Sol,Cost)|NewSols],
       merge(Cost,InBnds,NewBnds1,Bnds2,Sols1,Sols2,NewSols).
merge(Limit,InBnds,Bnds1,Bnds2,[(Sol,Cost)|Sols1],Sols2,Sols)
    :- Cost>=Limit
    |  merge(Limit,InBnds,Bnds1,Bnds2,Sols1,Sols2,Sols).
merge(Limit,InBnds,Bnds1,Bnds2,Sols1,[(Sol,Cost)|Sols2],Sols)
    :- Cost>=Limit
    |  merge(Limit,InBnds,Bnds1,Bnds2,Sols1,Sols2,Sols).
merge(Limit,InBounds,Bounds1,Bounds2,[],Sols2,Sols)
    :- Sols=Sol2, Bounds2=InBounds.
merge(Limit,InBounds,Bounds1,Bounds2,Sols1,[],Sols)
    :- Sols=Sols1, Bounds1=InBounds.
```

To avoid repeated calculations of the cost associated with a state, costs are passed around in pairs with solutions. The result of executing the program will be to create a tree of **merge** actors, each of which will have one incoming stream of lower bounds, two outgoing streams of lower bounds, two incoming streams of solution/cost pairs and one outgoing stream of solution/cost pairs. All streams will be in decreasing cost order. Note the use of **unknown** to check that the latest available bound from the stream of incoming bounds is being used – when this is the case, **unknown** will succeed when it takes as argument the channel storing the rest of the stream.

6.11 Game Tree Search

Chapter 1 emphasized the role which games played in early Artificial Intelligence. Programs that play games like chess are another form of state-space search in which we have a tree of states with the root being the initial state. The root's descendants are generated by all possible actions from this state. The descendants of its descendants are generated from them recursively. In a complete game tree, the leaves represent board positions where no further actions may be made. Ignoring the possibility of games with draw positions, the leaves ofthe game tree may be labeled "win" or "lose". If it is not a leaf, the root of the game tree is labeled "win" if at least one of its descendant states is labeled "win". By taking the actions that lead to that leaf a winning position can be reached. The root is labeled "lose" if none of the descendants is labeled "win". Then, whatever actions are taken, it is not possible to reach a winning position. The labeling of the subtrees of the root differs since they represent positions in which it is the opponent trying to force a "lose" position. A subtree is labeled "lose" if it has a subtree labeled "lose." It is labeled "win" if it has no subtree labeled "lose". The next level down is labeled as the root level and so on alternately down to the leaves. For this reason, game trees are a form of AND/OR tree. If win/lose are treated as Booleans we have trees of logic terms where the odd level branches are conjunctions and the even level disjunctions.

In the search of a complete game tree, it can be seen that when labeling nodes at an odd level in the tree, as soon as search of one subtree returns a "win" it is unnecessary to search the rest; a path that leads to a certain win has already found. Similarly, at even levels as soon as one subtree returns "lose" it is unnecessary to search the rest. If it is decided to search more than one branch of the tree in parallel we are engaging in speculative computation since it is not known whether the search of the second and subsequent branches will be necessary or not to return a solution. However, search of them is initiated anyway to take advantage of parallelism.

This is a similar situation to that with standard search for a solution in a tree. Either we take a cautious approach and lose all opportunity for parallelism, since all the parallelism in the problem is speculative, or we ignore the fact that the parallelism is speculative and run into the problem of overwhelming the system with speculative computations.

The simple solution, with all speculative search possible, but cutting off no speculative computation found unnecessary, is:

```
player(State, Val)
    :- isleaf(State, L), playeraction(L, State, Val).
playeraction(true, State, Val) :- eval(State, Val).
playeraction(false, State, Val)
    :- successors(State, Succs), or(Succs, Val).
```

```
or([], Val) :- Val=lose.
or([State|Siblings], Val)
    :- opponent(State, Val1),
       or(Siblings, Val2),
       either(Val1, Val2, Val).

either(win, _, Val) :- Val=win.
either(_, win, Val) :- Val=win.
either(lose, lose, Val) :- Val=lose.

opponent(State, Val)
    :- leaf(State, L), opponentaction(L, State, Val).

opponentaction(true, State, Val) :- eval(State, Val).
opponentaction(false, State, Val)
    :- successors(State, Succs), and(Succs, Val).

and([], Val) :- Val=win.
and([State|Siblings], Val)
    :- player(State, Val1),
       and(Siblings, Val2),
       both(Val1, Val2, Val).

both(lose, _, Val) :- Val=lose.
both(_, lose, Val) :- Val=lose.
both(win, win, Val) :- Val=win.
```

An alternative formulation of game tree search labels nodes "win" or "lose" depending on whether they represent a win or lose state for the player who is next to move at the node itself, rather than always for the player at the root of the tree. In this case a non-leaf node is labeled "win" if any of its successors are labeled "lose" and is labeled "lose" if none of its successors are labeled "lose". This leads to a simpler algorithm and program, as it is no longer necessary to consider two different sorts of nodes, though it is perhaps not so intuitive:

```
search(State, Val)
    :- isleaf(State, L), expand(L, State, Val)

expand(true, State, Val) :- eval(State, Val)
expand(false, State, Val)
    :- successors(State, Succs), branch(Succs, Val)

branch([], Val) :- Val=win.
branch([State|Siblings], Val)
    :- game(State, Val1),
       branch(Siblings, Val2),
       combine(Val1, Val2, Val).
```

combine(lose, _, Val) :- Val=win.
combine(_, lose, Val) :- Val=win.
combine(win, win, Val) :- Val=lose.

It can be seen that this program is a version of the generic search program (Section 6.5). Thus, termination channels may be used as previously to halt speculative search that is found to be redundant.

6.12 Minimax and Alpha-Beta Search

In practice, apart from that subfield of games playing concerned with end-game situations, game trees are usually too large for a complete exposition. Rather a state which is not an end position in the game may be treated as a leaf and assigned a heuristic value which represents an estimate of the likelihood of that state being a win position in a full analysis. Naively, all states at a given depth in the tree will be taken as leaves and assigned a numerical value. On similar principles to full game trees above, a value for the root node and every non-leaf node at an even depth in the tree is determined by selecting the maximum value of its descendants. The value for every non-leaf node at odd depth is determined by selecting the minimum value of its descendants. Hence the name *minimax* search. At the root, the action corresponding to the subtree with highest value is given as the next move to make since this value is the maximum value which the player can force the opponent to concede to.

For example, Figure 6.12.1 shows a complete tree, assuming nodes at depth 3 are treated as leaves and evaluated according to the evaluation function. The values of the internal nodes are worked out using the minimax procedure. The convention is that square boxes represent maximizing nodes and round boxes minimizing nodes:

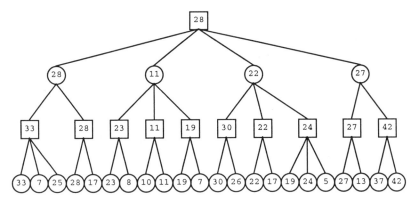

Fig. 6.12.1 A minimax tree

As the leftmost branch of Figure 6.12.1 supplies the highest value at the root, the action represented by the leftmost branch is the estimated the best action to make. Estimating the position three plays ahead, this is the action that can guarantee leaving the player in the best position whatever actions the opponent makes.

It is not, however, necessary to search the whole tree. In Figure 6.12.1, consider the case where a sequential depth-first left-to right evaluation of the tree takes place. When the leftmost subtree of the root has been found to return a value of 28, it cannot return a value greater than 28. This is because the root node is maximizing and its descendants are minimizing. If any of the descendants of the descendants should evaluate to less than 28, its parent is minimizing so its value cannot be picked as the maximum. When the first sub-branch of the second branch returns a value of 23, it is not necessary to search the rest of the branch since at most it will return a value of 23, which will not exceed the 28 already established. With the third branch, its third sub-branch's return of 30 indicates a possibility of a better choice, but when the second sub-branch of the third branch returns 22 the possibility that the actions represented by the third branch is better is lost. The tree only needs to be searched to the extent shown in Figure 6.12.2.

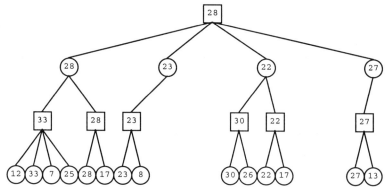

Fig. 6.12.2 Alpha-beta pruned game tree

A formalization of these considerations of cutoffs in game-tree search, together with a change to the formulation similar to that with complete game-trees, avoids having to distinguish between maximizing and minimizing nodes and gives the well-known alpha-beta algorithm [Knuth and Moore, 1975] for estimated game-tree search. This may be described in pseudo-code:

```
function alphabeta(p: position; α,β: valuation):valuation= {
    if leaf(p) then return(value(p)) else {
    for each successor position of p, p₁ to pw do {
    α:=max(α,–alphabeta(pᵢ,–β,–α));
    if α≥β then return(α)
};
    return(α)
    }
}
```

The evaluation is initialized with α and β set to $-\infty$ and ∞ respectively. The value of α may be increased by recursive calls but if it is increased to the value of β or beyond, a cutoff position has been reached and no further evaluation is done as it is unnecessary. When α is increased, a reduced value for β is passed to recursive calls, which again may cause cutoffs. The difference between α and β is described as the *alpha-beta window*.

A GDC version of the alpha-beta algorithm is:

```
alphabeta(Position, Alpha, Beta)
    :- isleaf(Position,Flag),
       expand(Flag, Position, Alpha, Beta, Eval).

expand(true, Position, _, _, Eval)
    :- evaluate(Position, Eval).
expand(false, Position, Alpha, Beta, Eval)
    :- successors(Position, Succs),
       branch(Alpha, Beta, Succs, Eval).

branch(Alpha, Beta, [], Eval) :- Eval=Alpha.
branch(Alpha, Beta, _, Eval) :- Alpha>=Beta | Eval=Alpha.
branch(Alpha, Beta, [Pos|Siblings], Eval)
    :- NAlpha:=0-Alpha, NBeta:=0-Beta,
       alphabeta(Pos, NBeta, NAlpha, PosEval),
       max(PosEval, Alpha, Alpha1),
       branch(Alpha1, Beta, Siblings, Eval).
```

Like the pseudo-code algorithm, this program will be sequential since the evaluation of any branch is not started until the evaluation of its left sibling has completed and returned an alpha value. In fact, it can be seen that the program follows the general pattern of the previous linear search programs.

6.13 Parallel Game-Tree Search

The sequential nature of alpha-beta search comes from the desire to avoid speculative computation. Since search of any one branch is likely to narrow the alpha-beta window, it makes sense to wait until it has completed before searching the next branch. This is particularly so because in most cases the branches in a game tree search can be ordered so that there is a strong likelihood that search of the initial few branches will reduce the alpha-beta window so as to make search of the rest unnecessary [Marsland and Campbell, 1982]. It is thus particularly important that the parallelism in parallel game tree search is ordered so that that most likely to contribute to a solution is given priority.

The usual approach to parallel alpha-beta search is described as *tree-splitting* [Finkel and Fishburn, 1983], which works in a similar way to the parallel tree search considered previously, setting up actors to search every subtree in parallel. A different approach to parallel alpha-beta search which will not be considered here divides the alpha-beta window among processors and sets up multiple searches of the complete tree with the different subwindows [Baudet, 1978]. In tree-splitting alpha-beta search, when one subtree terminates and returns an alpha value, if this results in an updating of alpha, the new alpha-beta window is sent to those branch searches which have not yet terminated. This means that search actors also have to take account of the possibility that they may receive updated alpha-beta windows from their parents. If so, they have to be passed down to their children and search is halted if they cause alpha to exceed beta. Huntbach and Burton [1988] develop the tree-splitting algorithm of Fishburn and Finkel [1983] by moving away from an approach that depends on a particular tree structured architecture towards a more abstract virtual tree [Burton and Huntbach, 1984] in which a tree of potentially parallel actors matching the search tree is constructed. It is left to the underlying system to map it onto a physical architecture. The algorithm is described in a pseudo-code style using asynchronous remote procedure calls:

```
process alphabeta(p:position; α,β:valuation):valuation = {
    asynchronous procedure report(α1:valuation)= {
        if α1≥α then {
            α:=α1;
            for all remaining children do child.update(-β,-α);
            if α≥β then terminate
        }
    }

    asynchronous procedure update(α1,β1:valuation)= {
        α:=max(α,α1);
        β:=min(β,β1);
        for all remaining children do child.update(-β,-α);
        if α≥β then terminate
    }

    for each successor position of p, p₁ to p_w do
        setup new process alphabeta(pi,-β,-α);
    wait until no remaining children;
    parent.report(-α);
    terminate
}
```

In this program, report is the procedure that sends new alpha values upwards only when all children have terminated. The procedure update sends new alpha and beta values downwards and is executed whenever new alpha or alpha and beta values are received. The following gives a direct translation of this algorithm into GDC:

```
alphabeta(Pos,_,Alpha,Beta,Eval) :- Alpha>=Beta
    | Eval=Alpha.
alphabeta(Pos,[(Alpha1,Beta1)|Upds],Alpha,Beta,Eval)
    :- max(Alpha,Alpha1,Alpha2),
       min(Beta,Beta1,Beta2),
       alphabeta(Pos,Upds,Alpha2,Beta2,Eval).
```

```
alphabeta(Pos,Upds,Alpha,Beta,Eval)
    :-  unknown(Upds), Alpha<Beta
    |   isleaf(Position,Flag),
        expand(Flag,Position,Upds,Alpha,Beta,Eval).


expand(true,Position,_,_,_,Eval)
    :-  evaluate(Position,Eval).
expand(false,Position,Upds1,Alpha,Beta,Eval)
    :-  successors(Position,Succs),
        branch(Upds1,Alpha,Beta,Succs,Reports),
        manager(Upds,Alpha,Beta,Reports,Upds1,Eval).


branch(Upds,Alpha,Beta,[],Reports)
    :-  Reports=[].
branch(Upds,Alpha,Beta,[Pos|Siblings],Reports)
    :-  heuristic(Pos,H),
        alphabeta(Pos,Upds,Alpha,Beta,Report)@priority(H),
        branch(Upds,Alpha,Beta,Siblings,Reports1),
        insert(Report,Reports1,Reports).


insert(Alpha,Alphas,Alphas1) :- wait(Alpha)
    |   Alphas1=[Alpha|Alphas].
insert(Alpha,[Alpha1|Alphas],Alphas1)
    :-  Alphas1=[Alpha1|Alphas2],
        insert(Alpha,Alphas,Alphas2).
insert(Alpha,[],Alphas) :- Alphas=[Alpha].


manager(InUpds,Alpha,Beta,[Alpha1|Reports],OutUpds,Eval)
    :-  Alpha1>Alpha
    |   NAlpha:=0-Alpha1,
        NBeta:=0-Beta,
        OutUpds = [(NBeta,NAlpha)|OutUpds1],
        manager(InUpds,Alpha1,Beta,Reports,OutUpds1,Eval).
manager(InUpds,Alpha,Beta,[Alpha1|Reports],OutUpds,Eval)
    :-  Alpha1<=Alpha
    |   reports(InUpds,Alpha,Beta,Reports,OutUpds,Eval).
manager([(Alpha1,Beta1)|InUpds],Alpha,Beta,Reports,OutUpds,Eval)
    :-  max(Alpha,Alpha1,Alpha2),
        min(Beta,Beta1,Beta2),
        NBeta:=0-Beta2,
        NAlpha:=0-Alpha2,
        OutUpds = [(NBeta,NAlpha)|OutUpds1],
        manager(InUpds,Alpha2,Beta2,Reports,OutUpds1,Eval).
manager(InUpds,Alpha,Beta,[],OutUpds,Eval) :- Eval=Alpha
    |   OutUpds=[]
```

Note again the use of **unknown** and **wait** to ensure the latest alpha and beta values are used. Some improvements can be made at the cost of a rather more complex program (but one, which is not such a direct translation of the concurrent algorithm). For example, checks on update values could ensure that update messages are not forwarded when they do not change the alpha-beta window.

The actor structure is complicated by the use of a single one-to-many stream used to pass updates down the tree from the **manager** actor and a merger of results using **insert** to insert individual reports into the stream of reports passed upwards into the manager. The situation after the expansion of an individual **alphabeta** actor and before the expansion of any of its descendants is shown in Figure 6.13.1.

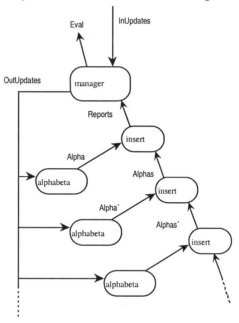

Fig. 6.13.1 The alpha-beta actor structure

If the heuristic used is the depth in the tree, the search will revert to standard alpha-beta search on a single processor. As suggested in [Huntbach and Burton, 1988], ordering of the tree as in [Marsland and Campbell, 1982] can be obtained if the priority is a real number, composed of the sum of an integer representing the depth and a number between 0 and 1 representing the ordering evaluation of the position. Alternatively, if the integer part of the priority is a heuristic evaluation and the mantissa based on the depth to distinguish between positions of the same heuristic at differing depths, a parallel version of the SSS* algorithm [Stockman, 1979] is obtained. In fact, Kumar and Kanal [1983] give a general formulation which indicates that both alpha-beta search and SSS* can be fitted into the branch-and-bound model. Wilson [1987] also notes that in a concurrent logic program alpha-beta search and SSS* are simply variants of a common game-tree search program which depend on scheduling, though his program does not make use of priorities. Instead it relies on an explicit oracle actor as part of the program which interacts with the search.

6.14 Parallel Search and Cooperative Distributed Problem Solving

Lesser [1990] considers distributed state space search, as considered in this chapter, to be the model on which more complex schemes of co-operative problem-solving may be based. Many of the problems and tradeoffs that are encountered in distributed search are simple forms of things that recur throughout attempts to distribute problem solving across a network of agents. For example, the decision over when to pass bounds in branch-and-bound search that may cause cutoffs generalizes to the problem of trading off communication of information on the global problem between agents, with its inevitable overhead, and allowing agents to pursue their own subtask untrammeled by communication from elsewhere. Such communications may show the subtask to be redundant, or give information that could help solve it, but they may be merely unnecessary interference. The distribution of tasks to agents in a multi-agent system, involving the recognition of potential interactions and the possibility of interference both beneficial and disadvantageous (as with the search anomalies discussed in Section 6.9) is met in a simple form in distributed search.

Lesser was involved in a large-scale project called the *Distributed Vehicle Monitoring Testbed* (DVMT) which served as an exemplar for distributed problem solving leading towards multi-agent systems [Lesser and Corkhill, 1983]. The basis of this system was that sensors distributed over an environment collected acoustic data at discrete sensed times. Sensors were attached to local processors that were linked into a global network. The global problem was to interpret the data as vehicle tracks.

In our distributed search, distribution of subtasks occurs in order to obtain speedup by dividing the work. There is some of this in the DVMT as well: actors situated in part of the environment where there is a lot of data picked up may pass some of their interpretation work to processors situated in quiet areas which would otherwise be idle. However, in this case the distribution also maps a physical distribution in the data collection. The partial interpretation of raw sensory data at local level into patterns, which may be more concisely represented, avoids the communications costs associated with one central processor. One processor may advise another of those parts of its data on which it would be advisable to concentrate work when the first has discovered a vehicle track that leads into the sensing area of the second. This is similar to the way in which in parallel alpha-beta search the passing of alpha-beta bounds from the search of one subtree advises another search agent of those parts of its subtree on which it would be most beneficial to concentrate search. In the DVMT the sharing of partial results and the putting together of local plans into a global interpretation of the data is built into a framework called *Partial Global Planning* [Durfee and Lesser, 1991]. A partial global plan (PGP) is the knowledge of the global situation a node has locally, based on its partial information and information received from other nodes, plus a proposed plan of action. As problem solving proceeds, nodes exchange PGPs gradually building up a more coherent global picture. Experiments with this framework show there is a fine balance in the trade-off of communication overhead against focussing on more relevant processing.

Chapter 7

Distributed Constraint Solving

When spider webs unite they can tie up a lion.

Ethiopian proverb

Combinatorial search algorithms of the type discussed in Chapter 6 are usually described in terms of a single agent manipulating or traversing a representation of the search space. As shown, however, when the constraint that the search algorithm is run sequentially is removed, they may be viewed as a collection of agents, organized in a tree-shaped network, which co-operate in finding an optimal solution, passing suggested solutions upwards and bounds to solutions downwards. There is no centralized representation of the search space or overall central planner.

The field of *Distributed Artificial Intelligence* (DAI) [Bond and Gasser, 1988] extends the idea of AI problem solving by dividing the work into a number of co-operating modules. In particular it places an emphasis on problem solving which from the outset is seen in terms of multiple agents. Gasser and Bond distinguish this from *Parallel Artificial Intelligence* (PAI), by which they mean using parallel architectures and languages simply to improve performance in existent AI systems. With DAI the aim is as much to advance understanding of the nature of reasoning and intelligent behavior among multiple agents as to improve performance.

The origin of DAI lies with early, largely speculative, work in computer science that looked for alternative models of computation to the single-thread von Neumann model. The work centered on Hewitt at MIT, which saw computation in terms of message passing [Hewitt, 1977], is an important early component. Hewitt himself acknowledged the influence of work by Newell [1962]. A particularly important motivating early work in DAI was the *Hearsay-II* system [Erman et al., 1980] for understanding spoken speech. This evolved from the production-system approach by considering multiple threads of control operating on a single database of information. A striking metaphor was used, that each thread of control could be considered as an expert in some aspect of speech understanding. The database could be considered as a blackboard (Newell [1962] also used the blackboard metaphor) which these experts used to communicate their partial solutions to the problem between each other. For example, one expert might have knowledge of phonetics and would write hypotheses to the blackboard based on grouping sounds into syllables. Another expert might have knowledge of grammar and would work at putting together words into sentences. This could also be viewed as coroutining. The method of co-operatively developing hypotheses was claimed to overcome some of the problems of combinatorial explosion associated with a single-thread control search with backtracking.

Hearsay's metaphor of a community of experts clustered around a blackboard has led to a range of speculative work in which human social systems are taken as a model for the development of computational systems based around co-operating distributed processes. Kornfeld and Hewitt [1980] compared problem solving in a parallel language they developed called *Ether* [Kornfeld, 1979] with the way communities of scientists develop answers to scientific questions. Hewitt [1986] compared a human office structure with a computational open system. Miller and Drexler [1988] considered that the arguments of economists who preferred a free-market economy to a centrally planned system might also apply to computational systems. The way in which societies of animals exhibit complex behavior emerging from individual animals obeying fairly simple rules has also been inspirational in the development of DAI systems [Drogoul and Ferber, 1992].

At its limit, the development of DAI leads to an "open system" characterized as a large collection of computational services which use each other without central coordination, trust or complete knowledge of each other. They need to act concurrently and asynchronously. Kahn and Miller [1988] note that few programming languages are adequate as foundations on which to program large-scale open systems, but suggest that actor languages and concurrent logic languages are exceptions.

The Hearsay-II system fell some way short of the open-system model, as its communication between computational components, or knowledge sources, was through the centralized blackboard rather than directly between individual knowledge sources. In fact although the knowledge sources were conceptually independent they did not compute concurrently. Rather, there was a single coordinating mechanism which dictated a priority order [Hayes-Roth and Lesser, 1977]. Given the lack of real parallelism and its associated indeterminism, this mechanism meant that in reality Hearsay was centrally controlled. Attempts to introduce real parallelism [Fernel and Lesser, 1977] were hampered by the need for strong coordination to manage multiple accesses to the single blackboard (approximately half the processing time was taken up in coordinating the blackboard) and resulted in limited speedup. This illustrates the point made above that a conceptual distribution into independent entities as a design issue to structure an AI system is not necessarily related to a physical distribution to speed performance. The introduction of multiple blackboards was suggested by Lesser and Erman [1980]. But Hewitt and Lieberman [1984] argued against the use of blackboards on the grounds that a single one is a bottleneck but multiple blackboards are an unnecessary complication that can be dispensed with altogether in favor of a completely distributed message-passing system. Taking this further, any central coordinating mechanism can be seen as a bottleneck acting against the efficiency of a large-scale distributed system.

Blackboard systems may therefore be seen as an intermediate step on the way to full distributed processing. Another intermediate step was various simple models for distributing parallel computations over networks of processors. The virtual tree machine concept of Huntbach and Burton [1984; 1988] for instance, used a simple mechanism in which individual processors swapped information on their workload with their neighbors. Based on this information a decision was made on whether to offload work from one processor to another. There was no overall central coordinating mechanism and each processor made decisions based only on knowledge received from its neighbor. With no global view available, very simple protocols for the exchange of work proved sufficient to maintain a fair share of work between processors leading to significant speedups in search problems similar to those discussed in Chapter 6.

The virtual tree machine, however, assumed homogeneity both in processes and processors. Each processor in the network could be considered identical to every other; each process would run the same program, with a copy of that program available on every processor. Clearly, the component processes of Hearsay-II were heterogeneous. Allocation of processes to processors would be a considerably more complex problem if different processors had different programs on them so that each would have its own problem solving abilities. In these circumstances communication between the processes to decide where and when a computation is to be executed is considerably more complex. Davis and Smith [1983] use the metaphor of negotiation to describe the interchange of information and agreement on distribution of work. They devised a formal notation, the *contract net protocol* [Smith, 1980], by which when a new task is created its existence may be made known to the various processing elements and those able to execute it could then decide whether to do so. If several decided to do so, a decision on which to use is made using a bidding system. The analogy was drawn between this and business management in which contracts may be put out to tender and the best bid accepted. Subsequent work made further use of this analogy [Malone et al., 1988]. Growth in these ideas during the 1980s may be linked with the interest expressed in free market economics and the use of market mechanisms generally during this time. (In Britain, for example, a range of Acts of Parliament passed in that time either put previously centrally controlled government services out to tender or introduced internal markets [Chartered Institute for Public Finance and Accountancy, 1995]). Kraus [1993], among others, has taken the metaphor so far as to introduce a pseudo-money scheme to reward agents that have been contracted to do others' work or to barter for future contracts. The distinction between processors and processes was also broken down since a conceptual processor may itself be an abstract software entity provided by an interpreter (Chapter 8), leading to the idea of a network of software agents negotiating and competing with each other.

The extent to which agents co-operate is an issue in this style of distributed processing. Early work in DAI assumed that agents would have common or non-conflicting actors. Rosenschein and Genesereth [1985] called this the *benevolent agent assumption* and suggested that it was unrealistic in a large-scale system with a highly complex degree of interaction. They suggested that in such a system it might be better to have a framework that recognizes and resolves sub-actor conflict. This is an extension of the software engineering principle of trying to minimize the dependency between modules. Breaking with the assumption that all components will co-operate perfectly increases the robustness of a system, as it is no longer necessary to have to take into account explicitly every possible interaction. It also means the system can be changed by adding or deleting agents without having to reprogram them. On the other hand, there is an overhead associated with having to establish links through negotiation. Jennings [1995] gives some experimental results exploring different degrees of co-operation in an industrial multi-agent system.

At the minimum, agents need to have a common language by which they communicate, whether they communicate directly or through the medium of a blackboard. Agents with a communication link to other agents (acquaintances in the Actor terminology) may be said to "know" those other agents, the extent to which the code for one can rely on assumptions about the behavior for another can be described as its "knowledge" of it. This knowledge may increase in run time as agents co-operate. Continuing the metaphor with human society, the set of assumptions about other agents under which individual agents operate may be referred to as "social laws" [Shoham and Tennenholtz, 1995] and compared with human conceptions of knowledge and actions [Gasser, 1991]. It has also been suggested that these social laws could themselves emerge through negotiation between agents [Shoham and Tennenholtz, 1992]. In this case, there would need to be a set of social metalaws to describe how interactions would occur to lay down the social laws. (The issue of laws and metalaws are discussed in Chapter 8). Partial evaluation, covered in Chapter 9, is of relevance here too. The overhead of a loose control resolved at run-time in order to give a flexible system may in some cases be overcome by partially evaluating that system with respect to some particular circumstances. In which case, the negotiation would take place during partial evaluation time and the resulting residual program would have a fixed pattern of interaction as in a more traditional system.

7.1 All-Pairs Shortest Path Problem

While there is not space here to give GDC programs for a full multi-agent system, with heterogeneous agents interacting, some idea of the possibilities can be given by a family of graph programs in GDC which work on a distributed principle, with no overall control or global data structure. These programs have in common the representation of each vertex in a graph by a GDC actor and each arc by a shared channel. The principle of using recursion to turn ephemeral actors to long-lived actors and partial binding to turn use-once channels to long-lived channels is used.

The first problem considered is the all-pairs shortest-path problem on a directed graph. Initially, each vertex is represented by an actor that has as data: a unique identifier, a list of channel/cost pairs representing outward directed arcs and a list of channel/cost pairs representing incoming arcs. An undirected graph would have to be represented by having two channels for each arc, one for each direction. An example graph is shown in Figure 7.1.1 where the letters are vertex names and the numbers arc costs. The network of actors represents this figure:

```
:-  vertex(a, [a(BA,7),a(GA,9)],[a(AC,5),a(AD,3),a(AF,8)]),
    vertex(b, [a(DB,4),a(FB,6)], [a(BA,7)]),
    vertex(c, [a(AC,5),a(DC,2)], [a(CE,4)]),
    vertex(d, [a(AD,3),a(ED,1)],[a(DB,4),a(DC,2),a(DG,2),a(DF,6)]),
    vertex(e, [a(CE,4),a(GE,5)], [a(ED,1),a(EF,10)]),
    vertex(f, [a(AF,8),a(EF,10),a(DF,6)],[a(FB,6),a(FG,7)]),
    vertex(g, [a(FG,7),a(DG,2)], [a(GA,9),a(GE,5)]).
```

Note that for convenience of reference, the channels have been given names that correspond to the arcs they represent.

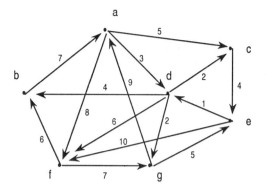

Fig. 7.1.1 An example graph for the shortest path problem

The distributed solution to the shortest path problem requires channels representing arcs to be used as streams. Messages are sent in the *reverse* direction to their direction in the graph, since messages received *from* another node contain the path and cost *to* that node. The algorithm is initialized by each actor representing the vertex named x sending a message down its outgoing streams of the form p(x,[x],N) where N is the associated cost of the arc. Each actor also merges its incoming streams and sets up a table. When an actor representing vertex y receives a message of the form p(x,P,N) it checks its table to see if it has a record of a path to x of lower cost than N. If it has, it does nothing more until it receives its next message. If it does not, it updates its table and sends on each of its outgoing streams a message of the form p(x,[y|P],N′) where N′ is obtained from N by adding the cost paired with the arc represented by the stream. So actors receive messages containing a destination, a route leading to that destination and the cost of that route. If no other route is known to that destination or an existing known route is of higher cost, the new route is stored as the lowest cost route. Messages are sent out to each further node, z, proposing a new route to x through y as the shortest route from z to x.

The code to initialize **vertex/3** is:

```
vertex(Id,InArcs,OutArcs)
    :- mergeall(OutArcs,InStream),
       emptytable(Table),
       addtotable(p(Id,[],0),Table,Table1),
       sendouts(Id,[],0,InArcs,OutStreams),
       vertex(Id,InStreams,OutStreams,Table1).

mergeall([],M) :- M=[].
mergeall([a(Stream,Cost)|Arcs],M)
    :- mergeall(Arcs,M1), merge(Stream,M1,M).
```

where **mergeall** uses standard stream merger to merge all the incoming streams into one stream. The actor **emptytable** sets up a new table of paths and lowest costs and **addtotable** adds an entry to this table. The code for **sendouts** is given below.

The code for an actor representing a vertex is:

```
vertex(Id,[p(To,Path,Cost)|Ins],Outs,Table)
   :- lowerCostPathExists(To,Cost,Table,Flag),
      vertex1(Flag,Id,To,[Id|Path],Cost,Ins,Outs,Table).

vertex1(true,Id,To,Path,Cost,Ins,Outs,Table)
   :- vertex(Id,Ins,Outs,Table).
vertex1(false,Id,To,Path,Cost,Ins,Outs,Table)
   :- addToTable(p(To,Path,Cost),Table,Table1),
      sendouts(To,Path,Cost,Outs,Outs1),
      vertex(Id,Ins,Outs1,Table1).

sendouts(From,Path,Cost,[],Outs)
   :- Outs=[].
sendouts(From,Path,Cost,[a(Out,Cost1)|Outs],Outs1)
   :- Cost2:=Cost+Cost1,
      Out=[p(From,Path,Cost2)|Out1],
      sendouts(From,Path,Cost,Outs,Outs2),
      Outs1=[a(Out1,Cost1)|Outs2].
```

where **lowerCostPathExists**(From,Cost,Table,Flag) binds Flag to true if a path to From of cost lower than Cost exists in table Table and to false otherwise.

At any time a vertex will hold an approximation to the lowest cost paths to other vertices. This approximation will improve as more messages are sent. When the whole system reaches a quiescent state when no more messages are being sent, the all-pairs shortest path problem is solved. In practice, there would also be a way of querying vertices to find the solutions held in them.

Consider the graph in Figure 7.1.1 and assume that the tables of paths are just lists, following initialization, the actor network becomes:

```
:- merge([p(c,[c],5)|AC],[p(d,[],3)|AD],M0),
   merge(M0,[p(f,[f],8)|AF],A),
   vertex(a,A,[a(BA,7),a(GA,9)],[p(a,[],0)]),
   vertex(b,[p(a,[a],7)|BA],[a(DB,4),a(FB,6)],[p(b,[],0)]),
   vertex(c,[p(e,[e],4)|CE],[a(AC,5),a(DC,2)],[p(c,[],0)]),
   merge([p(b,[b],4)|DB],[p(d,[],2)|DC],M1),
   merge([p(g,[g],2)|DG],M1,M2),
   merge([p(f,[f],6)|DF],M2,D),
   vertex(d,D,[a(AD,3),a(ED,1)],[p(d,[],0)]),
   merge([p(d,[d],1)|ED],[p(f,[],10)|EF],E),
   vertex(e,E,[a(CE,4),a(GE,5)],[p(e,[],0)]),
   merge([p(b,[b],6)|FB],[p(g,[],7)|FG],F),
   vertex(f,F,[a(AF,8),a(EF,10),a(DF,6)],[p(f,[],0)]),
   merge([p(a,[a],9)|GA],[p(e,[],5)|GE],G),
   vertex(g,G,[a(FG,7),a(DG,2)],[p(g,[],0)]).
```

The next step will depend on which actors are chosen for reduction (no commitment was made to these existing on separate processors so they will not necessarily reduce in parallel) and how the indeterminism of **merge** is resolved. Note that the actors for vertices b and c have no inward merger of streams as b and c each have only one outgoing arc (and hence only one incoming stream of messages). Suppose that these are chosen for reducing. Then b, having received a message from a will record that it now knows a path to a and will send messages to d and f proposing that they use this path to access a. Vertex c, having received a message from e, will similarly record that it knows a path to e and will send a message to a and d, resulting in:

```
:-  merge([p(c,[c],5),p(e,[c,e],9)|AC],[p(d,[],3)|AD],M0),
    merge(M0,[p(f,[f],8)|AF],A),
    vertex(a,A,[a(BA,7),a(GA,9)],[p(a,[],0)]),
    vertex(b,BA,[a(DB,4),a(FB,6)],[p(a,[a],7),p(b,[],0)]),
    vertex(c,CE,[a(AC,5),a(DC,2)],[p(c,[],0),p(e,[e],4)]),
    merge([p(b,[b],4),p(a,[b,a],11)|DB],[p(d,[],2),p(e,[c,e],6)|DC]M1),
    merge([p(g,[g],2)|DG],M1,M2),
    merge([p(f,[f],6)|DF],M2,D),
    vertex(d,D,[a(AD,3),a(ED,1)],[p(d,[],0)]),
    merge([p(d,[d],1)|ED],[p(f,[],10)|EF],E),
    vertex(e,E,[a(CE,4),a(GE,5)],[p(e,[],0)]),
    merge([p(b,[b],6),p(a,[b,a],13)|FB],[p(g,[],7)|FG],F),
    vertex(f,F,[a(AF,8),a(EF,10),a(DF,6)],[p(f,[],0)]),
    merge([p(a,[a],9)|GA],[p(e,[],5)|GE],G),
    vertex(g,G,[a(FG,7),a(DG,2)],[p(g,[],0)]).
```

Suppose that all mergers are resolved by passing on the head of the first stream, the actor network will then become:

```
:-  merge([p(e,[c,e],9)|AC],[p(d,[],3)|AD],M0),
    merge([p(c,[c],5)|M0],[p(f,[f],8)|AF],A),
    vertex(a,A,[a(BA,7),a(GA,9)],[p(a,[],0)]),
    vertex(b,BA,[a(DB,4),a(FB,6)],[p(a,[a],7),p(b,[],0)]),
    vertex(c,CE,[a(AC,5),a(DC,2)],[p(c,[],0),p(e,[e],4)]),
    merge([p(a,[b,a],11)|DB],[p(d,[],2),p(e,[c,e],6)|DC],M1),
    merge(DG,[p(b,[b],4)|M1],M2),
    merge(DF,[p(g,[g],2)|M2],D),
    vertex(d,[p(f,[f],6)|D],[a(AD,3),a(ED,1)],[p(d,[],0)]),
    merge(ED,[p(f,[],10)|EF],E),
    vertex(e,[p(d,[d],1)|E],[a(CE,4),a(GE,5)],[p(e,[],0)]),
    merge([p(a,[b,a],13)|FB],[p(g,[],7)|FG],F),
    vertex(f,[p(b,[b],6)|F],[a(AF,8),a(EF,10),a(DF,6)],[p(f,[],0)]),
    merge(GA,[p(e,[],5)|GE],G),
    vertex(g,[p(a,[a],9)|G],[a(FG,7),a(DG,2)],[p(g,[],0)]).
```

resulting in the actors for vertices d, e, f and g having messages to deal with. From these messages they will record that they now know paths to f, d, b and a respectively and send further messages and the system will continue in this way.

Although the code is simple, it shows some elements of the DAI paradigm. There is no overall coordinator or global record of information as there is in more standard forms of solving shortest path problems (for example Dijkstra's method [1959]).

Actors negotiate on finding an overall solution by sending messages proposing routes to each other. The language used for communication is very simple, just the agreement that messages have the three arguments, destination, path and cost in that order. Actors have knowledge of the rest of the graph in the form of the table of routes, which grows as computation proceeds. It would be possible to extend this framework leading to a more complete DAI system, allowing a variety of different messages to be exchanged, with individual actors being heterogeneous, each holding different sorts of information and having different sorts of problem-solving abilities.

7.2 The Graph Coloring Problem

The graph-coloring problem is another example of a graph-oriented problem, which is often used as an example of constraint solving. Mackworth [1977] notes that many Artificial Intelligence tasks can be formulated as constraint solving problems and solved by backtracking. Agreeing with Sussmann and McDermott's criticisms of the inclusion of backtracking as a feature in programming languages [1972], he notes that crude backtracking solutions to constraint problems are often inefficient at solving them. Forms of constraint propagation, such as that proposed by Waltz [1975] for the interpretation of line drawings, can drastically cut the search space. Yokoo [1998] discusses the connection between distributed constraint solving and multi-agent systems.

The k-graph-coloring problem is to find a labeling of the vertices of a graph with labels chosen from a set of k colors, such that no two vertices labeled with the same color are connected by a single edge. The chromatic number of a graph is the minimum value of k such that a k-coloration of the graph can be found. The famous 4-color theorem [Appel and Haken, 1989] is related to this problem. Many practical resource allocation problems are variations of the graph-coloring problem [Chaitin, 1982], [Wood, 1969]. For most graphs, it is in fact easy either to find a k-coloration or to show that no such k-coloration exists [Turner, 1988] although the problem can shown in general to be NP-complete [Gibbons, 1985]. Cheeseman et al. [1991] note that the reason for this seeming contradiction is that graph coloring is an example of a problem where there is only a small distance between examples which are easy to solve and examples which are easy to show insoluble. The really hard problems are those that fall in this band, in the case of graph coloring within a small range of density.

Since solutions are easy to find, brute-force search methods, such as those programmed in Chapter 6, oriented towards problems where it is difficult to find a solution are often not the most appropriate way to solve them. (In other problems, such as chess playing, brute-force search methods continue to outperform others [Hsu et al., 1990]). In some cases, while the problem of finding the optimal solution is NP-complete, acceptable sub-optimal solutions can be found in polynomial time. Korf [1990], for example, finds solutions to sliding-tile puzzles like the 8-puzzle of Chapter 6, which are too large to be found by the branch-and-bound search methods. Improved solutions can be found by applying modifications to the original sub-optimal solution [Minton et al., 1990]. The simulated annealing method [Kirkpatrick et al., 1983] is a variant of this.

A concurrent algorithm for finding a k-coloration of a graph, which is particularly suitable for us, was published by Bhandari, Krishna and Siewiork [1988] (henceforth called the *BKS algorithm*). It is approximate, as it cannot be guaranteed to find a k-coloration if one exists. But in most cases it converges quickly on a solution. It is described in terms of communicating actors representing one vertex of the graph and communicating with other actors representing nearest neighbors. Hence the problem falls into the same family as our all-pairs shortest path algorithm. As there is no concept of direction in edge coloring and the algorithm requires two-way communication between vertices connected by an edge, each edge must be represented by two channels, one for sending messages one way, the other for sending them the other.

The algorithm assumes that the actors representing vertices are each uniquely numbered. Each holds a list of the colors it may choose from, initially of length k, but it may be reduced as coloration of neighboring vertices constrains the possibilities that may be chosen. The algorithm is synchronous. On each cycle each actor selects a color from its list of possibilities and informs the actors representing neighboring nodes of the color chosen. Then any actor labeled i, which has chosen a color not chosen by any of its neighbors labeled j, where j>i, makes the choice permanent, informing its neighbors that it has done so. Following this, all processors delete from their list of possible colors, any of which has been chosen and made permanent by any of their neighbors. The next cycle proceeds with only those actors, which have not made permanent choices. If any actor has the number of colors it can choose from reduced to 0 then the algorithms has failed to find a k-coloration. It must eventually terminate either with a failure or with a k-coloration. This is because on each cycle the actor who is active with the highest index number will always be able to make its choice permanent and so the number of active actors is reduced by at least one on every cycle.

Some elements of negotiation may be observed in this algorithm. Actors may be said to negotiate on colors by making tentative choices and discussing them with their neighbors. There is a "social law" expressing a strict order of precedence on the actors establishing when one must defer to another should both choose the same color.

In GDC the assumption that each actor is on its own processor need not be maintained. A node represents an actor and the mapping of actors to vertices is orthogonal to the abstract description of the algorithm in terms of actors. Although there is no direct synchronization in GDC, the synchronization of the algorithm will arise through the exchange of messages in the system. As messages pass both ways between actors representing vertices connected by an arc, a pair of channels must represent each arc. These will be represented by C_{ij}/C_{ji} being the pair of channels linking the actors representing vertices i and j. The convention will be that the first channel in the pair is used for input, the second for output, the / is just an infix tupling operator. Each actor will store its links to other actors in two lists, one representing arcs linking to lower numbered vertices, the other representing arcs linking to higher numbered vertices. For example the initial setup for the graph in Figure 7.2.1 (similar to the one used for shortest path problem, but the numbers are vertex labels and the graph is undirected) is:

```
:-  vertex(1,C,[C12/C21,C13/C31,C14/C41,C16/C61,C17/C71],[],S1),
    vertex(2,C,[C24/C42,C26/C62],[C21/C12],S2),
    vertex(3,C,[C34/C43,C35/C53],[C31/C13],S3),
    vertex(4,C,[C45/C54,C46/64,C47/C74],[C41/C14,C42/C24,C43/C34],[],S4),
    vertex(5,C,[C56/C65,C57/C75],[C53/C35,C54/C45],[],S5),
    vertex(6,C,[C67/C76],[C61/C16,C62/C26,C64/C46,C65/C56],[],S6),
    vertex(7,C,[],[C71/C17,C74/C47,C76/C67],S7).
```

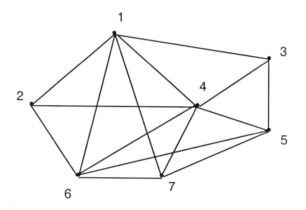

Fig. 7.2.1 An example graph for the graph coloring problem

Here C is bound to the list of possible colors, while the channel Si is used to return the color eventually chosen for vertex i.

A direct implementation of the BKS algorithm works by having each actor send a message of the form mess(Color,Accepted) on all of its output channels. The channel Color will be bound to the color it has selected from its list of possibilities. The channel Accepted will be initially unbound, but will later be bound to either true or false depending on whether the color is accepted permanently (which is not known until it has received and analyzed all incoming messages). A test is made on all incoming messages from actors with higher numbered labels and Accepted is bound to true if none of them has the same color as that selected by the actor, false otherwise. If Accepted is bound to true, the actor halts and records the color chosen. Otherwise it goes through its list of incoming messages again, removing from its list of possible colors any color that has been permanently accepted by any neighbor. The code for this is:

```
vertex(V,Cols,HiChans,LoChans,Sol)
   :- select(Cols,Col),
      sendCol(Col,Accepted,HiChans),
      sendCol(Col,Accepted,LoChans),
      accepted(Col,HiChans,Accepted),
      retry(Accepted,V,Col,Cols,HiChans,LoChans,Sol).

sendCol(Col,Accepted,[]).
sendCol(Col,Accepted,[I/O|Chans])
   :- O=[mess(Col,Accepted)|Chan],
      sendCol(Col,Accepted,Chans).

accepted(Col,[],Accepted)
   :- Accepted=true.
accepted(MyCol,[[mess(Col,A)|Chan]/O|Chans],Accepted)
   :- Col=MyCol
   |  Accepted=false.
accepted(MyCol,[[mess(Col,A)|Chan]/O|Chans],Accepted)
   :- Col=/=MyCol
   |  accepted(MyCol,Chans,Accepted).

retry(false,V,Col,Cols,HiChans,LoChans,Solution)
   :- restrictCols(Cols,HiChans,NewCols1,HiChans1),
      restrictCols(NewCols1,LoChans,NewCols,LoChans1),
      vertex(V,NewCols,HiChans1,LoChans1,Solution).
retry(true,V,Col,Cols,HiChans,LoChans,Solution)
   :- Solution=node(V,Col).

restrictCols(Cols,[[mess(Col,true)|I]/[Mess|O]|Chans],
          NewCols,NewChans)
   :- removeCol(Col,Cols,NewCols1),
      restrictCols(NewCols1,Chans,NewCols,NewChans).
restrictCols(Cols,[[mess(Col,false)|I]/[Mess|O]|Chans],
          NewCols,NewChans)
   :- restrictCols(Cols,Chans,NewCols,NewChans1),
      NewChans=[I/O|NewChans1].
restrictCols(Cols,[],NewCols,NewChans)
   :- NewCols=Cols,
      NewChans=[].
```

This will completely implement the BKS algorithm, given the initial vertex setup, needing only code for **select** to be added. One possibility is always to take the first color from the list, which will lead to a vertex choosing color n from a list of k colors only if it cannot choose any of colors 1 to n−1 due to neighbors having permanently accepting each of them. Note that although there is no central synchronization mechanism, the fact that each actor must read every message from its neighbors before sending out a further message acts to synchronize them.

Although the code given above directly reflects the original BKS algorithm, an inefficiency is apparent. The list of channels from higher numbered vertices on any particular vertex is traversed twice. It is first traversed to find if any of them has chosen the same color as chosen by the vertex in question. It is again traversed in **restrictCols** to see if any of the colors chosen by higher numbered vertices has been accepted permanently. The list of channels from lower numbered vertices is traversed only in **restrictCols**. But **restrictCols** requires the Accepted argument in the messages to be bound, which can only take place when the lower indexed actor has received and read all the messages from its higher indexed neighbors. Thus it is not necessary for two neighboring actors to send messages to each other simultaneously. The lower indexed actor can wait until it has received a message from the higher and reply by back-communication without affecting the amount of potential parallelism.

This leads to an improved algorithm in which arcs are represented by a single channel. Messages between actors take the form mess(Col,Accepted,Return). Here Col is the color chosen by the higher indexed actor; Accepted indicates whether it has been accepted permanently (as before, it may be unbound at the time the original message is sent) and Return is used for the return communication from the lower indexed actor. Return is set to none if that actor does not make a permanent choice of color in that cycle, or to the color chosen if it does. The initial actor setup for the graph shown previously is:

```
:-  vertex(1,C,[C12,C13,C14,C16,C17],[],S1),
    vertex(2,C,[C24,C26],[C12],S2),
    vertex(3,C,[C34,C35],[C13],S3),
    vertex(4,C,[C45,C46,C47],[C14,C24,C34],[],S4),
    vertex(5,C,[C56,C57],[CC35,CC45],[],S5),
    vertex(6,C,[C67],[C16,C26,C46,C56],[],S6),
    vertex(7,C,[],[C17,C47,C67],S7).
```

where C is the list of possible colors. The revised program (less **restrictCol**, which remains unchanged) is:

```
vertex(V,Cols,HiChans,LoChans,Solution)
    :-  select(Cols,Col),
        sendCol(Col,Accepted,LoChans),
        accepted(Col,HiChans,Accepted),
        retry(Accepted,V,Col,Cols,HiChans,LoChans,Solution).

sendCol(Col,Accepted,[]).
sendCol(Col,Accepted,[X|Chans])
    :-  X=[mess(Col,Accepted,YourCol)|Chan],
        sendCol(Col,Accepted,Chans).

accepted(Col,[],Accepted) :- Accepted=true.
accepted(MyCol,[[mess(Col,A,Ret)|Chan]|Chans],Accepted)
    :-  Col=MyCol |
        Accepted=false.
```

```
accepted(MyCol,[[mess(Col,A,Ret)|Chan]|Chans],Accepted)
   :- Col=/=MyCol |
      accepted(MyCol,Chans,Accepted).

retry(false,V,Col,Cols,HiChans,LoChans,Solution)
   :- hiResCols(Cols,HiChans,NewCols1,HiChans1),
      loResCols(NewCols1,LoChans,NewCols,LoChans1),
      vertex(V,NewCols,HiChans1,LoChans1,Solution).
retry(true,V,Col,Cols,HiChans,LoChans,Solution)
   :- cutoff(Col,HiChans),
      Solution=Col(V,Col).

cutoff(Col,[]).
cutoff(Col,[[mess(Col,Accepted,Ret)|Chan]|Chans])
   :- Ret=Col,
      cutoff(Col,Chans).

hiResCols(Cols,[[mess(Col,true,Ret)|I]|Chans],NewCols,NewChans)
   :- removeCol(Col,Cols,NewCols1),
      hiResCols(NewCols1,Chans,NewCols,NewChans).
hiResCols(Cols,[[mess(Col,false,Ret)|I]|Chans],NewCols,NewChans)
   :- Ret=none,
      hiResCols(Cols,Chans,NewCols,NewChans1),
      NewChans=[I|NewChans1].
hiResCols(Cols,[],NewCols,NewChans)
   :- NewCols=Cols,
      NewChans=[].

loResCols(Cols,[[mess(MyCol,false,Col)|I]|Chs],NewCols,NewChs)
   :- Col=/=none |
      removeCol(Col,Cols,NewCols1),
      loResCols(NewCols1,Chs,NewCols,NewCs).
loResCols(Cols,[[mess(MyCol,false,none)|I]|Chs],NewCols,NewChs)
   :- loResCols(Cols,Chs,NewCols,NewChs1),
      NewChs=[I|NewChs1].
loResCols(Cols,[],NewCols,NewChs)
   :- NewCols=Cols,
      NewChs=[].
```

Thus, single channels now represents arcs, and carry a stream of messages running from a higher to a lower numbered vertex. Each actor representing a vertex chooses a color from its list of available colors and sends a message to the actors representing its lower-numbered connections only. The message takes the form mess(Col,Accepted,Return). Here, Col is the color chosen, Accept is an unbound channel shared between all the messages to be used to send a further message, but Return is a separate unbound channel for each message sent to be used to receive a reply. The actor then reads the Col argument of the messages it has received from the actors representing its higher-numbered connections. If none of the colors chosen by its higher-numbered connections are the same as the color it has chosen, it sends a message indicating that it has permanently accepted its color to its lower-numbered connections by binding the previously unbound Accepted to true. Only then, it informs its higher-numbered connections by binding the Return argument in each of the messages it received from them to the color. Otherwise, it indicates that it has not permanently accepted its color by binding the Accepted channel in the messages it previously sent out to false and binding the Return channel in each of the messages it has received to none. If any of the messages it has received has its Accepted channel bound to true, it removes the color in the Col channel of the message from its own list of colors and removes the channel the message was received on from its list of input channels. It also reviews the Return channels in each of the messages it has sent out. If any of them has been bound to a color rather than none it removes that color from its list and removes the channel the message was sent out on from its list of output channels.

As an example of the algorithm in execution, let us consider using it to find a 4-coloration of the graph given in Figure 7.2.1 with initially each vertex having the list red, green, yellow and blue (initialized in the trace below) as possible colors. The selection rule used is that every vertex chooses the first color from its list. Cycles of the algorithm are broken into three stages:

1. Choose colors and inform lower numbered neighbors of choice.
2. Decide whether to make choice permanent depending on messages received from higher numbered neighbors. Inform lower numbered neighbors of permanency of previously communicated choice and higher numbered neighbors of choice or none by back-communication.
3. Receive information on permanent choices and restrict list of colors and channels accordingly.

The trace is:

```
Cycle 1a
Vertex  1: [r,g,y,b]    Chooses r
Vertex  2: [r,g,y,b]    Chooses r, informs 1 of choice
Vertex  3: [r,g,y,b]    Chooses r, informs 1 of choice
Vertex  4: [r,g,y,b]    Chooses r, informs 1,2,3 of choice
Vertex  5: [r,g,y,b]    Chooses r, informs 3,4 of choice
Vertex  6: [r,g,y,b]    Chooses r, informs 1,2,4,5 of choice
Vertex  7: [r,g,y,b]    Chooses r, informs 1,4,5,6 of choice

Cycle 1b
Vertex  1: Receives messages:
             2 chose r, 3 chose r, 4 chose r, 6 chose r, 7 chose r
           Does not make its choice of r permanent
           Replies to 2,3,4,6 and 7: no permanent choice made
       Vertex  2: Receives messages: 4 chose r, 6 chose r
           Does not make its choice of r permanent
           Replies to 4 and 6: no permanent choice made
           Further message to 1: choice not permanently accepted
```

Vertex   3: Receives messages: 4 chose r, 5 chose r
　　　　　Does not make its choice of r permanent
　　　　　Replies to 4 and 5: no permanent choice made
　　　　　Further message to 1: choice not permanently accepted
Vertex   4: Receives messages: 5 chose r, 6 chose r, 7 chose r
　　　　　Does not make its choice of r permanent
　　　　　Replies to 5, 6 and 7: no permanent choice made
　　　　　Further message to 1,2,3: choice not permanently accepted
Vertex   5: Receives messages: 6 chose r, 7 chose r
　　　　　Does not make its choice of r permanent
　　　　　Replies to 6 and 7: no permanent choice made
　　　　　Further message to 3,4: choice not permanently accepted
Vertex   6: Receives message: 7 chose r
　　　　　Does not make its choice of r permanent
　　　　　Replies to 7: no permanent choice made
　　　　　Further message to 1,2,4,5 choice not permanently accepted
Vertex   7: Receives no messages
　　　　　Makes its choice of r permanent
　　　　　Further message to 1,4,5,6: choice made permanent

Cycle 1c
　　Vertex   1: Informed by 2,3,4,6 previous choice not accepted
　　　　　Receives message from 7 of permanent choice of r
　　　　　Closes channel with 7
　　　　　Restricts color list to [g,y,b]
　　Vertex   2: Informed by 1 no permanent choice made
　　　　　Informed by 4,6 previous choice not accepted
　　Vertex   3: Informed by 1 no permanent choice made
　　　　　Informed by 4,5 previous choice not accepted
　　Vertex   4: Informed by 1,2,3 no permanent choice made
　　　　　Informed by 5,6 previous choice not accepted
　　　　　Receives message from 7 of permanent choice of r
　　　　　Closes channel with 7
　　　　　Restricts color list to [g,y,b]
　　Vertex   5: Informed by 3,4 no permanent choice made
　　　　　Informed by 6 previous choice not accepted
　　　　　Receives message from 7 of permanent choice of r
　　　　　Closes channel with 7
　　　　　Restricts color list to [g,y,b]
　　Vertex   6: Informed by 1,2,4,5 no permanent choice made
　　　　　Receives message from 7 of permanent choice of r
　　　　　Closes channel with 7
　　　　　Restricts color list to [g,y,b]
　　Vertex   7: COLORED r

Cycle 2a
Vertex 1: [g,y,b]   Chooses g
Vertex 2: [r,g,y,b]   Chooses r, informs 1 of choice
Vertex 3: [r,g,y,b]   Chooses r, informs 1 of choice
Vertex 4: [g,y,b]   Chooses g, informs 1,2,3 of choice
Vertex 5: [g,y,b]   Chooses g, informs 3,4 of choice
Vertex 6: [g,y,b]   Chooses g, informs 1,2,4,5 of choice

Cycle 2b
Vertex 1: Receives messages: 2 chose r, 3 chose r, 4
                chose g, 6 chose g
           Does not make its choice of g permanent
           Replies to 2,3,4 and 6: no permanent choice made
Vertex 2: Receives messages: 4 chose g, 6 chose g
           Makes its choice of r permanent
           Replies to 4 and 6: permanent choice made of r
           Further message to 1: choice made permanent
Vertex 3: Receives messages: 4 chose g, 5 chose g
           Makes its choice of r permanent
           Replies to 4 and 5: permanent choice made of r
           Further message to 1: choice made permanent
Vertex 4: Receives messages: 5 chose g, 6 chose g
           Does not make its choice of g permanent
           Replies to 5 and 6: no permanent choice made
           Further message to 1,2,3: choice not permanently accepted
Vertex 5: Receives message: 6 chose g
           Does not make its choice of g permanent
           Replies to 6: no permanent choice made
           Further message to 3,4: choice not permanently accepted
Vertex 6: Receives no messages
           Makes its choice of g permanent
           Further message to 1,2,4,5: choice made permanent

Cycle 2c
Vertex 1: Receives message from 2 of permanent choice of r
           Receives message from 3 of permanent choice of r
           Informed by 4 previous choice not accepted
           Receives message from 6 of permanent choice of g
           Closes channels with 2,3,6
           Restricts color list to [y,b]
Vertex 2: COLORED r
Vertex 3: COLORED r

Vertex 4: Informed by 1 no permanent choice made
        Receives message from 2 of permanent choice of r
        Receives message from 3 of permanent choice of r
        Informed by 5 previous choice not accepted
        Receives message from 6 of permanent choice of g
        Closes channels with 2,3,6
        Restricts color list to [y,b]
Vertex 5: Receives message from 3 of permanent choice of r
        Informed by 4 no permanent choice made
        Receives message from 6 of permanent choice of g
        Closes channels with 3,6
        Restricts color list to [y,b]
Vertex 6: COLORED g

Cycle 3a
    Vertex 1: [y,b] Chooses y
    Vertex 4: [y,b] Chooses y, informs 1 of choice
    Vertex 5: [y,b] Chooses y, informs 4 of choice

Cycle 3b
    Vertex 1: Receives message: 4 chose y
        Does not make its choice of y permanent
    Vertex 4: Receives message: 5 chose y
        Does not make its choice of y permanent
        Replies to 1: no permanent choice made
    Vertex 5: Receives no message
        Makes its choice of y permanent
        Further message to 4: choice made permanent

Cycle 3c
    Vertex 1: Informed by 4 previous choice not accepted
    Vertex 4: Informed by 1 no permanent choice made
        Receives message from 5 of permanent choice of y
        Closes channel with 5
        Restricts color list to [b]
    Vertex 5: COLORED y

Cycle 4a
    Vertex 1: [y,b] Chooses y
    Vertex 4: [b] Chooses b, informs 1 of choice

Cycle 4b
    Vertex 1: Receives message: 4 chose b
        Makes its choice of y permanent
    Vertex 4: Receives no messages
        Makes its choice of b permanent
        Further message to 1: choice made permanent

Cycle 4c
  Vertex 1: COLORED y
  Vertex 4: COLORED b

Thus the final result, achieved after four cycles is that vertices 2, 3 and 7 are colored red, vertices 1 and 5 are colored yellow, vertex 6 is colored green and vertex 4 is colored blue. Note that the select mechanism used meant that even if more than four colors were available initially, a 4-coloration would have been found since any vertex would only have considered a fifth color had the first four been excluded from it during the course of the algorithm execution.

Now consider how this is represented in GDC. The initial setup is as before, with C bound to [r,g,y,b]. Following the first sending of messages after stage 1a, the situation is:

:-   **accepted**(r,[C12,C13,C14,C16,C17],A1a),
     retry(A1a,1,r,[r,g,y,b],[C12,C13,C14,C16,C17],[],S1),
     C12=[mess(r,A2a,R12a)|C12a],
     accepted(r,[C24,C26],A2a),
     retry(A2a,2,r,[r,g,y,b],[C24,C26],[C12],S2),
     C13=[mess(r,A3a,R13a)|C13a],
     accepted(r,[C34,C35],A31a),
     retry(A3a,3,r,[r,g,y,b],[C34,C35],[C13],S3),
     C14=[mess(r,A4a,R14a)|C14a],
     C24=[mess(r,A4a,R24a)|C24a],
     C34=[mess(r,A4a,R34a)|C34a],
     accepted(r,[C45,C46,C47],A4a1),
     retry(A4a,4,r,[r,g,y,b],[C45,C46,C47],[C14,C24,C34],[],S4),
     C35=[mess(r,A5a,R35a)|C35a],
     C45=[mess(r,A5a,R45a)|C45a],
     accepted(r,[C56,C57],A5a),
     retry(A5a,5,r,[r,g,y,b],[C56,C57],[C35,C45],[],S5),
     C16=[mess(r,A6a,R16a)|C16a],
     C26=[mess(r,A6a,R26a)|C26a],
     C46=[mess(r,A6a,R46a)|C46a],
     C56=[mess(r,A6a,R56a)|C56a],
     accepted(r,[C67],A6a),
     retry(A6a,r,[r,g,y,b],[C67],[C16,C26,C46,C56],[],S6),
     C17=[mess(r,A7a,R17a)|C17a],
     C47=[mess(r,A7a,R47a)|C47a],
     C67=[mess(r,A7a,R67a)|C67a],
     accepted(r,[],A7a),
     retry(A7a,7,r,[r,g,y,b],[],[C17,C47,C67],S7).

Following this, each **accepted** actor will bind its final argument to false except **accepted**(r,[],A7a) which binds A7a to true. Each **retry** actor, except the one for vertex 7 will then reduce to a **hiResCols** and a **loResCols** actor, with the **hiResCols** actors reducing and sending the return messages which are used in the

loResCols actors. This corresponds to the end of stage 1b and the beginning of 1c, leaving the actor situation:

```
:-  R12a=none, R13a=none, R14a=none, R16a=none,
    vertex(1,[g,y,b],[C12a,C13a,C14a,C16a],[],S1),
    R24a=none, R26a=none,
    loResCols([r,g,y,b],[[mess(r,false,R12a)|C12a]],Col2,Lo2),
    vertex(2,Col2,[C24a,C26a],Lo2,S2),
    R34a=none, R35a=none,
    loResCols([r,g,y,b],[[mess(r,false,R13a)|C13a]],Col3,Lo3),
    vertex(3,Col3,[C34a,C35a],Lo3,S3),
    R45a=none, R46a=none, R47a=none,
    loResCols([g,y,b],
        [[mess(r,false,R14a)|C14a],
        [mess(r,false,R24a)|C24a],
        [mess(r,false,R34a)|C34a]],
        Col4,Lo4),
    vertex(4,Col4,[C45a,C46a],Lo4,S4),
    R56a=none, R57a=none,
    loResCols([g,y,b],
        [[mess(r,false,R35a)|C35a],[mess(r,false,R45a)|C45a]],
        Col5,Lo5),
    vertex(5,Col5,[C56a],Lo5,S5),
    R671=none,
    loResCols([g,y,b],
        [[mess(r,false,R16a)|C16a],[mess(r,false,R26a)|C26a],
        [mess(r,false,R46a)|C46a],[mess(r,false,R56a)|C56a]],
        Lo6,S6),
    vertex(6,Col6,[],Lo6,S6),
    S7=col(7,r).
```

At this point only vertex 7 has made a permanent choice and all the none reply messages shown above indicate that there is no case where a low numbered vertex has been able to make a permanent choice. This leads to the situation following the second round of color choices (stage 2a):

```
:-  accepted(g,[C12a,C13a,C14a,C16a],A1b),
    retry(A1b,1,g,[g,y,b],[C12a,C13a,C14a,C16a],[],S1),
    C12a=[mess(r,A2b,R12b)|C12b],
    accepted(r,[C24a,C26a],A2b),
    retry(A2b,2,r,[r,g,y,b],[C24a,C26a],[C12a],S2),
    C13a=[mess(r,A3b,R13b)|C13b],
    accepted(r,[C34a,C35a],A3b),
    retry(A3b,3,r,[r,g,y,b],[C34a,C35a],[C13a],S3),
    C14a=[mess(g,A4b,R14b)|C14b],
    C24a=[mess(g,A4b,R24b)|C24b],
    C34a=[mess(g,A4b,R34b)|C34b],
    accepted(g,[C45a,C46a,C47a],A4b),
    retry(A4a,4,g,[g,y,b],[C45a,C46a],[C14a,C24a,C34a],[],S4),
```

```
C35a=[mess(g,A5b,R35b)|C35b],
C45a=[mess(g,A5b,R45b)|C45b],
accepted(g,[C56a],A5b),
retry(A5b,5,g,[g,y,b],[C56a,C57a],[C35a,C45a],[],S5),
C16a=[mess(g,A6b,R16b)|C16b],
C26a=[mess(g,A6b,R26b)|C26b],
C46a=[mess(g,A6b,R46b)|C46b],
C56a=[mess(g,A6b,R56b)|C56b],
accepted(g,[],A6b),
retry(A6b,g,[g,y,b],[],[C16a,C26a,C46a,C56a],[],S6).
```

This time vertices 2 and 3 are able to make their choice permanent, as well as the highest numbered vertex, 6. Thus, each of them has their acceptance channel A2b, A3b and A6b respectively bound to true (these channel names are given purely for demonstration purposes, here the b indicating that it is a second attempt to try for acceptance). The actor scenario then is:

```
:-  R12b=none, R13b=none, R14b=none, R16b=none,
    vertex(1,[y,b],[C14b],[],S1),
    R24b=r, R26b=r,
    S2=col(2,r),
    R34b=r, R35b=r,
    S3=col(3,r),
    R45b=none, R46b=none,
    loResCols([y,b],[[mess(g,false,R14b)|C14b],
        [mess(g,false,R24b)|C24b],
        [mess(g,false,R34b)|C34b]],
        Col4,Lo4),
    vertex(4,Col4,[C45b,],Lo4,S4),
    R56b=none,
    loResCols([y,b],
        [[mess(g,false,R35b)|C35b],[mess(g,false,R45b)|C45b]],
        Col5,Lo5),
    vertex(5,Col5,[],Lo5,S5),S6=col(6,g).
```

So the information that vertices 2 and 3 have each chosen color r is passed through the reply channels R24b, R26b, R34b, and R35b to their remaining higher numbered neighbors. The tracing of this problem will be left at this stage.

It might be questioned why in this algorithm a vertex cannot permanently accept a color if the only thing stopping it is a higher-numbered vertex which has chosen that color, but has not permanently accepted it itself. The reason is that to introduce a wait-to-see whether each of the colors chosen by its higher-numbered connections is accepted, would destroy the parallelism of the algorithm, since its own lower-numbered connections would then have to wait in sequence and so on. Yokoo and Hirayama's [1998] algorithm for multi-agent graph-coloring has some similarities to the one above. This includes the use of an improved priority on agents and a multistage process where colors are chosen, communicated and then either accepted and confirmed or rejected. Yokoo and Hirayama's algorithm appears to require many more cycles to come to a solution than the one presented here.

The second program for graph coloring illustrates how GDC may be used as an executable specification language to develop parallel algorithms. The initial program was a GDC representation of an algorithm that had been described in the abstract in the initial reference. An improved version of the algorithm was obtained by noting and correcting inefficiencies in the GDC program and then describing the underlying algorithm of the improved program in abstract terms again. In the next section an algorithm for the minimal spanning tree graph problem is discussed that was arrived at by similar means [Huntbach, 1993].

7.3 Minimal Spanning Trees

The minimal spanning tree problem may be stated as follows:

> An undirected graph $G = <V,E>$ consists of a vertex set V and an edge set E. Associated with each edge $\{u,v\}$ is a cost $c(u,v)>0$. A minimal spanning tree of G is a connected subgraph $<V,E'>$ such that $\sum_{\{u,v\}\in E'}c(u,v)$ is minimal. Such a subgraph must be a tree, since if not there exists a circuit and by removing an edge a lower cost spanning tree can be derived.

The following concept can be used to produce a minimal spanning tree algorithm:

> A linked *minimal spanning forest* of a graph $<V,E>$ is a set of triplets $\{<V_1,E_1,L_1>,...,<V_n,E_n,L_n>\}$ where $V_1,...,V_n$ partitions V; $E_i,L_i \subseteq E$; $<V_i,E_i>$ is a minimal spanning tree over $<V_i,\{\{u,v\}\in E|u,v\in V_i\}>$, $L_i=\{\{u,v\}\in E|u\in V_i,v\in V_j,j\neq i\}$, $1\leq l\leq n$. That is, the vertices of the graph $<V,E>$ are divided up among the trees of the forest, each tree in the forest is a minimal spanning tree over its vertices With each tree is a set of linking edges, which are those edges in E which link vertices in the tree with vertices in other trees.

Given a linked minimal spanning forest, if $\{u,v\}$ is the lowest cost member of L_i with $u\in V_i$, $v\in V_j$, trees $[V_i,E_i,L_i]$ and $[V_j,E_j,L_j]$ can be removed from the forest and replace them by $[V_k,E_k,L_k]$ where

$$V_k=V_i\cup V_j, \ E_k=E_i\cup E_j\cup\{(u,v)\}, \ L_k=L_i\cup L_j-\{\{x,y\}|x\in V_i,y\in V_j\}$$

The result will also be a linked minimal spanning forest. That is two trees in the forest have been simply linked by their lowest cost linking edge and any other edges that also join these trees deleted. Starting with the linked minimal spanning forest $\{<\{v\},\{\},L_v>|v\in V,L_v=\{\{v,y\}\in E\}\}$, where each tree consists of just a single vertex, every time the above replacement is applied it will reduce the number of trees in the forest by one. Eventually the stage where the forest has the single element $<V,E',\{\}>$ will be reached, which since it covers all the vertices is a minimal spanning tree for $<V,E>$.

The above algorithm is presented in a slightly unorthodox manner. By explicitly partitioning the set of edges into linking edges for each tree an algorithm is produced which is more general than those usually presented. The idea of linking edges is implicit, though not stressed in the algorithm of Lavallée and Roucairol [1986], which is discussed below. It is also found in the work of Yao [1975] and Gabow et al [1989], but not usually in texts introducing the minimal spanning tree problem.

The algorithm as described leaves open the question of which trees are merged at any stage. At any time, if F is the forest, there will be at least $|F|/2$ mergers possible since each tree will have a minimum cost linking edge to use. But it is possible for a pair of trees to mutually agree on merger – this will occur when the minimum cost linking edge of V_i is {x,y} and that of V_j is {y,x}. (Although these refer to the same edge, the convention that a tree refers to its linking edges by the node that occurs in the tree first is used). The solution to the problem is indeterminate if edge costs are not unique. If there are two or more edges of minimum cost linking two trees in the forest and the cost is minimal for both trees any of the edges may be used leading to a different solution for each. A protocol needs to be established to prevent not just simultaneous attempts at merger using the same edge, but the case where one attempts to merge using one of the edges and the other simultaneously attempts to merge using another. This is discussed in further detail below. At most there will be $|F|-1$ mergers possible – this will occur when there is some tree with which each minimum cost linking edge of all the other subtrees links. The classical algorithms of Prim and Kruskal [Barr et al., 1989] can be considered special cases of this algorithm.

Prim's algorithm [1957] (also attributed to Dijkstra [1959]) works by continually adding edges to one subtree until it encompasses all the vertices in the graph. Keeping the trees in the above algorithm in a list, always trying to link the first tree with another and always putting the resulting merged tree at the head of the list gives Prim's algorithm. Sollin's algorithm [Berge and Ghouila-Houri, 1965] can be obtained by putting the resulting merged tree at the end of the list. The equivalent to Kruskal's algorithm [1956] can be obtained by linking whichever two trees in the forest can be linked by the shortest link of any possible merger. As conventionally described however, Kruskal's algorithm delays deleting edges, working instead by considering the edges one by one in order of cost and deleting those which link vertices already in the same tree due to a previous merger.

Barr, Helgaon and Pennington [1989] present a concurrent version of Prim's algorithm in which the parallelism comes in the search for the lowest cost link from the first subtree. Our presentation of the minimal spanning tree problem makes it clear that there is a large source of parallelism in the minimal spanning tree problem apart from this. The main source being the fact, shown above, that at any stage at least $|F|/2$ mergers are possible. Rather than pick between them they can all be carried out in parallel. The present description of the problem in terms of a linked minimal spanning forest removes all global data structures and the consequent need to co-ordinate access to global structures. It suggests a distributed approach to the problem in which agents represent the trees in the forest. Mergers take place through negotiation between these agents. Although further parallelism is available in the bookkeeping associated with merging two trees, our concern is with the more fundamental parallelism of allowing several trees to merge at one time.

An actor that contains lists of the vertices and edges that form the tree may represent each tree in the linked minimal spanning forest. The links are represented as a list of channel/cost pairs. Thus if trees T_i and T_j are linked by edge $\{x,y\}$ on T_i (and hence $\{y,x\}$ on T_j) there will be a shared channel between the actors representing the trees T_i and T_j. The merger of T_i and T_j can be accomplished by the actor T_i sending a message containing its edges, vertices and links to the actor for T_j on the channel representing the link $\{x,y\}$ and terminating. On receiving the message, the actor for T_j will adjust its records accordingly to become the actor for the new merged tree. This model therefore assumes that the initiative for a merger is taken by the tree which is to merge. The initial state of the actor system represents the initial graph, with vertices represented by actors and edges represented by channels. This is similar to the initial state in the graph-coloring algorithm above. However whereas in the graph-coloring algorithm the actor and communications structure remains static, here it alters as the algorithm progresses.

Consider what happens when the lowest cost link on T_i is $\{x,y\}$ and the lowest cost link on T_j is $\{y,x\}$. A protocol needs to be established so that both trees do not send merger messages to each other and terminate. Supposing the cost of each edge in the graph is distinct, there is the more general problem of a circuit of trees mutually attempting to merge with each other. Consider the case where one of the lowest cost links (there may be several with the same cost) on T_i is the link to T_{i+1}. One of the lowest cost links on T_{i+1} is a link to T_{i+2} and so on to T_{i+k} and the lowest cost links on T_{i+k} include a link to T_i. This circuit can only exist if each of its links has an identical cost. Assuming a method for mutual merging across a link, two linked trees can mutually agree to merge at any edge in the circuit, but this will still leave a smaller circuit. Without a circuit-breaking mechanism, the potential problem of each of the trees in the circuit attempting to merge with the next one remains.

Ignoring for now the circuit problem, the case of T_i merging with T_j at the same time as T_j merges with T_k can be easily resolved. It may be noted that the merger operation is associative, so it does not matter if T_i first merges with T_j then the resulting tree merges with T_k, or T_j merges with T_k and T_i merges with the result. So if T_j merges with T_k without waiting for the incoming message from T_i, since the merger operation causes the channels of T_j to be included among the channels of the new merged actor, the incoming message will simply be passed on to this new merged actor. Note that it is not possible for a merger to replace the lowest cost link with a lower cost one. A tree always merges using its lowest cost link (which must be one of the existing links in the tree to which it is merging since the graph is non-directional). A tree can only bring in more links of equal or greater cost, so at most merger can only introduce additional lowest cost links.

The algorithm as described so far originates from attempts to implement the algorithm of Lavallée and Roucairol [1986]. The principal difference is that Lavallée and Roucairol keep the initial actor/channel state throughout the computation. In their case, when a tree merges its actor remains in existence, explicitly passing further merger messages onto the actor representing the merged tree. Their description of the algorithm in a CSP-like notation does not allow for channels to be passed in messages and, hence, the necessity for these explicit message passing actors. In GDC, channels are recursive and may easily be passed around in messages. The effect of passing a channel in actor P to actor Q is that messages intended for P will be received by Q.

Lavallée and Roucairol make the assumption that each vertex is identified by a unique integer. The lowest valued identifier in a tree is referred to as its *root*. Thus the actors representing the roots of the trees at any time can be considered to be the "real" actors of the algorithm, other actors being simply methods of passing information between roots. The circuit problem is resolved by allowing a tree T_i to send its edge and link details and merge with T_j only if the root of T_i is greater than the root of T_j. It follows that no circuit of mergers can occur.

The difficulty with the algorithm is that an actor T_i cannot simply decide to merge across its lowest cost link, because it does not know the root of T_j, the actor with which it is attempting to merge. Instead it must first send a request to merge containing its own root identifier. On receiving the request, T_j will send back either an acceptance or a refusal depending on the root values. (In fact, the algorithm as described in the reference is slightly different: the message-passing actors answer queries directly and can do so as they hold a record of their root which is updated when mergers take place). Only when an acceptance has been received will T_i send its full details for merger to take place. While waiting for acceptance or refusal of its merger request T_i will accept or refuse any requests it receives and modify its records if it receives any full mergers (which clearly can only come from trees with higher roots than its own, so will not affect its own root value).

If T_i's request for a merger is refused, it may be the case that T_j has requested a merger which T_i will accept and which will cause its lowest cost link to be deleted when the merger is completed. Otherwise, T_i has no alternative but to repeat the request in the hope that in the meantime T_j has merged with another tree T_k whose root is low enough for the request to be accepted. A modification to the algorithm is suggested in which if T_i's merger request is refused, T_i will not make any further requests until it has itself received a request from its lowest cost link indicating that T_j has indeed merged with some T_k.

It may be noted that even when the complexities due to the existence of explicit message-passing nodes have been stripped out, the algorithm still requires the interchange of at least three messages to accomplish a merger. Nevertheless, Lavallée and Roucairol claim that their algorithm improves on that of Gallagher, Humblet and Spira [1983] in terms of the number of message exchanges. The algorithm for coordinating tree merger, given below, improves on both, requiring just one message to accomplish each tree merger. The algorithm solves the problem of circuits by making channels between actors representing edges unidirectional. Thus, Lavallée and Roucairol's imposition of an ordering on potential mergers through root identities may be replaced by an imposition of ordering on individual edges. Unidirectional channels simplify the representation in GDC, since a single shared channel can represent such a channel. The convention that a unique integer identifier represents each vertex is adopted. A channel representing the link between the vertex identified x and the vertex identified y, where x>y is set to be unidirectional, outgoing from the actor containing the vertex x and incoming at the actor containing vertex y. It should be stressed that the graph itself is still nondirectional – a nondirectional edge is simply represented by a unidirectional channel. It can be seen that this is a similar approach to that adopted in the graph-coloring problem.

At any time during the algorithm's execution any actor whose lowest cost link is represented by an incoming channel will remain passive waiting for a merger message to arrive. Any actor whose lowest cost link is represented by an outgoing channel will send a message containing its vertices, edges and linking channels (both incoming and outgoing) down this lowest cost channel and terminate. Note that when an actor receives a message, it is not necessarily on its own lowest cost incoming link, so we require the ability to receive on any incoming channel.

When a passive actor receives a merger message from one of its incoming channels, it appends the vertices and edges to its own and adds the new edge from which the merger message was received. It then deletes from its links any links, incoming or outgoing, which link to the newly added vertices. It adds to its links any of the new links, which do not link to any of its existing vertices. These new links retain their status unchanged as incoming or outgoing. If the result is that the lowest cost link is still represented by an incoming channel, the actor remains passive. Otherwise it merges and terminates using its lowest cost link, as above. Execution continues until there is only one actor left with no links – the edges on this actor then form the minimal spanning tree. When there is an incoming link and an outgoing link of the same cost and no links of lower cost, the actor remains passive if the vertex of the actor to which the incoming link joins has a lower identifier than the vertex which the outgoing link joins. (The vertex must be in a different actor and hence must have a different identifier.) Otherwise the actor is active. If an actor is active and has more than one outgoing link of the same cost and this cost is the lowest cost, the choice of which to use for merging is non-determinate.

The algorithm is a version of the more general algorithm stated initially, so it must terminate with a minimal spanning tree providing it does not deadlock and we do not get a circuit of actors simultaneously merging and terminating. At any stage in the computation there will be a link between two actors whose cost is less than or equal to the cost of any other link and whose destination vertex has an identifier less than or equal to that of any links of equal cost. The actor which has this link as an outgoing edge will always be able to use it to send a merge message and terminate, reducing the number of actors by one. Its destination actor must always be passive and thus will eventually receive the message, hence the algorithm cannot deadlock.

Channels are unidirectional, so for any potential circuit every actor in the circuit will have one incoming channel forming part of the circuit and one outgoing channel. Unless all links in the circuit are of the same cost, there must be one actor which will not participate in the circuit merger since its incoming circuit channel represents a lower cost link than its outgoing circuit channel. It therefore remains passive or, should it have outgoing links to non-circuit actors of lower cost than its incoming circuit link, merges with an actor not part of the circuit. The circuit may shrink but will never totally merge and cause every one of its actors to terminate. The point will eventually be reached where the circuit consists of two actors, each linked to the other, one active and one passive. The active one will terminate, sending a merger message. The passive one will receive the message and delete its link to the former active actor before becoming active itself.

Consider, now, a potential circuit all of whose links are of the same cost. Taking into account the unidirectionality of links, such a circuit cannot exist in the original graph, since that would imply that every vertex in the circuit has an identifier greater than the identifier of the vertex at the destination of its outgoing link in the circuit. However, once merges take place circuits can form. If this occurs, there must be one actor for which the incoming link that forms part of the circuit has the destination vertex with the lowest identifier of any incoming link in the circuit. This actor will not participate in the circuit merger, since its outgoing circuit link must be to a vertex with a higher identifier.

As an example, the graph on the left of Figure 7.3.1 does not contain a circuit because of the directionality imposed. However when the actors representing the vertices 1 and 5 are merged, giving the graph on the right, there is a potential circuit. Assuming all edge costs are the same, there would not be a complete circuit merger. Because the actor representing the vertices {1,5} has incoming edge {1,2}, destination 1 and outgoing edge {5,4}, destination 4, it will remain passive as the vertex to which its lowest cost incoming link connects has a lower identifier than the vertex to which its lowest cost outgoing edge connects. In Figure 7.3.1, the bold integers are the vertex identifiers, the italic integer pairs are the edge identifiers at their destinations. The section enclosed within dotted lines on the left may be considered shrunk to a single actor on the right (it should be noted that this shrinking records the edge used but would delete any additional links if they existed).

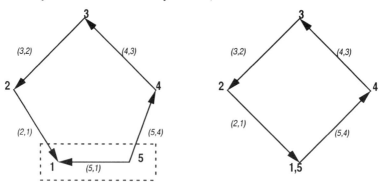

Fig. 7.3.1 Merging two subtrees

Below is a simple implementation in this in GDC. The initial state of the system is assumed to be a collection of actors, one for each vertex. Each actor contains a list of links to other actors, with their costs. A shared channel named Xij represents a link.

This setup could easily be generated from a more basic description of the graph. In the case of the graph in Figure 7.3.2 (in this case the bold integers are vertex identifiers, the italic integers edge costs; no directionality is assumed at this stage),

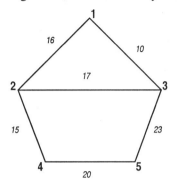

Fig. 7.3.2 Implemented example of minimal spanning tree

the initial set-up of actors will be as given:

```
:-  vertex(1,[l(2,16,X12),l(3,10,X13)]),
    vertex(2,[l(1,16,X12),l(3,17,X23),l(4,15,X24)]),
    vertex(3,[l(1,10,X13),l(2,17,X23),l(5,23,X35)]),
    vertex(4,[l(2,15,X24),l(5,20,X45)]),
    vertex(5,[l(3,23,X35),l(4,20,X45)]).
```

The initialization must divide the links into incoming and outgoing links. The incoming channels are merged, using the standard non-deterministic merge, to give one channel that delivers all incoming messages to the actor. The outgoing channels are kept separate with the record of the edges which each implements. The **insertout** and **insertin** actors put the links in order of their cost (lowest cost first), in order of destination vertex for those of equal cost:

```
vertex(V,Links) :- initialize(V,Links,[],[],[]).

initialize(V,[l(U,Cost,X)|Links],InChan,InLinks,OutLinks)
    :- V>U
    |   insertout(out(V,U,Cost,X),OutLinks,OutLinks1),
        initialize(V,Links,InChan,InLinks,OutLinks1).
initialize(V,[l(U,Cost,X)|Links],InChan,InLinks,OutLinks)
    :- V<U
    |   merge(X,InChan,InChan1),
        insertin(in(V,U,Cost),InLinks,InLinks1),
        initialize(V,Links,InChan1,InLinks1,OutLinks).
initialize(V,[],InChan,InLinks,OutLinks)
    :- active([V],[],InChan,InLinks,OutLinks).
```

This would convert the representation of the graph above to:

```
:-  merge(C12,C13,In1),
    active([1],[],In1,[in(1,3,10),in(1,2,16)],[]),
    merge(C23,C24,In2),
    active([2],[],In2,[in(2,4,15),in(2,3,17)],[out(2,1,16,C12)]),
    active([3],[],C35,[in(3,5,23)],[out(3,1,10,C13),out(3,2,17,C23)]),
    active([4],[],C45,[in(4,5,20)],[out(4,2,15,C24)]),
    active([5],[],[],[],[out(5,4,20,C45),out(5,3,23,C35)]).
```

Having initialized the system in this way, **active** checks whether an actor should merge and terminate, or become passive and wait for a merger from another actor. In the latter case, the clause for **passive** causes the actor to suspend until a merger message arrives on its input. The **append** in **passive**'s subactors is standard list append. The **mergeinlinks** and **mergeoutlinks** actors merge two sorted lists of links, giving a sorted list as output. The **deletein** and **deleteout** actors take a list of links and a list of vertices and delete from the list of links all those edges whose second vertex is in the list of vertices. Merge messages take the form of a tuple containing the vertices, edges, incoming links and outgoing links of the merging actor. The following is the code for **active** and **passive** actors:

```
// Lowest cost link outgoing - send merge message:
active(Verts,Edges,InChan,[in(X1,Y1,N1)|InLinks],
        [out(X2,Y2,N2,OutChan)|OutLinks])
    :-  N2<N1
    |   OutChan=[mergemess(Verts,[edge(X2,Y2)|Edges],
            [in(X1,Y1,N1)|InLinks],OutLinks)|InChan].
// Lowest cost link incoming - wait for merge message:
active(Verts,Edges,InChan,[in(X1,Y1,N1)|InLinks],
        [out(X2,Y2,N2,OutChan)|OutLinks])
    :-  N2>N1
    |   passive(Verts,Edges,InChan,[in(X1,Y1,N1)|InLinks],
            [out(X2,Y2,N2,OutChan)|OutLinks]).
// Equal cost incoming and outgoing, outgoing has lowest
// destination vertex:
active(Verts,Edges,InChan,[in(X1,Y1,N1)|InLinks],
        [out(X2,Y2,N2,OutChan)|OutLinks])
    :-  N2=N1,Y2<X1
    |   OutChan=[mergemess(Verts,[edge(X2,Y2)|Edges],
            [in(X1,Y1,N1)|InLinks],OutLinks)|InChan].
// Equal cost incoming and outgoing, incoming has lowest
// destination vertex:
active(Verts,Edges,InChan,[in(X1,Y1,N1)|InLinks],
        [out(X2,Y2,N2,OutChan)|OutLinks])
    :-  N2=N1,Y2>X1
    |   passive(Verts,Edges,InChan,[in(X1,Y1,N1)|InLinks],
            [out(X2,Y2,N2,OutChan)|OutLinks]).
```

```
// No more outgoing links:
active(Verts,Edges,InChan,[in(X,Y,N)|InLinks],[])
    :-  passive(Verts,Edges,InChan,[in(X,Y,N)|InLinks],[]).
// No more incoming links:
active(Verts,Edges,InChan,[],
            [out(X,Y,N,OutChan)|OutLinks])
    :-  OutChan=[mergemess(Verts,[edge(X,Y)|Edges],
            [],OutLinks)|InChan].
// No links at all: finished - print solution:
active(Verts,Edges,InChan,[],[])
    :-  write('Solution : '), writeln(Edges).


// Wait for message and carry out merger:
passive(Verts,Edges,[mergemess(VertsM,EdgesM,InLinksM,
            OutLinksM)|InChan],InLinks,OutLinks)
    :-  append(Edges,EdgesM,NewEdges),
        append(Verts,VertsM,NewVerts),
        deletein(VertsM,InLinks,InLinks1),
        deletein(Verts,InLinksM,InLinks2),
        mergeinlinks(InLinks1,InLinks2,NewInLinks),
        deleteout(VertsM,OutLinks,OutLinks1),
        deleteout(Verts,OutLinksM,OutLinks2),
        mergeoutlinks(OutLinks1,OutLinks2,NewOutLinks),
        active(NewVerts,NewEdges,InChan,NewInLinks,NewOutLinks).
```

This is sufficient to describe the algorithm. Note that when an actor terminates and sends a merge message, it appends its input stream to the merge message and thus any further messages to it will be directed to the actor with which it merges. As a convenience, the active actor adds its linking edge to the list of edges sent in its merge message, rather than leaving it to the passive actor to add. It should be noted that when **deleteout** deletes a link of the form **out**(X,Y,N,OutChan) it should set OutChan to [] to cause the **merge** actor which takes OutChan as input to terminate rather than remain indefinitely suspended. The linking edges are stored in simple cost-ordered lists in order to give a simple program that emphasizes the methods that have been introduced for avoiding circuits. Data structures such as those described by Gabow et al. [1989] could be used to give a more efficient implementation.

In the example of Figure 7.3.2, once the conversion to **passive** of all those actors with the lowest cost edge incoming is made, the situation is:

```
    :-  merge(C12,C13,In1),
        passive([1],[],In1,[in(1,3,10),in(1,2,16)],[]),
        merge(C23,C24,In2),
        passive([2],[],In2,[in(2,4,15),in(2,3,17)],[out(2,1,16,C12)]),
        active([3],[],C35,[in(3,5,23)],[out(3,1,10,C13),out(3,2,17,C23)]),
        active([4],[],C45,[in(4,5,20)],[out(4,2,15,C24)]),
        active([5],[],[],[],[out(5,4,20,C45),out(5,3,23,C35)]).
```

Note that unlike the graph-coloring problem, the program does not impose synchronization; there is no concept of a cycle of execution during which a particular change is made to the graph. At any time during execution any active actor will be able to execute and contribute a tree merger. The actual order of mergers is not determined at program level, but is instead dependent on the underlying scheduling of the language implementation. Thus, the actual solution obtained may vary as the architecture is changed (for example, changing the number of processors used) as this will change the scheduling. There was no such indeterminacy in the graph-coloring problem, thus the solution given there was architecture independent.

In the example, any one of the three active actors could have ended and sent its information as a message, or any two of them or all three simultaneously. For simplicity, let us assume that just the first, as listed does. The information in the process is packaged into a message and sent out on the channel representing the lowest cost outwards link and linking this channel with its inwards channel, giving:

:- **merge**(C12,C13,In1),
    passive([1],[],In1,[in(1,3,10),in(1,2,16)],[]),
    merge(C23,C24,In2),
    passive([2],[],In2,[in(2,4,15),in(2,3,17)],[out(2,1,16,C12)]),
    C13=[mergemess([3],[edge(3,1)],[in(3,5,23)],out(3,2,17,C23))|C35],
    active([4],[],C45,[in(4,5,20)],[out(4,2,15,C24)]),
    active([5],[],[],[],[out(5,4,20,C45),out(5,3,23,C35)]).

The message is passed on to the actor with which it merged, representing a merger of the tree containing just node 3 with the tree containing just node 1, to give a tree containing nodes {1,3} and one edge, {1,3}. Following reception of the message and its passing through the **merge** actors, the situation is:

:- **merge**(C12,C35,In11),
    passive([1],[],In11,[mergemess([3],[edge(3,1)],[in(3,5,23)],
        [out(3,2,17,C23)])|In11],[in(1,3,10),in(1,2,16)],[]),
    merge(C23,C24,In2),
    passive([2],[],In2,[in(2,4,15),in(2,3,17)],[out(2,1,16,C12)]),
    active([4],[],C45,[in(4,5,20)],[out(4,2,15,C24)]),
    active([5],[],[],[],[out(5,4,20,C45),out(5,3,23,C35)]).

And after completion of the merger (note the removal from the list of input vertices of the {1,3} edge), with the receiving actor becoming active, the situation becomes:

:- **merge**(C12,C35,In11),
    active([1,3],[edge(3,1)],In11,[in(1,2,16),in(3,5,23)],[out(3,2,17,C23)]),
    merge(C23,C24,In2),
    passive([2],[],In2,[in(2,4,15),in(2,3,17)],[out(2,1,16,C12)]),
    active([4],[],C45,[in(4,5,20)],[out(4,2,15,C24)]),
    active([5],[],[],[],[out(5,4,20,C45),out(5,3,23,C35)]).

However, as the new merged actor's lowest cost link is incoming, it becomes passive again, leading to a situation in which there are two active actors which may merge:

:- **merge**(C12,C35,In11),
    passive([1,3],[edge(3,1)],In11,[in(1,2,16),in(3,5,23)],[out(3,2,17,C23)]),
    merge(C23,C24,In2),
    passive([2],[],In2,[in(2,4,15),in(2,3,17)],[out(2,1,16,C12)]),
    active([4],[],C45,[in(4,5,20)],[out(4,2,15,C24)]),
    active([5],[],[],[],[out(5,4,20,C45),out(5,3,23,C35)]).

Suppose the first of these merges takes place:

:- **merge**(C12,C35,In11),
    passive([1,3],[edge(3,1)],In11,[in(1,2,16),in(3,5,23)],[out(3,2,17,C23)]),
    merge(C23,C24,In2),
    passive([2],[],In2,[in(2,4,15),in(2,3,17)],[out(2,1,16,C12)]),
    C24=[mergemess([4],[edge(4,2)],[in(4,5,20)],[])|C45],
    active([5],[],[],[],[out(5,4,20,C45),out(5,3,23,C35)]).

But this time, suppose the other active actor turns itself into a message at the same time, giving:

:- **merge**(C12,C35,In11),
    passive([1,3],[edge(3,1)],In11,[in(1,2,16),in(3,5,23)],[out(3,2,17,C23)]),
    merge(C23,C24,In2),
    passive([2],[],In2,[in(2,4,15),in(2,3,17)],[out(2,1,16,C12)]),
    C24=[mergemess([4],[edge(4,2)],[in(4,5,20)],[])|C45],
    C45=[mergemess([5],[edge(5,4)],[],[out(5,3,23,C35)])].

The result will be that the second passive actor will have two incoming messages to deal with. In this case, one follows the other on a single incoming stream, so there is no indeterminacy. In another case the situation may arise where there are two separate messages coming from different channels, in which case which is dealt with first is resolved in the indeterminacy handling of **merge**. In this case, the situation is:

:- **merge**(C12,C35,In11),
    passive([1,3],[edge(3,1)],In11,[in(1,2,16),in(3,5,23)],[out(3,2,17,C23)]),
    passive([2],[],[mergemess([4],[edge(4,2)],[in(4,5,20)],[]),
            mergemess([5],[edge(5,4)],[],[out(5,3,23,C35)])|C23],
            [in(2,4,15),in(2,3,17)],[out(2,1,16,C12)]).

Dealing with the first merger gives:

:- **merge**(C12,C35,In11),
    passive([1,3],[edge(3,1)],In11,[in(1,2,16),in(3,5,23)],[out(3,2,17,C23)]),
    active([2,4],[edge(4,2)],
            [mergemess([5],[edge(5,4)],[],[out(5,3,23,C35)])|C23],
            [in(2,3,17),in(4,5,20)],[out(2,1,16,C12)]).

Here the lowest cost link is outgoing, at a cost of 16, so the second input message in fact is not dealt with, but is placed on the channel behind the message which the active actor turns itself into:

```
:-  merge(C12,C35,In11),
    passive([1,3],[edge(3,1)],In11,
         [in(1,2,16),in(3,5,23)],[out(3,2,17,C23)]),
         C12= [mergemess([2,4],[edge(2,1),edge(4,2)],
              [in(2,3,17),in(4,5,20)],[]),
         mergemess([5],[edge(5,4)],[],[out(5,3,23,C35)])]|C23].
```

This leads to the situation where there is a single actor left with two merge messages to deal with:

```
:-  merge(C23,C35,In12),
    passive([1,3],[edge(3,1)],
         [mergemess([2,4],[edge(2,1),edge(4,2)]),
         [in(2,3,17),in(4,5,20)],[]),
         mergemess([5],[edge(5,4)],[],[out(5,3,23,C35)])]|In12],
         [in(1,2,16),in(3,5,23)],[out(3,2,17,C23)]).
```

When the first of these messages is dealt with, joining the tree containing vertices {1,3} with the tree containing vertices {2,4} along edge(2,1), the higher cost edge(2,3) which links these two trees is deleted and the channel representing it, C23, set to []. The result is:

```
:-  merge([],C35,In12),
    active([1,3,2,4],[edge(3,1),edge(2,1),edge(4,2)],
         [mergemess([5],[edge(5,4)],[],[out(5,3,23,C35)])]|In12],
         [in(4,5,20),in(3,5,23)],[]).
```

It can be seen that the setting of the channel representing the deleted edge to [] is necessary to cause the **merge** to terminate correctly. Handling the final merger message causes the tree containing just the node 5 to be linked with the tree containing the nodes {1,2,3,4} along edge(5,4) and deletes the other edge linking these two trees, edge(3,5). This gives the final situation:

```
:-  active([1,3,2,4,5],[edge(3,1),edge(2,1),edge(4,2),edge(5,4)],[],[],[]).
```

which reports the set of edges:

```
[edge(3,1),edge(2,1),edge(4,2),edge(5,4)]
```

as a minimal spanning tree for the graph.

The dynamic handling of channels was important in this program. Merger messages themselves contain channels which could be used to send further merger messages. Messages that are sent to one actor could be dynamically sent on to another as the progress of the algorithm changes the actor structure. For example, note how the merger of the tree containing just the node 5 was originally sent to the actor representing the tree containing just the node 4, but was eventually dealt with by the combined actor representing the nodes {1,2,3,4}.

7.4 Conclusion

This chapter began with a brief discussion of Distributed Artificial Intelligence. Underlying a DAI system is the idea of a network of actors linked by communication channels, which together work towards finding a solution. There is no overall co-ordination actor, nor do actors interact in any way except through an exchange of messages in a way dictated by some form of message language and "social laws" of interaction. There are various reasons for taking this approach. In some cases it may be built on top of a system which is physically distributed. In some cases, the most natural way of approaching a problem may be to break it up into distributed loosely linked components. This is the motivation behind object-oriented programming. In a deeper way it is behind Brooks' [1991] criticisms of symbolic AI which argues that artificial intelligence is better built not from a top-down approach but seen as a property which emerges from a chaotic collection of competing behaviors. (A Russian team [Okhotsimski 79] had this insight earlier, complete the idea later popularized by Brooks of building artificial insect-like robots.) In other cases, the main motivation behind seeking a distributed way of solving a problem is to use it to exploit the potential of speedup obtainable by mapping it onto a distributed architecture. Given the high costs of communication in a distributed architecture it is important to be able to minimize communication by avoiding any form of central structure, whether that be a centralized control mechanism or a shared memory, which would act as a bottleneck.

It is not possible in a work of this size whose main purpose is to describe a particular programming language to give extensive details on large-scale distributed systems. However, something of the nature of a distributed problem solving approach has been demonstrated by considering three graph problems. A common approach to these problems is a solution involving an actor mechanism that directly reflects the graph itself: actors represent vertices and communication channels between actors represent arcs between vertices. The programs for each of these problems were simple enough to be given in their entirety and for traces of the problem being solved with a small graph to be given. The fact that these programs do not have a central bottleneck means that scaling them up is less of a problem than often has been the case for AI programs.

Kahn and Miller [1988] argue that the concurrent logic languages are one of the few programming language paradigms which are capable of effectively tackling the problems associated with large-scale open distributed systems, supporting the definition of robust servers and dynamic ways of creating, removing, synchronizing and linking them together. They define the terms:

omniscience – the ability to access all of some category of information defined without reference to where the information originates or is stored and

omnipotence – the similar ability to modify such categories of information

as properties which most programming languages attempt to implement but must fail in a distributed open system. Global name spaces are given as the major culprit in preventing scalability to large scale distributed systems and collections of agents. It can be seen that what at first seem to be the weaknesses of concurrent logic programming – its failure to offer any form of omniscience or omnipotence is in fact its strength. Its additional strength is the ease with which it expresses dynamic behavior of multi-actor systems without the need for large amounts of heavy syntax.

The graph programs presented above were simple to express in GDC, indeed the simplicity of the programs enabled us to improve the algorithms by working on improving the efficiency of the programs. They demonstrate different aspects of the language. The first two problems, shortest paths and graph coloring have a static actor structure, but the shortest-path problem is asynchronous whereas graph-coloring is synchronous. The graph-coloring problem demonstrates synchronization achieved not by a central synchronizing mechanism but by the protocol of the individual actors for the interchange of messages. The third problem, minimal-spanning trees, demonstrates a dynamic actor structure and, in particular, shows an example of a program where the ability to treat channels as first class values, which may themselves be passed as arguments in messages is crucial to success.

Chapter 8

Meta-Interpretation

> *I can play with the chessmen according to certain rules. But I can invent a game in which I play with the rules themselves. The pieces in my game are now the rules of chess, and the rules of the game are, say, the laws of logic. In that case I have yet another game and not a metagame.*
>
> Ludwig Wittgenstein, *Philosophical Remarks*

Quis custodiet ipsos custodes? Anyone familiar with the distinction between theory and metatheory will answer instantly that of course the metaguards guard the guards. "Meta-X is X about X" and from the time of Russell's paradox dividing X up into levels of X, meta-X, meta-meta-X and so on has been a useful aid to thought. If you have experienced an argument change (as they often do!) from arguing about something to arguing about the argument, you will have experienced a meta-argument. If you have ever wondered who trains the people who teach in teacher-training school, you will have started considering the possibility of an infinite number of levels in the tower of meta-X. If the answer to this question is that the teachers in teacher training school teach teaching in general and thus are perfectly capable of teaching how to teach teaching you will have encountered the idea of metacircular-X. You will, as well, experience the sort of convoluted sentence to which prolonged thought on metalevels leads to.

Barklund and Hamfelt [1994], quoting Hart [1961], note that a correspondence can be drawn between the different layers of reasoning in a system involving metalogic with the different layers of law in a legal system. Some laws regulate behavior, while others regulate the practice of law itself; these latter could be termed "metalaws". The constitution of a state or organization may be regarded as a formalization of the concept of metalaws. A person may be judged guilty or innocent under the laws of the land, but a constitution which contains a Bill of Rights in effect may judge a law to be guilty or innocent according to this Bill of Rights and rule out laws which conflict with it. Since there is, in general, no higher level constitution against which a constitution may be judged, a constitution may be deemed metacircular. A constitution defines in itself how it operates, but one could separate those clauses of a constitution which deal with how it operates or may be amended as a "metaconstitution" or "meta-metalaw".

The British constitution is, unusually, "unwritten". This does not mean, as some suppose, that there is no such thing as a British constitution. Rather, that no formal distinction is made between constitutional law and any other law: a law affecting or amending the way the constitution works may be made in the same way as any other law may be made, there is no special qualified voting or referendum. Ultimately, British law rests on the absolute authority of the Sovereign (a legal concept that may have originally meant literally the sovereign as a living human being, but at a later date was taken to mean the sovereign acting through Parliament). A comparison may be drawn between the British legal system and programming languages that do not have a metalanguage or mix in arbitrarily metaprogramming concepts with the language itself: the ultimate authority is the hardware. Arguments for and against the unwritten constitution sound rather like arguments for and against a programming language without a strong and distinct metaprogramming layer: it is defended for its efficiency and power and attacked for its inherent lack of safety. Bagehot [1861] in comparing the UK and USA constitutions, attacks the latter for unnecessary layers of complexity and defends the former as acceptable since relying on the "reasonableness of the British middle classes".

8.1 Metalanguage as Language Definition and Metacircular Interpreters

The concept of a metalanguage as a "language about language" is a vague one and has led to it being used with several different meanings. The comment that "metalogical has often been used where extralogical would be more appropriate" has been made [Weyrauch, 1980]. This point will be returned to later in this chapter. With programming languages, the term was used early on to describe languages that could formally describe the meaning or behavior of the first high-level languages, inspired in particular by Algol [Naur, 1960], one of the first attempts to define a language formally first and practically second. It was also inspired by concern (see, for instance, [Feldman, 1966]) that others of the then newly developed high-level languages could only be genuinely considered "high-level" and could be safely ported between machines if they could be described in terms other than the assembly languages into which they compiled. If they could not and the assembly languages in turn could only be described in terms of the physical electronics of the machines, the languages were really only defined by the hardware. An important early conference on metalanguage for programming language description held in Vienna in 1964 [Steel, 1966] was considered then as "among the most valuable and productive scientific meetings ever held on a subject pertaining to information processing". Note that the vagueness of the term metalanguage was already apparent at this stage. Some of the papers described metalanguages, which built on *BNF* (Backus Naur Form) and some explicitly noted the distinction between syntax and semantics. Our interest here will only be on the semantics side.

As mentioned in Chapter 2, Landin noted a correspondence between Algol and Church's lambda calculus [Landin, 1965] and expounded further on it at this Vienna conference. At the same conference, McCarthy [1965] chose the different approach of describing Algol in terms of a mini-language he called "Micro-Algol". Programs in this language consist only of assignments and conditional **goto**s of the form **if** *p* **then goto** *a*. McCarthy later developed this into a full metacircular interpreter; the idea was that since the interpreter was written in Micro-Algol and could interpret Micro-Algol, Micro-Algol was a language, which defined itself. Algol and any other high-level language that could be translated to Micro-Algol were thus fully defined. The definition did not have to resort to a lowest-level description in terms of machine hardware (just as the self-interpreting USA constitution means that the USA legal system does not ultimately rely on the whims of a monarch or the reasonableness of the middle classes).

The following is McCarthy's [1965] Micro-Algol metacircular interpreter:

```
micro: n:=c(s,ξ);
       if beyond(π,m) then goto done;
       s:=statement(n,π);
       ξ:=if assignment(s) then a(sn,n+1,a(left(s),value(right(s),ξ),ξ))
          else if value(proposition(s),ξ) then a(sn,numb(destination(s),π),ξ)
          else a(sn,n+1,ξ);
       goto micro;
done:
```

This requires some explanation. ξ is the state vector of the program π being interpreted. The state gives the value of all the variables and all other information that together with the program itself determines the future course of the computation. Today this would be called a *continuation*. The pseudo-variable sn, whose value is included in ξ, gives the number of the statement, which is currently being executed. a(var,value,ξ) gives the new state resulting from assigning value to variable var; left(s) gives the variable on the left hand side of an assignment s, right(s) gives the expression on the right-hand side; value(e,ξ) evaluates expression e when the current state is ξ; proposition(s) gives p when s is **if** p **then goto** a while destination(s) gives a; numb(L,π) gives the statement number corresponding to label L in program π.

Landin's compilation into lambda calculus was the more immediately practical. Since lambda calculus could be considered the machine code of the abstract SECD machine which Landin had also developed [Landin, 1963], this could in turn be implemented on a real machine, thus the approach could be the basis of a practical compiler. The important thing was the introduction of clarity into what was then something of a "black-art" of compiler writing through this division into layers. The division was somewhat spoilt by the necessity to add further facilities to the SECD machine to cope with those aspects of Algol that could not easily be represented in lambda calculus. The development of programming languages that were purely sugared lambda calculus came later [Turner, 1979].

McCarthy's approach was not designed to lead to a practical compiler, or even to an impractical one that could nevertheless be put forward as a working model to define the semantics of a language operationally; it was more an operation in defining semantics abstractly. An important distinction is that McCarthy's interpreter makes the machine state of the language an explicit object in the metalanguage, whereas in Landin's approach the implicit machine state of the language is translated to an implicit machine state in the metalanguage. In the discussions following the presentations of the papers Landin [1963] links McCarthy's approach with a paper presented by Strachey at the same conference, which in retrospect may be seen as introducing ideas that led to the concept of denotational semantics [Scott and Strachey, 1971]. (Helpfully for computer science historians, fairly full accounts of these discussions are included in the proceedings.)

8.2 Introspection

The idea of a programming language being able to handle an explicit representation of its own state was of interest to workers in Artificial Intelligence. It was argued that a crucial component of an intelligent system is the ability to reason about itself, or to introspect. Maes [1986] gives a simple introduction to the subject. Introspection is first clearly defined in the language *3-Lisp* [Smith, 1984], although features that may be regarded as introspective are provided in a more ad hoc manner in earlier languages. The idea is that facilities exist in the language to take objects that may be assumed to exist at the interpreter or metalanguage level and make them first-class entities in the language level. In McCarthy's micro-Algol meta-interpreter, for example, the pseudo-variable sn might be considered such an object, as indeed might any part of the state ξ. Object level decisions may be made on the basis of their value and new values for them constructed and put back into the meta-interpreter. The term *reification* came to be used to refer to taking metalevel objects from the program and making them data, while *reflection* referred to the reverse process of putting data objects into the program [Friedman and Wand, 1984].

Introspection was promoted not only as a way for allowing programs to reflect on themselves, but also as a way for programmers to tailor the programming language for their own needs, changing the evaluation order, adding traces for debugging and so on. It was particularly influential in object-oriented programming [Maes, 1987]. In Smalltalk [Goldberg and Robson, 1989], the idea that "everything is an object", including the classes that describe objects and hence the concept of a metaclass as the class which describes classes, means that introspection is a natural part of the language. In Prolog, the system predicate **clause** is a reification predicate, making an aspect of the program into data, while **assert** is a reflection predicate. Prolog's **retract** may be regarded as a combination of reification and reflection. Even the cut (and more so many proposed variants of it) may be regarded as a stereotyped combination of reification and reflection, giving the program access to the abstract search space of the interpreter and modifying it, though with severe restrictions on the modifications possible. This is the connection between extralogical and metalogical promised earlier.

The key to introspection in programming languages is that it relies on an abstract interpreter, which is in fact a virtual interpreter. There is no requirement that the meta-interpreter, which it assumes exists, actually does exist. Indeed it cannot always, since reflection is often recursive: it is possible for the metalayer to introspect on a meta-metalayer and so on infinitely, producing what is described as the "tower of interpreters". The real interpreter or compiler, which actually implements the language, is something different and remains unreachable by the programmer. The concepts in the meta-interpreters are produced lazily as required. If introspection were introduced into McCarthy's Micro-Algol, for instance, it would be possible to access and change sn, the statement position indicator. But there is a clear distinction between this, an abstract concept and the program counter of the underlying assembly language. However deep you got into the tower of meta-interpreters, you would never hit the real program counter.

The problem with introspection in programming languages is that it gives both the power and the danger of self-modifying code. In 3-Lisp it is possible to access and change variable bindings and function definitions using introspection. Thus the barrier between language and metalanguage is broken down, it becomes a notational convenience, but not one that can be relied on. If we can change the environment at whim, we have lost the valuable declarative properties of functional programming. As Hofstadter [1979] puts it: "below every tangled hierarchy lies an inviolate level." The only real metalanguage when we have unlimited reflection (perhaps we could call it the hyper-language) is the inviolate machine code which implements the system. In our constitutional analogy, we are back to the position where the only absolute power lies with the whim of the sovereign; there are no hard constitutional safeguards. The reasonableness of the programmer in not misusing reflection can be compared to the reasonableness of the British middle classes in Bagehot's defense of the unwritten constitution.

8.3 Amalgamating Language and Metalanguage in Logic Programming

As mentioned above, the introduction of a meta-interpretation layer enables us to reason explicitly about programs and their execution. In logic programming terms, it enables one to reason explicitly about theories (collections of clauses) and about the inference mechanism used to make derivations from these theories. We expressed concern, however, about the lack of control when we had an implicit meta-interpreter and an undisciplined approach to manipulating it. This can be overcome by making an interpreter explicit, but explicit in a limited way. Only those elements of the interpreter that we want to reason about are made explicit, while other elements remain implicit. For example, if we want a program that adds or deletes clauses from the set of clauses but does not make any changes to the inference mechanism, we can write an interpreter with an explicit representation of the clauses, but the inference mechanism remaining implicit and inviolate. In doing so, we limit the amount of damage caused by work at the metalevel. As mentioned above, the metalevel and object-level are in fact almagamated by giving the programmer control of both. But if the communication between the two is limited as much as possible in the program it is good software engineering principle, akin to other ways of dividing up programs into modules and limiting and making explicit the communication between the modules.

Bowen and Kowalski [1982] formalized discussion of metaprogramming in logic by introducing two rules that describe the interactions between the object-level and metalevel:

$$\frac{\text{Pr} \vdash_M \text{demo}(A',B')}{A \vdash_L B} \qquad \frac{A \vdash_L B}{\text{Pr} \vdash_M \text{demo}(A',B')}$$

These are referred to as *reflection rules*, the terminology coming from Feferman [1962] via Weyhrauch [1981]; it is related but not identical to the use of the term reflection in introspective systems. Here $\vdash_M$ represents proof at the metalevel, while $\vdash_L$ represents proof at the object language level. So the first rule states that if it is possible to prove that demo(A´,B´) follows from the program Pr at the metalevel, then it can be inferred that B can be proved from A at the object level, while the second rule states the reverse. A´ is the representation of the object-level theory A at the metalevel and similarly B´ is the representation of the object-level expression B at the metalevel. This relationship is specified formally by a *naming relationship* [van Harmelen, 1992]. The naming relationship is a formalization of McCarthy's packaging of program state into the "state vector" ξ in his meta-interpreter.

The classic "vanilla" meta-interpreter of Prolog is simpler than Bowen and Kowalski's **demo**:

solve(true).
solve((A,B)) :- **solve**(A), **solve**(B).
solve(Goal) :- **clause**(Goal,Body), **solve**(Body).

because it makes no distinction between object-level and metalevel clauses. Here the object level and the metalevel language are identical, except that object-level predicate names are represented by metalevel function names. The blurring of object and metalevel in **clause** confuses even this. A particularly important point is that object-level variables are represented by metalevel variables.

We can remove the problem caused by Prolog's **clause** by having the object-level program represented as an explicit value in the metalevel program, then we can define a **demo** which works as indicated by Bowen and Kowalski's rules:

demo(Pr,[]).
demo(Pr,[A|B]) :- **body**(Pr,A,Body), **demo**(Pr,Body), **demo**(Pr,B).

The exact metalevel representation of object-level clauses will be further defined by **body**, which it can be assumed selects a clause from the object-level program Pr, whose head matches with A and returns in Body the body of that clause, importantly with variables re-named as necessary. The interpreter does require that an object-level clause body is represented by a metalevel list of metalevel representations of goals or by the empty list if it is **true** at the object-level.

What is crucial is that object-level control is represented implicitly by metalevel control. There is nothing in the interpreter that indicates that it is Prolog's depth-first left-to-right with backtracking control. We could build a tower of such meta-interpreters and the control would remain in the underlying Prolog system (the inviolate hyper-interpreter, introduced earlier). Indeed, if it were running on top of GDC or some other non-Prolog logic language, it would inherit that language's control mechanism. We can note therefore that contrary to McCarthy's intentions with his Mini-Algol meta-interpreter, this metacircular interpreter does not fully define the logic language, indeed in amalgamating language with metalanguage it leaves it undefined.

The use of such a meta-interpreter comes when we do not wish to interfere with the control, but wish to add some extra processing alongside inheriting the control mechanism of the underlying language. The following meta-interpreter adds to the "vanilla" interpreter a mechanism for counting the number of object-level goal reductions:

```
demo(Pr,[],N) :- N=0.
demo(Pr,[A|B],N) :-
    body(Pr,A,Body), demo(Pr,Body,N1), demo(Pr,B,N2),
    N is N1+N2.
```

Another use might be an interpreter that simply prints each goal as it is reduced. This could thus be used as a simple tracer. A useful aspect of this interpreter is that in making the object-level program explicit we can handle program-altering primitives like **assert** and **retract** in a way which viewed from the metalevel does not violate the logical basis of the program:

```
demo(Pr,[]).
demo(Pr,[assert(C)|Rest]) :- !,
    insert(C,Pr,Pr1), demo(Pr1,Rest).
demo(Pr,[retract(C)|Rest]) :- !,
    delete(C,Pr,Pr1), demo(Pr1,Rest).
demo(Pr,[A|B]) :- body(Pr,A,Body), demo(Pr,Body), demo(Pr,B).
```

Some measure of the extent to which a primitive is merely extra-logical as opposed to metalogical may be gained by the ease with which it can be incorporated into a metacircular interpreter. Prolog's cut performs badly on this front, since it is certainly not possible to represent an object-level cut by a metalevel cut; to implement it correctly would require a large amount of the underlying control to be made explicit in the meta-interpreter so that it can be manipulated. On the other hand, negation by failure is trivial to implement in the meta-interpreter; it requires just the addition of the following clause to the vanilla **demo**:

```
demo(Pr,[not(G)|Rest]) :- not(demo(Pr,[G])), demo(Pr,Rest).
```

The version of **demo** suggested by Bowen and Kowalski enables greater control to be exercised at the metalevel over the object level:

```
demo(Prog, Goals) :- empty(Goals).
demo(Prog, Goals) :-
    select(Goals, Goal, Rest),
    member(Clause, Prog),
    rename(Clause, Goals, VariantClause),
    parts(VariantClause, Head, Body),
    match(Head, Goal, Substitution),
    join(Body, Rest, NewGoals1),
    apply(Substitution, NewGoals1, NewGoals),
    demo(Prog, NewGoals).
```

Here the selection of the particular object-level goal to reduce is determined by the metalevel procedure **select** and **match** determines the sort of matching of goal against clause head. It would be possible for **select** and **join** which adds the new goals to the existing waiting goals to be written so that the control regime provided at object-level is not Prolog's depth-first left-to-right, but something else. For example, if **join** joined the new goals to the rear of the rest of the goals and **select** chose the first goal from the front, the result would be breadth-first expansion of the search tree.

Although **match** could be written as GDC style input matching rather than full
unification, this interpreter still inherits Prolog's underlying assumption of sequential
execution. Note for example, it is assumed that a complete set of goals to be executed
is passed sequentially from each goal reduction, with Prolog's global substitution on
unification assumed.

8.4 Control Metalanguages

In the interpreters discussed above, control is fixed, whether inherited implicitly from
the underlying hyper-interpreter, or provided explicitly through procedures such as
select. However, another strand of work in metalevel reasoning concerns the
definition of separate languages for programming control. Confusingly, these
languages are also referred to as "metalanguages". In the Bowen and Kowalski
[1982], brief mention is made of a four argument **demo** predicate, whose first two
arguments are the theorem and expression to be proved as above, but whose third
argument is an input control value and whose fourth argument is an unspecified
output. The idea of a proof argument to **demo** is expanded in a further paper by
Bowen and Weinberg [1985]. With the four-argument **demo**, we can extend the
reflection rules:

$$\frac{Pr \vdash_M demo(A',B',C',D')}{A \vdash_{LC} B,D} \qquad \frac{A \vdash_{LC} B,D}{Pr \vdash_M demo(A',B',C',D')}$$

Clearly, the proof argument C here could have a very simple structure, consisting
perhaps of just a single word indicating that search should be depth-first or breadth-
first. The existence of infinite trees means that something may be provable when
proof is specified as breadth-first but not when depth-first. Gallaire and Lassere
[1982] and Dincbas and Le Pape [1984] have proposed considerably more complex
metalanguages for control in logic programming. Trinder et al [1998] introduce a
meta-programming strategy argument to parallelize lazy functional programming.

Although control metalanguages are expressed here in terms of a second input along
with the object-level program to an explicit meta-interpreter, the more common
situation is that the meta-interpreter they control is implicit and as with introspection
may be considered a virtual concept. Just as with introspection, what the language
designer chooses to make reifiable and what remains inviolate is not fixed. It depends
on the way in which the language is intended to be viewed. What a control
metalanguage may actually control depends on what the language designer who
makes the control metalanguage available chooses to reveal as controllable. For
example, whereas the control metalanguages for logic programming mentioned above
view logic programming in terms of an abstract resolution model, another proposed
control metalanguage for Prolog [Devanbu et al., 1986] views Prolog in procedural
terms. Thus it gives the programmer the ability to alter the control pattern of Prolog
as expressed by the Byrd four port model [Byrd, 1980].

As noted in Section 1.8, the idea of explicit metalevel control systems which may themselves be programmed first arose in the context of production rule systems, where it was possible that in a given situation more than one rule could fire. In this case, the potential set of rules that can fire is termed the *conflict resolution set* and the mechanism for picking one rule to fire from these is termed *conflict resolution*. Early production systems had simple built-in implicit strategies, just as Prolog had a built-in control order. *OPS* [Forgy and McDermott, 1977], for example, gives a preference to the rule which matches with the most recent additions to working memory and then to the rule with the greatest number of conditional elements. One of the first systems to give an explicit control over selection of rules in conflict resolution was *TEIRESIAS* [Davis and Buchanan, 1977; Davis, 1980], which gave the ability to specify which rule to select by a set of metarules. As these metarules took the same format as the object-level rules, the possibility of meta-metalevel rules to govern them and so on existed, though Davis did not find any need for levels of rules above the metalevel.

The idea of structuring knowledge into multiple layers, with separate layers of metaknowledge for reasoning about control is now commonplace. The *KADS* methodology for developing expert systems [Schreiber et al., 1993], for example, specifies four distinct layers [van Harmelen and Balder, 1992]:

- Domain layer – knowledge about the specific domain of the expert system.

- Inference Layer – how to use the knowledge from the domain layer.

- Task layer – specifies control over the execution of the inference steps.

- Strategy layer – concerned with task selection: how to choose between various tasks that achieve the same goal.

In intelligent agent systems, multiple layers of control are also a common form of structuring [Malec, 1994]. For example, a system developed in Sweden to give intelligent assistance to drivers [Morin et al., 1992] has three layers:

- A process layer, which receives input from the environment and translates continuous data to discrete values.

- An intermediate discrete response layer, which computes a response to events forwarded from the process layer.

- An analysis layer, which deals with planning and reasoning.

We consider the idea of layering in agents in more detail in Chapter 10

Metalevel control systems can be divided into those that make use of domain information and those that are purely concerned with the metalevel. In TEIRESIAS, for example, a typical metarule will suggest that rules containing one specified object-level property should be preferred over rules containing another: this is domain level information. A medical expert system might, for example, have a metarule that states that rules indicating the presence of an infectious disease should always be tried before other rules. This sort of control rule may be considered essentially as a structuring of the domain knowledge. An example of a metarule that does not involve domain knowledge would be one that stated that the rule with the largest number of conditions to match should always be tried first. Metarules like this, which simply specify a search order without reference to the domain or solely in terms of the representation at the metalevel, may be considered essentially as a way of structuring the interpreter. In a concurrent language, an important application of this layering of interpreters is to have an interpreter which provides an abstract layer of virtual parallelism [Burton and Huntbach, 1984]. The applications program interpreted itself by a meta-interpreter maps the virtual parallelism onto a real parallel architecture [Taylor et al., 1987]. Annotations such as those we have described for priority and codemapping may be considered as a simple metalanguage that breaks through to the mapping meta-interpreter. Prolog's cut may be considered a similar sort of notation which breaks through the control-free model of clause resolution in logic to a separate control mechanism, thus accounting for the difficulty of modeling it in a meta-interpreter.

Clancey argues the case for keeping domain knowledge out of metalevel control rules [Clancey, 1983], saying that doing so keeps systems easier to debug and modify, ensures that they are reusable in a variety of domains and also enables systems to easily generate explanations for their actions. He demonstrated this by extracting the domain-independent control strategy that was implicit in the MYCIN medical expert system [Shortliffe, 1976] and making it separate and explicit in a new expert system called NEOMYCIN [Clancey and Letsinger, 1981].

8.5 A Classification of Metalevel Systems

Drawing on the discussion above, we can now attempt a classification of metalevel systems. The classification is based on that suggested by van Harmelen [1991]. The first class of metalevel systems may be termed *definitional* and uses a metalanguage in order to define another language. This may be purely in order to give a semantics, which is operational if the metalanguage is executable, but it may also be part of a practical implementation. Symbolic processing languages are particularly suited to implementing other languages. In artificial intelligence, building a higher-level knowledge-representation language on top of a lower-level declarative language is a common practice, recommended in textbooks on artificial intelligence programming in both Lisp [Charniak et al., 1987] and Prolog [Bratko, 1986].

A second class may be termed *enhanced metacircular interpreters*. In this class the metalanguage is the same as the object language and the purpose of the interpreter is to provide an additional output alongside the interpretation. Among the additional outputs that can be provided are certainty factors for use in expert systems applications [Shapiro, 1983] and computation trees for use in debugging [Huntbach, 1987]. The chapter on meta-interpreters in Sterling and Shapiro's Prolog textbook [Sterling and Shapiro, 1986] is largely confined to this sort of meta-interpreter and provides numerous examples. Use of this sort of meta-interpreter occurs mainly among logic programmers because they are easy to write in logic languages: complex issues like control and variable handling are simply passed implicitly from object level to metalevel to the underlying system.

The most varied class of metalevel systems, however, is that class of systems where the aim is to separate control issues from declarative issues, but to provide the ability to program both. This follows from Kowalski's [1979] dictum "Algorithm = Logic + Control." Multiple layers of meta-interpreters means that it is possible to break down control into metalogic and metacontrol and so on.

It might be possible to alter the flow of control in some procedural languages, but in general these languages are such that logic and control are so intertwined as to be inseparable. Declarative languages, however, are built around the idea that control is left to the underlying system and the program is simply a declaration of the possible set of solutions. This opens the question as to why the programmer should have any control over control, since it is just an implementation detail. There is, however, a group of languages that are neither procedural nor declarative. As suggested above, production rule systems fall into this group and are the paradigm in which the issue of metalevel control first received practical attention.

The reason why control arises as an issue in declarative languages is the question of efficiency. In functional languages the only control issue is reduction order. The Church–Rosser theorem [Barendregt, 1984] tells us that if it terminates, whatever way we reduce a functional expression we will get the same result. It is possible for one reduction order to return a result quicker than another is, or for one reduction order to return a result while another does not terminate. Additional questions of efficiency arise when implementing a functional language on a multi-processor system when a decision has to be made as to whether the overhead of moving a subexpression to another processor to be evaluated in parallel is outweighed by the benefits of parallel execution. These considerations have led to suggestions for simple control annotations controlling reduction order and parallel processing in functional languages [Burton, 1987].

In logic languages, there is greater scope for order of reduction to affect efficiency. Whereas in a functional language control is generally considered something for the system to sort out, in logic languages there have been many proposals for methods to give the user control over control. Smith and Genesereth [1985] analyze in detail the effect that the ordering of conjunctive queries can have. The practical Prolog programmer always has to be aware of Prolog's left-to-right reduction order, writing programs such that the optimal ordering of queries matches this built-in order. However, the optimal order may only be determinable at run-time and often depends on the mode in which a predicate is called. The lack of ability to change query order dynamically is one of the reasons why Prolog's multi-mode facility is rarely useful in any but trivial programs. Metalevel annotations to give the programmer control over query order were among the earliest suggestions to improve Prolog [Clark et al., 1982; Colmerauer et al., 1982]. Cohen [1985] gives a metacircular interpreter to implement Prolog II's **freeze**. This is a metalevel procedure where **freeze**(X,G) with X a variable and G a goal causes G to be removed from the list of goals waiting for execution if X is unbound, but to be placed at the head of it as soon as X becomes bound. Owen [1988] gives a metacircular interpreter that was used to allow flexible goal ordering, which was used in the domain of protein topology. As we have seen, in GDC there is a built-in suspension mechanism which works in a similar way to

freeze and otherwise obviates the need for further goal ordering mechanisms until we consider the speculative computation issues in Chapter 6.

Van Harmelen classifies metalevel systems on the basis on combinatorial soundness and completeness. A metalevel inference system is combinatorially complete if it derives *all* results derivable from the object level theory and combinatorially sound if it derives *only* results derivable from the object level theory. Goal re-ordering will not affect the soundness or completeness of a logic program (except that it may make solutions obtainable that would be unobtainable due to being beyond infinite branches). Metarules that prune the search tree by cutting out some clauses from being considered will make a metalevel system incomplete, which is not a problem in GDC, as it does not attempt to be complete. The **unknown** test in a guard is an example of a metalevel feature that prunes the results possible. Prolog's **assert** is an example of a metalevel feature that introduces unsoundness. The distinction commonly made in Prolog between "red cuts" and "green cuts" distinguishes those usages of cut which affect the completeness of a Prolog program and those usages where the cut is used purely to cut out search, which the programmer knows will not lead to solutions and thus will not affect the completeness. The red/green distinction could usefully be extended to other extra-logical notations: usages that affect the soundness or completeness being termed red, those which do not being termed green. A green **assert** in Prolog, for example, would be one which simply asserts a lemma for efficiency reasons that could be proved form the existing clauses for the predicate. A useful general rule in considering proposed metalevel control annotations would be to accept only those that are capable of just green use.

Van Harmelen's main classification of metalevel systems, however, concerns the *locus of action*: the place in which the system is active at any one point in time. A metalevel system with object-level inference is one where the main activity is in the object-level interpreter. This covers those systems where the metalevel interpreter is implicit and programmer control over it is limited to annotations, such as the various examples above of Prolog control languages. A metalevel system with metalevel inference is one where the computation takes place mainly in the metalevel interpreter. This covers those systems where a full interpreter is available for inspection and modification, and the attention is on this interpreter manipulating the object-level program. An intermediate class covers those systems where the locus of action shifts between the object-level and the metalevel. An example of the intermediate class is those production systems where control jumps to the metalevel for conflict resolution. In parallel logic programming, *Pandora* [Bahgat and Gregory, 1989] is an example of a mixed-level inference system. It behaves in a similar way to the concurrent logic languages, but if it hits a deadlock, control jumps to a metalevel deadlock handler [Bahgat, 1992] which resolves the situation by making a non-deterministic choice.

The final distinction that van Harmelen makes is to distinguish between *monolingual* and *bilingual* metalevel systems. A monolingual system is one where the language at the metalevel is the same as at the object-level, in particular object-level variables are mapped into metalevel variables. A bilingual system is one where the object-level and metalevel languages are distinct, in particular object-level variables are represented by ground terms at the metalevel. Van Harmelen argues strongly in favor of bilingual systems on the grounds of clarity. The argument is both informal, considering the practical and conceptual difficulties of mixing the two levels, and formal, after Hill and Lloyd's analysis [1988] which suggested that semantics for metalevel programs could not be derived while there was a confusion between metalevel and object-level variables. Hill and Lloyd followed this by introducing a logic language, *Gödel* [Hill and Lloyd, 1994], in which there are built-in object-level and metalevel variables, with predicates at the metalevel operating on object-level variables which replace the extra-logical predicates of Prolog. The counter-argument is the simplicity of monolingual interpreters due to not having to make explicit that which they do not change from the underlying system. Martens and de Schreye [1995] argue that it *is* possible to come up with a formal semantics for monolingual systems.

8.6 Some GDC Monolingual Interpreters

Having discussed the background behind the idea of meta-interpreters and given a classification, we can now consider the subject on a practical level by considering a few examples. The following is the vanilla meta-interpreter for GDC:

```
reduce(X=Y) :- X=Y.
reduce(Actor) :- otherwise
    |   behavior(Actor, Body), reducelist(Body).
reducelist([]).
reducelist([H|T]) :- reduce(H), reducelist(T).
```

Since GDC does not have built-in operations for manipulating the behaviors that form a program, the object level behaviors must be represented in a form that explicitly marks them out as object-level behaviors. The following would be the representation for quicksort:

```
behavior(qsort([],Sorted),Body)
    :- Body=[Sorted=[]].
behavior(qsort([Pivot|List],Sorted), Body)
    :- Body=[part(List,Pivot,Lesser,Greater),
             qsort(Lesser,Lsorted),qsort(Greater,Gsorted),
             concatenate(Lsorted,[Pivot|Gsorted],Sorted)].
behavior(part([],Pivot,Lesser,Greater),Body)
    :- Body=[   Lesser=[],Greater=[]].
behavior(part([Item|List],Pivot,Lesser,Greater),Body)
    :- Pivot=<Item
    |   Body=[   Greater=[Item|Upper],part(List,Pivot,Lesser,Upper)].
behavior(part([Item|List],Pivot,Lesser,Greater),Body)
    :- Item=<Pivot
    |   Body=[Lesser=[Item|Lower],part(List,Pivot,Lower,Greater)].
behavior(concatenate([],List,Total), Body)
    :- Body=[Total=List].
behavior(concatenate([Item|List1],List2,Total), Body)
```

```
:-  Body=[Total=[Item|List],concatenate(List1,List2,List)].
```

Note that in this interpreter the concurrency of the object level maps implicitly onto the concurrency of the metalevel, the concurrency of the second behavior for **reducelist** giving the concurrency of the object level. Behavior commitments at the object level map implicitly onto the commitment of the actor in the second behavior of **reduce**. Object level guards represent metalevel guards. The unification primitive at the object-level maps onto the unification primitive of the first behavior for **reduce**. Further primitive operations could be covered in a similar way to unification by adding behaviors to **reduce**.

A number of simple interpreters may be derived from the above meta-interpreter [Safra and Shapiro, 1986]. The following, for example, uses the "short-circuit" technique to report when execution of an actor has completed:

```
reduce(X=Y,Left,Right)
    :-  (X,Right)=(Y,Left).
reduce(Actor,Left,Right) :- otherwise
    |   behavior(Actor,Body),
        reducelist(Body,Left,Right).
reducelist([],Left,Right)
    :-  Right=Left.
reducelist([H|T],Left,Right)
    :-  reduce(H,Left,Middle),
        reducelist(T,Middle,Right).
```

The initial call to the interpreter will take the form :- **reduce**(Actor,done,Flag). The message done is sent on the channel Flag only when execution of all actors spawned by the actor execution has completed. Note the assumption in the first behavior for **reduce** is that the component parts of the unification can be assumed to be done simultaneously (atomic unification). If this is not the case, we need to ensure that the short-circuit is closed only when the unification of the two object level messages has been completed. In this case we will need to use a system primitive which performs unification on its first two arguments and binds a flag channel given as its third argument, the message being sent only when the unification is complete. Assuming the message done is sent on the flag channel following unification, this will give us the following:

```
reduce(X=Y,Left,Right)
    :-  unify(X,Y,Flag), close(Flag,Left,Right).

close(done,Left,Right) :- Left=Right.
```

Similar flag-message sending versions of any other system primitives will be required.

The short-circuit technique can be used to give sequential execution. If we want a pair of actors to execute sequentially, we will not start execution of the second until execution of the first has completely finished. The following meta-interpreter enforces sequential execution:

```
reduce(X=Y,Flag)
```

```
    :-  (X,Flag)=(Y,done).
reduce(Actor,Flag)
    :-  otherwise
    |   behavior(Actor, Body),
        reducelist(Body,Flag).

sequential_reducelist(List,done,Flag)
    :-  reducelist(List,Flag).

reducelist([],Flag)
    :-  Flag=done.
reducelist([H|T],Flag)
    :-  reduce(H,Flag1),
        sequential_reducelist(T,Flag1,Flag).
```

The initial call is :- **reduce**(Actor,Flag) where Flag is an unbound channel.

In the GDC meta-interpreter above, the selection of a behavior to execute an actor was mapped implicitly onto GDC's own behavior selection mechanism. If, however, we wish to override the built-in behavior-selection mechanism we must explicitly program in a replacement behavior-selection mechanism. As an example, consider a meta-interpreter where GDC's indeterminism is resolved by offering a choice between the behaviors, which may reduce an actor. Interpreters like this may be used for debugging purposes letting the human user who is investigating different ways of resolving the indeterminacy make the choice. Alternatively, we could have another layer of meta-interpreter that selects between behaviors, essentially the same idea as the conflict-resolution mechanism in production systems.

The following gives the top level:

```
reduce(X=Y)
    :-  X=Y.
reduce(Actor)
    :-  otherwise
    |   behaviors(Actor, Behaviors),
        possbodies(Actor, Behaviors, Possibilities),
        select(Actor, Possibilities, Body),
        reducelist(Body).
reducelist([]).
reducelist([H|T])
    :-  reduce(H),
        reducelist(T).
```

Here **behaviors**(Actor,Behaviors) is intended to give all behaviors for a possible actor. The actor **possbodies**(Actor,Behaviors,Possibilities) will return in Possibilities the bodies of all behaviors in Behaviors to which Actor may commit. The actor **select**(Actor,Possibilities,Body) will select one of these possibilities.

In this conflict-resolution interpreter, it will be assumed, for convenience, that each behavior in the list of behaviors given by **behaviors** contains distinct channels and only behaviors with empty guards will be handled. Behaviors are represented by

(Head, Body) pairs. Thus the program for non-deterministic merge would be represented by:

behaviors(merge(X0,Y0,Z0), Behaviors)
  :- Behaviors=[
        (merge(X1,[],Z1),[Z1=X1]),(merge([],Y2,Z2),[Z2=Y2]),
        (merge([H3|T3],Y3,Z3),[merge(T3,Y3,Z13), Z3=[H3|Z13]]),
        (merge(X4,[H4|T4],Z4),[merge(X4,T4,Z14), Z4=[H4|Z14]])].

In order to gain a list of possible behavior bodies in **possbodies,** the OR-parallelism of the object-level needs to be simulated by AND-parallelism at the metalevel as described in Chapter 6. The behavior selection mechanism is made explicit, involving an explicit call to a **match** actor which performs the matching which is done implicitly in GDC execution. In this case, **match** as well as receiving messages in the behavior head also sends on a flag channel the message true if the match succeeds and false otherwise:

possbodies(Actor, [(Head,Body)|Rest], Poss)
  :- **match**(Actor, Head, Flag),
      possbodies(Actor, Rest, RPoss),
      addposs(Flag, Body, RPoss, Poss).
possbodies(Actor, [], Poss) :- Poss=[].

The actor **addposs** simply adds a behavior body (with channels appropriately bound) to the list of possibilities if matching succeeds:

addposs(false,_,RPoss,Poss)
  :- Poss=RPoss.
addposs(true,Body,RPoss,Poss)
  :- Poss=[Body|Poss].

Although it would be possible to provide a version of **match** as a system primitive, it may be programmed directly:

match(X, Y, V) :- **unknown**(Y) | Y=X,V=true.
match(X, Y, V) :- X=Y | V=true.
match(X, Y, V) :- X=/=Y | V=false.
match(X, Y, V) :- **list**(X), **list**(Y) | **matchlist**(X, Y, V).
match(X, Y, V) :- **tuple**(X), **tuple**(Y)
    | X=..LX, Y=..LY, **matchlist**(LX, LY, V).

matchlist([], [], V) :- V=true.
matchlist([H1|T1], [H2|T2],V)
    :- **match**(H1, H2, VH), **matchlist**(T1, T2, VT) and(VH, VT, V).
matchlist(X, Y, V) :- **unknown**(Y) | Y=X, V=true.

and(true, true, V) :- V=true.
and(false, _, V) :- V=false.
and(_, false, V) :- V=false.

While this meta-interpreter is more complex than previous ones, a large amount of the object-level GDC still maps implicitly onto metalevel GDC. In particular there is no direct reference to the scheduling of actors or the suspension mechanism. The scheduling of the object-level GDC is whatever is provided by the metalevel GDC. A suspension in the object-level GDC will map into a suspension of the metalevel GDC in the **match** actor of the meta-interpreter, when X is unbound but Y is bound so the guards X==Y and X=/=Y are both suspended until X becomes sufficiently bound for them to resolve. It is assumed that **select** will only present a menu of possible bodies to resolve an actor when there are no suspensions for that actor. Note that it is a context free selection as the set of actors awaiting execution remains implicit, so it is not an explicit object that can be viewed when making a behavior selection. The order in which the selection menus are presented will in effect be the scheduling order, which is not under user control.

A further development would be to introduce an explicit scheduling list. This could be used to give a meta-interpreter that implements the actor priorities of Chapter 6. The following meta-interpreter does this. The idea is that the top-level actor network is:

   :-   **reduce**(Actor/Priority,S), **scheduler**(S)

where S is a stream of messages of the form req(Priority,Go). These messages are generated by the **reduce** actor and consumed by the **scheduler** actor. As generated Go is unbound in the messages. The **scheduler** binds these channels in the order determined by Priority. It is assumed that a behavior body consists of a list of actor/priority pairs. A priority could be a constant or a channel which is bound during execution.

The scheduler actor will keep an explicit list of priority requests, which will in effect form the explicit scheduling list. The **wait** actor will ensure that behavior selection is suspended until allowed by the scheduler since it cannot proceed until the request channel is bound. Streams of requests are merged using conventional stream merging:

```
reduce(X=Y, S) :- X=Y, S=[].
reduce(Actor/Priority, S)
      :-  S=[req(Priority,Go)|S1],
          behaviors(Actor,Behaviors),
          wait(Go,Actor,Behaviors,Body),
          reducelist(Body,S1).

reducelist([],S) :- S=[].
reducelist([H|T],S)
      :-  reduce(H,S1), reducelist(T,S2), merge(S1,S2,S).

wait(go,Actor,Behaviors,Body)
      :-  possbodies(Actor,Behaviors,Possibilities),
          select(Actor,Possibilities,Body).
```

This interpreter is deficient because there are no limits on the scheduler. The scheduler could just authorize every actor to proceed to behavior selection as soon as it receives the actor's request. This defeats the purpose of the interpreter, since given a limited number of processors scheduling would default to whichever order is decided by the underlying system. In order to give user-defined scheduling we need to authorize only enough actors to keep the processors busy. To do this, the scheduler would need to know how many of the current set of actors are suspended on all their possible messages and thus not consuming any processor resources. This could be done with a version of **match**, but would require an explicit handling of suspensions rather than the implicit mapping of objectlevel suspensions to metalevel suspensions. Rather than suspend, **match** would terminate and return a list of channels and messages to which they must be bound for the actor to be woken.

An interpreter that explicitly handled suspensions could either use *busy-waiting*, continually testing whether a channel whose value is required has become bound, or *non-busy-waiting*, in which a list of suspended actors is associated with each unbound channel and the actors woken when the channel becomes bound. Such a meta-interpreter would be considerably more complex than the simple meta-interpreters with which we started, but it still relies on implicit mapping from metalevel to object level of store allocation and garbage collection.

Another variant of the meta-interpreter that explicitly gives a selection between behaviors to resolve an actor is one that illustrates the effect of choosing each possible behavior. This is referred to as an *all-solutions* interpreter since it will give all possible bindings of some channel in an actor. For a more detailed discussion of this problem see [Ueda, 1987]. The way the all-solutions interpreter below works is to maintain a list of actors and a list of partial solutions. When an actor may be resolved in one of several ways a duplicate of these lists, or continuation, is made to represent the position in the computation that would be obtained by choosing each alternative. The continuation will rename each channel (so that, for example, the list [X,X,Y] would become [X1,X1,Y1]), we will assume we have a primitive **copy** which creates such a copy with renamed channels. The list of possible solutions is obtained by appending together the list of solutions obtained from each continuation.

```
allsols(Actor,TermSols) :- reduce([Actor],[Term],Sols).

reduce([],Terms,Sols) :- Sols=Terms.
reduce([X=Y|Actors],Terms,Sols)
    :- X=Y, reduce(Actors,Terms,Sols).
reduce([Actor|Actors],Terms,Sols)
    :- otherwise
    |   behaviors(Actor,Behaviors),
        reducewith(Actor,Actors,Behaviors,Terms,Sols).

reducewith(Actor,Actors,[(Head,Body)|Rest],Terms,Sols)
    :- match(Actor,Head,Flag),
       reduceon(Flag,Actors,Body,Rest,Terms,Sols1),
       reducewith(Actor,Actors,Rest,Terms,Sols2),
       append(Sols1,Sols2,Sols).
reducewith(Actor,Actors,[],Terms,Sols) :- Sols=[].
```

```
reduceon(true,Actors,Body,Rest,Terms,Sols)
  :-  append(Body,Actors,Actors1),
      copy([Terms,Actors1],[Terms2,Actors2]),
      reduce(Actors2,Terms2,Sols).
reduceon(false,Actors,Body,Rest,Terms,Sols) :- Sols=[].
```

The effect of a call **allsols**(Actor,Term,Sols) is to bind Sols to a list of the different instances of Term given by all possible evaluations of Actor. For example, a call **allsols**(merge([a,b],[c],X),X,Sols) will cause Sols to become bound to [[a,b,c],[a,c,b],[c,a,b]], assuming we have the representation of non-deterministic merge given previously.

In the interpreter **reducewith** matches an actor against the heads of each of the behaviors for that actor. If matching succeeds, **reduceon** sets up a **reduce** actor to construct all solutions which involve this particular matching. Note that the code interpreted by this interpreter is limited to examples which do not require any suspensions since **reduceon** which initiates solution of the remaining actors remains suspended until matching has completed and sent the message true or false on the channel Flag. Since matching does not bind channels in the actor, it is safe to leave the construction of a continuation until after matching has completed successfully, thus avoiding unnecessary copying for cases where matching fails.

8.7 GDC Bilingual Interpreters

The problems with monolingual interpreters became more apparent in Section 8.6. The mapping of object-level variables to metalevel variables resulted in the need to introduce a variety of extra-logical primitives, culminating in **copy** in the all-solutions interpreter for general logic programs. The problem is that a single GDC variable with its single-assignment property cannot be used to model a variable in a logic language with non-deterministic backtracking as such a variable can be reassigned its value on backtracking. What is needed is a separate representation of object-level variables by ground terms at the metalevel, that is a bilingual interpreter.

In fact we have already seen a range of bilingual interpreters in Chapter 6. Search programs specifically for the 8-puzzle were generalized generic search programs that could be used for any system where a state is rewritten non-deterministically by a set of rewrite rules. We could therefore consider the rules by which the successors to a state are generated in the **successors** actor in Chapter 6 to be the object level program and the various search programs to be metalevel programs.

While the object-level rules in Chapter 6 could be simple rules for showing the possible changes of state in something like the 8-puzzle, they could equally well be a complete set of rewrite rules specifying how a set of sentences in logic could be changed using resolution. This would then make these rules themselves a metaprogram, with the logic sentences being the object-level programs and the search programs meta-metaprograms. If the search program used involved priorities and these were implemented using a meta-interpreter as suggested above, this interpreter would be a meta-meta-metalevel interpreter for the logic sentences. Note that this

four-leveled layering of interpreters corresponds to the proposed four layers in the
KADS methodology for knowledge-based systems development noted previously.

Below is a simple implementation of Chapter 6's **successors** for the case where the
state stored in a node in the search tree is a list of Goals in a Prolog-like language,
together with an environment giving the values of variables in the Goals. It is
assumed that variables in the Goals are represented by ground terms in GDC:

```
successors(state([Goal|Goals],Env), Succs)
    :- Goal=..[Functor|Args],
       clauses(Functor,Clauses),
       expandGoal(Args,Goals,Env,Clauses,Succs).


expandGoal(Args,Goals,Env,[],Succs) :- Succs=[].
expandGoal(Args,Goals,Env,[clause(Head,Body,Vars)|Clauses],Succs)
    :- append(Vars,Env,Env2),
       unify(Args,Head,Env2,Env1,Flag),
       expandGoal1(Flag,Args,Goals,Body,Env,Env2,Clauses,Succs).


expandGoal1(false,Args,Goals,Body,Env,Env1,Clauses,Succs)
    :- expandGoal(Args,Goals,Env,Clauses,Succs).
expandGoal1(true,Args,Goals,Body,Env,Env1,Clauses,Succs)
    :- append(Body,Goals,Goals1),
       expandGoal(Args,Goals,Env,Clauses,Succs1),
       Succs=[state(Goals1,Env1)|Succs1].
```

Here, the actor **clauses** returns a representation of the clauses associated with the
input goal name in the form of a list of triples. Each of these contains the head
arguments in list form, the body of the clause and a separate environment for the
variables in the clause (assuming a mechanism to make these fresh variables) each
linked with the value unbound. Clearly the **issol** required in the search programs in
Chapter 6 returns a solution found when the list of outstanding goals becomes empty:

```
issol(state([],Env),Flag) :- Flag=true.
issol(state([Goal|Goals],Env),Flag) :- Flag=false.
```

It can be seen that this version of **successors** always takes the first goal from the
list of outstanding goals and appends the body of any clause which it matches to the
front of the remaining goals. Therefore the goal ordering of Prolog is built-in. The
clause ordering is not, however, built-in since it will depend on the order in which the
search tree is searched. The search order also is not built-in and is determined at the
level of the search program.

The GDC code for **unify** sends true in its fifth argument if its first and second
arguments unify with the variable bindings of the environment of its the third
argument, giving the updated variable bindings as output in the fourth argument. If
unification is not possible, false is returned in the fifth argument, otherwise true is
returned here. This flag value is passed into **expandGoal1**, which adds a successor
state to the list of successor states if a successful unification was achieved.

If a variable at the object level is represented by the ground term var(<name>) where <name> is some constant unique for each separate variable and environment is a list of <name>/<value> pairs, the following code will implement **unify**:

```
unify([H1|T1],[H2|T2],IEnv,OEnv,Flag)
    :-  unify(H1,H2,IEnv,MEnv,Flag1),
        unify1(Flag1,T1,T2,MEnv,OEnv,Flag).
unify(X1,X2,IEnv,OEnv,Flag) :- X1==X2 | OVars=IVars, Flag=true.
unify(var(A),var(B),IEnv,OEnv,Flag)
    :-  lookup(A,IEnv,AVal), lookup(B,IEnv,BVal),
        unifyvars(A,B,IEnv,AVal,BVal,OVars,Flag).
unify(var(A),X2,IEnv,OEnv,Flag) :- X2=/=var(B)
    |  lookup(A,IEnv,AVal), setvar(A,AVal,X2,IVars,OVars,Flag).
unify(X1,var(A),IEnv,OEnv,Flag) :- X1=/=var(B)
    |  lookup(A,IVars,AVal), setvar(A,AV,X1,IEnv,OEnv,Flag).
unify(X1,X2,IEnv,OEnv,Flag) :- X1=/=var(A), X2=/=var(B), X1=/=X2
    |  Flag:=false, OEnv=IEnv.


unify1(false,X1,X2,IEnv,OEnv,Flag) :- Flag=false.
unify1(true,X1,X2,IEnv,OEnv,Flag)
    :-  unify(X1,X2,IEnv,OEnv,Flag).


unifyvars(A,B,IEnv,unbound,BVal,OEnv,Flag) :- BVal=/=unbound
    |  bind(A,BVal,IEnv,OEnv), Flag=true.
unifyvars(A,B,IEnv,AVal,unbound,OEnv,Flag) :- AVal=/=unbound
    |  bind(B,AVal,IEnv,OEnv), Flag=true.
unifyvars(A,B,IEnv,unbound,unbound,OEnv,Flag) :- A<B
    |  bind(B,var(A),IEnv,OEnv), Flag=true.
unifyvars(A,B,IVars,unbound,unbound,OEnv,Flag) :- A>B
    |  bind(A,var(B),IEnv,OEnv), Flag=true.
unifyvars(A,B,IEnv,AVal,BVal,OEnv,Flag)
    :-  AVal=/=unbound, BVal=/=unbound
    |  unify(AVal,BVal,IEnv,OEnv,Flag).


lookup(A,[B/Val|Env],AVal) :- A==B | AVal=Val.
lookup(A,[B/Val|Env],AVal) :- A=/=B | lookup(A,Env,AVal).


setvar(A,unbound,X,IEnv,OEnv,Flag)
    :-  Flag=true, bind(A,X,IEnv,OEnv).
setvar(A,var(B),X,IEnv,OEnv,Flag)
    :-  lookup(B,IVars,BVal), setvar(B,BVal,X,IEnv,OEnv,Flag).
setvar(A,V,X,IEnv,OEnv,Flag) :- V==X
    |  Flag=true, OEnv=IEnv.
setvar(A,[HV|TV],[HX|TX],IEnv,OEnv,Flag)
    :-  unify(HV,HX,IEnv,MEnv,Flag1),
        unify1(Flag1,TV,TX,MEnv,OEnv,Flag).
```

```
setvar(A,[H|T],X,IEnv,OEnv,Flag) :- X=/=[HX|TX]
    |    Flag=false, OEnv=IEnv.
setvar(A,V,[HX|TX],IEnv,OEnv,Flag) :- V=/=[HV|TV], V=/=var(B)
    |    Flag=false, OEnv=IEnv.
setvar(A,V,X,IEnv,OEnv,Flag) :- X=/=[HX|TX], X=/=V, V=/=var(B)
    |    Flag=false, OEnv=IEnv.

bind(A,AVal,[B/BVal|Env],Env1) :- A==B
    |    Env1=[A/AVal|Env].
bind(A,AVal,[B/BVal|Env],Env1) :- A=/=B
    |    bind(A,AVal,Env,Env2), Env1=[B/BVal|Env2].
```

The cost of the bilingual interpreter in having to implement unification completely rather than inheriting any unification from the underlying system is apparent. However, the division into layers means that once we have constructed this layer implementing the resolution and unification, it may be incorporated with any of the search programs in Chapter 6 which will add more control and also give the precise nature of the output. For example, it could be used to give a single solution or all solutions. One point to note is that the bilingual nature of the interpreter means that it avoids use of extra-logical primitives, such as the **copy** that was needed in our all-solutions interpreter above and is also needed in the OR-parallel Prolog interpreter proposed by Shapiro [1987]. The importance of this will become more apparent when partial evaluation of meta-interpreters is considered in Chapter 9.

In order to duplicate exactly Prolog's search order though, a search program is required that searches in depth-first order on demand, which was not given in Chapter 6. The following version of **search** will do this:

```
search(State,[],OutSlots) :- OutSlots=[].
search(State,[Slot|InSlots],OutSlots)
    :- issol(State,Flag),
        expand(Flag,State,[Slot|InSlots],OutSlots).

expand(true,State,[Slot|InSlots],OutSlots)
    :- solution(State,Slot), OutSlots=InSlots.
expand(false,State,InSlots,OutSlots)
    :- successors(State,States),
        branch(States,InSlots,OutSlots).
branch([],InSlots,OutSlots) :- OutSlots=InSlots.
branch([H|T],InSlots,OutSlots)
    :- search(H,InSlots,MidSlots),
        branch(T,MidSlots,OutSlots).
```

Here the second input to **search** is a list of unbound channels or slots. Prolog-like sequential clause will occur because no expansion of the right branch of the search tree will take place until search of the left branch has completed and failed to fill the slots available by binding them. An OR-parallel effect can be gained if this condition is relaxed and search of the right-branch is allowed when it is not known whether a solution will be found in the left branch. Adding the following clause:

search(State,InSlots,OutSlots)
  :- **unknown**(InSlots)
  | **issol**(State,Flag), **expand**(Flag,State,InSlots,OutSlots).

will achieve this, since it means that a node in the search tree will be expanded when the binding status of the slots passed to it is unknown.

8.8 An Interpreter for Linda Extensions to GDC

As a final example of a meta-interpreter for a guarded definite clause language, an interpreter is described which adds *Linda extensions* [Gelernter, 1985] to GDC. According to Gelerntner, the Linda notation is a set of simple primitives, which may be added to any programming language to introduce concurrency into it. The basis of these notations is that a dynamic database of tuples exists. Actors communicate by asserting, reading and retracting tuples from this database, it may therefore be considered a blackboard system [Engelmore and Morgen, 1988]. The Linda extensions are eval(P), which sets up P as an actor, out(T) which adds the tuple T to the database, in(T) which removes the tuple T from the database and rd(T) which reads the tuple T from the database. In the case of in and rd, the tuple argument may contain unbound variables and there will be a search for a matching tuple in the database; when a match is found the variables in the argument will be bound to the matching values. If no match is found for in or rd the actor which made the call is suspended until another actor adds a matching tuple using out, the suspended in or rd call is then evaluated and the actor which made the in or rd call restarted.

The reason for paying particular attention to implementing Linda extensions to GDC is that Linda has been proposed as a competitor [Carriero and Gelernter, 1989] to GDC. It has achieved popularity in use as a concurrent programming paradigm, though this may be because it can be grafted onto existing languages and thus there is less of a barrier to using it than changing to a novel concurrent language. Nevertheless, the simplicity of the conceptual model of Linda has led to it being put forward as another way of introducing concurrency into logic programming [Brogi and Cincanini, 1991]. The use of interpreters moves away from "language wars" to the idea of multi-paradigm programming in which different parts of a program may be expressed in whichever paradigm is most suitable for them. Correspondingly, GDC equipped with a range of interpreters is a multi-paradigm language. The next section shows how functional programming may be embedded in GDC using an interpreter while in Chapter 9 an interpreter for an imperative language is given.

Linda extensions may be added to GDC by using an interpreter that passes on a stream of the database handling commands to a database-handling actor. Each actor that is interpreted will produce a stream of requests to the database. Non-primitive actors will merge the streams from the subactors into which they reduce. The Linda primitives will produce a stream consisting of a single database request. Other primitives will produce an empty stream. Since in GDC all actors are concurrent, there is no need for an explicit eval primitive. The following is the interpreter:

```
reduce(X=Y,S) :- X=Y, S=[].
reduce(in(M),S) :- S=[in(M)].
reduce(rd(M),S) :- S=[rd(M)].
reduce(out(M),S) :- S=[out(M)].
reduce(Actor,S)
    :- otherwise
    |  behavior(Actor,Body), reducelist(Body,S).

reducelist([], S) :- S=[].
reducelist([H|T],S)
    :- reduce(H, S1), reducelist(T,S2), merge(S1,S2,S).
```

The top level actor network would be

```
:-  reduce(Actor,Stream), database(Stream).
```

The database handler needs to keep two lists of tuples. One will be tuples currently in the database. The other will be a list of in and rd requests that are suspended waiting for a tuple to be added. When a tuple is added it is matched against all the suspended in and rd requests. If it matches a suspended in request, it is not taken any further since this in request will cause it to be removed from the database. The matching used is similar to the matching we used in the meta-interpreters previously, except that we need to overcome the problem that matching could fail after binding some channels. The interpreter is monolingual, so if the binding took place it could not be undone if matching failed later. We reduce the problem by using a version of **match** which rather than bind any channels returns a list of channels which would be bound and values to which they would be bound if the matching succeeds. If matching does succeed, these bindings take place. This gives the following as the complete database handler:

```
// Handle an out message by checking against all waiting in and rd
// messages. If it has not been matched with a waiting in message,
// the tuple is added to the database of tuples.
database([out(M)|S],Waits,Tuples)
    :- checkwaits(M, Waits,OutWaits,Found),
       addtuple(Found,S,M,OutWaits,Tuples).
// Handle an in message by checking against the database of
// tuples. If there are no matches, the in message is added to the
// list of waiting in and rd requests.
database([in(M)|S],Waits,Tuples)
    :- checktuples(M,Tuples,OutTuples,Found),
       addwait(Found,S,M,Waits,OutTuples).
// Handle a rd message similarly to an in message.
database([rd(M)|S],Waits,Tuples)
    :- check(M,Tuples,Found), addrd(Found, S, M, Waits, Tuples).

addtuple(no,S,M,Waits,Tuples)
    :- database(S,Waits,[M|Tuples]).
addtuple(yes,S,M,Waits,Tuples)
    :- database(S,Waits,Tuples).
```

```
addwait(no,S,M,Waits,Tuples)
    :- database(S,[in(M)|Waits],Tuples).
addwait(yes,S,M Waits,Tuples)
    :- database(S,Waits,Tuples).

addrd(no,S,M,Waits,Tuples)
    :- database(S,[rd(M)|Waits],Tuples).
addrd(yes,S,M,Waits,Tuples)
    :- database(S,Waits,Tuples).
```

// Check a tuple against waiting in and rd requests. If it is
// matched successfully against an in request Found is bound to
// "yes", the in request is removed from the list of waiting
// requests and no further checking is done. If it is successfully
// matched against a waiting rd request, the request is removed
// but checking against further requests continues. If all
// requests are checked and no successful matching with an in
// request occurs, Found is bound to "no".

```
checkwaits(M,[in(N)|Waits],OutWaits,Found)
    :- match(M,N,Flag,Matches),
       isinmatch(Flag,Matches,M,N,Waits,OutWaits,Found).
checkwaits(M,[rd(N)|Waits],OutWaits,Found)
    :- match(M,N,Flag,Matches),
       isrdmatch(Flag,Matches,M,N,Waits,OutWaits,Found).
checkwaits(M,[],OutWaits,Found)
    :- Found=no, OutWaits=[].

isinmatch(true,Matches,M,N,Waits,OutWaits,Found)
    :- Found=yes, domatches(Matches), OutWaits=Waits.
isinmatch(false,Matches,M,N,Waits,OutWaits,Found)
    :- checkwaits(M,Waits,OutWaits1,Found),
            OutWaits=[in(N)|OutWaits1].

isrdmatch(true,Matches,M,N,Waits,OutWaits,Found)
    :- domatches(Matches), checkwaits(M,Waits,OutWaits,Found).
isrdmatch(false,Matches,M,N,Waits,OutWaits,Found)
    :- checkwaits(M,Waits,OutWaits1,Found),
            OutWaits=[rd(N)|Outwaits1].
```

// Check an in request against the database of tuples.
// If a match is found the matching tuple is taken from the
// database of tuples and Found is bound to "yes". Otherwise
// Found is bound to "no".

```
checktuples(M,[N|Tuples],OutTuples,Found)
    :- match(N,M,Flag,Matches),
       ismatch(Flag,Matches,M,N,Tuples,OutTuples,Found).
```

```
checktuples(M,[],OutTuples,Found)
    :- Found=no, OutTuples=[].


// Perform the channel binding if matching succeeds.
ismatch(true,Matches,M,N,Tuples,OutTuples,Found)
    :- domatches(Matches), OutTuples=Tuples, Found=yes.
ismatch(false,Matches,M,N,Tuples,OutTuples,Found)
    :- checktuples(M,Tuples,OutTuples1,Found),
        OutTuples=[N|OutTuples1].


domatches([Y/X|Matches]) :- Y=X, domatches(Matches).
domatches([]).


// Check a rd request against the database of tuples, bind Found
// to "yes" if a match is found, to "no" otherwise.
check(M,[N|Tuples],Found)
    :- match(N,M,Flag,Matches),
        isfound(Flag,Matches,M,Tuples,Found).
check(M,[],Found) :- Found=no.


isfound(true,Matches,M,Tuples,Found)
    :- Found=yes, domatches(Matches).
isfound(false,Matches,M,Tuples,Found) :- check(M,Tuples,Found).


// A version of match which binds V to "true" if matching
// succeeds, "false"otherwise and which returns a list of
// channel bindings to be performed only if the complete match
// succeeds.
match(X,Y,V,Matches) :- unknown(Y) | Matches=[Y/X], V=true.
match(X,Y,V,Matches) :- X==Y | V=true, Matches=[].
match(X,Y,V,Matches) :- X=/=Y | V=false, Matches=[].
match(X,Y,V,Matches) :- list(X), list(Y)
    | matchlist(X,Y,V,Matches).
match(X,Y,V,Matches) :- tuple(X), tuple(Y)
    | X=..LX, Y=..LY, matchlist(LX,LY,V,Matches).


matchlist([],[],V,Matches) :- V=true, Matches=[].
matchlist([H1|T1],[H2|T2],V,Matches)
    :- match(H1,H2,VH,Matches1), matchlist(T1,T2,VT,Matches2),
        andp(VH,VT,V), merge(Matches1,Matches2,Matches).
matchlist(X,Y,V,Matches) :- unknown(Y)
    | Matches=[Y/X], V=true.


andp(true,true,V) :-V=true.
andp(false,_,V) :- V=false.
andp(_,false,V) :- V=false.
```

The behavior representation below will reduce the Dining Philosophers problem (Section 4.12) in a way similar to that described in [Carriero and Gelernter, 1989]. The idea is that a chopstick available for use is represented by a tuple in the database. When a philosopher actor wishes to use a chopstick, an in command for the chopstick is issued. If the chopstick is already in use by another philosopher the philosopher actor will suspend until that other philosopher has finished with the chopstick and issued an out command on it, putting it into the tuple database and awakening the in command. To avoid deadlock, only four philosophers are allowed in the dining room at any time. Initially, this is represented by having four meal tickets in the database. A philosopher must issue an in command on a meal ticket and receive it before entering the dining room, the ticket is put out again when the philosopher finishes eating. Philosophers are represented by the indices of the chopsticks they use to eat.

```
behavior(hungryphil(hungry,F1,F2),Body)
    :-  Body=[in(ticket(T)),enteringphil(T,F1,F2)].
behavior(enteringphil(ticket,F1,F2),Body)
    :-Body=[in(chopstick(F1,T1)),in(chopstick(F2,T2)),
            eatingphil(T1,T2,F1,F2)].
behavior(eatingphil(chopstick,chopstick,F1,F2), Body)
    :-  Body=[eat(E), exitingphil(E,F1,F2)].
behavior(exitingphil(full,F1,F2), Body)
    :-  Body=[out(chopstick(F1,chopstick)),
            out(chopstick(F2,chopstick)),
            out(ticket(ticket)), thinkingphil(F1,F2)].
behavior(thinkingphil(F1,F2), Body)
    :-  Body=[think(H),hungryphil(H,F1,F2)].
behavior(init, Body)
    :-  Body=[out(chopstick(1,chopstick)),
            out(chopstick(2,chopstick)),out(chopstick(3,chopstick)),
            out(chopstick(4,chopstick)),out(chopstick(5,chopstick)),
            out(ticket(ticket)),out(ticket(ticket)),
            out(ticket(ticket)),out(ticket(ticket)),
            thinkingphil(1,2),thinkingphil(2,3),thinkingphil(3,4),
            thinkingphil(4,5),thinkingphil(5,1)].
```

Note that here it has been necessary to include explicit sequencing in the interpreted program. For example a meal ticket is represented by the 1-tuple ticket(ticket) rather than the 0-tuple ticket. A message in(ticket(T)) will bind T to ticket when a tuple ticket(ticket) is in the database. The actor **enteringphil**(T,F1,F2) will suspend until T is bound. Without this sequencing the calls in(ticket) and **enteringphil**(F1,F2) would proceed in parallel. That is, a philosopher would not wait for the meal ticket to become available. Similarly, the n-th chopstick is represented by the tuple chopstick(n,chopstick) rather than just chopstick(n). It is assumed that think(H) will bind H to hungry after a suitable interval of time and eat(E) will similarly bind E to full.

A more complex form of the interpreter would make the sequencing implicit, using a similar technique to that we used to introduce sequentiality previously. In this case, it is necessary to introduce the explicit primitive eval for the cases where we want a concurrent actor to be spawned:

```
reduce(X=Y,S,Flag) :- unify(X,Y,Flag), S=[].
reduce(in(M),S,Flag) :- S=[in(M,Flag)].
reduce(rd(M),S,Flag) :- S=[rd(M,Flag)].
reduce(out(M),S,Flag) :- S=[out(M,Flag)].
reduce(eval(T),S,Flag) :- reduce(T,S,_), Flag=done.
reduce(Actor,S,Flag) :- otherwise
    |  behavior(Actor,Body), reducelist(done,Body,S,F).

reducelist(Flag1,[],S,Flag2) :- S=[], Flag2=Flag1.
reducelist(done,[H|T],S,Flag)
    :- reduce(H,S1,Flag1),
       reducelist(Flag1,T,S2,Flag),
       merge(S1,S2,S).
```

Note that the Flag channel is added to the in, rd and out messages passed to the database handler. It is assumed that the database handler will bind Flag to done when the operation is completed. In the case of in and rd messages if there is no matching tuple in the database, the requests will be queued as before, each with its associated flag and the flag eventually will be bound when a matching tuple is added by an out message.

Using this interpreter the program for the dining philosophers is:

```
behavior(hungryphil(F1,F2),Body)
    :-  Body=[in(ticket),enteringphil(F1,F2)].
behavior(enteringphil(F1,F2),Body)
    :-  Body=[in(chopstick(F1)),in(chopstick(F2)),eatingphil(F1,F2)].
behavior(eatingphil(F1,F2),Body)
    :-  Body=[eat,exitingphil(F1,F2)].
behavior(exitingphil(F1,F2),Body)
    :-  Body=[out(chopstick(F1)),out(chopstick(F2)),out(ticket),
            thinkingphil(F1,F2)].
behavior(thinkingphil(F1,F2),Body)
    :-  Body=[think,hungryphil(F1,F2)].
behavior(init,Body)
    :-  Body=[out(chopstick(1)), out(chopstick(2)),
            out(chopstick(3)), out(chopstick(4)),
            out(chopstick(5)), out(ticket), out(ticket), out(ticket),
            out(ticket), eval(thinkingphil(1,2)),
            eval(thinkingphil(2,3)), eval(thinkingphil(3,4)),
            eval(thinkingphil(4,5)), eval(thinkingphil(5,1))].
```

8.9 Parallelization via Concurrent Meta-interpretation

As the Linda extension interpreter indicates, the underlying parallelism in GDC may be used through interpreters to provide parallelism in a form which is not directly provided in GDC itself. Huntbach, [1991] gives an interpreter which models in GDC the explicit message-passing parallelism of Occam, the transputer language based on Dijkstra's CSP [Dijkstra, 1975]. But the implicit parallelism in GDC may be used to realize parallelism which exists implicitly in another language, through the use of a GDC interpreter for that language.

Landin's usage of lambda calculus as a metalanguage for describing the semantics of Algol and the more direct basis of the functional languages on lambda calculus was noted in Section 8.1. Landin proposed the abstract *SECD* machine to evaluate lambda calculus expressions. The SECD machine reifies much of the control aspects of lambda calculus evaluation by using explicit stacks, which can be seen as a sacrifice of generality for the sake of efficiency. Because the control of the SECD machine is explicit, it does not parallelize without modification.   McCarthy's *Eval/Apply* interpreter [McCarthy, 1960] is more general. As a Lisp-like interpreter for Lisp, it can be seen as another part of his interest in meta-interpreters discussed with respect to Algol, in this case mapping the recursion of the functional language implicitly onto the recursion of the interpreter. A GDC version of the Eval/Apply interpreter will automatically parallelize lambda calculus evaluation, since the control is minimally specified. Incorporation of such an interpreter for those problems where the power of functional programming, particularly higher order functions, is useful, may be seen as an alternative to developing a new language which explicitly combines logic and functional programming [Belia and Levy, 1986].

The lambda calculus interpreter given below is based on one given by Field and Harrison [1988]. Variables are stored in an explicit environment, similar to the environments used to build an interpreter for a backtracking logic language in Section 8.7. The beta-reduction mechanism is implemented by adding the bindings for the bound variable to the environment rather than actual textual substitution. Correct binding of variables is achieved by the standard method of constructing a closure in which an abstraction is linked with an environment giving values for any free variables within it.

The interpreter works for expressions in lambda calculus, with $\lambda x.E$, where E is any expression, represented by lambda(x,E), the expression E1 E2, that is E1 applied to E2 represented by apply(E1,E2) and the variable x represented by vbl(x). Arithmetic and other built-in operators are represented in their curried form by op(p) where p is the operator, or op1(p,E) where E is an expression for the partially applied form:

```
eval(apply(E1,E2),Env,R)
    :- eval(E1,Env,R1), eval(E2,Env,R2), apply(R1,R2,R).
eval(lambda(X,Exp),Env,R) :- R=closure(X,Exp,Env).
eval(vbl(X),Env,R) :- lookup(X,Env,R).
eval(Exp,Env,R) :- otherwise | R=Exp.

apply(closure(X,Exp1,Env),Exp2,R)
    :- eval(Exp1,[X/Exp2|Env],R).
apply(op(P),Exp,R) :- R=op1(P,Exp).
apply(op1(P,Exp1),Exp2,R) :- dobuiltin(P,Exp1,Exp2,R).
```

dobuiltin(plus,Exp1,Exp2,R) :- R:=Exp1+Exp2.

// plus code for other built-in operations

If actors were executed sequentially, this interpreter would give us eager evaluation, since both function and argument expressions in an application are evaluated before applying the function. However, as we have unrestricted parallelism, initiation of the evaluation of the function, evaluation of its argument and the function application itself is concurrent. The effect is that if the function evaluates to a closure, the function application may take place even though computation of its argument is still in progress. With an actor network

:-   **eval**(Exp2,Env,R2), **apply**(closure(X,Exp,Env1),R2,R).

applying the closure gives:

:-   **eval**(Exp2,Env,R2), **eval**(Exp,[X/R2|Env2],R).

Although the value of R2 is still being computed we may proceed with the evaluation of Exp. The channel R2 plays a role similar to MultiLisp's "future" construct [Halstead, 1985]: a place-holder which may be manipulated as a first-class object while its final value is being computed. Application of strict operators however will be suspended until their arguments are evaluated, for example, an arithmetic operation will reduce to a call to GDC's built-in arithmetic and suspend until its arguments are ground.

If a curried operator implements conditional expressions, we will end up by computing both branches of the conditional even though only one is needed since computation of both branches will commence in parallel. To inhibit this, as in Field and Harrison's eager interpreter, we can treat conditionals as a special case by including an additional constructor in the definition of expressions to accommodate them. So "if E1 then E2 else E3" is parsed to cond(E1,E2,E3) rather than apply(apply(apply(op(cond),E1),E2),E3). We then need to add additional behaviors:

eval(cond(E1,E2,E3),Env,R)
    :-   **eval**(E1,Env,TruthVal), **branch**(TruthVal,E2,E3,Env,R).

branch(true,E2,E3,Env,R) :- **eval**(E2,Env,R).
branch(false,E2,E3,Env,R) :- **eval**(E3,Env,R).

The dependency in **branch** means that evaluation of the branches of the conditional will not take place until the condition has been fully evaluated to a Boolean constant.

Full lazy evaluation, as used in modern functional languages, may be obtained by passing the argument in an application in the form of a suspension containing the unevaluated expression and its environment to ensure that if it is eventually evaluated its channels are correctly bound. This gives us the following rule to replace the rule for evaluating applications:

eval(apply(E1,E2),Env,R)
    :-   **eval**(E1,EnvR1), **apply**(E1,susp(E2,Env),R).

We also need a rule to evaluate suspensions when necessary:

eval(susp(E,Env1),Env2,R) :- **eval**(E,Env1,R).

Since the environment may contain suspensions, when we look up an identifier we may need to evaluate it further, so we alter the rule for variable lookup to:

:- **eval**(vbl(X),Env,R) :- **lookup**(X,Env,V), **eval**(V,Env,R).

Since some primitives such as the arithmetic functions require their arguments to be fully evaluated before the operation can be completed (that is, the primitives are strict), we must add this to the code for executing the primitive, for example:

dobuiltin(plus,Exp1,Exp2,R)
     :- **eval**(Exp1,[],R1), **eval**(Exp2,[],R2), R:=R1+R2.

Parallelism is limited in the lazy interpreter but not completely excised. We no longer evaluate the function application and the argument simultaneously since evaluation of the argument is suspended. However evaluation of the arguments to strict primitives, such as plus above, does take place in parallel. The effect is to give conservative parallelism: we only do those computations in parallel whose results we know are definitely needed. A more sophisticated combination of lazy functional programming could be obtained by using operators such as those proposed by Trinder et al [1998].

The interpreters given here for lambda calculus are not the most efficient that could be achieved and are given mainly for illustration of the technique of using interpreters to embed one language in another. One major issue we have not dealt with in lazy evaluation is that in practice call-by-need is essential to ensure that suspensions are evaluated once with the evaluation shared by all references to them, rather than re-evaluated every time they are referenced. An efficient way of dealing with recursion, used by Field and Harrison [1988], is to build circular environments rather than rely on the fact that the fixpoint operator can be represented directly in lambda calculus [Barendregt, 1984]. (These issues can be dealt with in GDC, but there is not space for further detail here.) Circular environments can be represented directly if we take up Colmerauer's proposal [Colmeraurer, 1982] to recognize the lack of the occur check as a language feature which can be interpreted as the logic of circular or infinite structures. A more efficient way however would be to dispense with environments altogether and use a combinator [Turner, 1979] or super-combinator [Hughes, 1982] based evaluator.

8.10 Conclusion

The use of meta-interpreters may be seen as both a way of structuring programs and a way of avoiding cluttering a programming language with a variety of features. It has been recognized that programs are clearer if the logic of the program is separated from the control. This was one of the guiding principles in the development of logic programming languages. For efficiency reasons a detailed user-defined control mechanism may be necessary, but this should not be mixed in with the specification of the logic of the program. A meta-interpreter may be regarded as the third element of a program that combines the logic and the control. It may be an implicit part of the language or the programmers may themselves provide it. It is often the case that program clarity is aided by writing the program in a simple problem-oriented language and implementing that language in a language closer to the underlying machine. Recursively, the implementation language may itself be similarly implemented. This is a technique already familiar under the name structured programming [Dahl et al., 1972]. But metaprogramming provides a clear division between the levels of structure and the potential separation of logic and control at each layer means that the top-level layer is not constrained to inherit directly the control of the machine level, or to be cluttered with explicit control structures to subvert it.

On language features, meta-interpretation provides a facility to add features or change aspects of that language as required through the use of an interpreter specifically designed to add or change a particular feature. This compares with complex single-level languages where every feature a programmer may at any time have to use must be added as part of the language definition. This creates an unwieldy language that is difficult to learn, use safely and debug. It should be recalled that every new feature added to a language must not only be considered in its own terms but also in terms of its impact on other features.

One important use of interpreters (not considered in detail) here is their use to assist in the problem of mapping the abstract parallelism of a language like GDC onto a real parallel architecture. Such an interpreter would deal with problems like load-balancing and deciding when the increased communication costs involved in moving some computation to another processor are balanced by an increased utilization of parallelism.

The biggest barrier against the use of meta-interpreters as a program or language-definition structuring device is the overhead. A program, which must work through several layers of interpreter before getting to the machine level, will not be as efficient as one that directly controls the machine level. To some extent this can be overcome, as we have shown, through the use of interpreters in which much of the lower level is inherited implicitly by the upper level rather than explicitly reimplemented. However, even the "vanilla meta-interpreter" of logic programming which inherits almost everything from the underlying level has been shown in practice to increase execution time by an order of magnitude. A solution to the problem is to use partial evaluation to flatten out the layers of interpretation into a single-level program. This technique will be explored in detail in the next chapter.

Chapter 9

Partial Evaluation

> *There are three rules for writing a novel. Unfortunately, no one knows what they are.*
>
> Somerset Maugham

The use of meta-interpreters offers a principled way to tailor a language to a programmer's needs. Adding another layer of meta-interpretation can produce any additional information that is required during the computation or any additional control over the computation. Sterling and Beer [1986] make a strong appeal for structuring programs into multiple layers of meta-interpreters for expert system construction. Each layer of interpretation has its own clear semantics and the boundary between the layers is clearly defined. This is unlike the confusion that occurs if extensive use is made of reflective constructs within languages to move between conceptual layers of meta-interpreters.

To add k extra behaviors to an actor, another actor can be constructed in which there is a layer of meta-interpreters each adding one behavior. If the meta-interpreters interpret using the actors **actor1, actor2,..., actork**, the top level actor will be:

:- **actor1**(actor2(...actork(Actor)...))

Note that at this level, only the outer layer, **actor1**, is represented by an explicit actor. The others are represented by messages at the object-level and the code for them may similarly have to be represented by separate messages

:- **actor1**(actor2(...actork(Actor,P)...),P2)

where Pi is the object-level representation of the behavior for the i-th meta-interpreter in the layer of meta-interpreters and P the behavior for Actor. A meta-interpreter may also take in its own information, such as a control directive and return its own output, such as trace information. If each of the meta-interpreters has its own input and output the top-level actor will be:

:- **actor1**(actor2(...actork(Actor,Ik,Ok,PG)...),I1,O1,P2)

The drawback to this method of program structuring is the overhead of meta-interpretation. The literature has tended to suggest that an overhead of an order of magnitude for each layer of meta-interpretation can be expected. Van Harmelen [1991] gives some analysis that suggests this is a considerable underestimate. Particularly in bilingual systems where object-level concepts are not represented directly by their equivalent meta-level concepts, there is a great amount of bookkeeping and meta-level inference required to make one object-level behavior. Clearly the multiplication of the overhead caused by one meta-interpreter interpreting another rules out as impractical the use of the method of deploying programs as layers of meta-interpreters. A way of overcoming the problem is to use methods of program transformation [Partsch and Steinbruggen, 1983]. This changes the initial layered program into one which is more efficient at the cost of lacking the structure of the initial one, but which has the same semantics in terms of observable behavior.

Ad hoc methods for composing meta-interpreters have been considered [Lakhotia and Sterling, 1988] based on the idea that many meta-interpreters have similar structures developing from the vanilla meta-interpreter. If two meta-interpreters both perform a search of the proof tree, the separate searches can be fused into a single search. While this method may be satisfactory for simple meta-interpreters, such as those discussed by Safra [Safra and Shapiro, 1986], which essentially add information to the vanilla meta-interpreter, it is less easy to find the correspondences necessary for composing meta-interpreters when they are more complex and make alterations to the control. A more systematic approach to reducing the overhead of meta-interpreters involves the use of partial evaluation. Research into partial evaluation in logic programming, started in the 1980s by Komorowski [1981], has been led principally by the possibilities given by the combination of partial evaluation and meta-interpretation. Important early work on partial evaluation of logic meta-interpreters was done by Gallagher [1986] in Ireland and Takeuchi [1986] in Japan.

9.1 Partial Evaluation

Partial evaluation is a systematic form of program transformation based on the insight that many programs contain considerable portions of code whose execution is common to all runs of the program. Most commonly, there will be procedure calls $p(a_1, \ldots, a_n)$ where some of the a_i are constants rather than variables. The reason for this is that it may aid program clarity to have one general procedure p rather than several specialized to the various arguments p may take. Any computation which is dependent only on values which will in fact always be set to some constant on any execution (termed *static*, whereas those dependent on the input to be provided at run-time are termed *dynamic*) may in fact be carried out in advance. Another way of thinking of it is as *program specialization*: programs may be generated for particular purposes from a generalized template by setting some of the variables in that template to constants and then applying partial evaluation.

The aim of partial evaluation is to separate out that part of the program that does not depend on any input parameters and execute it, returning a revised form of the program in which these non-variant parts are simplified. For example, assuming an imperative style language, an assignment a:=b+c, where b and c are both static variables, may be replaced by a:=n where n is the integer which is the sum of the static values in b and c. Preprocessors (e.g. the C language) can do such simple transformations. Similarly, if a and b are static, an expression of the form if a>b then code1 else code2 endif may be replaced simply by code1 or code2 depending on how the comparison evaluates. Clearly the transformation here means that the summing or testing of a and b takes place once and for all during partial evaluation and is not re-evaluated unnecessarily each time the code is used, as it would be if the original code were used.

In the examples given above, partial evaluation reduces the size of the code. In other circumstances it can increase the size of the code. A single procedure or block of code that may be entered several times during the evaluation of a program may be partially evaluated into a separate procedure or block of code specialized for each of the circumstances in which it is entered. If we have $a:=f(a_1,...,a_n)$ and $b:=f(b_1,...,b_n)$ where a_1 to a_p are static and b_1 to b_q are static $p,q<n$, we can replace them by $a:=fa(a_{p+1},...,a_n)$ and $b:=fb(b_{q+1},...,b_n)$ where fa and fb are separate new procedures representing f specialized to each of the different partially static parameter lists. Thus, code for fa and fb, as well as code for any other circumstances in which f might be called will replace the code for the procedure f. Although in these examples consecutive arguments in the parameter list are static, this is not a necessity since any subset of the parameter list could be static.

Ershov [1980], who did early research in partial evaluation of imperative programs, called this *mixed computation*. His aim was that a program with static and dynamic variables should be executed as far as possible, with assignments whose right-hand sides were expressions containing dynamic variables being written to a residual program and the variable on the left-hand side being treated as dynamic. Procedure calls may be specialized as explained above. When dealing with conditional expressions of the form if cond then code1 else code2 endif, where cond is dynamic, mixed computation must partially evaluate both code1 and code2, returning residual code1´ and code2´ respectively and returning as residual code for the whole expression:

    if cond then code1´ else code2´ endif

Note, the presence of loops and recursion can lead to partial evaluation as described above generating a program of infinite size. For example, consider the simple procedure:

```
procedure f(a,b)=
    begin
        if a then return b else return f(g(a),b+1) endif
    end
```

specialized for the case $b=1$, but a dynamic. The call $f(a,b)$ would specialize to $f1(a)$ where $f1$ is defined by:

```
procedure f1(a)=
    begin
        if a then return 1 else return f2(g(a)) endif
    end
```

where $f2$ is f specialized to the case where its second argument is statically 2. Clearly the code for $f2$ would require $f3$ and so on. The method to decide when to halt partial evaluation to prevent this sort of infinite expansion of the code is one of the major aspects of partial evaluation, referred to as the *stop criterion* [van Harmelen, 1991]. In fact finding the ideal solution is impossible, as it would require solving the halting problem. For safety's sake a partial evaluation algorithm must always err on the cautious side. To avoid a partial evaluation that has the possibility of non-termination it is necessary to have residual programs that could be further evaluated.

Partial evaluation became an identifiable field in computer science at a conference in Denmark in 1987 that brought together many of those working in the area. Ershov gave an opening speech [Ershov, 1988] to this conference that took a retrospective look at his own work. He noted his insight was a key idea whose importance had been hidden by being scattered among various researchers many of whom were unaware of each others' work and thus used different terminology for what was in fact the same concept. A similar point is made in an early paper on partial evaluation by Beckman and colleagues [Beckman et al., 1976] who noted several even earlier pieces of work that could be identified as partial evaluation.

Ershov's own interest in partial evaluation stemmed from a desire to overcome the technical limitations of Soviet computers by clever compiling techniques. The detection of elements of computation that are not dependent on run-time information by tracing through dependency links is known as *constant propagation* in the field of compiling and when continued through into conditional branches [Wegman and Zadeck, 1991] is very similar to the partial evaluation techniques discussed above. Partial evaluation may be distinguished from clever compilation by the fact that it is generally a source-to-source transformation rather than a translation to an object code.

In lambda calculus and functional languages the technique known as *currying* (after the logician Curry who used it extensively in combinator theory [Curry et al., 1958]) may be considered as a form of partial evaluation. Currying causes a function which is conceptually of the form $f(x,y)$ to be written as $(f(x))(y)$ and similarly for functions of more arguments. An application of f to a single argument m returns a function f_m which may be regarded as a specialization of f with its first argument fixed to m, since $f_m(y)$ is equal to $f(m,y)$ using the non-curried f for any y. Landin [1963] used the term "partial evaluation" when noting that the reduction order of an applicative expression could be altered so that a function may be evaluated as far as possible before all of its arguments are fully evaluated. Holst and Gomard [1991] further explore the connection between partial evaluation and lazy evaluation. Although currying does not directly enable us to specialize the function f above by fixing its second argument y so that it can be applied to a variety of xs, this can be done indirectly. If we define C as the function C f y x = f x y (Turner's [1979] C combinator), then C f n will evaluate to the partial evaluation of f with its second argument set to n.

The earliest work to fully consider partial evaluation in a practical environment was that of Lombardi in the 1960s [Lombardi, 1967]. Lombardi preferred the term *incremental computation* and was particularly concerned with the then new idea of computers where the user had on-line access and could then partially supply input data over time, rather than have all the input for a program presented at one time as in a batch processor. His incremental computation was designed to formalize in a programming language the concept of computations that could go as far as possible with the data they had and then suspend until new data was available from the on-line supplier. So in fact this first use of partial evaluation came in response to the first reactive systems in computers. The affinity between reactive systems and partial evaluation will be discussed later in this chapter.

Perhaps the most important early work on partial evaluation, particularly in the context of its use in conjunction with meta-interpreters, was a short paper by Futamura [1971]. In his opening speech to the first partial evaluation conference,

Ershov singled out this paper as a classic example of a major concept buried in an obscure journal. Ershov was responsible for promoting the name *Futamura projections* [Ershov, 1982] for the idea of applying a partial evaluator to meta-interpreters. Partial evaluation of an interpreter with respect to a program was called the first Futamura projection. Partial evaluation of the partial evaluator with respect to an interpreter was called the second Futamura projection. Partial evaluation of the partial evaluator with respect to itself was called the third Futamura projection. These will be discussed in detail in the next section.

9.2 Futamura Projections

The Futamura projections are best explained diagrammatically. A transformational view of a program is a *black box*, Figure 9.2.1, into which input enters and from which output exits:

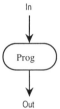

In

Prog

Out

Fig 9.2.1 Simple black-box view of a program

This can be seen as an abstraction of a system in which a program runs on a machine. Making the machine $Mach_P$ explicit, the program is input to the machine, which executes code written in the language P. In Figure 9.2.2, dotted lines indicate how the view above is obtained by seeing the program and machine as a single system.

This is still an abstraction. In practice, a machine directly executes a different language from the one a program is written in. Call the machine language M and the machine that executes it $Mach_M$. A compiler is a program that takes a program written in P as input and returns a program in M as output. For any input, the compiled program running on $Mach_M$ gives the same output as the program would if directly run on $Mach_P$. Alternatively, an interpreter, which is a program written in M, that takes two inputs, a program written in P and an input to that program and returns the same output that would be given if the program were run on $Mach_P$. These two approaches are shown in Figure 9.2.3. The dotted lines show a way of grouping the machine and the interpreter or compiler together so that the programmer need not be aware whether the program is interpreted or compiled.

The compiler itself could be broken down into a compilation program running on a machine, but this step is not needed here. The advantage of using a compiler over using an interpreter is that it makes explicit the intermediate stage of the compiled program. Being made explicit, we can store it and re-use it when needed with other inputs. Some of the work that the interpreter would have to do each time the program is run is done once and for all when the compiled version is produced. This is illustrated in Figure 9.2.4.

In diagrammatic notation, partial evaluation may be defined as an equivalence between two diagrams in Figure 9.2.5, where Peval is the partial evaluator program (which again may be broken down into program and machine).

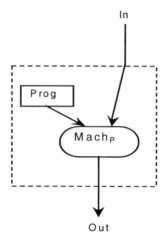

Fig. 9.2.2 Program and machine as a single system

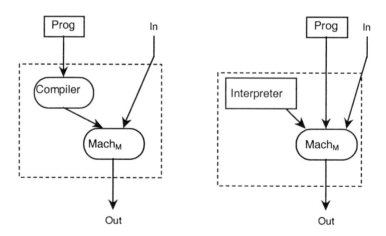

Fig. 9.2.3 Compilation and interpretation

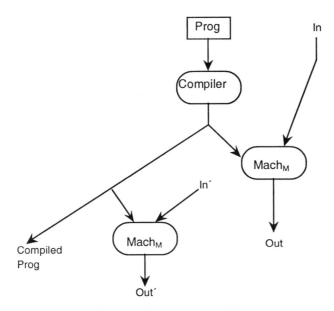

Fig. 9.2.4 Repeated runs of a compiled program

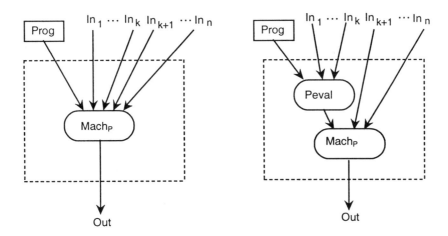

Fig. 9.2.5 Definition of partial evaluation

This holds for any value of **Prog**, the n inputs In_1 to In_n and the appropriate output **Out** for Prog with the given inputs. The advantage is that the partially evaluated program output from **Peval** may be saved and used again. In particular, if we set the input In_1 to In_k to static values a_1 to a_k, partial evaluation separates out an intermediate form of the input program described as "**Prog** partially evaluated with respect to $In_1=a_1,... In_k=a_k$", in which those elements of the computation specific to these static values are executed once and for all. That is, the intermediate form is a program written in P which requires n-k inputs and runs on $Mach_P$ giving the same results if it has inputs b_{k+1}, ..., b_n as Prog would have if it were run on $Mach_P$ with inputs a_1, ..., a_k, b_{k+1}, ..., b_n.

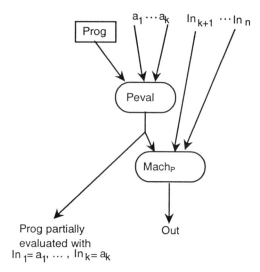

Fig. 9.2.6 The use of partial evaluation

Kleene [1952] shows that such a partial function can always be found as his s-m-n Theorem. It is assumed here that Peval is a P to P transformer and that we have a $Mach_P$ machine to run P programs on. We can always substitute a compiler or interpreter and a $Mach_M$ as above for $Mach_P$ where necessary.

The first Futamura projection refers to partially evaluating an interpreter with respect to a particular program. Note that in this case the partial evaluator must be an M to M transformer. Otherwise this is just a special case of our more general partial evaluation with n=2, Interpreter the program being partially evaluated and In_1 being set to the program being interpreted, Prog. The input to Prog is left dynamic. The result of the partial evaluation is a program written in M which when given input In runs on machine $Mach_M$ and gives the same output as Prog gives when run on $Mach_P$ with input In. In other words, the combination of partial evaluator and interpreter can be regarded as a compiler taking the program Prog written in P and returning a program which has the same behavior but is written in M; Figure 9.2.7 illustrates this. On the left-hand side of the figure the original use of the interpreter to run a P program on $Mach_M$ is shown. The middle of the figure shows the use of partial evaluation to give a version of the interpreter specialized to the particular P program. The right hand side of the figure shows the use of a compiler, with the dotted lines indicating the equivalence.

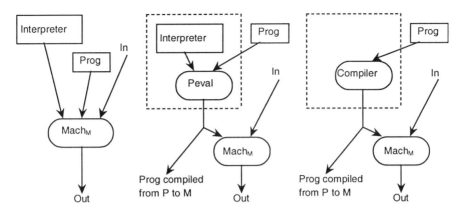

Fig. 9.2.7 The First Futamura Projection

The second Futamura projection recognizes that Peval itself may be regarded as a program running on Mach$_M$, rather than a machine-program system as regarded up till now. The second projection takes a program and some partial input and produces a specialized program. When specializing an interpreter with respect to a program, the two inputs are the interpreter and the program, and the output is the compiled program (Figure 9.2.8).

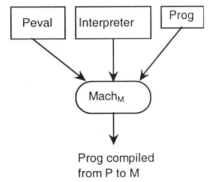

Fig. 9.2.8 Inputs of the Second Futamura Projection

The second Futamura projection is the use of the partial evaluator on itself to give a version of the partial evaluator specialized with respect to a particular program P running on M interpreter. In Figure 9.2.9, a distinction is made between the angled-box Peval, which is the partial evaluator program itself and the rounded-box Peval, which can be seen as a simplification standing for the combination of the program Peval and the machine Mach$_M$.

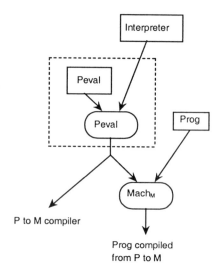

Fig. 9.2.9 The Second Futamura Projection

The combination of partial evaluator applied to itself, enclosed within dotted lines Figure 9.2.9, can be seen to take a P running on M interpreter and produce a program which when applied to some program Prog, written in P, runs on $Mach_M$ and produces a version of Prog compiled from P to M. In other words, a partial evaluator applied to itself gives a program, which takes a P to M interpreter and produces a P to M compiler. Since this will work for any interpreter, P can be considered a variable. The self-application of a partial evaluator may be considered a compiler generator, generating an equivalent compiler given an interpreter.

The third Futamura projection takes the second projection one stage further, expanding the program-machine Peval combination and then bringing in a further Peval, so that partially evaluating a partial evaluator with respect to itself gives an explicit compiler generator program. The complete system showing the three Futamura projections is shown in Figure 9.2.10.

In order to build such a system, a partial evaluator is required which is sufficiently powerful to be able to be applied to itself. The first such self-applicable partial evaluator was constructed by Jones, Sestoft and Søndergaard [1985]. The problem with self-applicable partial evaluators is that every aspect of the language that is used to program the partial evaluator must also be capable of being effectively treated in the partial evaluation. This is a particular difficulty in languages like Lisp and Prolog, which add to their basic declarative framework a lot of non-declarative features which require special handling during partial evaluation. One solution is to build a self-applicable partial evaluator in the declarative subset of the full language and then use a meta-interpreter to mix in the features of the full language.

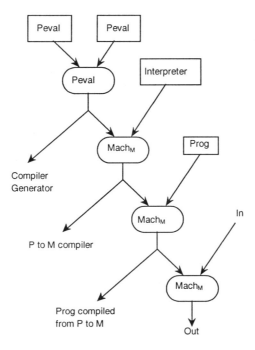

Fig. 9.2.10 The Third Futamura Projection

9.3 Supercompilation

The informal method of partial evaluation described above was formalized under the name *supercompilation* by another Russian researcher, Turchin [1986]. Turchin's idea was that a program execution could be described as a graph of machine configurations. An arc between nodes represents each possible step in a program's execution. In normal execution of a program, the configurations are ground and the graph is simply a chain from the initial configuration to the final one. In a partial execution, at any point where a program could transform to a number of states depending on some dynamic information, child states for each possibility are created. The arcs leading to these child states are labeled with the value required for the dynamic data required for execution to follow that arc.

The above process is described as *driving* and would result in forming a decision tree. If the decision tree were finite, a program could be reconstructed from it. The program would amount to a partial evaluation of the original program specialized for those values of data that were initially provided. In most cases, however, the decision tree would be infinite. Supercompilation is described as a specialized form of driving in which to prevent the attempted construction of infinite trees, loops in the graph are allowed. In particular, an arc to an existing configuration may be constructed if a configuration is found to be identical to another one in all but variable name. It can also be a specialization of it, that is, identical to the other one in all but variable name or in having identified values at points that are variable in the other. This means that arcs have to be labeled not only with the conditions necessary for execution to take a particular arc, but also to which any variables in the destination configuration would be bound if execution went down that route. To ensure against the construction of infinite graphs, supercompilation also involves the concept of *generalization*. Generalization occurs when two configurations are found to be "nearly identical". When this occurs, both are combined into one more general configuration with the values where they differ replaced by a variable and the arcs leading into it having bindings for this variable depending on which original configuration they led to.

For example, the graph in Figure 9.3.1 represents a version of insertion sort.

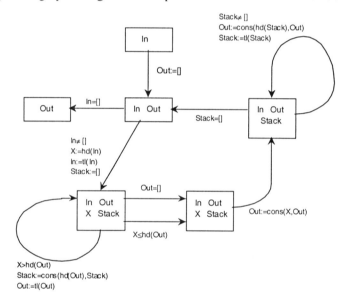

Fig. 9.3.1 Graph of insertion sort

Here, the machine configurations are labeled with the sets of variables that represent the dynamic data of those configurations. Each configuration would also have static data representing the machine state, but this data can be discarded in the final diagram, leaving something similar to a finite state machine. The conditions on the arcs are labeled by comparison operators and equalities, the binding of variables by the := operator. The initial configuration has the single variable In, the final configuration the single variable Out. From this graph, a simple imperative program could be reconstructed:

```
0: read(In); Out:=[]; goto 1;
1: if In=[] then goto 5
     else X:=hd(In); In:=tl(In); Stack:=[]; goto 2
   endif
```

```
2: if Out=[] then goto 3
      else if X≤hd(Out) then goto 3
      else Stack:=cons(hd(Out),Stack); Out:=tl(Out);
         goto 2
      endif
3: Out:=cons(X,Out); goto 4;
4: if Stack=[] then goto 1
      else Out:=cons(hd(Stack),Out);
         Stack:=tl(Stack); goto 4
      endif
5: write(Out)
```

However, it would also be possible to construct a GDC program, having a separate actor for each state:

state0(In) :- **state1**(In,[]).

state1([],Out) :- **state5**(Out).
state1([X|In],Out) :- **state2**(In,Out,X,Stack).

state2(In,[],X,Stack) :- **state3**(In,Out,X,Stack).
state2(In,[H|Out],X,Stack) :- X≤H
    | **state3**(In,Out,X,Stack).
state2(In,[H|Out],X,Stack) :- X>H
    | **state2**(In,Out,X,Stack).

state3(In,Out,X,Stack) :- **state4**(In,[X|Out],Stack).

state4(In,Out,[]) :- **state1**(In,Out).
state4(In,Out,[H|Stack]) :- **state4**(In,[H|Out],Stack).

state5(Out) :- **write**(Out).

Note that the bodies of the clauses all have just one actor, making the program what is called a *binary program*. However, it can be shown that non-binary logic programs can be transformed to binary logic programs [Demoen, 1992].

Turchin's supercompilation can be explained as manipulations of the graphical notation. Firstly, if the static information of two states is identical, they can be merged into a single state, with changes in variable names on the incoming arcs as necessary:

Figure 9.3.2 represents the case where the first state with dynamic information X, Y and Z has already been produced, with appropriate outgoing arcs and the second state with dynamic information A, B and C is being produced and so has no outgoing arcs. The second state is identified as equivalent to the first in all its static information and is merged with the first state, leaving the original outgoing arcs.

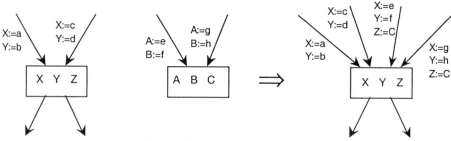

Fig. 9.3.2 Graph transformation

Secondly, if the static information in one state is a specialization of another, it can be merged with the other with the addition of arc labeling setting the variable value. For example, suppose the middle state below represents a situation where the static information is the same as the left state except that A and B are used for variables in the place of X and Z and that where the left state has dynamic Y it has constant n. Then the right state represents the merger:

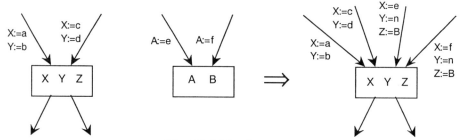

Fig. 9.3.4 Merging states

In the case where the more specialized state had been encountered first and outgoing arcs from it explored, these would have to be replaced by developing the new outgoing arcs for the more general state. So a decision has to be made: either to go ahead with the merger and abandon this previous work as "overspecialization", or whether to keep it at the cost of a more complex graph.

A similar problem occurs when two states are found which differ only in one part of their static information. Generalization refers to making this static information where they differ dynamic. New outgoing arcs for the more general state must be developed. Deciding when this generalization and merging of states is the preferable step to take is a key issue in partial evaluation. Figure 9.3.5 represents a situation where two states are found to represent identical static states except that one uses the variable names X and Y, the other A and B and also that at one point in the static information the first has information m while the second has n. The merger makes this static information difference dynamic, representing it by a new variable K. No outgoing arcs are given for the merged state, because new ones have to be developed to take account of this generalization.

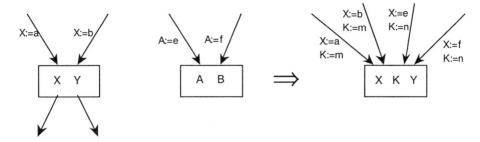

Fig. 9.3.5 Generalization

Specialization is the opposite process to the above merging of states in the graph. In specialization, if an arc leading into a state assigns a value to a dynamic value in that state, a separate node making that value static is created. Figure 9.3.6 shows the effect of specializing the top state by instantiating its dynamic value V to static n. Arcs to the descendant states of the original state are copied, with the assignment passed down into these arcs:

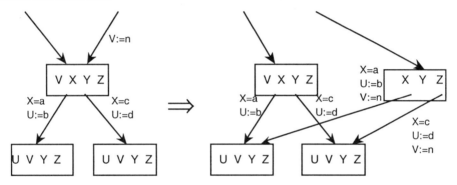

Fig. 9.3.6 Specialization

This specialization may be repeated by pushing it down to the next level. Specialized versions of the descendant states are created in the same way. The specialization can continue until all specializations are recognized as variants of previous states and ended in loops, in the way described above. Figure 9.3.7 shows the result of pushing specialization down one level.

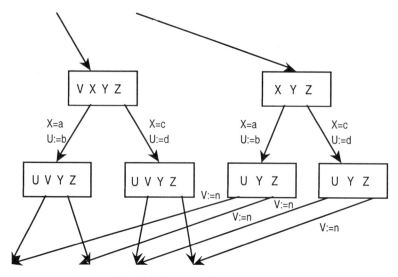

Fig. 9.3.7 Repeated specialization

A further transformation is possible when specializing in this way. When a state is specialized and the assignment making the specialization is passed to its outgoing arcs, any arc with an assignment setting a variable to one value and a condition requiring it to have another may be removed as contradictory. Figure 9.3.8 represents the specialization of a state with dynamic values W, X, Y and Z. By setting Y to n, the specialized state has no arc leading to the middle descendant state of the original state, as that arc requires Y to have the value m;

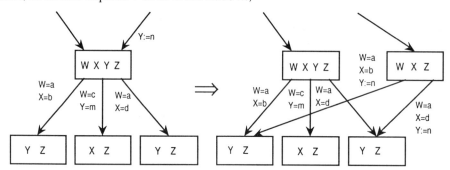

Fig. 9.3.8 Specialization evaluating satisfied conditions

Given a program represented in the graphical form used here, a partial evaluation can be performed by adding a link leading to the state representing the initial state of the program which sets some of the variables in it to static values. Then the specializations can be passed down as indicated above, generalizing to form loops where necessary to ensure the process of specialization terminates. Having done this, any state in the transformed graph, which is not reachable from the initial specialized state, is removed. This will lead us to a graph representing the specialized program alone, which can be converted back to standard program form.

Although explained graphically here, the techniques described may be found using different terminology in most partial evaluation systems and, indeed generally, in program transformation systems. The combining of nodes may be regarded as a form of folding and the specialization and hence multiplication of nodes as a form of unfolding [Burstall and Darlington, 1977]. Good explanations of partial evaluation in terms of specialization and generalization may be found for functional languages in the work of Weise et al. [1991] and for Prolog in the work of Sahlin [1993].

9.4 Partial Deduction

The above view of partial evaluation was based on an imperative view of programming. An alternative way of considering partial evaluation of logic programs based on their logic foundation has been given by Lloyd and Shepherdson [1991]. Because of its basis in logical deduction, this has been termed *partial deduction*.

In the abstract view of logic programming, unbound variables require no special treatment, since terms which contain unbound variables form a natural part of logic programming. It could be considered therefore that there is no distinction between partial evaluation and ordinary evaluation in logic programming. The fully expanded SLD tree for any query gives the full set of possible answers for that query, each of the non-failure leaves representing an answer which can be found by tracing down the branches accumulating variable unifications. For an incomplete query, though, an SLD tree will often be infinite. For example, consider the specialization of the standard list append to the case where we are appending a list to the fixed list [x,y,z]. If we were to run the query append(A,[x,y,z],B) on Prolog, we would get the answers:

```
A=[], B=[x,y,z]
A=[V1], B=[V1,x,y,z]
A=[V1,V2],B=[V1,V2,x,y,z]
A=[V1,V2,V3,x,y,z]
```

and so on. This could be seen as specializing the query to the infinite set of facts:

```
appendtoxyz([],[x,y,z]).
appendtoxyz([V1],[V1,x,y,z]).
appendtoxyz([V1,V2],[V1,V2,x,y,z]).
appendtoxyz([V1,V2,V3],[V1,V2,V3,x,y,z]).
```

and so on.

What is needed is a way of halting this infinite expansion so that we are left with a program of the form:

```
appendtoxyz([],[x,y,z]).
appendtoxyz([V|L],[V|A]) :- appendtoxyz(L,A).
```

Lloyd and Shepherdson's solution to this is to note that a partially expanded SLD tree may be regarded as a definition of a program. A leaf node in a partially expanded SLD tree may be neither a success node nor a failure node but one which stores a goal or goals, which would be further expanded in the full SLD tree. Such a leaf node may be regarded as a "qualified answer" [Vasey, 1986]: the goal at the root of the SLD tree holds if, following the substitutions on the branches to reach the leaf, the goals at the leaf hold. Given an incomplete SLD tree, the partially evaluated program for the query at the root of tree is the set of clauses $p(Vars)\theta_i\text{:-}G_i$ where Vars are the variables in the original query, the G_is are the goals at the leaves of the tree and the θ_is the unifications on the branches to those goals. Any clauses from the original program required to answer any of the G_is are also included in the partially evaluated program. Full evaluation is a special case of this where G_i is always true. Lloyd and Shepherdson showed the soundness and completeness of using these incomplete SLD trees.

Following from this, a method is needed to decide when to halt expansion of the SLD tree. Techniques to prune infinite branches from SLD trees were considered early on in the logic programming field [Brough and Walker, 1984]. The technique of *tabulation* was developed [Tamaki and Sato, 1986] which stores goals as they are encountered in the SLD tree in a table. Then, when any goal is found later which is a variant of one already in the table, its branch of the tree can be replaced by a link to the branch for the existing node. Using the idea of qualified answers, a node in the search tree which has a looping link into it may be returned as a clause giving a qualified answer to the query at the root of the tree, with the looping link represented by a recursive call. We can see that this is essentially the same process that Turchin [1986] was using with his building of loops in the supercompilation to overcome the problem of an infinite computation tree derived by driving the computation.

Generally, the SLD tree for partial deduction is larger than that for full evaluation of a goal, because partial deduction implies that some variables that are intended by the programmer to be bound are left unbound. Therefore, the SLD tree must give the possibilities for every possible binding of those variables, whereas in full evaluation the variable bindings act as constraints and only those bindings compatible with the given bindings are considered. In an SLD tree, as in the tree resulting from Turchin's driving, each node represents a complete state of computation. The efficiency of Horn clauses stems from the fact that it is possible to retain soundness and completeness (ignoring the possibility of infinite trees) while having a single computation rule which selects for expansion a single goal from the set of goals forming the state of computation [Lloyd, 1984]. In standard Prolog this is the leftmost goal.

An alternative way of viewing the search tree of a logic program is to divide each computation state into separate goals, leading to an AND-OR tree [Kowalski, 1979]. In this case OR-nodes are labeled with single goals and the arcs leading from them are labeled with the variable bindings required for the goal to be rewritten by each of the possible clauses whose head matches with it. Each of these arcs leads to an unlabelled AND-node, with arcs leading to a node for each of the goals in the body of the clause. The advantage of the AND-OR tree representation for partial evaluation is that it makes finding loops easier. Rather than building a loop only when two entire computation states are found to match, it is only necessary to find a match between individual goals. It is easier to find a correspondence between two atomic goals than two complete computation states.

9.5 Partial Evaluation and Reactive Systems

A GDC program may in fact be represented by an AND-OR tree, with the OR-arcs labeled as above and the AND-arcs labeled with the argument assignments. For instance, the AND-OR graph in Figure 9.5.1.

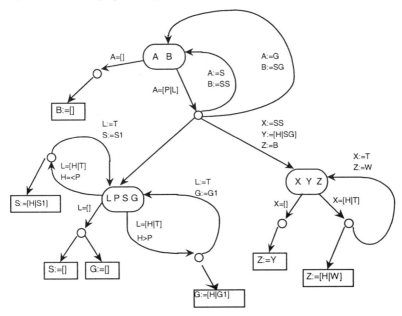

Fig. 9.5.1 AND-OR representation of quicksort

represents the GDC quick-sort program:

```
qsort([],B) :- B=[].
qsort([P|L],B)
    :- part(L,P,S,G), append(SS,[H|SG],B),
       qsort(S,SS), qsort(G,GG).

part([],P,S,G) :- S=[], G=[].
part([H|T],P,S,G) :- H=<P | part(T,P,S1,G), S=[H|S1].
part([H|T],P,S,G) :- H>P | part(T,P,S,G1), G=[H|G1].

append([],Y,Z) :- Z=Y.
append([H|T],Y,Z) :- append(T,Y,W), Z=[H|W].
```

The small round nodes in Figure 9.5.1 are the AND-nodes and the rectangular leaves represent system primitives. The node labeled with the variable arguments A B represents the **qsort** actor, the node labeled L P S G the part actor and the one labeled X Y Z the append actor.

Partial evaluation may proceed in a similar way to that described with the purely OR-graphs used previously. However, a problem occurs when considering individual actors in isolation from the context in which they occur. Evaluation of one actor may bind variables in its siblings. To partially evaluate an actor without taking account of bindings made by siblings means that a large amount of unnecessary evaluation is done. Partial evaluation takes account of every possible value allowed for in the behaviors for the actor rather than the limited set of values that its context dictates. It is for this reason that in full evaluation of Prolog only the leftmost goal is expanded, with the trust that the programmer has arranged the goal order so as to provide maximum benefit from one goal constraining its siblings. In GDC only those actors that are sufficiently bound so as not to require any information from their siblings in order to commit to a clause are expanded. In partial evaluation a technique is often used to limit partial evaluation of components occurring in some context to the finite set of values which some dynamic variable may have in that context, treating it as static for each of its possible values. This technique is so common that in their survey work on partial evaluation, Jones, Gomard and Sestoft [1993] refer to it simply as *the trick*.

One way of dealing with this issue in partial deduction is to use a method that is intermediate between having nodes representing full computation states and nodes representing individual actors. AND-OR trees are used, but an OR-node may represent a group of more than one actor. This is done in particular in cases where one actor is *dependent* on another. That is, its reduction depends on the value of some variable local to the behavior in which it occurs which is set by another actor in that behavior. If a0 is the actor which sets the variable V and a1 is the actor whose rewriting depends on the value of V, then a node representing a0&a1 can be set up. In GDC, since a1 is dependent on a0, it cannot rewrite until a0 has committed to a behavior and reduced. So the a0&a1 combination can only alter through a0 reduction. The OR-arcs descending from it are therefore labeled only with the channel values required for a0 to commit and the descendants from the AND-node include a1 (possibly with further channel bindings as it may contain other shared channels with a0 which need to be bound for a0 to commit). The a1 actor may again be combined in a single node with other actors and any further combination may be checked for correspondence and hence node merger with the original a0&a1 combination. On recreating the GDC program from the graph, the a0&a1 combination will become a single actor. The result is a form of goal fusion [Furukawa and Ueda, 1985]. This will be discussed in further detail and more formally below in Section 9.7.

Partial evaluation has been described as a transformation of some program P with respect to some arguments $a_1, \ldots a_k$, to give a residual program P′ such that the result of executing $P'(i_{k+1}, \ldots i_n)$ is the same as executing $P(a_1, \ldots, a_k, i_{k+1}, \ldots, i_n)$ for any $i_{k+1}, \ldots, i_n$. It has already been mentioned that this disregards the case that there is no necessity that the specialization is with respect only to the first k arguments to P rather than any selection of k arguments. Another simplification in this explanation is that it ignores the possibility that any of the a_i may be a compound term which itself contains further dynamic variables. This is of particular importance in the partial evaluation of meta-interpreters. Generally an actor of the form

:-   **reduce**(Actor,Prog,InfoIn,InfoOut)

is partially evaluated by binding Actor to some tuple $f(v_1, \ldots ,v_n)$ where $v_1, \ldots ,v_n$ are variables and Prog to some ground representation of a program (InfoIn and InfoOut being optional additional information input and output from the meta-interpreter), resulting in an actor **reduce_f**($v_1, \ldots ,v_n$,InfoOut) together with a program for **reduce_f**. For GDC, partial evaluation may be seen as "flattening out" the arguments of an actor, returning an actor and a partially evaluated program for it whose arguments are just the channels that occurred in the original argument list, less the constants and any surrounding functors.

Recall that an actor in a reactive system is a program execution which "reacts" when it receives a message or partial message. The actor reacts by reducing itself as far as it can to the point where it is suspended waiting for messages (which may include the further channels). It can be seen that this activity of transformation to a new process following the reception of input (but not enough input to fully bind all input channels) is almost the same as partial evaluation. The difference is that partial evaluation stores the result of the transformation in response to partial input so that instead of being used just once in response to the next partial message, it may be re-used any number of times.

To some extent the program evaluator for any reactive system language is a partial evaluator. In the parallel functional language *Multilisp* [Halsted, 1985], for example, *futures* are first-class entities in the language which represent locations into which computations are concurrently putting results. A computation in Multilisp may proceed putting futures into compound structures and suspending only when the actual value that is stored in a future is required. Suppose a Multilisp computation were run with no concurrent computation putting results into some futures it took as input. A stored version of the program as it finally suspended waiting for the futures to be evaluated could be regarded as a partial evaluation in which the futures are the dynamic variables.

The difference between partial evaluation and general evaluation in a reactive system is that as the result of partial evaluation is to be saved for repeated future use, it is worthwhile spending a fair amount of time on it. In the normal evaluation mechanism in a reactive system it would generally not be cost-effective to spend large amounts of processor time fully transforming process code in response to its latest input. However, one could imagine in a large-scale distributed system that a processor which would otherwise be idle could spend its time partially evaluating an actor which is waiting for further mesages, with respect to the messages that it has already received.

9.6 An Algorithm for Partial Evaluation of GDC Programs

The first stage of partial evaluation would be to execute the program under normal GDC evaluation. This leads to the point where a computation will consist entirely of actors suspended due to insufficient variable binding and may be considered a form of unfolding. GDC evaluation suspends an actor if expansion depends on the value of some variable that at the time of evaluation is undefined. This is similar to Ershov's [1980] mixed computation suspending a computation and adding it to the residual program if it depends on information that is dynamic.

In partial evaluation, rather than just suspend the actors we make specialized programs for them. For example, if we had an actor :- p(a,b,c,4,A,B) and behaviors:

p(a,V,W,X,Y,Z) :- q(V,X,M,N), r(M,Y,P), s(W,N,P,Z).

q(b,A,B,C) :- f(A,B,C).

r(c,Y,Z) :- g(Y,Z).
r(d,Y,Z) :- h(Y,Z).

s(W,X,Y,Z) :- X>5 | t(W, Z).
s(W,X,Y,Z) :- X≤5 | u(X,Y,Z).

f(I,J,K) :- I>3 | m(J,K).
f(I,J,K) :- I=<3 | n(J,K).

the actor can be reduced to the point where we have the subactors :- m(M,N),r(M,A,P),s(c,N,P,B), but no further since none of the actors at this point is sufficiently bound to allow further reduction. However, the actor s(c,N,P,B) has its first variable bound, so we can specialize it to some new actor sc(N,P,B) with a program giving the behavior of s when restricted to the cases where its first argument is c.

One distinction between unfolding and normal evaluation in event driven languages is that noted by Furukawa et al. [1988], who developed a set of rules for unfolding programs in the concurrent logic language *GHC*, that no assignment to variables in the initial actor should take place. This is because in these languages, for example, a clause p(X,Y) :- X=a, q(X,Y) will cause the actor p(U,V) when executed to send a message a to the channel U, q(X,Y) will be executed simultaneously, not necessarily waiting for its first argument to be bound to a unless this binding is needed for it to proceed further) whereas a clause p(a,Y) :- q(a,Y) will cause the actor p(U,V) to be suspended waiting for message a to arrive at channel U so that it can match. During unfolding, any assignment to a variable that occurred in the initial actor is left suspended since otherwise the semantics of the program would be changed, but the right-hand side of the assignment replaces occurrences of that variable in other actors being unfolded. Another way of thinking of it is to ensure that output assignments occur during final evaluation rather than prematurely during partial evaluation.

The unfolding mechanism described above means that non-deterministic choices made in commitment in event driven languages are made during partial evaluation when possible. This means that the residual program will not be equivalent to the initial program in terms of the solutions which it is possible it may give, since some may have been lost during partial evaluation. If this is undesirable, it may be avoided by restricting the unfolding to actors where there is only one possible commitment, suspending for the next stage of partial evaluation those actors where an indeterministic choice is possible.

The next stage is the specialization of individual suspended actors, referred to as *reparametrization* in Sahlin's [1993] work on partial evaluation of Prolog. It means constructing a set of behaviors specialized to the particular bindings in an actor. The process of specialization can be broken down to the following steps:

1. Remove any behaviors with which the actor cannot match.

2. Pass through any bindings in the actor to the remaining behaviors.

3. Rename the actor, restrict its argument to the actor's variables.

4. Partially evaluate the bodies of the behaviors.

Stage 4 is a recursive call on the entire partial evaluation algorithm, except that when we partially evaluate a set of actors, message sends to channels which occur in the head of the behavior are not executed for the reasons noted. The whole process is similar to the specialization process described diagrammatically above in supercompilation. The removal of behaviors which cannot match in Stage 1 is equivalent to the removal of arcs with assignments of a variable to one value and a condition requiring it to have another. Stage 2 is the pushing down of the messages, or *constant propagation*. Note that when the messages are passed through, conditions in the guard of a behavior may become further bound, a guard condition being removed if it evaluates true, the whole behavior being removed if it evaluates false. The diagrammatic notation of supercompilation did not directly name the nodes, but the renaming of stage 3 is equivalent to the establishment of a separate node.

As an example of specialization, consider the initial actor: **g**([A,3|B],C,4,D) with behaviors:

g([W],X,Y,Z) :- **a**(W,X,Y,Z).
g([H|T],6,Y,Z) :- **b**(H,T,Y,Z).
g([U,V|W],X,Y,Z) :- V>5 | **c**(U,W,X,Y,Z).
g([U,V|W],7,Y,Z) :- V=<5 | **d**(U,W,Y,A,B), **e**(A,B,X,Z).
g([H|T],X,Y,Z) :- X>=8 | **f**(H,Y,U,V), **g**([U|T],V,Y,Z).

The steps in specialization are as follows:

1. Behavior removal

first behavior removed

g([H|T],6,Y,Z) :- **b**(H,T,Y Z).
g([U,V|W],X,Y,Z) :- V>5 | **c**(U,W,X,Y,Z).
g([U,V|W],7,Y,Z) :- V=<5 | **d**(U,W,Y,A,B), **e**(A,B,X,Z).
g([H|T],X,Y,Z) :- X>=8 | **f**(H,Y,U,V), **g**([U|T],V,Y,Z).

2.   Passing through messages

    g([H,3|B],6,4,Z) :- **b**(H,[3|B],4,Z).
    g([U,3|W],X,4,Z) :- 3>5 | **c**(U,W,X,4,Z).

*guard becomes **false***

    g([U,3|W],7,4,Z) :- 3=<5 | **d**(U,W,4,A,B), **e**(A,B,X,Z).

*guard becomes **true***

    g([H,3|B],X,4,Z) :- X>=8 | **f**(H,4,U,V), **g**([U,3|B],V,4,Z).

3.   Rename predicate giving actor **g1**(A, B, C, D)

    g1(H,B,6,Z) :- **b**(H,[3|B],4,Z).
    g1(U,W,7,Z) :- **d**(U,W,4,A,B), **e**(A,B,X,Z).
    g1(H,B,X Z) :- X>=8 | **f**(H,4,U,V), **g**([U,3|B],V,4,Z).

4.   Partially evaluating behavior bodies

    g1(H,B,6,Z) :- **b1**(H,B,Z).
    g1(U,W,7,Z) :- **d1**(U,W,A,B), **e**(A,B,X,Z).
    g1(H,B,X Z) :- X$\geq$8 | **f1**(H,U,V), **g2**(U,B,V,Z).

At Stage 4 in the above example, it was assumed that during the specialization of the actor **g**([A,3|B],C,4,D) to **g1**(A,B,C,D) the actor **g**([U,3|B],V,4,Z) would be found in the body of the third behavior and the algorithm applied recursively giving some new actor **g2**(U,B,V,Z). However **g**([U,3|B],V,4,Z) is identical to **g**([A,3|B],C,4,D) in all but variable name. If specialization were to proceed it would do so identically as above except for variable names, resulting in the need to specialize **g**([U′,3|B],V′,4,Z′) and so on infinitely.

Clearly it is possible to specialize **g**([U,3|B],V,4,Z) to a recursive call **g1**(U,B,V,Z). This is a case where we are looking for equivalences, in our diagrammatic notation making a loop which turns an infinite tree into a graph. In this case, the equivalence is simple, as the two calls are identical in all but variable name. However, the stop criterion "equivalent except for variable names" is too weak and will not prevent infinite unfolding in all cases. Consider specialization of a program that performs list reversing with an accumulator and also applies a function with argument n to items in the list.

The original program is:

    freverse(N,[],Acc,R) :- R=Acc.
    freverse(N,[H|T],Acc,R)
       :-   **f**(N,H,X), **freverse**(N,T,[X|Acc] R).

If we specialize **freverse**(n,A,[] B) with these behaviors we get, before constant propagation:

    freverse1([],R) :- R=[].
    freverse1([H|T],R) :- **f**(n,H,X), **freverse**(n,T,[X],R).

The actor **f**(n,H,X)   will specialize to some actor **fn**(H,X). The second actor here requires specialization and is not equivalent in all but channel names to the previous actor1 **freverse**(n,A,[],B),   so   we   can   specialize   **freverse**(n,T,[X],R)   to **freverse2**(T,X,R) with behaviors:

> **freverse2**([],X,R) :- R=[X].
> **freverse2**([H|T],X,R) :- **f**(n,H,X1), **freverse**(T,[X1,X],R).

The actor **f**(n,H,X1) specializes to **fn**(H,X1) but **freverse**(T,[X1,X], R) is not identical in all but variable names to a previously specialized actor so it becomes **freverse3**(T,X1,X,R) and so on. We end up constructing a separate actor for every possible length of the accumulator and specialization continues without terminating.

What is needed is a recognition that **freverse**(n,A,[],B) and **freverse**(n,T,[X],R) are related. In the place of separate specializations, we specialize **freverse**(n,A,Acc,B) to **freverse0**(A,Acc,B), replacing **freverse**(n,A,[],B) by **freverse0**(A,[],B) and **freverse**(n,T,[X],R) by **freverse0**(T,[X],R). That is, we are generalizing by abstracting out an argument that is diverging on recursive calls. This is a formalization of Turchin's generalization in his supercompilation.

In general, if specializing an actor a_B and we have previously specialized an actor of the same predicate name and arity a_A, we check for recursion by matching the arguments of a_A with those of a_B. A divergence is found where a constant in a_A matches against a variable or tuple in a_B, two differing constants match, or where two tuples A and B of differing name or arity match, such that there is no well-founded ordering $\succ$ such that A$\succ$B. Bruynooghe et al. [1992] have given a detailed consideration of the use of well-founded orderings for avoiding infinite specialization in partial evaluation. Consideration of suitable well-founded orderings for actor languages is currently a matter under investigation.

We need to find an actor which generalizes a_A and a_B, that is an actor a such that there are substitutions θ and ψ where aψ=a_A and aθ=a_B. The actor should be the least general generalization, that is such that there is no ψ', θ' and a$'$ where a$'\psi'$=a_A and a$'\theta'$=a_B and $|\psi'|<|\psi|$. Plotkin [1970] first described this process under the name anti-unification.

Following generalization we specialize a to give a$'$, return a$'\theta$ as the residual actor for a_B and replace the original specialized version of a_A by a$'\psi$. It should be recalled that the specialization of a_B and hence generalization may occur within the attempt to construct behaviors specialized for a_A, if this is the case the specialization of a_A, referred to as "overspecialization", is abandoned. This is referred to as *generalized restart* by Sahlin [1993].

In the special case where ψ is empty, we can use the behaviors originally obtained from the specialization of a_A and replace by a recursive call to the actor introduced then (i.e. $a_A\theta$). This covers cases where no generalization is required and actors are equivalent except for variable names.

An algorithm that may be used for generalization is given in Figure 9.6.1.

```
set θ, ψ and ξ to { }; A to the list of arguments in aₐ
set B to the list of arguments in aB; C to the list of arguments in g₀
repeat
    let hₐ = head(A), hB = head(B), hC = head(C),
    let tₐ = tail(A), tB = tail(B), tC = tail(C)
    if hB is a variable then
        if hₐ is a variable then
            set θ to θ∪{hₐ:=hB}, ξ to ξ∪{hC:=hₐ}, A to tₐ, B to tB, C to tC
            else set ψ to ψ∪{hB:=hₐ}, ξ to ξ∪{hC:=hB}, A to tₐ, B to tB, C to tC
        else if hₐ is a variable then
            if hB a tuple or hₐ is a result of a previous generalization then
                set ξ to ξ∪{hC:=hₐ}, θ to θ∪{hC:=hB}, A to tₐ, B to tB, C to tC
            else exit, convergence found
        else if hₐ and hB are tuples then
            if the names and arities of hB and hₐ are the same then
                let M be the most general term of hB in
                    set A to the arguments of hₐ appended to tₐ
                    set B to the arguments of hB appended to tB
                    set C to the arguments of M appended to tC
                    set ξ to ξ∪{hC:=M}
            else if hₐ ≻ hB for some ≻ then exit, convergence found
            else set θ to θ∪{hC:=hB}, ψ to ψ∪{hC:=hₐ}, A to tₐ, B to tB, C to tC
        else if hₐ is a tuple then exit, convergence found
        else if hₐ=hB then set ξ to ξ∪{hC:=hB}, A to tₐ, B to tB, C to tC
        else
            set θ to θ∪{hC:=hB}, ψ to ψ∪{hC:=hₐ}, A to tₐ, B to tB, C to tC
until A is empty
```

Figure 9.6.1 Generalization algorithm

On exit from this algorithm, the generalization a is given by $a_0\xi$ where a_0 is the most general actor for a_A and a_B that is, an actor of the same name and arity but with each argument a new distinct variable. If the algorithm exits early with convergence, then it is shown that no looping is occurring, a_A is left alone and a_B specialized to a new actor. It is necessary to check that this convergence is not in fact a reintroduction of an over-specialization, so if a variable matches against a non-variable, it is only treated as a convergence if the variable did not arise from a previous generalization. Unless a definite convergence is found, the algorithm will always convert a_A and a_B to calls on instances of an actor for $a_0\xi$, or convert the call a_B to a recursive call on the actor for a_A when ψ is empty. In the latter case, no more partial evaluation is done. In the former case, since $a_0\xi$ is a generalization and since it is not possible to infinitely generalize (the most general actor will eventually be reached), partial evaluation will always terminate.

Sahlin [1993] uses for his version of our test of convergence $h_A \succ h_B$ the test

termsize(h_A) > termsize(h_B), where termsize(x) is defined on Prolog terms as:

$$
\text{termsize}(x) = \begin{cases} 1 \text{ if } x \text{ is a constant or variable} \\ 1 + \displaystyle\sum_{i=1}^{\text{arity}(x)} \text{termsize}(\text{argument}(x,i)) \text{ otherwise} \end{cases}
$$

This generalization algorithm, however, is not sufficient to partially evaluate many meta-interpreters. Consider the case where we have

reduce(Actor) :- **rule**(Actor,Body), **reduce**(Body)
rule(f(X),Body) :- Body:=g(X).

Partial evaluation of **reduce**(f(X)), to give a new actor **reducef**(X) with appropriate behaviors, will come across the partial evaluation of **reduce**(g(X)) and since it is not the case that termsize(f(X))>termsize(g(X)), both generalize back to the original **reduce**(f(X)) and **reduce**(g(X)). So we fail to evaluate away the interpreter.

In fact, two tuples with differing names or arities are only possibly diverging if we have an infinite number of names. If we cannot generate any new tuple names, that is there is no use of the Prolog **univ** (=..) or its equivalents which can convert from a list to a tuple whose functor is the item at the head of a list and whose arguments are the items on its tail, we can safely take a matching of tuples with differing names or arities as a convergence, since we cannot have an infinite chain of actors each differing from the previous ones in matched tuple name.

Going further, if it is not possible to generate new constants (that is there is no use of list to string primitives) we can safely assume a convergence has been found if two actors differ only in matching constants and it follows that if we cannot generate any new names at all, we cannot generate any new tuple names.

9.7 Actor Fusion

As noted previously, we can represent a GDC program as an AND-OR graph, with individual nodes representing individual actor states, but we also considered a variant where a node might represent the state of a network of actors. The limit of this is Turchin's original system where each node represented the network, all actors together making a complete system state. In the representation, a node in the AND-OR graph is labeled with the variables representing the dynamic information, which is the unbound variables in an individual actor. The static information attached to the node is the complete set of arguments, which is not required in the final AND-OR graph, but is required to detect possible node mergers.

An OR-node represents an actor, with the arcs leading from it labeled with the variable unifications (which are taken to include guard conditions) necessary for a node to commit to a particular behavior. An AND-node represents an individual behavior, the arcs leading from it leading to the nodes representing the actors in the behavior and labeled with bindings for the dynamic variables of these nodes. So a complete actor **A**, which may rewrite using a different behaviors is represented by Figure 9.7.1 where vars(**A**) are the variables in **A** and θ_i is the binding of these variables necessary for A to commit to the behavior represented by the i-th AND-node.

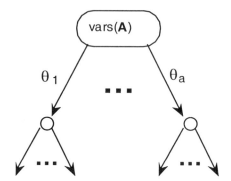

Fig. 9.7.1 Representation of a single actor

A node representing two actors, **A** and **B**, will be labeled with the union of the variables in **A** and **B**. It may reduce either by **A** becoming sufficiently bound to rewrite or by **B** becoming sufficiently bound to rewrite. Suppose there are b behaviors to which **B** can commit, with ϕ_1 to ϕ_b being the substitutions required for commitment to each behavior. Then there are a+b ways in which the **A**&**B** combination may reduce. If the ith behavior for **A** has the form $A\theta_i:-G_{i1},...,G_{in_i}$, then the effect of **A** becoming bound to commit by this behavior changes the **A**&**B** combination to a $G_{i1}\&...\&G_{in_i}\&B\theta_i$ combination. Note the bindings on **B** occur because **B** may share some channels with **A** which are required to be bound for **A** to commit using this behavior. We can represent this by adding a new arc to each of the AND-nodes representing the possibly further bound actor out of **A**&**B** which did not commit first. The subsection of the AND-OR graph for the **A**&**B** combination is given in Figure 9.7.2.

Note that some variables in **A** and **B** occur only in **A** and **B**, that is they are used to convey information into or out of the **A**&**B** combination but only between **A** and **B** within this combination. We will call these channels links(**A**,**B**). If all the bindings required for **B** to commit, ϕ_1 to ϕ_b, include a binding for one of links(**A**,**B**) then **B** cannot commit before **A** and the only arcs that need be included in the node for **A**&**B** are those representing **A** committing. In addition, links(**A**,**B**) are purely internal in **A**&**B** and thus need not be represented in the root node for **A**&**B**. This leads to a simpler structure for **A**&**B** given in Figure 9.7.3.

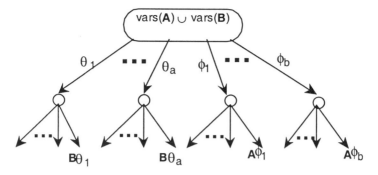

Fig. 9.7.2 Representation of two actors combined

The rules for comparing nodes in the graph and forming loops apply to nodes formed by actor fusion as to any other. Before any behaviors are developed for the fused node with variables vars(**A**)∪vars(**B**)-links(**A**,**B**), they should be checked against other actors formed by fusing actors of the same name and arity as **A** and **B**, using the same generalization algorithm used previously for specialization. Should a correspondence be found, as before the fused call is turned into a call to the previously defined actor if it is identical except for variable names to a previous fused call, or if the only correspondences are between non-variables in **A&B** and variables in the previous fusion. Otherwise, if a more general correspondence is found, the previous predicate is abandoned as over-specialized and a more general one in which there is less constant propagation is produced.

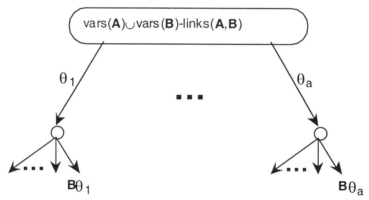

Fig. 9.7.3 Simpler representation of two actors combined

The technique of searching for correspondences between conjunctions of goals in the SLD tree was described formally, extending Tamaki and Sato's work on tabulation, by Boulanger and Bruynooghe [1992]. Their work is a generalization of previous work on goal fusion, particularly that of Proietti and Pettorossi [1991; 1993]. Proietti and Pettorossi were particularly interested in using the technique to eliminate unnecessary variables. As shown above, variables linking the two fused actors are eliminated, although it may seem that the communication using these variables has simply been pushed down a level. However, it should be recalled that a similar actor fusion may take place among actors in the bodies of the new behaviors developed for **A&B**. It is when such a fusion can be identified as a version of **A&B** and converted in a recursive call that the elimination of unnecessary channels occurs. Restriction of actor fusion to cases where one actor is dependent on another ensures there is no loss of potential parallelism.

9.8 Actor Fusion Examples

Actor fusion in GDC constructs a set of behaviors for **A&B** as follows. For each behavior of the predicate for **A**, which will take the form A_i:-<guard>$_i$|<body>$_i$, a new behavior for **A&B** is constructed. Unifications θ_i and ψ_i are found such that $A\theta_i = A_i\psi_i$ = the most general unification of **A** and A_i, with θ_i extended to rename all channels in **A** to their matching channels in A_i and also to rename all channels in **B** with new names. The arguments in the head of the new behavior are those of A_i, less the linking channels link(**A**,**B**), appended to a copy of all those channels in $B\theta_i$ but not in $A\theta_i$. The body of the new behavior is initially the conjunction of <body>$_i$ and $B\theta_i$ but $B\theta_i$ is unfolded to give a set of suspended actors <bodyg>$_i$. Unfolding is, as described above, similar to normal evaluation with channels in the head of the new behavior treated as channels in the initial actor in the top-level unfolding. Assignments are not executed, but occurrences of the channel on the left-hand side of the assignment in the body of the behavior are replaced by the right-hand side of the assignment; if this should cause any actor in <body>$_i$ to become further bound, it too is unfolded. Following this unfolding, each of the actors in <bodyg>$_i$ is tested for fusion with those in <body>$_i$ and any which do not fuse is specialized using the method given above, actor fusion being applied recursively to those which are fuseable.

As a specific example, consider the fusion of **append**(L1,L2,L3) and **length**(L3,N) to give a new actor **append_length**(L1,L2,N), eliminating channel L3. If initially:

```
append([],L,L1) :- L1=L.
append_length([H|T],L,L1)
    :- append(T,L,L2), L1=[H|L2].

length([],N) :- N=0.
length([H|T],N)
    :- append(T,L,L2), L1=[H|L2], length(L1,N).
```

the initial behaviors for **append_length** are:

```
append_length([],L,N) :- L1=L, length(L1,N).
append_length([H|T],N)
    :- length(T,N1) ), add(1,N1,N).
```

Following execution of message sends to non-head channels, we have:

append_length([],L,N) :- **length**(L N).
append_length([H|T],L,N)
    :- **append**(T,L,L2), **length**([H|L2],N).

After unfolding the second actor in the body of the second behavior we have:

append_length([],L,N) :- **length**(L,N).
append_length([H|T],L,N)
    :- **append**(T,L,L2), **length**(L2 N1), **add**(1,N1,N).

The fusion of actors **append**(T,L,L2) and **length**(L2,N1) in the second behavior is identical in all but variable name to the previous fusion, so we can convert it to a call to the previously defined predicate **append_length**, giving behaviors:

append_length([],L,N) :- **length**(L,N).
append_length([H|T],L,N)
    :- **append_length** (T,L,N1), **add**(1,N1,N).

A general rule is that no attempts are made to fuse actors which are recursive calls. In this case, **append_length**(T,L,N1) being recursive is not fused with **add**(1,N1,N).

Folding to eliminate a channel (and the consequent building up of a data structure which is passed in this channel and then broken down again) is similar to the functional programming transformation technique of *deforestation* [Wadler, 1988]. Where in logic programming the goals to be combined have the form

$$\textbf{f}(a_1,...,a_n,V), \; \textbf{g}(V,b_1,...,b_m)$$

in functional programming the form would be f a_1 ... a_n (g b_1 ... b_m). As can be seen, in functional programming the communication between f and g may be implicit rather than through an explicit variable. The correspondence is rather more obvious if the nested function call is abstracted out:

let $V = g \; b_1$ ... b_m in f a_1 ... a_n V.

While it has been suggested that in general actor fusion should be restricted to those cases where one actor is dependent on another, there are other circumstances where the method may be of benefit. In particular, it may be used to combine multiple traversals of a single data structure into one traversal. Consider, for example, finding both the sum and product of the leaves of a tree:

sum_product(T,S,P) :- **sum**(T,S), **prod**(T,P).
sum(tip(N),S) :- S=N.
sum(tree(L,R),S) :- **sum**(L,SL), **sum**(R,SR), **add**(SL,SR,S).

prod(tip(N),P) :- P=N.
prod(tree(L,R),) :- **prod**(L,PL), **prod**(R,PR), **mult**(PL,PR,S).

To combine these into a single traversal of the tree, first push **prod**(T,P) into the behaviors for **sum** giving:

sumprod(tip(N),S,P) :- S=N, **prod**(tip(N),P).
sumprod(tree(L,R),S,P)
    :- **sum**(L,SL), **sum**(R,SR), **add**(SL,SR,S), **prod**(tree(L,R),P).

Unfolding the calls to **prod** in the behavior bodies gives:

sumprod(tip(N),S,P) :– S=N, P=N.
sumprod(tree(L,R),S,P)
   :- **sum**(L,SL), **sum**(R,SR), **add**(SL, R,),
       prod(L,PL), **prod**(R,PR), **mult**(PL,PR,S).

Folding (that is noting two possible actor combines which are identical in all but variable name to the original one) in the body of the second behavior gives:

sumprod(tip(N),S,P) :- S=N, P=N.
sumprod(tree(L,R),S,P)
   :- **sumprod**(L,SL,PL), **sumprod**(R,SR,PR),
       add(SL,SR,S), **mult**(PL,PR,S).

Two actors are considered identical during the fusion if they are identical in actor name, arity and in input channels, differing only in channels which are only used for output. If during fusion two actors are identical then one of the actors can be removed and all occurrences of its output channels replaced in the rest of the body of the behavior with the equivalent channels from the other actor. In this case, it acts to remove computations, which are redundant, as they act simply to reproduce results obtained elsewhere.

Lakhotia and Sterling [1988] refer to this technique of combining several traversals into one as *clausal join*. As suggested earlier, their methods are fairly ad hoc and they failed to note it as just one form of a more general method of goal fusion.

9.9 Partial Evaluation of an Interpreter

As an extended example of partial evaluation, we consider the use of the techniques we have described on a GDC interpreter for a simple imperative language. The effect is to translate programs written in that language to GDC and also to partially evaluate them should they be supplied with partial input. As we have mentioned, some early work in partial evaluation, such as that of Ershov [1980] did consider the direct partial evaluation of imperative languages. Later work has tended to go through a declarative language as a meta-language. Ross, for example [1988] uses Prolog.

It is possible and useful, to define an imperative language using predicate logic, in terms of the values held by variables, or environment, before and after the execution of statements in the language [Hehner et al., 1986]. If the logic used is in the form of a logic program, the definition serves a dual purpose. Firstly it is a specification of the semantics of the imperative language, but secondly, as it is executable, it serves also as an interpreter for the imperative language.

Here an interpreter for an imperative language written in a actor language is partially evaluated with respect to some program in that imperative language. This gives us a actor program that has the same semantics as the original imperative program. If we partially supply the input data to the imperative program, this data will further specialize the residual program. This is a different approach from Ross, who uses a separate translator from an imperative language to a logic program and then uses the full partial evaluation algorithm on the resulting program.

Adding a back-end which converts the final logic program back to the imperative language would complete the process whereby an logic language is used to partially evaluate an imperative language, although this last stage is not covered here (it has been considered in [Huntbach, 1990]).

The present use of an actor language rather than Ross's Prolog gains several advantages. Firstly, where the sequentiality of a standard imperative language does not effect its semantics, the sequentiality disappears in the concurrent specification. As a result, the conversion process automatically introduces parallelism into the program. This has the potential of reverse engineering [Chikofsky and Cross, 1990] "dusty deck" imperative programs into versions that can exploit the new generation of parallel architectures. Secondly, it extends the techniques to imperative languages that already embody parallel processing.

The idea of using a meta-language as the basis for a program manipulation system is also a part of the *Programmer's Apprentice* project [Waters, 1985]. In [Huntbach, 1990] an equivalence was shown between the plan notation of the Programmer's Apprentice and logic programming. The present method of language translation through partial evaluation is similar to the abstraction and reimplementation method of Waters [1988], though whereas the Programmer's Apprentice uses an ad hoc library of programming clichés to transform its meta-language version of the program, a rather more systematic transformation method is used.

Statements in an imperative language are specified in terms of a relation between an input environment and an output environment, where an environment is simply a list of name-value pairs. The figure below gives a BNF for a simple imperative language involving just assignments, loops and conditionals. Actual symbols of the language are given in bold type, non-terminal symbols within angled brackets. The BNF is such that programs in the language are also valid terms in an actor language, therefore no parser is required (it is assumed that, as in Prolog, certain operators, such as the arithmetic operators, are predefined as infix). For simplicity, the BNF suggests that arithmetic expressions may only take a simple <Variable> <Operator> <Variable> form, though it would not be difficult to extend it to cover full arithmetic expressions. Variables are represented by strings beginning with *lower case* letters and are thus distinct from the channels of the meta-language. This is, of course, essential, since imperative variables may be reassigned values, whereas channels have a single-assignment property. It is also assumed that the language provides simple list handling primitives. There is no type checking.

```
<Program> :      := <Block>
<Block> :        := []
<Block> :        := [ <Statement> {, <Statement> } ]
<Statement> :    := if(<Condition>,<Block>,<Block>)
<Statement> :    := while(<Condition>,<Block>)
<Statement>      ::= <Variable> := <Expression>
<Expression> :   := <Variable> <ArithOp> <Variable>
<Expression> :   := hd(<Variable>)
```

```
<Expression>     := tl(<Variable>)
<Expression> :   := cons(<Variable>,<Variable>)
<Expression>     := []
<Condition>      := empty(<Variable>)
<Condition>      := <Variable> <CompOp> <Variable>
```

The semantics for the language are given by the GDC interpreter for it. The semantics for an assignment statement give an output environment in which the variable on the left-hand-side of the assignment is linked with the result obtained from evaluating the expression on the right-hand-side of the assignment in the input environment, with all other elements of the environment unchanged. A conditional statement has the semantics of either of its two substatements depending on how its condition evaluates in the input environment. The semantics for a while statement involve the standard logic programming conversion of iteration to recursion. Sequencing is achieved by taking the output environment of the first statement as the input for the rest. In the GDC interpreter below code for arithmetic operators and comparison operators other than plus and greater then is not given, but will follow the same pattern as plus and greater than. It would be possible to extend the interpreter considerably to give a more realistic imperative language, or to add other desired features. In [Huntbach, 1991], for example, a version of it is given which includes Occam-style guarded commands.

```
block(InEnv,[],OutEnv) :- OutEnv=InEnv.
block(InEnv,[Stat|Statements],OutEnv)
    :-  statement(InEnv,Stat,MidEnv),
        block(MidEnv,Statements,OutEnv).

statement(InEnv,Var:=Expr,OutEnv)
    :-  evalinenv(InEnv,Expr,Val), replace(Var,Val,InEnv,OutEnv).
statement(InEnv,while(Cond,Block),OutEnv)
    :-  evalinenv(InEnv,Cond,TruthVal),
        loop(TruthVal,InEnv,Cond,Block,OutEnv).
statement(InEnv,if(Cond,Block1,Block2),OutEnv)
    :-  evalinenv(InEnv,Cond,TruthVal),
        switch(TruthVal,InEnv,Block1,Block2,OutEnv).

switch(true,InEnv,Block1,Block2,OutEnv)
    :-  block(InEnv,Block1,OutEnv).
switch(false,InEnv,Block1,Block2,OutEnv)
    :-  block(InEnv,Block2,OutEnv).

loop(false,InEnv,Cond,Block,OutEnv) :- OutEnv=InEnv.
loop(true,InEnv,Cond,Block,OutEnv)
    :-  block(InEnv,Block,MidEnv),
        evalinenv(MidEnv,Cond,TruthVal),
        loop(TruthVal, MidEnv, Cond, Block, OutEnv).

evalinenv(Env,N,V) :- integer(N) | V:=N.
evalinenv(Env,N,V) :- string(N) | lookup(N,Env,V).
```

```
evalinenv(Env,E1+E2,V)
    :-  evalinenv(Env,E1,V1), evalinenv(Env,E2,V2),
        V:=V1+V2.
evalinenev(Env,E1>E2,V)
    :-  evalinenv(Env,E1,V1), evalinenv(Env,E2,V2),
        gt(V1,V2,V).
evalinenv(Env,not(E),V)
    :-  evalinenv(Env,E,V1), negate(V1,V).
evalinenv(Env,hd(E),V)
    :-  evalinenv(Env,E,V1), head(V1,V).
evalinenv(Env,tl(E),V)
    :-  evalinenv(Env,E,V1), tail(V1,V).
evalinenv(Env,cons(E1,E2),V)
    :-  evalinenv(Env,E1,V1),
        evalinenv(Env,E2,V2), cons(V1,V2,V).
evalinenv(Env,empty(E),V)
    :-  evalinenv(Env,E,V1), null(V1,V).


gt(V1,V2,V) :- V1>V2 | V=true.
gt(V1,V2,V) :- V1=<V2 | V=false.


negate(true,V) :- V=false.
negate(false,V) :- V=true.


cons(H,T,L) :- L=[H|T].


head([H|T],X) :- X=H.


tail([H|T],X) :- X=T.


null([],V) :- V=true.
null([H|T],V) :- V=false.


lookup(Var,[(Var1,Val1)|Env],Val) :- Var=Var1
    |   Val=Val1.
lookup(Var,[(Var1,Val1)|Env], Val) :- Var=\=Var1
    |   lookup(Var,Env,Val).


replace(Var,Val,[(Var1,Val1)|Env1],Env) :- Var=\=Var1
    |   replace(Var,Val,Env1,Env2),
        Env=[(Var1,Val1)|Env2].
replace(Var,Val,[(Var1,Val1)|Env1], Env) :- Var==Var1
    |   Env=[(Var,Val)|Env1].
```

As an example of partial evaluation of this interpreter, a simple list reversal program is used which uses a loop that builds up on an accumulator. The imperative code is:

```
while(not(empty(in), [
    acc:=cons(hd(in),acc),
    in:=tl(in)
]
```

with in the input list, acc initially set to the empty list and the final value of acc returned as output. This can be achieved by adding the behavior:

> **reverse**(L,R)
> :- **block**([[(in,L),(acc,[])],
>   [while(not(empty(in)),
>   [acc:=cons(hd(in),acc), in:=tl(in)])]], Env),
>   **lookup**(acc,Env,R).

to the interpreter and then partially evaluating the actor **reverse**(L, R).

The actor will unfold to the set of actors:

> :- **null**(L,V),
>   **negate**(V,V1),
>   **loop**(V1,[(in,L),(acc,[])],not(empty(in)),
>   [acc:=cons(hd(in),acc),in:=tl(in)],Env),
>   **lookup**(acc,Env,R).

The **null** actor is suspended because it cannot rewrite further while L is unbound. The **negate** actor is suspended as V is unbound. The **loop** actor is suspended as V1 is unbound and the **lookup** actor is suspended as Env is unbound. The **loop** actor can be specialized, but as it is dependent on the **negate** actor we leave it for fusion. At this stage the **null** actor and **negate** actor are fused to remove the variable V. This gives the new actor **null_negate**(L,V1), with behaviors (before the partial evaluation of their bodies):

> **null_negate**([],V1) :- V=true, **negate**(V,V1).
> **null_negate**([H|T],V1) :- V=false, **negate**(V,V1).

In both cases, as the channel V does not occur in the head of the behaviors, so we can go ahead with sending the message, then unfold the **negate** actor, giving:

> **null_negate**([],V1) :- V1=false.
> **null_negate**([H|T],V1) :- V =true.

The next stage fuses **null_negate**(L,V1) with the **loop** actor. This will give the actor **null_negate_loop**(L,Env) with behaviors, before partial evaluation of their bodies:

> **null_negate_loop**([],Env)
> :- V1=true,
>   **loop**(V1,[(in,[]),(acc,[])],not(empty(in)),
>   [acc:=cons(hd(in),acc),in:=tl(in)],Env).
> **null_negate_loop**([H|T], Env)
> :- V1=false,
>   **loop**(V1,[(in,[H|T]),(acc,[])],not(empty(in)),
>   [acc:=cons(hd(in),acc),in:=tl(in)],Env).

Note how the L in the **loop** actor has been bound in the first behavior to [] and in the second to [H|T] as this channel was shared with the **null_negate** actor and the arguments with which it matches in the behaviors for **null_negate** are so bound. As with the formation of **null_negate**, the assignments within the bodies may take place and this enables the **loop** actors within the bodies to be unfolded until the point is reached where they have unfolded to actors which are all suspended:

```
null_negate_loop([],Env)
    :- Env=[(in,[]),(acc,[])].
null_negate_loop([H|T],Env)
    :- null(T,V),
       negate(V, V1),
       loop(V1,[(in,T),(acc,[H])],not(empty(in))),
       [acc:=cons(hd(in),acc),in:=tl(in)],Env).
```

Note in the second behavior that the **lookup** and **replace** actors altering the environments are completely evaluated in the unfolding. This gives an environment in which in is paired with the tail of the initial list and acc is paired with a list of one element, the head of the initial list.

At this point, **null**(T,V) and **negate**(T,V1) are fused in the second behavior and this is found to be equivalent in all but channel names to the previous fusion of a **null** and **negate** actor, so it becomes **null_negate**(T,V1) with no further definition of behaviors. When **null_negate**(T,V1) is fused with the **loop** actor, however, a divergence is found. It is equivalent to the previous fusion of a **null_negate** with a **loop** actor, except that the channel T occurs in the place of the previous L and also in the place of [] there is now [H]. This latter condition means that the previous fusion is abandoned as an over-specialization. In the place of **null_negate_loop**(L,Env), put:

```
null_negate_loop1(L,[],Env)
```

where the behaviors for **null_negate_loop1**(L,A,Env) are obtained from the fusion of **null_negate**(L,V1) and

```
loop(V1, [(in,T),(acc,A)], not(empty(in))),
    [acc:=cons(hd(in),acc), in:=tl(in)], Env)
```

That is, we have abstracted out the specific value of the accumulator.

The behaviors for **null_negate_loop1**, following unfolding of the actors in their bodies but not actor fusion in the bodies are:

```
null_negate_loop1([],A,Env)
    :- Env=[(in,[]),(acc,A)].
null_negate_loop1([H|T],A,Env)
    :- null(T,V),
       negate(V,V1),
       loop(V1,[(in,T),(acc,[H|A])],not(empty(in))),
       [acc:=cons(hd(in),acc),in:=tl(in)],Env).
```

As previously, **null**(T,V) and **negate**(V,V1) will fuse to give **null_negate**(T,V1) but this time when this is fused with the **loop** actor, it will be detected as a version of the previous fusion to form **null_negate_loop1** with [H|A] matching against A. A channel matching against a tuple in this way does not require further generalization so the fusion becomes the recursive call:

:-   **null_negate_loop1**([H|T],[H|A],Env),

with no further need to define behaviors.

So the position we are now in is that we have top level actors:

:-   **null_negate_loop1**(L,[],Env),
    lookup(acc, Env, R)

with the behaviors for **null_negate_loop1**:

null_negate_loop1([],A,Env)
    :- Env=[(in,[]),(acc,A)].
null_negate_loop1([H|T],A, nv)
    :- **null_negate_loop1**(T,[H|A],Env).

At the top level we can now fuse the two actors, removing the variable Env. This leaves us with the single actor **null_negate_loop1_lookup**(L,[],R) with behaviors, initially:

null_negate_loop1_lookup([],A,R)
    :- Env=[(in,[]),(acc,A)], **lookup**(acc,Env,R).
null_negate_loop1_lookup([H|T],A,Env)
    :- **null_negate_loop1**(T,[H|A],Env),
        lookup(acc,Env,R).

In the first of these behaviors, the assignment can be executed and:

lookup(acc,[(in,[]),(acc,A)],R)

unfolds completely to R=A. In the second behavior, the fusion of **null_negate_loop1**(T,[H|A],Env) and **lookup**(acc,Env,R) matches the previous fusion and so becomes the actor:

null_negate_loop1_lookup(T,[H|A],R).

This leaves **null_negate_loop1_lookup**(L,[],R) as the residual actor with behaviors:

null_negate_loop1_lookup([],A,R) :- R=A.
null_negate_loop1_lookup([H|T],A,R)
    :- **null_negate_loop1_lookup**(T,[H|A],R).

It can be seen that we have the standard logic program for reverse with an accumulator. The interesting point is that the handling of the environment took place entirely within the partial evaluation. Partial evaluation has had the effect of compiling away the overhead associated with managing an environment.

Also note that the interpreter for the imperative language detects any implicit potential parallelism and converts it to the real parallelism of GDC. This implicit parallelism respects the data dependency of the sequencing of statements giving parallelism only where it has no effect on the result of the execution. Consider the execution of the assignments x:=exp1, y:=exp2, z:=exp3 where exp1, exp2 and exp3 are arbitrary expressions. The call

:-   **block**(Env1,[x:=exp1,y:=exp2,z:=exp3],OutEnv)

will unfold to:

```
:-  V1 = evaluation of exp1 in Env1,
    V2 = evaluation of exp2 in Env2,
    V3 = evaluation of exp3 in Env3,
    replace(x,V1,Env1,Env2),
    replace(y,V2,Env2,Env3),
    replace(z,V3,Env3,OutEnv)
```

Suppose the initial environment (Env1) is:

$$[(x,1),(y,2),(z,3),(a,4),(b,5),(c,6)]$$

then the calls to **replace** will unfold giving:

```
:-  V1 = evaluation of exp1 in Env1,
    V2 = evaluation of exp2 in Env2,
    V3 = evaluation of exp3 in Env3,
    Env2 = [(x,V1),(y,2),(z,3),(a,4),(b,5),(c,6)],
    Env3 = [(x,V1),(y,V2),(z,3),(a,4),(b,5),(c,6)],
    OutEnv = [(x,V1),(y,V2),(z,V3),(a,4),(b,5),(c,6)]
```

If exp1, exp2 and exp3 contain references to a, b and c only, they may be evaluated in parallel. If however, exp2 contains references to x it will use V1 for x and evaluation will be suspended until V1 is bound by evaluation of exp1. Similarly, evaluation of exp3 will be halted if it contains references to x or y. In contrast a purely parallel execution of the assignments which does not respect data dependency could have indeterminate effect if exp2 contains references to x or exp3 contains references to x or y. The effect is as if the assignments were carried out in any order. If the assignments were [x:=y,y:=9,z:=2*x+y], the result would be that x is linked with either 2 or 9 and z any of 4, 6, 13 or 27.

The interpreter presented retains those elements of the sequential execution which are a necessary part of the semantics, but not those which are not, hence the process of partial evaluation into actors may also be used as an automated paralleliser. We have separated out what has been termed the kernel from the semantically unnecessary control [Pratt, 1987].

Chapter 10

Agents and Robots

Civilization advances by extending the number of important operations that we can perform without thinking about them.

AN Whitehead (1861–1947)

Stemming from several sources, the notion of a *computational agent* came to prominence in the 1990s. The multiple parentage of the concept meant that there was no clear definition as to what the terminology meant. The rapid growth of interest led to many using the term as a buzzword in the hope of gaining a foothold on the bandwagon. As this book has indicated, agents have been a common theme in the sociology of artificial intelligence. At the 13th International Conference on Distributed AI, Hewitt remarked that the question "what is an agent?" is as embarrassing for the agent-based computing community as the question "what is intelligence?" Underlying the development of the concept of agent is the move away from computers as stand-alone systems that are used to model aspects of the world towards being active participants in the world. One of the dictionary definitions of agent is "a person or thing, which exerts power or has the power to act" and this sense lies behind the use of the word in computing.

As Gelernter and Carriero [1992] and many others have noted, computing has developed with the processing of data seen as paramount and the transmission of data and results as secondary or superficial. AI systems used for problem solving or expert systems illustrate this. They provide output when given input, the output reflecting how a human would approach the same mental task. They do not attempt to interfere with the world itself. This is left to humans. Such systems have a complete and closed model of the world, working on the assumption that manipulating this model will parallel manipulating the real world. This will work perfectly in real world situations like game playing where strict rules are obeyed. It is not surprising that the playing of games like chess has been one of the most successful applications of AI. However, the capturing of uncertainty has been a major theme in moving beyond simple microworlds like this. Systems are soon engulfed by the amount of information needed and combinatorial explosion when every possible result of attempting an action in the real world is considered.

10.1 Reactive Agents: Robots and Softbots

Concerns of this sort led Brooks [1991a] to challenge the Artificial Intelligence community, claiming it had gone down a blind alley. Brooks was concerned with building robots that could cope with ordinary physical environments [Brooks, 1986]. He wanted his robots to be robust, able to deal with inconsistency in sensor readings and able to achieve a modicum of sensible behavior if the environment changed, rather than fail and halt or engage in irrational behavior. His response to this challenge was to drop the *good old-fashioned AI* approach involving detailed planning and knowledge representation and build robots that worked purely on reaction to sensor input. He argued that this was how real animals worked (or, as he put it, "Elephants don't play chess" [Brooks, 1990]). This harks back to the behavioral psychology, Section 1.6. Thus, an artificial intelligence should be constructed by first building a base with animal-like behavior with simple reactive rules and then adding to it layers of more intelligent control. Experiments with real animals, for example [Arbib and Liaw, 1995], have been used to show that much animal behavior can be accounted for by simple reactive mechanisms.

The lowest level of control of Brooks' robots led them simply to avoid collision (bearing in mind they had to exist in environments where other objects might be moving) by sending appropriate messages to movement motors when the sensors detected the approach of an object. The next level of control caused the robots to move independently but aimlessly by sending messages to move and turn at random. A level above this gave some direction to the movement, sending the robot towards areas that its sensors detected had free space. Only at levels above this (which were not included in Brooks' original robots) would the robot store maps it had constructed of its environment and plan movement around these maps. Each layer of control in the robots worked independently of the higher layers. Higher levels could take control from the lower levels by issuing instructions that the lower level messages be ignored, but the lower levels would continue issuing the messages regardless. This was called a *subsumption architecture*.

Agre and Chapman [1987] made a similar use of a purely reactive architecture in their influential *PENGI* system. This system was designed to play an arcade computer game involving moving an object in an environment where points may be gained by reaching certain positions. Hostile moving objects have to be avoided and the player may set other objects in motion. Unlike Brooks' robots, the PENGI system was working with an artificial and thus strictly limited world. The large numbers of objects in this world, their unpredictable behavior and the time-dependent nature of the game, meant that tackling the game in a way involving detailed modeling and planning was unfeasible. Rather, the approach used was for the artificial player to react immediately based on simple rules involving the immediate surroundings of the manipulable object.

The most obvious aspect of the move of computing away from standalone systems is the development of the Internet, making all connected machines one large distributed system. The term *agent* has been associated with systems designed to work with the Internet. Reading email or directly requesting the transfer of remote files, the Internet is an infrastructure driven by human actions. Systems designed to explore the Internet in order to discover information, or to filter email to reduce information overload [Maes, 1994] are agents in a second dictionary sense of the word "ones entrusted with the business of another". Clearly such systems may be simple and we would resist describing a mail filter that simply throws away all email not from a given list of addresses as "intelligent". Higher levels of intelligence might include making use of some set of rules and an inference engine in order to make decisions, build user models, learn and adapt in response to feedback and so on.

The connection of these software agents with agents in the Brooks' sense is argued by Etzioni [Etzioni, 1993]. He suggests that a system operating in a real software environment shared by other users faces much the same problems as a robot working in a physical environment. These are: lack of complete knowledge of what the environment contains; the need to be able to handle whatever is encountered in the environment without failing; the dynamic nature of the environment; the ability of the agent to change the environment. To emphasize the similarity with physical robots, Etzioni uses the term *softbot*. The pragmatic convenience of softbots over robots for agent research is noted. It is cheaper and quicker to build and experiment with software artifacts rather than physical artifacts, but such experimentation is not simply games-playing as it has obvious commercial potential [Tenenbaum, 1997].

10.2 A Simple Robot Program

As shown in Chapter 5, an actor can be represented by a system where (mutually) recursive calls represent a continuation of a state. Single assignment variables and terms can be interpreted as recursively defined messages. Consider an input stream connected to a sensor which converts messages to the single assignment form while an output stream connected to an effector which converts values to commands to a robot's motors. A robot working in an environment may then be programmed. This has been done with real robots by Nishiyama et al. [1998]. To demonstrate this, consider a simple world consisting of a two-dimensional grid (similar to the tile world [Pollack and Ringuette, 1990] that has been used as the basis for a number of agent experiments). We have a robot situated in this world which can face one of the four compass points. Squares in the grid are either clear or blocked and the robot may only move to clear squares. The robot has one sensor that returns the message clear if the square it is facing is clear, blocked otherwise. Its one effector may be sent the messages move to move forward one square, clock to turn a quarter-turn clockwise (without changing square) and anti to similarly turn anticlockwise.

The state of the robot will consist of the streams connected to the sensor and effector, the direction it is facing and the x and y coordinate. Additionally, differences between the square in which the robot is located and a goal square (positive if the robot is to the south/west of the goal, negative if it is to the north/east) can be stored. The program will simply cause the robot to move towards the goal square avoiding blocked squares.

The algorithm may be represented by a finite state machine as in Table 10.2.1. Here State 0 is the state the robot is in before making a move. Recalling that on a square grid, two of the compass directions will be facing towards the goal location and two away, States 2 and 4 represent the robot turning in the alternative direction to the goal if its initial direction is blocked. If the second direction is also blocked, the double turn after this to States 3 and 5 means the robot only returns the way it has entered a square if all other adjoining squares are blocked. States 6 and 8 represent a robot, which is not initially facing the goal turning to face it. States 7 and 9 represent it turning back to the original direction if the new direction is blocked. If the original direction is also blocked, again it turns to the third facing, returning the way it came only if that too is blocked.

Table 10.2.1 Finite state machine robot

State 0:   If clear and facing goal: move forward, goto state 0.
                            If blocked and facing goal and a clockwise turn faces
                                goal: turn clockwise, goto state 2.
                            If blocked and facing goal and an anticlockwise turn
                                faces goal: turn anticlockwise, goto state 4.
                            If not facing goal and a clockwise turn faces goal: turn
                                clockwise, goto state 6.
                            If not facing goal and an anticlockwise turn faces goal:
                                turn anticlockwise, goto state 8.
State 1:   If clear: move forward, goto state 0.
                            If blocked:goto state 0.
State 2:   If clear: move forward, goto state 0.
                            If blocked:turn clockwise twice, goto state 3.
State 3:   If clear: move forward, goto state 0.
                            If blocked: turn anticlockwise, goto state 1.
State 4:   If clear: move forward, goto state 0.
                            If blocked: turn anticlockwise twice, goto state 5.
State 5:   If clear: move forward, goto state 0.
                            If blocked: turn clockwise, goto state 1.
State 6:   If clear: move forward, goto state 0.
                            If blocked: turn anticlockwise, goto state 7.
State 7:   If clear: move forward, goto state 0.
                            If blocked: turn anticlockwise, goto state 3.
State 8:   If clear: move forward, goto state 0.
                            If blocked: turn clockwise, goto state 9.
State 9:   If clear: move forward, goto state 0.
                            If blocked: turn clockwise, goto state 5.

Note that in State 1, representing the robot returning the way it came, a check is made to see whether the way is blocked and if so the robot returns to checking other directions. This is because the robot program is intended to operate in a dynamic environment, so the way may have become blocked since the robot moved from it and other ways may become unblocked.

The code for this is tedious, but not complex:

```
robot0(north,Xd,Yd,[clear|S],E) :- Yd>=0
    |  E=[move|E1], Yd1:=Yd+1,
       robot0(north,Xd,Yd1,S,E1).
robot0(south,Xd,Yd,[clear|S],E) :- Yd<0
    |  E=[move|E1], Yd1:=Yd-1,
       robot0(south,Xd,Yd1,S,E1).
```

```
robot0(east,Xd,Yd,[clear|S],E) :- Xd>=0
    |   E=[move|E1], Xd1:=Xd-1,
        robot0(east,Xd1,Yd,S,E1).
robot0(west,Xd,Yd,[clear|S],E) :- Xd<0
    |   E=[move|E1], Xd1:=Xd+1,
        robot0(west,Xd1,Yd,S,E1).
robot0(north,Xd,Yd,[block|S],E) :- Yd>=0, Xd>=0
    |   E=[clock|E1], robot2(east,Xd,Yd,S,E1).
robot0(south,Xd,Yd,[block|S],E) :- Yd<0, Xd<0
    |   E=[clock|E1], robot2(west,Xd,Yd,S,E1).
robot0(east,Xd,Yd,[block|S],E) :- Xd>=0, Yd<0
    |   E=[clock|E1], robot2(south,Xd,Yd,S,E1).
robot0(west,Xd,Yd,[block|S],E) :- Xd<0, Yd>=0
    |   E=[clock|E1], robot2(north,Xd,Yd,S,E1).
robot0(north,Xd,Yd,[block|S],E) :- Yd>=0, Xd<0
    |   E=[anti|E1], robot4(west,Xd,Yd,S,E1).
robot0(south,Xd,Yd,[block|S],E) :- Yd<0, Xd>=0
    |   E=[anti|E1], robot4(east,Xd,Yd,S,E1).
robot0(east,Xd,Yd,[block|S],E) :- Xd>=0, Yd>=0
    |   E=[anti|E1], robot4(north,Xd,Yd,S,E1).
robot0(west,Xd,Yd,[block|S],E) :- Xd<0, Yd<0
    |   E=[anti|E1], robot4(south,Xd,Yd,S,E1).
robot0(north,Xd,Yd,[_|S],E) :- Yd<0, Xd>=0
    |   E=[clock|E1], robot6(east,Xd,Yd,S,E1).
robot0(south,Xd,Yd,[_|S],E) :- Yd>=0, Xd<0
    |   E=[clock|E1], robot6(west,Xd,Yd,S,E1).
robot0(east,Xd,Yd,[_|S],E) :- Xd<0, Yd<0
    |   E=[clock|E1], robot6(south,Xd,Yd,S,E1).
robot0(west,Xd,Yd,[_|S],E) :- Xd>=0, Yd>=0
    |   E=[clock|E1], robot6(north,Xd,Yd,S,E1).
robot0(north,Xd,Yd,[_|S],E) :- Yd<0, Xd<0
    | E=[anti|E1], robot8(west,Xd,Yd,S,E1).
robot0(south,Xd,Yd,[_|S],E) :- Yd>=0, Xd>=0
    |   E=[anti|E1], robot8(east,Xd,Yd,S,E1).
robot0(east,Xd,Yd,[_|S],E) :- Xd<0, Yd>=0
    |   E=[anti|E1], robot8(north,Xd,Yd,S,E1).
robot0(west,Xd,Yd,[_|S],E) :- Xd>=0, Yd<0
    |   E=[anti|E1], robot8(south,Xd,Yd,S,E1).

robot1(Face,Xd,Yd,[clear|S],E)
    :-  E=[move|E1], move(Face,Xd,Yd,Xd1,Yd1),
        robot0(Face,Xd1,Yd1,S,E1).
robot1(Face,Xd,Yd,[block|S],E)
    :-  robot0(Face,Xd,Yd,[block|S],E).
```

```
robot2(Face,Xd,Yd,[clear|S],E)
   :- E=[move|E1], move(Face,Xd,Yd,Xd1,Yd1),
      robot0(Face,Xd1,Yd1,S,E1).
robot2(Face,Xd,Yd,[block|S],E)
   :- E=[clock,clock|E1], reverse(Face,Face1),
      consume(S,S1),
      robot3(Face1,Xd,Yd,S1,E1).

robot3(Face,Xd,Yd,[clear|S],E)
   :- E=[move|E1], move(Face,Xd,Yd,Xd1,Yd1),
robot0(Face,Xd1,Yd1,S,E1).
robot3(Face,Xd,Yd,[blocked|S],E)
   :- E=[anti|E1], anti(Face,Face1),
      robot1(Face1,Xd,Yd,S,E).

robot4(Face,Xd,Yd,[clear|S],E)
   :- E=[move|E1], move(Face,Xd,Yd,Xd1,Yd1),
      robot0(Face,Xd1,Yd1,S,E1).
robot4(Face,Xd,Yd,[block|S],E)
   :- E=[anti,anti|E1], reverse(Face,Face1),
      consume(S,S1), robot5(Face1,Xd,Yd,S1,E1).

robot5(Face,Xd,Yd,[clear|S],E)
   :- E=[move|E1], move(Face,Xd,Yd,Xd1,Yd1),
      robot0(Face,Xd1,Yd1,S,E1).
robot5(Face,Xd,Yd,[blocked|S],E)
   :- E=[clock|E1], clock(Face,Face1),
      robot1(Face1,Xd,Yd,S,E).

robot6(Face,Xd,Yd,[clear|S],E)
   :- E=[move|E1], move(Face,Xd,Yd,Xd1,Yd1),
      robot0(Face,Xd1,Yd1,S,E1).
robot6(Face,Xd,Yd,[block|S],E)
   :- E=[anti|E1], anti(Face,Face1),
      robot7(Face1,Xd,Yd,S,E1).

robot7(Face,Xd,Yd,[clear|S],E)
   :- E=[move|E1], move(Face,Xd,Yd,Xd1,Yd1),
      robot0(Face,Xd1,Yd1,S,E1).
robot7(Face,Xd,Yd,[block|S],E)
   :- E=[anti|E1], anti(Face,Face1), robot3(Face1,Xd,Yd,S,E1).

robot8(Face,Xd,Yd,[clear|S],E)
   :- E=[move|E1], move(Face,Xd,Yd,Xd1,Yd1),
      robot0(Face,Xd1,Yd1,S,E1).
robot8(Face,Xd,Yd,[block|S],E)
   :- E=[clock|E1], clock(Face,Face1), robot9(Face1,Xd,Yd,S,E1).
```

```
robot9(Face,Xd,Yd,[clear|S],E)
    :- E=[move|E1], move(Face,Xd,Yd,Xd1,Yd1),
       robot0(Face,Xd1,Yd1,S,E1).
robot9(Face,Xd,Yd,[block|S],E)
    :- E=[clock|E1], clock(Face,Face1), robot5(Face1,Xd,Yd,S,E1).

consume([_|S],S1) :- S1=S.

move(north,Xd,Yd,Xd1,Yd1) :- Xd1=Xd, Yd1:=Yd-1.
move(south,Xd,Yd,Xd1,Yd1) :- Xd1=Xd, Yd1:=Yd+1.
move(east,Xd,Yd,Xd1,Yd1) :- Xd1:=Xd-1, Yd1=Yd.
move(west,Xd,Yd,Xd1,Yd1) :- Xd1:=Xd+1, Yd1=Yd.


clock(north,Face) :- Face=east.
clock(east,Face) :- Face=south.
clock(south,Face) :- Face=west.
clock(west,face) :- Face=north,

anti(north,Face) :- Face=west.
anti(west,Face) :- Face=south.
anti(south,Face) :- Face=east.
anti(east,Face) :- Face=north.

reverse(north,Face) :- Face=south.
reverse(south,Face) :- Face=north.
reverse(east,Face) :- Face=west.
reverse(west,Face) :- Face=east.
```

Stopping the robot from turning back the way it has come is necessary to prevent it from reaching a situation where it is forced to move away from the goal because all ways to it are blocked. But then, having moved one square away, it immediately returns to the blocked square and repeats this until the blocks disappear. An initial situation is shown in Figure 10.2.2 with the robot initially at <e,3> and facing west, moving towards the goal at <b,1>. It will move to <d,3> and finding <c,3> blocked, turn first south (entering State 4), then finding <d,2> blocked, turn north (State 5). Finding <d,4> clear, it will move to <d,4> (returning to State 0). At this point, the robot will turn again towards the goal (entering State 8) rather than proceed in the clear direction in front of it. As it then faces blocked <c,4> it turns back north (State 9) and proceeds to <d,5>. It does this, rather than turn to face the goal in the way it has come and returns to <d,3>. At <d,5> the process of turning west, finding the way blocked and proceeding north is repeated, moving to <d,6>. At <d,6>, again it turns west, this time the way is not blocked and it proceeds to <c,6>. At <c,6>, it is facing towards the goal, so moves to <b,6>. Here the west direction is no longer facing towards the goal, so it turns south (entering State 8) and finding the way clear continues to move to the goal.

The program as given, however, will not always avoid going into a loop (in this case causing the robot actually traverse a loop of squares indefinitely). Consider the arrangement in Figure 10.2.3. Here the robot will proceed as before until it reaches <d,4>. At this point, in State 9 facing north, it finds the way ahead blocked, so turns east (entering State 5) and finding the way clear moves to <e,4>. At <e,4> it turns south to face the goal and moves to <e,3>. Finding the way ahead blocked, it turns to the alternative direction for the goal (State 2) and finding the way ahead clear moves forward. It is now in an identical position to a previous state and unless there are any changes in the blocks will continue to move around the four squares <d,3>, <d,4>, <e,4> and <e,3>.

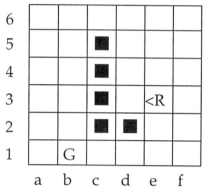

Fig. 10.2.2 Initial state of robot and environment

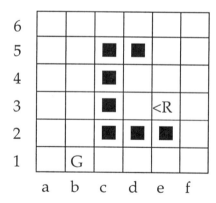

Fig. 10.2.3 An arrangement which causes the robot to loop

10.3 Reaction and Intelligence

In the case of the above robot, a more sophisticated set of rules could be devised to enable it to correctly manoeuver around an obstacle to reach its goal. However, another tactic could be to use a technique similar to *simulated annealing* [Kirkpatrick et al., 1993]. In this technique an agent occasionally (using a random choice mechanism) makes a move which according to its heuristics is not the best one available. This enables it to escape from situations that are local but not global best positions. Treating the concept of hill-climbing literally, a robot whose goal is to move to the highest point on a landscape would have the heuristic that it generally moves in whichever direction takes it upwards, but at random can make the occasional downward move. Without such downward moves, it would stay put at the top of a small hill once it reached it and never explore larger hills. Similarly in any situation where an agent inhabits a world which is too complex for its simple heuristics to bring it inevitably to its goal, some random antiheuristic behavior may help. Such behavior can avoid it getting stuck in situations where rigidly obeying its rules causes it to continually repeat a sequence of behavior without real progression.

Another approach for the agent would be to physically alter the environment. Imagine a robot with a supply of pebbles, the ability to drop a pebble in a square, and the ability to detect the presence of a pebble in a square (and possibly pick it up). Periodically the robot drops a pebble on the square it is in. A robot entering a square containing a pebble might choose the second best exit route on the grounds that choosing the best exit route has simply led it returning to the same location.

In both these approaches, no attempt is made to model the world in which the robot moves as part of its internal state and use this to reason about routes through the world. (It may be argued that dropping pebbles is using the environment as its own model.) Brooks proposed originally that such modeling and planning behavior would exist as a higher level layer in his robots, though he became the champion of the purely reactive approach. In practice, a layered approach [Müller, 1996; Chaib-Draa and Levesque, 1996] combining reaction and planning has become common in building agents. The balance of planning and reaction employed will depend on the characteristics of the environment. In an environment which is largely static, planning may be used generally, with a resort to reactive techniques only when changes render the planning inaccurate. This enables an agent to get over the brittleness of a planning system that can take no account at all of changes to the environment. As an analogy, consider the case where one is driving one's car along a route planned in advance. It would be foolish to plan in advance for every possible roadblock that might occur. It would be dangerous to have no way of reacting should the planned route be blocked at some point. The usual approach taken to divert from the planned route and feel one's way using a sense of direction until a position of the planned route is found again and the plan is resumed, is a mixture of planning and reaction. The fact that while driving a car it is not always possible to stop, consult a map and replan the route indicates the real-time constraints that might favor a reactive approach. It is better to make a quick decision on which direction to take, even though that may not turn out to have been the best one, than halt to ponder the decision and cause a pile-up!

The argument as to whether reactive systems are intelligent falls at the heart of the question "what is intelligence?" Traditional artificial intelligence has tried to model behavior which in a human we would regard as signs of high intelligence. Thus, ability to play a good game of chess, or to solve logical puzzles is often considered the sign of an intelligent person, indeed IQ tests are based on problem solving. A computer system, which can solve puzzles or play games, is deemed intelligent on a subjective basis because it seems to behave as a human would. Intensive media comment on "computers becoming human" was generated by the first computer to beat the world chess champion and was not dimmed by explanations of the fairly simple nature of computer chess-playing algorithms. Similarly, fairly simple reactive systems can look alive on a subjective human view. For example, a few rules of attraction and repulsion have been used to model a system which can be viewed as an animal risking approaching a waterhole while avoiding predators [Kearny, 1992]. A human viewer is led to believe two predator agents are acting in planned coordination, though there is no real communication between them. The appearance of planned cooperative behavior in a system with multiple reactive agents is taken further in simulations of social insects like ants [Drogoul and Ferber, 1992], where the behavior extends to different social roles being taken by the agents similar to that in a real ants' nest. Drogoul calls this *Eco-Problem Solving*.

It may be better to use the term *Artificial Life* [Langton, 1989] for those systems whose approach to the goal of Artificial Intelligence is to model general life-like behavior in an unpredictable environment and build upwards from this platform. The name "Artificial Intelligence" could be reserved for the approach of building systems that behave intelligently in a more restricted realm. The former could be seen as building using horizontal layers, while the latter uses vertical layers. The emergence of intelligent behavior from a collection of reactive agents is a further approach to building intelligence. Drogoul [1993a] discusses this issue and demonstrates a chess playing system whose behavior derives from the joint behavior of a collection of agents, each representing an individual chess piece. This system plays chess to the point where it can beat weak amateurs, but not a standard search-based computer chess machine. Drogoul [1993b] has also shown that other classic planning problems, such as the N-puzzle, can be tackled by collections of agents each of which has no goal itself and works as a finite state automaton, making just tropistic movements.

Brooks' robots are themselves collections of agents, since their behavior emerges from the collective behavior of their layers. Taken further, with the reactive components within an agent becoming simpler, we eventually reach the neural-network architecture. Brooks [1991b] is however, careful to distinguish his work from neural networks. He notes that neural networks consist of undifferentiated components without a detailed design, whereas his robots are designed and built from distinguishable components. However, the human brain can be considered as a network of networks of neurons [Minsky, 1986] with different functions.

Brooks' approach to building artificial intelligence without the use of representation is criticized by Kirsh [1991]. Kirsh argues that the lack of internal representational methods in reactive agents means they will always remain limited to animal-like behavior. Without a representational language, agents are restricted to simply hardwired goals and thus cannot define their own goals. Reactive agent communication is on a simple basis, either attractant-repellant behavior, or indirectly through mechanisms like the robot pebble-dropping involve changing the environment (called *stigmergy* [Holland, 1996]).

10.4 Objects, Actors and Agents

Reactive agents, as described above, are similar in some ways to objects in the computational sense. A reactive agent reacts to messages received on its input sensors by changing its state and sending messages on its output effectors. An object reacts on receiving messages by changing its state and sending messages to other objects. The internal appearance is the same – to the agent the environment it works in as it interacts through its sensors and effectors might be just another agent. Where it differs is that agents have autonomy and seek primarily to satisfy their own goals rather than simply respond to orders in a fixed way. The robot described previously had the goal of reducing the x and y differences in its state to 0, while avoiding crashing into blocks and responded to its inputs with whatever outputs would assist in satisfying this goal. A computational object, however, would not vary its output depending on its own desires, it simply responds in a predictable manner

Additionally, an agent is embodied not only in the sense of its physical presence in and interaction with its environment, but also in having its own processor dedicated to its own use. That is why an object can easily create new objects, since they are just software entities that can be created by copying and instantiation, whereas robots don't usually create complete new bodies for new robots. (This excludes industrial robots.) An actor in a concurrent object-oriented system, however, could be considered as being created with its own processor, using the principle of virtual parallelism discussed in Chapter 6. That is, the assumption that there are always enough spare processors for any computations declared as running concurrently (with the practical resource allocation hidden from view). So another approach to multi-agent systems is to consider agents as a development from concurrent object-oriented systems, with the addition of further autonomy built into the objects. This should be distinguished from the use of parallelism for speedup purely to improve response time. Here the division of tasks between objects is done on a conceptual basis. In general, the emphasis is on separate objects with separate tasks in the solving of problems, whereas parallel AI tends to be concerned with large numbers of similar objects dividing out the work pragmatically.

Object-oriented programming emerged as a *silver bullet* [Brooks, 1987], as the next attempt after structured programming to tackle the complexity barrier [Winograd, 1973] whereby computer systems become increasingly risky as their size increases: difficult to construct, difficult to maintain and difficult to guarantee error-free. A large part of the complexity is due to the complex nature of possible interactions (planned and accidental) between different components of a computer program. Structured programming partitioned code into blocks, thus limiting the range of control transfers possible, but it left the data unconnected with the control structure.

The key idea of object-oriented programming was encapsulating the data with code, so that data access too is limited. Concurrent object-oriented programming maps the logical distribution of the object paradigm onto the physical distribution of parallel processors. As we have seen, GDC programming can be seen in terms of concurrent object-oriented programming.

Miller and Drexler [1988] compare the encapsulation of data with the human ownership of property: both establish protected spheres in which entities can plan the use of their resources free of interference from unpredictable external influences. This enables entities to act despite having limited local knowledge, aiding the division of labor. They take the concept of encapsulation further and propose it be extended to physical computational resources such as memory blocks or processor time slices. Clearly this is necessary for a truly autonomous agent, since such an agent needs to have assurance that it will have the physical resources necessary for it to remain in active existence responding to inputs in real time. A robot has by definition its own physical resources but a softbot would need ownership of a share on the machine on which it resides.

Currently, concurrent languages work on a "socialist" planned economy where resources are shared out as needed by a central planner or on an "anarchist" basis where there is a free-for-all (as with human anarchism its success depends on the assumption that all agents are benevolent towards each other). Miller and Drexler [1988] propose a "capitalist" ownership of property, in which absolute ownership rights are protected even where, for example, a planner might see cases where a reallocation of resources would improve efficiency in reaching the overall goal. While an agent which is currently idle cannot be forced to give room on a processor it owns to another which needs the processing capacity, it is suggested that agents may trade their ownership rights amongst themselves. Ideally, each agent is programmed to fulfil its own goals and trades resources it has but does not need for resources it needs but does not have (for example, time slices on a processor could be traded for memory). The result, it is claimed, will be a better allocation of resources overall than could be obtained by a global allocation algorithm once the overall system becomes so complex that it is not possible to operate a simple global resource allocation algorithm. This is the classic free market economy argument, associated with Adam Smith [1776] and later economists. The emergence of what from a global perspective seems a planned algorithm from what on closer inspection seems unplanned chaos is similar to that which has already been noted with eco-problem solving, except here there is no suggestion that the components be restricted to simple reactive agents.

As can be seen, once agents become truly autonomous, the ease with which discussions on the organization of multi-agent systems slip into analogies with the organization of human societies becomes irresistible. Fox [1991] suggests that such analogies are not cute anthropomorphisms, but an inevitable response to the growing complexity of computer systems and in particular to the problem of bounded rationality [Simon, 1957], when the complexity of a problem exceeds the capacity of a single agent to solve it. Organizational techniques to distribute problems amongst human teams can be applied to distributed computer systems. For example, an alternative to arranging multi-agent systems on a flat market-type basis is to construct hierarchies similar to management hierarchies in large organizations. Quoting Galbraith [1973], Fox claims that in both human and computer systems, whereas complexity suggests the market approach, uncertainty, defined as the difference between the information available and the information necessary to make the best decision, suggests the hierarchical approach. In the hierarchical approach, managers can switch tasks and resources between employees as new information becomes available, whereas the market approach requires the striking of contracts that cannot be so easily altered.

Another way in which multi-agent systems develop from concurrent object-oriented systems by employing human metaphors concentrates on the design of individual agents, ascribing to them mental components such as beliefs, capabilities, choices and commitments, standing in rough correspondence to their common sense counterparts in human life. Such an agent is termed an *intentional system* [Dennett, 1987]. The idea is most clearly developed by Shoham [1993] who describes a framework called *agent-oriented programming* which may be considered a specialization of object-oriented programming. Agent-oriented programming is a form of object-oriented programming where the state of objects is restricted to parameters which can be labeled as mental states and the messages between objects consist of "speech acts" [Searle, 1969], informing, requesting, offering, promising and so on. The exact mental attributes that should be given to an agent are a matter of contention. Following McDermott [1978], Shoham stresses that the decision should not be arbitrary but should enable the development of a theory that may be used non-trivially to analyze a system. Beliefs, desires and intentions, leading to the terminology *BDI architecture* [Rao and Georgeff, 1991] are a popular set of mental attributes used, but Shoham prefers beliefs, obligations and capabilities. The values of the mental attributes within the states are built up using knowledge representation formalism, often a form of temporal logic.

The beliefs of an agent refer to the model of its environment it has built up. This model may be incomplete and/or incorrect. In a multi-agent system it may include beliefs about other agents, indeed in some multi-agent systems the environment may consist solely of other agents. Desires are the overall goals of an agent, while intentions are the elements of plans it has made to reach its desires. Shoham's system enables a stronger relationship between agents in a multi-agent system to be modeled, since an obligation is a relationship between one agent and another, with one committed to the other to bring about some situation. An intention in this case is an obligation of an agent to itself. The capabilities of an agent are its physical abilities in the environment it shares with the other agents.

Agents in Shoham's system are programmed in a language called *AGENT-0*, which constrains them to follow certain behaviors. Mental states may not be changed arbitrarily, but only as a fixed response to speech acts. For example, an agent may not drop its commitment to another agent, but an agent A may release another agent B from a commitment that B has to A. An agent will always update its own beliefs in response to a message informing it of new facts from another agent. In effect, every agent believes every other agent is telling it the truth. The internal knowledge representation language of Shoham's agents is restricted so that checking consistency when new knowledge is added is tractable. A strong assumption of AGENT-0 is that all internal updating in response to messages and execution of any commitments for a particular time can be made in a single real-time interval. The whole system depends on this cycle being performed each time a real-time system clock emits a signal, which it does at fixed intervals.

10.5 Objects in GDC

As demonstrated in this book, programming concurrent objects can easily be done in GDC. The behaviors below define an object of type **xyobj** that has just two simple elements to its state, which may be set using messages setx and sety to set each individually, and setxy to set both to the same value. The values of the components of the state of the object may be obtained by sending it the messages valx and valy with an unbound variable argument as a "reply slot". A new **xyobj** object with the same state values as the original may be obtained by sending the message new to the object, with a reply slot for the reference to the new object:

```
xyobj([setx(V)|S],X,Y) :- xyobj(S,V,Y).
xyobj([sety(V)|S],X,Y) :- xyobj(S,X,V).
xyobj([setxy(V)|S],X,Y) :- xyobj(S,V,V).
xyobj([valx(V)|S],X,Y) :- xyobj(S,X,Y), V=X.
xyobj([valy(V)|S],X,Y) :- xyobj(S,X,Y), V=Y.
xyobj([new(A)|S],X,Y) :- xyobj(S,X,Y), xyobj(A,X,Y).
```

To create a new object of type **xyobj** with initial state values a and b the object **xyobj**(S,a,b) is required. S may refer to the object, except that we can only safely have one writer to a channel. To have several we need to write to separate channels and merge. If it is necessary to share references to **xyobj**, we set up objects **p** and **q**

```
:-  p(...,S1,...), q(...,S2,...), merge(S1,S2,S), xyobj(S,a,b)
```

which both have the **xyobj** as an acquaintance. In concurrent object-oriented languages, all first-class values in a state are themselves objects, but this is not so in GDC. Here the two values in the state of the **xyobj** are just values. If they were to be objects, the behaviors for **xyobj** would be more complex:

```
xyobj([setx(V)|S],X,Y) :- xyobj(S,V,Y), X=[].
xyobj([sety(V)|S],X,Y) :- xyobj(S,X,V), Y=[].
xyobj([setxy(V)|S],X,Y)
    :-  xyobj(S,V1,V2), X=[], Y=[], merge(V1,V2,V).
xyobj([valx(V)|S],X,Y)
    :-  xyobj(S,X1,Y), merge(V,X1,X).
xyobj([valy(V)|S],X,Y)
    :-  xyobj(S,X,Y1), merge(V,Y1,Y).
xyobj([new(A)|S],X,Y)
    :-  xyobj(S,X1,Y1), xyobj(A,X2,Y2), merge(X1,X2,X),
        merge(Y1,Y2,Y).
xyobj([],X,Y) :- X=[], Y=[].
```

An object which is input is represented by a channel used as a stream to output messages, an object which is output is represented by a channel used as a stream to input messages. Using an object as an argument in a recursive behavior counts as outputting it. References to an object are tied together by merging all the input streams, representing each place the object is output into one stream that is sent to the input occurrence of the object. If there are no output occurrences of an object which is input, the variable used for its input is sent the empty list value, as in the first three behaviors above where the input objects X and Y are no longer referred to, being replaced by V. The final behavior which has been added above is similar to a destructor operator in conventional object-oriented programming, detailing the behavior of an object when it no longer has any references. In this case, **xyobj** terminates itself and also terminates its references to its acquaintance objects. This would give automated garbage collection of unreferenced objects were it not for the problem of self-reference. As an object may have a reference to itself as an acquaintance, or to an acquaintance which has itself as an acquaintance, or so on, so a clique of objects with only internal references could remain in existence.

To give an example of a behavior in which messages are sent in response to messages received, consider additional messages, copyx and copyy, similar to valx and valy. However, the object returns a reference to new copies of the X and Y acquaintances rather than references to the original object. If we assume X and Y are programmed to respond to new messages similarly to an xyobj object, the following will give this effect:

xyobj([copyx(A)|S],X,Y) :- X=[new(A)|X1], **xyobj**(S,X1,Y).
xyobj([copyx(A)|S],X,Y) :- Y=[new(A)|Y1], **xyobj**(S,X,Y1).

The flexible nature of GDC means that many techniques, which in dedicated object-oriented languages require special language features, may be programmed without introducing new primitives. For example, consider a version of our original **xyobj** (with non-object X and Y values) in which we want two classes of access, one of which may rewrite the values in the state of the object, but the other of which may only read them. This can be done by having two output streams as references to an **xyobj** object, one with privileged access (able to use the setting operations), the other without:

xyobj(S,[setx(V)|P],X,Y) :- **xyobj**(S,P,V,Y).
xyobj(S,[sety(V)|P],X,Y) :- **xyobj**(S,P,X,V).
xyobj(S,[setxy(V)|P],X,Y) :- **xyobj**(S,P,V,V).
xyobj([valx(V)|S],P,X,Y) :- **xyobj**(S,P,X,Y), V=X.
xyobj([valy(V)|S],P,X,Y) :- **xyobj**(S,P,X,Y), V=Y.
xyobj(S,[valx(V)|P],X,Y) :- **xyobj**(S,P,X,Y), V=X.
xyobj(S,[valy(V)|P],X,Y) :- **xyobj**(S,P,X,Y), V=Y.
xyobj(S,[new(A)|P],X,Y) :- **xyobj**(S,P,X,Y), **xyobj**(B,A,X,Y), B=[].
xyobj([new(A)|S],P,X,Y) :- **xyobj**(S,P,X,Y), **xyobj**(A,B,X,Y), B=[].
xyobj([],[],X,Y).

The two behaviors for the new message show how either privileged or normal access may be granted. A new message received on the privileged stream causes a new **xyobj** object to be created and returns the privileged reference to that object. A new message on the standard stream returns a standard reference to the new **xyobj** object. Clearly, in a complex system, any number of classes of access rights could be programmed in.

In a similar way, express mode message passing, as employed in the concurrent object-oriented language *ABCL/1* [Yonezawa et al., 1986] may be programmed by having a separate stream for express messages:

xyobj(S,[setx(V)|E],X,Y) :- **xyobj**(S,E,V,Y).
xyobj(S,[sety(V)|E],X,Y) :- **xyobj**(S,E,X,V).
xyobj(S,[setxy(V)|E],X,Y) :- **xyobj**(S,E,V,V).
xyobj(S,[valx(V)|E],X,Y) :- **xyobj**(S,E,X,Y), V=X.
xyobj(S,[valy(V)|E],X,Y) :- **xyobj**(S,E,X,Y), V=Y.
xyobj(S,[new(A,B)|E],X,Y) :- **xyobj**(S,E,X,Y), **xyobj**(A,B,X,Y).
xyobj([valx(V)|S],E,X,Y) :- **unknown**(E)
  | **xyobj**(S,U,X,Y), V=X.
xyobj([valy(V)|S],E,X,Y) :- **unknown**(E)
  | **xyobj**(S,E,X,Y), V=Y.
xyobj([setx(V)|S],E,X,Y) :- **unknown**(E)
  | **xyobj**(S,E,V,Y).
xyobj([sety(V)|S],E,X,Y) :- **unknown**(E)
  | **xyobj**(S,E,X,V).
xyobj([setxy(V)|S],E,X,Y) :- **unknown**(E)
  | **xyobj**(S,E,V,V).
xyobj([new(A,B)|S],E,X,Y) :- **unknown**(E)
  | **xyobj**(S,E,X,Y), **xyobj**(A,B,X,Y).
xyobj([],[],X,Y).

A message is taken from the non-express stream only when there are no messages available on the express stream, so it is an unbound channel. Here, new **xyobj** objects are returned with both their normal and express streams available. As an alternative to the use of **unknown**, the **alternatively** construct of KL1 could be used to separate behaviors dealing with handling messages from the express stream (which would be placed before the **alternatively**) from behaviors dealing with handling messages from the standard stream.

The creation of new **xyobj** objects by sending a new message to an existing **xyobj** object indicates a form of prototyping [Borning, 1986], that is new objects being created by cloning old ones. Prototyping is associated with delegation [Lieberman, 1986] where several objects may delegate responsibility to a single shared parent object. In our cloning of objects, new objects shared the acquaintances of old ones, through streams, which are merged to a single object. This would give delegation as Lieberman explained it. For example, a royal elephant is an elephant identical to the prototype elephant except that its color is white. If E is a reference to a prototype elephant object, a reference to a royal elephant object could be obtained in R by the object **royal**(R,E) where the behaviors for **royal** are:

royal([color(C)|R],E)
  :- C=white, **royal**(R,E).
royal([new(A)|R],E)
  :- **royal**(A,E1), **royal**(R,E2), **merge**(E1,E2,E).
royal([M|R],E) :- **otherwise**
  | E=[M|E1], **royal**(R,E).

Any message other than a new message or a color message is passed on to the prototype to deal with. However, a closer correspondence to inheritance, as conventionally understood in the object-oriented programming paradigm, is obtained by cloning the acquaintances of a new object when creating one by cloning, thus:

royal([color(C)|R],E)
  :- C=white, **royal**(R,E).
royal([new(A)|R],E)
  :- **royal**(A,E1), **royal**(R,E2), E=[new(E1)|E2].
royal([M|R],E) :- **otherwise**
  | E=[M|E1], **royal**(R,E).

so each **royal** object has its own **elephant** object to send messages to other than new and color messages. In this case, sharing of delegation is not wanted, since otherwise a change in an attribute a royal elephant has by virtue of it being a form of elephant would be propagated to every royal elephant. Note that, circular acquaintance references give problems here as they did with garbage collection, since if there was a rule that on cloning all acquaintances were cloned, a circular reference would cause an infinite production of new messages as the circle was continuously cycled.

The fact that stream merging is explicit in the GDC form of object-oriented programming means programmers can alter the merge procedures as desired. For example, a biased merge gives priority access to an object, so

  :- **p**(...,S1,...), **q**(...,S2,...), **bmerge**(S1,S2,S), **xyobj**(S,a,b)

where **bmerge** passes on values from its second stream only when it has none on its first stream causes the object **p** to have priority access to the **xyobj** object and

  :- **p**(...,S1,...), **q**(...,S2,...), **append**(S1,S2,S), **xyobj**(S,a,b)

locks the **xyobj** object to the **p** object. Messages from the **q** object will only be passed on to the **xyobj** object after all messages from the **p** object (assuming the convention that objects close their references to acquaintances when they terminate by sending the empty list, so S1 is a finite list).

Huntbach [1995] has considered proposals for a syntactic sugar or preprocessor so that programs written in an object-oriented like notation may be translated to GDC in the way described here. Although the approach considered in this preprocessor is a compiler into GDC, rather than an interpreter written in GDC which interprets object-oriented code, the results of the compilation could benefit from the program transformation techniques outlined in Chapter 9. These would produce code that is more efficient, but less obviously built on the object-oriented principle than code directly output by the translator.

Note that a difference between GDC and classic object-oriented programming as found in Smalltalk and the concurrent object-oriented languages, is that GDC does not work on the basis that all entities in the language are themselves objects. In GDC, a client receiving a message knows which arguments are objects and which are simple atomic values or tuples. Kahn and Miller [1988] point out this is an advantage in avoiding *Trojan horses*. They consider a service that computes some mathematical function according to a proprietary algorithm. If the numbers the client sends are objects that report back the tests and operations performed on them, the secrecy of the algorithm is compromised. There are no such problems if the numbers are known by the receiver of the message to be just atomic numeric values.

10.6 Agents in GDC

Moving the concurrent object-oriented style of programming in GDC towards agent-oriented programming in Shoham's sense could be partly just a matter of scale. The restriction that object states be seen in terms of attributes of mind and messages be seen in terms of speech acts reacted to appropriately by objects, could simply be adopted as a code of practice by programmers. Suppose one element of an object's state is defined to be its beliefs and another its obligations. Then, an insistence on a common semantics could be made, such that for example when an object receives a message inform(B) it adds belief B to its set of beliefs, while when it receives a message request(C) it adds commitment C to its obligations. But there is nothing in the semantics of GDC to stop it from idiosyncratically treating the messages the other way round. Alternatively, a compilation approach could be used so that an agent language like Shoham's AGENT-0, with its semantics for these messages and for object states, is translated into GDC. Note that there is no necessity for an agent to be represented by a single GDC actor. As we indicated with the royal elephant example, something, which is conceptually a single object, may be represented by more than one GDC actor. So several actors could in fact represent an agent, with one managing each component of the mental state. The beliefs of an agent could be represented rather like the Linda tuple space we covered in Section 8.8. Hewitt and Inman [1991] discuss a method by which collections of actors may be composed and viewed as a single actor.

A successor to AGENT-0 is a language called *PLACA* [Thomas, 1994]. PLACA works similarly to AGENT-0, with a propositional temporal logic language used to construct the mental states of agents and a language for inter-agent communication of beliefs and requests to take actions. It differs from AGENT-0 in allowing an agent to request that another agent takes an action which requires planning to achieve, whereas AGENT-0 allows requests only of primitive capabilities. The fact that higher-level goals may be communicated in the place of a stream of actions planned by one agent but requested of another agent to perform, cuts down on the communication overhead. It is also assumed an agent will be able to do a better job of planning for itself (including recovering from any unforeseen failures in the plan) on the basis of an allocated high level goal than following a plan drawn up for it by another agent.

An agent in PLACA has an input buffer for both messages from other agents and information from its sensors. It has two output buffers: one for messages intended for other agents and one for commands to its own effectors. It can be seen to combine the robot concept, with its sensors and effectors reacting with the physical environment and the actor concept, with its interactions with the virtual environment of other actors. In GDC, a mapping mechanism would be needed to map the logical goals onto the physical architecture. The fact that GDC has a separate output stream for messages to each acquaintance is a minor matter of difference. What GDC lacks, however, to fully implement PLACA is real-time facilities.

At its most basic level, a PLACA agent's computation consists of the following:

1.   Collect messages received from other agents

2.   Update its mental state as specified in its program

3.   If sufficient time remains before the next tick of the clock, refine its plans

4.   Begin execution of the action to be performed next and return to step 1.

Step 3 relies on a global clock and can be compared to the behavior of layered agents considered above. So long as there is time available, an agent plans by refining its goals, but it reacts when forced to, in this case by the clock. There is also a facility to ignore input messages, leaving them in the buffer while planning continues. The handling of express messages in GDC using **unknown** or **alternatively** as described previously, suggests a clock mechanism could be handled by converting clock ticks to messages on an express stream. Note that, if the actors performing the planning share a processor with the process suspended waiting for the planning to finish or for a clock tick to be received, the waiting process needs to have priority over the planning processes. As soon as the clock tick is received, it can take action to shut off further planning.

The physical architecture of guarded definite clause languages is currently not well developed, not merely by accident but as a matter of principle. The languages developed on the basis that a declarative style of programming gave programmers the opportunity to break away from the architecture of the machines on which their programs ran and to think purely in abstract terms. Parallel architectures were merely a convenience, which enabled declarative languages to be implemented efficiently. Since they were not based around the single processor architecture of the von Neumann machine and since the declarative style involves breaking programs down into discrete components with well-defined limited methods of communication, concurrent declarative languages could, it was thought, easily be mapped onto parallel architectures. It was in the interest of programmers not to have to be concerned with this mapping. Just as it was in the interest of programmers in high-level imperative languages not to be concerned with mapping variables onto registers, core memory and backup store, but instead to leave the operating system to work it out, while maintaining the illusion of a single store with infinite capacity.

It would not be desirable to depart from this principle of abstract parallelism where it is not necessary to do so. When an algorithm is AND-parallel it should be enough to break down the problem into pieces and leave the underlying system to decide where and when to run each piece, as when one is run relative to another does not affect the algorithm. The guarded definite clause languages have an AND-parallel basis, but as we saw with search algorithms can be used to model OR-parallel algorithms. At this point, the assumption that we need not bother with the physical mapping of process to processor broke down. The introduction of the priority operator recognized that computational resources are not infinite and that in some cases the programmer needs to ensure that finite computational resources are used in an effective manner.

The connection of processes to processors matters in multi-agent systems when as shown, those agents are connected to the environment through physical sensors and effectors, needing to make decisions in real time, with a process running an agent. Miller and Drexler's ideas of encapsulated control of physical resources may offer a clean way to incorporate architectural considerations in GDC in a more sophisticated manner than the simple priority mechanism and thus to construct agents in the sense where an agent is an actor plus its physical embodiment. A priority attached to a GDC actor has a meaning only in the global context of an entire GDC computation, giving privileged access of a process to a processor only if other processes competing for the processor have not been given higher priorities. However, "ownership" of a processor or a time-slice on a processor due to resource encapsulation guarantees access to it. The need for such a guarantee becomes more important as we move away from systems of benevolent agents where all agents can be assumed to be working towards a common goal, to competitive systems where agents are pursuing their own, possibly conflicting, goals.

Waldspurger et al. [1992] describe an experimental system, called *Spawn*, which implements market-based access to computational resources based on Miller and Drexler's ideas. The system of prioritizing they use is based on one developed for Actor languages, but which could easily be adapted to guarded definite clause languages. In it, every transaction must be sponsored by a *tick*, the basic unit of computational resource. A global sponsor provides a flow of ticks which is divided amongst lower level sponsors responsible for individual threads of computation. A sponsor may either grant a number of ticks to a computation or deny further funding, in which case the thread is aborted, rather like academic research. Funds may be allocated in any manner, but may neither be created nor destroyed (unlike GDC priorities, which can be set at any level arbitrarily). The Spawn system refines this notion of sponsorship by replacing the straight matching of ticks against resources by an auction system in which agents bid for time slices on idle processors. The allocation system used is a sealed-bid second-price auction. That is, bidding agents cannot access information about other agents' bids, the agent bidding highest wins the time-slice but pays the amount offered by the second-highest bidder. If there is no second bidder, the time slice is given free. The Spawn system was used to implement a Monte Carlo algorithm running on a network of processors, with figures indicating some success in establishing a computational market.

10.7 Top-Down and Bottom-Up Multi-Agent Systems

From the discussion so far, two approaches to multi-agent systems are emerging. One approach, which could be called bottom-up, develops from work on robots and softbots and focuses on the individual agent working in its environment. As we have suggested, an intelligent agent might construct a partial model of its environment noting the existence of other agents in the environment. The agent may have to exist in an environment where other agents make changes to the detriment of its own attempt to reach its goals. On the other hand, other agents may make changes, which benefit it. We have discussed multi-agent behavior which simply emerges from reaction rules, but more sophisticated agents may communicate with other agents in their environment in order to minimize harmful interferences and maximize beneficial interferences. A team at the Hebrew University in Jerusalem have given extensive study to the topic of negotiation between agents which may not necessarily share goals [Zlotkin and Rosenschein, 1991].

The second approach takes multi-agent systems as a development from object-oriented systems, seeing the concept as a step in an evolutionary process of programming methodologies forced by the growing complexity of problems tackled by computer systems. In this case, the environment in which the agents work may be a network of computers, the agent concept being used as a way to handle computational resources efficiently without the need for a central planning mechanism. The environment may also be the other agents, each agent communicating directly with those it has as acquaintances, or as an alternative, it may be some blackboard or tuple space so that the agents communicate only indirectly by adding to and taking from the blackboard. This approach is top-down in that we are concentrating on seeing a collection of agents working together to achieve a common goal of the overall system.

In the top-down approach, agents may generally be assumed to be benevolent towards each other. That is, since the agents in the system exist only to pursue some overall system goal, an agent can assume that other agents it interacts with will not deliberately set out to harm or mislead them and agents will willingly help each other achieve their respective goals. For example, Shoham's agents accept that when other agents send them information that information will be true or at least believed by the other agent to be true and accept requests from other agents without expecting a trade in return. Such benevolence cannot be expected in systems where there is no overall goal. We could imagine an automatic trading system in which agents are software entities acting on behalf of human traders, each of whom has the separate goal of maximizing his profit. Some trades may be beneficial to both parties: a trader who has X and needs Y to complete some goal will trade with one who has Y and needs X. Other trades will be seeking to make a profit at the expense of some other agent's loss. Consider two traders who both need X interacting with a third trader that has a single X to exchange.

The top-down approach moves towards the bottom-up approach when we consider dividing a problem into self-interested agents as a means of simplifying coordination. At the cost of needing to resolve local conflict, we lose the need to consider complex global coordination. In a simple way, OR-parallel search in GDC works in this way. We need a problem solved, but we are not sure which is the best way to solve it. So we divide it amongst several agents each trying to solve it in a different way. These agents compete for computational resources, the processors in a limited multiprocessor system. Coordination is resolved purely at local level using the rule that whichever of several agents competing for control of a processor can present the most promising partial solution (given by its heuristic value) wins. "Competition of the fittest" ensures that the best solution tends to win out. Jennings [1995] points out that some degree of "social concern" amongst competing agents is beneficial. He suggests that agents that ultimately have a common goal be under an obligation to inform other agents if that goal has become obsolete, or conditions for reaching it have changed, or it has itself changed in some way. Again, this can be seen as just a more complex form, befitting a more complex problem, of the passing of bounds in our distributed search programs which are used to inform search goals of limitations on the search required of them.

The bottom-up approach moves towards the top-down approach as agents become more sophisticated, using intelligent techniques to combine goals and develop plans to work together to achieve them. It has already been noted that an agent may be layered with a reactive component and a planning component. A third layer is used in several systems (for example by Müller [1996]) to deal with the multi-agent coordination work.

A third "middle-out" approach to multi-agent systems comes from distributed systems. A distributed system is one that consists of several physically distributed processors. Such processors may store separately maintained databases for example, with the distributed system involving bringing together information from several databases. Other forms of distributed systems link together processors containing sensors and effectors distributed over a physical environment. Such systems move into the field of *distributed artificial intelligence* (DAI) when artificial intelligence techniques are incorporated either in the individual processors, or in their overall coordination. DAI is sometimes used as a synonym for *multi-agent systems* (MAS), but many researchers distinguish between the two [Stone and Velso, 1996]. MAS is seen as a specialization of DAI which is only applicable when the components of a DAI system achieve "agenthood" through a high degree of autonomy and possibly through being constructed on an intentional basis and/or communicating with an agent communication language.

Ygge and Akkermans [1997] give a critical discussion of the value of bringing agent techniques into distributed systems. They discuss a classic distributed system application, the control of air-conditioning in a building. They compare systems constructed using standard control engineering methods, with systems constructed on the basis of a collection of agents bidding in a market system for cooling power. Surprisingly, their conclusion, based on empirical results, is that the multi-agent approach is at least as effective as the more traditional approach.

Distributed systems may be constructed because of the need to bring together physically distributed computational mechanisms dealing with a physical problem or environment. More generally, it has been suggested [Tokoro, 1993] that there will be an increasing tendency for computing systems to be constructed by making use of remote services over networks. This can be seen as an extension of the object-oriented idea of reusability. In object-oriented programming, programmers are encouraged to make use of existing libraries of code rather than program from scratch. In the network computer, programmers make use of existing services in a more direct way, not by copying their code but by accessing their actual instances, using an agent in the sense of code embodied by a processor, rather than an object in the sense of just code. Gelernter and Carriero [1992] suggest that programmers will move from being concerned mainly with the computational aspects of programming to being concerned with the coordination aspects, with asynchronous ensembles of computational entities being brought together by coordination languages becoming the dominant model of computer systems in the future.

Programmers of such ensembles have the advantage of being able to use expensive computational mechanisms and extensive databases without the expense of having to maintain their personal copies. Rather they need only a network computer and access rights for the limited time-share of the larger system they need. Miller and Drexler [1988] describe the economic advantages of this "charge-per-use" as opposed to "charge-per-copy" approach to the use of software. One major advantage is the inhibition of software piracy. When Miller and Drexler wrote their paper, this could be seen as an idealistic view of the future, but with the development of the Web it has moved closer to reality. Currently, Web services tend to be offered free of charge (in fact free access is exchanged for expected real-world publicity) or are available with unrestricted access once a real-world agreement to exchange passwords has been made. Most users of the Web offer little back in return. Miller and Drexler envisage a world where a personal computer connected to a network may be offered to be used by any large application, which needs computational resources. The active offering and exchanging may be done by an agent rather than by the human computer owner. A computer used intermittently by its owner for domestic tasks, such as playing games or writing letters might be used (in exchange for real money, or some computational access rights) by a computationally-bound service (say, a weather forecasting system). The service searches (again through agents) for computational power being offered, dividing its computations up as resources are located and bid for.

10.8 GDC as a Coordination Language

As noted by Gelernter and Carriero [1989], the move towards multi-agent systems emphasizes the need for coordination or composition [Nierstrasz and Meijler 1994] languages, acting as the "glue" for joining diverse computational entities together. In conventional languages, the only coordination activity built into the language is that which binds the computation to the input/output devices attached to the computer on which it runs and such I/O is often added grudgingly as an afterthought to a computational model. Declarative languages can be even worse, since I/O is dismissed as part of the dirty imperative stuff, which the languages are trying to escape from. Recently [Wadler, 1997], the concept of monads has been popularized for obtaining imperative effects cleanly in functional languages. Logic languages would seem to fall into this trap, since in their abstract form their only means of communicating with the outside world is through the variables in the arguments to logic goals. The inductively defined messages of guarded definite clause languages rescues them from the solipsism of the classic declarative language. As shown in Chapter 4, partially bound channels bring the ability for conversational information exchange into guarded definite clause languages. All that is required is for a protocol to be developed so that channels are connected to external devices, which obey the "once-only" assignment rule (with the flexibility of partial binding) and guarded definite clause languages become effective coordination languages. Such a mechanism is already used in KLIC to provide I/O and links with the underlying Unix system [Chikayama, 1995]. To print a value x for example from KLIC, it is necessary to send a message of the fwrite(x) to a stream which has been linked to the standard output via a primitive defined as making that link. There is no primitive actors of the form **write**(x) which simply writes x.

This has some similarity to the monadic approach in functional programming where a program evaluates to a stream of instructions to some external machine. However, in the monadic approach there is just a single link between the "mind" of the program and the "body" of the machine, the analogue of Descartes' pineal gland as Wadler [1997] puts it. The use of channels in GDC allows arbitrary numbers of linkages between the program and the machine, each linkage representing a separate sense organ or limb.

As noted in Chapter 8, the basis of the Linda mechanism proposed by Gelernter and Carriero as a coordination language is that a few simple primitives may be added to any language X to produce the parallel language Linda-X. One primitive, eval, sparks a new parallel process and parallel processes communicate only through a global shared database, with the primitive out putting data-objects called "tuples" into this database, while rd and in read tuples from it (the former leaving it unchanged, the latter consuming the tuple read). An in or rd statement may contain variables which are matched against constants in the database, but if no matching tuple is found, the process containing the statement suspends until another process introduces one with an out. The system is multi-lingual since systems written in Linda-X may share a database with systems written in some other language Linda-Y.

An obvious criticism of this approach is that the global database offers no security. A tuple put out by one process intended for coordination with another may be removed by a third process using an in inadvertently due to a programming mistake, or by design if a hostile agent is attempting to "hack" into the system. Various ways of tackling this problem, generally involving multiple tuple spaces [Gelernter, 1989; Minsky and Leichter, 1994], have been proposed. Hewitt and Lieberman (1984) note, however, that once one has got into the complexity of multiple blackboards, one has lost the conceptual simplicity of the blackboard idea. The argument against using straight message passing has been lost – a blackboard can be seen as just a complicated form of message channel.

Primitives of similar simplicity to Linda's could be added to existing languages, but which, rather than use a global data base, communicate through shared single-assignment variables. Such variables have one writer and may have several readers and only the process initializing the concurrency (and any process to which access has been granted recursively) grants access to them. Any reader who needs to access the value of a variable will suspend until it has been assigned one by its writer, but unbound variables may otherwise be passed as first-class values. The variables may be termed single assignments but could also be termed *futures*, as used in parallel functional [Halstead, 1985] and object-oriented [Lieberman, 1987] languages. We use the term future in the discussion below to emphasize the fact that the computations being coordinated do not themselves have to be written in a logic language. The use of single-assignment variables as a way of coping with parallelism has also been considered in imperative languages [Thornley, 1995].

Any language which is to be used to build a component of a system coordinated in this approach needs a way in which a program in that language may be invoked with input and output futures and a way of reading and writing futures. A future may be bound to a constant or to a tuple with a fixed number of arguments each of which are further futures, which may be bound then or at a later stage. Some sort of error condition may be raised if there is an attempt to bind a future that has already been bound. Similarly, when a future is read, it is read as a name and a fixed-length list of further futures, which is empty if the future is bound to a constant and stores the arguments to a tuple otherwise. No guarantee can be given as to when or in which order these further futures may be bound to. For simplicity, assume there is no back-communication; that is, a reader of a variable is always a reader of arguments of a tuple to which it becomes bound; a writer is always a writer to the arguments of any tuple to which it binds a variable. Back communication could be added at the expense of needing a slightly more complex protocol. Coordination is provided by giving primitives in languages which provide this reading and writing of tuples; we shall leave it to others to fit such primitives into existing languages, but they should be no more difficult to incorporate than Linda's in, rd and out.

This leaves the need for the equivalent of Linda's eval. A process named p, which is a reader of m futures and a writer of n could be set up by $eval(p(x_1,...,x_m) \rightarrow (y_1,...,y_n))$. Each $x_1,...x_m$ is either a new future or one to which the originating process is a reader or writer, while each $y_1,...,y_n$ is either a future to which the originating process is a writer or a new future. Any of $x_1,...x_m$ which is a new future becomes an output future in the calling process, while all $y_1,...y_n$ whether new or existing output futures become input futures.

We could also allow a form of eval which sets up multiple processes, possibly communicating with each other through new futures. In this case, k concurrent processes are set up by

$$\mathbf{eval}(p_1(x_{11},...,x_{1m_1}) \rightarrow (y_{11},...,y_{1n_1}),...p(x_{k1},...x_{km_k}) \rightarrow (y_{k1},...y_{kn_k})).$$

Here, any x_{ij} must be either an existing future to which the originating process is a reader or writer, or a new future and similarly any y_{ij} must be either an existing future to which the originating process is a writer or a new future. No future may occur more than once in a y_{ij} position, a new future occurring in a y_{ij} position becomes an input future in the originating process, any new future occurring in an x_{ij} position but not a y_{ij} position becomes an output future in the originating process. An error condition occurs if the originating process terminates without binding all its output futures. This keeps the property that every future has exactly one writer and one or more readers.

The eval construct allows GDC computations to be set up within foreign language programs. These computations may use their variables as communication between these programs and others similarly equipped with a GDC link. Note that for simplicity of handling a mode is assigned either input or output, to channels used in non-logic programs, with the $\rightarrow$ symbol separating those variables used for input from those used for output.

It has been described how an interface to a guarded definite clause program can be defined in another language X with similar ease to the addition of a few primitives to make Linda-X. The channel binding coordination method removes the insecure tuple-space blackboard. It fits in with the object-oriented concept, with modularity guaranteed by the limited means of communication between objects. There is in fact no way in which a guarded definite clause actor, communicating through a shared single assignment can know whether that single assignment is shared with another actor, or is in fact joined to a non-logic process viewing it as a "future" through the protocol described above.

Kahn and Miller [1988] suggest that guarded definite clause languages have many of the features required in a language for programming "open systems", defined as "a large collection of computational services that use each other without central coordination, trust or complete knowledge of each other". Guarded definite clause actors react to a simultaneous influx of information received asynchronously, because they must be able to deal with channels being bound by other actors on an unpredictable timescale. Because channels are both the means of communication and first-class citizens in the language, guarded definite clause systems have the property of evolvability, allowing the dynamic linking of names to object and the transfer of access to a server. Complete encapsulation of data, allowing services to interact with untrustworthy clients is guaranteed in the guarded definite clause languages since the only means by which a client may interact with a server is by putting a message on an channel, which it takes as input and handles itself. The merging of input streams gives safe mutual reference to objects.

Kahn and Miller note some points where guarded definite clause languages do not work in a way ideal for open systems. The main one is that they do not have any mechanisms for dealing with failure, either hardware or software. It is not reasonable for a service to break because it receives a malformed request, but an actor can only deal with an input pattern that matches with one of its behaviors. When failure occurs because no behavior matches, the complete system fails, there is no simple way to isolate and recover from failure. The guarded definite clause languages assume that a computation moved to another processor will eventually complete, they do not allow backtracking and reassignment of a partially completed computation. As noted by Waldo et al. [1996] partial failure is a central reality of distributed computing caused when a machine crashes or a network link goes down. Given the lack of central coordination, there may not be any agent able to determine that a component has failed and inform other components of that failure. Clearly this is an area where more work needs to be done on the guarded definite clause languages if they are to be used on large-scale distributed networks.

10.9 Networks and Mobile Agents

As an example of the use of GDC for coordination, let us consider a simple setup that simply coordinates two systems. Suppose we start with:

```
:-  setup(AB,BA,ArgsA)@systemA,
    setup(BA,AB,ArgsB)@systemB.
```

Here systemA and systemB could be considered separate processors or separate networks of parallel processors. We assume the underlying setup is such that no actor is moved from systemA to systemB as part of the built-in load balancing of GDC, though if both are systems of parallel processors, actors may be moved about freely between them without the programmer giving explicit instructions for it. The arguments ArgsA and ArgsB could in fact be large numbers of arguments, including links to sensors and effectors, single arguments are given here for the sake of simplicity.

Let **setup** set up two processes, one to manage the system, the other to run a program on the system:

```
setup(Out,In,Args)
    :-  split(Args,SysArgs,ProgArgs),
        manager(Out,In,ForSelf,ForOther,SysArgs),
        program(ForSelf,ForOther,ProgArgs).
```

The result of this is that two programs will be running, one on systemA, the other on systemB and any communication between the two has to pass through a manager. The stream ForSelf is intended to be used for messages to the system running the program and ForOther for messages to the other system. Such messages could be used to access services provided by the systems. The streams are separated and merged as usual, so:

```
program(ForSelf,ForOther,Args)
    :-  split(Args,Args1,Args2),
        merge(ForSelf1,ForSelf2,ForSelf),
        merge(ForOther1,ForOther2,ForOther),
        program1(ForSelf1,ForOther1,Args1),
        program2(ForSelf2,ForOther2,Args2).
```

The manager may choose not to pass on messages intended for the other system, thus we could have the behavior:

```
manager(Out,In,ForSelf,[Message|ForOther],Args)
    :-  acceptable(Message,Args,Flag),
        manager1(Flag,Message,Out,In,ForSelf,ForOther,Args).
```

where **manager1** is defined as:

```
manager1(true,Message,Out,In,ForSelf,ForOther,Args)
    :- Out=[Message|Out1],
        manager(Out1,In,ForSelf,ForOther,Args).
manager1(false,Message,Out,In,ForSelf,ForOther,Args)
    :- handle(Message,Args,Args1),
        manager(Out,In,ForSelf,ForOther,Args1).
```

The second behavior for **manager1** indicates the case where the manager decides to handle the message itself rather than pass it on. Handling the message may cause its own arguments to change and may also bind return channels in the message. The presence of return channels in a message means that if it is accepted for sending to the other system, a direct means of communication between two processes in the two different systems, which does not go through the manager, is established. It is assumed that the messages accepted by the manager are those that conform to a protocol that limits the format of messages passed over.

The managers may need to negotiate about the extent to which they are willing to accept messages from each other. Negotiations about shared work could be formalized, for example in the way suggested by Zlotkin and Rosenschein [1989]. Let us assume an agreement less complex than that, in which the systems simply agree to charge each other one nominal unit for each transferred message handled, with the proviso that one system may not go into a debt of 10 or more units to the other. The **manager** actor will have an extra argument recording its credit level, so the initial call to **manager** in **setup** is:

```
    :- manager(0,Out,In,ForSelf,ForOther,SysArgs).
```

To maintain the credits, we have the following behaviors for **manager** to deal with sending and receiving messages from the other system:

```
manager(Credit,Out,In,ForSelf,[Message|ForOther],Args)
    :- acceptable(Credit,Message,Args,Flag),
        manager1(Flag,Message,Credit,Out,In,ForSelf,ForOther,Args).
manager(Credit,Out,[Message|In],ForSelf,ForOther,Args)
    :- Credit<10
    |  handle(Message,Args,Args1),
        Credit1:=Credit+1,
        manager(Credit1,Out,In,ForSelf,ForOther,Args1).
```

with **manager1** defined by:

```
manager1(true,Credit,Message,Credit,Out,In,ForSelf,ForOther,Args)
    :- Out=[Message|Out1],
        Credit1:=Credit-1,
        manager(Credit1,Out1,In,ForSelf,ForOther,Args).
manager1(false,Message,Credit,Out,In,ForSelf,ForOther,Args)
    :- handle(Message,Args,Args1),
        manager(Credit,Out,In,ForSelf,ForOther,Args1).
```

The second behavior for **manager1** deals with the case where a message is not sent but is instead handled locally. If the credit level reaches 10, messages from the other system are not received but in effect left in a buffer. The system waits until it receives messages to send and thus reduce its credit level, when they can be received in the order sent. Note that the credit level is given as an argument to **acceptable**, as it may be used as a factor in deciding whether to transfer a message. A behavior to allow actors to check the credit level of their system may be useful as an actor's own decision on whether to send a message for the other system may depend on the credit level:

```
manager(Credit,Out,In,[credit(C)|ForSelf],ForOther,Args)
   :- C=Credit, manager1(Credit,Out,In,ForSelf,ForOther,Args1).
```

Clearly, the system management described here could be extended to more complex arrangements than just two systems communicating with each other. A whole network of systems can be envisaged, each with its own manager process managing communication between processes on the system and processes on other systems.

An actor can move itself from one system to the other by converting itself into a message and sending itself on the ForOther stream. The following behavior will do this for the actor **actor**:

```
actor(ForSelf,ForOther,Args)
   :- ForSelf=[], ForOther=[actor(Args)].
```

The actor has to trust it will be unpacked and turned back into an actor once it has been sent to the other system. The following behavior will do this:

```
manager(Credit,Out,[actor(PArgs)|In],ForSelf1,ForOther1,Args)
   :- Credit<10
   |   actor(ForSelf2,ForOther2,PArgs),
       Credit1:=Credit+1,
       manager(Credit1,Out,In,ForSelf,ForOther,Args),
       merge(ForSelf1,ForSelf2,ForSelf),
       merge(ForOther1,ForOther2,ForOther).
```

It is assumed here that the charge for running **actor** on the new system will be one credit unit, though a more complex system of charging based on estimated resource usage could be developed. Note that the arguments to **actor** will be the same ones as on the old system including variables which may be used as channels for communication without going through the manager. The ForSelf and ForOther streams however refer to the new situation, so ForSelf sends messages intended for the new system that **actor** has migrated to and ForOther sends messages to the old one. Alternatively the ForSelf and ForOther arguments to the new actor could be put the other way round so that references to systemA and systemB in the code for **actor** remain linked to those systems independently of where the code is executing.

The above gives some ideas as to how *mobile agents* [Knabe, 1996] may be implemented in GDC. In this case, the idea that agents are autonomous is maintained, since the **actor** has to take the initiative to migrate, the first moves towards migration are not made by the system calling a process over. The migrating process is dependent on the system it migrates to willingly accepting it, if it were somehow to trick the system into giving it space and processing time to run, it would be a virus. In a system involving resource encapsulation the process would have to be assigned resources, possibly involving some degree of negotiation between systems. The giving of a limited amount of resources would act as a protection against the migrating process taking over the system to which it has migrated.

However, mobile agents are generally objects that contain their own code. The code must be in a form such that it is executable on the system migrated to. We have so far assumed that every processor in a distributed system has access to a copy of the same GDC code. Clearly this is not an assumption that can be made if we are considering open systems. We cannot assume the code for **actor** on systemA is identical to the code for **actor** on systemB. A mechanism for attaching code to messages could be introduced in GDC. Alternatively, a meta-interpreter approach could be used. If systemA and systemB both have copies of the behaviors for some meta-interpreter, a message exchanged between them could consist of data representing code that runs on this meta-interpreter, plus an initial meta-interpreter goal.

The abstract nature of GDC means it has the platform independence that is essential for a language for mobile agents. In addition, its declarative nature means there are no problems with name conflicts, external references and the like. A goal and its behaviors are a self-contained unit, with shared variables providing all necessary communication. Knabe [1996] argues for a functional based language to be used for mobile agents on similar grounds. We have suggested ways in which resource awareness may be incorporated into GDC, as for example proposed in the Java-extension *Sumatra* [Acharya et al., 1996]. Although Java [Gosling and McGilton, 1995] has attracted much attention as a language for Internet applications, it is limited in its scope for programming truly mobile agents, classified as at best a weakly mobile code language [Cugola et al., 1996]. Java lacks built-in communication primitives and agents are unable to initiate migration themselves. The authors of the Sumatra language claim that truly mobile agents need three properties:

1. awareness – the ability of a computational agent to monitor the availability and quality of computational resources in its environment;

2. agility – the ability to react quickly to asynchronous events such as changes in the computational environment

3. authority – the ability of agents to control the way in which resources are used on their behalf by system support.

The distributed computational environment in a mobile agent system is like the physical environment in a multiple robot system. The system manager in our example above works like Sumatra's resource monitor.

10.10 Conclusion

We have moved a long way from the origin of guarded definite clause programming with the Japanese Fifth Generation Initiative. The aim initially was to produce a "parallel Prolog", on the grounds that this would be the most suitable way to implement intelligence programs on parallel architectures. Prolog was based not on the architecture of a computer, but on a knowledge representation system, predicate logic, tried and tested by generations of philosophers. Computation in Prolog was reasoning with logic and knowledge, plus reasoning was thought to equal intelligence. In addition, the lack of a basis on computer architecture meant that Prolog was not dependent on the single-processor von Neumann machine, unlike standard high-level languages, which had been built up in an evolutionary manner from machine code.

The Fifth Generation Initiative was buried by developments that were visible at its start, but became much more prominent as it went on. The limitations of predicate logic as a knowledge representation system became more obvious as logicians struggled with problems (often involving Tweety the bird who may or may not be a non-flying penguin) caused by the closed world assumption. Radical critiques of the knowledge based approach to AI, such as the revived neural network community and Brooks with his reactive robots, gathered forces. The cycle of hype and inevitable disappointment at ambitious goals not being reached was seen, as it had been before and undoubtedly will be again in AI. In the computer world, the standalone mainframe was succeeded by the networked personal computer. While declarative languages failed to find much of a market outside their academic developers, object-oriented programming, in the shape of C++, boomed. The language C++ moved from initial release to the language of choice for many new developments in a matter of months, before a satisfactory description of it could be put together. Part of the reason for its success was that it was a hybrid language, combining high-level object-oriented principles with low-level control of physical computer architecture. Java followed on its heels, claiming machine independence but not in the way dreamed of by the declarative programmers. The first lesson to be learnt from this is the importance of commercial backing in programming language adoption. The second lesson was that ideas on programming languages originating in academic research labs can eventually make it into commercial computing, but we should not underestimate the timescale required for them to do so. C/C++/Java can be seen as representing the ultimate triumph of Algol in the 1960s Algol v FORTRAN/Cobol war.

The Fifth Generation Project concluded viewing the language it developed as its main achievement [Shapiro and Takeuchi, 1993]. It was flexible [Huntbach and Ringwood, 1995], implementable [Rokusawa et al., 1996] and recognized by some [Kahn and Miller, 1988] as having potential unmet by most other current languages. However, it was not a "parallel Prolog". Prolog turned out to be far more dependent on a single processor and global structures than was thought when it was adopted as the base for the Fifth Generation. In making compromises necessary to map the logic paradigm onto parallel architecture, many considered the guarded definite clause languages had lost those aspects of logic programming which made it attractive. The Holy Grail of a language in which programs were logical statements continued to be pursued elsewhere [Hill and Lloyd, 1994; Wetzel, 1997].

What had been achieved was an abstract concurrent language. The clarity of this achievement was clouded by arguments over whether it was really logical and differences over minor matters [Shapiro, 1989] which hid the fact that several teams, not only the Japanese one but elsewhere, had converged on essentially the same language. The symbol-processing nature of this language inherited from its logic background made it suitable for the symbol processing of representational AI. Its simple operational semantics and declarative nature made it suitable for program tools such as debuggers, code transformers and abstract interpreters. It enabled the programmer to think in terms of abstract concurrency while ignoring the real architectural details of parallel machines.

Almost accidentally, the guarded definite clause languages were found to correspond closely to the concurrent object-oriented paradigm. This looks less accidental when one considers that object-oriented programming owes its origins to thinking in parallel. The ancestor of object-oriented programming, SIMULA [Birtwistle et al., 1973], was devised as a language to program simulations of systems of several components working in parallel. The power of object-oriented programming may be seen as lying in the way it enables the programmer to relax from the restrictions of having to think about the data of the program being manipulated as a single object in a purely sequential way. Rather, it exists in discrete parts that can be guaranteed to remain unchanged in parallel with other parts changing. In performing an action on A and leaving B unchanged then performing an action on B and leaving A unchanged we are saved from having to think in terms of performing two sequential actions on AB. Having to think of an order at all is an unnecessary complexity forced on us by a purely sequential language. In parallel processing the division into discrete parts is necessity in order to exploit the parallel capacity and the guarantee of non-interference between the parts means we do not have to consider how to implement the interference. In object-oriented programming it is imposed as a good software engineering principle.

An alternative way into object-oriented programming is through the stream starting with Hewitt's [1977] Actors. Whereas the approach which starts from SIMULA is evolutionary, following the move from assembly languages, through the early high-level languages and through languages designed for structured programming, the actors principle was revolutionary. It started from the first principle that computation could be organized as a set of autonomous components exchanging messages rather than as a variation on the single-processor von Neumann machine. Smalltalk can be seen as an implementation of that principle, though adjusted to fit on to a sequential architecture and influenced also by ideas on knowledge representation in AI [Minsky, 1975].

GDC being based on an abstract model and having broken away from Prolog's reliance on a global stack and strict sequential ordering of goals and clauses, has a close affinity with Actors. Spurred by this, the authors have investigated its use to implement algorithms viewed in an actors-like way, that is as collections of object exchanging messages. The additional flexibility caused by the fact that communications channels are first-class values in the language, rather than implicit in a built-in communications structure, is useful in many cases. The logic programming background gives GDC a firmer semantics than proposed actors languages have had, aiding the development of programming tools. We considered one such tool, a partial evaluator, in detail. The affinity logic programming has with meta-interpreters provides further scope for methods of program development, indeed GDC can be used a base language to implement other programming language paradigms.

The final chapter on agents challenges GDC to move beyond the abstract parallelism of the Fifth Generation to the open systems that have transformed computer science in recent years. As we have seen, the idea of building systems in terms of combining intelligent agents builds on the actors version of object-oriented programming. Interestingly, having moved away from direct control of the computer architecture, our discussion of the suitability of GDC for implementing intelligent agents leads to suggestions that reincorporate architectural control. However, they do so in a disciplined high-level way. Access to lower level resource usage should be used only where necessary and not forced on the programmer as a consequence of moving from sequential systems. Annotations to control resource usage should not be entirely orthogonal to those used to express the behavior of the program. There needs to be some simple mechanism for reflection. In many cases, separating the two into programs and meta-programs helps make the distinction clear. Programming parallel, distributed and multi-agent systems is difficult as it involves coordinating several activities happening at once. A language which enables the programmer to concentrate on those aspects which are necessary to control – the behavior of the algorithm, the design of individual agents, the control of resources where limited resources are an issue – does much to simplify the problem.

References and Bibliography

Abelson H, Sussmann GJ and Sussmann J (1985) *Structure and Interpretation of Computer Programs*, MIT Press

Acharya A, Ranganathan M and Saltz J (1996) Sumatra: a language for resource-aware mobile programs, in Vitek J and Tschudin C eds, *Mobile Object Systems,* Springer-Verlag *LNCS* **1222**:111–30

Adams DA (1968) *A Computation Model with Dataflow Sequencing*, TR **CS 117** Stanford U

Agha, G (1986) *Actors: A Model of Cconcurrent Computation in Distributed Systems*, MIT Press

Agha G (1990) Concurrent object-oriented programming, *CACM* **33**(9)125–141

Agre P and Chapman D (1987) PENGI: an implementation of a theory of activity, *Proc Sixth Nat Conf on Artificial Intelligence, AAAI–87:*268–72

Aiello L and Levi G (1984) The uses of metaknowledge in AI systems, in O'Shea T ed, *Advances in Artificial Intelligence (ECA–I84)*, Elsevier, 705–17

Ait-Kaci H (1991) *Warren's Abstract Machine*, MIT Press

Aleksander I (1988) Logical connectionist system, in Eckmiller R and Malsburg CH eds, *Neural Computers*, Springer-Verlag, 189–197

Alexander WG and Wortman DB (1975) Static and dynamic characteristics of XPL programs, *IEEE Computer* **8**:41–46

Amdahl GM (1967) Validity of the single processor approach to achieving large scale computing capabilities, *Proc AFIPS Spring Joint Computer Conf 30*, Atlantic City, 483–485

Amerding GW (1962) FORTAB: *A Decision Table Language for Scientific Computing Applications*, TR **RM–3306–PR** RAND Corp

America P(1987) Inheritance and subtyping in a parallel object-oriented language, *ECOOP'87*, Springer-Verlag *LNCS* **276**:234–242

America P (1990) A parallel object-oriented programming language with inheritance and subtyping, *Proc OOPSLA '90, SIGPLAN Notices*, ACM Press, 161–68

Anderson JADW ed (1989) *POP-11 Comes of Age: The Advancement of an AI Programming Language*, Ellis Horwood

Andrews GR (1991) *Concurrent Programming*, Benjamin–Cummings

Anzai Y (1987) Ninshiki to suiron no jyouhoushori mekanizumu, *Kagaku* (Japan), (April)210–219,

Appel K and Haken W (1989) Every planar map is four colorable, *Contemporary Mathematics* **98**, Am Math Soc

Apt KR (1994) Logic programming and negation: a survey, *J Logic Programming* **19–20**:9–71

Apt and van Emden (1982) Contributions to the theory of logic programming, *JACM* **29**(3)841–62

Arbib MA (1988) *The Metaphorical Brain: An Introduction to Schemes and Brain Theory*, Wiley

Arbib MA and Liaw J-S (1995) Sensorimotor transformations in the world of frogs and toads, *Artificial Intelligence* **72**:53–79

Armstrong J, Virding R and Williams M (1993) *Concurrent Programming in Erlang*, Prentice-Hall

Arvind K, Gostelow KP and Plouffe W (1977) Indeterminacy, monitors and dataflow, Proc Sixth ACM Symp on Operating Systems Principles, *Operating System Rev*iews **11**(5)159–69

Arvind VK and Ianucci RA (1987) Two fundamental issues in multiprocessing, *DFVLR Proc Conf on Parallel Processing in Science and Engineering*, Bonn–Bad Godesberg, 61–68

Ashby WR (1956) *An Introduction to Cybernetics*, Wiley

Ashcroft EA and Wadge WW (1975) Proving programs without tears, *Proc IRIA Symp on Proving and Improving Programs*, 99–111

Ashcroft EA, Jagannathan R, Faustini AA and Huey B (1985) Eazyflow engines for Lucid – a family of supercomputer architectures based upon demand-driven and data-driven computation, *Proc First Int Conf on Supercomputing*

Asimov I (1942) Runaround, *Astounding Science Fiction*, March:94–103

Astrahan MM, Blasgen MW, Chamberlain DD, Eswaran KP, Gray JN, Griffiths PP, King WF, Lorie RA, McJones PR, Mehl JW, Putzolo GR, Traiger IL, Wade BW and Watson V (1976) System R: relational approach to database management, *ACM TODS* **1**(2)97–137

Attwood JW (1976) Concurrency in operating systems, *IEEE Computer* **9**:18–26

Austin JL (1962) *How to Do Things with Words*, Oxford UP

Axelrod R (1984) *The Evolution of Cooperation*, Basic Books

Baader F and Siekmann JH (1994) Unification theory, in Gabbay DM, Hogger CJ and Robinson JA eds, *Handbook of Logic in Artificial Intelligence and Logic Programming*, Clarendon Press, 41–125

Backus J (1978) Can programming be liberated from the von Neumann style? A functional style and its algebra of programs, ACM Turing Lecture, *CACM* **21**:613–41

Backus J (1982) Function-level computing, *IEEE Spectrum* **19**:22–7

Backus JW, Beeber RJ, Best S, Goldberg R, Haibt LM, Herrick HL, Nelson RA, Syare D, Sheridan PB, Stern H, Ziller I, Hughes RA nd Nutt R (1957) The Fortran automatic coding system, *Western Joint Computer Conference*, 188–98

Bagehot W (1861) The American constitution at the present crisis, *National Review vol XIII*, (1861)465–93 Reprinted in St John-Stevas N ed, *The Collected Works of Walter Bagehot vol IV*, The Economist

Bahgat R (1992) The Pandora deadlock handler metalevel relation, *Metaprogramming in Logic (META–92)*, Springer-Verlag *LNCS* **649**:162–176

Bahgat R and Gregory S (1989) Pandora: non-deterministic parallel logic programming, *Proceedings Sixth Int Conf on Logic Programming*, 471–86

Bal HE (1991) Heuristic search in Parlog using replicated worker style parallelism, *Future Generation Computer Systems* **6**(4)303–15

Bal HE, Steiner JG and Tanenbaum AS (1989) Programming languages for distributed systems, *ACM Computing Surveys* **21**:261–322

Ballard D H (1986) *Parallel Logical Inference and Energy Minimization*, TR **142**, CS Dept, U Rochester, NY

Bar-Hillel Y (1960) The present status of automatic translation of languages, *Advances in Computers* **1**:91–163

Barendregt HP (1984) *The Lambda Calculus – its Syntax and Semantics*, North-Holland

Barklund J and Hamfelt A (1994) Hierarchical representation of legal knowledge with metaprogramming in logic, *New Generation Computing* **13**(3)55–80

Barlett FC (1932) *Remembering*, Cambridge UP

Baron RV et al. (1987) *MACH Kernel Interface Manual*, TR Dept CS, CMU

Barr A and Feigenbaum EA (1982) *The Handbook of Artificial Intelligence vol 2*, Pitman

Barr RS, Helgaon RV and Kennington JL (1989) Minimal spanning trees: an empirical investigation of parallel algorithms, *Parallel Computing* **12**:45–52

Baudet G (1978) *The Design and Analysis of Algorithms for Asynchronous Multiprocessors*, PhD Dissertation, Carnegie Mellon U

Beckman L, Haraldson, Oskarsson O and Sandewall E (1976) A partial evaluator and its use as a programming tool, *Artificial Intelligence* 7:319–57

Bellia M, Degano P and Levi G (1980) A functional plus predicate logic language, in Tärnlund S-Å ed, *Proc Logic Programming Workshop*, Debrecen (Hungary), 334–347

Bellia M and Levy G (1986) The relationship between logic and functional languages: a survey, *J Logic Programming* 3(3)217–36

Bell CG (1985) Multis: A new class of multiprocessor computers, *Science* **228**:462–67

Berge C and Ghouila-Houri A (1965) *Programming, Games and Transportation Networks*, Methuen, 179–180

Berliner HJ (1989) Hitech chess: From master to senior master with no hardware change, *MIV–89, Proc Int Workshop on Industrial Applications of Machine Intelligence and Vision* (Seiken Symposium) 12–21

Bhandari IS, Krishna CM and Siewiorek DP (1988) A parallel algorithm for coloring graphs, *Proc Eighth IEEE Conf on Distributed Computing Systems*, San Jose, CA

Birtwistle G, Dahl O-J, Myrhaug B and Nygaard K (1973) *Simula Begin*, Van Nostrand Reinhold

Bitner J and Reingold EM (19750 Backtrack programming techniques, *CACM* **18**:651–55

Bledsoe WW and Loveland DW eds (1984) *Automated Theorem Proving: after 25 Years*, Contemporary Mathematics **29**, AMS

Bobrow DG (1967) Natural language input for a computer problem solving system, in Minsky ML ed, *Semantic Information Processing*, MIT Press, 135–215

Bobrow DG and Raphael B (1974) New programming languages for artificial intelligence research, *Computing Surveys* **6**:153–74

Bohm C and Jacopini G (1966) Flow diagrams, Turing machines, and languages with only two formation rules, *CACM* **9**:336–71

Bond AH and Gasser L (1988) *Readings in Distributed Artificial Intelligence*, Morgan Kaufmann

Boole G (1847) *The Mathematical Analysis of Logic: Being an Essay Towards a Calculus of Deductive Reasoning*, Macmillan

Borning AH (1986) Classes versus prototypes in object-oriented languages, *Proc ACM/IEEE Fall Joint Computer Conference*, Dallas, 36–40

Bouknight WJ, Denberg SA, McIntyre DE, Randall JM, Sameh AH and Slotnick DL (1972) The ILLIAC system, Proc IEEE **60**:369–79

Boulanger D and Bruynooghe M (1992) Deriving transformations of logic programs using abstract interpretation, in Lau K-K and Clements T eds, *Logic Program Synthesis and Transformation (LOPSTR'92)*, Workshops in Computer Science, Springer-Verlag, 99–117

Bowen D, Byrd L, Pereira LM, Pereira FCN and Warren DHD (1981) *PROLOG on the DEC System–10 user's manual*, TR Dept AI, U Edinburgh

Bowen KA and Kowalski RA (1982) Amalgamating language and metalanguage in logic programming, in Clark KL and Tärnlund S-Å eds, *Logic Programming* 153–172

Bowen KA and Weinberg T (1985) A metalevel extension of Prolog, *Symp Logic Programming*, 48–52

Boyer RS and Moore J (1972) The sharing of structure in theorem proving programs, *Machine Intelligence* **7**, Meltzer B and Michie D eds, Edinburgh UP

Brachmann RJ (1983) What IS-A is and isn't: An analysis of taxonomic links in semantic networks, *IEEE Computer* **16**:30–6

Brachmann RJ (1985) I lied about the trees or defaults and definitions in knowledge representation, *AI Magazine* **6**:60–93

Brachmann RJ and Leveque HJ (1985) *Readings in Knowledge Representation*, Morgan Kaufmann

Brachmann RJ and Smith BC eds (1980) *Special Issue on Knowledge Representation*, SIGART **70**

Brachmann RJ (1990) The future of knowledge representation, *Proc Eighth Nat Conf on AI*, MIT Press

Braitenberg V (1984) *Vehicles*, MIT Press

Bratko I (1986) *Prolog Programming for Artificial Intelligence* 2/e, Addison-Wesley

Bratman ME (1987) *Intentions, Plans and Practical reason*, Harvard UP

Breal M (1900) *Semantics: Studies in the Science of Meaning*, Henry Holt and Co

Briggs R (1985) Knowledge representation in Sanskrit and artificial intelligence, *AI Magazine* **6**(1)32–9

Brinch-Hansen P (1970) The nucleus of a multiprogramming system, *CACM* **13**:238–41

Brinch-Hansen P (1972) Structured multiprogramming, *CACM* **15**:574–78

Brinch-Hansen P (1973) *Operating System Principles*, Prentice-Hall

Briot JP and Yonezawa A (1987) Inheritance and synchronization in concurrent OOP, *ECOOP'87*, Springer-Verlag *LNCS* **276**, 33–40

Briot JP (1989) Acttalk: a testbed for classifying and designing actor languages in the Smalltalk–80 environment, *Proc ECOOP'89*, Cambridge UP, 109–29

Britton KH, Parker RA and Parnas DL (1981) A procedure for designing abstract interfaces for device interface modules, *Proc Fifth Int Conf on Software Engineering*, IEEE Comp Soc Press, 195–204

Brock JD and Ackermann WB (1981) Scenario: A model of nondeterministic computation, in Diaz J and Ramos I eds, *Formalisation of Programming Concepts,* Springer-Verlag *LNCS* **107**:252–59

Brogi A and Ciancarini P (1991) The concurrent language Shared Prolog, *ACM Trans Prog Lang Sys* **13**(1)99–123

Bromley AG (1987) Charles Babbage's calculating engines, *Ann History of Computing*, **9**(2)113–36

Brooks F (1987) No silver bullet: essence and accidents of software engineering, *Computer* **20**

Brooks FP (1962) Architectural philosophy, in Buchholz W ed, *Planning a Computer System*, McGraw-Hill, 5–16

Brooks FP Jr (1975) *The Mythical Man Month*, Addison-Wesley

Brooks RA (1986) A robust layered control system for a mobile robot, *IEEE J Robotics and Automation* **RA–2**(1)14–23

Brooks RA (1990) Elephants don't play chess, *Robotics and Autonomous Systems* **6**:3–15

Brooks RA (1991a) Intelligence without representation, *Artificial Intelligence* **47**:139–59

Brooks RA (1991b) Intelligence without reason, *IJCAI–91*, 569–95

Brown LM (1962) Decision table experience on a file maintenance system, *Proc Decision Tables Symp*, ACM, 75–80

Brown GW (1962) *Computers and the World of the Future*, MIT Press

Brown T (1820) *Lectures on the Human Mind*, Tait

Brough DR and Walker A (1984) Some practical properties of logic programming interpreters, *Proc Int Conf on Fifth Generation Computer Systems 1984*, Tokyo

Bruynooghe M (1991) Intelligent backtracking revisited, in Lassez JL and Plotkin G eds, *Computational Logic*, MIT Press

Bruynooghe M, de Schreye D and Martens B (1992) A general stop criterion for avoiding infinite unfolding during partial evaluation, *New Generation Computing* **11**(1)47–79

Bryson AE and Ho YC (1969) *Applied Optimal Control*, Blaisdell

Buchanan BG, Feigenbaum EA, Lederberg J (1971) *Proc Second IJCAI*, London, 40–8

Buchanan BG and Mitchell TM (1978) Model directed learning of production rules, in Waterman DA and Hayes-Roth F eds, *Pattern-directed Inference Systems*, Academic Press

Bundy A and Welham B (1981) Using metalevel inference for selective application of multiple rewrite rule sets in algebraic manipulation, *AI Journal* **16**:189–212

Bunemann P and Clemons E (1979) Efficiently monitoring relational databases, *ACM TODS*

Burstall RM and Darlington J (1977) A transformation system for developing recursive programs, *JACM* **24**(1)44–67

Burt A and Ringwood GA (1988) *The Binding Conflict Problem in Concurrent Logic Languages*, TR Dept Computing, Imperial College, London

Burton FW (1985) Speculative computation, parallelism and functional programming, *IEEE Trans Computers* **C34**(12)1190–93

Burton FW (1987) Functional programming for concurrent and distributed computing *Computer J* **30**(5)437–50

Burton FW (1988) Nondeterminism with referential transparency in functional programming languages, *Computer J* **31**(3)243–47

Burton FW and Huntbach MM (1984) Virtual tree machines, *IEEE Trans Computers* **C33**(3)278–80

Byrd L (1980) Understanding the control flow of Prolog programs, *Logic Programming Workshop*, Debrecen (Hungary)

Carnap R (1928) *Aufbau der Welt*, George RA tr (1967) *The Logical Structure of the World*, Routledge

Carriero N and Gelerntner D (1989) Linda in context, *CACM* **32**(4)444–58

Chaib-Draa B and Levesque P (1996) Hierarchy and communication in multi-agent environment, *J Theoretical and Experimental AI* **8**(1)7–20

Chaitin GJ (1982) Register allocation and spilling via coloring, *SIGPLAN Notices* **17**(6)

Chan D (1988) Constructive negation based on the completed database, in Kowalski R and Bowen D eds, *Proc the Fifth Int Conf and Symp on Logic Programming*, Seattle, MIT Press

Chandrasekaran B (1983) Towards a taxonomy of problem-solving types, *AI Magazine* **4**:9–17

Chandrasekaran B (1985a) Expert systems: matching techniques to tasks, in Reitman W ed, *Artificial Intelligence Applications for Business*, Ablex Corp

Chandrasekaran B (1985b) Generic tasks in expert systems and their role in explanation of problem solving, *NAS/ONR Workshop on AI and Distributed Problem Solving*

Chandy KM and Kesselman C (1992) Compositional C++: Compositional parallel programming, **CS–92–13** Caltech

Chandy M and Misra J (1988) *Parallel Program Design*, Addison-Wesley

Chang C (1970) The unit proof and the input proof in theorem proving, *JACM*, 698–707

Charniak E, Riesbeck CK, McDermott DV and Meehan JR (1987) *Artificial Intelligence Programming* 2/e, Lawrence Erlbaum

Chartered Institute for Public Finance and Accountancy (1995) *Code of Conduct for Compulsory Competition – January 1995 Consolidated Edition*, CIPFA, London

Checkland P (1981) *Systems Thinking, Systems Practice*, Wiley

Cheeseman P, Kanefsky B and Taylor WM (1991) Where the really hard problems are, *IJCAI–91*, 331–37

Chen PP (1976) The entity relationship model: toward a unified view of data, *ACM Trans on Database Sys* **1**:9–37

Chen PP (1977) The entity relationship model: a basis for the enterprise view of data, *Proc IFIPS NCC* **46**:76–84

Cheriton DR (1987) *The V Distributed System*, TR Dept CS, Stanford U

Chikofsky EJ and Cross JH II (1990) Reverse engineering and design recovery, *IEEE Software* **7**:13–17

Chikayama T (1993a) The Fifth Generation Project: personal perspectives, *CACM* **36**(3)82–90

Chikayama T (1993b) ICOT Research Center, in Shapiro E and Warren DHD eds, The Fifth Generation Project: personal perspectives, *CACM* **36**(3)82–90

Chikayama T (1995) *KLIC User's Manual*, Institute for New Generation Technology, Tokyo, Japan

Chikayama T, Satoh H and Miyazaki T (1988) Overview of the Parallel Inference Machine Operating System (PIMOS) *Proc Int Conf on Fifth Generation Computing Systems 1988*, Tokyo

Chilvers I and Osborne H (1988) *The Oxford Dictionary of Art*, Oxford UP

Church A (1936) An unsolvable problem of elementary number theory, *American J Mathematics* **58**:345–63

Clancey W (1983) The advantage of abstract control knowledge in expert systems, *Proc AAAI–83*:74–8

Clancey WJ and Letsinger R (1981) NEOMYCIN: reconfiguring a rule-based expert system for application to teaching, *IJCAI–***8**:829–936

Clark KL (1978) Negation as failure, in Gallaire H and Minker J, *Logic and Databases*, Plenum

Clark KL and Gregory S (1981) A relational language for parallel programming, *Proceedings ACM Conference on Functional Programming Languages and Computer Architecture* (Portsmouth, NH) ACM, 171–178

Clark KL and Gregory S (1983) *Parlog: a Parallel Logic Programming Language*, TR **83/5** Dept Computing, Imperial College and improved version with set predicates (1986) ACM *Transactions on Programming Languages and Systems* **8**:1–49

Clark KL and Gregory S (1985) Notes on the implementation of Parlog, *J Logic Prog* **2**:17–42

Clark KL and Gregory S (1986) Parlog: parallel programming in logic, *ACM TOPLAS* **8**:1–49

Clark KL and Gregory S (1987) Parlog and Prolog united, *Fourth Int Conf on Logic Prog*, 243–47

Clark KL, McCabe FG (1979) The control facilities of IC-Prolog, in Michie D ed, *Expert Systems in the Micro-electronic Age*, Edinburgh UP

Clark KL, McCabe FG and Gregory S (1982) IC-Prolog language features, in Clark KL and Tärnlund S-Å eds, *Logic Programming*, Academic Press253–66

Clark KL and Tärnlund S-Å (1977) A first-order theory of data and programs, in *Information Processing 77: Proc IFIP Congress*, 939–44

Clark KL and Tärnlund S-Å eds (1982) *Logic Programming*, Academic Press, 189–98

Clarke LA, Wileden JC and Wolf AL (1980) Nesting in ADA programs is for the birds, Proc *SIGPLAN Symp on the ADA Prog Language*, 139–45

Chomsky N (1957) *Syntactic Structures*, Mouten and Co

Clancey W (1983) The advantage of abstract control knowledge in expert systems, *Proc AAAI–83*:74–8

Clocksin FW and CS (1981) Programming in Prolog, Springer-Verlag

Clowes MB (1971) On seeing things, *Artificial Intelligence* **2**:79–116

CODASYL (1962) Preliminary specifications for a decision table structured language, *CODASYL Systems Group*

CODASYL (1978) *Report of the CODASYL Data Description Language Committee*, Pergamon Press

Codd EF (1970) A relational model of data for large shared databases, *CACM* **13**(6)377–87

Codd EF and Date CJ (1974) Interactive support for non-programmers: the relational and network approaches, in Randall and Rustin eds, *Data Models: Structure Set vs Relational, Proc ACM SIGMOD Workshop on Data Description, Access and Control*, vol II

Codish M and Shapiro E (1987) Compiling OR-parallelism into AND-parallelism, *New Generation Computing* **5**(1)45–61

Cohen J (1985) Describing Prolog by its interpretation and compilation, *CACM* **28**(12)1311–24

Cohen D, Huntbach MM and Ringwood GA (1992) Logical Occam, in Kacsuk P and Wise MJ eds, *Implementations of Distributed Prolog*, Wiley

Cohen D and Ringwood GA (1993) Distributed databases tied with StrIng, *Advances in Databases*, Springer-Verlag *LNCS* **696**:76–92

Cohen H (1979) What is an image? *Proc Sixth IJCAI*, Tokyo

Cohen P (1988) A view of the origins and development of Prolog, *CACM* **31**:26–36

Cohen PR and Leveque HL (1990) *Intention is Choice with Commitment*, Morgan Kaufmann

Cohen PR and Leveque HL (1995) Communicative actions for artificial agents, in Lesser V ed, *Proc First Int Conf on Multi-agent Systems* (ICMAS–95) 65–72

Cohen PR and Perrault CR (1979) Elements of a plan based theory of speech acts, *Cognitive Science* **3**:177–212

Cohen PM (1965) *Universal Algebra*, Harper and Row

Colmerauer A (1973) *Les Systems-Q ou un Formalisme pour Analyser et Synthetiser des Phrases sur Ordinateur*, TR **43** Dept d'Informatique, U de Montreal

Colmerauer A (1975) *Les Grammaires de Metamorphose*, TR Groupe d'Intelligence Artificielle, U Grenoble, translated into English (1978) Metamorphosis grammars, in Bolc L ed, *Natural Language Communication with Computers*, Springer-Verlag

Colmerauer A (1982) Prolog and infinite trees, in Clark KL and Tärnlund S-Å eds, *Logic Programming*, Academic Press, 231–251

Colmerauer A, Kanoui H and van Caneghem M (1982) *Prolog II Manuel de Référence et Modèle Théorique*, Groupe Intelligence Artificielle, Univ d'Aix-Marseille II

Colmerauer A and Roussel P (1992) The birth of Prolog, *History of Programming Languages II, ACM SIGPLAN Notices* **28**(3)37–52

Colouris G, Dollimore J and Kindberg T (1993) *Distributed Systems: Concepts and Design* 2/e, Addison-Wesley

Condon JH and Thompson K (1982) Belle chess hardware, in Clarke MRB ed, *Advances in Computer Chess 3*, Pergamon, 45–54

Conery JS (1987) *Parallel Execution of Logic Programs*, Kluwer

Conery JS and Kibler DF (1981) Parallel interpretation of logic programming, *Proc Conf on Functional Programming, Languages and Computer Architecture*, 163–70

Conway ME (1963) Design of a separable transition diagram compiler, *CACM* **6**(7)396–408

Copleston F (1985) *A History of Philosophy*, Image Books

Courtois PJ, Heymans F and Parnas DL (1971) Concurrent control with readers and writers, *CACM* **14**(10)667–8

Coyne R (1988) *Logic Models of Design*, Pitman

Craig ID (1991) *Formal Specification of Advanced AI Architectures*, Ellis Horwood

Craik KJW (1943) *The Nature of Explanation*, Cambridge UP

Crick FH and Asanuma C (1986) Certain aspects of the anatomy and physiology of the cerebral cortex, in Rumelhart DE and McClelland JL eds, *Parallel Distributed Processing* 2, MIT Press, 333–371

Crockett L (1994) *The Turing Test and the Frame Problem: AI's Mistaken Understanding of Intelligence*, Ablex

Cugola G, Ghezzi C, Picco GP and Vigna G (1996) Analyzing mobile code languages, in Vitek J and Tschudin C eds, *Mobile Object Systems*, Springer-Verlag *LNCS* **1222**:93–109

Curry HB, Feys R and Craig W (1958) *Combinatory Logic, Vol I*, North-Holland

Dahl O-J, Myrhaug B and Nygaard K (1970) (Simula 67) *Common Base Language*, TR S–22 Norwegian Computing Center, Oslo

Dahl O-J (1972) Hierarchical program structures, in Dahl OJ, Dijkstra EW and Hoare CAR eds, *Structured Programming*, Academic Press

Dahl O-J, Dijkstra EW and Hoare CAR (1972) *Structured Programming*, Academic Press

Dasgupta S (1989) *Computer Architecture: A Modern Synthesis* (2 vols), Wiley

Dausmann M, Perch G and Winterstein G (1979) Concurrent logic, *Proc Fourth Workshop on Artificial Intelligence*, Bad Honnef

Davis AL (1978) The architecture and system method of DDM1: A recursively structured data driven machine, *Proc Fifth Ann Symp on Comp Arch*, ACM, 210–15

Davis M (1957) A computer program for Presburger's Algorithm, in Robinson A ed, *Proving Theorems, (as Done by Man, Logician, or Machine)*, Cornell U, 215–233

Davis M (1963) Eliminating the irrelevant from mechanical proofs, *Proc Symp App Math, XV*, 15–30

Davis M (1973) Hilbert's tenth problem is unsolvable, *American Mathematical Monthly*, 80

Davis MD (1983) The prehistory and early history of automated deduction, in Siekmann J and Wrightson G eds, *Automation of Reasoning*, Springer-Verlag, 1–28

Davis M and Putnam H (1960) A computing procedure for quantification theory, *JACM*, 201–15

Davis PJ and Hersh R (1981) Lakatos and the philosophy durability, in Davis PJ and Hersh R eds, *The Mathematical Experience*, Harvester Press

Davis R (1980a) Metarules: reasoning about control, *Artificial Intelligence* **15**:179–222

Davis R (1980b) Report on the workshop distributed AI, *SIGART Newsletter* **73**:42–52

Davis RE (1982) Runnable specification as a design tool, in, Clark KL and Tärnlund S-Å eds, *Logic Programming*, Academic Press, 141–149

Davis R and Buchanan BG (1977) Metalevel knowledge: overview and applications, *IJCAI-77*:920–27

Davis R and Smith RG (1983) Negotiation as a metaphor for distributed problem solving, *Artificial Intelligence* **20**:63–109

Davison A (1992) Object-oriented databases in Polka, in Valduriez P ed, *Parallel Processing and Data Management*, Chapman Hall, 207–223

de Groot AD (1946) *Het Denken van den Schaker*, Elsevier/North-Holland, translated in de Groot AD (1978) *Thought and Choice in Chess 2/e*, Mouten

Delgado-Rannauro SA (1992a) Restricted AND and AND/OR-parallel logic computational models, in Kacsuk P and Wise M eds, *Implementations of Distributed Prolog*, Wiley

Delgado-Rannauro SA (1992b) Or-parallel logic computation models, in Kacsuk P and Wise M eds, *Implementations of Distributed Prolog*, Wiley

De Marco T (1979) *Structured Analysis and Systems Specification*, Prentice-Hall

Demoen B (1992) On the transformation of a Prolog program to a more efficient binary program, in Lau K-K and Clements T eds, *Logic Program Synthesis and Transformation (LOPSTR) '92*, Springer-Verlag, 242–52

de Morgan A (1847) *Formal Logic, or the Calculus of Inference, Necessary and Probable*, Taylor and Walton

Dennett DC (1987) *The Intentional Stance*, Bradford Books/MIT Press

Dennis JB and Misunas DP (1975) A preliminary architecture for a basic dataflow computer, *Proc Second Annual Symp on Comp Architecture*, ACM

Dennis JB (1976) A language for structured concurrency, in Williams JH and Fischer DA eds, *LNCS* **54**:453–57

Derthick M (1988) *Mundane Reasoning by Parallel Constraint Satisfaction*, PhD thesis, Dept CS, CMU

Devanbu P, Freeland M and Naqvi S (1986) A procedural approach to search control in Prolog, *European Conference on AI 1986 Vol II*, 53–57

Devine DJ (1965) Decision Tables as the basis of a programming language, *Data Processing* **8**:461–466

Devlin K (1987) A clever little number, *The Guardian*, July 16:16

Dijkstra EW (1959) A note on two problems in connection with graphs, *Numerische Mathematik* **1**:269–271

Dijkstra EW (1965) Solution of a problem in concurrent programming control, *CACM* **8**, 569

Dijkstra EW (1968a) The structure of the THE multiprogramming system *CACM* **11**:341–46

Dijkstra EW (1968b) Cooperating sequential processes in Genuys F ed, *Programming Languages*, Academic Press, 43–112

Dijkstra EW (1968c) Goto statement considered harmful, *CACM* **11**:147–8

Dijkstra EW (1971) Hierarchical ordering of sequential processes, *Acta Informatica* **1**:115–38

Dijkstra EW (1972) Notes on structured programming, in Dahl OJ, Dijkstra EW and Hoare CAR eds, *Structured Programming*, Academic Press

Dijkstra EW (1975) Guarded commands, nondeterminacy and formal derivation of programs, *CACM* **18**:453–57

Dijkstra EW (1976) *A Discipline of Programming*, Prentice-Hall

Dincbas M (1980) The Metalog problem-solving system, an informal presentation, *Proc Logic Programming Workshop*, Debrecen (Hungary), 80–91

Dincbas M and Le Pape J-P (1984) Meta control of logic programs, Metalog, *Int Conf Fifth Generation Systems*, 361–370

Dolev D (1982) The Byzantine generals strike again, *J Algorithms* **3**(1)14–30

Doran RW (1979) *Computer Architecture: A Structured Approach*, Academic Press

Dowson M (1984) A note on Micro-Planner, in Campbell JA ed, *Implementations of Prolog*, Ellis Horwood

Doyle J (1983) What is rational psychology, toward a modern mental philosophy, *AI Magazine* **4**(3)50–3

Dreben B and Denton J (1966) A supplement to Herbrand, *J Symbolic Logic* **31**:393–98

Dreyfus HL (1972) *What Computers Can't Do: A Critique of Artificial Reason*, Harper and Row

Dreyfus HL and Dreyfus SE (1988) Making a mind versus modeling the brain, in Graubard SR ed, *The Artificial Intelligence Debate*, MIT Press

Drogoul A (1993a) When ants play chess (or can strategies emerge from tactical behaviors), in Castelfranchi C and Werner E eds, *From Reaction to Cognition*, 5th European Conf on Modeling Autonomous Agents in a Multi-Agent World (MAAMAW–93), Springer-Verlag *LNAI* **957**:13–27

Drogoul A (1993b) *De la simulation multi-agents à la résolution collective de problèmes. Une étude de l'émergence de structures d'organisation dans les systèmes multi-agents*, Thèse de Doctorat, Université P and M Curie, Paris (6)

Drogoul A and Ferber J (1992) Multi-agent simulation as a tool for modeling societies: application to social differentiation in ant colonies, in Castelfranchi C and Werner E eds, *Artificial Social Systems,* Fourth European Conf on Modeling Autonomous Agents in a Multi-Agent World (MAAMAW–92), Springer-Verlag *LNAI* **830**:3–23

Duda RO, Gasching JG and Hart PE (1979) Model design in the PROSPECTOR consultant system for mineral exploration, in Michie D ed, *Expert Systems in the Microelectronic Age*, Edinburgh UP, 153–67

Dung PM (1995) On the Acceptability of arguments and its fundamental role in nonmonotonic reasoning, logic programming and n-person games, *Artificial Intelligence* **77**:321–57

Durfee EH (1988) *Coordination of Distributed Problem Solvers*, Kluwer

Durfee EH and Lesser VR (1991) Partial global planning: a coordination framework for distributed hypothesis formation, *IEEE Trans Sys Man and Cyb* **21**(5)1167–83

Dyer M (1983) *In-Dpeth Understanding*, MIT Press

Eckert JP (1945) Disclosure of a magnetic calculating machine, unpublished typescript reprinted (1980) as The ENIAC in *A History of Computing in the Twentieth Century*, Academic Press

Egan GK (1980) *FLO, a Decentralised Dataflow System, Parts 1 and 2*, TR Dept Comp Sci, Univ Manchester

Elcock EW (1968) Descriptions, in Michie D ed, *Machine Intelligence* **3**, Edinburgh UP, 173–80

Elcock EW (1991) Absys, the first logic programming language: a view of the inevitability of logic programming, in Lassez J-L and Plotkin G eds, *Computational Logic: Essays in Honor of Alan Robinson*, MIT Press

Engelmore R and Morgan T eds (1988) *Blackboard Systems*, Addison-Wesley

Eriksson L-H and Rayner M (1984) Incorporating mutable arrays into logic programming, in Tärnlund S-Å ed, *Proc Second Int Logic Programming Conf*, Uppsala UP

Erman LD, Fennel R, Lesser VR and Reddy R (1976) System organization for speech understanding implications of network and multiprocessor computer architectures for AI, *IEEE Trans on Computers* **C25**:414–21

Erman LD, Hayes-Roth FA, Lesser VR and Reddy DR (1980) The Hearsay-II speech-understanding system: integrating knowledge to resolve uncertainty, *Computing Surveys* **12**:213–53

Ershov AP (1980) Mixed computation: potential applications and problems for study, in (Russian) *Mathematical Logic Methods in AI Problems and Systematic Programming, Part 1*, Vil'nyus, USSR, 26–55, in (English) *Theoretical Computer Science* **18**:41–67

Ershov AP (1982) On Futamura projections, *BIT (Japan)* **12**(14)4–5

Ershov AP (1988) Opening key-note speech, *New Generation Computing* **6**:9–86

Etzioni O (1993) Intelligence without robots (a reply to Brooks), *AI Magazine* **14**(4)7–13

Evans C (1989) *Negation as Failure as an Approach to the Hanks and McDermott Problem*, TR Imperial College, Dept Computing

Evans TG (1968) A program for the solution of a class of geometric-analogy intelligence-test questions, in Minsky ML ed, *Semantic Information Processing*, MIT Press, 271–353

Fahlman SE (1974) A planning system for robot construction tasks, *Artificial Intelligence* **5**(1)1–49

Fahlman SE (1979) *NETL: A System for Representing and Using Real-world Knowledge*, MIT Press

Fahlman S (1981) Computing facilities for AI: a survey of present and near-future options, *AI Magazine* (Winter)16–23

Feferman S (1962) Transfinite recursive progressions of axiomatic theories, *J Symbolic Logic* **27**(3)259–316

Feigenbaum EA (1977) *The Art of Artificial Intelligence: Themes and Case Studies of Knowledge Engineering*, TR **STAN–CS–77–621** Dept CS, Stanford U

Feigenbaum EA (1980) *Knowledge Engineering: the Applied Side of Artificial Intelligence*, TR **STAN–CS–80–812** Dept CS, Stanford U

Feigenbaum EA and McCorduck P (1984) *The Fifth Generation*, Addison-Wesley

Feldman JA (1966) A formal semantics for computer languages and its application in a compiler-compiler, *CACM* **9**(1)3–9

Fennel RD and Lesser VR (1977) Parallelism in artificial intelligence problem solving: a case study of Hearsay-II, *IEEE Trans on Comp* **C26**(2)98–111

Ferbrache D (1992) *A Pathology of Computer Viruses*, Springer-Verlag

Fikes RE, Hart PE and Nilsson NJ (1971) STRIPS: a new approach to the application of theorem proving to problem solving, *Artificial Intelligence* 3(4)251–88

Field AJ and Harrison PG (1988) *Functional Programming*, Addison-Wesley

Filman RE and Friedman DP (1984) *Coordinate Computing*, McGraw-Hill

Findler NV ed (1979) *Associative Networks*, Academic Press

Finger JJ (1987) *Exploiting Constraints in Design Synthesis*, PhD Thesis, Stanford U, CA

Finkel R and Fishburn J (1983) Parallelism in alpha-beta search, *Artificial Intelligence* **19**:89–106

Firby, RJ (1987) An investigation into reactive planning in complex domains, *AAAI* **87**:202–206

Fitting M (1987) *Computability Theory, Semantics and Logic Programming*, OUP

Flavell JH (1963) *The Developmental Psychology of Piaget*, Van Nostrand

Floyd RW (1967a) Nondeterminsitic algorithms, *JACM* **14**:636–44

Floyd RW (1967b) Assigning meanings to programs, *Proc American Math Soc Symp in Applied Maths* **19**:19–31

Floyd RW (1979) The paradigms of programming, 1978 Turing lecture award, *CACM* (August)455–60

Flynn MJ (1966) Very high speed computing systems, Proc IEEE **54**:1901–9

Forgy CL (1981) OPS5 *Reference Manual*, TR **CMU–CS–81–135** Carnegie Mellon U

Forgy CL (1982) A fast algorithm for the many pattern many object match problem, *Artificial Intelligence* **19**:17–37

Forgy C and McDermott J (1977) OPS, a domain-independent production system language, *IJCAI–77*, 933–39

Foster IT, Gregory S, Ringwood GA and Satoh K (1986) A sequential implementation of Parlog, *Third International Conference on Logic Programming*, Springer-Verlag *LNCS* **225**:149–156

Foster IT and Taylor S (1989) *Strand: a Practical Parallel Programming Language*, TR Math and Comp Science Div, Argonne National Labs

Foster IT and Taylor S (1990) *Strand: New Concepts in Parallel Programming*, Prentice-Hall

Foster JM (1968) Assertions: programs written without specifying unnecessary order, in Michie D ed, *Machine Intelligence* **3**, Edinburgh UP, 387–92

Foster JM and Elcock EW (1969) Absys1: An incremental compiler for assertions – an introduction, in Michie D ed, *Machine Intelligence* **4**, Edinburgh UP

Fox MS (1991) An organizational view of distributed systems, *IEEE Trans on Systems, Man and Cybernetics* **11**(1)70–80

Frank EH and Sproull RF (1981) Testing and debugging custom purpose VLSI chips, *ACM Computing Surveys* **13**:425–51

Frege G (1879) *Bergriffsschrift eine der Arithmetischen Nachgebildete Formelsprache des Reinen Denkens*, Halle, English tr van Heijenoort [1967]

Friedman DP and Wand M (1984) Reification: reflection without metaphysics, *Proc ACM Symp on Lisp and Functional Programming*, 348–355

Friedman D and Wise D (1976) CONS should not evaluate its arguments, in Michaelson D ed, *Automata, Languages and Programming*, Edinburgh UP, 256–284

Fuchi K and Furukawa K (1986) The role of logic programming in the Fifth Generation Computer Project, *Proc Third Int Conf on Logic Programming*, Springer-Verlag *LNCS* **526**:1–24

Furukawa K, Okumura A and Murukami M (1988) Unfolding rules for GHC programs, *New Generation Computing* **6**:211–25

Furukawa K and Ueda K (1985) GHC process fusion by program transformation, *Proc Second Annual Conf Japan Soc Software Science and Technology*, 89–92

Futamura Y (1971) Partial evaluation of computation process – an approach to a compiler-compiler, *Systems, Computers, Controls* **2**(5)45–50

Gabow HN, Galil Z and Spencer TH (1989) Efficient implementation of graph algorithms using contractions, *JACM* **36**(3)540–72

Galbraith J (1973) *Designing Complex Organizations*, Addison-Wesley

Gallagher J (1986) Transforming logic Programs by specialising interpreters, in du Boulay B, Hogg D and Steels L eds, *Advances in Artificial Intelligence II*, North-Holland, 313–326

Gallagher RG, Humblet PA and Spira PM (1983) A distributed algorithm for minimum weight spanning trees, *ACM TOPLAS* **5**(1)66–77

Gallaire H and Lassere C (1980) A control metalanguage for logic programming, *Proc Logic Programming Workshop*, Debrecen (Hungary), 73–79

Gallaire H and Lassere C (1982) Metalevel control for logic programs, in Clark KL and Tärnlund S-Å eds, *Logic Programming*, 173–185

Gane C and Sarson T (1979) *Structured Systems Analysis: Tools and Techniques*, Prentice-Hall

Gardner M (1970) John Horton Conway's "Life" game, *Scientific American* **223**

Gardner M (1982) *Logic Machines and Diagrams 2/e*, Chicago UP

Gasser L, Brazganza C and Herman N (1987) MACE: A flexible testbed for distributed AI research, in Huhns MN ed, *Distributed Artificial Intelligence*, Pitman–Morgan Kaufmann, 119–152

Gasser L (1991) Social conceptions of knowledge and action: DAI foundations and open systems semantics, *Artificial Intelligence* **47**:107–138

Gasser L (1992) Boundaries, aggregation and identity: Plurality issues for multi-agent systems, in Demazeau Y and Werner E eds, *Decentralized Artificial Intelligence 3*, Elsevier

Gasser L and Briot J-P (1992) Object based concurrent programming in DAI, in Avouris NA and Gasser L eds, *Distributed Artificial Intelligence: Theory and Praxis*, Kluwer, 81–107

Gelernter D (1985) Generative communication in Linda, *ACM Trans Prog Lang Sys* **7**(1)80–112

Gelernter D (1989) Multiple tuple spaces in Linda, in Odijk E, Rem M, Syre J-C eds, *Parallel Languages and Architectures Europe (PARLE–89)*, Springer-Verlag *LNCS* **366**:20–7

Gelernter D and Carriero N (1992) Coordination languages and their significance, *CACM* **35**(2)97–107

Gelerntner H (1963) Realization of a geometry theorem-proving machine, in Feigenbaum EA and Feldman J eds, *Computers and Thought*, McGraw-Hill, 134–52

Gelerntner H, Hansen JR and Gererrich CL (1960) A Fortran compiled list processing language, *JACM* **7**: 87–101

Genlebe E (1989) *Multiprocessor Performance*, Wiley

Gentzen G (1934) Untersuchungen uber das logische schliessen, *Mathematische Zeitschrift*, **39**:176–210,405–431

Gibbons A (1985) *Algorithmic Graph Theory*, Cambridge UP

Giloi WK (1983) Towards a taxonomy of computer architectures based on the machine data type view, *Proc 10th Symp on Computer Architecture*, IEEE, 6–15

Gingras A (1990) Dining Philosophers revisited, *ACM SIGCSE Bulletin* **22**(4)21–24

Gödel K (1931) Uber formal unentscheidbare satze der principia mathematica und verwandte systeme, *Monats Math Phys* **38**:137–198 [English tr Meltzer B, *Kurt Gödel (2 vols)*, Basic Books

Goldberg A and Robson D (1983) *Smalltalk–80, the Language and its Implementation*, Addison-Wesley

Goldberg A and Robson D (1989) *Smalltalk–80: The Language,* Addison-Wesley

Golomb SW and Baumbert LD (1965) Backtracking programming, *JACM* **12**:516–24

Gosling J and McGilton H (1995) *The Java Language Environment White Paper*, Sun Microsystems

Gray R, Kotz D, Nog S, Rus D and Cybenko G (1976) *Mobile Agents for Mobile Computing*, *TR* **PCS–TR96–285** Dept CS, Dartmouth College, http://www.cs.dartmouth.edu/reports/abstracts/TR96–285/

Green C (1969) Theorem proving by resolution as a basis for question-answering systems, *Machine Intelligence* **4**:183–205

Gregory G (1988) *Decision Analysis*, Pitman

Gregory S (1987) *Parallel Logic Programming in PARLOG,* Addison-Wesley

Griesmer JH and Jenks RD (1971) SCRATCHPAD/1 – an interactive facility for symbolic mathematics, in Petrick S ed, *Proc Second Symp on Symbolic and Algebraic Manipulation*, NY

Grit GH and Page RL (1981) Deleting irrelevant tasks in an expression-oriented multiprocessor system, *ACM Trans Prog Lang Sys* **3**(1)49–59

Gudeman D and Miller S (1992) *User Manual for jc, a Janus Compiler*, TR U Arizona

Halstead RH (1985) Multi-Lisp – a language for concurrent symbolic computation, *ACM Trans on Prog Lang Syst* **7**(4)501–38

Hanks S and McDermott DV (1986) Default reasoning, nonmonotonic logics and the frame problem, *Proc AAAI*, Morgan Kaufmann, 328–33

Hanks S and McDermott DV (1987) Nonmonotonic logics and temporal projection, *Artificial Intelligence* **33**:165–95

Hansson A, Haridi and Tärnlund S-Å (1980) Some aspects of a logic machine prototype, in Tärnlund S-Å ed, *Proc of Logic Programming Workshop*, Debrecen (Hungary)

Harel A and Pnueli A (1985) On the development of reactive systems, in Apt KR ed, *Logics and Models of Concurrent Systems*, Springer-Verlag

Haridi S (1990) A logic programming language based in the Andorra model, *New Generation Computing* **7**:109–25

Harris R (1986) *The Origin of Writing*, Harper and Row

Hart HLA (1961) *The Concept of Law,* Oxford UP

Hasegawa R and Mammiya M (1984) Parallel execution of logic programs based on the dataflow concept, *Proc Int Conf Fifth Generation computer Systems*, 507–516

Hatley DJ and Pirbhai IA (1987) *Strategies for Real-time Systems Specification*, Dorset House

Hayes JE and Levy DNL (1974) *The World Computer Chess Championship*, Edinburgh UP

Hayes PJ (1973) Computation and deduction, *Proc Symp Math Found Computer Science*, Czechoslovakian Academy of Sciences, 105–17

Hayes PJ (1977) In defense of logic, *Proc Fifth IJCAI*, Morgan Kaufmann, 559–65

Hayes PJ (1985) The naive physics manifesto, in Hobbs JR and Moore RC eds, *Formal Theories of the Commonsense World*, Norwood

Hayes-Roth F and Lesser VR (1977) FOCUS of attention in the Hearsay-II speech understanding system, *IJCAI-77*, 27–35

Hearn AC (1971) REDUCE-2 – a system and language for algebraic manipulation, in Petrick S ed, *Proc Second Symp on Symbolic and Algebraic Manipulation*, NY

Hebb DO (1949) *The Organization of Behavior*, Wiley

Hehner ECR (1984) *The Logic of Programming*, Prentice-Hall

Hehner HCR, Gupta LE and Malton AJ (1986) Predicative methodology, *Acta Informatica* 23:487–505

Hendler JA (1989) Marker-passing over microfeatures: towards a hybrid symbolic-connectionist model, *Cognitive Science* 13:79–106

Henkin L (1959) (1961) Some remarks on infinitely long formulas, *Infinitistic Methods*, Pergamon Press, 167–83

Henkin L (1961) Some remarks on infinitely long formulas, *Infinitistic Methods*, *Proc Symp on Foundations of Mathematics*, Warsaw 1959, Pergamon Press

Hennesy JL and Patterson DA (1990) *Computer Architecture A Quantitative Approach*, Morgan Kaufmann

Henz M (1997) Objects in Oz, PhD Thesis, U Saarlandes

Herbrand J (1930) *Recherches sur la theorie de la demonstration*, Thesis, U Paris, in Goldfarb GW ed (1971) *Logical Writings*, Reidel

Hewitt CE (1969) Planner: a language for manipulating models and proving theorems in robots, *Proc IJCAI-1*, 295–301

Hewitt C (1972) *Description and Theoretical Analysis (using schemata) of Planner: A Language for Proving Theorems and Manipulating Models in a Robot*, PhD Thesis MIT, also TR **AI-258** MIT

Hewitt CE (1977) Viewing control structures as patterns of passing messages *Artificial Intelligence* 8:323–364

Hewitt CE (1984) Design issues in parallel architectures for artificial intelligence, *Proc COMPCON S'83, IEEE* 418–23

Hewitt CE (1985) The challenge of open systems, *BYTE*(Apr)223–42

Hewitt CE (1986) Offices are open systems, *ACM Trans on Office Information Systems* 4(3)271–87

Hewitt CE and Agha G (1988) Guarded horn clause languages; are they deductive and logical? *Proc Int Conf Fifth Generation Computer Systems*, ICOT, 650–57

Hewitt CE, Bishop P and Steiger R (1973) *Proc Third IJCAI*, Stanford, 235–43

Hewitt CE and Inman J (1991) DAI betwixt and between: from intelligent agent to open system science, *IEEE Transactions on System, Machines and Cybernetics* 21(6)1409–19

Hewitt CE and Lieberman H (1984) Design issues in parallel architectures for artificial intelligence, *Proc 28th IEEE Computer Society Int Conf*, SF, 418–23

Hewitt CE and Kornfeld WA (1980) Message passing semantics, *SIGART Newsletter*, **48**

Hewitt CE and Liebermann (1984) Design issues in parallel architectures for artificial intelligence, *Proc COMPCON S'84*, 418–23

Hill R (1974) *LUSH-Resolution and its Completeness*, TR **78** Dept Artificial Intelligence, U Edinburgh

Hill PM and Lloyd JW (1988) Analysis of metaprograms, *Metaprogramming in Logic Programming META–88*, MIT Press, 23–51

Hill PM and Lloyd JW (1994) *The Gödel Programming Language,* MIT Press

Hillis DW (1988) Intelligence as emergent behavior; or The Songs of Eden, in Graubard SR ed, *The Artificial Intelligence Debate*, MIT

Hintikka J (1973) Logic, *Language-Games and Information: Kantian Themes in the Philosophy of Logic*, Clarendon Press

Hoare CAR (1969) An axiomatic basis for computer programming, *CACM* **12**:576–83

Hoare CAR (1974) Monitors: an operating system structuring concept, *CACM* **17**:549–57

Hoare CAR (1978) Communicating sequential processes, *CACM* **21**:666–77

Hoare CAR (1981) The Emperor's Old Clothes, *CACM* **24**(2)75–83

Hoare CAR (1982) *Specifications, Programs and Implementations*, TR **PRG–29** Oxford U

Hoare CAR (1985) *Communicating Sequential Processes,* Prentice-Hall

Hoare CAR (1988) *Essays in Computing Science*, Prentice-Hall

Hodges W (1992) Horn clauses 1992, in Broda K ed, *Fourth UK Conference on Logic Programming, London*, Springer-Verlag,

Hodges W (1993) *Model Theory*, Cambridge UP

Hodges W (1994) *Games in Model Theory*, TR Dept Mathematics, Queen Mary and Westfield College

Hodges W (1997) *A Shorter Model Theory*, Cambridge UP

Hofstadter DR (1979) *Gödel, Escher and Bach: an Eternal Golden Braid*, Harvester Press

Holland J (1975) *Adaptation in Natural and Artificial Systems*, Michigan UP

Holland O (1996) Multi-agent systems: lessons from social insects and collective robotics, *Adaption, Coevolution and Learning in Multi-agent Systems: Papers from the 1996 AAAI Spring Symposium* (Menlo Park, CA), 57–62

Holyer I (1991) *Functional Programming with Miranda*, Pitman

Holst CK and Gomard CK (1991) Partial evaluation is fuller laziness, *ACM Symp on Partial Evaluation and Semantics-based Program Manipulation (PEPM'91), SIGPLAN Notices* **26**(9)223–33

Holt RC (1983) *Concurrent Euclid, The Unix System, and Tunis*, Addison-Wesley

Hopfield JJ (1982) Neural networks and physical systems with emergent computational abilities, *Proc National Academy of Sciences USA*, **79**:2554–8

Hord RM (1982) ILLIAC IV: *The First Supercomputer*, Computer Science Press

Horn A (1951) On sentences which are true of direct unions of algebras, *J Symbolic Logic* **16**:14–21

Horvitz EJ, Breese JS and Henrion M (1988) Decision theory in expert systems and artificial intelligence, *Int J Approximate Reasoning*, **2**:247–302

Hsu F-H, Anantharaman T, Campbell M and Nowatzyk A (1990) A grandmaster chess machine, *Scientific American* **263**(4)44–50

Hughes RJM (1982) Super-combinators: a new implementation technique for applicative languages, *Proc ACM Conf on Lisp and Functional Programming*

Huhns MN ed (1987) *Distributed Artificial Intelligence*, Pitman

Huntbach MM (1983) A single-message distributed algorithm for minimal spanning trees, in Lavallée I and Paker Y eds, *OPOPAC Actes des Journées Internationales sur les Problèmes Fondamentaux de l'Informatique Parallèle et Distribuée*, Hermès, Paris

Huntbach MM (1987) Algorithmic Parlog debugging, *Fourth Symposium on Logic Programming (San Francisco)*, IEEE, 288–297

Huntbach MM (1988) *Parlog as a Language for Artificial Intelligence*, TR Parlog Group, Dept Computing, Imperial College

Huntbach MM (1989a) Meta-interpreters and partial evaluation in Parlog, *Formal Aspects of Computing* 1:193–211

Huntbach MM (1989b) Implementing a graph-coloring algorithm in Parlog, *SIGPLAN Notices* 24:80–85

Huntbach MM (1990) *Interactive Program Synthesis and Debugging*, DPhil Thesis, U Sussex

Huntbach MM (1991a) Speculative computation and priorities in concurrent logic languages, in Wiggins GA, Mellish C and Duncan T eds, *Third UK Annual Conference on Logic Programming*, Springer-Verlag, 23–35

Huntbach MM (1991b) Automated translation of Occam to a concurrent logic language, in Clements TP and Lau K-K eds, *Logic Program Synthesis and Transformation LOPSTR–91*, Springer-Verlag, 254–75

Huntbach MM (1991c) *A Single-Message Distributed Algorithm for Minimal Spanning Trees*, TR Queen Mary and Westfield College, Dept CS

Huntbach MM (1995) The concurrent object-oriented language Briad, *ACM Symp on Applied Computing*, Nashville, 140–46

Huntbach MM and Burton FW (1988) Alpha-beta search on virtual tree machines, *Information Sciences* 44:3–17

Huntbach MM and Ringwood GA (1995) Programming in concurrent logic languages, *IEEE Software* 12(6)71–82

Hutchins WJ (1986) *Machine Translation: Past, Present and Future*, Ellis Horwood

Huffman DA (1971) Impossible objects as nonsense sentences, *Machine Intelligence* 6:295–323

Ichbiah JD, Barnes JGP, Heliard JC, Krieg-Brueckner B, Roubine O and Wichman BA (1979) Rationale for the design of the Ada programming language, *ACM SIGPLAN Notices* 14(6B)

Ingalls D (1978) The Smalltalk–76 programming system: design and implementation, *Fifth Ann ACM Symp POPL*, ACM

Ingerman PZ (1967) Panini–Backus form suggested, *CACM* 10(3):137

INMOS Ltd (1988) *Transputer Reference Manual*, Prentice-Hall

Ito N, Mausda K and Shimizu H (1983) *Parallel Prolog Machine Based on the Dataflow Model*, TR 035 ICOT, Tokyo

Ito N, Mausda K and Shimizu H (1985) Dataflow based execution mechanisms of parallel and concurrent Prolog, *New Generation Computing* 3:15–41

Jackson P (1986) *Introduction to Expert Systems*, Addison-Wesley

Jaffar J and Lassez J-L (1987) Constraint logic programming, *Proc SIGACT–SIGPLAN Symp on Princ Prog Langs*, ACM, 111–19

Jaffar JJ and Maher MJ (1994) Constraint logic programming: a survey, *J Logic Programming* 19–29:503–81

Janson S (1994) *AKL–A Multiparadigm Programming Language*, PhD Thesis, Swedish Institute of Computer Science

Jennings NR (1995) Controlling cooperative problem solving in an industrial multi-agent system using joint intentions, *Artificial Intelligence* 75:195–240

Jennings NR, Sycara K and Wooldrige M (1998) A roadmap of agent research and development, *Autonomous Agents and Multi-Agent Systems* **1**:7-38

Jevons WS (1870) On the mechanical performance of logical inference, *Philos Trans* **160**:497–518

Jevons WS (1879) *Principles of Science 2/e*, Macmillan

Jones ND, Gomard CK and Sestoft P (1993) *Partial Evaluation and Automatic Programming*, Prentice-Hall

Jones ND, Sestoft P and Søndergaard H (1985) An experiment in partial evaluation: the generation of a compiler-compiler, *Conf on Rewriting Techniques and Applications*, Springer-Verlag *LNCS* **202**:124–40

Kafura DG and Lee KH (1989) Inheritance in Actor based concurrent object-oriented languages, *Proc ECOOP'89*, Cambridge UP, 131–45

Kahn G (1974) The semantics of a simple language for parallel programming, *Information Threading: Proc IFIP Congress* **74**:471–475

Kahn G and MacQueen DB (1977) Coroutines and networks of parallel threads, *Information Threading* **77**:993–997

Kahn K (1989) Objects – a fresh look, in Cook S, ed, *Proc ECOOP* **89**, Cambridge UP

Kahn KM and Miller MS (1988) Language design and open systems, in Huberman BA ed, *The Ecology of Computation*, North-Holland, 291–313

Kahn KM, Tribble ED, Miller MS and Bobrow DG (1986) Vulcan: logical concurrent objects, *OOPSLA–86, SIGPLAN Notices* **21**(11) reprinted in Shapiro E ed (1987) *Concurrent Prolog Volume 2*, MIT Press, 274–303

Kant I (1787) *Critique of Pure Reason 2/e,* (reprinted 1963) Macmillan

Karp RM and Miller RE (1966) Properties of a model for parallel computation: Determinacy, termination and queuing, *SIAM J Applied Mathematics* **14**(6)1390–1411

Kautz H (1986) The logic of persistence, *AAAI–86*:401–5

Kavanagh TF (1960) TABSOL – A fundamental concept for systems-oriented languages, *Proc East Joint Comput Conf* **18**, Spartan Books, 117–136

Kay A (1972) A personal computer for children of all ages, *Proc ACM Nat Conf*, Boston

Kay A (1973) *Smalltalk Notebook*, Xerox Palo Alto Research Center

Kay A (1984) Computer software, *Scientific American* **251**(3)53–59

Kay A (1993) The early history of Smalltalk, *ACM SIGPLAN Notices* **28**:69–200

Kearney PJ (1992) Experiments in multi-agent system dynamics, in Castelfranchi C and Werner E eds, *Artificial Social Systems*, Fourth European Conf on Modeling Autonomous Agents in a Multi-Agent World (MAAMAW–92), Springer-Verlag *LNAI* **830**:24–40

Keller RM (1977) Denotational models for parallel programs with indeterministic operators, in Neuhold EJ ed, *Formal Description of Programming Concepts*, North-Holland, 337–366

Kemp RS and Ringwood GA (1990) Algebraic framework for abstract interpretation of definite programs, in Debray S and Hermenegildo M eds, *Logic Programming, Proc 1990 North American*, MIT Press, 516–30

Kiczales G, Rivieres J des and Bobrow DG (1991) *The Art of the Meta-object Protocol*, MIT Press

Kilmer WL McCulloch WS and Blum J (1969) A model of the vertebrate central command system, *Int J Man Machine Studies* **1**, 279–309

Kirkpatrick S, Gelatt CD and Vecchi MP (1983) Optimization by simulated annealing, *Science* **220**:671–680

Kirsh D (1991) Today the earwig, tomorrow man? *Artificial Intelligence* **47**:161–84

Kleene SC (1936) Lambda-definability and recursiveness, *Duke Mathematical J* **2**:340–53

Kleene SC (1952) *Introduction to Metamathematics*, van Nostrand

Knabe F (1996) An overview of mobile agent programming, in Dam M ed, *Analysis and Verification of Multiple-Agent Languages (5th LOMAPS Workshop)*, Springer-Verlag *LNCS* **1192**:100–16

Knuth (1969) *The Art of Computer Programming vol 1: Fundamental Algorithms*, Addison-Wesley

Knuth DE (1974) Structured programming with goto statements, *Computing Surveys* **6**(4)261–301

Knuth D and Moore R (1975) An analysis of alpha-beta pruning, *Artificial Intelligence* **6**:293–326

Kolodner J (1983) Reconstuctive memory: a computer model, *Cognitive Science* **7**:281–328

Kolmogorov AN and Yushkevich AP eds (1992) *Mathematics of the 19h Century*, Birkhauser

Komorowski HJ (1981) *A Specification of an Abstract Prolog Machine and its Application to Partial Evaluation*, TR **LSST 69**, Linkoping U, Sweden

Korf KF (1990) Real time heuristic search, *Artificial Intelligence* **42**:189–211

Kornfeld WA (1979) *Using Parallel Processing for Problem Solving*, TR **561**, MIT Artificial Intelligence Lab

Kornfeld WA (1982) Combinatorially implosive algorithms, *CACM* **22**(10)734–38

Kornfeld WA and Hewitt CE (1980) The scientific community metaphor, *IEEE Trans Syst, Man and Cyb* **11**(1)24–33

Kosinski PR (1978) A straight forward denotational semantics for nodeterministic data flow programs, *Proc Symp on Principles Programming Languages*, ACM, 214–21

Kowalski RA (1974) Predicate logic as a computational formalism, *Proc IFIP*, North-Holland, 569–74

Kowalski RA (1979a) Algorithm = logic + control, *CACM* **22**(7)424–36

Kowalski RA (1979b) *Logic for Problem Solving*, Elsevier

Kowalski RA (1984a) The relation between logic programming and logic specification, *Phil Trans R Soc Lond* **A312**, 345–61

Kowalski RA (1988) The early history of Logic Programming, *CACM* **31**, 38–43

Kowalski RA (1989) SNL is not SLD, *Logic Programming Newsletter*, **2**(1)

Kowalski RA (1995) *Using Meta-logic to Reconcile Reactive with Rational Agents*, TR Imperial College, U London

Kowalski RA and Kuehner D (1971) Linear resolution with selection function, *Artificial Intelligence* **2**:227–60

Kowalski RA and van Emden M (1976) The semantics of predicate logic as a programming language, *JACM* **22**:733–42

Kozato F (1988) *Modeling Neural Networks Parlog*, MSc Thesis, Imperial College, London, UK

Kozato F and Ringwood GA (1990) Virtual neural networks, *Proc Logic Programming Conference '90 (Tokyo)*, ICOT, 199–208

Kozato F and Ringwood GA (1992) How slow processes can think fast in concurrent logic, in Soucek B, ed, *Fast Learning and Invariant Object Recognition: the Sixth–Generation Breakthrough*, Wiley, 47–60

Kraus S (1993) Agents contracting tasks in non-collaborative environments, *AAAI–93*:243–48

Kruskal JB (1956) On the shortest spanning subtree of a graph and the travelling salesman problem, *Proc Am Math Soc* **7**:48–50

Kuehner D (1972) Some special purpose resolution systems, *Machine Intelligence* **7**, Edinburgh UP, 117–28

Kuehner D and Kowalski RA (1971) Linear resolution with selection function, *Artificial Intelligence* **2**:227–60

Kuhn TS (1962) *Structure of Scientific Revolution*, Chicago UP

Kumar V and Kanal LN (1983) A general branch-and-bound formulation for understanding and synthesizing and/or search procedures, *Artificial Intelligence* **21**:179–98

Kung HT (1982) Why Systolic Architectures? *IEEE Computer* **15**:37–46

Lai T-H and Sahni S (1984) Anomalies in parallel branch-and-bound algorithms, *CACM* **27**(6)594–602

Lakhotia A and Sterling L (1988) Composing recursive logic programs with clausal join, *New Generation Computing* **6**:211–25

Lakoff G (1987) *Women, Fire and Dangerous Things*, Chicago UP

Lalement R (1993) *Computation as Logic*, Prentice-Hall

Lamport L, Shostak R and Pease M (1982) The Byzantine generals problem, *ACM Transactions on Programming Languages and Systems* **4**(3)382–401

Lampson BW (1983) Hints for computer systems design, *ACM Operating System Review*, **17**(5)33–48

Landin PJ (1963) The mechanical evaluation of expressions, *Computer J* **6**(4)308–20

Landin PJ (1965) A correspondence between Algol 60 and Church's Lambda calculus, *CACM* **8**:89–101;158–65

Landin PJ (1966) The next 700 programming languages, *CACM* **9**: 157–66

Langton C ed (1989) *Artificial Life: Proceedings of an Interdisciplinary Workshop on the Synthesis and Simulation of Living Systems*, SFI Studies in Sciences of Complexity, Reading MA, Addison-Wesley

Lavallée I and Roucairol G (1986) A fully distributed (minimal) spanning tree algorithm, *Information Processing Letters* **23**:55–62

Lawler E and Wood D (1966) Branch-and-bound methods: a survey, *Oper Res* **14**:699–719

Leibniz GW (1765) *New essays on the human understanding*, in Remnant P and Burnett G (translators and editors, 1981), Cambridge UP

Laird JE, Newell A and Rosenbloom PS (1987) SOAR: an architecture for general intelligence, *Artificial Intelligence* **33**(1)1–64

Lenat DB (1995) CYC: a large scale investment in knowledge infrastructure, *CACM* **38**(11)32–38

Lenat DB and Guha RV (1990) *Building Large Knowledgebased Systems*, Addison-Wesley

Lescaudron L, Briot JP and Bouabsa, (1991) Prototyping programming environments for object-oriented concurrent languages: a Smalltalk base experience, *Proc Fifth Conf on Technology of Object-Oriented Languages and Systems* (Tools, Usa'91), Prentice-Hall, 449–62

Lesser VR (1990) An overview of DAI: viewing distributed AI as distributed search, *J Japanese Society for Artificial Intelligence* **5**(4)

Lesser VR and Corkill DD (1983) The Distributed Vehicle Monitoring Testbed: a tool for investigating distributed problem solving, *AI Magazine* **4**(3)15–33

Lesser VR and Erman LD (1980) Distributed interpretation: a model and experiment, *IEEE Trans Comp* **C–29**(12)1144–63

Levy DNL (1976) *Chess and Computers*, Computer Science Press

Levy D and Newborn M (1991) *How Computers Play Chess*, Computer Science Press

Levesque HJ and Brachmann RJ (1987) Expressiveness, tractability in knowledge representation, and reasoning, *Computational Intelligence* **3**(2)78–93

Lie G-J and Wah BW (1984) How to cope with anomalies in parallel approximate branch-and-bound search, *AAAI-84*:212–15

Lieberman H (1986) Using prototypical objects to implement shared behavior in object-oriented systems, *OOPSLA-86, SIGPLAN Notices* **21**(11)214–23

Lieberman (1987) Concurrent object-oriented programming in Act 1, in Yonezawa A and Tokoro M eds, *Object-Oriented Concurrent Programming* MIT Press, 9–36

Lighthill J (1973) Artificial intelligence: a general survey, *Artificial Intelligence: A Paper Symposium*, UK Science Research Council

Lindsay R, Buchanen B, Feigenbaum EA and Lederberg J (1980) *Applications of Artificial Intelligence for Organic Chemistry: The Dendral Project*, McGraw-Hill

Linney J (1991) *Review of Reactive Planning Literature*, TR Queen Mary and Westfield College, U of London

Linney J and Ringwood GA (1991) *Life Yet in Concurrent Logic*, TR Queen Mary and Westfield College, U London

Liskov B, Herlihy M and Gilbert L (1986) Limitations of remote procedure call and static process structure for distributed computing, *Proc 13th ACM Symp on Princ Prog Langs*, 150–9

Liskov B, Snyder A and Atkinson R (1977) Abstraction mechanisms in {CLU}, *CACM* **20**(8)564–76

Liskov B and Zilles S (1975) Specification techniques for data abstraction, *IEEE Transactions on Software Engineering*, **SE–1**(1)7–19

Lloyd JW (1984) *Foundations of Logic Programming*, Springer-Verlag

Lloyd JW and Shepherdson JC (1991) Partial evaluation in logic programming, *J Logic Programming* **11**:217–42

Lombardi LA (1967) Incremental computation, in Alt FL and Rubinoff M eds, *Advances in Computers* **8**:247–333

Longuet-Higgins HC et al. (1972) *The Nature of Mind*, Edinburgh UP

Loveland DW (1968) Mechanical theorem proving by model elimination, *JACM* **15**(2)236–51

Loveland DW (1984) Automated theorem-proving: a quarter-century review, in Bledsoe WW and Loveland DW eds, *Automated Theorem Proving: After 25 Years*, Contemporary Mathematics **29**, Am Math Soc, 1–45

Luger GF (1995) *Computation and Intelligence: Collected Reasoning*, AAAI/MIT Press

Lusk E, Warren DHD, Haridi et al. (1990) The Aurora or-parallel system, *New Generation Computing* **7**:243–271

Mackworth AK (1977) Consistency in networks of relations, *Artificial Intelligence* **8**:99–118

Maekawa M, Oldehoeft AE and Oldehoeft RR (1987) *Operating Systems: Advanced Concepts*, Benjamin-Cummings

Maes P (1986) Introspection in knowledge representation, *European Conference on AI 1986*:256–69

Maes P (1987) Concepts and experiments in computational reflection, *OOPSLA-87*:147–55

Maes P (1988) Computational reflection, *Knowledge Engineering Review* **3**(1)1–19

Maes P (1994) Agents that reduce work and information overload, *CACM* **37**(7)31–40

Malec J (1994) A unified approach to intelligent agency, in Wooldridge MJ and Jennings NR eds, *ECAI–94 Workshop on Agent Theories, Architectures and Languages*, Springer-Verlag *LNCS* **890**:233–244

Malcev AI (1958) Certain classes of models, in Malcev AI (1971) *The Metamathematics of Algebraic Systems, Collected Papers 1936–1967*, North-Holland

Maher MJ (1987) Logic semantics for a class of committed-choice programs, in *Proc Fourth Int Conf on Logic Programming*, MIT Press

Malone TW, Fikes RE, Grant KR and Howard MT (1988) Enterprise; a market-like task scheduler for distributed computing environments, in Huberman BA ed, *The Ecology of Computation*, North-Holland

Man T-L (1993) Real-time concurrent logic programming, PhD Thesis, Imperial College

March L (1976) *The Architecture of Form*, Cambridge UP

Markov AA (1951) The Theory of Algorithms, *Trudy Mathematicheskogo Instituta Immeni V A Steklova* **38**:176–89

Markov AA (1954) *A Theory of Algorithms*, USSR National Academy of Sciences

Martens B and de Schreye D (1995) Why untyped nonground metaprogramming is not (much of) a problem, *J Logic Programming* **21**:47–99

Marsland TA and Campbell M (1982) Parallel search of strongly ordered game trees, *Computing Surveys* **14**(4)533–51

Martelli A and Montonari U (1982) An efficient unification algorithm, *ACM Transactions on Programming Languages and Systems* **4**(2)258–282

Maslov SY (1987) *Theory of Deductive Systems and Its Applications*, MIT Press

Mates B (1953) *Stoic Logic*, California UP

Matsuoka S and Yonezawa A (1993) Analysis of inheritance anomaly in object oriented concurrent programming languages, in Agha G, Wegner P and Yonezawa A eds, *Research Directions in Concurrent Object-Oriented Programming*, MIT Press

Mazurkiewicz AW (1971) Proving algorithms by tail functions, *Information and Control* **18**:220–226

McBrien P et al. [1991] A rule language to capture and model business policy specifications, *Proc Third Nordic Conference on Advanced Information Systems Engineering*, Springer-Verlag *LNCS* **498**

McBurney DL and Sleep MR (1987) Transputer-based experiments with the ZAPP architecture, *Parallel Architectures and Languages Europe '87 (PARLE 87)*, Springer-Verlag *LNCS* **258**:242–59

McCarthy J (1958) Programs with common sense, *Proc Symp On the Mechanization of Thought Processes*, National Physics Lab, Teddington, UK

McCarthy, JM (1960) Recursive functions of symbolic expressions and their computation by machine, *CACM* **3**(4)184–95

McCarthy J (1965) Problems in the theory of computation, *Proc IFIP Congress* **65**(I)219–22

McCarthy JM (1977) Epistemological problems of Artificial Intelligence, *IJCAI* **5**:1038–44

McCarthy JM (1978) History of Lisp, *SIGPLAN Notices* **13**:217–23

McCarthy JM (1988) Mathematical Logic and Artificial Intelligence, in Graubard SR ed, *The Artificial Intelligence Debate*, MIT Press

McCarthy JM (1980) Circumscription – a form of nonmonotonic reasoning, *Artificial Intelligence* **26**(3)89–116

McCulloch WS and Pitts W (1943) A logical calculus of the ideas immanent in nervous activity, *Bull Math Biophysics* **5**:115–33

McCarthy J and Hayes PJ (1969) Some philosophical problems from the standpoint of artificial intelligence, in Meltzer B and Michie D eds, *Machine Intelligence* **4**, Edinburgh UP

McCorduck P (1991) *Aaron's Code: Meta-art, Artificial Intelligence and the Work of Harold Cohen*, WH Freeman

McCulloch WS, Arbib MA and Cowan JD (1962) Neurological models and integrative processes, in Yovits MC, Jacobi GT and Goodstein eds, *Self-Organizing Systems,* Spartan Books, 49–59

McDermott D (1976) Artificial intelligence meets natural stupidity, *SIGART Newsletter* **57**

McDermott D (1980) The PROLOG phenomenon, *SIGART Newsletter* **7**:16–20

McDermott D (1988) A critique of pure reason, J *Computational Intelligence* 3(30)151–237

McDermott J (1981) R1's formative years, *AI Magazine* **2**:2

McDermott J (1982) R1: a rule based configurer of computer systems, *Artificial Intelligence* **19**

McDermott J (1984) R1 revisited: Four years in the trenches, *AI Magazine,* Fall:21–32

McDermott DV (1987) Tarskian semantics, or no notation without denotation! *Cognitive Science* 2(3)277–282

McGraw JR, Skedzielewski SK, Allan S, Oldehoeft R, Glauert J, Kirkham C, Noyce W and Thomas, R (1985) SISAL: *Streams and Iteration in a Single Assignment Language,* TR **M–146** Lawrence Livermore National Laboratory

McKinsey JJ (1943) The decision problem for some classes of sentences without quantifiers, *J Symbolic Logic* **8**:61–76

Mead CA and Mahowald MA (1988) A silicon model of early visual processing, neural networks **1**:91–7

Mead GH (1934) *Mind, Self and Society,* Chicago UP

Metropolis N and Worlton J (1980) A trilogy of errors in the history of computing, *Annals Hist Comp* 2(1)49–59

Metropolis N, Howlett J and Rota G-C eds (1990) *A History of Computing in the 20th Century,* Academic Press

Metzner JR and Barnes BH (1977) *Decision Table Languages and Systems,* ACM Monograph Series, Academic Press

Mierkowsky C, Taylor S, Shapiro E, Levy J and Safra S (1985) *The Design and Implementation of Flat Concurrent Prolog,* TR **CS85–09,** Weizmann Inst

Miller MS and Drexler KE (1988) Markets and computations: agoric open systems, in Huberman BA ed, *The Ecology of Computation,* Elsevier, 133–76

Milne R and Strachey C (1976) *A Theory of Programming Language Semantics,* 2 vols, Chapman Hall

Milner AJRG (1980) *A Calculus of Communicating Agents,* Springer-Verlag *LNCS* **92**

Milner AJRG, Parrow J and Walker D (1989) *A Calculus of Mobile Processes,* TR **ECS–LFCS–89–85 and 86,** LFCS, U Edinburgh

Milner AJRG, Tofte M and Harper R (1990) *The Definition of Standard ML,* MIT Press

Miller GA (1956) The magical number seven, plus or minus two, *The Psychological Review* 63(2)81–97

Minsky M L(1956) Notes on the geometry problem I and II, *Artificial Intelligence Project,* Dartmouth College

Minsky ML (1967) *Computation: Finite and Infinite Machines,* Prentice-Hall

Minsky M (1975) A framework for representing knowledge, in Winston PH ed, *The Psychology of Computer Vision,* McGraw-Hill 211–17

Minsky M (1986) *The Society of Mind,* Simon and Schuster

Minsky M and Papert S (1969 revised 1987) *Perceptrons: An introduction to computational geometry,* MIT Press

Minsky NH and Leichter J (1994) Law-governed Linda as a coordination model, in Ciancarini P, Nierstrasz O and Yonezawa A eds, *Object-Based Models and Languages for Concurrent Systems,* Springer-Verlag *LNCS* **924**:125–46

Minton S, Johnston MD, Philips AB and Laird P (1990) Solving large-scale constraints satisfaction and scheduling problems using a heuristic repair method, *AAAI–90*:17–24

Mitchell WJ (1990) *The Logic of Architecture*, MIT Press

Montalbano M (1962) Tables, flow charts and program logic, *IBM Syst J* 1:51–63

Moon D (1986) Object-oriented programming with Flavors, *Proc ACM Conf Object-Oriented Systems, Languages and Applications*

Moon DA (1987) Symbolics architecture, *IEEE Computer* (January)43–52

Moore GE (1903) *Principia Ethica*, Cambridge UP

Moravec HP (1981) *Robot Rover Visual Navigation*, UMI Research, Ann Arbor, MI

Morin M, Nadjm-Tehrani S, Österling P and Sandewall E (1992) Real-time hierarchical control, *IEEE Software* 9(5)51–7

Morris PH (1980) A dataflow interpreter for logic programs, *Logic Programming Workshop*, Debrecen (Hungary), 148–59

Morrison P and Morrison E eds (1961) *Charles Babbage on the Principles and Development of the Calculator: and Other Seminal Writings*, Dover

Mortimer H (1988) *The Logic of Induction*, Ellis Horwood

Moses (1967) *Symbolic Integration*, TR **MIT–LCS//MIT/LCS/TR–47** MIT

Mostow J (1985) Models of the design process, *AI Magazine* (Spring):44–57

Moto–oka T (1982) Challenge for knowledge information processing systems, *Proc Int Conf on Fifth Generation Computer Systems*, North-Holland

Müller JP (1996) *The Design of Intelligent Agents*, Springer-Verlag *LNCS* **1177**

Myers C and Aleksander I (1988) *Learning Algorithms for Probabilistic Neural Nets*, TR Imperial College, Dept Computing

Naish L (1985) *Negation and Control in Prolog*, PhD thesis, U Melbourne, Australia

Naur P (1960) Report on the algorithmic language ALGOL 60, *CACM* **3**:299–314

Naur P (1966) Proof algorithms by general snapshots, *BIT* **6**:310–16

Neisser U (1967) *Cognitive Psychology*, Appleton-Century-Crofts

Nelson G and Oppen D (1980) Fast Decision Procedures Based on Congruence Closure, *JACM* **27**(2) 356–64

Newell A (1962) Some problems of basic organization in problem solving programs, in Yovits MC, Jacobi GT and Goldstein GD eds, *Conference on Self-Organizing Systems*, Spartan Books, 393–423

Newell A (1981) *Duncker on thinking: An enquiry into progress in cognition*, TR **CMU–CS–80–151,** Carnegie Mellon U

Newell A (1983) Intellectual issues in the history of artificial intelligence, in Machlup F and Mansfield U eds, *The Study of Information: Interdisciplinary Messages*, Wiley

Newell A (1990) *Unified Theories of Cognition*, Harvard UP

Newell A and Ernst G (1965) The search for generality, *Information Processing* 1:17–24

Newell A, Shaw JC and Simon HA (1956) The Logic Theory Machine: a complex information processing system, *IRE Trans on Information Theory* 2:61–79

Newell A and Simon HA (1963) GPS A program that simulates human thought, in Feigenbaum EA and Feldman E eds, *Computers and Human Thought*, McGraw-Hill, 279–93

Newell A and Simon HA (1972) *Human Problem Solving*, Prentice-Hall

Newell A and Simon HA (1976) Computer science as empirical inquiry: symbols and search, *CACM* **19**(3)113–26

Newman JD (1990) *Logic Programming: Prolog and Stream Parallel Languages*, Prentice-Hall

Nierstrasz O and Meijler TD (1994) Requirements for a composition language, in Ciancarini P, Nierstrasz O and Yonezawa A eds, *Object-Based Models and Languages for Concurrent Systems*, Springer-Verlag *LNCS* **924**:147–61

Nilsson NJ (1971) *Problem Solving Methods in Artificial Intelligence*, McGraw-Hill

Nilsson NJ ed (1984) *Shakey the Robot*, TR **323** SRI

Nilsson NJ (1998) *Artificial Intelligence: A New Synthesis*, Morgan Kaufmann

Nishiyama H, Ohwada H and Mizoguchi F (1998) Multi-agent robot language for communication and concurrency control, *in Third Int Conf Multi-agent Systems, IEEE Computer Society*, 372–9

Norvig P (1992) *Paradigms of Artificial Intelligence Programming: Case Studies in Common Lisp*, Morgan Kaufmann

Ogden CK and Richards IA (1932) *The Meaning of Meaning*, Kegan Paul

Ohki M Takeuchi A and Furukawa K (1987) An object-oriented programming language based on parallel logic programming, in Lassez J-L ed, Proc Fourth Int Conf on Logic Programming, Melbourne, MIT Press, 894–909

Oikkonen J (1965) How to obtain interpolation for Lk+k, in Drake FR and Truss eds, *Logic Colloquium '86*, Elsevier, 175–208

O'Keefe, R (1990) *The Craft of Prolog*, MIT Press

Okhotsimski DE, Gurfinkel VS, Devyanin EA and Platonov AK (1979) Integrated walking robot, in Hayes JE, Michie D and Mikulich LI eds, *Machine Intelligence* **9**, Ellis Horwood, 313–29

Okumura A and Matsumoto Y (1987) Parallel Programming with layered streams, *IEEE Symp on Logic Programming*, San Francisco, 224–33

Owen S (1988) Issues in the partial evaluation of meta-interpreters, *Metaprogramming in Logic Programming META–88*, MIT Press, 319–39

Palfreman J and Doron S (1991) *The Dream Machine*, BBC Books

Papathomas M (1989) Concurrency issues in object-oriented programming languages, in Tsichritzis ed, *Object-Oriented Development*, Geneva UP, 207–245

Papert S (1988) One AI or many, in Graubard SR ed, *The Artificial Intelligence Debate*, MIT Press

Park D (1980) On the semantics of fair parallelism, in Bjorner D ed, Springer-Verlag *LNCS* **86**:504–26

Parker DS (1990) Stream data analysis in Prolog, in Sterling LS ed, *The Practice of Prolog*, MIT Press, 249–301

Parnas DL (1972a) A technique for software module specification with examples, *CACM* **15**(5)330–36

Parnas DL (1972b) On the criteria to be used in decomposing systems into modules, *CACM* **5**:1053–58

Parnas DL, Clements PC and Weiss DM (1985) The modular structure of complex systems, *IEEE Transactions on Software Engineering*, SE–**11**:259–66

Partsch H and Steinbrüggen R (1983) Program transformation systems, *ACM Computer Surveys* **15**(33)199–236

Patterson DA and Dietzel D (1980) The case for reduced instruction set computers, *Computer Architecture News (SIGARCH)* **8**:25–33

Peano (1889) Arithmetices Principia, Novo Methodo Exposita, Frates Boca, English tr van Heijenoort [1967])

Pearl J (1984) *Heuristics: Intelligent Search Strategies for Computer Problem Solving*, Addison-Wesley

Pereira LM, Pereira F and Warren D (1979) *User's Guide to DEC System–10 Prolog*, Occasional Paper 15, Dept Artificial Intelligence, Edinburgh U

Pereira FCN and Warren DHD (1980) Definite clause grammars for language analysis: a survey of the formalism and a comparison with augmented transitions networks, *Artificial Intelligence* **13**:231–278

Peterson JL (1973) Petri Nets, *Computing Surveys* **9**(3)223–52

Petri CA (1962a) *Kommunikation mit Automaton*, PhD thesis, Inst Intrumentelle Mathematik, Bonn

Petri CA (1962b) *Communication with Automata*, TR U Bonn, tr by Green CH Jr, TR **65–377** Rome Air Develop Cent

Pitts WH and McCulloch WS (1947) How we know universals: the perception of auditory visual forms, *Bulletin of Mathematical Biophysics* **9**:127–47

Plotkin GD (1970) A note on inductive generalization, in Meltzer B and Michie D eds, *Machine Intelligence* **5**, American Elsevier

Pnueli A (1986) Applications of temporal logic to the specification and verification of reactive systems: a survey of current trends, in de Bakker JW, de Roever WP and Rozenberg G eds, *Trends in Concurrency, Overviews and Tutorials*, Springer-Verlag *LNCS* **224**:510–84

Pollack ME and Ringuette M (1990) Introducing the tileworld: experimentally evaluating agent architectures, in *Proc Eighth Nat Conf on Artificial Intelligence, AAAI*–**90**:183–89

Pollard GH (1981) *Parallel Execution of Horn Clause Programs*, Phd Thesis, Imperial College, London

Popper KR (1972) *Objective Knowledge: An Evolutionary Approach*, Clarendon Press

Post EL (1936) Finite combinatory processes formulation I, *J Symbolic Logic*, **1**:103–5

Post EL (1943) Formal reductions of the general combinatorial problem, *Am J Maths*, **65**:197–268

Pratt T (1987) Program analysis and optimization through kernel-control decomposition, *Acta Informatica* **9**:195–216

Prawitz D (1960) An improved proof procedure, *Theory*, 102–39

Prawitz D (1965) *Natural deduction: a proof theoretical study*, PhD thesis, Almqvist and Wiksell, Stockholm

Prim RC (1957) Shortest connection network and some generalizations, *Bell Syst Tech J* **36**:1389–401

Pritchard HA (1968) Descartes' "Meditations", in Doney W ed, *Descartes: A Collection of Critical Essays*, Macmillan: London

Proietti M and Pettorossi A (1993a) Unfolding – definition – folding, in this order for avoiding unnecessary variables in logic programming, *Proc Conf on Programming language implementation and logic programming (PLILP '91)*, Springer-Verlag *LNCS* **528**

Proietti M and Pettorossi A (1993b) The loop absorption and the generalization strategies for the development of logic programs and partial deduction, *J Logic Programming* **16**:123–61

Przymusinski T (1991) Three-valued nonmonotonic formalisms and semantics of logic programs, *Artificial Intelligence* **49**:309–43

Pullham GK (1991) *The Great Eskimo Vocabulary Hoax*, Chicago UP

Quillian MR (1968) Semantic Memory in Minsky M ed, *Semantic Information Processing*, MIT Press, 227–70

Quinlan JR (1982) Semi-autonomous acquisition of pattern-based knowledge, in Michie D ed, *Introductory Readings in Expert Systems*, Gordon and Breach, 192–207

Rabin J (1971) Conversion of limited entry decision tables into optimal decision trees: fundamental concepts, *SIGPLAN Notices* **6**:125–151

Ramamritham K and Stankovic JA (1984) Dynamic task scheduling in hard-real-time distributed systems, *IEEE Software* **1**(3)65–75

Rao AS and Georgeff MP (1991) Modeling rational agents within a BDI architecture, in Allen J, Fikes R and Sandewall E eds, *Proc Second Int Conf on Principles of Knowledge Representation and Reasoning*, Morgan Kaufmann

Raphael B (1968) SIR: Semantic information retrieval, in Minsky ML ed, *Semantic Information Processing*, MIT Press, 33–134

Rashid RF (1988) From Rig to Accent to Mach: The evolution of a network operating system, in Huberman BA (1988) *The Ecology of Computation*, North-Holland, 207–230

Rawling MW (1989) *GHC on the CSIRAC II Dataflow Computer*, TR **118–90R** Dept Comm and Elec Eng, Royal Melbourne Inst Technology,

Raynal M (1986) *Algorithms for Mutual Exclusion*, MIT Press

Raynal M (1988) *Distributed Algorithms and Protocols*, MIT Press

Rayward-Smith VJ, McKeown GP and Burton FW (1988) The general problem solving algorithm and its implementation, *New Generation Computing* **6**(1)41–66

Reddy US (1994) Higher-order aspects of logic programming, in Van Hentenryck P ed, *Logic Programming – Proc Eleventh International Conference on Logic Programming*, MIT Press, 402–18

Reggia J (1983) Diagnostic expert systems based on a set-covering model, *Int J Man Machine Studies* **19**:437–60

Reid C (1970) *Hilbert*, Springer-Verlag

Reinwald LT (1966) *An Introduction to TAB40: a Processor for Table-written Fortran IV Programs*, TR **TP–229** Research and Analysis Corporation

Reisig W (1985) *Petri Nets*, Springer-Verlag

Reiter R (1971) Two results on ordering for resolution with merging and linear format, *JACM* **15**:630–46

Reiter R (1978) On closed world data bases, in Galliare H and Minker J eds, Logic and Databases, Plenum

Reiter R (1980) A logic for default reasoning, *Artificial Intelligence* **13**:81–132

Reynolds J (1970) Transformation systems and the algebraic structure of atomic formulas, in Meltzer B and Michie D eds, *Machine Intelligence* **5**, Edinburgh UP, 135-52

Reynolds J (1972) Definitional interpreters for higher order programming languages, *ACM Fifth National Conference*, 717–40

Rieger C (1976) An organization of knowledge for problem solving and language comprehension, *Artificial Intelligence* **7**:89–127

Ringwood GA (1986a) *Parlog86 and the Dining Logicians*, TR Imperial College and (1988) *CACM* **31**:10–25

Ringwood GA (1986b) *Flat Parlog with Assignment*, unpublished seminar series delivered at Imperial College UK, April 1986

Ringwood GA (1987) *Pattern-Directed, Markovian, Linear Guarded Definite Clause Resolution*, TR Imperial College, Dept Computing

Ringwood GA (1988a) Metalogic machines: a retrospective rationale for the Japanese Fifth Generation, *Knowledge Engineering Review* **3**:303–20

Ringwood GA (1988b) SLD: A Folk Acronym? *Logic Programming Newsletter* **2**(1)5–8 and *SIGPLAN Notices* **24**(5)71–5

Ringwood GA (1989a) A comparative exploration of concurrent logic languages, *Knowledge Engineering Review* **4**:305–32

Ringwood GA (1989b) Predicates and pixels, *New Generation Computing* **7**:59–80

Ringwood GA (1994) A brief history of stream parallel logic programming, *Logic Programming Newsletter* **7**(2)2–4

Roberts DD (1973) *The Existential Graphs of Charles S Peirce*, Mouton

Roberts ES, Evans A, Morgan CR and Clarke EM (1981) Task management in Ada – a critical evaluation for real-time multiprocessors, *Software-Practice and Experience* **11**:365–75

Roberts GM (1977) *An implementation of Prolog*, Master's Thesis, Dept CS, U Waterloo

Robinson JA (1965) A machine-oriented logic based on the resolution principle, *JACM* **12**: 23–41

Robinson JA (1983) Logic programming: past present and future, *New Generation Computing* **1**(2)107–24

Rochester N, Holland JH Haibt LH and Duda WL (1956) Test on a cell assembly theory of the action of the brain, using a large digital computer, *IRE Transaction on Information Theory*, **IT**–2(3)80–93

Rodriguez JE (1967) *A Graph Model for Parallel Computation*, PhD Thesis, MIT

Rogers H Jr (1967) *Theory of Recursive Functions and Effective Computability*, McGraw-Hill

Rokusawa K, Nakase A and Chikayama T (1996) Distributed memory implementation of KLIC, *New Generation Computing* **14**:261–80

Rosenblatt F (1962) *Principles of Neurodynamics: Perceptrons and the Theory of Brain Mechanisms*, Sparta Books

Rosenbleuth A, Wiener N and Bigelow J (1943) Behavior, purpose and teleology, *Philosophy of Science* **10**:18–24

Rosenschein JS and Genesereth MR (1985) Deals among rational agents, *IJCAI–85*:91–9

Ross BJ (1988) The partial evaluation of imperative programs using Prolog, in Abramson H and Rogers MH eds, *Meta-Programming in Logic Programming*, MIT Press

Rozier M and Martins L (1987) The Chorus distributed operating system: some design issues, in Paker Y et al. eds, *Distributed Operating Systems: Theory and Practice*, NATO ASI series, vol F28, Springer-Verlag, 261–87

Rumelhart DE, Hinton GE and Williams RJ (1986) Learning internal representations by error propagation, in Rumelhart DE and McClelland JL eds, *Parallel Distributed Processing* **1**:318–62

Russell B (1945) *A History of Western Philosophy*, Simon and Schuster

Russell S and Norvig P (1995) *Artificial Intelligence: A Modern Approach*, Prentice-Hall

Rydehead DE and Burstall RM (1986) *Computational Category Theory*, Prentice-Hall

Sacks O (1985) *The Man Who Mistook His Wife for a Hat*, Duckworth

Safra S and Shapiro E (1986) Meta-interpreters for real, in Kugler H-J ed, *Proc IFIP–86*:271–78

Sahlin D (1993) Mixtus: an automatic partial evaluator for pure Prolog, *New Generation Computing* **12**(1)7–51

Saletore VA (1990) *Machine Independent Parallel Execution of Speculative Computations*, PhD Thesis, U Illinois at Urbana–Champaign

Samuel AL (1959) Some studies in machine learning using the game of checkers, *IBM J Res and Development* **3**(3)210–29

Samelson K and Bauer FL (1959) Sequential formula translation, *CACM* **3**:76–83

Saraswat VA (1986) *Problems with Concurrent Prolog*, TR **86–100**, CMU

Saraswat VA (1987a) The concurrent logic programming language CP: definition and operational semantics, *Proc of SIGACT–SIGPLAN Symposium on Principles of Programming Languages*, ACM, 49–63

Saraswat VA (1987b) Merging many streams efficiently: the importance of atomic commitment, *Concurrent Prolog: Collected Papers, MIT,* vol **1**:421–45

Saraswat VA (1987c) GHC: operational semantics, problems and relationship with CP, *IEEE Int Symp on Logic Programming,* San Francisco, 347–358

Saraswat VA (1987c) Usenet, *comp.lang.prolog* contribution

Saraswat VA (1989) *Concurrent Constraint Programming Languages,* PhD thesis, CMU

Schank RC (1972) Conceptual dependency: a theory of natural language understanding, *Cognitive Psychology* **3**:552–631

Schank RC and Abelson RP (1977) *Scripts, Plans, Goals and Understanding,* Erlbaum

Schank RC and Riesbeck CK (1981) *Inside Computer Understanding: Five Programs Plus Minatures,* Erlbaum

Schreiber G, Weilinga B and Breuker J (1993) *KADS: A Principled Approach to Knowledge-Based System Development,* Academic Press

Scott DS and Strachey C (1971) Towards a mathematical semantics for computer languages, *Symp on Computers and Automata,* NY Polytechnic Press, 19–46

Searle JR (1969) *Speech Acts: An Essay in the Philosophy of Language,* Cambridge UP

Selz O (1922) *Uber die Gesetze des geordneten Denkverlaufs II,* Cohen

Sejnowski TJ (1981) Skeleton filters in the brain, in Hinton GE and Anderson JA eds, *Parallel Models of Associative Memory,* Lawrence Erlbaum Associates, 49–82

Sejnowski TJ and Rosenberg CR (1985) *NETtalk: a Parallel Network that Learns to Read Aloud,* TR **13**, John Hopkins U, Cognitive Neuropsychology Laboratory

Sejnowski TE and Rosenberg CR (1987) Parallel networks that learn to pronounce English text, *Complex Systems* **1**:145–68

Selfridge OG (1955) Pattern recognition and modern computers, Proc 1955 Western Joint Computer Conference, 91–93

Shannon CE (1950a) Automatic chess player, *Scientific American* **182**:48–51

Shannon CE (1950b) Programming a digital computer for playing chess, *Philosophical Magazine* **41**:256–75

Shannon CE (1948) A mathematical theory of communication, *Bell System Tech J* **27**:379–423; 623–656

Shannon CE and McCarthy J eds (1956) *Automata Studies,* Princeton UP

Shannon CE and Weaver W (1949) *The Mathematical Theory of Communication,* Illinois UP

Shapiro EY (1983) Logic programs with uncertainties, *IJCAI–83*:529–532

Shapiro EY (1983) *A Subset of Concurrent Prolog and its Interpreter,* TR–**003**, ICOT, Tokyo

Shapiro EY (1984) Systolic programming a paradigm for parallel processing, *Proc Int Conf Fifth Generation Computer Systems,* Tokyo, 458–471

Shapiro EY (1986) *Concurrent Prolog: A Progress Report,* TR **CS86–10**, *Weizmann Institute,* Dept Applied Maths,

Shapiro EY (1987a) ed, *Concurrent Prolog: Collected Papers (2 vols),* MIT Press

Shapiro EY (1987b) Or-parallel Prolog in Flat Concurrent Prolog, in Shapiro E ed, *Concurrent Prolog vol 2,* MIT Press, 415–441

Shapiro EY (1989) The family of concurrent logic programming languages, *ACM Computing Surveys* **21**(3)413–510

Shapiro EY and Takeuchi A (1983) Object-oriented programming in Concurrent Prolog, *New Generation Computing* **1**(1)25–48, reprinted in Shapiro E ed (1987) *Concurrent Prolog vol 2,* MIT Press

Shapiro EY and Takeuchi A eds (1993) The Fifth Generation project: personal perspectives, *CACM* **36**(3)46–101

Shastri L (1988) A connectionist approach to knowledge representation and limited inference, *Cognitive Science* **12**:311–392

Shastri L (1989) *A Connectionist System for Rule Based Reasoning with Multi-Place Predicates and Variables*, TR U Pennsylvania, Philadelphia, Computer and Information Science Department

Shoham Y (1990) *Agent-oriented Programming*, TR **STAN–CS–1335–90**, Stanford U, CA

Shoham Y (1993) Agent-oriented programming, *Artificial Intelligence* **60**:51–92

Shoham Y and Tennenholtz M (1992) Emergent conventions in multi-agent systems: initial experimental results and observations, *Proc KR–92*, Cambridge, MA

Shoham Y and Tennenholtz T (1995) On social law for artificial agent societies: off-line design, *Artificial Intelligence* **73**:231–52

Shortliffe E (1976) *Computer Based Medical Consultation: MYCIN*, American Elsevier

Shortliffe EH, Axline SG, Buchanan BG, Merigan TC and Cohen SN (1973) An artificial intelligence program to advise physicians regarding antimicrobial therapy, *Computers and Biomedical Research* **6**:544–60

Siekmann JH (1989) The history of deductions systems and some applications, *Deduction Systems in Artificial Intelligence*, Ellis Horwood, 11–36

Simon HA (1957) *Models of Man*, Wiley

Simon HA (1981) *The Sciences of the Artificial* 2/e, MIT Press

Simon HA (1982) *Models of Bounded Rationality* (2 vols), MIT Press

Simon H and Newell A (1958) Heuristic problem solving: the next advance in operations research, *Operations Research* **6**:6

Skinner BF (1953) *Science and Human Behaviour*, Macmillan

Skolem T (1920) Logico-combinatorial investigations in the satisfiability or provability of mathematical propositions: a simplified proof of a theorem by L Lowenheim and generalizations of the theorem, in van Heijenoort [1967]

Skyttner L (1996) *General Systems Theory*, Macmillan

Slagle JR (1963) A heuristic program that solves symbolic integration problems in freshman calculus, *JACM* **10**(4)

Slagle JR (1971) *Automatic Theorem-Proving for Theories of Partial and Total Ordering*, TR Nat Inst for Health, *Bethesda*, Div Comput Res and Tech

Sleator DD and Tarjan RE (1985) Self-adjusting binary search trees, *JACM* **32**(3)652–686

Smith A (1776) *The Wealth of Nations*

Smith DE and Genesereth MR (1985) Ordering conjunctive queries, *Artificial Intelligence* **26:171**–215

Smith BC (1984) Reflection and Semantics in Lisp, *Eleventh ACM Symp on Principles of Programming Languages*, 23–35

Smith RG (1980) The contract net protocol: high-level communication and control in a distributed problem solver, *IEEE Trans Comp* **C29**(12)1104–13

Smolka G (1995) The Oz programming model, in Leeuwen J van ed, *Computer Science Today*, Springer-Verlag *LNCS* **1000**:1104-1113

Smullyan RM (1956a) Elementary formal systems (abstract), *Bull Am Math Soc* **62**:600

Smullyan RM (1956b) On definability by recursion (abstract), *Bull Am Math Soc* **62**:601

Smullyan RM (1961) *Theory of Formal Systems*, Princeton UP

Smyth MB (1982) *Finitary Relations and their Fair Merge*, TR **CSE–107–82**, U Edinburgh, Dept Comp Science

Sowa, J ed (1991) *Principles of Semantic Networks: Explorations in the Representation of Knowledge*, Morgan Kaufmann, CA

Stankovic JA, Ramamritham K, and Cheng S (1985) Evaluation of a flexible task-scheduling algorithm for distributed hard real-time systems, *IEEE Transactions on Computers*, **C34**(12)1130–43

Steele GL Jr (1976) *LAMBDA: The Ultimate Imperative*, TR **353**, *MIT*, AI Lab

Steel TB Jr (1966) *Formal Language Description Languages for Computer Programming*, North-Holland

Stefik M and Bobrow D (1986) Object-oriented programming: themes and variations, *AI Magazine* **6**(4)40–64

Sterbenz RF (1971) TABSOL decision table preprocessor, *SIGPLAN Notices* **6**(8)33–40

Sterling L and Shapiro E (1986a) *The Art of Prolog*, MIT Press

Sterling L and Beer RD (1986b) Incremental flavor-mixing of meta-interpreters for expert system construction, *Proc Third International Logic Programming Symposium*, Salt Lake City, 20–7

Stickel ME (1982) A nonclausal connection-graph resolution theorem proving program, *Proc Nat Conf on AI*, Pittsburgh, 229–23

Stickel ME (1986) Schubert's steamroller problem: formulations and solutions, *J Automated Reasoning*, 89–101

Stockman GC (1979) A minimax algorithm better than alpha-beta? *Artificial Intelligence* **12**:179–96

Stolfo SJ and Miranker DP (1986) The DADO production system machine, *J Parallel and Distributed Computing* **3**:269–96

Stone P and Veloso M (1996) Multi-agent systems: a survey from a machine learning perspective, submitted to *IEEE Trans on Knowledge and Data Engineering*

Stoy JE (1981) *Denotational Semantics: The Scott Strachey Approach to Programming Language Theory*, MIT Press

Strachey C and Wadsworth CP (1974) *Continuations, a Mathematical Semantics for Handling Full Jumps*, TR **PRG–11** Oxford U

Steer K (1988) Testing data flow diagrams with Parlog, in Kowalski RA and Bowen KA eds, *Proc Fifth Int Conf and Symp on Logic Programming*, MIT Press, 96–109

Subramanian GH, Nosek J, Ragunathan SP and Kanitar SS (1992) A comparison of decision table and tree, *CACM* **35**(3)89–94

Sutherland IE (1963) SKETCHPAD: A Man-machine graphical communication system, *IFIP Proc of Springs Joint Comp Conf*

Sussmann GJ and McDermott DV (1972) From Planner to CONNIVER – a genetic approach, *Proc AFIPS Fall Conference*, 1171–79

Sussmann GJ, Winograd T and Charniak (1971) *Micro Planner Reference Manual*, TR **AIM–203A**, MIT

Szabo ME (1970) *The Collected Papers of Gerhard Gentzen*, Studies in Logic, Elsevier

Szeredi P (1991) Solving optimization problems in the Aurora Or-parallel Prolog system, in Beaumont A and Gupta G eds, *ICLP'91 Pre-Conference Workshop on Parallel Execution of Logic Programs*, Springer-Verlag *LNCS* **569**:39–53

Takeuchi A (1983) *How to Solve it in Concurrent Prolog*, unpublished note, ICOT, Tokyo

Takeuchi A (1986) Affinity between meta-interpreters and partial evaluation, in Kugler H-J ed, *Information Processing 86*, Dublin (Ireland), 279–282

Tamaki H and Sato T (1986) OLD resolution with tabulation, *Third Int Conf on Logic Programming*, Springer-Verlag *LNCS* **225**:84–98

Tanaka J (1993) *Visual Input System for GHC Programs*, TR Tsukuba, Japan

Tanaka J and Matono F (1992) Constructing and collapsing a reflective tower in Reflective Guarded Horn Clauses, *Proc Int Conf Fifth Generation Computer Systems*, ICOT

Tanenbaum AS (1987) *Operating Systems: Design and Implementation*, Prentice-Hall

Tenenbaum JM, Chowdhry TS and Hughes K (1997) Eco system: an internet commerce architecture, *Computer* **30**(5)48–55

Tarau P and Boyer M (1990) Elementary logic programs, in Deransart P and Maluszynski J eds, *Proc Programming Language Implementation and Logic Programming*, Springer-Verlag *LNCS* **456**

Taylor S, Av-Ron E and Shapiro E (1987) A layered method for thread and code mapping, *New Generation Computing*, 185–205 and in Shapiro E ed, *Concurrent Prolog vol 2*, MIT Press, 78–100

Tesler LG and Enea HJ (1968) A language design for concurrent threads, *AFIPS Conf Proc*, **32**:403–8

Thomas SR (1994) The PLACA agent programming language, *Intelligent Agents (ECAI–94 Workshop on Agent Theories, Architectures and Languages)*, Springer-Verlag *LNAI* **890**:355–70

Thornley J (1995) Declarative Ada: parallel dataflow programming in a familiar context, *ACM Computer Science Conf*, Nashville TN, 73–80

Thornton C and du Boulay B (1992) *Artificial Intelligence Through Search*, Intellect

Tick E (1991) *Parallel Logic Programming*, MIT Press

Tick E and Ichiyoshi N (1990) Programming techniques for efficiently exploiting parallelism in logic programming languages, *Second ACM Symp on Princ and Pract of Parallel Programming, SIGPLAN Notices* **25**(3)31–3

Toffoli T and Margolis N (1987) *Cellular Automata Machines*, MIT Press

Tokoro M (1993) The society of objects, *Addendum to OOPSLA–9, OOPS Messenger* **5**(2)3–12

Tomlinson C and Scheevel M (1989) Concurrent object-oriented programming languages, in Kim W and Lochovsky FH eds, *Object-Oriented Concepts, Databases, and Applications*, Addison-Wesley

Tomlinson C And Singh V (1989) Inheritance and synchronization with enabled-sets, OOPSLA'89, *Special Issue SIGPLAN Notices*, (10)24

Touretzky D S & Hinton G E (1988) A Distributed Connectionist Production System, *Cognitive Science* **12**:423–466

Treleavan PC (1983) The new generation of computer architecture, *Proc Tenth Int Symp on Computer Architecture*, ACM, 402–9

Trinder PW, Hammond K, Loidl HW and Peyton SL (1998) Algorithm+strategy=parallelism, *J Functional Programming* **8**(1)

Turchin VF (1986) The concept of a supercompiler, *ACM TOPLAS* **8**(3)292–325

Turing A (1936) On computable numbers, with an application to the Entsheidungsproblem, *Proc London Mathematical Soc 2*, **42**:230–65

Turing A (1949) Checking a large routine, *Report of the Conference on High Speed Automatic Calculating Machines*, Mathematical Laboratory, U Cambridge, 67

Turing AM (1950) Computing machinery and intelligence, *Mind* **59**:433–60

Turner DA (1979) A new implementation technique for applicative languages, *Soft Pract Exp* **9**:31–49

Turner JS (1988) Almost all k-colorable graphs are easy to color, *J Algorithms* **9**:63–82

Ueda K (1985a) *Concurrent PROLOG Re-examined*, TR **102**, ICOT, Tokyo

Ueda K (1985b) *Guarded Horn Clauses*, TR **103**, ICOT Tokyo

Ueda K (1986) *Guarded Horn Clauses*, EngD Thesis, U Tokyo, Japan

Ueda K (1987) Making exhaustive search programs deterministic, *New Generation Computing* **5**(1)29–44

Ueda K and Chikayama T (1990) Design of the kernel language for the parallel inference machine, *Computer J* **33**(6)494–500

Ungar D and Patterson D (1987) What price Smalltalk, *IEEE Computer* **20**:67–72

Unger J (1987) *The Fifth Generation Fallacy*, OUP

van Emden MH and de Luceana GJ (1979) *Predicate Logic as a Language for Parallel Programming*, TR **CS 79–15**, U Waterloo and in Clark KL and Tärnlund S-Å eds (1982) *Logic Programming*, Academic Press, 189–98

van Harmelen F (1991) *Metalevel Inference Systems*, Pitman

van Harmelen F (1992) Definable naming relations in metalevel systems, *Metaprogramming in Logic 92*, Springer-Verlag *LNCS* **649**:89–104

van Harmelen F and Balder J (1992) (ML)^2: a formal language for KADS models of expertise, *Knowledge Acquisition* **4**(1)127–61

van Heijenoort J ed (1967) *From Frege to Gödel: A Source book in Mathematical Logic, 1879–1931*, Harvard UP

Vasey P (1986) Qualified answers and their application to program transformation, *Third Int Conf on Logic Programming*, Springer-Verlag *LNCS* **225**:425–32

von Bertalanffy L (1940) The organism considered as a physical system, in von Bertalanffy [1968]

von Bertalanffy L (1956) General systems theory, in von Bertalanffy [1968]

von Bertalanffy L (1968) *General Systems Theory*, Braziller

von Neumann J and Morgenstern O (1944) *The Theory of Games and Economic Behavior*, Princeton UP

von Neumann J (1945) First draft of a report on EDVAC, in Randell B ed (1975) *Origins of Digital Computers*, Springer-Verlag, 355–64

von Neumann J (1951) The general and logical theory of automata, *Cerebral Mechanisms in Behavior: The Hixon Symposium*, Wiley

von Neumann J (1966) *Theory of Self-Reproducing Automata* (ed and completed by Burks AW), Illinois UP

Wadler P (1988) Deforestation: transforming programs to eliminate trees, *Second European Symp on Programming*, Springer-Verlag *LNCS* **300**:344–358

Wadler PL (1997) How to declare an imperative, *ACM Computing Surveys* **29**(3)240–63

Wah BW ed (1987) New AI systems: harnessing the combinatorial explosion, *IEEE Computer* (Special Issue) **20**

Wah BW and Li G-J eds (1986) *Computers for Artificial Intelligence Applications*, IEEE

Waldo J, Wyant G, Wollrath A and Kendall S (1996) A note on distributed computing, in Vitek J and Tschudin C eds, *Mobile Object Systems,* Springer-Verlag *LNCS* **1222**:49–66

Waldspurger CA et al. (1992) Spawn: a distributed computational economy, *IEEE Trans Soft Eng* **18**(2)103–16

Walker RL (1960) An enumerative technique for a class of combinatorial problems, *Amer Math Soc Proc Symp Appl Math* **10**:91–4

Walther C (1984) A mechanical solution of Schubert's steamroller by many-sorted resolution, *AAAI–84*

Walter G (1950) An imitation of life, *Scientific American*, **182**:42–45

Walter G (1951) A machine that learns, *Scientific American*, **185**:60–63

Waltz DL (1972) *Generating Semantic Descriptions from Drawings of Scenes with Shadows*, TR **AI–271**, *MIT*

Waltz D (1975) Understanding line drawings of scenes with shadows, in Winston PH ed, *The Psychology of Computer Vision*, McGraw-Hill

Wang H (1960) Toward mechanical mathematics, *IBM J of Research and Development*, 2–22

Warren DHD (1977) *Implementing Prolog – Compiling Predicate Logic Programs*, TR **DAI** 39/40 Dept Artificial Intelligence, Edinburgh U,

Warren DHD (1983) *An Abstract Prolog Instruction Set*, TR **309**, SRI International

Waterman D and Hayes-Roth F eds, (1978) *Pattern Directed Inference Systems*, Academic Press

Waters R (1979) A method for analysing loop programs, *IEEE Transactions on Software Engineering* **5**(3)237–247

Waters RC (1985) The Programmer's Apprentice: a session with KBEmacs, *IEEE Trans Soft Eng* **11**:1296–320

Waters RC (1988) Program transformation via abstraction and reimplementation, *IEEE Trans Soft Eng* **SE–14**(8)1207–228

Wathansian S (1978) *Proposed Language for the Multiprocessor System*, TR U Manchester, Dept Comp Sci

Wegman MN and Zadeck FK (1991) Constant propagation with conditional branches, *ACM Trans Prog Lang Sys* **13**:180–210

Weise D, Conybeare R, Ruf E and Seligman S (1991) Automatic online partial evaluation, *Fifth ACM Conf on Functional Programming Languages and Computer Architecture*, Springer-Verlag *LNCS* **523**:165–191

Weitzenfeld A and Arbib MA (1991) A concurrent object-oriented framework for the simulation of neural networks, *OOPSLA/ECOOP'90 Workshop on Object-Oriented Concurrent Programming*, OOPS Messenger, *ACM SIGPLAN* **2**(2)120–24

Wertheimer M (1945) *Productive Thinking*, Harper

Wetzel G (1997) *Abductive and Constraint Logic Programming*, PhD thesis, Dept Computing, Imperial College, London

Wexelblat RL (1981) *History of Programming Languages*, Academic Press

Weyrauch R (1980) Prologemena to a theory of mechanical formal reasoning, *Artificial Intelligence* **13**:133–70

Whitehead AN and Russell B (1910–13) *Principia Mathematica* (3 vols), Cambridge UP

Whorf BL (1956) *Language, Thought and Reality*, MIT Press

Widrow B and Hoff ME (1960) Adaptive switching circuits, *IRE WESCON Convention Record*, 96–104

Wiener N (1948) *Cybernetics*, Wiley

Wikstrom MC, Prabhu GM and Gustafson JL (1992) Myths of load balancing, in Evans DJ, Joubert GR and Liddell H eds, *Parallel Computing '91*, Elsevier

Wilensky R (1983) *Planning and Understanding*, Addison-Wesley

Wilkes MV (1968) Computers then and now: 1967 Turing Lecture, *JACM* **15**(1)1–7

Wilson WG (1987) Concurrent alpha-beta, a study in concurrent logic programming, *IEEE Symp on Logic Programming*, San Francisco, 360–7

Winograd T (1972) *Understanding Natural Language*, Academic Press

Winograd T (1973a) A procedural model of language understanding, in Schank R and Colby K eds, *Computer Models of Thought and Language*, Freeman

Winograd T (1973b) Breaking the complexity barrier (again), *Proc ACM SIGIR–SIGPLAN Interface Meeting*

Winograd T (1985) [Computer Section] *The Guardian* 23 May

Winograd T and Flores F (1986) *Understanding Computers and Cognition*, Addison-Wesley

Winston PH (1975) Learning Structural Descriptions from Examples, in Winston PH ed, *Psychology of Computer Vision*, McGraw-Hill, 157–209

Wirth N (1974) On the design of programming languages, *Proc IFIP Congress 74*, North-Holland, 386–93

Wirth N (1976) *Algorithms + Data Structures = Programs*, Prentice-Hall

Wirth N and Jensen K (1974) *The Pascal User Manual and Report*, Springer-Verlag

Wise MJ (1986) *Prolog Multiprocessors*, Prentice-Hall

Wittgenstein L (1922) *Tractatus Logico-Philosophicus*, Kegan Paul

Wittgenstein L (1953) *Philosophical Investigations*, Blackwell

Wolfram DA (1986) Intractable unifiability problems and backtracking, *Third Int Conf on Logic Programming*, Springer-Verlag *LNCS* **225**:107–21

Woods W (1972) Progress in natural language understanding: an application to lunar geology, *AFIPS Conf Proc* **42**

Wooldrige D (1968) *Mechanical Man*, McGraw-Hill

Wood DC (1969) A technique for coloring a graph applicable to large-scale timetabling problems, *Computer J* **12**(4)

Woods W (1975) What's in a link: foundations of semantic networks, in Bobrow DG and Collins A eds, *Representation and Understanding*, Academic Press

Wos L and Veroff R (1994) Logical basis for the automation of reasoning: case studies, in Gabbay DM, Hogger CJ and Robinson JA eds, *Handbook of Logic in Artificial Intelligence and Logic Programming*, Clarendon Press, 41–125

Yang R and Aiso H (1986) P-Prolog, a parallel logic language based on exclusive relation, *Proc Third Int Logic Prog Conf*, Springer-Verlag, 255–269

Yao AC (1975) An O(|E| log log |V|) algorithm for finding minimal spanning trees, *Information Processing Letters* **4**(1)21–3

Yardeni E, Kliger S, and Shapiro E (1990) The languages FCP(:) and FCP(:,?), *New Generation Computing* **7**:89–107

Yasui T (1972) *Conversion of Decision Tables into Decision Trees*, PhD Thesis UIUCDCS–R–72–501, U Illinois at Urbana-Champaign

Ygge F and Akkermans H (1997) Making a case for multi-agent systems, in Boman M and van de Velde W eds, *Multi Agent Rationality (MAAMAW–97)*, Springer-Verlag *LNAI* **1237**

Yokoo M (1998) Distributed constraint satisfaction: foundation and application, *Third Int Conf Multi-agent Systems,* IEEE Computer Society, 14–5

Yokoo M and Hirayama K (1998) Distributed constraint satisfaction for complex local problems, *Third Int Conf Multi-agent Systems,* IEEE Computer Society, 372–9

Yonezawa A ed (1990) *ABCL: An Object-Oriented Concurrent System*, MIT Press

Yonezawa A, Briot J-P and Shibayama E (1986) Object-oriented programming in ABCL/1, *OOPSLA–86, SIGPLAN Notices* **21**(11)258–268

Yuba T, Shimada T, Yamguchi Y, Hiraki K and Sakai S (1990) Dataflow computer development in Japan, *Proc ACM Int Conf on Supercomputing*, 140–7

Zlotkin G and Rosenschein JS (1989) Negotiation and task sharing among autonomous agents in cooperative domains, *Eleventh Int Joint Conf on Art Int (IJCAI–91)*, 912–917

Zlotkin G and Rosenschein JS (1991) Incomplete information and deception in multi-agent negotiation, *Twelveth Int Joint Conf on Art Int (IJCAI-91)*

Zuse K (1945) *Der Plankalkül*, TR **175** Gesellschaft für Mathematik und Datenverarbeitung, Bonn

Lecture Notes in Artificial Intelligence (LNAI)

Vol. 1574: N. Zhong, L. Zhou (Eds.), Methodologies for Knowledge Discovery and Data Mining. Proceedings, 1999. XV, 533 pages. 1999.

Vol. 1582: A. Lecomte, F. Lamarche, G. Perrier (Eds.), Logical Aspects of Computational Linguistics. Proceedings, 1997. XI, 251 pages. 1999.

Vol. 1585: B. McKay, X. Yao, C.S. Newton, J.-H. Kim, T. Furuhashi (Eds.), Simulated Evolution and Learning. Proceedings, 1998. XIII, 472 pages. 1999.

Vol. 1599: T. Ishida (Ed.), Multiagent Platforms. Proceedings, 1998. VIII, 187 pages. 1999.

Vol. 1600: M. J. Wooldridge, M. Veloso (Eds.), Artificial Intelligence Today. VIII, 489 pages. 1999.

Vol. 1604: M. Asada, H. Kitano (Eds.), RoboCup-98: Robot Soccer World Cup II. XI, 509 pages. 1999.

Vol. 1609: Z. W. Ras, A. Skowron (Eds.), Foundations of Intelligent Systems. Proceedings, 1999. XII, 676 pages. 1999.

Vol. 1611: I. Imam, Y. Kodratoff, A. El-Dessouki, M. Ali (Eds.), Multiple Approaches to Intelligent Systems. Proceedings, 1999. XIX, 899 pages. 1999.

Vol. 1612: R. Bergmann, S. Breen, M. Göker, M. Manago, S. Wess, Developing Industrial Case-Based Reasoning Applications. XX, 188 pages. 1999.

Vol. 1617: N.V. Murray (Ed.), Automated Reasoning with Analytic Tableaux and Related Methods. Proceedings, 1999. X, 325 pages. 1999.

Vol. 1620: W. Horn, Y. Shahar, G. Lindberg, S. Andreassen, J. Wyatt (Eds.), Artificial Intelligence in Medicine. Proceedings, 1999. XIII, 454 pages. 1999.

Vol. 1621: D. Fensel, R. Studer (Eds.), Knowledge Acquisition Modeling and Management. Proceedings, 1999. XI, 404 pages. 1999.

Vol. 1623: T. Reinartz, Focusing Solutions for Data Mining. XV, 309 pages. 1999.

Vol. 1630: M. M. Huntbach, G. A. Ringwood, Agent-Oriented Programming. XIV, 386 pages. 1999.

Vol. 1632: H. Ganzinger (Ed.), Automated Deduction – CADE-16. Proceedings, 1999. XIV, 429 pages. 1999.

Vol. 1634: S. Džeroski, P. Flach (Eds.), Inductive Logic Programming. Proceedings, 1999. VIII, 303 pages. 1999.

Vol. 1637: J.P. Walser, Integer Optimization by Local Search. XIX, 137 pages. 1999.

Vol. 1638: A. Hunter, S. Parsons (Eds.), Symbolic and Quantitative Approaches to Reasoning and Uncertainty. Proceedings, 1999. IX, 397 pages. 1999.

Vol. 1640: W. Tepfenhart, W. Cyre (Eds.), Conceptual Structures: Standards and Practices. Proceedings, 1999. XII, 515 pages. 1999.

Vol. 1647: F.J. Garijo, M. Boman (Eds.), Multi-Agent System Engineering. Proceedings, 1999. X, 233 pages. 1999.

Vol. 1650: K.-D. Althoff, R. Bergmann, L.K. Branting (Eds.), Case-Based Reasoning Research and Development. Proceedings, 1999. XII, 598 pages. 1999.

Vol. 1652: M. Klusch, O.M. Shehory, G. Weiss (Eds.), Cooperative Information Agents III. Proceedings, 1999. XI, 404 pages. 1999.

Vol. 1669: X.-S. Gao, D. Wang, L. Yang (Eds.), Automated Deduction in Geometry. Proceedings, 1998. VII, 287 pages. 1999.

Vol. 1674: D. Floreano, J.-D. Nicoud, F. Mondada (Eds.), Advances in Artificial Life. Proceedings, 1999. XVI, 737 pages. 1999.

Vol. 1688: P. Bouquet, L. Serafini, P. Brézillon, M. Benerecetti, F. Castellani (Eds.), Modeling and Using Context. Proceedings, 1999. XII, 528 pages. 1999.

Vol. 1692: V. Matoušek, P. Mautner, J. Ocelíková, P. Sojka (Eds.), Text, Speech, and Dialogue. Proceedings, 1999. XI, 396 pages. 1999.

Vol. 1695: P. Barahona, J.J. Alferes (Eds.), Progress in Artificial Intelligence. Proceedings, 1999. XI, 385 pages. 1999.

Vol. 1699: S. Albayrak (Ed.), Intelligent Agents for Telecommunication Applications. Proceedings, 1999. IX, 191 pages. 1999.

Vol. 1701: W. Burgard, T. Christaller, A.B. Cremers (Eds.), KI-99: Advances in Artificial Intelligence. Proceedings, 1999. XI, 311 pages. 1999.

Vol. 1704: Jan M. Żytkow, J. Rauch (Eds.), Principles of Data Mining and Knowledge Discovery. Proceedings, 1999. XIV, 593 pages. 1999.

Vol. 1705: H. Ganzinger, D. McAllester, A. Voronkov (Eds.), Logic for Programming and Automated Reasoning. Proceedings, 1999. XII, 397 pages. 1999.

Vol. 1706: J. Hatcliff, T. Æ. Mogensen, P. Thiemann (Eds.), Lectures on Partial Evaluation. Proceedings, 1998. IX, 433 pages. 1999.

Vol. 1711: N. Zhong, A. Skowron, S. Ohsuga (Eds.), New Directions in Rough Sets, Data Mining, and Granular-Soft Computing. Proceedings, 1999. XIV, 558 pages. 1999.

Vol. 1712: H. Boley, A Tight, Practical Integration of Relations and Functions. XI, 169 pages. 1999.

Vol. 1714: M.T. Pazienza (Eds.), Information Extraction. IX, 165 pages. 1999.

Vol. 1715: P. Perner, M. Petrou (Eds.), Machine Learning and Data Mining in Pattern Recognition. Proceedings, 1999. VIII, 217 pages. 1999.

Vol. 1721: S. Arikawa, K. Furukawa (Eds.), Discovery Science. Proceedings, 1999. XI, 374 pages. 1999.

Lecture Notes in Computer Science